CITE THIS VOLUME:

42 USCS §—

UNITED STATES CODE SERVICE
Lawyers Edition

★ ★ ★ ★ ★ ★ ★ ★ ★

All federal laws of a general and permanent nature arranged in accordance with
the section numbering of the United
States Code and the supplements
thereto.

42 USCS

Public Health and Welfare

§§ 13601–15800

2012

LexisNexis®

www.lexisnexis.com

Editorial Offices
701 East Water Street, Charlottesville, VA 22902 (800) 446-3410

For information about United States Code Service, call
1-800-446-3410 (8 a.m. – 5 p.m. EST), and ask for the USCS
Hotline, or contact:
Derrick Wilborn, J.D., *Derrick.Wilborn@lexisnexis.com*
Elizabeth Evans, J.D., *Elizabeth.Evans@lexisnexis.com*

Library of Congress Catalog Card Number 72-76254

ISBN: 978-0-327-13469-5

47191-12

(Pub.46902)

PUBLICATION EDITOR:
Elizabeth Evans, J.D.

CONSULTING EDITOR:
Derrick R. Wilborn, J.D.

CONTRIBUTING EDITOR:
Brian Cooley, J.D.

TECHNICAL SUPPORT STAFF:
Jonathan Shiff
Heather Towe
Ellen Weeden

ABBREVIATIONS

Reporters, Texts, Etc.

A	Atlantic Reporter
A2d	Atlantic Reporter, Second Series
ACMR	Army Court of Military Review
AD	Appellate Division Reports (NY)
AD2d	Appellate Division Reports, Second Series (NY)
AD Cas.	BNA Americans with Disabilities Cases
ADD	Americans With Disabilities Decisions
AdL2d	Pike and Fischer Administrative Law, Second Series
ADVA	Administrator's Decisions, Veterans' Administration
AFCMR	Air Force Court of Military Review
AFTR	American Federal Tax Reports
AFTR2d	American Federal Tax Reports, Second Series
AGBCA	Department of Agriculture Board of Contract Appeals
Agric Dec	Agriculture Decisions
ALAB	NRC Atomic Safety and Licensing Appeal Board
ALR	American Law Reports
ALR2d	American Law Reports, Second Series
ALR3d	American Law Reports, Third Series
ALR4th	American Law Reports, Fourth Series
ALR5th	American Law Reports, Fifth Series
ALR6th	American Law Reports, Sixth Series
ALR Fed.	American Law Reports, Federal
ALR Fed 2d	American Law Reports, Federal, Second Series
Am Bankr NS	American Bankruptcy, New Series
AMC	American Maritime Cases
Am Disab	Americans With Disabilities: Practice and Compliance Manual
Am Jur 2d	American Jurisprudence, Second Edition
Am Jur Legal Forms 2d	American Jurisprudence Legal Forms, Second Edition
Am Jur Pl & Pr Forms (Rev ed)	American Jurisprudence Pleading and Practice Forms, Revised Edition

Am Jur Proof of Facts.....	American Jurisprudence Proof of Facts
Am Jur Proof of Facts 2d..	American Jurisprudence Proof of Facts, Second Series
Am Jur Proof of Facts 3d..	American Jurisprudence Proof of Facts, Third Series
Am Jur Trials.............	American Jurisprudence Trials
Am Law Prod Liab 3d.....	American Law of Products Liability, Third Edition
App DC	United States Court of Appeals for the District of Columbia
Appx....................	Appendix
ASBCA..................	Armed Services Board of Contract Appeals
ATF Qtrly Bull............	Quarterly Bulletin, Alcohol, Tobacco and Firearms Bureau, U.S. Dept. Treas.
ATR Rul.................	Ruling of Alcohol, Tobacco and Firearms Bureau, U.S. Dept. Treas.
BAMSL..................	Bankruptcy Reporter of the Bar Association of Metropolitan St. Louis
BCA	Board of Contract Appeals
BCD	Bankruptcy Court Decisions
Bd App.................	Patent & Trademark Office Board of Appeals
Bd Imm App	Board of Immigration Appeals
Bd Pat Inter..............	Board of Patent Appeals and Interferences
BIA	Board of Immigration Appeals
Bkr L Ed................	Bankruptcy Service, Lawyers Edition
BLR....................	BRBS Black Lung Reporter
BNA EBC................	Employee Benefits Cases
BNA FEP Cas............	Fair Employment Practices Cases
BNA IER Cas	Individual Employment Rights Cases
BNA Intl Trade Rep	International Trade Reporter
BNA LRRM	Labor Relations Reference Manual
BNA OSHC	Occupational Safety and Health Cases
BNA WH Cas	Wage and Hour Cases
BR.....................	Bankruptcy Reporter
BRBS	Benefits Review Board Service
BTA....................	Board of Tax Appeals
BTA Mem...............	Board of Tax Appeals Memorandum Decisions
CA.....................	United States Court of Appeals
CAB Adv Dig............	Civil Aeronautics Board Advance Digest
CAD	Customs Appeals Decisions
Cal Rptr................	California Reporter
CB.....................	Cumulative Bulletin of the Internal Revenue Service
CBC	Clark Boardman Callaghan or Collier Bankruptcy Cases
CBCA..................	Civilian Board of Contract Appeals
CBD	Customs Bulletin and Decisions, Customs Service, Department of the Treasury
CCF	CCH Contract Cases Federal

CCG	Consumer Credit Guide
CCH Bankr L Rptr	Bankruptcy Law Reporter
CCH BCA Dec	Board of Contract Appeals Decisions
CCH CCG	Consumer Credit Guide
CCH Comm Fut L Rep	Commodity Futures Law Reporter
CCH EEOC Dec	Decisions of the Equal Employment Opportunity Commission
CCH EPD	Employment Practice Decisions
CCH Fed Secur L Rep	Federal Securities Law Reporter
CCH FERC	Federal Energy Regulatory Commission Reports
CCH LC	Labor Cases
CCH NLRB	National Labor Relations Board Decisions
CCH OSHD	Occupational Safety and Health Decisions
CCH SEC Doc	CCH Securities Exchange Commission Docket
CCH TCM	Tax Court Memorandum Decisions
CCH Trade Cas	Trade Cases
CCH Trade Reg Rep	Trade Regulation Reports
CCH Unemployment Ins Rep	Unemployment Insurance Reporter
CCPA	Court of Customs and Patent Appeals
CD	Customs Decisions
CDOS	California Daily Opinion Service
CFR	Code of Federal Regulations
CFTC	Commodity Futures Trading Commission
CGCMR	Coast Guard Court of Military Review
CGLB	Coast Guard Law Bulletin
CIT	Court of International Trade
CLI	Commission Licensing Issuance
CMA	Court of Military Appeals
CMR	Court-Martial Reports
COGSA	Carriage of Goods by Sea Act
Colo J C A R	Colorado Journal, Colorado Appellate Reports
Comm Fut L Rep	Commodity Futures Law Reporter
Comp Gen	Decisions of the U.S. Comptroller General
Comp Gen Unpub Dec	Unpublished decisions of the U.S. Comptroller General
Comr Pat	Commissioner of Patents and Trademarks
Copy L Rep	CCH Copyright Law Reporter
CPD	Customs Penalty Decisions
CPSC Advisory Op No	Consumer Product Safety Commission Advisory Opinion Number
CRD	Customs Rules Decisions
CR L	Criminal Law Reporter
CSD	Customs Service Decisions
Ct Cl	Court of Claims
Cust Bull	Customs Bulletin and Decisions, US Department of Treasury
Cust Ct	Customs Court

Cust & Pat App (Cust).....	U.S. Court of Customs and Patent Appeals (Customs)
Cust & Pat App (Pat)......	U.S. Court of Customs and Patent Appeals (Patents)
Daily Journal DAR........	California Daily Journal Daily Appellate Reports
DC.....................	United States District Court
DCAB..................	Department of Commerce Contract Appeals Board
DCO	Department of Commerce Orders
Dist Col App	District of Columbia Court of Appeals
DOA	Department of Agriculture
DOC	Department of Commerce
DOE	Department of Energy
DOHA..................	Department of Defense Office of Hearings and Appeals
DOT CAB................	Department of Transportation Contract Appeals Board
DPRM..................	Denial of Petition for Rulemaking, NRC Decision
EBC	Employee Benefits Cases
EBCA..................	Department of Energy Board of Contract Appeals
ECAB	Employees' Compensation Appeals Board, U.S. Department of Labor
EEOC DEC	Equal Employment Opportunity Commission Decisions
ELR....................	Environmental Law Reporter
Em Ct App..............	Emergency Court of Appeals
EMP COORD	Employment Coordinator
ENG BCA	Corps of Engineers Board of Contract Appeals
EPD	Employment Practices Decisions
ERA	Economic Regulatory Administration
Envt Rep Cas............	Environmental Reporter Cases
ERISA Op Letters	Employee Retirement Income Security Act Opinion Letters
Ex Or	Executive Order
F	Federal Reporter
F2d....................	Federal Reporter, Second Series
F3d	Federal Reporter, Third Series
F Cas	Federal Cases
FCC	Federal Communications Commission
FCC2d	Federal Communications Commission Reports, Second Series
FCSC	Foreign Claims Settlement Commission
FCSC 1981 Ann Rpt......	FCSC Annual Report for 1981
FCSC Dec & Anno (1968) .	FCSC Decisions and Annotations, 1968 edition
FDA....................	Food and Drug Administration
FDA Dec	Food and Drug Administration Decisions
FEA....................	Federal Energy Administration
Fed Appx	Federal Appendix

Fed Cl...................	Court of Federal Claims Reporter
Fed Evid Rep............	Federal Rules of Evidence Service
Fed Proc L Ed...........	Federal Procedure, Lawyers Edition
Fed Procedural Forms, L Ed.....................	Federal Procedure Forms, Lawyers Edition
Fed Reg.................	Federal Register
Fed Rules Evid Serv......	Federal Rules of Evidence Service
FEP Case...............	Fair Employment Practice Cases (BNA)
FEPC...................	Fair Employment Practice Cases
FERC...................	Federal Energy Regulatory Commission Reports
Fed Secur L Rep.........	Federal Securities Law Reporter
FHLBB.................	Federal Home Loan Bank Board
FLRA..................	Federal Labor Relations Authority
FLRA GCO.............	Federal Labor Relations Authority, General Counsel Opinions
FLRC..................	Federal Labor Relations Council
FLW Fed...............	Florida Law Weekly Federal
FMC...................	Federal Maritime Commission
FMSHRC...............	Federal Mine Safety and Health Review Commission
FOIA..................	Freedom of Information Act
FPC...................	Federal Power Commission
FR....................	Federal Register
FRB..................	Federal Reserve Bulletin
FRCP.................	Federal Rules of Civil Procedure
FRCrP................	Federal Rules of Criminal Procedure
FRD..................	Federal Rules Decisions
FRE..................	Federal Rules of Evidence
FRS..................	Federal Reserve System
FR Serv...............	Federal Rules Service
FR Serv 2d.............	Federal Rules Service, Second Series
FR Serv 3d.............	Federal Rules Service, Third Series
FSIP..................	Federal Service Impasses Panel
F Supp.................	Federal Supplement
F Supp 2d..............	Federal Supplement, Second Series
FTC...................	Federal Trade Commission
GAO...................	Government Accountability Office
GSBCA.................	General Services Administration Board of Contract Appeals
HEW...................	Department of Health, Education and Welfare
HHS...................	Department of Health and Human Services
HUD...................	Department of Housing and Urban Development
HUD BCA..............	Department of Housing and Urban Development Board of Contract Appeals
IBCA..................	Interior Department Board of Contract Appeals
IBIA..................	Interior Board of Indian Appeals (Dept. of the Interior)
IBLA..................	Interior Board of Land Appeals (Dept. of Interior)

ICC	Interstate Commerce Commission
ID	Decisions of the Department of the Interior
I & N Dec	Immigration and Naturalization Service Decisions
ILS	Immigration Law Service
INS	Immigration and Naturalization Service
IRB	Internal Revenue Bulletin
IRS	Internal Revenue Service
ITRD	Internal Trade Reporter Decisions
JAG	Judge Advocate General
Jud Pan Mult Lit	Rulings of the Judicial Panel on Multidistrict Litigation
LBCA	Department of Labor Board of Contract Appeals
LC	Labor Cases
LD	Land Decisions
L Ed	Lawyers Edition U.S. Supreme Court Reports
L Ed 2d	Lawyers Edition U.S. Supreme Court Reports, Second Series
LRRM	Labor Relations Reference Manual
MA	Maritime Administration
MCC	Motor Carrier Cases (decided by ICC)
Media L R	Media Law Reporter
Mich	Michigan Reports
Mich App	Michigan Appeals Reports
Misc	Miscellaneous Reports (NY)
Misc 2d	Miscellaneous Reports, Second Series (NY)
MJ	Military Justice Reporter
MMLR	Medicare and Medicaid Law Reporter
MSB	Maritime Subsidy Board
MSPB	Merit Systems Protection Board
MSPR	United States Merit Systems Protection Board Reporter
Mun Ct App Dist Col	Municipal Court of Appeals for District of Columbia
NASA BCA	National Aeronautics and Space Administration Board of Contract Appeals
NCMR	Navy Court of Military Review
NE	North Eastern Reporter
NE2d	North Eastern Reporter, Second Series
NITA	The National Institute for Trial Advocacy
NLRB	Decisions and Orders of the National Labor Relations Board
NLRB Advice Mem Case No	National Labor Relations Board Advice Memorandum Case Number
NMCMR	U.S. Navy-Marine Corps Court of Military Review
NOAA	National Oceanic and Atmospheric Administration
NRC	Nuclear Regulatory Commission

NTSB	National Transportation Safety Board
NW	North Western Reporter
NW2d	North Western Reporter, Second Series
NY	New York Reports
NY2d	New York Reports, Second Series
NYS	New York Supplement
NYS2d	New York Supplement, Second Series
nt	note
nts	notes
OAG	Opinions of the Attorney General
OCSLA	Outer Continental Shelf Lands Act
OFCCP	Office of Federal Contract Compliance Programs
OHA	Office of Hearings and Appeals
Op Atty Gen	Opinions of Attorney General
Op Comp Gen	Opinions of Comptroller General
OPM	Office of Personnel Management
ORW	Ocean Resources and Wildlife Reporter
OSAHRC	Occupational Safety and Health Review Commission (Official Reports)
OSHRC	Occupational Safety and Health Review Commission
P	Pacific Reporter
P. L.	Public Law
P2d	Pacific Reporter, Second Series
PBGC Op No	Pension Benefit Guaranty Corporation Opinion Number
PRD	Protest Review Decisions
prec	preceding
Proc	Proclamation
PSBCA	Postal Service Board of Contract Appeals
PS Docket	Postal Service Docket
PTE	Prohibited Transaction Exemption Decisions of the Office of Pension and Welfare Benefit Programs, Department of Labor
PUR3d	Public Utilities Reports, Third Series
PUR4th	Public Utilities Reports, Fourth Series
RD	Reappraisement Decision, U. S. Customs Court
RESPA	Real Estate Settlement Procedures Act
Rev Proc	Revenue Procedure
Rev Rul	Revenue Ruling
RIA	Research Institute of America
RIA Benefits Coord	RIA Benefits Coordinator
RIA Corp Capital Trans Coord	RIA Corporate Capital Transaction Coordinator
RIA Employee Ben Comp Coord	RIA Employee Benefits Compliance Coordinator
RIA Employment Coord	RIA Employee Coordinator
RIA Employ Discrim Coord	RIA Employment Discrimination Coordinator
RIA Estate Plan & Tax Co-	

ord.	RIA Estate Planning & Taxation Coordinator
RIA Exec Comp & Tax Co-ord.	RIA Executive Compensation & Taxation Coordinator
RIA Fed Tax Coord 2d	RIA Federal Tax Coordinator 2d
RIA Partnership & S Corp Coord	RIA Partnership & S Corporation Coordinator
RIA Pension Coord	RIA Pension Coordinator
RIA Real Estate Coord	RIA Real Estate Coordinator
RIA Tax Action Coord	RIA Tax Action Coordinator
RIA TC Memo	Tax Court Memorandum Decisions
RICO Bus Disp Guide	RICO Business Disputes Guide
RRRA	Regional Rail Reorganization Act
R.S.	Revised Statutes
RUSCC	Rules of United States Claims Court
S Ct.	United States Supreme Court Reporter
SE	South Eastern Reporter
SE2d.	South Eastern Reporter, Second Series
SEC	Securities and Exchange Commission Reports
So	Southern Reporter
So 2d	Southern Reporter, Second Series
Soc Sec LP	Social Security Law and Practice
Soc Sec Rep Serv	Social Security Reporter Service
Soc Sec & Unemployment Ins Rep.	Social Security and Unemployment Insurance Reporter
Sp Ct RRRA	Special Court, Regional Rail Reorganization Act
SSA	Social Security Administration
SSR	Social Security Rulings
Stat	Statutes at Large
STB.	Surface Transportation Board
SW	South Western Reporter
SW2d	South Western Reporter, Second Series
TC.	United States Tax Court Reports
TCM	Tax Court Memorandum
T Ct.	United States Tax Court
TD	Treasury Decisions
TD ATF.	Treasury Decisions concerning matters of Alcohol, Tobacco and Firearms Bureau
TIAS	Treaties and International Agreements Series
TMT & App Bd	Trademark Trial and Appeal Board
TNT	Tax Notes Today
UCCRS	Uniform Commercial Code Reporting Service
UCCRS2d	Uniform Commercial Code Reporting Service, Second Series
US.	United States Reports
USC	United States Code
USCMA	United States Court of Military Appeals

USCS	United States Code Service
USEPA GCO	United States Environmental Protection Agency, General Counsel Opinions
USEPA RCO	United States Environmental Protection Agency, Regional Counsel Opinions
USEPA NPDES	United States Environmental Protection Agency, National Pollutant Discharge Elimination System
USLW	United States Law Week
USPQ	United States Patents Quarterly
USSG	United States Sentencing Guidelines
UST....................	United States Treaties and Other International Agreements
USTC	United States Tax Cases
VA CAB	Veterans Administration Contract Appeals Board
VA GCO	Veterans Administration, General Counsel Opinions
Vet Apps	Court of Veterans Appeals Reporter
Vet App R	Rules of Veterans Appeals
WAB	Wage Appeals Board Decision, Dept. of Labor
WGL	Warren Gorham Lamont
WGL Employee Ben Comp Coord	WGL Employee Benefits Compliance Coordinator
WGL Employment Coord ..	WGL Employee Coordinator
WGL Employ Discrim Coord.....................	WGL Employment Discrimination Coordinator
WH Cases	Wage and Hour Cases
WH2d	Wage and Hour Cases, Second Series
WH Op Letter	Wage and Hour Opinion Letter

Legal Periodicals

ABA J	American Bar Association Journal
ABIJ	American Bankruptcy Institute Journal
Admin LJ Am U	Administrative Law Journal of American University
Admin L Rev	Administrative Law Review
Advoc (Boise)	Advocate (Boise, Id.)
AF L Rev	Air Force Law Review
AIPLA QJ................	AIPLA Quarterly Journal
Ak Bar Rag	Alaska Bar Rag
Akron L Rev	Akron Law Review
Akron Tax J	Akron Tax Journal
Ala Law	Alabama Lawyer
Ala L Rev...............	Alabama Law Review
Alaska L Rev............	Alaska Law Review
Alb L Envtl Outlook	Albany Law Environmental Outlook
Alb LJ Sci & Tech........	Albany Law Journal of Science and Technology
Alb L Rev...............	Albany Law Review

Am Bankr Inst L Rev......	American Bankruptcy Institute Law Review
Am Bankr LJ.............	American Bankruptcy Law Journal
Am B Found Res J	American Bar Foundation Research Journal
Am Bus LJ..............	American Business Law Journal
Am Crim L Rev..........	American Criminal Law Review
Am Indian L Rev	American Indian Law Review
Am J Comp L............	American Journal of Comparative Law
Am J Crim L	American Journal of Criminal Law
Am J Fam L	American Journal of Family Law
Am J Int'l L	American Journal of International Law
Am J L and Med..........	American Journal of Law and Medicine
Am J Legal Hist	American Journal of Legal History
Am J Tax Pol'y	American Journal of Tax Policy
Am J Trial Advoc	American Journal of Trial Advocacy
Am L Rev...............	American Law Review
Am U Int'l L Rev..........	American University International Law Review
Am U J Gender & L.......	American University Journal of Gender & the Law
Am UJ Gender Soc Pol'y & L	American University Journal of Gender, Social Policy & the Law
Am U J Int'l L & Pol'y	American University Journal of International Law and Policy
Am UL Rev	American University Law Review
Am U Modern Am	The Modern American
Animal L................	Animal Law
Ann Health L.............	Annals of Health Law
Antitrust Bull	Antitrust Bulletin
Antitrust LJ	Antitrust Law Journal
Arb J..................	Arbitration Journal
Ariz Atty	Arizona Attorney
Ariz J Int'l & Comp L......	Arizona Journal of International and Comparative Law
Ariz L Rev	Arizona Law Review
Ariz St LJ...............	Arizona State Law Journal
Ark L Rev...............	Arkansas Law Review
Army Law...............	Army Lawyer
Bank Dev J	Bankruptcy Developments Journal
Banking LJ..............	Banking Law Journal
Barry L Rev.............	Barry Law Review
Baylor L Rev............	Baylor Law Review
BBJ...................	Boston Bar Journal
BC Envtl Aff L Rev........	Boston College Environmental Affairs Law Review
BC Ind & Com LR	Boston College Industrial and Commercial Law Review
BC Int'l & Comp L Rev	Boston College International and Comparative Law Review

BC L Rev................	Boston College Law Review
BC Third World LJ........	Boston College Third World Law Journal
Behav Sci & L............	Behavior Sciences & the Law
Benefits LJ	Benefits Law Journal
Berkeley Bus LJ..........	Berkeley Business Law Journal
Berk J Afr-Am L & Pol'y ...	Berkeley Journal of African-American Law & Policy
Berkeley J Emp & Lab L...	Berkeley Journal of Employment and Labor Law
Berkeley J Int'l L.........	Berkeley Journal of International Law
Berkeley Tech LJ	Berkeley Technology Law Journal
Brook L Rev	Brooklyn Law Review
Brooklyn J Int'l L..........	Brooklyn Journal of International Law
Buff Intell Prop LJ	Buffalo Intellectual Property Law Journal
Buff L Rev	Buffalo Law Review
Buff Pub Interest LJ.......	Buffalo Public Interest Law Journal
BU Int'l LJ	Boston University International Law Journal
BU J Sci & Tech L	Boston University Journal of Science and Technology Law
BU L Rev................	Boston University Law Review
BU Pub Int LJ............	Boston University Public Interest Law Journal
Bus Law.................	Business Lawyer
BYU Educ & LJ	Brigham Young University Education and Law Journal
BYU J Pub L.............	Brigham Young University Journal of Public Law
BYU L Rev	Brigham Young University Law Review
Cal Bankr J..............	California Bankruptcy Journal
Cal Intl Prac	California International Practitioner
Cal Law	California Lawyer
Cal L Rev................	California Law Review
Cal Real Prop J	California Real Property Journal
Cal St BJ................	California State Bar Journal
Cal W Int'l LJ	California Western International Law Journal
Cal W L Rev.............	California Western Law Review
Campbell L Rev	Campbell Law Review
Cap Def J	Capital Defense Journal
Cap U L Rev.............	Capital University Law Review
Cardozo Arts & Ent LJ	Cardozo Arts and Entertainment Law Journal
Cardozo J Int'l & Comp L..	Cardozo Journal of International and Comparative Law
Cardozo JL & Gender.....	Cardozo Journal of Law & Gender
Cardozo L Rev	Cardozo Law Review
Cardozo Pub L Pol'y & Eth-ics J	Cardozo Public Law, Policy & Ethics Journal
Case W Res	Case Western Reserve Law Review
Case W Res J Int'l L......	Case Western Reserve Journal of International Law
Case W Res L Rev	Case Western Reserve Law Review

Cath Law	The Catholic Lawyer
Cath UL Rev	Catholic University Law Review
Champion	The Champion
Chap L Rev	Chapman Law Review
Chi B Rec	Chicago Bar Record
Chi J Int'l L	Chicago Journal of International Law
Chi-Kent L Rev	Chicago-Kent Law Review
Children's Legal Rts J	Children's Legal Rights Journal
Clearinghouse Rev	Clearinghouse Review
Clev St L Rev	Cleveland State Law Review
Colo J Int'l Envtl L & Pol'y	Colorado Journal of Environmental Law and Policy
Colo Law	Colorado Lawyer
Colum Bus L Rev	Columbia Business Law Review
Colum Human Rights L Rev	Columbia Human Rights Law Review
Colum J Envtl L	Columbia Journal of Environmental Law
Colum J Eur L	Columbia Journal of European Law
Colum J Gender & L	Columbia Journal of Gender and Law
Colum JL & Arts	Columbia Journal of Law & the Arts
Colum JL & Soc Probs	Columbia Journal of Law and Social Problems
Colum J Transnat'l L	Columbia Journal of Transnational Law
Colum L Rev	Columbia Law Review
Colum Sci & Tech L Rev	Columbia Science and Technology Law Review
Colum-VLA JL & Arts	Columbia-VLA Journal of Law and the Arts
Com LJ	Commercial Law Journal
Comm & L	Communications and the Law
Comm L & Pol'y	Communications Law & Policy
CommLaw Conspectus	CommLaw Conspectus: Journal of Communications Law and Policy
Comp Lab L & Pol'y J	Comparative Labor Law and Policy Journal
Comp Lab LJ	Comparative Labor Law Journal
Comp L Rev & Tech J	Computer Law Review and Technology Journal
Computer Internet Law	Computer & Internet Lawyer
Computer Law	Computer Lawyer
Computer LJ	Computer Law Journal
Conn BJ	Connecticut Bar Journal
Conn Ins LJ	Connecticut Insurance Law Journal
Conn J Int'l L	Connecticut Journal of International Law
Conn L Rev	Connecticut Law Review
Conn Pub Int LJ	Connecticut Public Interest Law Journal
Const Commentary	Constitutional Commentary
Copyright L Symp	Copyright Law Symposium
Copyright World	Copyright World
Cornell Int'l LJ	Cornell International Law Journal
Cornell J L & Pub Pol'y	Cornell Journal of Law and Public Policy
Cornell L Rev	Cornell Law Review
Corp L Rev	Corporation Law Review
Corp Prac Comment	Corporate Practice Commentator

Court Review	Court Review
Creighton L Rev	Creighton Law Review
Crim Def.	Criminal Defense
Crim L Bull.	Criminal Law Bulletin
Crim LQ	Criminal Law Quarterly
Cumb L Rev	Cumberland Law Review
Cum-Sam L Rev.	Cumberland-Samford Law Review
Dayton L Rev	University of Dayton Law Review
DCL J Int'l L & Prac.	Journal of International Law and Practice
DC L Rev.	University of the District of Columbia Law Review
Def Couns J	Defense Counsel Journal
Del J Corp L	Delaware Journal of Corporate Law
Del L Rev.	Delaware Law Review
Denver LJ	Denver Law Journal
Denv J Int'l L & Pol'y	Denver Journal of International Law and Policy
Denv UL Rev	Denver University Law Review
DePaul Bus & Com LJ	DePaul Business and Commercial Law Journal
DePaul Bus LJ	DePaul Business Law Journal
DePaul J Health Care L ...	DePaul Journal of Health Care Law
DePaul J Sports L Contemp Probs	DePaul Journal of Sports Law & Contemporary Problems
DePaul-LCA J Art & Ent L .	DePaul-LCA Journal of Art and Entertainment Law
DePaul L Rev	DePaul Law Review
Det CL Rev	Detroit College of Law Review
Dick J Int'l L	Dickinson Journal of International Law
Dick L Rev.	Dickinson Law Review
Drake J Agric L.	Drake Journal of Agricultural Law
Drake L Rev	Drake Law Review
Duke Env L & Pol'y F	Duke Environmental Law & Policy Forum
Duke J Comp & Int'l L.	Duke Journal of Comparative and International Law
Duke L & Tech Rev	Duke Law & Technology Review
Duke LJ	Duke Law Journal
Duq BLJ.	Duquesne Business Law Journal
Duq L Rev	Duquesne Law Review
Ecology LQ	Ecology Law Quarterly
Elder LJ	Elder Law Journal
E Min L Inst.	Eastern Mineral Law Institute
Emory Int'l L Rev	Emory International Law Review
Emory LJ	Emory Law Journal
Empl Rel LJ.	Employee Relations Law Journal
Empl Rts & Employ Pol'y J	Employee Rights and Employment Policy Journal
Energy LJ	Energy Law Journal
Ent L Rev.	Entertainment Law Review

Envtl Claims J.	Environmental Claims Journal
Envtl L	Environmental Law
Est Plan	Estate Planning
Fam Adv	Family Advocate
Fam LQ	
FCLR	Federal Courts Law Review
Fed BJ	Federal Bar Journal
Fed B News & J	Federal Bar News and Journal
Fed Cir BJ	Federal Circuit Bar Journal
Fed Comm LJ	Federal Communications Law Journal
Fed Cts L Rev	Federal Courts Law Review
Fed Law	Federal Lawyer
Fed L Rev	Federal Law Review
Fed Sent R	Federal Sentencing Reporter
Fed'n Def & Corp Couns Q	Federation of Defense & Corporate Counsel Quarterly
Fed'n Ins Couns Q	Federation of Insurance Counsel Quarterly
First Amend L Rev	First Amendment Law Review
Fla Bar J	Florida Bar Journal
Fla J Int'l L	Florida Journal of International Law
Fla L Rev	University of Florida Law Review
Fla St UL Rev	Florida State University Law Review
Fla Tax Rev	Florida Tax Review
Fl Coastal LJ	Florida Coastal Law Journal
Food Drug Cosm LJ	Food Drug and Cosmetic Law Journal
Food Drug Cosm & Med Device L Dig	Food, Drug, Cosmetic and Medical Device Law Digest
Food Drug LJ	Food and Drug Law Journal
Fordham Intell Prop Media & Ent LJ	Fordham Intellectual Property, Media & Entertainment Law Journal
Fordham Int'l LJ	Fordham International Law Journal
Fordham J Corp & Fin L . . .	Fordham Journal of Corporate & Financial Law
Fordham L Rev	Fordham Law Review
Fordham Urb LJ	Fordham Urban Law Journal
Ga BJ	Georgia Bar Journal
Ga J Int'l & Comp L	Georgia Journal of International and Comparative Law
Ga L Rev	Georgia Law Review
Ga St UL Rev	Georgia State University Law Review
Geo Immigr LJ	Georgetown Immigration Law Journal
Geo Int'l Envtl L Rev	Georgetown International Environmental Law Review
Geo J Gender & L	Georgetown Journal of Gender and the Law
Geo J Int'l L	Georgetown Journal of International Law
Geo JL & Pub Pol'y	Georgetown Journal of Law & Public Policy
Geo J Legal Ethics	Georgetown Journal of Legal Ethics

Geo J Poverty Law & Pol'y	Georgetown Journal on Poverty Law & Policy
Geo LJ	Georgetown Law Journal
Geo Mason L Rev	George Mason Law Review
Geo Mason U Civ Rts LJ	George Mason University Civil Rights Law Journal
Geo Wash Int'l L Rev	George Washington International Law Review
Geo Wash L Rev	George Washington Law Review
Golden Gate U L Rev	Golden Gate University Law Review
Gonz L Rev	Gonzaga Law Review
Green Bag 2d	Green Bag, Second Series
GW J Int'l L & Econ	George Washington Journal of International Law & Economics
Hamline J Pub L & Pol'y	Hamline Journal of Law and Public Policy
Hamline L Rev	Hamline Law Review
Harv BlackLetter J	Harvard BlackLetter Journal
Harv CR-CL L Rev	Harvard Civil Rights and Civil Liberties Law Review
Harv Envtl L Rev	Harvard Environmental Law Review
Harv Hum Rts J	Harvard Human Rights Journal
Harv Int'l LJ	Harvard International Law Journal
Harv J L & Gender	Harvard Journal of Law & Gender
Harv JL & Pub Pol'y	Harvard Journal of Law and Public Policy
Harv J Law & Tec	Harvard Journal of Law and Technology
Harv J on Legis	Harvard Journal on Legislation
Harv Latino L Rev	Harvard Latino Law Review
Harv L Rev	Harvard Law Review
Hastings Bus LJ	Hastings Business Law Journal
Hastings Comm & Ent LJ	Hastings Communications and Entertainment Law Journal
Hastings Const LQ	Hastings Constitutional Law Quarterly
Hastings Int'l & Comp L Rev	Hastings International and Comparative Law Review
Hastings LJ	Hastings Law Journal
Hastings W-NW J Envtl L & Pol'y	Hastings West-Northwest Journal of Environmental Law and Policy
Health Matrix	Health Matrix: Journal of Law Medicine
Hofstra Lab & Emp LJ	Hofstra Labor and Employment Law Journal
Hofstra Lab LJ	Hofstra Labor Law Journal
Hofstra L Rev	Hofstra Law Review
Hous Bus & Tax LJ	Houston Business and Tax Law Journal
Hous J Int'l L	Houston Journal of International Law
Hous L Rev	Houston Law Review
How LJ	Howard Law Journal
Idaho L Rev	Idaho Law Review
IDEA	IDEA: The Journal of Law and Technology
IFLR	International Financial Law Review
Ill BJ	Illinois Bar Journal

ILSA J Int'l & Comp L	ILSA Journal of International & Comparative Law
ILSA J Int'l L	ILSA Journal of International Law
Immigr Brief.	Immigration Briefings
Ind Health L Rev	Indiana Health Law Review
Ind Int'l & Comp L Rev	Indiana International and Comparative Law Review
Ind J Global Leg Stud	Indiana Journal of Global Legal Studies
Ind LJ	Indiana Law Journal
Ind L Rev	Indiana Law Review
Indus Rel LJ	Industrial Relations Law Journal
Ins Counsel J	Insurance Counsel Journal
Inst on Sec Reg	Institute on Securities Regulation (Practicing Law Institute)
Int'l & Comp LQ	International and Comparative Law Quarterly
Int'l Company & Com L Rev	International Company and Commercial Law Review
Int'l Law	International Lawyer
Int'l Legal Persp	International Legal Perspectives
Iowa J Corp L	The Journal of Corporation Law
Iowa L Rev	Iowa Law Review
ISJLP	I/S: Journal of Law and Policy for the Information Society
Issues L & Med	Issues in Law and Medicine
J Am Acad Matrimonial Law	Journal of the American Academy of Matrimonial Lawyers
J Agr Tax & L	Journal of Agricultural Taxation & Law
J Air L & Com	Journal of Air Law and Commerce
J App Prac & Proc	Journal of Appellate Practice and Process
J Arts Mgmt & Law	Journal of Arts Management and Law
J Bankr L & Prac	Journal of Bankruptcy Law and Practice
J Bus L	Journal of Business Law
J Contemp Health L & Pol'y	Journal of Contemporary Health Law & Policy
J Contemp L	Journal of Contemporary Law
J Copyright Soc'y USA	Journal of the Copyright Society of the USA
J Corp Tax'n	Journal of Corporate Taxation
J Crim L & Criminology. . . .	Journal of Criminal Law & Criminology
J Crim LC & PS	Journal of Criminal Law, Criminology, and Police Science
JC & UL	Journal of College and University Law
J Disp Resol	Journal of Dispute Resolution
J Envtl L & Litig	Journal of Environmental Law and Litigation
J Envtl Mgmt.	Journal of Environmental Management
J Fam L	Journal of Family Law
J Gender Race & Just.	Journal of Gender, Race and Justice
J Health & Biomed Law . . .	Journal of Health & Biomedical L
J Health & Hosp L	Journal of Health and Hospital Law
J Health L	Journal of Health Law

J High Tech L	Journal of High Technology Law
JICL	Journal of International & Comparative Law
J Intell Prop L	Journal of Intellectual Property Law
J Internet L	Journal of Internet Law
J Juv L	Journal of Juvenile Law
J Kan BA	Journal of the Kansas Bar Association
JL & Com.	Journal of Law and Commerce
JL & Econ	Journal of Law & Economics
J L & Educ.	Journal of Law & Education
J L & Politics	Journal of Law and Politics
JL & Pol'y	Journal of Law and Policy
J Land Use & Envtl L	Journal of Land Use and Environmental Law
J Law & Pub Pol'y	Florida Journal of Law and Public Policy
J Legal Aspects of Sport. . .	Journal of Legal Aspects of Sport
J Legal Med	Journal of Legal Medicine
J Legal Prof.	Journal of the Legal Profession
J Legal Stud	Journal of Legal Studies
J Legis	Journal of Legislation
J L Fam Stud	Journal of Law and Family Studies
JL Med & Ethics	Journal of Law, Medicine and Ethics
J L Soc'y	Journal of Law in Society
J Mar L & Com.	Journal of Maritime Law and Commerce
J Marshall J Computer & Info Law	John Marshall Journal of Computer and Information Law
J Marshall L Rev	John Marshall Law Review
J Mo B	Journal of the Missouri Bar
J NAALJ.	Journal of the National Association of Administrative Law Judges
J Nat Resources & Envtl L.	Journal of Natural Resources and Environmental Law
J NY State Bar Assoc	Journal (New York State Bar Association)
J Online L	Journal of Online Law
J Pat & Trademark Off Soc'y.	Journal of Patent and Trademark Office Society
J Psych & L.	Journal of Psychiatry & Law
J Real Est Tax'n	Journal of Real Estate Taxation
J Small & Emerging Bus L.	Journal of Small & Emerging Business Law
J St Taxn	Journal of State Taxation
J Tax'n	Journal of Taxation
J Tax'n Invest	Journal of Taxation of Investments
J Tech L & Pol'y	Journal of Technology Law & Policy
J Transnat'l L & Pol'y	Florida State University Journal of Transnational Law & Policy
J Transp L Logist & Pol'y . .	Journal of Transportation Law, Logistics and Policy
Judges' Journal	The Judges' Journal
Jurimetrics J	Jurimetrics Journal

Kan JL & Pub Pol'y	Kansas Journal of Law & Public Policy
Ky LJ	Kentucky Law Journal
La BJ	Louisiana Bar Journal
Lab LJ	Labor Law Journal
Lab Law	Labor Lawyer
La L Rev	Louisiana Law Review
Land & Water L Rev	Land and Water Law Review
L & Philosophy	Law and Philosophy
Law & Bus Rev Am	Law & Business Review of the Americas
Law & Contemp Probs	Law and Contemporary Problems
Law & Hist Rev.	Law and History Review
Law & Hum Behav.	Law and Human Behavior
Law & Ineq J.	Law and Inequality Journal of Theory and Practice
Law & Pol'y Int'l Bus	Law and Policy in International Business
Law & Sex.	Law and Sexuality A Review of Lesbian and Gay Legal Issues
Law & Soc Inquiry	Law and Social Inquiry
Law & Soc'y Rev	Law and Society Review
Law Libr J	Law Library Journal
Law Med & Health Care . . .	Law, Medicine & Health Care
Law Sea Inst Proc	Law of the Sea Institute Proceedings
Lawyers J	Lawyers Journal
Legal Ref Serv Q	Legal Reference Services Quarterly
Lewis & Clark L Rev	Lewis & Clark Law Review
Lincoln L Rev	Lincoln Law Review
Litig	Litigation
Loy Intell Prop & High Tech J.	Loyola Intellectual Property & High Technology Journal
Loy J Pub Int L.	Loyola Journal of Public Interest Law
Loy LA Ent LJ.	Loyola of Los Angeles Entertainment Law Journal
Loy LA Int'l & Comp LJ. . . .	Loyola of Los Angeles International and Comparative Law Journal
Loy LA Int'l & Comp L Rev.	Loyola of Los Angeles International & Comparative Law Review
Loy LA L Rev	Loyola of Los Angeles Law Review
Loy L Rev	Loyola Law Review
Loy Mar LJ	Loyola Maritime Law Journal
Loy U Chi LJ.	Loyola University Chicago Law Journal
L Rev MSU-DCL	Law Review of Michigan State University - Detroit College of Law
Maine BJ	Maine Bar Journal
Marq L Rev	Marquette Law Review
Marq Sports LJ.	Marquette Sports Law Journal
Marq Sports L Rev.	Marquette Sports Law Review
Mass L Rev.	Massachusetts Law Review

Mass LQ	Massachusetts Law Quarterly
McGeorge L Rev	McGeorge Law Review
Md BJ.	Maryland Bar Journal
Md J Int'l L & Trade.	Maryland Journal of International Law and Trade
Md L Rev.	Maryland Law Review
Me BJ.	Maine Bar Journal
Media L & Pol'y	Media Law and Policy
Med Trial Tech Q	Medical Trial Technique Quarterly
Me L Rev.	Maine Law Review
Mem St UL Rev	Memphis State University Law review
Mercer L Rev	Mercer Law Review
MI Bar Jnl	Michigan Bar Journal
Mich J Int'l L	Michigan Journal of International Law
Mich J Race & L.	Michigan Journal of Race & Law
Mich L Rev	Michigan Law Review
Mich St J Med & Law	Michigan State University Journal of Medicine and Law
Mich St L Rev.	Michigan State Law Review
Mich Telecomm Tech L Rev	Michigan Telecommunications and Technology Law Review
Mich YB Int'l Legal Stud . . .	Michigan Yearbook of International Legal Studies
Mil L Rev	Military Law Review
Minn Intell Prop Rev	Minnesota Intellectual Property Review
Minn J Global Trade	Minnesota Journal of Global Trade
Minn JL Sci & Tech	Minnesota Journal of Law, Science & Technology
Minn L Rev	Minnesota Law Review
Miss C L Rev	Mississippi College Law Review
Miss LJ.	Mississippi Law Journal
Mod L Rev.	Modern Law Review
Mo Envtl L & Pol'y Rev. . . .	Missouri Environmental Law and Policy Review
Mo L Rev.	Missouri Law Review
Mont L Rev	Montana Law Review
MSU-DCL J Int'l L	Michigan State University-DCL Journal of International Law
Mun Fin J.	Municipal Finance Journal
NAFTA L & Bus Rev Am. . .	NAFTA: Law & Business Review of the Americas
Nat'l Black LJ	National Black Law Journal
Nat'l J Crim Def	National Journal of Criminal Defense
N Atl Reg Bus L Rev.	North Atlantic Regional Business Law Review
Nat Resources & Envt.	Natural Resources and Environment
Nat Resources J.	Natural Resources Journal
Navy L Rev	Naval Law Review
NC Cent LJ	North Carolina Central Law Journal
NC J Int'l L & Com Reg . . .	North Carolina Journal of International Law and Commercial Regulation

NC L Rev...............	North Carolina Law Review
ND L Rev...............	North Dakota Law Review
Neb L Rev..............	Nebraska Law Review
NE J on Crim & Civ Con ..	New England Journal on Criminal and Civil Confinement
New Eng L Rev	New England Law Review
New LJ.................	New Law Journal
Nev LJ	Nevada Law Journal
NH BJ.................	New Hampshire Bar Journal
N Ill U L Rev.............	Northern Illinois University Law Review
NJ Law.................	New Jersey Lawyer
N Ky L Rev	Northern Kentucky Law Review
NM L Rev	New Mexico Law Review
Notre Dame Law	Notre Dame Lawyer
Notre Dame L Rev........	Notre Dame Law Review
Nova L Rev.............	Nova Law Review
Nw J Int'l L & Bus	Northwestern Journal of International Law and Business
Nw U L Rev..............	Northwestern University Law Review
NY Int'l L Rev	New York International Law Review
NY LF..................	New York Law Forum
NYL Sch J Hum Rts	New York Law School Journal of Human Rights
NYL Sch J Int'l & Comp L .	New York Law School Journal of International and Comparative Law
NYL Sch L Rev...........	New York Law School Law Review
NY St BJ	New York State Bar Journal
NYU Ann Surv Am L	New York University Annual Survey of American Law
NYU Conf on Lab.........	NYU Conference on Labor
NYU Envtl LJ	New York University Environmental Law Journal
NYU J Int'l L & Pol........	New York University Journal of International Law and Politics
NYU J Legis & Pub Pol'y..	New York University School of Law Journal of Legislation and Public Policy
NYU L Rev	New York University Law Review
NYU Rev L & Soc Change.	New York University Review of Law and Social Change
Ohio NU L Rev...........	Ohio Northern University Law Review
Ohio St J Crim L	Ohio State Journal of Criminal Law
Ohio St J on Disp Resol...	Ohio State Journal on Dispute Resolution
Ohio St LJ	Ohio State Law Journal
Oil & Gas Tax Q..........	Oil and Gas Tax Quarterly
Okla City UL Rev.........	Oklahoma City University Law Review
Okla L Rev	Oklahoma Law Review
Or L Rev	Oregon Law Review
Pa BAQ	Pennsylvania Bar Association Quarterly
Pace Envtl L Rev.........	Pace Environmental Law Review
Pace Int'l L Rev	Pace International Law Review

Pace L Rev	Pace Law Review
Pac LJ	Pacific Law Journal
Pac Rim L & Pol'y	Pacific Rim Law & Policy Journal
Pat World.	Patent World
Penn St L Rev	Pennsylvania State Law Review
Pepp L Rev	Pepperdine Law Review
Pierce L Rev	Pierce Law Review
Prac Law	Practical Lawyer
Prac Litig	Practical Litigator
Prac Real Est Law.	Practical Real Estate Lawyer
Prac Tax Law	Practical Tax Lawyer
Priv Inv Abroad.	Private Investments Abroad
Pub Cont LJ	Public Contract Law Journal
Pub Land and Resources L Reg.	Public Land and Resources Law Register
Pub Land L Rev	Public Land Law Review
Public Law.	Public Law
Quinnipiac L Rev	Quinnipiac Law Review/Bridgeport Law Review
Real Est LJ	Real Estate Law Journal
Real Prop Prob & Tr J.	Real Property, Probate and Trust Journal
Regent J Int'l L.	Regent Journal of International Law
Regent UL Rev.	Regent University Law Review
Res Gestae	Res Gestae
Rev Jur UPR.	Revista Juridica Universidad de Puerto Rico
Rev Litig.	Review of Litigation
Rev Tax Indiv	Review of Taxation of Individuals
RI Bar Jnl.	Rhode Island Bar Journal
Rich J L & Tech	Richmond Journal of Law & Technology
Rocky Mt Min L Inst.	Rocky Mountain Mineral Law Institute
Roger Williams U L Rev . . .	Roger Williams University Law Review
RRGC.	University of Maryland Law Journal of Race, Religion, Gender & Class
Rut Cam LJ	Rutgers-Camden Law Journal
Rutgers Computer & Tech LJ	Rutgers Computer and Technology Law Journal
Rutgers J Law & Relig	Rutgers Journal of Law and Religion
Rutgers LJ.	Rutgers Law Journal
Rutgers L Rec.	Rutgers Law Record
Rutgers L Rev.	Rutgers Law Review
Rutgers Race & L Rev	Rutgers Race and the Law Review
San Diego L Rev	San Diego Law Review
Santa Clara Computer & High Tech LJ	Santa Clara Computer and High Technology Law Journal
Santa Clara Law.	Santa Clara Lawyer
Santa Clara L Rev	Santa Clara Law Review
S Cal Interdis LJ.	Southern California Interdisciplinary Law Journal

S Cal L Rev..............	Southern California Law Review
S Carolina Lawyer........	South Carolina Lawyer
Sch L Bull	School Law Bulletin
SCHOLAR...............	Scholar: St. Mary's Law Review on Minority Issues
SC L Rev...............	South Carolina Law Review
S Ct Econ Rev	Supreme Court Economic Review
SD L Rev...............	South Dakota Law Review
Seattle Univ L R.........	Seattle University Law Review
Sec Reg LJ..............	Securities Regulation Law Journal
Sedona Conf J...........	The Sedona Conference Journal
Seton Hall Const LJ.......	Seton Hall Constitutional Law Journal
Seton Hall J Sports L	Seton Hall Journal of Sports Law
Seton Hall L Rev	Seton Hall Law Review
Seton Hall Legis J	Seton Hall Legislative Journal
S Ill U LJ	Southern Illinois University Law Journal
SMU L Rev	SMU (Southern Methodist) Law Review
Sports Law J.............	Sports Lawyers Journal
Stan Envtl LJ.............	Stanford Environmental Law Journal
Stan JCR & CL..........	Stanford Journal of Civil Rights and Civil Liberties
Stan J Int'l L	Stanford Journal of International Law
Stan JL Bus & Fin	Stanford Journal of Law, Business & Finance
Stan L Rev	Stanford Law Review
Stetson L Rev............	Stetson Law Review
S Tex L Rev.............	South Texas Law Review
St John's L Rev	St John's Law Review
St John's JL Comm.......	St John's Journal of Legal Commentary
St Louis U LJ	Saint Louis University Law Journal
St Louis U Pub L Rev	St. Louis University Public Law Review
St Mary's LJ	St Mary's Law Journal
St Thomas L Rev.........	St Thomas Law Review
Suffolk J Trial & App Adv ..	Suffolk Journal of Trial and Appellate Advocacy
Suffolk Transnat'l LJ	Suffolk Transnational Law Journal
Suffolk U L Rev	Suffolk University Law Review
SU L Rev................	Southern University Law Review
Sup Ct Rev	Supreme Court Review
Sw JL & Trade Am........	Southwestern Journal of Law and Trade in the Americas
Sw LJ..................	Southwestern Law Journal
Sw U L Rev..............	Southwestern University Law Review
Syracuse J Int'l L & Com ..	Syracuse Journal of International Law and Commerce
Syracuse L Rev	Syracuse Law Review
Taxes	CCH Taxes—The Tax Magazine
Tax L Rev	Tax Law Review
Temp Envtl L & Tech J	Temple Environmental Law and Technology Journal

Temp L Rev..............	Temple Law Review
Temp Pol & Civ Rts L Rev.	Temple Political and Civil Rights Law Review
Tenn BJ	Tennessee Bar Journal
Tenn L Rev	Tennessee Law Review
Tex BJ	Texas Bar Journal
Tex F on CL & CR........	Texas Forum on Civil Liberties & Civil Rights
Tex Hisp JL & Pol'y	Texas Hispanic Journal of Law and Policy
Tex Intell Prop LJ........	Texas Intellectual Property Law Journal
Tex Int'l LJ..............	Texas International Law Journal
Tex J Women & L	Texas Journal of Women and the Law
Tex L Rev	Texas Law Review
Tex Rev Ent & Sports L ...	Texas Review of Entertainment & Sports Law
Tex Rev Law & Pol	Texas Review of Law and Politics
Tex Tech J Tex Admin L ...	Texas Tech Journal of Texas Administrative Law
Tex Tech L Rev...........	Texas Tech Law Review
Tex Wesleyan L Rev	Texas Wesleyan Law Review
Theoretical Inq L	Theoretical Inquiries in Law
The Record..............	Record of the Association of Bar of the City of New York
T Jefferson L Rev.........	Thomas Jefferson Law Review
T Marshall L Rev	Thurgood Marshall Law Review
TM Cooley L Rev.........	Thomas M Cooley Law Review
Tort & Ins LJ.............	Tort and Insurance Law Journal
Touro L Rev.............	Touro Law Review
Trademark Rep...........	Trademark Reporter
Trademark World	Trademark World
Transnat'l L & Contemp Probs	Transnational Law & Contemporary Problems
Transnat'l Law	Transnational Lawyer
Transp LJ................	Transportation Law Journal
Trial....................	Trial
Trial Law Guide	Trial Lawyer Guide
Tul Envtl LJ..............	Tulane Environmental Law Journal
Tul Eur & Civ LF	The Tulane European & Civil Law Forum
Tul J Int'l & Comp L.......	Tulane Journal of International and Comparative Law
Tul L Rev...............	Tulane Law Review
Tul Mar LJ..............	Tulane Maritime Law Journal
Tulsa J Comp & Int'l L	Tulsa Journal of Comparative and International Law
Tulsa LJ.................	Tulsa Law Journal
U Ark Little Rock L Rev ...	University of Arkansas Little Rock Law Review
U Balt Intell Prop LJ	University of Baltimore Intellectual Property Law Journal
U Balt J Envtl L	University of Baltimore Journal of Environmental Law
U Balt L Rev	University of Baltimore Law Review

UCC LJ	Uniform Commercial Code Law Journal
UC Davis Bus LJ	Business Law Journal, University of California, Davis
UC Davis J Juv L & Pol'y . .	UC Davis Journal of Juvenile Law & Policy
UC Davis L Rev	UC Davis Law Review
U Chi L Rev	University of Chicago Law Review
U Chi Legal F	University of Chicago Legal Forum
U Cin L Rev	University of Cincinnati Law Review
UCLA Alaska L Rev	UCLA Alaska Law Review
UCLA Ent L Rev	UCLA Entertainment Law Review
UCLA J Envtl L & Pol'y	UCLA Journal of Environmental Law and Policy
UCLA JL & Tech	UCLA Journal of Law & Technology
UCLA L Rev	UCLA Law Review
UCLA Pac Basin LJ	UCLA Pacific Basin Law Journal
UCLA Women's LJ	UCLA Women's Law Journal
U Colo L Rev	University of Colorado Law Review
U Dayton L Rev	University of Dayton Law Review
U Det J Urb L	University of Detroit Journal of Urban Law
U Det Mercy L Rev	University of Detroit Mercy Law Review
U Fla JL & Pub Pol'y	University of Florida Journal of Law and Public Policy
U Haw L Rev	University of Hawaii Law Review
U Ill JL Tech & Pol'y	University of Illinois Journal of Law, Technology and Policy
U Ill LF	University of Illinois Law Forum
U Ill L Rev	University of Illinois Law Review
U Kan L Rev	University of Kansas Law Review
U Mem L Rev	University of Memphis Law Review
U Miami Bus L Rev	University of Miami Business Law Review
U Miami Inter-Am L Rev . . .	University of Miami Inter-American Law Review
U Miami L Rev	University of Miami Law Review
U Mich JL Reform	University of Michigan Journal of Law Reform
UMKC L Rev	University of Missouri at Kansas City Law Review
U of Louisville J of Fam L .	University of Louisville Journal of Family Law
U Pa J Const L	University of Pennsylvania Journal of Constitutional Law
U Pa J Int'l Econ L	University of Pennsylvania Journal of International Economic Law
U Pa J Lab & Emp L	University of Pennsylvania Journal of Labor and Employment Law
U Pa L Rev	University of Pennsylvania Law Review
U Pitt L Rev	University of Pittsburgh Law Review
U Puget Sound L Rev	University of Puget Sound Law Review
Urb Law	The Urban Lawyer
U Rich L Rev	University of Richmond Law Review
USAFA J Leg Stud	United States Air Force Academy Journal of Legal Studies

USF L Rev...............	University of San Francisco Law Review
Utah L Rev	Utah Law Review
UTLJ....................	University of Toronto Law Journal
U Tol L Rev..............	University of Toledo Law Review
U West LA L Rev.........	University of West Los Angeles Law Review
Va Envtl LJ	Virginia Environmental Law Journal
Va J Int'l L...............	Virginia Journal of International Law
Va JL & Tech.............	Virginia Journal of Law and Technology
Va J Soc Pol'y & L........	Virginia Journal of Social Policy and the Law
Va J Sports & L	Virginia Journal of Sports and the Law
Va L Rev	Virginia Law Review
Val UL Rev	Valparaiso University Law Review
Va Tax Rev	Virginia Tax Review
Vand J Ent & Tech L......	Vanderbilt Journal of Entertainment & Technology Law
Vand J Transnat'l L	Vanderbilt Journal of Transnational Law
Vand L Rev	Vanderbilt Law Review
Va Sports & Ent LJ	Virginia Sports & Entertainment Law Journal
Vill Envtl LJ	Villanova Environmental Law Journal
Vill L Rev	Villanova Law Review
Vill Sports & Ent LJ	Villanova Sports and Entertainment Law Journal
Vt L Rev.................	Vermont Law Review
Wake Forest Intell Prop LJ.	Wake Forest Intellectual Property Law Journal
Wake Forest L Rev	Wake Forest Law Review
Wash & Lee J Civ Rts & Soc Just....................	Washington & Lee Journal of Civil Rights & Social Justice
Wash & Lee L Rev........	Washington and Lee Law Review
Washburn LJ.............	Washburn Law Journal
Wash L Rev..............	Washington Law Review
Wash St B News	Washington State Bar News
Wash U Global Stud L Rev	Washington University Global Studies Law Review
Wash U JL & Pol'y........	Washington University Journal of Law & Policy
Wash U J Urb & Contemp L	Washington University Journal of Urban and Contemporary Law
Wash U LQ	Washington University Law Quarterly
Wayne L Rev	Wayne Law Review
Westchester BJ	Westchester Bar Journal
Whittier L Rev............	Whittier Law Review
Widener J Pub L	Widener Journal of Public Law
Widener L Rev	Widener Law Review
Widener L Symp J	Widener Law Symposium Journal
Willamette J Int'l L & Dispute Res	Willamette Journal of International Law and Dispute Resolution
Willamette L Rev	Willamette Law Review

ABBREVIATIONS

Wis B Bull	Wisconsin Bar Bulletin
Wis Int'l LJ.	Wisconsin International Law Journal
Wis Law.	Wisconsin Lawyer
Wis L Rev	Wisconsin Law Review
Wis Women's LJ	Wisconsin Women's Law Journal
Wm & Mary Bill of Rts J. . .	William and Mary Bill of Rights Journal
Wm & Mary J Envtl L	William and Mary Journal of Environmental Law
Wm & Mary J of Women & L	William and Mary Journal of Women and the Law
Wm & Mary L Rev	William and Mary Law Review
Wm Mitchell L Rev.	William Mitchell Law Review
Women's Rts L Rep.	Women's Rights Law Reporter
W New Eng L Rev.	Western New England Law Review
W St U L Rev	Western State University Law Review
W Va L Rev.	West Virginia Law Review
Yale HR & Dev LJ	Yale Human Rights and Development Law Journal
Yale J Int'l L	Yale Journal of International Law
Yale JL & Feminism.	Yale Journal of Law & Feminism
Yale JL & Human.	Yale Journal of Law and the Humanities
Yale JL & Tech	Yale Journal of Law and Technology
Yale J on Reg.	Yale Journal on Regulation
Yale L & Pol'y Rev.	Yale Law and Policy Review
Yale LJ.	Yale Law Journal
Yearbook of Int'l Law.	Yearbook of International Law

TABLE OF CONTENTS

TITLE 42—Public Health and Welfare

[Chapters 135 through 148 are contained in this volume.]

TABLE OF CONTENTS

TABLE OF CONTENTS

TABLE OF CONTENTS

TABLE OF CONTENTS

THE CODE OF THE LAWS

OF THE

UNITED STATES OF AMERICA

TITLE 42 — THE PUBLIC HEALTH AND WELFARE

STANDARDS AND OBLIGATIONS OF RESIDENCY IN FEDERALLY ASSISTED HOUSING

CROSS REFERENCES

This subtitle (42 USCS §§ 13601 et seq.) is referred to in 12 USCS § 1701q; 42 USCS §§ 1437d, 1437f.

§ 13601. Compliance by owners as condition of Federal assistance

The Secretary of Housing and Urban Development shall require owners of federally assisted housing (as such term is defined in section 683(2) [42 USCS § 13641(2)]), as a condition of receiving housing assistance for such housing, to comply with the procedures and requirements established under this subtitle [42 USCS §§ 13601 et seq.].

(Oct. 28, 1992, P. L. 102-550, Title VI, Subtitle C, § 641, 106 Stat. 3820.)

HISTORY; ANCILLARY LAWS AND DIRECTIVES

Other provisions:
Application of section. Act Oct. 28, 1992, P. L. 102-550, Title VI, Subtitle F, § 684, 106 Stat. 3832, which appears as 42 USCS § 13642, provides that this section is applicable upon expiration of the 6-month period beginning on enactment.

§ 13602. Compliance with criteria for occupancy as requirement for tenancy

In selecting tenants for occupancy of units in federally assisted housing, an owner of such housing shall utilize the criteria for occupancy in federally assisted housing established by the Secretary, by regulation, under section 643 [42 USCS § 13603]. If an owner determines that an applicant for occupancy in the housing does not meet such criteria, the owner may deny such applicant occupancy.

(Oct. 28, 1992, P. L. 102-550, Title VI, Subtitle C, § 642, 106 Stat. 3821.)

HISTORY; ANCILLARY LAWS AND DIRECTIVES

Other provisions:
Application of section. Act Oct. 28, 1992, P. L. 102-550, Title VI, Subtitle F, § 684, 106 Stat. 3832, which appears as 42 USCS § 13642, provides that this section is applicable upon expiration of the 6-month period beginning on enactment.

§ 13603. Establishment of criteria for occupancy

(a) **Task force.** (1) Establishment. To assist the Secretary in establishing reasonable criteria for occupancy in federally assisted housing, the Secretary shall establish a task force to review all rules, policy statements, handbooks, technical assistance memoranda, and other relevant documents issued by the Department of Housing and Urban Development on the standards and obligations governing residency in federally assisted housing and make recommendations to the Secretary for the establishment of such criteria for occupancy.

(2) Members. The Secretary shall appoint members to the task force, which shall include individuals representing the interests of owners, managers, and tenants of federally assisted housing, public housing agencies, owner and tenant advocacy organizations, persons with disabilities and disabled families, organizations assisting homeless individuals, and social service, mental health, and other nonprofit servicer providers who serve federally assisted housing.

(3) Compensation. Members of the task force shall not receive compensation for serving on the task force.

(4) Duties. The task force shall—

(A) review all existing standards, regulations, and guidelines governing occupancy and tenant selection policies in federally assisted housing;

(B) review all existing standards, regulations, and guidelines governing lease provisions and other rules of occupancy for federally assisted housing;

(C) determine whether the standards, regulations, and guidelines reviewed under subparagraphs (A) and (B) provide sufficient guidance to owners and managers of federally assisted housing to—

(i) develop procedures for preselection inquiries sufficient to determine the capacity of applicants to comply with reasonable lease terms and conditions of occupancy;

(ii) utilize leases that prohibit behavior which endangers the health or safety of other tenants or violates the rights of other tenants to peaceful enjoyment of the premises;

(iii) assess the need to provide, and appropriate measures for providing, reasonable accommodations required under the Fair Housing Act [42 USCS §§ 3601 et seq.] and section 504 of the Rehabilitation Act of 1973 [29 USCS § 794] for persons with various types of disabilities; and

(iv) comply with civil rights laws and regulations;

(D) propose criteria for occupancy in federally assisted housing, standards for the reasonable performance and behavior of tenants of federally assisted housing, compliance standards consistent with the reasonable accommodation of the requirements of the Fair Housing Act [42 USCS §§ 3601 et seq.] and section 504 of the Rehabilitation Act of 1973 [29 USCS § 794], standards for compliance with other civil rights laws, and procedures for the eviction of tenants not complying with such standards consistent with sections 6 and 8 of the United States Housing Act of 1937 [42 USCS §§ 1437d and 1437f]; and

(E) report to the Congress and the Secretary of Housing and Urban Development pursuant to paragraph (7).

(5) Procedure. In carrying out its duties, the task force shall hold public hearings and receive written comments for a period of not less than 60 days.

(6) Support. The Secretary of Housing and Urban Development shall cooperate fully with the task force and shall provide support staff and office space to assist the task force in carrying out its duties.

(7) Reports. Not later than 3 months after the date of enactment of this Act [enacted Oct. 28, 1992], the task force shall submit to the Secretary and the Congress a preliminary report describing its initial actions. Not later than 6 months after the date of enactment of this Act [enacted Oct. 28, 1992], the task force shall submit a report to the Secretary and the Congress, which shall include—

(A) a description of its findings; and

(B) recommendations to revise such standards, regulations, and guidelines to provide accurate and complete guidance to owners and managers of federally assisted housing as determined necessary under paragraph (4).

(b) **Rulemaking.** (1) Authority. The Secretary shall, by regulation, establish criteria for selection of tenants for occupancy in federally assisted housing and lease provisions for such housing.

(2) Standards. The criteria shall provide sufficient guidance to owners and managers of federally assisted housing to enable them to (A) select tenants capable of complying with reasonable lease terms, (B) utilize leases prohibiting behavior which endangers the health or safety of others or violates the right of other tenants to peaceful enjoyment of the premises, (C) comply with legal requirements to make reasonable accommodations for persons with disabilities, and (D) comply with civil rights laws. The criteria shall be consistent with the requirements under subsections (k) and (l) of section 6 and section 8(d)(1) of the United States Housing Act of 1937 [42 USCS §§ 1437d(k), (l) and 1437f(d)(1)] and any similar contract and lease requirements for federally assisted housing. In establishing the criteria, the Secretary shall take into consideration the report of the task force under subsection (a)(7).

(3) Procedure. Not later than 90 days after the submission of the final report under subsection (a)(7), the Secretary shall issue a notice of proposed rulemaking of the regulations under this subsection providing for notice and opportunity for public comment regarding the regulations, pursuant to the provisions of section 553 of title 5, United States Code (notwithstanding subsections (a)(2), (b)(B), and (d)(3) of such section). The duration of the period for public comment under such section 553 shall not be less than 60 days. The Secretary shall issue final regulations under this subsection not later than the expiration of the 60-day period beginning upon the conclusion of the comment period, which shall take effect upon issuance.

(Oct. 28, 1992, P. L. 102-550, Title VI, Subtitle C, § 643, 106 Stat. 3821.)

HISTORY; ANCILLARY LAWS AND DIRECTIVES

References in text:
The "civil rights laws", referred to in subsecs. (a)(4)(C)(iv), (D), and (b)(2)(D), appear generally as 42 USCS §§ 1981 et seq.

Other provisions:
Application of section. Act Oct. 28, 1992, P. L. 102-550, Title VI, Subtitle F, § 684, 106 Stat. 3832, which appears as 42 USCS § 13642, provides that this section is applicable upon expiration of the 6-month period beginning on enactment.

CROSS REFERENCES
This section is referred to in 42 USCS § 13602.

§ 13604. Assisted applications

(a) Authority. The Secretary shall provide that any individual or family applying for occupancy in federally assisted housing may include in the application for the housing the name, address, phone number, and other relevant information of a family member, friend or social, health, advocacy, or other organization, and that the owner shall treat such information as confidential.

(b) Maintenance of information. The Secretary shall require the owner of any federally assisted housing receiving an application including such information to maintain such information for any applicants who become tenants of the housing for the purposes of facilitating contact by the owner with such person or organization to assist in providing any services or special care for the tenant and assist in resolving any relevant tenancy issues arising during the tenancy of such tenant.

(c) Limitations. An owner of federally assisted housing may not require any individual or family applying for occupancy in the housing to provide the information described in subsection (a).
(Oct. 28, 1992, P. L. 102-550, Title VI, Subtitle C, § 644, 106 Stat. 3823.)

HISTORY; ANCILLARY LAWS AND DIRECTIVES

Other provisions:
Application of section. Act Oct. 28, 1992, P. L. 102-550, Title VI, Subtitle F, § 684, 106 Stat. 3832, which appears as 42 USCS § 13642, provides that this section is applicable upon expiration of the 6-month period beginning on enactment.

AUTHORITY TO PROVIDE PREFERENCES FOR ELDERLY RESIDENTS AND UNITS FOR DISABLED RESIDENTS IN CERTAIN SECTION 8 ASSISTED HOUSING

CROSS REFERENCES
This subtitle (42 USCS §§ 13611 et seq.) is referred to in 42 USCS § 1437f.

§ 13611. Authority

Notwithstanding any other provision of law, an owner of a covered section 8 housing project (as such term is defined in section 659 [42 USCS § 13619]) designed primarily for occupancy by elderly families may, in selecting tenants for units in the project that become available for occupancy, give preference to elderly families who have applied for occupancy in the housing, subject to the requirements of this subtitle [42 USCS §§ 13611 et seq.].
(Oct. 28, 1992, P. L. 102-550, Title VI, Subtitle D, § 651, 106 Stat. 3823.)

HISTORY; ANCILLARY LAWS AND DIRECTIVES

Other provisions:
Application of section. Act Oct. 28, 1992, P. L. 102-550, Title VI, Subtitle F, § 684, 106 Stat. 3832, which appears as 42 USCS § 13642, provides that this section is applicable upon expiration of the 6-month period beginning on enactment.

CODE OF FEDERAL REGULATIONS
Office of the Assistant Secretary for Housing-Federal Housing Commissioner, Department of Housing and Urban Development (Section 8 Housing Assistance Programs, etc.)—Section 8 housing assistance payments program for new construction, 24 CFR 880.101 et seq.
Office of the Assistant Secretary for Housing-Federal Housing Commissioner, Department of Housing and Urban Development (Section 8 Housing Assistance Programs, etc.)—Section 8 housing assistance payments program for substantial rehabilitation, 24 CFR 881.101 et seq.

Office of the Assistant Secretary for Housing-Federal Housing Commissioner, Department of Housing and Urban Development (Section 8 Housing Assistance Programs, etc.)—Section 8 housing assistance payments program-State housing agencies, 24 CFR 883.101 et seq.

Office of the Assistant Secretary for Housing-Federal Housing Commissioner, Department of Housing and Urban Development (Section 8 Housing Assistance Programs, etc.)—Section 8 housing assistance payments program, new construction set-aside for Section 515 rural rental housing projects, 24 CFR 884.101 et seq.

Office of the Assistant Secretary for Housing-Federal Housing Commissioner, Department of Housing and Urban Development (Section 8 Housing Assistance Programs, etc.)—Section 8 housing assistance payments program-special allocations, 24 CFR 886.101 et seq.

CROSS REFERENCES

This section is referred to in 42 USCS §§ 13612, 13613, 13615.

§ 13612. Reservation of units for disabled families

(a) Requirement. Notwithstanding any other provision of law, for any project for which an owner gives preference in occupancy to elderly families pursuant to section 651 [42 USCS § 13611], such owner shall (subject to sections 653, 654, and 655 [42 USCS §§ 13613, 13614 and 13615]) reserve units in the project for occupancy only by disabled families who are not elderly or near-elderly families (and who have applied for occupancy in the housing) in the number determined under subsection (b).

(b) Number of units. Each owner required to reserve units in a project for occupancy under subsection (a) shall reserve a number of units in the project that is not less than the lesser of—

(1) the number of units equivalent to the higher of—

(A) the percentage of units in the project that were occupied by such disabled families upon the date of the enactment of this Act [enacted Oct. 28, 1992]; or

(B) the percentage of units in the project that were occupied by such families upon January 1, 1992; or

(2) 10 percent of the number of units in the project.

(Oct. 28, 1992, P. L. 102-550, Title VI, Subtitle D, § 652, 106 Stat. 3823.)

HISTORY; ANCILLARY LAWS AND DIRECTIVES

Other provisions:

Application of section. Act Oct. 28, 1992, P. L. 102-550, Title VI, Subtitle F, § 684, 106 Stat. 3832, which appears as 42 USCS § 13642, provides that this section is applicable upon expiration of the 6-month period beginning on enactment.

CROSS REFERENCES

This section is referred to in 42 USCS §§ 13613, 13615, 13616.

§ 13613. Secondary preferences

(a) Insufficient elderly families. If an owner of a covered section 8 housing project in which elderly families are given a preference for occupancy pursuant to section 651 [42 USCS § 13611] determines (in accordance with regulations established by the Secretary) that there are insufficient numbers of elderly families who have applied for occupancy in the housing to fill all the units in the project not reserved under section 652 [42 USCS § 13612], the owner may give preference for occupancy of such units to disabled families who are near-elderly families and have applied for occupancy in the housing.

(b) Insufficient non-elderly disabled families. If an owner of a covered section 8 housing project in which elderly families are given a preference for occupancy pursuant to section 651 [42 USCS § 13611] determines (in accordance with regulations established by the Secretary) that there are insufficient numbers of disabled families who are not elderly or near-elderly families and have applied for occupancy in the housing to fill all the units in the project reserved under section 652 [42 USCS § 13612], the owner may give preference for occupancy of units so reserved to disabled families who are near-elderly families and have applied for occupancy in the housing.

(Oct. 28, 1992, P. L. 102-550, Title VI, Subtitle D, § 653, 106 Stat. 3824.)

HISTORY; ANCILLARY LAWS AND DIRECTIVES

References in text:
"Covered section 8 housing", referred to in this section, is defined in 42 USCS § 13619.

Other provisions:
Application of section. Act Oct. 28, 1992, P. L. 102-550, Title VI, Subtitle F, § 684, 106 Stat. 3832, which appears as 42 USCS § 13642, provides that this section is applicable upon expiration of the 6-month period beginning on enactment.

CROSS REFERENCES
This section is referred to in 42 USCS §§ 13612, 13614, 13615.

§ 13614. General availability of units

If an owner of a covered section 8 housing project in which disabled families who are near-elderly families are given a preference for occupancy pursuant to subsection (a) or (b) of section 653 [42 USCS § 13613] determines (in accordance with regulations established by the Secretary) that there are an insufficient number of such families to fill all the units in the project for which the preference is applicable, the owner shall make such units generally available for occupancy by families who have applied, and are eligible, for occupancy in the housing, without regard to the preferences established pursuant to this subtitle [42 USCS §§ 13611 et seq.].

(Oct. 28, 1992, P. L. 102-550, Title VI, Subtitle D, § 654, 106 Stat. 3824.)

HISTORY; ANCILLARY LAWS AND DIRECTIVES
References in text:
"Covered section 8 housing", referred to in this section, is defined in 42 USCS § 13619.

Other provisions:
Application of section. Act Oct. 28, 1992, P. L. 102-550, Title VI, Subtitle F, § 684, 106 Stat. 3832, which appears as 42 USCS § 13642, provides that this section is applicable upon expiration of the 6-month period beginning on enactment.

CROSS REFERENCES
This section is referred to in 42 USCS § 13612.

§ 13615. Preference within groups

Among disabled families qualifying for occupancy in units reserved under section 652 [42 USCS § 13612], and among elderly families and near-elderly families qualifying for preference for occupancy pursuant to section 651 or 653 [42 USCS § 13611 or 13613], preference for occupancy in units that are assisted under section 8 of the United States Housing Act of 1937 [42 USCS § 1437f] shall be given to disabled families according to any preferences established under any system established under section 8(d)(1)(A) [42 USCS § 1437f(d)(1)(A)] by the public housing agency.
(Oct. 28, 1992, P. L. 102-550, Title VI, Subtitle D, § 655, 106 Stat. 3824; Jan. 26, 1996, P. L. 104-99, Title IV, § 402(d)(6)(C), 110 Stat. 43; Oct. 21, 1998, P. L. 105-276, Title V, Subtitle A, § 514(b)(2)(B), 112 Stat. 2548.)

HISTORY; ANCILLARY LAWS AND DIRECTIVES
Amendments:
1996. Act Jan. 6, 1996 (effective on enactment and only for fiscal years 1996, 1997, and 1998, and to cease to be effective 10/21/1998, as provided by § 402(f) of such Act, as amended, and § 514(f) of Act Oct. 21, 1998, P. L. 105-276, which appear as 42 § 1437a notes) substituted "any preferences" for "the preferences for occupancy referred to in section 8(d)(1)(A)(i) of the United States Housing Act of 1937 and the first sentence of section 8(o)(3)(B) of such Act, to elderly families according to such preferences, and to near-elderly families according to such preferences, respectively".

1998. Act Oct. 21, 1998 (effective on, and applicable beginning upon, 10/21/98, as provided by § 514(g) of such Act, which appears as 12 USCS § 1701s note) substituted "shall be given to disabled families according to any preferences established under any system established under section 8(d)(1)(A) by the public housing agency." for "shall be given to disabled families according to the preferences for occupancy referred to in section 8(d)(1)(A)(i) of the United States Housing Act of 1937 and the first sentence of section 8(o)(3)(B) of such Act, to elderly families according to such preferences, and to near-elderly families according to such preferences, respectively.".

Other provisions:
Application of section. Act Oct. 28, 1992, P. L. 102-550, Title VI, Subtitle F, § 684, 106 Stat. 3832, which appears as 42 USCS § 13642, provides that this section is applicable upon expiration of the 6-month period beginning on enactment.

CROSS REFERENCES
This section is referred to in 42 USCS § 13612.

§ 13616. Prohibition of evictions

Any tenant who, except for reservation of a percentage of the units of a project pursuant to section 652 [42 USCS § 13612] or any preference for occupancy established pursuant to this subtitle, is lawfully residing in a dwelling unit in a covered section 8 housing project, may not be evicted or otherwise required to vacate such unit because of the reservation or preferences or because of any action taken by the Secretary of Housing and Urban Development or the owner of the project pursuant to this subtitle [42 USCS §§ 13611 et seq.].
(Oct. 28, 1992, P. L. 102-550, Title VI, Subtitle D, § 656, 106 Stat. 3824.)

HISTORY; ANCILLARY LAWS AND DIRECTIVES

References in text:
"Covered section 8 housing", referred to in this section, is defined in 42 USCS § 13619.

Other provisions:
Application of section. Act Oct. 28, 1992, P. L. 102-550, Title VI, Subtitle F, § 684, 106 Stat. 3832, which appears as 42 USCS § 13642, provides that this section is applicable upon expiration of the 6-month period beginning on enactment.

§ 13617. Treatment of covered section 8 housing not subject to elderly preference

If an owner of any covered section 8 housing project designed primarily for occupancy by elderly families does not give preference in occupancy to elderly families as authorized in this subtitle, then elderly families (as such term was defined in section 3 of the United States Housing Act of 1937 [42 USCS § 1437a] before the date of the enactment of this Act [enacted Oct. 28, 1992]) shall be eligible for occupancy in such housing to the same extent that such families were eligible before the date of the enactment of this Act [enacted Oct. 28, 1992].
(Oct. 28, 1992, P. L. 102-550, Title VI, Subtitle D, § 657, 106 Stat. 3825.)

HISTORY; ANCILLARY LAWS AND DIRECTIVES

References in text:
"Covered section 8 housing", referred to in this section, is defined in 42 USCS § 13619.

Other provisions:
Application of section. Act Oct. 28, 1992, P. L. 102-550, Title VI, Subtitle F, § 684, 106 Stat. 3832, which appears as 42 USCS § 13642, provides that this section is applicable upon expiration of the 6-month period beginning on enactment.

§ 13618. Treatment of other federally assisted housing

(a) Restricted occupancy. An owner of any federally assisted project (or portion of a project) as described in subparagraphs (D), (E), and (F) of section 683(2) [42 USCS § 13641(2)(D), (E), and (F)] that was designed for occupancy by elderly families may continue to restrict occupancy in such project (or portion) to elderly families in accordance with the rules, standards, and agreements governing occupancy in such housing in effect at the time of the development of the housing.

(b) Prohibition of evictions. Any tenant who is lawfully residing in a dwelling unit in a housing project described in subsection (a) may not be evicted or otherwise required to vacate such unit because of any reservation or preferences under this subtitle [42 USCS §§ 13611 et seq.] or because of any action taken by the Secretary of Housing and Urban Development or the owner of the project pursuant to this subtitle [42 USCS §§ 13611 et seq.].

(Oct. 28, 1992, P. L. 102-550, Title VI, Subtitle D, § 658, 106 Stat. 3825.)

HISTORY; ANCILLARY LAWS AND DIRECTIVES

Other provisions:

Application of section. Act Oct. 28, 1992, P. L. 102-550, Title VI, Subtitle F, § 684, 106 Stat. 3832, which appears as 42 USCS § 13642, provides that this section is applicable upon expiration of the 6-month period beginning on enactment.

§ 13619.   "Covered section 8 housing" defined

For purposes of this subtitle [42 USCS §§ 13611 et seq.], the term "covered section 8 housing" means housing described in section 683(2)(G) [42 USCS § 13641(2)(G)] that was originally designed for occupancy by elderly families.

(Oct. 28, 1992, P. L. 102-550, Title VI, Subtitle D, § 659, 106 Stat. 3825.)

HISTORY; ANCILLARY LAWS AND DIRECTIVES

Other provisions:

Application of section. Act Oct. 28, 1992, P. L. 102-550, Title VI, Subtitle F, § 684, 106 Stat. 3832, which appears as 42 USCS § 13642, provides that this section is applicable upon expiration of the 6-month period beginning on enactment.

CROSS REFERENCES

This section is referred to in 42 USCS §§ 1437f, 13611.

§ 13620.   Study.

The Secretary of Housing and Urban Development shall conduct a study to determine the extent to which Federal housing programs serve elderly families, disabled families, and families with children, in relation to the need of such families who are eligible for assistance under such programs. The Secretary shall submit a report to the Congress describing the study and the findings of the study not later than the expiration of the 1-year period beginning on the date of the enactment of this Act [enacted Oct. 28, 1992].

(Oct. 28, 1992, P. L. 102-550, Title VI, Subtitle D, § 661, 106 Stat. 3825.)

HISTORY; ANCILLARY LAWS AND DIRECTIVES

Other provisions:

Application of section. Act Oct. 28, 1992, P. L. 102-550, Title VI, Subtitle

F, § 684, 106 Stat. 3832, which appears as 42 USCS § 13642, provides that this section is applicable upon expiration of the 6-month period beginning on enactment.

SERVICE COORDINATORS FOR ELDERLY AND DISABLED RESIDENTS OF FEDERALLY ASSISTED HOUSING

§ 13631. Requirement to provide service coordinators

(a) In general. To the extent that amounts are made available for providing service coordinators under this section, the Secretary shall require owners of covered federally assisted housing projects (as such term is defined in subsection (d)) receiving such amounts to provide for employing or otherwise retaining the services of one or more individuals to coordinate the provision of supportive services for elderly and disabled families residing in the projects (in this section referred to as a "service coordinator"). No such elderly or disabled family may be required to accept services.

(b) Responsibilities. Each service coordinator of a covered federally assisted housing project provided pursuant to this subtitle or the amendments made by this subtitle—

(1) shall consult with the owner of the housing, tenants, any tenant organizations, any resident management organizations, service providers, and any other appropriate persons, to identify the particular needs and characteristics of elderly and disabled families who reside in the project and any supportive services related to such needs and characteristics;

(2) shall manage and coordinate the provision of such services for residents of the project;

(3) may provide training to tenants of the project in the obligations of tenancy or coordinate such training;

(4) shall meet the minimum qualifications and standards required under section 802(d)(4) of the Cranston-Gonzalez National Affordable Housing Act [42 USCS § 8011(d)(4)]; and

(5) may carry out other appropriate activities for residents of the project.

(c) Included services. Supportive services referred to under subsection (b)(1) may include health-related services, mental health services, services for non-medical counseling, meals, transportation, personal care, bathing, toileting, housekeeping, chore assistance, safety, group and socialization activities, assistance with medications (in accordance with any applicable State laws), case management, personal emergency response, education and outreach regarding telemarketing fraud in accordance with the standards issued under subsection (f), and other appropriate services. The services may be provided through any agency of the Federal Government or any other public or private department, agency, or organization.

(d) Covered federally assisted housing. For purposes of this subtitle, the term "covered federally assisted housing" means housing that is federally assisted housing (as such term is defined in section 683(2) [42 USCS § 13641(2)]), except that such term does not include housing described in subparagraphs (C) and (D) of such section.

(e) Services for low-income elderly or disabled families residing in vicinity of certain projects. To the extent only that this section applies to service coordinators for covered federally assisted housing described in subparagraphs (B), (C), (D), (E), (F), and (G) of section 683(2) [42 USCS § 13641(2)], any reference in this section to elderly or disabled residents of a project shall be construed to include low-income elderly or disabled families living in the vicinity of such project.

(f) Protection against telemarketing fraud. (1) In general. The Secretary, in coordination with the Secretary of Health and Human Services, shall establish standards for service coordinators in federally assisted housing who are providing education and outreach to elderly persons residing in such housing regarding telemarketing fraud. The standards shall be designed to ensure that such education and outreach informs such elderly persons of the dangers of telemarketing fraud and facilitates the investigation and prosecution of telemarketers engaging in fraud against such residents.

(2) Contents. The standards established under this subsection shall require that any such education and outreach be provided in a manner that—

(A) informs such residents of—

(i) the prevalence of telemarketing fraud targeted against elderly persons;

(ii) how telemarketing fraud works;

(iii) how to identify telemarketing fraud;

(iv) how to protect themselves against telemarketing fraud, including an explanation of the dangers of providing bank account, credit card, or other financial or personal information over the telephone to unsolicited callers;

(v) how to report suspected attempts at telemarketing fraud; and

(vi) their consumer protection rights under Federal law;

(B) provides such other information as the Secretary considers necessary to protect such residents against fraudulent telemarketing; and

(C) disseminates the information provided by appropriate means, and in determining such appropriate means, the Secretary shall consider on-site presentations at federally assisted housing, public service announcements, a printed manual or pamphlet, an Internet website, and telephone outreach to residents whose names appear on "mooch lists" confiscated from fraudulent telemarketers.

(Oct. 28, 1992, P. L. 102-550, Title VI, Subtitle E, § 671, 106 Stat. 3826; Dec. 27, 2000, P. L. 106-569, Title VIII, Subtitle C, Part 3, § 851(b), (c)(2), 114 Stat. 3024.)

HISTORY; ANCILLARY LAWS AND DIRECTIVES

References in text:

"This subtitle", referred to in this section, is Subtitle E of Title VI of Act Oct. 28, 1992, P. L. 102-550. For full classification of such Subtitle, consult USCS Tables volumes.

Amendments:

2000. Act Dec. 27, 2000 (effective as provided by § 803 of such Act, which appears as 12 USCS § 1701q note), in subsec. (a), substituted "for providing service coordinators under this section" for "to carry out this subtitle pursuant to the amendments made by this subtitle"; in subsec. (c), inserted "education and outreach regarding telemarketing fraud in accordance with the standards issued under subsection (f),"; in subsec. (d), inserted a close parenthesis following "683(2)"; and added subsecs. (e) and (f).

Other provisions:

Application of section. Act Oct. 28, 1992, P. L. 102-550, Title VI, Subtitle F, § 684, 106 Stat. 3832, which appears as 42 USCS § 13642, provides that this section is applicable upon expiration of the 6-month period beginning on enactment.

CROSS REFERENCES

This section is referred to in 12 USCS § 1701q; 42 USCS § 13632.

§ 13632. Grants for costs of providing service coordinators in certain federally assisted housing

(a) Authority. The Secretary may make grants under this section to owners of federally assisted housing projects described in subparagraphs (B), (C), (D), (E), (F), and (G) of section 683(2) [42 USCS § 13641(2)]. Any grant amounts shall be used for the costs of employing or otherwise retaining the services of one or more service coordinators under section 671 [42 USCS § 13631] to coordinate the provision of any services within the project for residents of the project who are elderly families and disabled families (as such terms are defined in section 683 of this Act [42 USCS § 13641]). A service coordinator funded with a grant under this section for a project may provide services to low-income elderly or disabled families living in the vicinity of such project.

(b) Application and selection. The Secretary shall provide for the form and manner of applications for grants under this section and for selection of applicants to receive such grants.

(c) Eligible project expense. For any federally assisted housing project described in subparagraph (B), (C), (D), (E), (F), or (G) of section 683(2) [42 USCS § 13641(2)] that does not receive a grant under this section, the cost of employing or otherwise retaining the services of one or more service coordinators under section 671 [42 USCS § 13631] and not more than 15 percent of the cost of providing services to the residents of the project shall be considered an eligible project expense, but only to the extent that amounts are available from project rent and other income for such costs.

(Oct. 28, 1992, P. L. 102-550, Title VI, Subtitle E, § 676, 106 Stat. 3828; Dec. 27, 2000, P. L. 106-569, Title VIII, Subtitle C, Part 3, § 851(a), 114 Stat. 3023.)

HISTORY; ANCILLARY LAWS AND DIRECTIVES

Amendments:

2000. Act Dec. 27, 2000 (effective as provided by § 803 of such Act, which appears as 12 USCS § 1701q note), in the section heading, substituted "certain federally assisted housing" for "multifamily housing assisted under National Housing Act"; in subsec. (a), substituted "(B), (C), (D), (E), (F), and (G)" for "(E) and (F)", substituted "section 671" for "section 661", and added the sentence beginning "A service coordinator . . ."; deleted subsec. (c), which read: "(c) Authorization of appropriations. There are authorized to be appropriated for fiscal years 1993 and 1994 such sums as may be necessary for grants under this section."; redesignated subsec. (d) as subsec. (c), and, in such section as redesignated, substituted "(B), (C), (D), (E), (F), or (G)" for "(E) or (F)", and substituted "section 671" for "section 661".

Other provisions:
Application of section. Act Oct. 28, 1992, P. L. 102-550, Title VI, Subtitle F, § 684, 106 Stat. 3832, which appears as 42 USCS § 13642, provides that this section is applicable upon expiration of the 6-month period beginning on enactment.

GENERAL PROVISIONS

§ 13641. Definitions

For purposes of this title:

(1) Elderly, disabled, and near-elderly families. The terms "elderly family", "disabled family", and "near-elderly family" have the meanings given the terms under section 3(b)(3) of the United States Housing Act of 1937 [42 USCS § 1437a(b)(3)].

(2) Federally assisted housing. The terms "federally assisted housing" and "project" mean—

(A) a public housing project (as such term is defined in section 3(b) of the United States Housing Act of 1937 [42 USCS § 1437a(b)]);

(B) housing for which project-based assistance is provided under section 8 of the United States Housing Act of 1937 [42 USCS § 1437f];

(C) housing that is assisted under section 202 of the Housing Act of 1959 [12 USCS § 1701q] (as amended by section 801 of the Cranston-Gonzalez National Affordable Housing Act [Act Nov. 28, 1990, P. L. 101-625]);

(D) housing that is assisted under section 202 of the Housing Act of 1959 [former 12 USCS § 1701q], as such section existed before the enactment of the Cranston-Gonzalez National Affordable Housing Act [enacted Nov. 28, 1990];

(E) housing financed by a loan or mortgage insured under section 221(d)(3) of the National Housing Act [12 USCS § 1715l(d)(3)] that bears interest at a rate determined under the proviso of section 221(d)(5) of such Act [12 USCS § 1715l(d)(5)];

(F) housing insured, assisted, or held by the Secretary or a State or State agency under section 236 of the National Housing Act [12 USCS § 1715z-1];

(G) housing constructed or substantially rehabilitated pursuant to assistance provided under section 8(b)(2) of the United States Housing Act of 1937 [former 42 USCS § 1437f(b)(2)], as in effect before October 1, 1983, that is assisted under a contract for assistance under such section; and

(H) housing that is assisted under section 811 of the Cranston-Gonzalez [National] Affording Housing Act (42 U.S.C. 8013).

(3) Housing assistance. The term "housing assistance" means, with respect to federally assisted housing, the grant, contribution, capital advance, loan, mortgage insurance, or other assistance provided for the housing under the provisions of law referred to in paragraph (2). The term also includes any related assistance provided for the housing by the Secretary, including any rental assistance for low-income occupants.

(4) Owner. The term "owner" means, with respect to federally assisted housing, the entity or private person, including a cooperative or public housing agency, that has the legal right to lease or sublease dwelling units in such housing.

(5) Secretary. The term "Secretary" means the Secretary of Housing and Urban Development.

(Oct. 28, 1992, P. L. 102-550, Title VI, Subtitle F, § 683, 106 Stat. 3831; March 11, 2009, P. L. 111-8, Div I, Title II, § 228, 123 Stat. 978.)

HISTORY; ANCILLARY LAWS AND DIRECTIVES

References in text:
"This title", referred to in this section, is Title VI of Act Oct. 28, 1992, P. L. 102-550, 106 Stat. 3802. For full classification of this Title, consult USCS Tables volumes.

Explanatory notes:
The bracketed word "National" has been inserted in para. (2)(H) to indicate the probable intent of Congress to include it.

Amendments:
2009. Act March 11, 2009, in para. (2), in subpara. (F), deleted "and" following the concluding semicolon, in subpara. (G), substituted "; and" for a concluding period, and added subpara. (H).

Other provisions:
Application of section. Act Oct. 28, 1992, P. L. 102-550, Title VI, Subtitle F, § 684, 106 Stat. 3832, which appears as 42 USCS § 13642, provides that this section is applicable upon expiration of the 6-month period beginning on enactment.

CROSS REFERENCES
This section is referred to in 12 USCS § 1701q-2; 42 USCS §§ 13601, 13618, 13619, 13631, 13632.

§ 13642. Applicability

Except as otherwise provided in subtitles B through F of this title and the amendments made by such subtitles, such subtitles and the amendments made by such subtitles shall apply upon the expiration of the 6-month period beginning on the date of the enactment of this Act.

(Oct. 28, 1992, P. L. 102-550, Title VI, Subtitle F, § 684, 106 Stat. 3832.)

HISTORY; ANCILLARY LAWS AND DIRECTIVES

References in text:
"Subtitles B through F of this title", referred to in this section, are Subtitles

B–F of Title VI of Act Oct. 28, 1992, P. L. 102-550, 106 Stat. 3812. For full classification of such Subtitles, consult USCS Tables volumes.

§ 13643.   Regulations

The Secretary shall issue regulations necessary to carry out subtitles B through F of this title and the amendments made by such subtitles not later than the expiration of the 6-month period beginning on the date of the enactment of this Act [enacted Oct. 28, 1992]. The regulations shall be issued after notice and opportunity for public comment pursuant to the provisions of section 553 of title 5, United States Code (notwithstanding subsections (a)(2), (b)(B), and (d)(3) of such section).

(Oct. 28, 1992, P. L. 102-550, Title VI, Subtitle F, § 685, 106 Stat. 3832.)

HISTORY; ANCILLARY LAWS AND DIRECTIVES

References in text:
"Subtitles B through F of this title", referred to in this section, are Subtitles B–F of Title VI of Act Oct. 28, 1992, P. L. 102-550, 106 Stat. 3812. For full classification of such Subtitles, consult USCS Tables volumes.

Other provisions:
Application of section. Act Oct. 28, 1992, P. L. 102-550, Title VI, § 684, 106 Stat. 3832, which appears as 42 USCS § 13642, provides that this section is applicable upon expiration of the 6-month period beginning on enactment.

SAFETY AND SECURITY IN PUBLIC AND ASSISTED HOUSING

§ 13661.   Screening of applicants for federally assisted housing

(a) Ineligibility because of eviction for drug crimes. Any tenant evicted from federally assisted housing by reason of drug-related criminal activity (as such term is defined in section 3(b) of the United States Housing Act of 1937 (42 U.S.C. 1437a(b)) shall not be eligible for federally assisted housing during the 3-year period beginning on the date of such eviction, unless the evicted tenant successfully completes a rehabilitation program approved by the public housing agency (which shall include a waiver of this subsection if the circumstances leading to eviction no longer exist).

(b) Ineligibility of illegal drug users and alcohol abusers. (1) In general. Notwithstanding any other provision of law, a public housing agency or an owner of federally assisted housing, as determined by the Secretary, shall establish standards that prohibit admission to the program or admission to federally assisted housing for any household with a member—

(A) who the public housing agency or owner determines is illegally using a controlled substance; or

(B) with respect to whom the public housing agency or owner determines that it has reasonable cause to believe that such household member's illegal use (or pattern of illegal use) of a controlled substance, or abuse (or pattern of abuse) of alcohol, may interfere with the health, safety, or right to peaceful enjoyment of the premises by other residents.

(2) Consideration of rehabilitation. In determining whether, pursuant to paragraph (1)(B), to deny admission to the program or federally assisted housing to any household based on a pattern of illegal use of a controlled substance or a pattern of abuse of alcohol by a household member, a public housing agency or an owner may consider whether such household member—

(A) has successfully completed a supervised drug or alcohol rehabilitation program (as applicable) and is no longer engaging in the illegal use of a controlled substance or abuse of alcohol (as applicable);

(B) has otherwise been rehabilitated successfully and is no longer engaging in the illegal use of a controlled substance or abuse of alcohol (as applicable); or

(C) is participating in a supervised drug or alcohol rehabilitation program (as applicable) and is no longer engaging in the illegal use of a controlled substance or abuse of alcohol (as applicable).

(c) **Authority to deny admission to criminal offenders.** Except as provided in subsections (a) and (b) of this section and in addition to any other authority to screen applicants, in selecting among applicants for admission to the program or to federally assisted housing, if the public housing agency or owner of such housing (as applicable) determines that an applicant or any member of the applicant's household is or was, during a reasonable time preceding the date when the applicant household would otherwise be selected for admission, engaged in any drug-related or violent criminal activity or other criminal activity which would adversely affect the health, safety, or right to peaceful enjoyment of the premises by other residents, the owner, or public housing agency employees, the public housing agency or owner may—

(1) deny such applicant admission to the program or to federally assisted housing; and

(2) after the expiration of the reasonable period beginning upon such activity, require the applicant, as a condition of admission to the program or to federally assisted housing, to submit to the public housing agency or owner evidence sufficient (as the Secretary shall by regulation provide) to ensure that the individual or individuals in the applicant's household who engaged in criminal activity for which denial was made under paragraph (1) have not engaged in any criminal activity during such reasonable period.

(Oct. 21, 1998, P. L. 105-276, Title V, Subtitle F, § 576, 112 Stat. 2639.)

HISTORY; ANCILLARY LAWS AND DIRECTIVES

Explanatory notes:

Subsec. (d) of this section, which has been omitted, amended 42 USCS §§ 1437d and 1437n.

This section was enacted as part of Act Oct. 21, 1998, P. L. 105-276, and not as part of Act Oct. 28, 1992, P. L. 102-550, which generally comprises this chapter.

Other provisions:

Applicability of section. This section shall apply beginning upon October 1, 1999, pursuant to § 503(a) of Act Oct. 21, 1998, P. L. 105-276, which appears as 42 USCS § 1437 note.

CROSS REFERENCES

This section is referred to in 42 USCS § 1437d.

RESEARCH GUIDE

Law Review Articles:

Carey. No Second Chance: People with Criminal Records Denied Access to Public Housing. 36 U Tol L Rev 545, Spring 2005.

INTERPRETIVE NOTES AND DECISIONS

42 USCS §§ 13661(b) and 13663(a) targeted three populations that Congress wished to bar from federally assisted housing: lifetime registrants, illegal drug users, and alcohol abusers; however, when it came to termination from participation in program as opposed to admission into program, with respect to only illegal drug users and alcohol abusers, Congress, in 42 USCS § 13662(a), expressly required termination of their participation, and there was no counterpart to 42 USCS § 13662(a) for lifetime sex offender registrants that required their termination from participation once they had been admitted into program; moreover, there was no express provision in 24 CFR § 982.553 that authorized termination of participation for lifetime registrants; therefore, because by its own terms, 42 USCS § 13663(a) was directed to prohibiting admission of lifetime registrants, not to their removal from participation, court rejected magistrate's recommendation that it grant summary judgment for Maine State Housing Authority on convicted sex offender's claim that his Section 8 housing subsidy was unlawfully terminated in violation of his Fourteenth Amendment rights. Miller v McCormick (2009, DC Me) 605 F Supp 2d 296.

§ 13662. Termination of tenancy and assistance for illegal drug users and alcohol abusers in federally assisted housing

(a) In general. Notwithstanding any other provision of law, a public housing agency or an owner of federally assisted housing (as applicable), shall establish standards or lease provisions for continued assistance or occupancy in federally assisted housing that allow the agency or owner (as applicable) to terminate the tenancy or assistance for any household with a member—

(1) who the public housing agency or owner determines is illegally using a controlled substance; or

(2) whose illegal use (or pattern of illegal use) of a controlled substance, or whose abuse (or pattern of abuse) of alcohol, is determined by the public housing agency or owner to interfere with the health, safety, or right to peaceful enjoyment of the premises by other residents.

(b) Consideration of rehabilitation. In determining whether, pursuant to subsection (a)(2), to terminate tenancy or assistance to any household based on a pattern of illegal use of a controlled substance or a pattern of abuse of alcohol by a household member, a public housing agency or an owner may consider whether such household member—

(1) has successfully completed a supervised drug or alcohol rehabilitation program (as applicable) and is no longer engaging in the illegal use of a controlled substance or abuse of alcohol (as applicable);

(2) has otherwise been rehabilitated successfully and is no longer engaging in the illegal use of a controlled substance or abuse of alcohol (as applicable); or

(3) is participating in a supervised drug or alcohol rehabilitation program (as applicable) and is no longer engaging in the illegal use of a controlled substance or abuse of alcohol (as applicable).

(Oct. 21, 1998, P. L. 105-276, Title V, Subtitle F, § 577, 112 Stat. 2640.)

HISTORY; ANCILLARY LAWS AND DIRECTIVES

Explanatory notes:

This section was enacted as part of Act Oct. 21, 1998, P. L. 105-276, and not as part of Act Oct. 28, 1992, P. L. 102-550, which generally comprises this chapter.

Other provisions:

Applicability of section. This section shall apply beginning upon October 1, 1999, pursuant to § 503(a) of Act Oct. 21, 1998, P. L. 105-276, which appears as 42 USCS § 1437 note.

CROSS REFERENCES

This section is referred to in 42 USCS § 1437d.

INTERPRETIVE NOTES AND DECISIONS

42 USCS §§ 13661(b) and 13663(a) targeted three populations that Congress wished to bar from federally assisted housing: lifetime registrants, illegal drug users, and alcohol abusers; however, when it came to termination from participation in program as opposed to admission into program, with respect to only illegal drug users and alcohol abusers, Congress, in 42 USCS § 13662(a), expressly required termination of their participation, and there was no counterpart to 42 USCS § 13662(a) for lifetime sex offender registrants that required their termination from participation once they had been admitted into program; moreover, there was no express provision in 24 CFR § 982.553 that authorized termination of participation for lifetime registrants; therefore, because by its own terms, 42 USCS § 13663(a) was directed to prohibiting admission of lifetime registrants, not to their removal from participation, court rejected magistrate's recommendation that it grant summary judgment for Maine State Housing Authority on convicted sex offender's claim that his Section 8 housing subsidy was unlawfully terminated in violation of his Fourteenth Amendment rights. Miller v McCormick (2009, DC Me) 605 F Supp 2d 296.

§ 13663. Ineligibility of dangerous sex offenders for admission to public housing

(a) In general. Notwithstanding any other provision of law, an owner of federally assisted housing shall prohibit admission to such housing for any household that includes any individual who is subject to a lifetime registration requirement under a State sex offender registration program.

(b) Obtaining information. As provided in regulations issued by the Secretary to carry out this section—

(1) a public housing agency shall carry out criminal history background checks on applicants for federally assisted housing and make further inquiry with State and local agencies as necessary to determine whether an applicant for federally assisted housing is subject to a lifetime registration requirement under a State sex offender registration program; and

(2) State and local agencies responsible for the collection or maintenance of criminal history record information or information on persons required to register as sex offenders shall comply with requests of public housing agencies for information pursuant to this section.

(c) Requests by owners for PHAs to obtain information. A public housing agency may take any action under subsection (b) regarding applicants for, or tenants of, federally assisted housing other than federally assisted housing described in subparagraph (A) or (B) of section 579(a)(2) [42 USCS § 13664(a)(2)], but only if the housing is located within the jurisdiction of the agency and the owner of such housing has requested that the agency take such action on behalf of the owner. Upon such a request by the owner, the agency shall take the action requested under subsection (b). The agency may not make any information obtained pursuant to the action under subsection (b) available to the owner but shall perform determinations for the owner regarding screening, lease enforcement, and eviction based on criteria supplied by the owner.

(d) Opportunity to dispute. Before an adverse action is taken with respect to an applicant for federally assisted housing on the basis that an individual is subject to a lifetime registration requirement under a State sex offender registration program, the public housing agency obtaining the record shall provide the tenant or applicant with a copy of the registration information and an opportunity to dispute the accuracy and relevance of that information.

(e) Fee. A public housing agency may be charged a reasonable fee for taking actions under subsection (b). In the case of a public housing agency taking actions on behalf of another owner of federally assisted housing pursuant to subsection (c), the agency may pass such fee on to the owner making the request and may charge an additional reasonable fee for making the request on behalf of the owner.

(f) Records management. Each public housing agency shall establish and implement a system of records management that ensures that any criminal record or information regarding a lifetime registration requirement under a State sex offender registration program that is obtained under this section by the public housing agency is—

  (1) maintained confidentially;
  (2) not misused or improperly disseminated; and
  (3) destroyed, once the purpose for which the record was requested has been accomplished.

(Oct. 21, 1998, P. L. 105-276, Title V, Subtitle F, § 578, 112 Stat. 2641.)

HISTORY; ANCILLARY LAWS AND DIRECTIVES

Explanatory notes:
This section was enacted as part of Act Oct. 21, 1998, P. L. 105-276, and not as part of Act Oct. 28, 1992, P. L. 102-550, which generally comprises this chapter.

Other provisions:
Applicability of section. This section shall apply beginning upon October 1, 1999, pursuant to § 503(a) of Act Oct. 21, 1998, P. L. 105-276, which appears as 42 USCS § 1437 note.

RESEARCH GUIDE

Annotations:
Validity of Statutes Imposing Residency Restrictions on Registered Sex Offenders. 25 ALR6th 227.

INTERPRETIVE NOTES AND DECISIONS

42 USCS §§ 13661(b) and 13663(a) targeted three populations that Congress wished to bar from federally assisted housing: lifetime registrants, illegal drug users, and alcohol abusers; however, when it came to termination from participation in program as opposed to admission into program, with respect to only illegal drug users and alcohol abusers, Congress, in 42 USCS § 13662(a), expressly required termination of their participation, and there was no counterpart to 42 USCS § 13662(a) for lifetime sex offender registrants that required their termination from participation once they had been admitted into program; moreover, there was no express provision in 24 CFR § 982.553 that authorized termination of participation for lifetime registrants; therefore, because by its own terms, 42 USCS § 13663(a) was directed to prohibiting admission of lifetime registrants, not to their removal from participation, court rejected magistrate's recommendation that it grant summary judgment for Maine State Housing Authority on convicted sex offender's claim that his Section 8 housing subsidy was unlawfully terminated in violation of his Fourteenth Amendment rights. Miller v McCormick (2009, DC Me) 605 F Supp 2d 296.

§ 13664. Definitions

[(a)] Definitions. For purposes of this subtitle, the following definitions shall apply:

(1) Drug-related criminal activity. The term "drug-related criminal activity" has the meaning given the term in section 3(b) of the United States Housing Act of 1937 (42 U.S.C. 1437a(b)).

(2) Federally assisted housing. The term "federally assisted housing" means a dwelling unit—

(A) in public housing (as such term is defined in section 3(b) of the United States Housing Act of 1937 (42 U.S.C. 1437a));

(B) assisted with tenant-based assistance under section 8 of the United States Housing Act of 1937 [42 USCS § 1437f];

(C) in housing that is provided project-based assistance under section 8 of the United States Housing Act of 1937 [42 USCS § 1437f], including new construction and substantial rehabilitation projects;

(D) in housing that is assisted under section 202 of the Housing Act of 1959 [12 USCS § 1701q] (as amended by section 801 of the Cranston-Gonzalez National Affordable Housing Act [Act Nov. 28, 1990, P. L. 101-625]);

(E) in housing that is assisted under section 202 of the Housing Act of 1959 [former 12 USCS § 1701q], as such section existed before the enactment of the Cranston-Gonzalez National Affordable Housing Act [enacted Nov. 28, 1990];

(F) in housing that is assisted under section 811 of the Cranston-Gonzalez National Affordable Housing Act [42 USCS § 8013];

(G) in housing financed by a loan or mortgage insured under section 221(d)(3) of the National Housing Act [12 USCS § 1715l(d)(3)] that bears interest at a rate determined under the proviso of section 221(d)(5) of such Act [12 USCS § 1715l(d)(5)];

(H) in housing insured, assisted, or held by the Secretary or a State or State agency under section 236 of the National Housing Act [12 USCS § 1715z-1]; or

(I) in housing assisted under section 514 or 515 of the Housing Act of 1949 [42 USCS § 1484 or 1485].

(3) Owner. The term "owner" means, with respect to federally assisted housing, the entity or private person (including a cooperative or public housing agency) that has the legal right to lease or sublease dwelling units in such housing.

(Oct. 21, 1998, P. L. 105-276, Title V, Subtitle F, § 579, 112 Stat. 2642.)

HISTORY; ANCILLARY LAWS AND DIRECTIVES

Explanatory notes:

The subsection designator "(a)" has been enclosed in brackets inasmuch as no subsec. (b) was enacted.

This section was enacted as part of Act Oct. 21, 1998, P. L. 105-276, and not as part of Act Oct. 28, 1992, P. L. 102-550, which generally comprises this chapter.

Other provisions:

Applicability of section. This section shall apply beginning upon October 1, 1999, pursuant to § 503(a) of Act Oct. 21, 1998, P. L. 105-276, which appears as 42 USCS § 1437 note.

CROSS REFERENCES

This section is referred to in 42 USCS § 13663.

CHAPTER 136. VIOLENT CRIME CONTROL AND LAW ENFORCEMENT

PRISONS

VIOLENT OFFENDER INCARCERATION AND TRUTH-IN-SENTENCING INCENTIVE GRANTS

CRIME PREVENTION

OUNCE OF PREVENTION COUNCIL

PRISONS

VIOLENT OFFENDER INCARCERATION AND TRUTH-IN-SENTENCING
INCENTIVE GRANTS

§ 13701. Definitions

Unless otherwise provided, for purposes of this subtitle [42 USCS §§ 13701 et
seq.]—

    (1) the term "indeterminate sentencing" means a system by which—

        (A) the court may impose a sentence of a range defined by statute; and

        (B) an administrative agency, generally the parole board, or the court,
controls release within the statutory range;

    (2) the term "part 1 violent crime" means murder and nonnegligent
manslaughter, forcible rape, robbery, and aggravated assault as reported to
the Federal Bureau of Investigation for purposes of the Uniform Crime
Reports; and

    (3) the term "State" means a State of the United States, the District of
Columbia, the Commonwealth of Puerto Rico, the United States Virgin
Islands, American Samoa, Guam, and the Northern Mariana Islands.

(Sept. 13, 1994, P. L. 103-322, Title II, Subtitle A, § 20101, as added April 26,
1996, P. L. 104-134, Title I, § 114(a), 110 Stat. 1321-15; May 2, 1996, P. L.
104-140, § 1(a), 110 Stat. 1327.)

HISTORY; ANCILLARY LAWS AND DIRECTIVES

Explanatory notes:

A prior § 13701 (Act Sept. 13, 1994, P. L. 103-322, Title II, Subtitle A,
§ 20101, 108 Stat. 1815) was omitted in the general amendment of this
subtitle (42 USCS §§ 13701 et seq.) by April 26, 1996, P. L. 104-134, Title
I, § 114(a), 110 Stat. 1321-14. Such section provided for grants for correctional facilities.

Act May 2, 1996, P. L. 104-140, § 1(a), 110 Stat. 1327, inserted the heading "TITLE I—OMNIBUS APPROPRIATIONS" after the enacting clause
of Act April 26, 1996, P. L. 104-134.

Short title:

Act Sept. 13, 1994, P. L. 103-322, § 1, 108 Stat. 1796, provides: "This Act
may be cited as the 'Violent Crime Control and Law Enforcement Act of
1994'.". For full classification of such Act, consult USCS Tables volumes.

Act Sept. 13, 1994, P. L. 103-322, Title III, Subtitle K, § 31101, 108 Stat.
1882, provides: "This subtitle [42 USCS §§ 13821 et seq.] may be cited as
the 'National Community Economic Partnership Act of 1994'.".

Act Sept. 13, 1994, P. L. 103-322, Title III, Subtitle S, § 31901, 108 Stat.
1892, provides: "This subtitle [42 USCS §§ 13881 et seq.] may be cited as
the 'Family Unity Demonstration Project Act'.".

Act Sept. 13, 1994, P. L. 103-322, Title IV, § 40001, 108 Stat. 1902,
provides: "This title may be cited as the 'Violence Against Women Act of
1994'.". For full classification of such Title, consult USCS Tables volumes.

Act Sept. 13, 1994, P. L. 103-322, Title IV, Subtitle A, § 40101, 108 Stat.
1903, provides: "This subtitle may be cited as the 'Safe Streets for Women

Act of 1994'.''. For full classification of such Subtitle, consult USCS Tables volumes.

Act Sept. 13, 1994, P. L. 103-322, Title IV, Subtitle B, § 40201, 108 Stat. 1925, provides: "This title may be cited as the 'Safe Homes for Women Act of 1994'.''. For full classification of such Title, consult USCS Tables volumes.

Act Sept. 13, 1994, P. L. 103-322, Title IV, Subtitle C, § 40301, 108 Stat. 1941, provides: "This subtitle may be cited as the 'Civil Rights Remedies for Gender-Motivated Violence Act'.''. For full classification of such Subtitle, consult USCS Tables volumes.

Act Sept. 13, 1994, P. L. 103-322, Title IV, Subtitle D, § 40401, 108 Stat. 1942, provides: "This subtitle [42 USCS §§ 13991 et seq.] may be cited as the 'Equal Justice for Women in the Courts Act of 1994'.''.

Act Sept. 13, 1994, P. L. 103-322, Title IV, Subtitle J, § 41001, as added Jan. 5, 2006, P. L. 109-162, Title I, § 105(a), 119 Stat. 2979, provides: "This subtitle [42 USCS §§ 14043 et seq.] may be cited as the 'Violence Against Women Act Court Training and Improvements Act of 2005'.''.

Act Sept. 13, 1994, P. L. 103-322, Title XX, Subtitle A, § 200101, 108 Stat. 2049, provides: This subtitle [42 USCS §§ 14091 et seq.] may be cited as the 'Police Corps Act'.''.

Act Sept. 13, 1994, P. L. 103-322, Title XX, Subtitle B, § 200201, 108 Stat. 2057, provides: This subtitle [42 USCS §§ 14111 et seq.] may be cited as the 'Law Enforcement Scholarships and Recruitment Act'.''.

Act Sept. 13, 1994, P. L. 103-322, Title XXI, Subtitle C, § 210301, 108 Stat. 2065, provides: "This subtitle may be cited as the 'DNA Identification Act of 1994'.''. For full classification of such Subtitle, consult USCS Tables volumes.

Act Sept. 13, 1994, P. L. 103-322, Title XXII, § 220001, 108 Stat. 2074, provides: "This title may be cited as the 'Motor Vehicle Theft Prevention Act'.''. For full classification of such Title, consult USCS Tables volumes.

Act May 17, 1996, P. L. 104-145, § 1, 110 Stat. 1345, provides: "This Act [amending 42 USCS § 14071(d)] may be cited as 'Megan's Law'.''.

Act Oct. 3, 1996, P. L. 104-236, § 1, 110 Stat. 3093, provides: "This Act may be cited as the 'Pam Lychner Sexual Offender Tracking and Identification Act of 1996'.''. For full classification of such Act, consult USCS Tables volumes.

Act Oct. 13, 2000, P. L. 106-297, § 1, 114 Stat. 1045, provides: "This Act [amending 42 USCS § 13704(a)] may be cited as the 'Death in Custody Reporting Act of 2000'.''.

Act Oct. 28, 2000, P. L. 106-386, Div B, § 1001, 114 Stat. 1491, provides: "This division may be cited as the 'Violence Against Women Act of 2000'.''. For full classification of such Division, consult USCS Tables volumes.

Act Dec. 19, 2000, P. L. 106-546, § 1, 114 Stat. 2726, provides: "This Act may be cited as the 'DNA Analysis Backlog Elimination Act of 2000'.''. For full classification of such Act, consult USCS Tables volumes.

Act Dec. 21, 2000, P. L. 106-560, § 1, 114 Stat. 2784, provides: "This Act [42 USCS §§ 13726 et seq.] may be cited as the 'Interstate Transportation of Dangerous Criminals Act of 2000' or 'Jeanna's Act'.''.

Act Oct. 30, 2004, P. L. 108-405, § 1(a), 118 Stat. 2260, provides: "This Act may be cited as the 'Justice for All Act of 2004'.''. For full classification of such Act, consult USCS Tables volumes.

Act Oct. 30, 2004, P. L. 108-405, Title II, § 201, 118 Stat. 2266, provides: "This title may be cited as the 'Debbie Smith Act of 2004'.". For full classification of such Title, consult USCS Tables volumes.

Act Oct. 30, 2004, P. L. 108-405, Title III, § 301, 118 Stat. 2272, provides: "This title may be cited as the 'DNA Sexual Assault Justice Act of 2004'.". For full classification of such Title, consult USCS Tables volumes.

Act Jan. 5, 2006, P. L. 109-162, § 1, 119 Stat. 2960; Aug. 12, 2006, P. L. 109-271, § 1(a), 120 Stat. 750, provides:

"(a) In general. This Act [for full classification, consult USCS Tables volumes] may be cited as the 'Violence Against Women and Department of Justice Reauthorization Act of 2005'.

"(b) Separate short titles. Section 3 and titles I through IX of this Act [for full classification, consult USCS Tables volumes] may be cited as the 'Violence Against Women Reauthorization Act of 2005'. Title XI of this Act [for full classification, consult USCS Tables volumes] may be cited as the 'Department of Justice Appropriations Authorization Act of 2005'.".

Act Jan. 5, 2006, P. L. 109-162, Title X, § 1001, 119 Stat. 3084, provides: "This title [amending 18 USCS §§ 3142 and 3297 and 42 USCS §§ 14132, 14135, and 14135a] may be cited as the 'DNA Fingerprint Act of 2005'.".

Act July 27, 2006, P. L. 109-248, Title VI, Subtitle B, § 611, 120 Stat. 632, provides: "This subtitle [amending 42 USCS § 13751 note] may be cited as the 'National Police Athletic League Youth Enrichment Reauthorization Act of 2006'.".

Act Oct. 8, 2008, P. L. 110-360, § 1, 122 Stat. 4008, provides: "This Act [amending 42 USCS §§ 14135, 14136(b), and 14136a(c)] may be cited as the 'Debbie Smith Reauthorization Act of 2008'.".

CODE OF FEDERAL REGULATIONS

Department of Justice—Grants for correctional facilities, 28 CFR 91.1 et seq.

CROSS REFERENCES

This section is referred to in 42 USCS §§ 13705, 14214.

RESEARCH GUIDE

Law Review Articles:

Landers. Prosecutorial Limits on Overlapping Federal and State Jurisdiction. 543 Annals 64, January 1996.

Simon. Sex Offender Legislation and the Antitherapeutic Effects on Victims. 41 Ariz L Rev 485, Summer 1999.

Weissman. Gender-Based Violence as Judicial Anomaly: Between "The Truly National and the Truly Local". 42 BC L Rev 1081, September 2001.

Teran. Barriers to Protection at Home and Abroad: Mexican Victims of Domestic Violence and the Violence Against Women Act. 17 BU Int'l LJ 1, Spring 1999.

Symposium: Violent Crime Control and Law Enforcement Act of 1994. 20 Dayton L Rev 557, Winter 1995.

Crais. Sixth Annual Review of Gender and Sexuality Law: II. Criminal Law Chapter: Domestic Violence and the Federal Government. 6 Geo J Gender & L 405, 2005.

Filler. Making the Case for Megan's Law: A Study in Legislative Rhetoric. 76 Ind LJ 315, Spring 2001.

Kelly. Stories from the front: seeking refuge for battered immigrants in the Violence Against Women Act, 92 Nw U L Rev 665, Winter 1998.

Pincus; Rosen. Fighting back: filing suit under the Violence Against Women Act, 33 Trial 20, December 1997.

Jacobs. Criminal Justice and other Programs: Legal and Political Impediments to Lethal Violence Policy. 69 U Colo L Rev 1099, Fall 1998.

Hearn. A thirteenth amendment defense of the Violence Against Women Act, 146 U Pa L Rev 1097, April 1998.

INTERPRETIVE NOTES AND DECISIONS

Ninth Amendment does not encompass enumerated, fundamental individual right to bear firearms, and plaintiff associations of individuals cannot show legal injury under 9th Amendment necessary for standing to challenge Crime Control Act, 42 USCS §§ 13701 et seq. San Diego County Gun Rights Comm. v Reno (1996, CA9 Cal) 98 F3d 1121, 96 CDOS 7760, 96 Daily Journal DAR 12811 (criticized in Jackson v City & County of San Francisco (2011, ND Cal) 2011 US Dist LEXIS 109812).

§ 13702. Authorization of grants

(a) In general. The Attorney General shall provide Violent Offender Incarceration grants under section 20103 [42 USCS § 13703] and Truth-in-Sentencing Incentive grants under section 20104 [42 USCS § 13704] to eligible States—

(1) to build or expand correctional facilities to increase the bed capacity for the confinement of persons convicted of a part 1 violent crime or adjudicated delinquent for an act which if committed by an adult, would be a part 1 violent crime;

(2) to build or expand temporary or permanent correctional facilities, including facilities on military bases, prison barges, and boot camps, for the confinement of convicted nonviolent offenders and criminal aliens, for the purpose of freeing suitable existing prison space for the confinement of persons convicted of a part 1 violent crime;

(3) to build or expand jails; and

(4) to carry out any activity referred to in section 2976(b) of the Omnibus Crime Control and Safe Streets Act of 1968 (42 U.S.C. 3797w(b)).

(b) Regional compacts. (1) In general. Subject to paragraph (2), States may enter into regional compacts to carry out this subtitle [42 USCS §§ 13701 et seq.]. Such compacts shall be treated as States under this subtitle [42 USCS §§ 13701 et seq.].

(2) Requirement. To be recognized as a regional compact for eligibility for a grant under section 20103 or 20104 [42 USCS § 13703 or 13704], each member State must be eligible individually.

(3) Limitation on receipt of funds. No State may receive a grant under this subtitle [42 USCS §§ 13701 et seq.] both individually and as part of a compact.

(c) Applicability. Notwithstanding the eligibility requirements of section 20104 [42 USCS § 13704], a State that certifies to the Attorney General that, as of the date of enactment of the Department of Justice Appropriations Act, 1996 [enacted April 26, 1996], such State has enacted legislation in reliance on subtitle A of title II of the Violent Crime Control and Law Enforcement Act [former 42 USCS §§ 13701 et seq.], as enacted on September 13, 1994, and would in fact qualify under those provisions, shall be eligible to receive a grant for fiscal year 1996 as though such State qualifies under section 20104 of this subtitle [42 USCS § 13704].

(Sept. 13, 1994, P. L. 103-322, Title II, Subtitle A, § 20102, as added April 26, 1996, P. L. 104-134, Title I, § 114(a), 110 Stat. 1321-15; May 2, 1996, P. L. 104-140, § 1(a), 110 Stat. 1327; April 9, 2008, P. L. 110-199, Title I, Subtitle A, § 104(a), 122 Stat. 669.)

HISTORY; ANCILLARY LAWS AND DIRECTIVES

Explanatory notes:

A prior § 13702 (Act Sept. 13, 1994, P. L. 103-322, Title II, Subtitle A, § 20102, 108 Stat. 1816) was omitted in the general amendment of this subtitle (42 USCS §§ 13701 et seq.) by April 26, 1996, P. L. 104-134, Title I, § 114(a), 110 Stat. 1321-14. Such section provided for truth in sentencing incentive grants.

Act May 2, 1996, P. L. 104-140, § 1(a), 110 Stat. 1327, inserted the heading "TITLE I—OMNIBUS APPROPRIATIONS" after the enacting clause of Act April 26, 1996, P. L. 104-134.

Amendments:

2008. Act April 9, 2008, in subsec. (a), in para. (2), deleted "and" following the concluding semicolon, in para. (3), substituted "; and" for a concluding period, and added para. (4).

Other provisions:

Construction of April 9, 2008 amendment. For construction of amendments by Act April 9, 2008, P. L. 110-199 and requirements for grants made under such amendments, see 42 USCS § 17504.

CROSS REFERENCES

This section is referred to in 42 USCS §§ 13705, 13706, 13707, 13708, 14214.

§ 13703. Violent offender incarceration grants

(a) Eligibility for minimum grant. To be eligible to receive a minimum grant under this section, a State shall submit an application to the Attorney General that provides assurances that the State has implemented, or will implement, correctional policies and programs, including truth-in-sentencing laws that ensure that violent offenders serve a substantial portion of the sentences imposed, that are designed to provide sufficiently severe punishment for violent offenders, including violent juvenile offenders, and that the prison time served is appropriately related to the determination that the inmate is a violent offender and for a period of time deemed necessary to protect the public.

(b) Additional amount for increased percentage of persons sentenced and time served. A State that received a grant under subsection (a) is eligible to receive additional grant amounts if such State demonstrates that the State has, since 1993—

(1) increased the percentage of persons arrested for a part 1 violent crime sentenced to prison; or

(2) increased the average prison time actually served or the average percent of sentence served by persons convicted of a part 1 violent crime.

Receipt of grant amounts under this subsection does not preclude eligibility for a grant under subsection (c).

(c) Additional amount for increased rate of incarceration and percentage of sentence served. A State that received a grant under subsection (a) is eligible to receive additional grant amounts if such State demonstrates that the State has—

(1) since 1993, increased the percentage of persons arrested for a part 1 violent crime sentenced to prison, and has increased the average percent of sentence served by persons convicted of a part 1 violent crime; or

(2) has increased by 10 percent or more over the most recent 3-year period the number of new court commitments to prison of persons convicted of part 1 violent crimes.

Receipt of grant amounts under this subsection does not preclude eligibility for a grant under subsection (b).

(Sept. 13, 1994, P. L. 103-322, Title II, Subtitle A, § 20103, as added April 26, 1996, P. L. 104-134, Title I, § 114(a), 110 Stat. 1321-16; May 2, 1996, P. L. 104-140, § 1(a), 110 Stat. 1327.)

HISTORY; ANCILLARY LAWS AND DIRECTIVES

Explanatory notes:
A prior § 13703 (Act Sept. 13, 1994, P. L. 103-322, Title II, Subtitle A, § 20101, 108 Stat. 1817) was omitted in the general amendment of this subtitle (42 USCS §§ 13701 et seq.) by April 26, 1996, P. L. 104-134, Title I, § 114(a), 110 Stat. 1321-14. Such section provided for Violent Offender Incarceration grants.

Act May 2, 1996, P. L. 104-140, § 1(a), 110 Stat. 1327, inserted the heading "TITLE I—OMNIBUS APPROPRIATIONS" after the enacting clause of Act April 26, 1996, P. L. 104-134.

Other provisions:
Implementation of controlled substance testing program for convicted offenders as requirement for grants. Act Sept. 30, 1996, P. L. 104-208, Div A, Title I, § 101(a) [Title I], 110 Stat. 3009-14, provides: "Beginning in fiscal year 1999, and thereafter, no funds shall be available to make grants to a State pursuant to section 20103 or section 20104 of the Violent Crime Control and Law Enforcement Act of 1994 [42 USCS §§ 13703, 13704] unless no later than September 1, 1998, such State has implemented a program of controlled substance testing and intervention for appropriate categories of convicted offenders during periods of incarceration and criminal justice supervision, with sanctions including denial or revocation of release for positive controlled substance tests, consistent with guidelines issued by the Attorney General.".

CROSS REFERENCES

This section is referred to in 42 USCS §§ 13702, 13705, 13706, 13708, 13709, 13712, 14214.

§ 13704. Truth-in-sentencing incentive grants

(a) Eligibility. To be eligible to receive a grant award under this section, a

State shall submit an application to the Attorney General that demonstrates that—

(1)(A) such State has implemented truth-in-sentencing laws that—

(i) require persons convicted of a part 1 violent crime to serve not less than 85 percent of the sentence imposed (without counting time not actually served, such as administrative or statutory incentives for good behavior); or

(ii) result in persons convicted of a part 1 violent crime serving on average not less than 85 percent of the sentence imposed (without counting time not actually served, such as administrative or statutory incentives for good behavior);

(B) such State has truth-in-sentencing laws that have been enacted, but not yet implemented, that require such State, not later than 3 years after such State submits an application to the Attorney General, to provide that persons convicted of a part 1 violent crime serve not less than 85 percent of the sentence imposed (without counting time not actually served, such as administrative or statutory incentives for good behavior); or

(C) in the case of a State that on the date of enactment of the Departments of Commerce, Justice, and State, the Judiciary, and Related Agencies Appropriations Act, 1996 [enacted April 26, 1996], practices indeterminate sentencing with regard to any part 1 violent crime—

(i) persons convicted of a part 1 violent crime on average serve not less than 85 percent of the prison term established under the State's sentencing and release guidelines; or

(ii) persons convicted of a part 1 violent crime on average serve not less than 85 percent of the maximum prison term allowed under the sentence imposed by the court (not counting time not actually served such as administrative or statutory incentives for good behavior); and

(2) such State has provided assurances that it will follow guidelines established by the Attorney General in reporting, on a quarterly basis, information regarding the death of any person who is in the process of arrest, is en route to be incarcerated, or is incarcerated at a municipal or county jail, State prison, or other local or State correctional facility (including any juvenile facility) that, at a minimum, includes—

(A) the name, gender, race, ethnicity, and age of the deceased;

(B) the date, time, and location of death; and

(C) a brief description of the circumstances surrounding the death.

(b) Exception. Notwithstanding subsection (a), a State may provide that the Governor of the State may allow for the earlier release of—

(1) a geriatric prisoner; or

(2) a prisoner whose medical condition precludes the prisoner from posing a threat to the public, but only after a public hearing in which representatives of the public and the prisoner's victims have had an opportunity to be heard regarding a proposed release.

(Sept. 13, 1994, P. L. 103-322, Title II, Subtitle A, § 20104, as added April 26, 1996, P. L. 104-134, Title I, § 114(a), 110 Stat. 1321-16; May 2, 1996, P. L.

104-140, § 1(a), 110 Stat. 1327; Oct. 13, 2000, P. L. 106-297, § 2, 114 Stat. 1045.)

HISTORY; ANCILLARY LAWS AND DIRECTIVES

Explanatory notes:

A prior § 13704 (Act Sept. 13, 1994, P. L. 103-322, Title II, Subtitle A, § 20101, 108 Stat. 1818) was omitted in the general amendment of this subtitle (42 USCS §§ 13701 et seq.) by April 26, 1996, P. L. 104-134, Title I, § 114(a), 110 Stat. 1321-14. Such section provided for matching requirement.

Act May 2, 1996, P. L. 104-140, § 1(a), 110 Stat. 1327, inserted the heading "TITLE I—OMNIBUS APPROPRIATIONS" after the enacting clause of Act April 26, 1996, P. L. 104-134.

Amendments:

2000. Act Oct. 13, 2000, in subsec. (a), redesignated para. (1) as para. (1)(A) and redesignated former subparas. (A) and (B) of such subdivision as cls. (i) and (ii), respectively, redesignated para. (2) as subpara. (B), redesignated para. (3) as subpara. (C) and redesignated former subparas. (A) and (B) of such subdivision as cls. (i) and (ii), respectively, and, in cl. (ii) as redesignated, substituted "; and" for a concluding period, and added new para. (2).

CROSS REFERENCES

This section is referred to in 42 USCS §§ 13702, 13705, 13706, 13708, 13709, 13712, 14214.

§ 13705. Special rules

(a) Sharing of funds with counties and other units of local government. (1) Reservation. Each State shall reserve not more than 15 percent of the amount of funds allocated in a fiscal year pursuant to section 20106 [42 USCS § 13706] for counties and units of local government to construct, develop, expand, modify, or improve jails and other correctional facilities.

(2) Factors for determination of amount. To determine the amount of funds to be reserved under this subsection, a State shall consider the burden placed on a county or unit of local government that results from the implementation of policies adopted by the State to carry out section 20103 or 20104 [42 USCS § 13703 or 13704].

(b) Use of truth-in-sentencing and violent offender incarceration grants. Funds provided under section 20103 or 20104 [42 USCS § 13703 or 13704] may be applied to the cost of—

(1) altering existing correctional facilities to provide separate facilities for juveniles under the jurisdiction of an adult criminal court who are detained or are serving sentences in adult prisons or jails;

(2) providing correctional staff who are responsible for supervising juveniles who are detained or serving sentences under the jurisdiction of an adult criminal court with orientation and ongoing training regarding the unique needs of such offenders; and

(3) providing ombudsmen to monitor the treatment of juveniles who are

detained or serving sentences under the jurisdiction of an adult criminal court in adult facilities, consistent with guidelines issued by the Assistant Attorney General.

(c) Funds for juvenile offenders. Notwithstanding any other provision of this subtitle [42 USCS §§ 13701 et seq.], if a State, or unit of local government located in a State that otherwise meets the requirements of section 20103 or 20104 [42 USCS § 13703 or 13704], certifies to the Attorney General that exigent circumstances exist that require the State to expend funds to build or expand facilities to confine juvenile offenders other than juvenile offenders adjudicated delinquent for an act which, if committed by an adult, would be a part 1 violent crime, the State may use funds received under this subtitle [42 USCS §§ 13701 et seq.] to build or expand juvenile correctional facilities or pretrial detention facilities for juvenile offenders.

(d) Private facilities. A State may use funds received under this subtitle [42 USCS §§ 13701 et seq.] for the privatization of facilities to carry out the purposes of section 20102 [42 USCS § 13702].

(e) "Part 1 violent crime" defined. For purposes of this subtitle [42 USCS §§ 13701 et seq.], "part 1 violent crime" means a part 1 violent crime as defined in section 20101(3) [20101(2)] [42 USCS § 13701(2)], or a crime in a reasonably comparable class of serious violent crimes as approved by the Attorney General.

(Sept. 13, 1994, P. L. 103-322, Title II, Subtitle A, § 20105, as added April 26, 1996, P. L. 104-134, Title I, § 114(a), 110 Stat. 1321-17; May 2, 1996, P. L. 104-140, § 1(a), 110 Stat. 1327; Oct. 21, 1998, P. L. 105-277, Div E, § 3, 112 Stat. 2681-760; Nov. 2, 2002, P. L. 107-273, Div A, Title III, § 307, 116 Stat. 1783.)

HISTORY; ANCILLARY LAWS AND DIRECTIVES

Explanatory notes:

The section reference "20101(2)" has been inserted in subsec. (e) to indicate the reference probably intended by Congress.

A prior § 13705 (Act Sept. 13, 1994, P. L. 103-322, Title II, Subtitle A, § 20105, 108 Stat. 1818) was omitted in the general amendment of this subtitle (42 USCS §§ 13701 et seq.) by April 26, 1996, P. L. 104-134, Title I, § 114(a), 110 Stat. 1321-14. Such section provided for rules and regulations.

Act May 2, 1996, P. L. 104-140, § 1(a), 110 Stat. 1327, inserted the heading "TITLE I—OMNIBUS APPROPRIATIONS" after the enacting clause of Act April 26, 1996, P. L. 104-134.

Amendments:

1998. Act Oct. 21, 1998, substituted subsec. (b) for one which read: "(b) Additional requirement. To be eligible to receive a grant under section 20103 or 20104, a State shall provide assurances to the Attorney General that the State has implemented or will implement not later than 18 months after the date of the enactment of this subtitle, policies that provide for the recognition of the rights and needs of crime victims.".

2002. Act Nov. 2, 2002, substituted subsec. (b) for one which read:

"(b) Additional requirements. (1) Eligibility for grant. To be eligible to receive a grant under section 20103 or section 20104, a State shall—

"(A) provide assurances to the Attorney General that the State has implemented or will implement not later than 18 months after the date of the enactment of this subtitle, policies that provide for the recognition of the rights of crime victims; and

"(B) subject to the limitation of paragraph (2), no later than September 1, 2000, consider a program of drug testing and intervention for appropriate categories of convicted offenders during periods of incarceration and post-incarceration and criminal justice supervision, with sanctions including denial or revocation of release for positive drug tests, consistent with guidelines issued by the Attorney General.

"(2) Use of funds. Beginning in fiscal year 1999, not more than 10 percent of the funds provided under section 20103 or section 20104 of this subtitle may be applied to the cost of offender drug testing and intervention programs during periods of incarceration and post-incarceration criminal justice supervision, consistent with guidelines issued by the Attorney General. Further, such funds may be used by the States to pay the costs of providing to the Attorney General a baseline study on their prison drug abuse problem. Such studies shall be consistent with guidelines issued by the Attorney General.".

CROSS REFERENCES
This section is referred to in 42 USCS § 14214.

§ 13706. Formula for grants

(a) Allocation of violent offender incarceration grants under section 20103.
(1) Formula allocation. 85 percent of the amount available for grants under section 20103 [42 USCS § 13703] for any fiscal year shall be allocated as follows (except that a State may not receive more than 9 percent of the total amount of funds made available under this paragraph):

(A) 0.75 percent shall be allocated to each State that meets the requirements of section 20103(a) [42 USCS § 13703(a)], except that the United States Virgin Islands, American Samoa, Guam, and the Commonwealth of the Northern Mariana Islands, if eligible under section 20103(a) [42 USCS § 13703(a)], shall each be allocated 0.05 percent.

(B) The amount remaining after application of subparagraph (A) shall be allocated to each State that meets the requirements of section 20103(b) [42 USCS § 13703(b)], in the ratio that the number of part 1 violent crimes reported by such State to the Federal Bureau of Investigation for the 3 years preceding the year in which the determination is made, bears to the average annual number of part 1 violent crimes reported by all States that meet the requirements of section 20103(b) [42 USCS § 13703(b)] to the Federal Bureau of Investigation for the 3 years preceding the year in which the determination is made.

(2) Additional allocation. 15 percent of the amount available for grants under section 20103 [42 USCS § 13703] for any fiscal year shall be allocated to each State that meets the requirements of section 20103(c) [42 USCS § 13703(c)] as follows:

(A) 3.0 percent shall be allocated to each State that meets the requirements of section 20103(c) [42 USCS § 13703(c)], except that the United States Virgin Islands, American Samoa, Guam, and the Commonwealth of the Northern Mariana Islands, if eligible under such subsection, shall each be allocated 0.03 percent.

(B) The amount remaining after application of subparagraph (A) shall be allocated to each State that meets the requirements of section 20103(c) [42 USCS § 13703(c)], in the ratio that the number of part 1 violent crimes reported by such State to the Federal Bureau of Investigation for the 3 years preceding the year in which the determination is made, bears to the average annual number of part 1 violent crimes reported by all States that meet the requirements of section 20102(c) [42 USCS § 13702(c)] to the Federal Bureau of Investigation for the 3 years preceding the year in which the determination is made.

(b) Allocation of truth-in-sentencing grants under section 20104. The amounts available for grants for section 20104 [42 USCS § 13704] shall be allocated to each State that meets the requirements of section 20104 [42 USCS § 13704] in the ratio that the average annual number of part 1 violent crimes reported by such State to the Federal Bureau of Investigation for the 3 years preceding the year in which the determination is made bears to the average annual number of part 1 violent crimes reported by States that meet the requirements of section 20104 [42 USCS § 13704] to the Federal Bureau of Investigation for the 3 years preceding the year in which the determination is made, except that a State may not receive more than 25 percent of the total amount available for such grants.

(c) Unavailable data. If data regarding part 1 violent crimes in any State is substantially inaccurate or is unavailable for the 3 years preceding the year in which the determination is made, the Attorney General shall utilize the best available comparable data regarding the number of violent crimes for the previous year for the State for the purposes of allocation of funds under this subtitle [42 USCS §§ 13701 et seq.].

(d) Regional compacts. In determining the amount of funds that States organized as a regional compact may receive, the Attorney General shall first apply the formula in either subsection (a) or (b) and (c) of this section to each member State of the compact. The States organized as a regional compact may receive the sum of the amounts so determined.

(Sept. 13, 1994, P. L. 103-322, Title II, Subtitle A, § 20106, as added April 26, 1996, P. L. 104-134, Title I, § 114(a), 110 Stat. 1321-18; May 2, 1996, P. L. 104-140, § 1(a), 110 Stat. 1327.)

HISTORY; ANCILLARY LAWS AND DIRECTIVES

Explanatory notes:
A prior § 13706 (Act Sept. 13, 1994, P. L. 103-322, Title II, Subtitle A, § 20106, 108 Stat. 1818) was omitted in the general amendment of this subtitle (42 USCS §§ 13701 et seq.) by April 26, 1996, P. L. 104-134, Title I, § 114(a), 110 Stat. 1321-14. Such section provided for technical assistance and training.

Act May 2, 1996, P. L. 104-140, § 1(a), 110 Stat. 1327, inserted the heading "TITLE I—OMNIBUS APPROPRIATIONS" after the enacting clause of Act April 26, 1996, P. L. 104-134.

CROSS REFERENCES

This section is referred to in 42 USCS §§ 13705, 14214.

§ 13707. Accountability

(a) Fiscal requirements. A State that receives funds under this subtitle [42 USCS §§ 13701 et seq.] shall use accounting, audit, and fiscal procedures that conform to guidelines prescribed by the Attorney General, and shall ensure that any funds used to carry out the programs under section 20102(a) [42 USCS § 13702(a)] shall represent the best value for the State governments at the lowest possible cost and employ the best available technology.

(b) Administrative provisions. The administrative provisions of sections 801 and 802 of the Omnibus Crime Control and Safe Streets Act of 1968 [42 USCS §§ 3782, 3783] shall apply to the Attorney General under this subtitle [42 USCS §§ 13701 et seq.] in the same manner that such provisions apply to the officials listed in such sections.
(Sept. 13, 1994, P. L. 103-322, Title II, Subtitle A, § 20107, as added April 26, 1996, P. L. 104-134, Title I, § 114(a), 110 Stat. 1321-19; May 2, 1996, P. L. 104-140, § 1(a), 110 Stat. 1327.)

HISTORY; ANCILLARY LAWS AND DIRECTIVES

Explanatory notes:
A prior § 13707 (Act Sept. 13, 1994, P. L. 103-322, Title II, Subtitle A, § 20107, 108 Stat. 1818) was omitted in the general amendment of this subtitle (42 USCS §§ 13701 et seq.) by April 26, 1996, P. L. 104-134, Title I, § 114(a), 110 Stat. 1321-14. Such section provided for evaluation.
Act May 2, 1996, P. L. 104-140, § 1(a), 110 Stat. 1327, inserted the heading "TITLE I—OMNIBUS APPROPRIATIONS" after the enacting clause of Act April 26, 1996, P. L. 104-134.

CROSS REFERENCES

This section is referred to in 42 USCS § 14214.

§ 13708. Authorization of appropriations

(a) In general. (1) Authorizations. There are authorized to be appropriated to carry out this subtitle [42 USCS §§ 13701 et seq.]—
    (A) $997,500,000 for fiscal year 1996;
    (B) $1,330,000,000 for fiscal year 1997;
    (C) $2,527,000,000 for fiscal year 1998;
    (D) $2,660,000,000 for fiscal year 1999; and
    (E) $2,753,100,000 for fiscal year 2000.
  (2) Distribution. (A) In general. Of the amounts remaining after the allocation of funds for the purposes set forth under sections 20110, 20111, and 20109 [42 USCS §§ 13710, 13711, 13709], the Attorney General shall,

from amounts authorized to be appropriated under paragraph (1) for each fiscal year, distribute 50 percent for incarceration grants under section 20103 [42 USCS § 13703], and 50 percent for incentive grants under section 20104 [42 USCS § 13704].

(B) Distribution of minimum amounts. The Attorney General shall distribute minimum amounts allocated for section 20103(a) [42 USCS § 13703(a)] to an eligible State not later than 30 days after receiving an application that demonstrates that such State qualifies for a Violent Offender Incarceration grant under section 20103 [42 USCS § 13703] or a Truth-in-Sentencing Incentive grant under section 20104 [42 USCS § 13704].

(b) Limitations on funds. (1) Uses of funds. Except as provided in section [sections] 20110 and 20111 [42 USCS §§ 13710, 13711], funds made available pursuant to this section shall be used only to carry out the purposes described in section 20102(a) [42 USCS § 13702(a)].

(2) Nonsupplanting requirement. Funds made available pursuant to this section shall not be used to supplant State funds, but shall be used to increase the amount of funds that would, in the absence of Federal funds, be made available from State sources.

(3) Administrative costs. Not more than 3 percent of the funds that remain available after carrying out sections 20109, 20110, and 20111 [42 USCS §§ 13709, 13710, 13711] shall be available to the Attorney General for purposes of—

(A) administration;

(B) research and evaluation, including assessment of the effect on public safety and other effects of the expansion of correctional capacity and sentencing reforms implemented pursuant to this subtitle;

(C) technical assistance relating to the use of grant funds, and development and implementation of sentencing reforms implemented pursuant to this subtitle; and

(D) data collection and improvement of information systems relating to the confinement of violent offenders and other sentencing and correctional matters.

(4) Carryover of appropriations. Funds appropriated pursuant to this section during any fiscal year shall remain available until expended. Funds obligated, but subsequently unspent and deobligated, may remain available, to the extent as may [be] provided in appropriations Acts, for the purpose described in section 20102(a)(4) [42 USCS § 13702(a)(4)] for any subsequent fiscal year. The further obligation of such funds by an official for such purpose shall not be delayed, directly or indirectly, in any manner by any officer or employee in the executive branch.

(5) Matching funds. The Federal share of a grant received under this subtitle [42 USCS §§ 13701 et seq.] may not exceed 90 percent of the costs of a proposal as described in an application approved under this subtitle [42 USCS §§ 13701 et seq.].

(Sept. 13, 1994, P. L. 103-322, Title II, Subtitle A, § 20108, as added April 26,

1996, P. L. 104-134, Title I, § 114(a), 110 Stat. 1321-19; May 2, 1996, P. L. 104-140, § 1(a), 110 Stat. 1327; April 9, 2008, P. L. 110-199, Title I, Subtitle A, § 104(b), 122 Stat. 669.)

HISTORY; ANCILLARY LAWS AND DIRECTIVES

Explanatory notes:

The bracketed word "sections" has been inserted in subsec. (b)(1) as the word probably intended by Congress.

The bracketed word "be" has been inserted in subsec. (b)(4) to indicate the probable intent of Congress to include it.

A prior § 13708 (Act Sept. 13, 1994, P. L. 103-322, Title II, Subtitle A, § 20108, 108 Stat. 1818) was omitted in the general amendment of this subtitle (42 USCS §§ 13701 et seq.) by April 26, 1996, P. L. 104-134, Title I, § 114(a), 110 Stat. 1321-14. Such section contained definitions.

Act May 2, 1996, P. L. 104-140, § 1(a), 110 Stat. 1327, inserted the heading "TITLE I—OMNIBUS APPROPRIATIONS" after the enacting clause of Act April 26, 1996, P. L. 104-134.

Amendments:

2008. Act April 9, 2008, in subsec. (b)(4), added the sentences beginning "Funds obligated . . ." and "The further obligation . . .".

CROSS REFERENCES

This section is referred to in 42 USCS §§ 13709, 13710, 13711, 14214.

§ 13709.　Payments for incarceration on tribal lands

(a) Reservation of funds. Notwithstanding any other provision of this part, of amounts made available to the Attorney General to carry out programs relating to offender incarceration, the Attorney General shall reserve $35,000,000 for each of fiscal years 2011 through 2015 to carry out this section.

(b) Grants to Indian tribes. (1) In general. From the amounts reserved under subsection (a), the Attorney General shall provide grants—

　(A) to Indian tribes for purposes of—

　　(i) construction and maintenance of jails on Indian land for the incarceration of offenders subject to tribal jurisdiction;

　　(ii) entering into contracts with private entities to increase the efficiency of the construction of tribal jails; and

　　(iii) developing and implementing alternatives to incarceration in tribal jails;

　(B) to Indian tribes for the construction of tribal justice centers that combine tribal police, courts, and corrections services to address violations of tribal civil and criminal laws;

　(C) to consortia of Indian tribes for purposes of constructing and operating regional detention centers on Indian land for long-term incarceration of offenders subject to tribal jurisdiction, as the applicable consortium determines to be appropriate.

(2) Priority of funding. [In] in providing grants under this subsection, the Attorney General shall take into consideration applicable—

(A) reservation crime rates;

(B) annual tribal court convictions; and

(C) bed space needs.

(3) Federal share. Because of the Federal nature and responsibility for providing public safety on Indian land, the Federal share of the cost of any activity carried out using a grant under this subsection shall be 100 percent.

(c) Applications. To be eligible to receive a grant under this section, an Indian tribe or consortium of Indian tribes, as applicable, shall submit to the Attorney General an application in such form and containing such information as the Attorney General may by regulation require.

(d) Long-term plan. Not later than 1 year after the date of enactment of this subsection [enacted July 29, 2010], the Attorney General, in coordination with the Bureau of Indian Affairs and in consultation with tribal leaders, tribal law enforcement officers, and tribal corrections officials, shall submit to Congress a long-term plan to address incarceration in Indian country, including—

(1) a description of proposed activities for—

(A) construction, operation, and maintenance of juvenile (in accordance with section 4220(a)(3) of the Indian Alcohol and Substance Abuse Prevention and Treatment Act of 1986 (25 U.S.C. 2453(a)(3)) and adult detention facilities (including regional facilities) in Indian country;

(B) contracting with State and local detention centers, on approval of the affected tribal governments; and

(C) alternatives to incarceration, developed in cooperation with tribal court systems;

(2) an assessment and consideration of the construction of Federal detention facilities in Indian country; and

(3) any other alternatives as the Attorney General, in coordination with the Bureau of Indian Affairs and in consultation with Indian tribes, determines to be necessary.

(Sept. 13, 1994, P. L. 103-322, Title II, Subtitle A, § 20109, as added April 26, 1996, P. L. 104-134, Title I, § 114(a), 110 Stat. 1321-20; May 2, 1996, P. L. 104-140, § 1(a), 110 Stat. 1327; July 29, 2010, P. L. 111-211, Title II, Subtitle D, § 244, 124 Stat. 2294.)

HISTORY; ANCILLARY LAWS AND DIRECTIVES

Explanatory notes:

The bracketed word "In" has been inserted in subsec. (b)(2) to indicate the capitalization probably intended by Congress.

Act May 2, 1996, P. L. 104-140, § 1(a), 110 Stat. 1327, inserted the heading "TITLE I—OMNIBUS APPROPRIATIONS" after the enacting clause of Act April 26, 1996, P. L. 104-134.

Amendments:

2010. Act July 29, 2010, substituted subsecs. (a) and (b) for ones which read:

"(a) Reservation of funds. Notwithstanding any other provision of this subtitle other than section 20108(a)(2), from amounts appropriated to carry out sections 20103 and 20104, the Attorney General shall reserve, to carry out this section—

"(1) 0.3 percent in each of fiscal years 1996 and 1997; and

"(2) 0.2 percent in each of fiscal years 1998, 1999, and 2000.

"(b) Grants to Indian tribes. From the amounts reserved under subsection (a), the Attorney General may make grants to Indian tribes for the purposes of constructing jails on tribal lands for the incarceration of offenders subject to tribal jurisdiction.";

in subsec. (c), inserted "or consortium of Indian tribes, as applicable,"; and added subsec. (d).

CROSS REFERENCES

This section is referred to in 42 USCS §§ 13708, 14214.

§ 13710. Payments to eligible States for incarceration of criminal aliens

(a) In general. The Attorney General shall make a payment to each State which is eligible under section 242(j) of the Immigration and Nationality Act in such amount as is determined under section 242(j), and for which payment is not made to such State for such fiscal year under such section.

(b) Authorization of appropriations. Notwithstanding any other provision of this subtitle [42 USCS §§ 13701 et seq.], there are authorized to be appropriated to carry out this section from amounts authorized under section 20108 [42 USCS § 13708], an amount which when added to amounts appropriated to carry out section 242(j) of the Immigration and Nationality Act for fiscal year 1996 equals $500,000,000 and for each of the fiscal years 1997 through 2000 does not exceed $650,000,000.

(c) Administration. The amounts appropriated to carry out this section shall be reserved from the total amount appropriated for each fiscal year and shall be added to the other funds appropriated to carry out section 242(j) of the Immigration and Nationality Act and administered under such section.

(d) Report to Congress. Not later than May 15, 1999, the Attorney General shall submit a report to the Congress which contains the recommendation of the Attorney General concerning the extension of the program under this section. (Sept. 13, 1994, P. L. 103-322, Title II, Subtitle A, § 20110, as added April 26, 1996, P. L. 104-134, Title I, § 114(a), 110 Stat. 1321-21; May 2, 1996, P. L. 104-140, § 1(a), 110 Stat. 1327.)

HISTORY; ANCILLARY LAWS AND DIRECTIVES

References in text:

"Section 242(j) of the Immigration and Nationality Act", referred to in this section, is § 242(j) of Act June 27, 1952, ch 477, which formerly appeared as 8 USCS § 1252(j), and was redesignated subsec. (i) of § 241 of such Act by § 306(a)(1) of Act Sept. 30, 1996, P. L. 104-208, and appears as 8 USCS § 1231(i).

Explanatory notes:

Act May 2, 1996, P. L. 104-140, § 1(a), 110 Stat. 1327, inserted the head-

ing "TITLE I—OMNIBUS APPROPRIATIONS" after the enacting clause
of Act April 26, 1996, P. L. 104-134.

CROSS REFERENCES

This section is referred to in 42 USCS § 13708.

§ 13711. Support of Federal prisoners in non-Federal institutions

(a) In general. The Attorney General may make payments to States and units
of local government for the purposes authorized in section 4013 of title 18,
United States Code.

(b) Authorization of appropriations. Notwithstanding any other provision of
this subtitle other than section 20108(a)(2) [42 USCS § 13708(a)(2)], there are
authorized to be appropriated from amounts authorized under section 20108 [42
USCS § 13708] for each of fiscal years 1996 through 2000 such sums as may
be necessary to carry out this section.
(Sept. 13, 1994, P. L. 103-322, Title II, Subtitle A, § 20111, as added April 26,
1996, P. L. 104-134, Title I, § 114(a), 110 Stat. 1321-21; May 2, 1996, P. L.
104-140, § 1(a), 110 Stat. 1327.)

HISTORY; ANCILLARY LAWS AND DIRECTIVES

Explanatory notes:
Act May 2, 1996, P. L. 104-140, § 1(a), 110 Stat. 1327, inserted the heading "TITLE I—OMNIBUS APPROPRIATIONS" after the enacting clause
of Act April 26, 1996, P. L. 104-134.

CROSS REFERENCES

This section is referred to in 42 USCS § 13708.

§ 13712. Report by the Attorney General

Beginning on October 1, 1996, and each subsequent July 1 thereafter, the Attorney General shall report to the Congress on the implementation of this
subtitle [42 USCS §§ 13701 et seq.], including a report on the eligibility of the
States under sections 20103 and 20104 [42 USCS §§ 13703, 13704], and the
distribution and use of funds under this subtitle [42 USCS §§ 13701 et seq.].
(Sept. 13, 1994, P. L. 103-322, Title II, Subtitle A, § 20112, as added April 26,
1996, P. L. 104-134, Title I, § 114(a), 110 Stat. 1321-21; May 2, 1996, P. L.
104-140, § 1(a), 110 Stat. 1327.)

HISTORY; ANCILLARY LAWS AND DIRECTIVES

Explanatory notes:
Act May 2, 1996, P. L. 104-140, § 1(a), 110 Stat. 1327, inserted the heading "TITLE I—OMNIBUS APPROPRIATIONS" after the enacting clause
of Act April 26, 1996, P. L. 104-134.

§ 13713. Aimee's Law

(a) Short title. This section may be cited as "Aimee's Law".

(b) Definitions. Pursuant to regulations promulgated by the Attorney General hereunder, in this section:

(1) Dangerous sexual offense. The term "dangerous sexual offense" means any offense under State law for conduct that would constitute an offense under chapter 109A of title 18, United States Code [18 USCS §§ 2241 et seq.], had the conduct occurred in the special maritime and territorial jurisdiction of the United States or in a Federal prison.

(2) Murder. The term "murder" has the meaning given the term in part I of the Uniform Crime Reports of the Federal Bureau of Investigation.

(3) Rape. The term "rape" has the meaning given the term in part I of the Uniform Crime Reports of the Federal Bureau of Investigation.

(c) Penalty. (1) Single State. Pursuant to regulations promulgated by the Attorney General hereunder, in any case in which a criminal-records-reporting State convicts an individual of murder, rape, or a dangerous sexual offense, who has a prior conviction for any one of those offenses in a State described in paragraph (3), it may, under subsection (d), apply to the Attorney General for $10,000, for its related apprehension and prosecution costs, and $22,500 per year (up to a maximum of 5 years), for its related incarceration costs with both amounts for costs adjusted annually for the rate of inflation.

(2) Multiple States. Pursuant to regulations promulgated by the Attorney General hereunder, in any case in which a criminal-records-reporting State convicts an individual of murder, rape, or a dangerous sexual offense, who has a prior conviction for any one or more of those offenses in more than one other State described in paragraph (3), it may, under subsection (d), apply to the Attorney General for $10,000, for its related apprehension and prosecution costs, and $22,500 per year (up to a maximum of 5 years), for its related incarceration costs with both amounts for costs adjusted annually for the rate of inflation.

(3) State described. Pursuant to regulations promulgated by the Attorney General hereunder, a State is described in this paragraph unless—

(A) the term of imprisonment imposed by the State on the individual described in paragraph (1) or (2), as applicable, was not less than the average term of imprisonment imposed for that offense in all States; or

(B) with respect to the individual described in paragraph (1) or (2), as applicable, the individual had served not less than 85 percent of the term of imprisonment to which that individual was sentenced for the prior offense.

For purposes of subparagraph (B), in a State that has indeterminate sentencing, the term of imprisonment to which that individual was sentenced for the prior offense shall be based on the lower of the range of sentences.

(d) State applications. In order to receive an amount under subsection (c), the chief executive of a State shall submit to the Attorney General an application, in such form and containing such information as the Attorney General may reasonably require, which shall include a certification that the State has convicted an individual of murder, rape, or a dangerous sexual offense, who has a prior conviction for one of those offenses in another State.

(e) Source of funds. (1) In general. Pursuant to regulations promulgated by the Attorney General hereunder, any amount under subsection (c) shall be derived by reducing the amount of Federal law enforcement assistance funds received by the State pursuant to section 505 of the Omnibus Crime Control and Safe Streets Act of 1968 [42 USCS § 3755] that convicted such individual of the prior offense before the distribution of the funds to the State. No amount described under this section shall be subject to section 3335(b) or 6503(d) of title 31, United States Code[.]

(2) Payment schedule. The Attorney General, in consultation with the chief executive of the State that convicted such individual of the prior offense, shall establish a payment schedule.

(f) Construction. Nothing in this section may be construed to diminish or otherwise affect any court ordered restitution.

(g) Exception. Pursuant to regulations promulgated by the Attorney General hereunder, this section does not apply if the individual convicted of murder, rape, or a dangerous sexual offense has been released from prison upon the reversal of a conviction for an offense described in subsection (c) and subsequently been convicted for an offense described in subsection (c).

(h) Report. The Attorney General shall—

(1) conduct a study evaluating the implementation of this section; and

(2) not later than October 1, 2006, submit to Congress a report on the results of that study.

(i) Collection of recidivism data. (1) In general. Beginning with calendar year 2002, and each calendar year thereafter, the Attorney General shall collect and maintain information relating to, with respect to each State (where practicable)—

(A) the number of convictions during that calendar year for—

(i) any dangerous sexual offense;

(ii) rape; and

(iii) murder; and

(B) the number of convictions described in subparagraph (A) that constitute second or subsequent convictions of the defendant of an offense described in that subparagraph.

(2) Report. The Attorney General shall submit to Congress—

(A) a report, by not later than 6 months after the date of enactment of this Act [enacted Jan. 5, 2006], that provides national estimates of the nature and extent of recidivism (with an emphasis on interstate recidivism) by State inmates convicted of murder, rape, and dangerous sexual offenses;

(B) a report, by not later than October 1, 2007, and October 1 of each year thereafter, that provides statistical analysis and criminal history profiles of interstate recidivists identified in any State applications under this section; and

(C) reports, at regular intervals not to exceed every five years, that include the information described in paragraph (1).

(j) Effective date. This section shall take effect on January 1, 2002.

(Oct. 28, 2000, P. L. 106-386, Div C, § 2001, 114 Stat. 1539; Jan. 5, 2006, P. L. 109-162, Title XI, Subtitle B, Ch. 5, § 1170, 119 Stat. 3122; Aug. 12, 2006, P. L. 109-271, § 8(m), 120 Stat. 767.)

HISTORY; ANCILLARY LAWS AND DIRECTIVES

Explanatory notes:

The period has been inserted in brackets in subsec. (e)(1) to indicate the probable intent of Congress to include such punctuation.

This section was enacted as part of Act Oct. 28, 2000, P. L. 106-386, and not as part of Act Sept. 13, 1994, P. L. 103-322, which generally comprises this chapter.

Amendments:

2006. Act Jan. 5, 2006, in subsec. (b), in the introductory matter, substituted "Pursuant to regulations promulgated by the Attorney General hereunder, in" for "In"; and, in subsec. (c), in paras. (1) and (2), substituted "Pursuant to regulations promulgated by the Attorney General hereunder, in" for "In", inserted "criminal-records-reporting", and substituted "it may, under subsection (d), apply to the Attorney General for $10,000, for its related apprehension and prosecution costs, and $22,500 per year (up to a maximum of 5 years), for its related incarceration costs with both amounts for costs adjusted annually for the rate of inflation" for "the Attorney General shall transfer an amount equal to the costs of incarceration, prosecution, and apprehension of that individual, from Federal law enforcement assistance funds that have been allocated to but not distributed to the State that convicted the individual of the prior offense, to the State account that collects Federal law enforcement assistance funds of the State that convicted that individual of the subsequent offense", and, in para. (3), in the introductory matter, substituted "Pursuant to regulations promulgated by the Attorney General hereunder, a" for "A", and substituted "unless—" for "if—", in subpara. (A), substituted "not less" for "convicted by the State is less", and, in subpara. (B), inserted "not" preceding "less".

Such Act further purported to amend subsec. (c)(3) by deleting "average", but did not specify which occurrence of the word was intended. In order to effectuate the probable intent of Congress, the amendment was executed by deleting only the first occurrence of the word; that is, preceding "term of imprisonment imposed by the State" in subpara. (A).

Such Act further purported to amend subsec. (c)(3) by deleting "individuals convicted of the offense for which,"; however, the amendment was executed by deleting "individuals convicted of the offense for which" preceding "the individual" in subpara. (A) in order to effectuate the probable intent of Congress.

Such Act further, in subsec. (d), deleted "transferred" preceding "under subsection (c)"; in subsec. (e)(1), substituted "Pursuant to regulations promulgated by the Attorney General hereunder, any" for "Any", deleted "transferred" preceding "under subsection (c)", inserted "pursuant to section 506 of the Omnibus Crime Control and Safe Streets Act of 1968", and substituted the sentence beginning "No amount . . ." for "The Attorney General shall provide the State with an opportunity to select the specific Federal law enforcement assistance funds to be so reduced (other than Federal crime victim assistance funds).''; in subsec. (g), substituted "Pur-

suant to regulations promulgated by the Attorney General hereunder, this"
for "This"; and, in subsec. (i), in para. (1), in the introductory matter,
inserted "(where practicable)", and substituted para. (2) for one which
read:

> "(2) Report. Not later than March 1, 2003, and on March 1 of each year
> thereafter, the Attorney General shall submit to Congress a report, which
> shall include—
>
> > "(A) the information collected under paragraph (1) with respect to
> > each State during the preceding calendar year; and
> >
> > "(B) the percentage of cases in each State in which an individual
> > convicted of an offense described in paragraph (1)(A) was previously
> > convicted of another such offense in another State during the preced-
> > ing calendar year.".

Act Aug. 12, 2006, in subsec. (e)(1), substituted "section 505" for "section 506".

MISCELLANEOUS PROVISIONS

§ 13721. Task force on prison construction standardization and techniques

(a) Task force. The Director of the National Institute of Corrections shall,
subject to availability of appropriations, establish a task force composed of
Federal, State, and local officials expert in prison construction, and of at least
an equal number of engineers, architects, and construction experts from the
private sector with expertise in prison design and construction, including the
use of cost-cutting construction standardization techniques and cost-cutting new
building materials and technologies.

(b) Cooperation. The task force shall work in close cooperation and communication with other State and local officials responsible for prison construction
in their localities.

(c) Performance requirements. The task force shall work to—

(1) establish and recommend standardized construction plans and techniques
for prison and prison component construction; and

(2) evaluate and recommend new construction technologies, techniques, and
materials,

to reduce prison construction costs at the Federal, State, and local levels and
make such construction more efficient.

(d) Dissemination. The task force shall disseminate information described in
subsection (c) to State and local officials involved in prison construction,
through written reports and meetings.

(e) Promotion and evaluation. The task force shall—

(1) work to promote the implementation of cost-saving efforts at the Federal,
State, and local levels;

(2) evaluate and advise on the results and effectiveness of such cost-saving
efforts as adopted, broadly disseminating information on the results; and

(3) to the extent feasible, certify the effectiveness of the cost-savings efforts.

(Sept. 13, 1994, P. L. 103-322, Title II, Subtitle D, § 20406, 108 Stat. 1826.)

§ 13722. Efficiency in law enforcement and corrections

(a) In general. In the administration of each grant program funded by appropriations authorized by this Act or by an amendment made by this Act, the Attorney General shall encourage—

(1) innovative methods for the low-cost construction of facilities to be constructed, converted, or expanded and the low-cost operation of such facilities and the reduction of administrative costs and overhead expenses; and

(2) the use of surplus Federal property.

(b) Assessment of construction components and designs. The Attorney General may make an assessment of the cost efficiency and utility of using modular, prefabricated, precast, and pre-engineered construction components and designs for housing nonviolent criminals.

(Sept. 13, 1994, P. L. 103-322, Title II, Subtitle D, § 20407, 108 Stat. 1826.)

HISTORY; ANCILLARY LAWS AND DIRECTIVES

References in text:

"This Act", referred to in this section, is Act Sept. 13, 1994, P. L. 103-322, 108 Stat. 1796, popularly known as the Violent Crime Control and Law Enforcement Act of 1994. For full classification of this Act, consult USCS Tables volumes.

§ 13723. Congressional approval of any expansion at Lorton and congressional hearings on future needs

(a) Congressional approval. Notwithstanding any other provision of law, the existing prison facilities and complex at the District of Columbia Corrections Facility at Lorton, Virginia, shall not be expanded unless such expansion has been approved by the Congress under the authority provided to Congress in section 446 of the District of Columbia Self-Government and Governmental Reorganization Act [District of Columbia Home Rule Act].

(b) Senate hearings. The Senate directs the Subcommittee on the District of Columbia of the Committee on Appropriations of the Senate to conduct hearings regarding expansion of the prison complex in Lorton, Virginia, prior to any approval granted pursuant to subsection (a). The subcommittee shall permit interested parties, including appropriate officials from the County of Fairfax, Virginia, to testify at such hearings.

(c) "Expanded" and "expansion" defined. For purposes of this section, the terms "expanded" and "expansion" mean any alteration of the physical structure of the prison complex that is made to increase the number of inmates incarcerated at the prison.

(Sept. 13, 1994, P. L. 103-322, Title II, Subtitle D, § 20410, 108 Stat. 1828.)

HISTORY; ANCILLARY LAWS AND DIRECTIVES

References in text:

"Section 446 of the District of Columbia Self-Government and Governmental Reorganization Act'', referred to in subsec. (a), is § 446 of Act Dec. 24, 1973, P. L. 93-198, which is not classified to the Code.

Explanatory notes:
The bracketed words "District of Columbia Home Rule Act" have been inserted in subsec. (a) on the authority of Act Aug. 5, 1997, P. L. 105-33, Title XI, Subtitle C, Ch 2, § 11717(b), 111 Stat. 786, which provides that any reference in law or regulation to the District of Columbia Self-Government and Governmental Reorganization Act shall be deemed to be a reference to the District of Columbia Home Rule Act.

§ 13724. Conversion of closed military installations into Federal prison facilities

(a) Study of suitable bases. The Secretary of Defense and the Attorney General shall jointly conduct a study of all military installations selected before the date of enactment of this Act [enacted Sept. 13, 1994] to be closed pursuant to a base closure law for the purpose of evaluating the suitability of any of these installations, or portions of these installations, for conversion into Federal prison facilities. As part of the study, the Secretary and the Attorney General shall identify the military installations so evaluated that are most suitable for conversion into Federal prison facilities.

(b) Suitability for conversion. In evaluating the suitability of a military installation for conversion into a Federal prison facility, the Secretary of Defense and the Attorney General shall consider the estimated cost to convert the installation into a prison facility and such other factors as the Secretary and the Attorney General consider to be appropriate.

(c) Time for study. The study required by subsection (a) shall be completed not later than the date that is 180 days after the date of enactment of this Act [enacted Sept. 13, 1994].

(d) Construction of Federal prisons. (1) In general. In determining where to locate any new Federal prison facility, and in accordance with the Department of Justice's duty to review and identify a use for any portion of an installation closed pursuant to title II of the Defense Authorization Amendments and Base Closure and Realignment Act (Public Law 100-526) [10 USCS § 2687 note] and the Defense Base Closure and Realignment Act of 1990 (part A of title XXIX of Public Law 101-510) [10 USCS § 2687 note], the Attorney General shall—

(A) consider whether using any portion of a military installation closed or scheduled to be closed in the region pursuant to a base closure law provides a cost-effective alternative to the purchase of real property or construction of new prison facilities;

(B) consider whether such use is consistent with a reutilization and redevelopment plan; and

(C) give consideration to any installation located in a rural area the closure of which will have a substantial adverse impact on the economy of the local communities and on the ability of the communities to sustain an economic recovery from such closure.

(2) Consent. With regard to paragraph (1)(B), consent must be obtained from the local re-use authority for the military installation, recognized and funded by the Secretary of Defense, before the Attorney General may proceed with plans for the design or construction of a prison at the installation.

(3) Report on basis of decision. Before proceeding with plans for the design or construction of a Federal prison, the Attorney General shall submit to Congress a report explaining the basis of the decision on where to locate the new prison facility.

(4) Report on cost-effectiveness. If the Attorney General decides not to utilize any portion of a closed military installation or an installation scheduled to be closed for locating a prison, the report shall include an analysis of why installations in the region, the use of which as a prison would be consistent with a reutilization and redevelopment plan, does not provide a cost-effective alternative to the purchase of real property or construction of new prison facilities.

(e) **"Base closure law" defined.** In this section, "base closure law" means—

(1) the Defense Base Closure and Realignment Act of 1990 (part A of title XXIX of Public Law 101-510; 10 U.S.C. 2687 note); and

(2) title II of the Defense Authorization Amendments and Base Closure and Realignment Act (Public Law 100-526; 10 U.S.C. 2687 note).

(Sept. 13, 1994, P. L. 103-322, Title II, Subtitle D, § 20413, 108 Stat. 1829.)

§ 13725. Correctional job training and placement

(a) **Purpose.** It is the purpose of this section to encourage and support job training programs, and job placement programs, that provide services to incarcerated persons or ex-offenders.

(b) **Definitions.** As used in this section:

(1) Correctional institution. The term "correctional institution" means any prison, jail, reformatory, work farm, detention center, or halfway house, or any other similar institution designed for the confinement or rehabilitation of criminal offenders.

(2) Correctional job training or placement program. The term "correctional job training or placement program" means an activity that provides job training or job placement services to incarcerated persons or ex-offenders, or that assists incarcerated persons or ex-offenders in obtaining such services.

(3) Ex-offender. The term "ex-offender" means any individual who has been sentenced to a term of probation by a Federal or State court, or who has been released from a Federal, State, or local correctional institution.

(4) Incarcerated person. The term "incarcerated person" means any individual incarcerated in a Federal or State correctional institution who is charged with or convicted of any criminal offense.

(c) **Establishment of Office.** (1) In general. The Attorney General shall establish within the Department of Justice an Office of Correctional Job Training and Placement. The Office shall be headed by a Director, who shall be appointed by the Attorney General.

(2) Timing. The Attorney General shall carry out this subsection not later than 6 months after the date of enactment of this section [enacted Sept. 13, 1994].

(d) Functions of Office. The Attorney General, acting through the Director of the Office of Correctional Job Training and Placement, in consultation with the Secretary of Labor, shall—

(1) assist in coordinating the activities of the Federal Bonding Program of the Department of Labor, the activities of the Department of Labor related to the certification of eligibility for targeted jobs credits under section 51 of the Internal Revenue Code of 1986 [26 USCS § 51] with respect to ex-offenders, and any other correctional job training or placement program of the Department of Justice or Department of Labor;

(2) provide technical assistance to State and local employment and training agencies that—

(A) receive financial assistance under this Act; or

(B) receive financial assistance through other programs carried out by the Department of Justice or Department of Labor, for activities related to the development of employability;

(3) prepare and implement the use of special staff training materials, and methods, for developing the staff competencies needed by State and local agencies to assist incarcerated persons and ex-offenders in gaining market-able occupational skills and job placement;

(4) prepare and submit to Congress an annual report on the activities of the Office of Correctional Job Training and Placement, and the status of cor-rectional job training or placement programs in the United States;

(5) cooperate with other Federal agencies carrying out correctional job train-ing or placement programs to ensure coordination of such programs through-out the United States;

(6) consult with, and provide outreach to—

(A) State job training coordinating councils, administrative entities, and private industry councils, with respect to programs carried out under this Act; and

(B) other State and local officials, with respect to other employment or training programs carried out by the Department of Justice or Department of Labor;

(7) collect from States information on the training accomplishments and employment outcomes of a sample of incarcerated persons and ex-offenders who were served by employment or training programs carried out, or that receive financial assistance through programs carried out, by the Department of Justice or Department of Labor; and

(8)(A) collect from States and local governments information on the devel-opment and implementation of correctional job training or placement programs; and

(B) disseminate such information, as appropriate.

(Sept. 13, 1994, P. L. 103-322, Title II, Subtitle D, § 20418, 108 Stat. 1835.)

HISTORY; ANCILLARY LAWS AND DIRECTIVES

References in text:
"This Act", referred to in this section, is Act Sept. 13, 1994, P. L. 103-322, 108 Stat. 1796, popularly known as the Violent Crime Control and Law Enforcement Act of 1994. For full classification of this Act, consult USCS Tables volumes.

§ 13726. Findings

Congress finds the following:

(1) Increasingly, States are turning to private prisoner transport companies as an alternative to their own personnel or the United States Marshals Service when transporting violent prisoners.

(2) The transport process can last for days if not weeks, as violent prisoners are dropped off and picked up at a network of hubs across the country.

(3) Escapes by violent prisoners during transport by private prisoner transport companies have occurred.

(4) Oversight by the Attorney General is required to address these problems.

(5) While most governmental entities may prefer to use, and will continue to use, fully trained and sworn law enforcement officers when transporting violent prisoners, fiscal or logistical concerns may make the use of highly specialized private prisoner transport companies an option. Nothing in this Act [42 USCS §§ 13726 et seq.] should be construed to mean that governmental entities should contract with private prisoner transport companies to move violent prisoners; however when a government entity opts to use a private prisoner transport company to move violent prisoners, then the company should be subject to regulation in order to enhance public safety.

(Dec. 21, 2000, P. L. 106-560, § 2, 114 Stat. 2784.)

HISTORY; ANCILLARY LAWS AND DIRECTIVES

Explanatory notes:
This section was enacted as part of Act Dec. 21, 2000, P. L. 106-560, and not as part of Act Sept. 13, 1994, P. L. 103-322, which generally comprises this chapter.

§ 13726a. Definitions

In this Act [42 USCS §§ 13726 et seq.]:

(1) Crime of violence. The term "crime of violence" has the same meaning as in section 924(c)(3) of title 18, United States Code.

(2) Private prisoner transport company. The term "private prisoner transport company" means any entity, other than the United States, a State, or an inferior political subdivision of a State, which engages in the business of the transporting for compensation, individuals committed to the custody of any State or of an inferior political subdivision of a State, or any attempt thereof.

(3) Violent prisoner. The term "violent prisoner" means any individual in the custody of a State or an inferior political subdivision of a State who has previously been convicted of or is currently charged with a crime of violence

or any similar statute of a State or the inferior political subdivisions of a State, or any attempt thereof.

(Dec. 21, 2000, P. L. 106-560, § 3, 114 Stat. 2784.)

HISTORY; ANCILLARY LAWS AND DIRECTIVES

Explanatory notes:
This section was enacted as part of Act Dec. 21, 2000, P. L. 106-560, and not as part of Act Sept. 13, 1994, P. L. 103-322, which generally comprises this chapter.

§ 13726b. Federal regulation of prisoner transport companies

(a) In general. Not later than 180 days after the date of enactment of this Act [enacted Dec. 21, 2000], the Attorney General, in consultation with the American Correctional Association and the private prisoner transport industry, shall promulgate regulations relating to the transportation of violent prisoners in or affecting interstate commerce.

(b) Standards and requirements. The regulations shall include the following:

(1) Minimum standards for background checks and preemployment drug testing for potential employees, including requiring criminal background checks, to disqualify persons with a felony conviction or domestic violence conviction as defined by section 921 of title 18, United States Code, for eligibility for employment. Preemployment drug testing will be in accordance with applicable State laws.

(2) Minimum standards for the length and type of training that employees must undergo before they can transport prisoners not to exceed 100 hours of preservice training focusing on the transportation of prisoners. Training shall be in the areas of use of restraints, searches, use of force, including use of appropriate weapons and firearms, CPR, map reading, and defensive driving.

(3) Restrictions on the number of hours that employees can be on duty during a given time period. Such restriction shall not be more stringent than current applicable rules and regulations concerning hours of service promulgated under the Federal Motor Vehicle Safety Act.

(4) Minimum standards for the number of personnel that must supervise violent prisoners. Such standards shall provide the transport entity with appropriate discretion, and, absent more restrictive requirements contracted for by the procuring government entity, shall not exceed a requirement of 1 agent for every 6 violent prisoners.

(5) Minimum standards for employee uniforms and identification that require wearing of a uniform with a badge or insignia identifying the employee as a transportation officer.

(6) Standards establishing categories of violent prisoners required to wear brightly colored clothing clearly identifying them as prisoners, when appropriate.

(7) Minimum requirements for the restraints that must be used when transporting violent prisoners, to include leg shackles and double-locked handcuffs, when appropriate.

(8) A requirement that when transporting violent prisoners, private prisoner transport companies notify local law enforcement officials 24 hours in advance of any scheduled stops in their jurisdiction.

(9) A requirement that in the event of an escape by a violent prisoner, private prisoner transport company officials shall immediately notify appropriate law enforcement officials in the jurisdiction where the escape occurs, and the governmental entity that contracted with the private prisoner transport company for the transport of the escaped violent prisoner.

(10) Minimum standards for the safety of violent prisoners in accordance with applicable Federal and State law.

(c) Federal standards. Except for the requirements of subsection (b)(6), the regulations promulgated under this Act [42 USCS §§ 13726 et seq.] shall not provide stricter standards with respect to private prisoner transport companies than are applicable, without exception, to the United States Marshals Service, Federal Bureau of Prisons, and the Immigration and Naturalization Service when transporting violent prisoners under comparable circumstances.

(Dec. 21, 2000, P. L. 106-560, § 4, 114 Stat. 2785.)

HISTORY; ANCILLARY LAWS AND DIRECTIVES

References in text:

The meaning of "Federal Motor Vehicle Safety Act", referred to in subsec. (b)(3), is unclear, as no such Act has been enacted. For provisions authorizing the Secretary of Transportation to prescribe requirements relating to hours of service of employees of a motor carrier, see 49 USCS §§ 31501 et seq.

Explanatory notes:

This section was enacted as part of Act Dec. 21, 2000, P. L. 106-560, and not as part of Act Sept. 13, 1994, P. L. 103-322, which generally comprises this chapter.

Transfer of functions:

For abolition of the Immigration and Naturalization Service, transfer of functions, and treatment of related references, see transfer of functions note under 8 USCS § 1551.

CROSS REFERENCES

This section is referred to in 42 USCS § 13726c.

§ 13726c. Enforcement

Any person who is found in violation of the regulations established by this Act [42 USCS §§ 13726 et seq.] shall—

(1) be liable to the United States for a civil penalty in an amount not to exceed $10,000 for each violation and, in addition, to the United States for the costs of prosecution; and

(2) make restitution to any entity of the United States, of a State, or of an inferior political subdivision of a State, which expends funds for the purpose of apprehending any violent prisoner who escapes from a prisoner transport company as the result, in whole or in part, of a violation of regulations promulgated pursuant to section 4(a) [42 USCS § 13726b(a)].

(Dec. 21, 2000, P. L. 106-560, § 5, 114 Stat. 2786.)

HISTORY; ANCILLARY LAWS AND DIRECTIVES

Explanatory notes:

This section was enacted as part of Act Dec. 21, 2000, P. L. 106-560, and not as part of Act Sept. 13, 1994, P. L. 103-322, which generally comprises this chapter.

CRIME PREVENTION

OUNCE OF PREVENTION COUNCIL

CROSS REFERENCES

This subtitle (42 USCS §§ 13741 et seq.) is referred to in 42 USCS § 13841.

§ 13741. Ounce of Prevention Council

(a) Establishment. (1) In general. There is established an Ounce of Prevention Council (referred to in this title as the "Council"), the members of which—

(A) shall include the Attorney General, the Secretary of Education, the Secretary of Health and Human Services, the Secretary of Housing and Urban Development, the Secretary of Labor, the Secretary of Agriculture, the Secretary of the Treasury, the Secretary of the Interior, and the Director of the Office of National Drug Control Policy; and

(B) may include other officials of the executive branch as directed by the President.

(2) Chair. The President shall designate the Chair of the Council from among its members (referred to in this title as the "Chair").

(3) Staff. The Council may employ any necessary staff to carry out its functions, and may delegate any of its functions or powers to a member or members of the Council.

(b) Program coordination. For any program authorized under the Violent Crime Control and Law Enforcement Act of 1994, the Ounce of Prevention Council Chair, only at the request of the Council member with jurisdiction over that program, may coordinate that program, in whole or in part, through the Council.

(c) Administrative responsibilities and powers. In addition to the program coordination provided in subsection (b), the Council shall be responsible for such functions as coordinated planning, development of a comprehensive crime prevention program catalogue, provision of assistance to communities and community-based organizations seeking information regarding crime prevention programs and integrated program service delivery, and development of strategies for program integration and grant simplification. The Council shall have the authority to audit the expenditure of funds received by grantees under programs administered by or coordinated through the Council. In consultation with the Council, the Chair may issue regulations and guidelines to carry out this subtitle [42 USCS §§ 13741 et seq.] and programs administered by or coordinated through the Council.

(Sept. 13, 1994, P. L. 103-322, Title III, Subtitle A, § 30101, 108 Stat. 1836.)

HISTORY; ANCILLARY LAWS AND DIRECTIVES

References in text:

"This title", referred to in this section, is Title III of Act Sept. 13, 1994, P. L. 103-322, 108 Stat. 1836, which appears generally as 42 USCS §§ 13741 et seq. For full classification of this Title, consult USCS Tables volumes.

The "Violent Crime Control and Law Enforcement Act of 1994", referred to in this section, is Act Sept. 13, 1994, P. L. 103-322, 108 Stat. 1796. For full classification of this Act, consult USCS Tables volumes.

CODE OF FEDERAL REGULATIONS

Department of Justice—Grants for correctional facilities, 28 CFR 91.1 et seq.

CROSS REFERENCES

This section is referred to in 42 USCS § 14214.

§ 13742. Ounce of prevention grant program

(a) **In general.** The Council may make grants for—

(1) summer and after-school (including weekend and holiday) education and recreation programs;

(2) mentoring, tutoring, and other programs involving participation by adult role models (such as D.A.R.E. America);

(3) programs assisting and promoting employability and job placement; and

(4) prevention and treatment programs to reduce substance abuse, child abuse, and adolescent pregnancy, including outreach programs for at-risk families.

(b) **Applicants.** Applicants may be Indian tribal governments, cities, counties, or other municipalities, school boards, colleges and universities, private non-profit entities, or consortia of eligible applicants. Applicants must show that a planning process has occurred that has involved organizations, institutions, and residents of target areas, including young people, and that there has been cooperation between neighborhood-based entities, municipality-wide bodies, and local private-sector representatives. Applicants must demonstrate the substantial involvement of neighborhood-based entities in the carrying out of the proposed activities. Proposals must demonstrate that a broad base of collaboration and coordination will occur in the implementation of the proposed activities, involving cooperation among youth-serving organizations, schools, health and social service providers, employers, law enforcement professionals, local government, and residents of target areas, including young people. Applications shall be geographically based in particular neighborhoods or sections of municipalities or particular segments of rural areas, and applications shall demonstrate how programs will serve substantial proportions of children and youth resident in the target area with activities designed to have substantial impact on their lives.

(c) **Priority.** In making such grants, the Council shall give preference to coalitions consisting of a broad spectrum of community-based and social service organizations that have a coordinated team approach to reducing gang membership and the effects of substance abuse, and providing alternatives to at-risk youth.

(d) Federal share. (1) In general. The Federal share of a grant made under this part may not exceed 75 percent of the total costs of the projects described in the applications submitted under subsection (b) for the fiscal year for which the projects receive assistance under this title.

(2) Waiver. The Council may waive the 25 percent matching requirement under paragraph (1) upon making a determination that a waiver is equitable in view of the financial circumstances affecting the ability of the applicant to meet that requirement.

(3) Non-Federal share. The non-Federal share of such costs may be in cash or in kind, fairly evaluated, including plant, equipment, and services.

(4) Nonsupplanting requirement. Funds made available under this title to a governmental entity shall not be used to supplant State or local funds, or in the case of Indian tribal governments, funds supplied by the Bureau of Indian Affairs, but shall be used to increase the amount of funds that would, in the absence of Federal funds received under this title, be made available from State or local sources, or in the case of Indian tribal governments, from funds supplied by the Bureau of Indian Affairs.

(5) Evaluation. The Council shall conduct a thorough evaluation of the programs assisted under this title.

(Sept. 13, 1994, P. L. 103-322, Title III, Subtitle A, § 30102, 108 Stat. 1837.)

HISTORY; ANCILLARY LAWS AND DIRECTIVES

References in text:

"This title", referred to in this section, is Title III of Act Sept. 13, 1994, P. L. 103-322, 108 Stat. 1836, which appears generally as 42 USCS §§ 13741 et seq. For full classification of this Title, consult USCS Tables volumes.

"This part", as used in this section, probably means Subtitle A of Title III of Act Sept. 13, 1994, P. L. 103-322, 108 Stat. 1836, which appears as 42 USCS §§ 13741 et seq.

CROSS REFERENCES

This section is referred to in 42 USCS § 14214.

§ 13743. "Indian tribe" defined

In this subtitle [42 USCS §§ 13741 et seq.], "Indian tribe" means a tribe, band, pueblo, nation, or other organized group or community of Indians, including an Alaska Native village (as defined in or established under the Alaska Native Claims Settlement Act (43 U.S.C. 1601 et seq.)[)], that is recognized as eligible for the special programs and services provided by the United States to Indians because of their status as Indians.

(Sept. 13, 1994, P. L. 103-322, Title III, Subtitle A, § 30103, 108 Stat. 1838.)

HISTORY; ANCILLARY LAWS AND DIRECTIVES

Explanatory notes:
The bracketed close parenthesis has been inserted to indicate the probable intention of Congress to include such punctuation.

CROSS REFERENCES
This section is referred to in 42 USCS § 14214.

§ 13744. Authorization of appropriations

There are authorized to be appropriated to carry out this subtitle [42 USCS §§ 13741 et seq.]—

    (1) $1,500,000 for fiscal year 1995;
    (2) $14,700,000 for fiscal year 1996;
    (3) $18,000,000 for fiscal year 1997;
    (4) $18,000,000 for fiscal year 1998;
    (5) $18,900,000 for fiscal year 1999; and
    (6) $18,900,000 for fiscal year 2000.

(Sept. 13, 1994, P. L. 103-322, Title III, Subtitle A, § 30104, 108 Stat. 1838.)

CROSS REFERENCES
This section is referred to in 42 USCS § 14214.

§ 13751. [Repealed]

HISTORY; ANCILLARY LAWS AND DIRECTIVES
This section (Act Sept. 13, 1994, P. L. 103-322, Title III, Subtitle B, § 30201, 108 Stat. 1838) was repealed by Act Jan. 5, 2006, P. L. 109-162, Title XI, Subtitle B, Ch. 5, § 1154(b)(1), 119 Stat. 3113. It provided for payments to local governments.

Other provisions:
Establishment of Boys and Girls Clubs. Act Oct. 11, 1996, P. L. 104-294, Title IV, § 401, 110 Stat. 3496; Dec. 2, 1997, P. L. 105-133, § 1, 111 Stat. 2568; Nov. 2, 2002, P. L. 107-273, Div B, Title I, § 1101, 116 Stat. 1791; Oct. 18, 2004, P. L. 108-344, § 1, 118 Stat. 1376, provides:

"(a) Findings and purpose. (1) Findings. The Congress finds that—

    "(A) the Boys and Girls Clubs of America, chartered by an Act of Congress on December 10, 1991, during its 90-year history as a national organization, has proven itself as a positive force in the communities it serves;

    "(B) there are 1,810 Boys and Girls Clubs facilities throughout the United States, Puerto Rico, and the United States Virgin Islands, serving 2,420,000 youths nationwide;

    "(C) 71 percent of the young people who benefit from Boys and Girls Clubs programs live in our inner cities and urban areas;

    "(D) Boys and Girls Clubs are locally run and have been exceptionally successful in balancing public funds with private sector donations and maximizing community involvement;

    "(E) Boys and Girls Clubs are located in 289 public housing sites across the Nation;

"(F) public housing projects in which there is an active Boys and Girls Club have experienced a 25 percent reduction in the presence of crack cocaine, a 22 percent reduction in overall drug activity, and a 13 percent reduction in juvenile crime;

"(G) these results have been achieved in the face of national trends in which overall drug use by youth has increased 105 percent since 1992 and 10.9 percent of the Nation's young people use drugs on a monthly basis; and

"(H) many public housing projects and other distressed areas are still underserved by Boys and Girls Clubs.

"(2) Purpose. The purpose of this section is to provide adequate resources in the form of seed money for the Boys and Girls Clubs of America to establish 1,500 additional local clubs where needed, with particular emphasis placed on establishing clubs in public housing projects and distressed areas, and to ensure that there are a total of not less than 5,000 Boys and Girls Clubs of America facilities in operation not later than December 31, 2010, serving not less than 5,000,000 young people.

"(b) Definitions. For purposes of this section—

"(1) the terms 'public housing' and 'project' have the same meanings as in section 3(b) of the United States Housing Act of 1937 [42 USCS § 1437a(b)]; and

"(2) the term 'distressed area' means an urban, suburban, rural area, or Indian reservation with a population of high risk youth as defined in section 517 of the Public Health Service Act (42 U.S.C. 290bb-23) of sufficient size to warrant the establishment of a Boys and Girls Club.

"(c) Establishment. (1) In general. For each of the fiscal years 2006, 2007, 2008, 2009, and 2010, the Director of the Bureau of Justice Assistance of the Department of Justice shall make a grant to the Boys and Girls Clubs of America for the purpose of establishing and extending Boys and Girls Clubs facilities where needed, with particular emphasis placed on establishing clubs in and extending services to public housing projects and distressed areas.

"(2) Applications. The Attorney General shall accept an application for a grant under this subsection if submitted by the Boys and Girls Clubs of America, and approve or deny the grant not later than 90 days after the date on which the application is submitted, if the application—

"(A) includes a long-term strategy to establish 1,500 additional Boys and Girls Clubs and detailed summary of those areas in which new facilities will be established, or in which existing facilities will be expanded to serve additional youths, during the next fiscal year;

"(B) includes a plan to ensure that there are a total of not less than 5,000 Boys and Girls Clubs of America facilities in operation before January 1, 2010;

"(C) certifies that there will be appropriate coordination with those communities where clubs will be located; and

"(D) explains the manner in which new facilities will operate without additional, direct Federal financial assistance to the Boys and Girls Clubs once assistance under this subsection is discontinued.

"(d) Report. Not later than May 1 of each fiscal year for which amounts are made available to carry out this Act [for full classification, consult

USCS Tables volumes], the Attorney General shall submit to the Committees on the Judiciary of the Senate and the House of Representatives a report that details the progress made under this Act in establishing Boys and Girls Clubs in public housing projects and other distressed areas, and the effectiveness of the programs in reducing drug abuse and juvenile crime.

"(e) Authorization of appropriations. (1) In general. There are authorized to be appropriated to carry out this section—

"(A) $80,000,000 for fiscal year 2006;

"(B) $85,000,000 for fiscal year 2007;

"(C) $90,000,000 for fiscal year 2008;

"(D) $95,000,000 for fiscal year 2009; and

"(E) $100,000,000 for fiscal year 2010.

"(2) [Deleted]

"(f) Role model grants. Of amounts made available under subsection (e) for any fiscal year—

"(1) not more than 5 percent may be used to provide a grant to the Boys and Girls Clubs of America for administrative, travel, and other costs associated with a national role-model speaking tour program; and

"(2) no amount may be used to compensate speakers other than to reimburse speakers for reasonable travel and accommodation costs associated with the program described in paragraph (1).".

Kids 2000 crime prevention and computer education initiative. Act Oct. 17, 2000, P. L. 106-313, Title I, § 112, 114 Stat. 1260, provides:

"(a) Short title. This section may be cited as the 'Kids 2000 Act'.

"(b) Findings. Congress makes the following findings:

"(1) There is an increasing epidemic of juvenile crime throughout the United States.

"(2) It is well documented that the majority of juvenile crimes take place during after-school hours.

"(3) Knowledge of technology is becoming increasingly necessary for children in school and out of school.

"(4) The Boys and Girls Clubs of America have 2,700 clubs throughout all 50 States, serving over 3,000,000 boys and girls primarily from at-risk communities.

"(5) The Boys and Girls Clubs of America have the physical structures in place for immediate implementation of an after-school technology program.

"(6) Building technology centers and providing integrated content and full-time staffing at those centers in the Boys and Girls Clubs of America nationwide will help foster education, job training, and an alternative to crime for at-risk youth.

"(7) Partnerships between the public sector and the private sector are an effective way of providing after-school technology programs in the Boys and Girls Clubs of America.

"(8) PowerUp: Bridging the Digital Divide is an entity comprised of more than a dozen nonprofit organizations, major corporations, and Federal agencies that have joined together to launch a major new initiative to help ensure that America's underserved young people acquire the skills, experiences, and resources they need to succeed in the digital age.

"(9) Bringing PowerUp into the Boys and Girls Clubs of America will be an effective way to ensure that our youth have a safe, crime-free environment in which to learn the technological skills they need to close the divide between young people who have access to computer-based information and technology-related skills and those who do not.

"(c) After-school technology grants to the Boys and Girls Clubs of America. (1) Purposes. The Attorney General shall make grants to the Boys and Girls Clubs of America for the purpose of funding effective after-school technology programs, such as PowerUp, in order to provide—

"(A) constructive technology-focused activities that are part of a comprehensive program to provide access to technology and technology training to youth during after-school hours, weekends, and school vacations;

"(B) supervised activities in safe environments for youth; and

"(C) full-time staffing with teachers, tutors, and other qualified personnel.

"(2) Subawards. The Boys and Girls Clubs of America shall make subawards to local boys and girls clubs authorizing expenditures associated with providing technology programs such as PowerUp, including the hiring of teachers and other personnel, procurement of goods and services, including computer equipment, or such other purposes as are approved by the Attorney General.

"(d) Applications. (1) Eligibility. In order to be eligible to receive a grant under this section, an applicant for a subaward (specified in subsection (c)(2)) shall submit an application to the Boys and Girls Clubs of America, in such form and containing such information as the Attorney General may reasonably require.

"(2) Application requirements. Each application submitted in accordance with paragraph (1) shall include—

"(A) a request for a subgrant to be used for the purposes of this section;

"(B) a description of the communities to be served by the grant, including the nature of juvenile crime, violence, and drug use in the communities;

"(C) written assurances that Federal funds received under this section will be used to supplement and not supplant, non-Federal funds that would otherwise be available for activities funded under this section;

"(D) written assurances that all activities funded under this section will be supervised by qualified adults;

"(E) a plan for assuring that program activities will take place in a secure environment that is free of crime and drugs;

"(F) a plan outlining the utilization of content-based programs such as PowerUp, and the provision of trained adult personnel to supervise the after-school technology training; and

"(G) any additional statistical or financial information that the Boys and Girls Clubs of America may reasonably require.

"(e) Grant awards. In awarding subgrants under this section, the Boys and Girls Clubs of America shall consider—

"(1) the ability of the applicant to provide the intended services;

"(2) the history and establishment of the applicant in providing youth activities; and

"(3) the extent to which services will be provided in crime-prone areas and technologically underserved populations, and efforts to achieve an equitable geographic distribution of the grant awards.

"(f) Authorization of appropriations. (1) In general. There is authorized to be appropriated $20,000,000 for each of the fiscal years 2001 through 2006 to carry out this section.

"(2) Source of funds. Funds to carry out this section may be derived from the Violent Crime Reduction Trust Fund.

"(3) Continued availability. Amounts made available under this subsection shall remain available until expended.".

National Police Athletic League Youth Enrichment Act of 2000. Act Oct. 27, 2000, P. L. 106-367, 114 Stat. 1412; July 27, 2006, P. L. 109-248, Title VI, Subtitle B, § 612–617, 120 Stat. 632, provides:

"Section 1. Short title.

"This Act may be cited as the 'National Police Athletic League Youth Enrichment Act of 2000'.

"Sec. 2. Findings.

"Congress makes the following findings:

"(1) The goals of the Police Athletic/Activities League are to—

"(A) increase the academic success of youth participants in PAL programs;

"(B) promote a safe, healthy environment for youth under the supervision of law enforcement personnel where mutual trust and respect can be built;

"(C) develop life enhancing character and leadership skills in young people;

"(D) increase school attendance by providing alternatives to suspensions and expulsions;

"(E) reduce the juvenile crime rate in participating designated communities and the number of police calls involving juveniles during nonschool hours;

"(F) provide youths with alternatives to drugs, alcohol, tobacco, and gang activity;

"(G) create positive communications and interaction between youth and law enforcement personnel; and

"(H) prepare youth for the workplace.

"(2) The Police Athletic/Activities League, during its 90-year history as a national organization, has proven to be a positive force in the communities it serves.

"(3) The Police Athletic/Activities League is a network of 1,700 facilities serving over 3,000 communities. There are 350 PAL chapters throughout the United States, the Virgin Islands, and the Commonwealth of Puerto Rico, serving 2,000,000 youths, ages 5 to 18, nationwide.

"(4) Based on PAL chapter demographics, approximately 85 percent of the youths who benefit from PAL programs live in inner cities and urban areas.

"(5) PAL chapters are locally operated, volunteer-driven organizations. Although most PAL chapters are sponsored by a law enforcement agency, PAL chapters rarely receive direct funding from law enforcement agencies and are dependent in large part on support from the private sector, such as individuals, business leaders, corporations, and foundations. PAL chapters have been exceptionally successful in balancing public funds with private sector donations and maximizing community involvement.

"(6) Today's youth face far greater risks than did their parents and grandparents. Law enforcement statistics demonstrate that youth between the ages of 12 and 18 are at risk of committing violent acts and being victims of violent acts between the hours of 3 p.m. and 8 p.m.

"(7) Greater numbers of students are dropping out of school and failing in school, even though the consequences of academic failure are more dire in 2005 than ever before.

"(8) Many distressed areas in the United States are still underserved by PAL chapters.

"Sec. 3. Purpose.

"The purpose of this Act is to provide adequate resources in the form of—

"(1) assistance for the 342 established PAL chapters to increase of services to the communities they are serving;

"(2) seed money for the establishment of 250 (50 per year over a 5-year period) additional local PAL chapters in public housing projects and other distressed areas, including distressed areas with a majority population of Native Americans, by not later than fiscal year 2010; and

"(3) support of an annual gathering of PAL chapters and designated youth leaders from such chapters to participate in a 3-day conference that addresses national and local issues impacting the youth of America and includes educational sessions to advance character and leadership skills.

"Sec. 4. Definitions.

"In this Act:

"(1) Assistant Attorney general. The term 'Assistant Attorney General' means the Assistant Attorney General for the Office of Justice Programs of the Department of Justice.

"(2) Distressed area. The term 'distressed area' means an urban, suburban, or rural area with a high percentage of high-risk youth, as defined in section 509A of the Public Health Service Act (42 U.S.C. 290aa-8(f)).

"(3) PAL Chapter. The term 'PAL chapter' means a chapter of a Police or Sheriff's Athletic/Activities League.

"(4) Police Athletic/activities League. The term 'Police Athletic/ Activities League' means the private, nonprofit, national representative organization for 320 Police or Sheriff's Athletic/Activities Leagues throughout the United States (including the Virgin Islands and the Commonwealth of Puerto Rico).

"(5) Public housing; project. The terms 'public housing' and 'project' have the meanings given those terms in section 3(b) of the United States Housing Act of 1937 (42 U.S.C. 1437a(b)).

"Sec. 5. Grants authorized.

"(a) In general. Subject to appropriations, for each of fiscal years 2006 through 2010, the Assistant Attorney General shall award a grant to the Police Athletic/Activities League for the purpose of establishing PAL chapters to serve public housing projects and other distressed areas, and expanding existing PAL chapters to serve additional youths.

"(b) Application. (1) Submission. In order to be eligible to receive a grant under this section, the Police Athletic/Activities League shall submit to the Assistant Attorney General an application, which shall include—

"(A) a long-term strategy to establish 250 additional PAL chapters and detailed summary of those areas in which new PAL chapters will be established, or in which existing chapters will be expanded to serve additional youths, during the next fiscal year;

"(B) a plan to ensure that there are a total of not fewer than 500 PAL chapters in operation before January 1, 2010;

"(C) a certification that there will be appropriate coordination with those communities where new PAL chapters will be located; and

"(D) an explanation of the manner in which new PAL chapters will operate without additional, direct Federal financial assistance once assistance under this Act is discontinued.

"(2) Review. The Assistant Attorney General shall review and take action on an application submitted under paragraph (1) not later than 120 days after the date of such submission.

"Sec. 6. Use of funds.

"(a) In general. (1) Assistance for new and expanded chapters. Amounts made available under a grant awarded under this Act shall be used by the Police Athletic/Activities League to provide funding for the establishment of PAL chapters serving public housing projects and other distressed areas, or the expansion of existing PAL chapters.

"(2) Program requirements. Each new or expanded PAL chapter assisted under paragraph (1) shall carry out not less than two programs during nonschool hours, of which—

"(A) not less than one program shall provide—

"(i) mentoring assistance;

"(ii) academic assistance;

"(iii) recreational and athletic activities;

"(iv) technology training; or

"(v) character development and leadership training; and

"(B) any remaining programs shall provide—

"(i) drug, alcohol, and gang prevention activities;

"(ii) health and nutrition counseling;

"(iii) cultural and social programs;

"(iv) conflict resolution training, anger management, and peer pressure training;

"(v) job skill preparation activities; or

"(vi) Youth Police Athletic/Activities League Conferences or Youth Forums.

"(b) Additional requirements. In carrying out the programs under subsection (a), a PAL chapter shall, to the maximum extent practicable—

"(1) use volunteers from businesses, academic communities, social organizations, and law enforcement organizations to serve as mentors or to assist in other ways;

"(2) ensure that youth in the local community participate in designing the after-school activities;

"(3) develop creative methods of conducting outreach to youth in the community;

"(4) request donations of computer equipment and other materials and equipment; and

"(5) work with State and local park and recreation agencies so that activities funded with amounts made available under a grant under this Act will not duplicate activities funded from other sources in the community served.

"Sec. 7. Reports.

"(a) Report to Assistant Attorney General. For each fiscal year for which a grant is awarded under this Act, the Police Athletic/Activities League shall submit to the Assistant Attorney General a report on the use of amounts made available under the grant.

"(b) Report to Congress. Not later than May 1 of each fiscal year for which amounts are made available to carry out this Act, the Assistant Attorney General shall submit to the Committees on the Judiciary of the Senate and the House of Representatives a report that details the progress made under this Act in establishing and expanding PAL chapters in public housing projects and other distressed areas, and the effectiveness of the PAL programs in reducing drug abuse, school dropouts, and juvenile crime.

"Sec. 8. Authorization of appropriations.

"(a) In general. There are authorized to be appropriated to carry out this Act $16,000,000 for each of fiscal years 2006 through 2010.

"(b) Funding for program administration. Of the amount made available to carry out this Act in each fiscal year—

"(1) not less than 2 percent shall be used for research and evaluation of the grant program under this Act;

"(2) not less than 1 percent shall be used for technical assistance related to the use of amounts made available under grants awarded under this Act; and

"(3) not less than 1 percent shall be used for the management and administration of the grant program under this Act, except that the total amount made available under this paragraph for administration of that program shall not exceed 6 percent.".

Youth violence reduction demonstration projects. Act Jan. 5, 2006, P. L. 109-162, Title XI, Subtitle C, § 1199, 119 Stat. 3132, provides:

"(a) Establishment of youth violence reduction demonstration projects. (1) In general. The Attorney General shall make up to 5 grants for the purpose of carrying out Youth Violence Demonstration Projects to reduce juvenile and young adult violence, homicides, and recidivism among high-risk populations.

"(2) Eligible entities. An entity is eligible for a grant under paragraph (1) if it is a unit of local government or a combination of local governments established by agreement for purposes of undertaking a demonstration project.

"(b) Selection of grant recipients. (1) Awards. The Attorney General shall award grants for Youth Violence Reduction Demonstration Projects on a competitive basis.

"(2) Amount of awards. No single grant award made under subsection (a) shall exceed $15,000,000 per fiscal year.

"(3) Application. An application for a grant under paragraph (1) shall be submitted to the Attorney General in such a form, and containing such information and assurances, as the Attorney General may require, and at a minimum shall propose—

"(A) a program strategy targeting areas with the highest incidence of youth violence and homicides;

"(B) outcome measures and specific objective indicia of performance to assess the effectiveness of the program; and

"(C) a plan for evaluation by an independent third party.

"(4) Distribution. In making grants under this section, the Attorney General shall ensure the following:

"(A) No less than 1 recipient is a city with a population exceeding 1,000,000 and an increase of at least 30 percent in the aggregated juvenile and young adult homicide victimization rate during calendar year 2005 as compared to calendar year 2004.

"(B) No less than one recipient is a nonmetropolitan county or group of counties with per capita arrest rates of juveniles and young adults for serious violent offenses that exceed the national average for nonmetropolitan counties by at least 5 percent.

"(5) Criteria. In making grants under this section, the Attorney General shall give preference to entities operating programs that meet the following criteria:

"(A) A program focusing on—

"(i) reducing youth violence and homicides, with an emphasis on juvenile and young adult probationers and other juveniles and young adults who have had or are likely to have contact with the juvenile justice system;

"(ii) fostering positive relationships between program participants and supportive adults in the community; and

"(iii) accessing comprehensive supports for program participants through coordinated community referral networks, including job opportunities, educational programs, counseling services, substance abuse programs, recreational opportunities, and other services.

"(B) A program goal of almost daily contacts with and supervision of participating juveniles and young adults through small caseloads and a coordinated team approach among case managers drawn from the community, probation officers, and police officers.

"(C) The use of existing structures, local government agencies, and nonprofit organizations to operate the program.

"(D) Inclusion in program staff of individuals who live or have lived in the community in which the program operates; have personal experiences or cultural competency that build credibility in relationships with program participants; and will serve as a case manager, intermediary, and mentor.

"(E) Fieldwork and neighborhood outreach in communities where the young violent offenders live, including support of the program from local public and private organizations and community members.

"(F) Imposition of graduated probation sanctions to deter violent and criminal behavior.

"(G) A record of program operation and effectiveness evaluation over a period of at least five years prior to the date of enactment of this Act.

"(H) A program structure that can serve as a model for other communities in addressing the problem of youth violence and juvenile and young adult recidivism.

"(c) Authorized activities. Amounts paid to an eligible entity under a grant award may be used for the following activities:

"(1) Designing and enhancing program activities.

"(2) Employing and training personnel.

"(3) Purchasing or leasing equipment.

"(4) Providing services and training to program participants and their families.

"(5) Supporting related law enforcement and probation activities, including personnel costs.

"(6) Establishing and maintaining a system of program records.

"(7) Acquiring, constructing, expanding, renovating, or operating facilities to support the program.

"(8) Evaluating program effectiveness.

"(9) Undertaking other activities determined by the Attorney General as consistent with the purposes and requirements of the demonstration program.

"(d) Evaluation and reports. (1) Independent evaluation. The Attorney General may use up to $500,000 of funds appropriated annually under this such section to—

"(A) prepare and implement a design for interim and overall evaluations of performance and progress of the funded demonstration projects;

"(B) provide training and technical assistance to grant recipients; and

"(C) disseminate broadly the information generated and lessons learned from the operation of the demonstration projects.

"(2) Reports to Congress. Not later than 120 days after the last day of each fiscal year for which 1 or more demonstration grants are awarded, the Attorney General shall submit to Congress a report which shall include—

"(A) a summary of the activities carried out with such grants;

"(B) an assessment by the Attorney General of the program carried out; and

"(C) such other information as the Attorney General considers appropriate.

"(e) Federal share. (1) In general. The Federal share of a grant awarded under this Act shall not exceed 90 percent of the total program costs.

"(2) Non-Federal share. The non-Federal share of such cost may be provided in cash or in-kind.

"(f) Definitions. In this section:

"(1) Unit of local government. The term 'unit of local government' means a county, township, city, or political subdivision of a county, township, or city, that is a unit of local government as determined by the Secretary of Commerce for general statistical purposes.

"(2) Juvenile. The term 'juvenile' means an individual who is 17 years of age or younger.

"(3) Young adult. The term 'young adult' means an individual who is 18 through 24 years of age.

"(g) Authorization of appropriations. There are authorized to be appropriated to carry out this section $50,000,000 for fiscal year 2007 and such sums as may be necessary for each of fiscal years 2008 through 2009, to remain available until expended.".

§ 13752. [Repealed]

HISTORY; ANCILLARY LAWS AND DIRECTIVES

This section (Act Sept. 13, 1994, P. L. 103-322, Title III, Subtitle B, § 30202, 108 Stat. 1841) was repealed by Act Jan. 5, 2006, P. L. 109-162, Title XI, Subtitle B, Ch. 5, § 1154(b)(1), 119 Stat. 3113. It authorized appropriations.

§ 13753. [Repealed]

HISTORY; ANCILLARY LAWS AND DIRECTIVES

This section (Act Sept. 13, 1994, P. L. 103-322, Title III, Subtitle B, § 30203, 108 Stat. 1841; Oct. 19, 1996, P. L. 104-316, Title I, § 122(u), 110 Stat. 3838) was repealed by Act Jan. 5, 2006, P. L. 109-162, Title XI, Subtitle B, Ch. 5, § 1154(b)(1), 119 Stat. 3113. It related to qualification for payment.

§ 13754. [Repealed]

HISTORY; ANCILLARY LAWS AND DIRECTIVES

This section (Act Sept. 13, 1994, P. L. 103-322, Title III, Subtitle B, § 30204, 108 Stat. 1842) was repealed by Act Jan. 5, 2006, P. L. 109-162, Title XI, Subtitle B, Ch. 5, § 1154(b)(1), 119 Stat. 3113. It related to allocation and distribution of funds.

§ 13755. [Repealed]

HISTORY; ANCILLARY LAWS AND DIRECTIVES

This section (Act Sept. 13, 1994, P. L. 103-322, Title III, Subtitle B, § 30205, 108 Stat. 1843) was repealed by Act Jan. 5, 2006, P. L. 109-162, Title XI, Subtitle B, Ch. 5, § 1154(b)(1), 119 Stat. 3113. It related to utilization of the private sector.

§ 13756. [Repealed]

HISTORY; ANCILLARY LAWS AND DIRECTIVES

This section (Act Sept. 13, 1994, P. L. 103-322, Title III, Subtitle B, § 30206, 108 Stat. 1843) was repealed by Act Jan. 5, 2006, P. L. 109-162, Title XI, Subtitle B, Ch. 5, § 1154(b)(1), 119 Stat. 3113. It provided for public participation.

§ 13757. [Repealed]

HISTORY; ANCILLARY LAWS AND DIRECTIVES

This section (Act Sept. 13, 1994, P. L. 103-322, Title III, Subtitle B,

§ 30207, 108 Stat. 1844) was repealed by Act Jan. 5, 2006, P. L. 109-162, Title XI, Subtitle B, Ch. 5, § 1154(b)(1), 119 Stat. 3113. It contained administrative provisions.

§ 13758. [Repealed]

HISTORY; ANCILLARY LAWS AND DIRECTIVES
This section (Act Sept. 13, 1994, P. L. 103-322, Title III, Subtitle B, § 30208, 108 Stat. 1844) was repealed by Act Jan. 5, 2006, P. L. 109-162, Title XI, Subtitle B, Ch. 5, § 1154(b)(1), 119 Stat. 3113. It defined terms.

MODEL INTENSIVE GRANT PROGRAMS

§ 13771. Grant authorization

(a) **Establishment.** (1) In general. The Attorney General may award grants to not more than 15 chronic high intensive crime areas to develop comprehensive model crime prevention programs that—

(A) involve and utilize a broad spectrum of community resources, including nonprofit community organizations, law enforcement organizations, and appropriate State and Federal agencies, including the State educational agencies;

(B) attempt to relieve conditions that encourage crime; and

(C) provide meaningful and lasting alternatives to involvement in crime.

(2) Consultation with the Ounce of Prevention Council. The Attorney General may consult with the Ounce of Prevention Council in awarding grants under paragraph (1).

(b) **Priority.** In awarding grants under subsection (a), the Attorney General shall give priority to proposals that—

(1) are innovative in approach to the prevention of crime in a specific area;

(2) vary in approach to ensure that comparisons of different models may be made; and

(3) coordinate crime prevention programs funded under this program with other existing Federal programs to address the overall needs of communities that benefit from grants received under this title.

(Sept. 13, 1994, P. L. 103-322, Title III, Subtitle C, § 30301, 108 Stat. 1844.)

HISTORY; ANCILLARY LAWS AND DIRECTIVES
References in text:
"This title", referred to in subsec. (b)(3), is Title III of Act Sept. 13, 1994, P. L. 103-322, which appears generally as 42 USCS §§ 13741 et seq. For full classification of such Title, consult USCS Tables volumes.

CROSS REFERENCES
This section is referred to in 42 USCS § 14214.

§ 13772. Uses of funds

(a) **In general.** Funds awarded under this subtitle [42 USCS §§ 13771 et seq.]

may be used only for purposes described in an approved application. The intent of grants under this subtitle [42 USCS §§ 13771 et seq.] is to fund intensively comprehensive crime prevention programs in chronic high intensive crime areas.

(b) Guidelines. The Attorney General shall issue and publish in the Federal Register guidelines that describe suggested purposes for which funds under approved programs may be used.

(c) Equitable distribution of funds. In disbursing funds under this subtitle [42 USCS §§ 13771 et seq.], the Attorney General shall ensure the distribution of awards equitably on a geographic basis, including urban and rural areas of varying population and geographic size.

(Sept. 13, 1994, P. L. 103-322, Title III, Subtitle C, § 30302, 108 Stat. 1845.)

CROSS REFERENCES

This section is referred to in 42 USCS § 14214.

§ 13773. Program requirements

(a) Description. An applicant shall include a description of the distinctive factors that contribute to chronic violent crime within the area proposed to be served by the grant. Such factors may include lack of alternative activities and programs for youth, deterioration or lack of public facilities, inadequate public services such as public transportation, street lighting, community-based substance abuse treatment facilities, or employment services offices, and inadequate police or public safety services, equipment, or facilities.

(b) Comprehensive plan. An applicant shall include a comprehensive, community-based plan to attack intensively the principal factors identified in subsection (a). Such plans shall describe the specific purposes for which funds are proposed to be used and how each purpose will address specific factors. The plan also shall specify how local nonprofit organizations, government agencies, private businesses, citizens groups, volunteer organizations, and interested citizens will cooperate in carrying out the purposes of the grant.

(c) Evaluation. An applicant shall include an evaluation plan by which the success of the plan will be measured, including the articulation of specific, objective indicia of performance, how the indicia will be evaluated, and a projected timetable for carrying out the evaluation.

(Sept. 13, 1994, P. L. 103-322, Title III, Subtitle C, § 30303, 108 Stat. 1845.)

CROSS REFERENCES

This section is referred to in 42 USCS § 14214.

§ 13774. Applications

To request a grant under this subtitle [42 USCS §§ 13771 et seq.] the chief local elected official of an area shall—

(1) prepare and submit to the Attorney General an application in such form, at such time, and in accordance with such procedures, as the Attorney General shall establish; and

(2) provide an assurance that funds received under this subtitle [42 USCS §§ 13771 et seq.] shall be used to supplement, not supplant, non-Federal funds that would otherwise be available for programs funded under this subtitle [42 USCS §§ 13771 et seq.].

(Sept. 13, 1994, P. L. 103-322, Title III, Subtitle C, § 30304, 108 Stat. 1845.)

CROSS REFERENCES

This section is referred to in 42 USCS § 14214.

§ 13775. Reports

Not later than December 31, 1998, the Attorney General shall prepare and submit to the Committees on the Judiciary of the House and Senate an evaluation of the model programs developed under this subtitle [42 USCS §§ 13771 et seq.] and make recommendations regarding the implementation of a national crime prevention program.

(Sept. 13, 1994, P. L. 103-322, Title III, Subtitle C, § 30305, 108 Stat. 1846.)

CROSS REFERENCES

This section is referred to in 42 USCS § 14214.

§ 13776. Definitions

In this subtitle [42 USCS §§ 13771 et seq.]—

"chief local elected official" means an official designated under regulations issued by the Attorney General. The criteria used by the Attorney General in promulgating such regulations shall ensure administrative efficiency and accountability in the expenditure of funds and execution of funded projects under this subtitle [42 USCS §§ 13771 et seq.].

"chronic high intensity crime area" means an area meeting criteria adopted by the Attorney General by regulation that, at a minimum, define areas with—

(A) consistently high rates of violent crime as reported in the Federal Bureau of Investigation's "Uniform Crime Reports", and

(B) chronically high rates of poverty as determined by the Bureau of the Census.

"State" means a State, the District of Columbia, the Commonwealth of Puerto Rico, the United States Virgin Islands, American Samoa, Guam, and the Northern Mariana Islands.

(Sept. 13, 1994, P. L. 103-322, Title III, Subtitle C, § 30306, 108 Stat. 1846.)

CROSS REFERENCES

This section is referred to in 42 USCS § 14214.

§ 13777. Authorization of appropriations

There are authorized to be appropriated to carry out this subtitle [42 USCS §§ 13771 et seq.]—

(1) $100,000,000 for fiscal year 1996;

(2) $125,100,000 for fiscal year 1997;
(3) $125,100,000 for fiscal year 1998;
(4) $125,100,000 for fiscal year 1999; and
(5) $150,200,000 for fiscal year 2000.
(Sept. 13, 1994, P. L. 103-322, Title III, Subtitle C, § 30307, 108 Stat. 1846.)

CROSS REFERENCES
This section is referred to in 42 USCS § 14214.

FAMILY AND COMMUNITY ENDEAVOR SCHOOLS GRANT PROGRAM

§ 13791. Community schools youth services and supervision grant program

(a) Short title. This section may be cited as the "Community Schools Youth Services and Supervision Grant Program Act of 1994".

(b) Definitions. In this section—

"child" means a person who is not younger than 5 and not older than 18 years old.

"community-based organization" means a private, locally initiated, community-based organization that—

(A) is a nonprofit organization, as defined in section 103(23) of the Juvenile Justice and Delinquency Prevention Act of 1974 (42 U.S.C. 5603(23)); and

(B) is operated by a consortium of service providers, consisting of representatives of 5 or more of the following categories of persons:

(i) Residents of the community.

(ii) Business and civic leaders actively involved in providing employment and business development opportunities in the community.

(iii) Educators.

(iv) Religious organizations (which shall not provide any sectarian instruction or sectarian worship in connection with an activity funded under this title).

(v) Law enforcement agencies.

(vi) Public housing agencies.

(vii) Other public agencies.

(viii) Other interested parties.

"eligible community" means an area identified pursuant to subsection (e).

"Indian tribe" means a tribe, band, pueblo, nation, or other organized group or community of Indians, including an Alaska Native village (as defined in or established under the Alaska Native Claims Settlement Act (43 U.S.C. 1601 et seq.)), that is recognized as eligible for the special programs and services provided by the United States to Indians because of their status as Indians.

"poverty line" means the income official poverty line (as defined by the Office of Management and Budget, and revised annually in accordance with section 673(2) of the Community Services Block Grant Act (42 U.S.C. 9902(2)[)] applicable to a family of the size involved.

"public school" means a public elementary school, as defined in section 101(i) of the Higher Education Act of 1965, and a public secondary school, as defined in section 101(d) of that Act.

"Secretary" means the Secretary of Health and Human Services, in consultation and coordination with the Attorney General.

"State" means a State, the District of Columbia, the Commonwealth of Puerto Rico, the Commonwealth of the Northern Mariana Islands, American Samoa, Guam, and the United States Virgin Islands.

(c) **Program authority.** (1) In general. (A) Allocations for States and Indian country. For any fiscal year in which the sums appropriated to carry out this section equal or exceed $20,000,000, from the sums appropriated to carry out this subsection, the Secretary shall allocate, for grants under subparagraph (B) to community-based organizations in each State, an amount bearing the same ratio to such sums as the number of children in the State who are from families with incomes below the poverty line bears to the number of children in all States who are from families with incomes below the poverty line. In view of the extraordinary need for assistance in Indian country, an appropriate amount of funds available under this subtitle [42 USCS §§ 13791 et seq.] shall be made available for such grants in Indian country.

(B) Grants to community-based organizations from allocations. For such a fiscal year, the Secretary may award grants from the appropriate State or Indian country allocation determined under subparagraph (A) on a competitive basis to eligible community-based organizations to pay for the Federal share of assisting eligible communities to develop and carry out programs in accordance with this section.

(C) Reallocation. If, at the end of such a fiscal year, the Secretary determines that funds allocated for community-based organizations in a State or Indian country under subparagraph (B) remain unobligated, the Secretary may use such funds to award grants to eligible community-based organizations in another State or Indian country to pay for such Federal share. In awarding such grants, the Secretary shall consider the need to maintain geographic diversity among the recipients of such grants. Amounts made available through such grants shall remain available until expended.

(2) Other fiscal years. For any fiscal year in which the sums appropriated to carry out this section are less than $20,000,000, the Secretary may award grants on a competitive basis to eligible community-based organizations to pay for the Federal share of assisting eligible communities to develop and carry out programs in accordance with this section.

(3) Administrative costs. The Secretary may use not more than 3 percent of the funds appropriated to carry out this section in any fiscal year for administrative costs.

(d) **Program requirements.** (1) Location. A community-based organization that receives a grant under this section to assist in carrying out such a program shall ensure that the program is carried out—

(A) when appropriate, in the facilities of a public school during nonschool hours; or

(B) in another appropriate local facility in a State or Indian country, such as a college or university, a local or State park or recreation center, church, or military base, that is—

(i) in a location that is easily accessible to children in the community; and

(ii) in compliance with all applicable local ordinances.

(2) Use of funds. Such community-based organization—

(A) shall use funds made available through the grant to provide, to children in the eligible community, services and activities that—

(i) shall include supervised sports programs, and extracurricular and academic programs, that are offered—

(I) after school and on weekends and holidays, during the school year; and

(II) as daily full-day programs (to the extent available resources permit) or as part-day programs, during the summer months;

(ii) [Not enacted]

(B) in providing such extracurricular and academic programs, shall provide programs such as curriculum-based supervised educational, work force preparation, entrepreneurship, cultural, health programs, social activities, arts and crafts programs, dance programs, tutorial and mentoring programs, and other related activities;

(C) may use—

(i) such funds for minor renovation of facilities that are in existence prior to the operation of the program and that are necessary for the operation of the program for which the organization receives the grant, purchase of sporting and recreational equipment and supplies, reasonable costs for the transportation of participants in the program, hiring of staff, provision of meals for such participants, provision of health services consisting of an initial basic physical examination, provision of first aid and nutrition guidance, family counselling, parental training, and substance abuse treatment where appropriate; and

(ii) not more than 5 percent of such funds to pay for the administrative costs of the program; and

(D) may not use such funds to provide sectarian worship or sectarian instruction.

(e) Eligible community identification. (1) Identification. To be eligible to receive a grant under this section, a community-based organization shall identify an eligible community to be assisted under this section.

(2) Criteria. Such eligible community shall be an area that meets such criteria with respect to significant poverty and significant juvenile delinquency, and such additional criteria, as the Secretary may by regulation require.

(f) Applications. (1) Application required. To be eligible to receive a grant under this section, a community-based organization shall submit an application to the Secretary at such time, in such manner, and accompanied by such information, as the Secretary may reasonably require, and obtain approval of such application.

(2) Contents of application. Each application submitted pursuant to paragraph (1) shall—

(A) describe the activities and services to be provided through the program for which the grant is sought;

(B) contain an assurance that the community-based organization will spend grant funds received under this section in a manner that the community-based organization determines will best accomplish the objectives of this section;

(C) contain a comprehensive plan for the program that is designed to achieve identifiable goals for children in the eligible community;

(D) set forth measurable goals and outcomes for the program that—
    (i) will—
        (I) where appropriate, make a public school the focal point of the eligible community; or
        (II) make a local facility described in subsection (d)(1)(B) such a focal point; and
    (ii) may include reducing the percentage of children in the eligible community that enter the juvenile justice system, increasing the graduation rates, school attendance, and academic success of children in the eligible community, and improving the skills of program participants;

(E) provide evidence of support for accomplishing such goals and outcomes from—
    (i) community leaders;
    (ii) businesses;
    (iii) local educational agencies;
    (iv) local officials;
    (v) State officials;
    (vi) Indian tribal government officials; and
    (vii) other organizations that the community-based organization determines to be appropriate;

(F) contain an assurance that the community-based organization will use grant funds received under this section to provide children in the eligible community with activities and services that shall include supervised sports programs, and extracurricular and academic programs, in accordance with subparagraphs (A) and (B) of subsection (d)(2);

(G) contain a list of the activities and services that will be offered through the program for which the grant is sought and sponsored by private nonprofit organizations, individuals, and groups serving the eligible community, including—
    (i) extracurricular and academic programs, such as programs described in subsection (d)(2)(B); and
    (ii) activities that address specific needs in the community;

(H) demonstrate the manner in which the community-based organization will make use of the resources, expertise, and commitment of private entities in carrying out the program for which the grant is sought;

(I) include an estimate of the number of children in the eligible community expected to be served pursuant to the program;

(J) include a description of charitable private resources, and all other resources, that will be made available to achieve the goals of the program;

(K) contain an assurance that the community-based organization will use competitive procedures when purchasing, contracting, or otherwise providing for goods, activities, or services to carry out programs under this section;

(L) contain an assurance that the program will maintain a staff-to-participant ratio (including volunteers) that is appropriate to the activity or services provided by the program;

(M) contain an assurance that the program will maintain an average attendance rate of not less than 75 percent of the participants enrolled in the program, or will enroll additional participants in the program;

(N) contain an assurance that the community-based organization will comply with any evaluation under subsection (m) [subsection (k)], any research effort authorized under Federal law, and any investigation by the Secretary;

(O) contain an assurance that the community-based organization shall prepare and submit to the Secretary an annual report regarding any program conducted under this section;

(P) contain an assurance that the program for which the grant is sought will, to the maximum extent possible, incorporate services that are provided solely through non-Federal private or nonprofit sources; and

(Q) contain an assurance that the community-based organization will maintain separate accounting records for the program.

(3) Priority. In awarding grants to carry out programs under this section, the Secretary shall give priority to community-based organizations who submit applications that demonstrate the greatest effort in generating local support for the programs.

(g) Eligibility of participants. (1) In general. To the extent possible, each child who resides in an eligible community shall be eligible to participate in a program carried out in such community that receives assistance under this section.

(2) Eligibility. To be eligible to participate in a program that receives assistance under this section, a child shall provide the express written approval of a parent or guardian, and shall submit an official application and agree to the terms and conditions of participation in the program.

(3) Nondiscrimination. In selecting children to participate in a program that receives assistance under this section, a community-based organization shall not discriminate on the basis of race, color, religion, sex, national origin, or disability.

(h) Peer review panel. (1) Establishment. The Secretary may establish a peer review panel that shall be comprised of individuals with demonstrated experience in designing and implementing community-based programs.

(2) Composition. A peer review panel shall include at least 1 representative from each of the following:

(A) A community-based organization.

(B) A local government.

(C) A school district.

(D) The private sector.

(E) A charitable organization.

(F) A representative of the United States Olympic Committee, at the option of the Secretary.

(3) Functions. A peer review panel shall conduct the initial review of all grant applications received by the Secretary under subsection (f), make recommendations to the Secretary regarding—

(A) grant funding under this section; and

(B) a design for the evaluation of programs assisted under this section.

(i) Investigations and inspections. The Secretary may conduct such investigations and inspections as may be necessary to ensure compliance with the provisions of this section.

(j) Payments; Federal share; non-Federal share. (1) Payments. The Secretary shall, subject to the availability of appropriations, pay to each community-based organization having an application approved under subsection (f) the Federal share of the costs of developing and carrying out programs described in subsection (c).

(2) Federal share. The Federal share of such costs shall be no more than—

(A) 75 percent for each of fiscal years 1995 and 1996;

(B) 70 percent for fiscal year 1997; and

(C) 60 percent for fiscal year 1998 and thereafter.

(3) Non-Federal share. (A) In general. The non-Federal share of such costs may be in cash or in kind, fairly evaluated, including plant, equipment, and services (including the services described in subsection (f)(2)(P)), and funds appropriated by the Congress for the activity of any agency of an Indian tribal government or the Bureau of Indian Affairs on any Indian lands may be used to provide the non-Federal share of the costs of programs or projects funded under this subtitle [42 USCS §§ 13791 et seq.].

(B) Special rule. At least 15 percent of the non-Federal share of such costs shall be provided from private or nonprofit sources.

(k) Evaluation. The Secretary shall conduct a thorough evaluation of the programs assisted under this section, which shall include an assessment of—

(1) the number of children participating in each program assisted under this section;

(2) the academic achievement of such children;

(3) school attendance and graduation rates of such children; and

(4) the number of such children being processed by the juvenile justice system.

(Sept. 13, 1994, P. L. 103-322, Title III, Subtitle D, § 30401, 108 Stat. 1846; Oct. 7, 1998, P. L. 105-244, § 102(a)(13)(N), 112 Stat. 1621.)

HISTORY; ANCILLARY LAWS AND DIRECTIVES

References in text:

"This title", referred to in this section, is Title III of Act Sept. 13, 1994, P. L. 103-322, 108 Stat. 1836, which appears generally as 42 USCS §§ 13741 et seq. For full classification of this Title, consult USCS Tables volumes.

The meaning of the references in subsec. (b) to sections 101(d) and (i) of the Higher Education Act of 1965 is unclear. Section 101 of that Act appears as 20 USCS § 1001, but includes no subsecs. (d) and (i). "Elementary school" and "secondary school" are defined for purposes of that Act in 20 USCS § 1003.

Explanatory notes:

The bracketed close parenthesis has been inserted in subsec. (b) to reflect the probable intent of Congress to include such punctuation.

The bracketed reference "subsection (k)" has been inserted in subsec. (f)(2)(N) as the reference probably intended by Congress.

Amendments:

1998. Act Oct. 7, 1998 (effective on 10/1/98, as provided by § 3 of such Act, which appears as 20 USCS § 1001 note), in subsec. (b), in the definition of "public school", substituted "101" for "1201" in two places and deleted "(20 U.S.C. 1141(i))" following "1965".

CROSS REFERENCES

This section is referred to in 42 USCS §§ 13793, 14214.

RESEARCH GUIDE

Federal Procedure:

15 Moore's Federal Practice (Matthew Bender 3d ed.), ch 101, Issues of Justiciability § 101.40.

§ 13792. [Repealed]

HISTORY; ANCILLARY LAWS AND DIRECTIVES

This section (Act Sept. 13, 1994, P. L. 103-322, Title III, Subtitle D, § 30402, 108 Stat. 1852) was repealed by Act Oct. 21, 1998, P. L. 105-277, Div A, § 101(f) [Title VIII, Subtitle III, § 301(d)], 112 Stat. 2681-410. It provided for a family and community endeavor schools grant program.

§ 13793. Authorization of appropriations

(a) In general. There are authorized to be appropriated to carry out this subtitle [42 USCS §§ 13791 et seq.]—

    (1) $37,000,000 for fiscal year 1995;

    (2) $103,500,000 for fiscal year 1996;

    (3) $121,500,000 for fiscal year 1997;

    (4) $153,000,000 for fiscal year 1998;

    (5) $193,500,000 for fiscal year 1999; and

    (6) $201,500,000 for fiscal year 2000.

(b) Programs. Of the amounts appropriated under subsection (a) for any fiscal year—

(1) 70 percent shall be made available to carry out section 30401 [42 USCS § 13791]; and

(2) 30 percent shall be made available to carry out section 30402 [former 42 USCS § 13792].

(Sept. 13, 1994, P. L. 103-322, Title III, Subtitle D, § 30403, 108 Stat. 1855.)

CROSS REFERENCES

This section is referred to in 42 USCS § 14214.

§ 13801.   [Repealed]

HISTORY; ANCILLARY LAWS AND DIRECTIVES

This section (Act Sept. 13, 1994, P. L. 103-322, Title III, Subtitle G, § 30701, 108 Stat. 1855) was repealed by Act Jan. 5, 2006, P. L. 109-162, Title XI, Subtitle B, Ch. 5, § 1154(b)(2), 119 Stat. 3113. It authorized grants to support the development and operation of projects to provide residential services to delinquent and at-risk youth.

§ 13802.   [Repealed]

HISTORY; ANCILLARY LAWS AND DIRECTIVES

This section (Act Sept. 13, 1994, P. L. 103-322, Title III, Subtitle G, § 30702, 108 Stat. 1856) was repealed by Act Jan. 5, 2006, P. L. 109-162, Title XI, Subtitle B, Ch. 5, § 1154(b)(2), 119 Stat. 3113. It authorized appropriations.

POLICE RECRUITMENT

§ 13811.   Grant authority

(a) Grants. (1) In general. The Attorney General may make grants to qualified community organizations to assist in meeting the costs of qualified programs which are designed to recruit and retain applicants to police departments.

(2) Consultation with the Ounce of Prevention Council. The Attorney General may consult with the Ounce of Prevention Council in making grants under paragraph (1).

(b) Qualified community organizations. An organization is a qualified community organization which is eligible to receive a grant under subsection (a) if the organization—

(1) is a nonprofit organization; and

(2) has training and experience in—

(A) working with a police department and with teachers, counselors, and similar personnel,

(B) providing services to the community in which the organization is located,

(C) developing and managing services and techniques to recruit individuals to become members of a police department and to assist such individuals in meeting the membership requirements of police departments,

(D) developing and managing services and techniques to assist in the retention of applicants to police departments, and

(E) developing other programs that contribute to the community.

(c) Qualified programs. A program is a qualified program for which a grant may be made under subsection (a) if the program is designed to recruit and train individuals from underrepresented neighborhoods and localities and if—

(1) the overall design of the program is to recruit and retain applicants to a police department;

(2) the program provides recruiting services which include tutorial programs to enable individuals to meet police force academic requirements and to pass entrance examinations;

(3) the program provides counseling to applicants to police departments who may encounter problems throughout the application process; and

(4) the program provides retention services to assist in retaining individuals to stay in the application process of a police department.

(d) Applications. To qualify for a grant under subsection (a), a qualified organization shall submit an application to the Attorney General in such form as the Attorney General may prescribe. Such application shall—

(1) include documentation from the applicant showing—

(A) the need for the grant;

(B) the intended use of grant funds;

(C) expected results from the use of grant funds; and

(D) demographic characteristics of the population to be served, including age, disability, race, ethnicity, and languages used; and

(2) contain assurances satisfactory to the Attorney General that the program for which a grant is made will meet the applicable requirements of the program guidelines prescribed by the Attorney General under subsection (i).

(e) Action by the Attorney General. Not later than 60 days after the date that an application for a grant under subsection (a) is received, the Attorney General shall consult with the police department which will be involved with the applicant and shall—

(1) approve the application and disburse the grant funds applied for; or

(2) disapprove the application and inform the applicant that the application is not approved and provide the applicant with the reasons for the disapproval.

(f) Grant disbursement. The Attorney General shall disburse funds under a grant under subsection (a) in accordance with regulations of the Attorney General which shall ensure—

(1) priority is given to applications for areas and organizations with the greatest showing of need;

(2) that grant funds are equitably distributed on a geographic basis; and

(3) the needs of underserved populations are recognized and addressed.

(g) Grant period. A grant under subsection (a) shall be made for a period not longer than 3 years.

(h) Grantee reporting. (1) For each year of a grant period for a grant under subsection (a), the recipient of the grant shall file a performance report with the Attorney General explaining the activities carried out with the funds received and assessing the effectiveness of such activities in meeting the purpose of the recipient's qualified program.

(2) If there was more than one recipient of a grant, each recipient shall file such report.

(3) The Attorney General shall suspend the funding of a grant, pending compliance, if the recipient of the grant does not file the report required by this subsection or uses the grant for a purpose not authorized by this section.

(i) Guidelines. The Attorney General shall, by regulation, prescribe guidelines on content and results for programs receiving a grant under subsection (a). Such guidelines shall be designed to establish programs which will be effective in training individuals to enter instructional programs for police departments and shall include requirements for—

(1) individuals providing recruiting services;

(2) individuals providing tutorials and other academic assistance programs;

(3) individuals providing retention services; and

(4) the content and duration of recruitment, retention, and counseling programs and the means and devices used to publicize such programs.

(Sept. 13, 1994, P. L. 103-322, Title III, Subtitle H, § 30801, 108 Stat. 1857.)

CROSS REFERENCES
This section is referred to in 42 USCS §§ 13812, 14214.

§ 13812. Authorization of appropriations

There are authorized to be appropriated for grants under section 30801 [42 USCS § 13811]—

(1) $2,000,000 for fiscal year 1996;

(2) $4,000,000 for fiscal year 1997;

(3) $5,000,000 for fiscal year 1998;

(4) $6,000,000 for fiscal year 1999; and

(5) $7,000,000 for fiscal year 2000.

(Sept. 13, 1994, P. L. 103-322, Title III, Subtitle H, § 30802, 108 Stat. 1858.)

CROSS REFERENCES
This section is referred to in 42 USCS § 14214.

NATIONAL COMMUNITY ECONOMIC PARTNERSHIP
Community Economic Partnership Investment Funds

CROSS REFERENCES
This chapter (42 USCS §§ 13821 et seq.) is referred to in 42 USCS § 13852.

§ 13821. Purpose

It is the purpose of this chapter [42 USCS §§ 13821 et seq.] to increase private investment in distressed local communities and to build and expand the capacity of local institutions to better serve the economic needs of local residents through the provision of financial and technical assistance to community development corporations.

(Sept. 13, 1994, P. L. 103-322, Title III, Subtitle K, Ch 1, § 31111, 108 Stat. 1882.)

CROSS REFERENCES

This section is referred to in 42 USCS §§ 13824, 13825, 14214.

§ 13822. Provision of assistance

(a) Authority. The Secretary of Health and Human Services (referred to in this subtitle [42 USCS §§ 13821 et seq.] as the "Secretary") may, in accordance with this chapter [42 USCS §§ 13821 et seq.], provide nonrefundable lines of credit to community development corporations for the establishment, maintenance or expansion of revolving loan funds to be utilized to finance projects intended to provide business and employment opportunities for low-income, unemployed, or underemployed individuals and to improve the quality of life in urban and rural areas.

(b) Revolving loan funds. (1) Competitive assessment of applications. In providing assistance under subsection (a), the Secretary shall establish and implement a competitive process for the solicitation and consideration of applications from eligible entities for lines of credit for the capitalization of revolving funds.

(2) Eligible entities. To be eligible to receive a line of credit under this chapter [42 USCS §§ 13821 et seq.] an applicant shall—

(A) be a community development corporation;

(B) prepare and submit an application to the Secretary that shall include a strategic investment plan that identifies and describes the economic characteristics of the target area to be served, the types of business to be assisted and the impact of such assistance on low-income, underemployed, and unemployed individuals in the target area;

(C) demonstrate previous experience in the development of low-income housing or community or business development projects in a low-income community and provide a record of achievement with respect to such projects; and

(D) have secured one or more commitments from local sources for contributions (either in cash or in kind, letters of credit or letters of commitment) in an amount that is at least equal to the amount requested in the application submitted under subparagraph (B).

(3) Exception. Notwithstanding the provisions of paragraph (2)(D), the Secretary may reduce local contributions to not less than 25 percent of the amount of the line of credit requested by the community development corporation if the Secretary determines such to be appropriate in accordance with section 31116 [42 USCS § 13826].

(Sept. 13, 1994, P. L. 103-322, Title III, Subtitle K, Ch 1, § 31112, 108 Stat. 1882.)

CROSS REFERENCES
This section is referred to in 42 USCS §§ 13823, 13824, 13825, 14214.

§ 13823. Approval of applications

(a) In general. In evaluating applications submitted under section 31112(b)(2)(B) [42 USCS § 13822(b)(2)(B)], the Secretary shall ensure that—

(1) the residents of the target area to be served (as identified under the strategic development plan) would have an income that is less than the median income for the area (as determined by the Secretary);

(2) the applicant community development corporation possesses the technical and managerial capability necessary to administer a revolving loan fund and has past experience in the development and management of housing, community and economic development programs;

(3) the applicant community development corporation has provided sufficient evidence of the existence of good working relationships with—

(A) local businesses and financial institutions, as well as with the community the corporation proposes to serve; and

(B) local and regional job training programs;

(4) the applicant community development corporation will target job opportunities that arise from revolving loan fund investments under this chapter so that 75 percent of the jobs retained or created under such investments are provided to—

(A) individuals with—

(i) incomes that do not exceed the Federal poverty line; or

(ii) incomes that do not exceed 80 percent of the median income of the area;

(B) individuals who are unemployed or underemployed;

(C) individuals who are participating or have participated in job training programs authorized under title I of the Workforce Investment Act of 1998 or the Family Support Act of 1988 (Public Law 100-485);

(D) individuals whose jobs may be retained as a result of the provision of financing available under this chapter; or

(E) individuals who have historically been under represented in the local economy; and

(5) a representative cross section of applicants are approved, including large and small community development corporations, urban and rural community development corporations and community development corporations representing diverse populations.

(b) Priority. In determining which application to approve under this chapter [42 USCS §§ 13821 et seq.] the Secretary shall give priority to those applicants proposing to serve a target area—

(1) with a median income that does not exceed 80 percent of the median for the area (as determined by the Secretary); and

(2) with a high rate of unemployment, as determined by the Secretary or in which the population loss is at least 7 percent from April 1, 1980, to April 1, 1990, as reported by the Bureau of the Census.

(Sept. 13, 1994, P. L. 103-322, Title III, Subtitle K, Ch 1, § 31113, 108 Stat. 1883; Oct. 21, 1998, P. L. 105-277, Div A, § 101(f) [Title VIII, Subtitle IV, § 405(d)(44), (f)(35)], 112 Stat. 2681-428, 2681-434.)

HISTORY; ANCILLARY LAWS AND DIRECTIVES

References in text:
"Title I of the Workforce Investment Act of 1998", referred to in this section, is Act Aug. 7, 1998, P. L. 105-220, 112 Stat. 936, which appears generally as 29 USCS §§ 2801 et seq. For full classification of such Title, consult USCS Tables volumes.

The "Family Support Act of 1988", referred to in this section, is Act Oct. 13, 1988, P. L. 100-485, 102 Stat. 2343. For full classification of such Act, consult USCS Tables volumes.

Amendments:
1998. Act Oct. 21, 1998 (effective on enactment as provided by § 405(g)(1) of Subtitle IV of Title VIII of § 101(f) of Division A of such Act, which appears as 5 USCS § 3502 note), in subsec. (a)(4)(C), substituted "authorized under the Job Training Partnership Act or title I of the Workforce Investment Act of 1998" for "authorized under the Job Training Partnership Act (29 U.S.C. 1501 et seq.)".

Such Act further (effective on 7/1/2000, as provided by § 405(g)(2)(B) of Subtitle VIII of Title IV of § 101(f) of Division A of such Act, which appears as 5 USCS § 3502 note), in subsec. (a)(4)(C), deleted "the Job Training Partnership Act or" preceding "title I".

CROSS REFERENCES
This section is referred to in 42 USCS §§ 13824, 14214.

§ 13824.   Availability of lines of credit and use

(a) Approval of application. The Secretary shall provide a community development corporation that has an application approved under section 31113 [42 USCS § 13823] with a line of credit in an amount determined appropriate by the Secretary, subject to the limitations contained in subsection (b).

(b) Limitations on availability of amounts. (1) Maximum amount. The Secretary shall not provide in excess of $2,000,000 in lines of credit under this chapter to a single applicant.

(2) Period of availability. A line of credit provided under this chapter [42 USCS §§ 13821 et seq.] shall remain available over a period of time established by the Secretary, but in no event shall any such period of time be in excess of 3 years from the date on which such line of credit is made available.

(3) Exception. Notwithstanding paragraphs (1) and (2), if a recipient of a line of credit under this chapter has made full and productive use of such line of credit, can demonstrate the need and demand for additional assistance, and can meet the requirements of section 31112(b)(2) [42 USCS § 13822(b)(2)], the amount of such line of credit may be increased by not more than $1,500,000.

(c) Amounts drawn from line of credit. Amounts drawn from each line of credit under this chapter [42 USCS §§ 13821 et seq.] shall be used solely for the purposes described in section 31111 [42 USCS § 13821] and shall only be drawn down as needed to provide loans, investments, or to defray administrative costs related to the establishment of a revolving loan fund.

(d) **Use of revolving loan funds.** Revolving loan funds established with lines of credit provided under this chapter may be used to provide technical assistance to private business enterprises and to provide financial assistance in the form of loans, loan guarantees, interest reduction assistance, equity shares, and other such forms of assistance to business enterprises in target areas and who are in compliance with section 31113(a)(4) [42 USCS § 13823(a)(4)].

(Sept. 13, 1994, P. L. 103-322, Title III, Subtitle K, Ch 1, § 31114, 108 Stat. 1884.)

CROSS REFERENCES
This section is referred to in 42 USCS § 14214.

§ 13825. Limitations on use of funds

(a) **Matching requirement.** Not to exceed 50 percent of the total amount to be invested by an entity under this chapter may be derived from funds made available from a line of credit under this chapter [42 USCS §§ 13821 et seq.].

(b) **Technical assistance and administration.** Not to exceed 10 percent of the amounts available from a line of credit under this chapter [42 USCS §§ 13821 et seq.] shall be used for the provision of training or technical assistance and for the planning, development, and management of economic development projects. Community development corporations shall be encouraged by the Secretary to seek technical assistance from other community development corporations, with expertise in the planning, development and management of economic development projects. The Secretary shall assist in the identification and facilitation of such technical assistance.

(c) **Local and private sector contributions.** To receive funds available under a line of credit provided under this chapter [42 USCS §§ 13821 et seq.], an entity, using procedures established by the Secretary, shall demonstrate to the community development corporation that such entity agrees to provide local and private sector contributions in accordance with section 31112(b)(2)(D) [42 USCS § 13822(b)(2)(D)], will participate with such community development corporation in a loan, guarantee or investment program for a designated business enterprise, and that the total financial commitment to be provided by such entity is at least equal to the amount to be drawn from the line of credit.

(d) **Use of proceeds from investments.** Proceeds derived from investments made using funds made available under this chapter may be used only for the purposes described in section 31111 [42 USCS § 13821] and shall be reinvested in the community in which they were generated.

(Sept. 13, 1994, P. L. 103-322, Title III, Subtitle K, Ch 1, § 31115, 108 Stat. 1884.)

CROSS REFERENCES
This section is referred to in 42 USCS § 14214.

§ 13826. Program priority for special emphasis programs

(a) In general. The Secretary shall give priority in providing lines of credit under this chapter [42 USCS §§ 13821 et seq.] to community development corporations that propose to undertake economic development activities in distressed communities that target women, Native Americans, at risk youth, farmworkers, population-losing communities, very low-income communities, single mothers, veterans, and refugees; or that expand employee ownership of private enterprises and small businesses, and to programs providing loans of not more than $35,000 to very small business enterprises.

(b) Reservation of funds. Not less than 5 percent of the amounts made available under section 31112(a)(2)(A) [31112(b)(1)] [42 USCS § 13852(b)(1)] may be reserved to carry out the activities described in subsection (a).

(Sept. 13, 1994, P. L. 103-322, Title III, Subtitle K, Ch 1, § 31116, 108 Stat. 1885.)

HISTORY; ANCILLARY LAWS AND DIRECTIVES

Explanatory notes:

The section reference "31112(b)(1)" has been inserted in subsec. (b) to indicate the reference probably intended by Congress.

CROSS REFERENCES

This section is referred to in 42 USCS §§ 13822, 14214.

Emerging Community Development Corporations

CROSS REFERENCES

This chapter (42 USCS §§ 13841 et seq.) is referred to in 42 USCS § 13852.

§ 13841. Community development corporation improvement grants

(a) Purpose. It is the purpose of this section to provide assistance to community development corporations to upgrade the management and operating capacity of such corporations and to enhance the resources available to enable such corporations to increase their community economic development activities.

(b) Skill enhancement grants. (1) In general. The Secretary shall award grants to community development corporations to enable such corporations to attain or enhance the business management and development skills of the individuals that manage such corporations to enable such corporations to seek the public and private resources necessary to develop community economic development projects.

(2) Use of funds. A recipient of a grant under paragraph (1) may use amounts received under such grant—

(A) to acquire training and technical assistance from agencies or institutions that have extensive experience in the development and management of low-income community economic development projects; or

(B) to acquire such assistance from other highly successful community development corporations.

(c) Operating grants. (1) In general. The Secretary shall award grants to community development corporations to enable such corporations to support an administrative capacity for the planning, development, and management of low-income community economic development projects.

(2) Use of funds. A recipient of a grant under paragraph (1) may use amounts received under such grant—

(A) to conduct evaluations of the feasibility of potential low-income community economic development projects that address identified needs in the low-income community and that conform to those projects and activities permitted under subtitle A [chapter 1] [42 USCS §§ 13821 et seq.];

(B) to develop a business plan related to such a potential project; or

(C) to mobilize resources to be contributed to a planned low-income community economic development project or strategy.

(d) Applications. A community development corporation that desires to receive a grant under this section shall prepare and submit to the Secretary an application at such time, in such manner, and containing such information as the Secretary may require.

(e) Amount available for community development corporation. Amounts provided under this section to a community development corporation shall not exceed $75,000 per year. Such corporations may apply for grants under this section for up to 3 consecutive years, except that such corporations shall be required to submit a new application for each grant for which such corporation desires to receive and compete on the basis of such applications in the selection process.

(Sept. 13, 1994, P. L. 103-322, Title III, Subtitle K, Ch 2, § 31121, 108 Stat. 1885.)

HISTORY; ANCILLARY LAWS AND DIRECTIVES

Explanatory notes:

The bracketed words "chapter 1" have been inserted in subsec. (c)(2)(A) to indicate the reference probably intended by Congress.

CROSS REFERENCES

This section is referred to in 42 USCS § 14214.

§ 13842. Emerging community development corporation revolving loan funds

(a) Authority. The Secretary may award grants to emerging community development corporations to enable such corporations to establish, maintain or expand revolving loan funds, to make or guarantee loans, or to make capital investments in new or expanding local businesses.

(b) Eligibility. To be eligible to receive a grant under subsection (a), an entity shall—

(1) be a community development corporation;

(2) have completed not less than one nor more than two community economic development projects or related projects that improve or provide job and employment opportunities to low-income individuals;

(3) prepare and submit to the Secretary an application at such time, in such manner, and containing such information as the Secretary may require, including a strategic investment plan that identifies and describes the economic characteristics of the target area to be served, the types of business to be assisted using amounts received under the grant and the impact of such assistance on low-income individuals; and

(4) have secured one or more commitments from local sources for contributions (either in cash or in kind, letters of credit, or letters of commitment) in an amount that is equal to at least 10 percent of the amounts requested in the application submitted under paragraph (2) [paragraph (3)].

(c) **Use of the revolving loan fund.** (1) In general. A revolving loan fund established or maintained with amounts received under this section may be utilized to provide financial and technical assistance, loans, loan guarantees or investments to private business enterprises to—

(A) finance projects intended to provide business and employment opportunities for low-income individuals and to improve the quality of life in urban and rural areas; and

(B) build and expand the capacity of emerging community development corporations and serve the economic needs of local residents.

(2) Technical assistance. The Secretary shall encourage emerging community development corporations that receive grants under this section to seek technical assistance from established community development corporations, with expertise in the planning, development and management of economic development projects and shall facilitate the receipt of such assistance.

(3) Limitation. Not to exceed 10 percent of the amounts received under this section by a grantee shall be used for training, technical assistance and administrative purposes.

(d) **Use of proceeds from investments.** Proceeds derived from investments made with amounts provided under this section may be utilized only for the purposes described in this subtitle [42 USCS §§ 13821 et seq.] and shall be reinvested in the community in which they were generated.

(e) **Amounts available.** Amounts provided under this section to a community development corporation shall not exceed $500,000 per year.

(Sept. 13, 1994, P. L. 103-322, Title III, Subtitle K, Ch 2, § 31122, 108 Stat. 1886.)

HISTORY; ANCILLARY LAWS AND DIRECTIVES

Explanatory notes:
The bracketed reference "paragraph (3)" has been inserted in subsec. (b)(4) as the reference probably intended by Congress.

CROSS REFERENCES
This section is referred to in 42 USCS § 14214.

Miscellaneous Provisions

§ 13851. Definitions
As used in this subtitle [42 USCS §§ 13821 et seq.]:

(1) Community development corporation. The term "community development corporation" means a private, nonprofit corporation whose board of directors is comprised of business, civic and community leaders, and whose principal purpose includes the provision of low-income housing or community economic development projects that primarily benefit low-income individuals and communities.

(2) Local and private sector contribution. The term "local and private sector contribution" means the funds available at the local level (by private financial institutions, State and local governments) or by any private philanthropic organization and private, nonprofit organizations that will be committed and used solely for the purpose of financing private business enterprises in conjunction with amounts provided under this subtitle [42 USCS §§ 13821 et seq.].

(3) Population-losing community. The term "population-losing community" means any county in which the net population loss is at least 7 percent from April 1, 1980 to April 1, 1990, as reported by the Bureau of the Census.

(4) Private business enterprise. The term "private business enterprise" means any business enterprise that is engaged in the manufacture of a product, provision of a service, construction or development of a facility, or that is involved in some other commercial, manufacturing or industrial activity, and that agrees to target job opportunities stemming from investments authorized under this subtitle to certain individuals.

(5) Target area. The term "target area" means any area defined in an application for assistance under this subtitle [42 USCS §§ 13821 et seq.] that has a population whose income does not exceed the median for the area within which the target area is located.

(6) Very low-income community. The term "very low-income community" means a community in which the median income of the residents of such community does not exceed 50 percent of the median income of the area.

(Sept. 13, 1994, P. L. 103-322, Title III, Subtitle K, Ch 3, § 31131, 108 Stat. 1887.)

CROSS REFERENCES
This section is referred to in 42 USCS § 14214.

§ 13852. Authorization of appropriations

(a) In general. There are authorized to be appropriated to carry out chapters 1 and 2 [42 USCS §§ 13821 et seq., 13841 et seq.]—

    (1) $45,000,000 for fiscal year 1996;

    (2) $72,000,000 for fiscal year 1997;

    (3) $76,500,000 for fiscal year 1998; and

    (4) $76,500,000 for fiscal year 1999.

(b) Earmarks. Of the aggregate amount appropriated under subsection (a) for each fiscal year—

    (1) 60 percent shall be available to carry out chapter 1 [42 USCS §§ 13821 et seq.]; and

(2) 40 percent shall be available to carry out chapter 2 [42 USCS §§ 13841 et seq.].

(c) **Amounts.** Amounts appropriated under subsection (a) shall remain available for expenditure without fiscal year limitation.
(Sept. 13, 1994, P. L. 103-322, Title III, Subtitle K, Ch 3, § 31132, 108 Stat. 1888.)

CROSS REFERENCES
This section is referred to in 42 USCS §§ 13826, 14214.

§ 13853. Prohibition

None of the funds authorized under this subtitle [42 USCS §§ 13821 et seq.] shall be used to finance the construction of housing.
(Sept. 13, 1994, P. L. 103-322, Title III, Subtitle K, Ch 3, § 31133, 108 Stat. 1888.)

CROSS REFERENCES
This section is referred to in 42 USCS § 14214.

COMMUNITY-BASED JUSTICE GRANTS FOR PROSECUTORS

§ 13861. Grant authorization

(a) **In general.** The Attorney General may make grants to State, Indian tribal, or local prosecutors for the purpose of supporting the creation or expansion of community-based justice programs.

(b) **Consultation.** The Attorney General may consult with the Ounce of Prevention Council in making grants under subsection (a).
(Sept. 13, 1994, P. L. 103-322, Title III, Subtitle Q, § 31701, 108 Stat. 1890.)

CROSS REFERENCES
This section is referred to in 42 USCS § 14214.

§ 13862. Use of funds

Grants made by the Attorney General under this section shall be used—
  (1) to fund programs that require the cooperation and coordination of prosecutors, school officials, police, probation officers, youth and social service professionals, and community members in the effort to reduce the incidence of, and increase the successful identification and speed of prosecution of, young violent offenders;
  (2) to fund programs in which prosecutors focus on the offender, not simply the specific offense, and impose individualized sanctions, designed to deter that offender from further antisocial conduct, and impose increasingly serious sanctions on a young offender who continues to commit offenses;
  (3) to fund programs that coordinate criminal justice resources with educational, social service, and community resources to develop and deliver violence prevention programs, including mediation and other conflict resolu-

tion methods, treatment, counseling, educational, and recreational programs that create alternatives to criminal activity;

(4) in rural States (as defined in section 1501(b) of title I of the Omnibus Crime Control and Safe Streets Act of 1968 (42 U.S.C. 3796bb(B)), to fund cooperative efforts between State and local prosecutors, victim advocacy and assistance groups, social and community service providers, and law enforcement agencies to investigate and prosecute child abuse cases, treat youthful victims of child abuse, and work in cooperation with the community to develop education and prevention strategies directed toward the issues with which such entities are concerned; and

(5) by a State, unit of local government, or Indian tribe to create and expand witness and victim protection programs to prevent threats, intimidation, and retaliation against victims of, and witnesses to, violent crimes.

(Sept. 13, 1994, P. L. 103-322, Title III, Subtitle Q, § 31702, 108 Stat. 1890; Jan. 7, 2008, P. L. 110-177, Title III, § 301(a), 121 Stat. 2538.)

HISTORY; ANCILLARY LAWS AND DIRECTIVES
Amendments:
2008. Act Jan. 7, 2008, in para. (3), deleted "and" following the concluding semicolon, in para. (4), substituted "; and " for a concluding period, and added para. (5).

CROSS REFERENCES
This section is referred to in 42 USCS §§ 13863, 14214.

§ 13863. Applications

(a) **Eligibility.** In order to be eligible to receive a grant under this part for any fiscal year, a State, Indian tribal, or local prosecutor, in conjunction with the chief executive officer of the jurisdiction in which the program will be placed, shall submit an application to the Attorney General in such form and containing such information as the Attorney General may reasonably require.

(b) **Requirements.** Each applicant shall include—
(1) a request for funds for the purposes described in section 31702 [42 USCS § 13862];
(2) a description of the communities to be served by the grant, including the nature of the youth crime, youth violence, and child abuse problems within such communities;
(3) assurances that Federal funds received under this part shall be used to supplement, not supplant, non-Federal funds that would otherwise be available for activities funded under this section; and
(4) statistical information in such form and containing such information that the Attorney General may require.

(c) **Comprehensive plan.** Each applicant shall include a comprehensive plan that shall contain—
(1) a description of the youth violence or child abuse crime problem;
(2) an action plan outlining how the applicant will achieve the purposes as described in section 31702 [42 USCS § 13862];

(3) a description of the resources available in the community to implement the plan together with a description of the gaps in the plan that cannot be filled with existing resources; and

(4) a description of how the requested grant will be used to fill gaps.

(Sept. 13, 1994, P. L. 103-322, Title III, Subtitle Q, § 31703, 108 Stat. 1891.)

HISTORY; ANCILLARY LAWS AND DIRECTIVES

References in text:
"This part", as used in this section, probably means Subtitle Q of Title III of Act Sept. 13, 1994, P. L. 103-322, 108 Stat. 1890, which appears as 42 USCS §§ 13861 et seq.

CROSS REFERENCES

This section is referred to in 42 USCS §§ 13864, 13865, 13866, 14214.

§ 13864. Allocation of funds; limitations on grants

(a) Administrative cost limitation. The Attorney General shall use not more than 5 percent of the funds available under this program for the purposes of administration and technical assistance.

(b) Renewal of grants. A grant under this part may be renewed for up to 2 additional years after the first fiscal year during which the recipient receives its initial grant under this part, subject to the availability of funds, if—

(1) the Attorney General determines that the funds made available to the recipient during the previous years were used in a manner required under the approved application; and

(2) the Attorney General determines that an additional grant is necessary to implement the community prosecution program described in the comprehensive plan required by section 31703 [42 USCS § 13863].

(Sept. 13, 1994, P. L. 103-322, Title III, Subtitle Q, § 31704, 108 Stat. 1891.)

HISTORY; ANCILLARY LAWS AND DIRECTIVES

References in text:
"This part", as used in this section, probably means Subtitle Q of Title III of Act Sept. 13, 1994, P. L. 103-322, 108 Stat. 1890, which appears as 42 USCS §§ 13861 et seq.

CROSS REFERENCES

This section is referred to in 42 USCS § 14214.

§ 13865. Award of grants

The Attorney General shall consider the following facts in awarding grants:

(1) Demonstrated need and evidence of the ability to provide the services described in the plan required under section 31703 [42 USCS § 13863].

(2) The Attorney General shall attempt, to the extent practicable, to achieve an equitable geographic distribution of grant awards.

(Sept. 13, 1994, P. L. 103-322, Title III, Subtitle Q, § 31705, 108 Stat. 1891.)

CROSS REFERENCES
This section is referred to in 42 USCS § 14214.

§ 13866. Reports

(a) Report to Attorney General. State and local prosecutors that receive funds under this subtitle shall submit to the Attorney General a report not later than March 1 of each year that describes progress achieved in carrying out the plan described under section 31703(c) [42 USCS § 13863(c)].

(b) Report to Congress. The Attorney General shall submit to the Congress a report by October 1 of each year in which grants are made available under this subtitle which shall contain a detailed statement regarding grant awards, activities of grant recipients, a compilation of statistical information submitted by applicants, and an evaluation of programs established under this subtitle.
(Sept. 13, 1994, P. L. 103-322, Title III, Subtitle Q, § 31706, 108 Stat. 1892.)

CROSS REFERENCES
This section is referred to in 42 USCS § 14214.

§ 13867. Authorization of appropriations

There are authorized to be appropriated $20,000,000 for each of the fiscal years 2008 through 2012 to carry out this subtitle [42 USCS §§ 13821 et seq.].
(Sept. 13, 1994, P. L. 103-322, Title III, Subtitle Q, § 31707, 108 Stat. 1892; Jan. 7, 2008, P. L. 110-177, Title III, § 301(b), 121 Stat. 2539.)

HISTORY; ANCILLARY LAWS AND DIRECTIVES
Amendments:
2008. Act Jan. 7, 2008, substituted the text of this section for one which read:
  "There are authorized to be appropriated to carry out this subtitle—
    "(1) $7,000,000 for fiscal year 1996;
    "(2) $10,000,000 for fiscal year 1997;
    "(3) $10,000,000 for fiscal year 1998;
    "(4) $11,000,000 for fiscal year 1999; and
    "(5) $12,000,000 for fiscal year 2000.".

CROSS REFERENCES
This section is referred to in 42 USCS § 14214.

§ 13868. Definitions

In this subtitle [42 USCS §§ 13821 et seq.]—
  "Indian tribe" means a tribe, band, pueblo, nation, or other organized group or community of Indians, including an Alaska Native village (as defined in or established under the Alaska Native Claims Settlement Act (43 U.S.C. 1601 et seq.)), that is recognized as eligible for the special programs and services provided by the United States to Indians because of their status as Indians.

"State" means a State, the District of Columbia, the Commonwealth of Puerto Rico, the Commonwealth of the Northern Mariana Islands, American Samoa, Guam, and the United States Virgin Islands.

"young violent offenders" means individuals, ages 7 through 22, who have committed crimes of violence, weapons offenses, drug distribution, hate crimes and civil rights violations, and offenses against personal property of another.

(Sept. 13, 1994, P. L. 103-322, Title III, Subtitle Q, § 31708, 108 Stat. 1892.)

CROSS REFERENCES
This section is referred to in 42 USCS § 14214.

FAMILY UNITY DEMONSTRATION PROJECT

§ 13881. Purpose

The purpose of this subtitle [42 USCS §§ 13881 et seq.] is to evaluate the effectiveness of certain demonstration projects in helping to—

(1) alleviate the harm to children and primary caretaker parents caused by separation due to the incarceration of the parents;

(2) reduce recidivism rates of prisoners by encouraging strong and supportive family relationships; and

(3) explore the cost effectiveness of community correctional facilities.

(Sept. 13, 1994, P. L. 103-322, Title III, Subtitle S, § 31902, 108 Stat. 1892.)

CROSS REFERENCES
This section is referred to in 42 USCS § 14214.

§ 13882. Definitions

In this subtitle [42 USCS §§ 13881 et seq.]—

"child" means a person who is less than 7 years of age.

"community correctional facility" means a residential facility that—

(A) is used only for eligible offenders and their children under 7 years of age;

(B) is not within the confines of a jail or prison;

(C) houses no more than 50 prisoners in addition to their children; and

(D) provides to inmates and their children—

(i) a safe, stable, environment for children;

(ii) pediatric and adult medical care consistent with medical standards for correctional facilities;

(iii) programs to improve the stability of the parent-child relationship, including educating parents regarding—

(I) child development; and

(II) household management;

(iv) alcoholism and drug addiction treatment for prisoners; and

(v) programs and support services to help inmates—

(I) to improve and maintain mental and physical health, including access to counseling;

(II) to obtain adequate housing upon release from State incarceration;

(III) to obtain suitable education, employment, or training for employment; and

(IV) to obtain suitable child care.

"eligible offender" means a primary caretaker parent who—

(A) has been sentenced to a term of imprisonment of not more than 7 years or is awaiting sentencing for a conviction punishable by such a term of imprisonment; and

(B) has not engaged in conduct that—

(i) knowingly resulted in death or serious bodily injury;

(ii) is a felony for a crime of violence against a person; or

(iii) constitutes child neglect or mental, physical, or sexual abuse of a child.

"primary caretaker parent" means—

(A) a parent who has consistently assumed responsibility for the housing, health, and safety of a child prior to incarceration; or

(B) a woman who has given birth to a child after or while awaiting her sentencing hearing and who expresses a willingness to assume responsibility for the housing, health, and safety of that child,

a parent who, in the best interest of a child, has arranged for the temporary care of the child in the home of a relative or other responsible adult shall not for that reason be excluded from the category "primary caretaker".

"State" means a State, the District of Columbia, the Commonwealth of Puerto Rico, the United States Virgin Islands, American Samoa, Guam, and the Northern Mariana Islands.

(Sept. 13, 1994, P. L. 103-322, Title III, Subtitle S, § 31903, 108 Stat. 1893.)

CROSS REFERENCES

This section is referred to in 42 USCS §§ 13893, 14214.

§ 13883. Authorization of appropriations

(a) Authorization. There are authorized to be appropriated to carry out this subtitle [42 USCS §§ 13881 et seq.]—

(1) $3,600,000 for fiscal year 1996;

(2) $3,600,000 for fiscal year 1997;

(3) $3,600,000 for fiscal year 1998;

(4) $3,600,000 for fiscal year 1999; and

(5) $5,400,000 for fiscal year 2000.

(b) Availability of appropriations. Of the amount appropriated under subsection (a) for any fiscal year—

(1) 90 percent shall be available to carry out chapter 1 [42 USCS §§ 13891 et seq.]; and

(2) 10 percent shall be available to carry out chapter 2 [42 USCS §§ 13901 et seq.].

(Sept. 13, 1994, P. L. 103-322, Title III, Subtitle S, § 31904, 108 Stat. 1894.)

CROSS REFERENCES

This section is referred to in 42 USCS §§ 13901, 14214.

Grants to States

CROSS REFERENCES

This chapter (42 USCS §§ 13891 et seq.) is referred to in 42 USCS §§ 13883, 13901.

§ 13891. Authority to make grants

(a) **General authority.** The Attorney General may make grants, on a competitive basis, to States to carry out in accordance with this subtitle [42 USCS §§ 13881 et seq.] family unity demonstration projects that enable eligible offenders to live in community correctional facilities with their children.

(b) **Preferences.** For the purpose of making grants under subsection (a), the Attorney General shall give preference to a State that includes in the application required by section 31912 [42 USCS § 13892] assurances that if the State receives a grant—

(1) both the State corrections agency and the State health and human services agency will participate substantially in, and cooperate closely in all aspects of, the development and operation of the family unity demonstration project for which such a grant is requested;

(2) boards made up of community members, including residents, local businesses, corrections officials, former prisoners, child development professionals, educators, and maternal and child health professionals will be established to advise the State regarding the operation of such project;

(3) the State has in effect a policy that provides for the placement of all prisoners, whenever possible, in correctional facilities for which they qualify that are located closest to their respective family homes;

(4) unless the Attorney General determines that a longer timeline is appropriate in a particular case, the State will implement the project not later than 180 days after receiving a grant under subsection (a) and will expend all of the grant during a 1-year period;

(5) the State has the capacity to continue implementing a community correctional facility beyond the funding period to ensure the continuity of the work;

(6) unless the Attorney General determines that a different process for selecting participants in a project is desirable, the State will—

(A) give written notice to a prisoner, not later than 30 days after the State first receives a grant under subsection (a) or 30 days after the prisoner is sentenced to a term of imprisonment of not more than 7 years (whichever is later), of the proposed or current operation of the project;

(B) accept at any time at which the project is in operation an application by a prisoner to participate in the project if, at the time of application, the remainder of the prisoner's sentence exceeds 180 days;

(C) review applications by prisoners in the sequence in which the State receives such applications; and

(D) not more than 50 days after reviewing such applications approve or disapprove the application; and

(7) for the purposes of selecting eligible offenders to participate in such project, the State has authorized State courts to sentence an eligible offender directly to a community correctional facility, provided that the court gives assurances that the offender would have otherwise served a term of imprisonment.

(c) Selection of grantees. The Attorney General shall make grants under subsection (a) on a competitive basis, based on such criteria as the Attorney General shall issue by rule and taking into account the preferences described in subsection (b).

(Sept. 13, 1994, P. L. 103-322, Title III, Subtitle S, Ch 1, § 31911, 108 Stat. 1894.)

CROSS REFERENCES

This section is referred to in 42 USCS §§ 13892, 14214.

§ 13892.   Eligibility to receive grants

To be eligible to receive a grant under section 31911 [42 USCS § 13891], a State shall submit to the Attorney General an application at such time, in such form, and containing such information as the Attorney General reasonably may require by rule.

(Sept. 13, 1994, P. L. 103-322, Title III, Subtitle S, Ch 1, § 31912, 108 Stat. 1895.)

CROSS REFERENCES

This section is referred to in 42 USCS §§ 13891, 14214.

§ 13893.   Report

(a) In general. A State that receives a grant under this title [chapter] [42 USCS §§ 13891 et seq.] shall, not later than 90 days after the 1-year period in which the grant is required to be expended, submit a report to the Attorney General regarding the family unity demonstration project for which the grant was expended.

(b) Contents. A report under subsection (a) shall—

(1) state the number of prisoners who submitted applications to participate in the project and the number of prisoners who were placed in community correctional facilities;

(2) state, with respect to prisoners placed in the project, the number of prisoners who are returned to that jurisdiction and custody and the reasons for such return;

(3) describe the nature and scope of educational and training activities provided to prisoners participating in the project;

(4) state the number, and describe the scope of, contracts made with public

and nonprofit private community-based organizations to carry out such project; and

(5) evaluate the effectiveness of the project in accomplishing the purposes described in section 31902 [42 USCS § 13882].

(Sept. 13, 1994, P. L. 103-322, Title III, Subtitle S, Ch 1, § 31913, 108 Stat. 1895.)

HISTORY; ANCILLARY LAWS AND DIRECTIVES

Explanatory notes:
The bracketed word "chapter" has been inserted in subsec. (a) to indicate the word probably intended by Congress.

CROSS REFERENCES
This section is referred to in 42 USCS § 14214.

Family Unity Demonstration Project for Federal Prisoners

CROSS REFERENCES
This chapter (42 USCS §§ 13901 et seq.) is referred to in 42 USCS § 13883.

§ 13901. Authority of the Attorney General

(a) In general. With the funds available to carry out this subtitle [42 USCS §§ 13881 et seq.] for the benefit of Federal prisoners, the Attorney General, acting through the Director of the Bureau of Prisons, shall select eligible prisoners to live in community correctional facilities with their children.

(b) General contracting authority. In implementing this title [subtitle] [42 USCS §§ 13881 et seq.], the Attorney General may enter into contracts with appropriate public or private agencies to provide housing, sustenance, services, and supervision of inmates eligible for placement in community correctional facilities under this title.

(c) Use of State facilities. At the discretion of the Attorney General, Federal participants may be placed in State projects as defined in chapter 1 [42 USCS §§ 13891 et seq.]. For such participants, the Attorney General shall, with funds available under section 31904(b)(2) [42 USCS § 13883(b)(2)], reimburse the State for all project costs related to the Federal participant's placement, including administrative costs.

(Sept. 13, 1994, P. L. 103-322, Title III, Subtitle S, Ch 2, § 31921, 108 Stat. 1896.)

HISTORY; ANCILLARY LAWS AND DIRECTIVES

Explanatory notes:
The bracketed word "subtitle" has been inserted in subsec. (b) to indicate the word probably intended by Congress.

CROSS REFERENCES
This section is referred to in 42 USCS §§ 13902, 14214.

§ 13902. Requirements

For the purpose of placing Federal participants in a family unity demonstration project under section 31921 [42 USCS § 13901], the Attorney General shall consult with the Secretary of Health and Human Services regarding the development and operation of the project.

(Sept. 13, 1994, P. L. 103-322, Title III, Subtitle S, Ch 2, § 31922, 108 Stat. 1896.)

CROSS REFERENCES
This section is referred to in 42 USCS § 14214.

PREVENTION, DIAGNOSIS, AND TREATMENT OF TUBERCULOSIS IN CORRECTIONAL INSTITUTIONS

§ 13911. Prevention, diagnosis, and treatment of tuberculosis in correctional institutions

(a) Guidelines. The Attorney General, in consultation with the Secretary of Health and Human Services and the Director of the National Institute of Corrections, shall develop and disseminate to appropriate entities, including State, Indian tribal, and local correctional institutions and the Immigration and Naturalization Service, guidelines for the prevention, diagnosis, treatment, and followup care of tuberculosis among inmates of correctional institutions and persons held in holding facilities operated by or under contract with the Immigration and Naturalization Service.

(b) Compliance. The Attorney General shall ensure that prisons in the Federal prison system and holding facilities operated by or under contract with the Immigration and Naturalization Service comply with the guidelines described in subsection (a).

(c) Grants. (1) In general. The Attorney General shall make grants to State, Indian tribal, and local correction authorities and public health authorities to assist in establishing and operating programs for the prevention, diagnosis, treatment, and followup care of tuberculosis among inmates of correctional institutions.

(2) Federal share. The Federal share of funding of a program funded with a grant under paragraph (1) shall not exceed 50 percent.

(3) Authorization of appropriations. There are authorized to be appropriated to carry out this section—

   (A) $700,000 for fiscal year 1996;

   (B) $1,000,000 for fiscal year 1997;

   (C) $1,000,000 for fiscal year 1998;

   (D) $1,100,000 for fiscal year 1999; and

   (E) $1,200,000 for fiscal year 2000.

(d) Definitions. In this section—

   "Indian tribe" means a tribe, band, pueblo, nation, or other organized group or community of Indians, including an Alaska Native village (as defined in or established under the Alaska Native Claims Settlement Act (43 U.S.C. 1601 et seq.)[)], that is recognized as eligible for the special programs and services provided by the United States to Indians because of their status as Indians.

"State" means a State, the District of Columbia, the Commonwealth of Puerto Rico, the Commonwealth of the Northern Mariana Islands, American Samoa, Guam, and the United States Virgin Islands.
(Sept. 13, 1994, P. L. 103-322, Title III, Subtitle V, § 32201, 108 Stat. 1901.)

HISTORY; ANCILLARY LAWS AND DIRECTIVES

Explanatory notes:
The bracketed close parenthesis has been inserted in subsec. (d) to reflect the probable intent of Congress to include such punctuation.

Transfer of functions:
For abolition of the Immigration and Naturalization Service, transfer of functions, and treatment of related references, see transfer of functions note under 8 USCS § 1551.

CROSS REFERENCES
This section is referred to in 42 USCS § 14214.

RESEARCH GUIDE

Other Treatises:
Cohen's Handbook of Federal Indian Law (Matthew Bender), ch 22, Government Services for Indians § 22.04.

GANG RESISTANCE EDUCATION AND TRAINING

§ 13921. Gang resistance education and training projects

(a) **Establishment of projects.** (1) In general. The Attorney General shall establish not less than 50 Gang Resistance Education and Training (GREAT) projects, to be located in communities across the country, in addition to the number of projects currently funded.

(2) Selection of communities. Communities identified for such GREAT projects shall be selected by the Attorney General on the basis of gang-related activity in that particular community.

(3) Amount of assistance per project; allocation. The Attorney General shall make available not less than $800,000 per project, subject to the availability of appropriations, and such funds shall be allocated—

(A) 50 percent to the affected State and local law enforcement and prevention organizations participating in such projects; and

(B) 50 percent to the Bureau of Alcohol, Tobacco, Firearms, and Explosives, Department of Justice for salaries, expenses, and associated administrative costs for operating and overseeing such projects.

(b) **Authorization of appropriations.** There is authorized to be appropriated to carry out this section—

(1) $20,000,000 for fiscal year 2006;
(2) $20,000,000 for fiscal year 2007;
(3) $20,000,000 for fiscal year 2008;
(4) $20,000,000 for fiscal year 2009; and
(5) $20,000,000 for fiscal year 2010.

(Sept. 13, 1994, P. L. 103-322, Title III, Subtitle X, § 32401, 108 Stat. 1902;
Nov. 25, 2002, P. L. 107-296, Title XI, Subtitle B, § 1112(p), 116 Stat. 2278;
Jan. 5, 2006, P. L. 109-162, Title XI, Subtitle C, § 1188, 119 Stat. 3128.)

HISTORY; ANCILLARY LAWS AND DIRECTIVES
Amendments:
2002. Act Nov. 25, 2002 (effective 60 days after enactment, as provided by
§ 4 of such Act, which appears as 6 USCS § 101 note), in subsec. (a), in
paras. (1) and (2), substituted "Attorney General" for "Secretary of the
Treasury", and, in para. (3), in the introductory matter, substituted "Attorney General" for "Secretary of the Treasury", and, in subpara. (B),
substituted "Bureau of Alcohol, Tobacco, Firearms, and Explosives, Department of Justice" for "Bureau of Alcohol, Tobacco and Firearms".
2006. Act Jan. 5, 2006, in subsec. (b), substituted paras. (1)–(5) for former
paras. (1)–(6), which read:
    "(1) $9,000,000 for fiscal year 1995;
    "(2) $7,200,000 for fiscal year 1996;
    "(3) $7,200,000 for fiscal year 1997;
    "(4) $7,200,000 for fiscal year 1998;
    "(5) $7,200,000 for fiscal year 1999; and
    "(6) $7,720,000 for fiscal year 2000.".
Although the Act purported to amend § 32401(b) of the Violent Crime
Control Act of 1994, the amendment was executed to § 32401(b) of the
Violent Crime Control and Law Enforcement Act of 1994 (subsec. (b) of
this section) in order to effectuate the probable intent of Congress.

CROSS REFERENCES
This section is referred to in 42 USCS § 14214.

VIOLENCE AGAINST WOMEN

§ 13925. Definitions and grant provisions

(a) Definitions. In this title:
    (1) Courts. The term "courts" means any civil or criminal, tribal, and Alaska
Native Village, Federal, State, local or territorial court having jurisdiction to
address domestic violence, dating violence, sexual assault or stalking,
including immigration, family, juvenile, and dependency courts, and the
judicial officers serving in those courts, including judges, magistrate judges,
commissioners, justices of the peace, or any other person with decisionmaking authority.
    (2) Child abuse and neglect. The term "child abuse and neglect" means any
recent act or failure to act on the part of a parent or caregiver with intent to
cause death, serious physical or emotional harm, sexual abuse, or exploitation, or an act or failure to act which presents an imminent risk of serious
harm. This definition shall not be construed to mean that failure to leave an
abusive relationship, in the absence of other action constituting abuse or
neglect, is itself abuse or neglect.
    (3) Community-based organization. The term "community-based organiza-
tion" means an organization that—

(A) focuses primarily on domestic violence, dating violence, sexual assault, or stalking;

(B) has established a specialized culturally specific program that addresses domestic violence, dating violence, sexual assault, or stalking;

(C) has a primary focus on underserved populations (and includes representatives of these populations) and domestic violence, dating violence, sexual assault, or stalking; or

(D) obtains expertise, or shows demonstrated capacity to work effectively, on domestic violence, dating violence, sexual assault, and stalking through collaboration.

(4) Child maltreatment. The term "child maltreatment" means the physical or psychological abuse or neglect of a child or youth, including sexual assault and abuse.

(5) Court-based and court-related personnel. The term "court-based" and "court-related personnel" mean persons working in the court, whether paid or volunteer, including—

(A) clerks, special masters, domestic relations officers, administrators, mediators, custody evaluators, guardians ad litem, lawyers, negotiators, probation, parole, interpreters, victim assistants, victim advocates, and judicial, administrative, or any other professionals or personnel similarly involved in the legal process;

(B) court security personnel;

(C) personnel working in related, supplementary offices or programs (such as child support enforcement); and

(D) any other court-based or community-based personnel having responsibilities or authority to address domestic violence, dating violence, sexual assault, or stalking in the court system.

(6) Domestic violence. The term "domestic violence" includes felony or misdemeanor crimes of violence committed by a current or former spouse of the victim, by a person with whom the victim shares a child in common, by a person who is cohabitating with or has cohabitated with the victim as a spouse, by a person similarly situated to a spouse of the victim under the domestic or family violence laws of the jurisdiction receiving grant monies, or by any other person against an adult or youth victim who is protected from that person's acts under the domestic or family violence laws of the jurisdiction.

(7) Dating partner. The term "dating partner" refers to a person who is or has been in a social relationship of a romantic or intimate nature with the abuser, and where the existence of such a relationship shall be determined based on a consideration of—

(A) the length of the relationship;

(B) the type of relationship; and

(C) the frequency of interaction between the persons involved in the relationship.

(8) Dating violence. The term "dating violence" means violence committed by a person—

117

(A) who is or has been in a social relationship of a romantic or intimate nature with the victim; and

(B) where the existence of such a relationship shall be determined based on a consideration of the following factors:

(i) The length of the relationship.

(ii) The type of relationship.

(iii) The frequency of interaction between the persons involved in the relationship.

(9) Elder abuse. The term "elder abuse" means any action against a person who is 50 years of age or older that constitutes the willful—

(A) infliction of injury, unreasonable confinement, intimidation, or cruel punishment with resulting physical harm, pain, or mental anguish; or

(B) deprivation by a person, including a caregiver, of goods or services with intent to cause physical harm, mental anguish, or mental illness.

(10) Indian. The term "Indian" means a member of an Indian tribe.

(11) Indian country. The term "Indian country" has the same meaning given such term in section 1151 of title 18, United States Code.

(12) Indian housing. The term "Indian housing" means housing assistance described in the Native American Housing Assistance and Self-Determination Act of 1996 (25 U.S.C. 4101 et seq., as amended).

(13) Indian tribe. The term "Indian tribe" means a tribe, band, pueblo, nation, or other organized group or community of Indians, including any Alaska Native village or regional or village corporation (as defined in, or established pursuant to, the Alaska Native Claims Settlement Act (43 U.S.C. 1601 et seq.)), that is recognized as eligible for the special programs and services provided by the United States to Indians because of their status as Indians.

(14) Indian law enforcement. The term "Indian law enforcement" means the departments or individuals under the direction of the Indian tribe that maintain public order.

(15) Law enforcement. The term "law enforcement" means a public agency charged with policing functions, including any of its component bureaus (such as governmental victim services programs), including those referred to in section 3 of the Indian Enforcement Reform Act (25 U.S.C. 2802).

(16) Legal assistance. The term "legal assistance" includes assistance to adult and youth victims of domestic violence, dating violence, sexual assault, and stalking in—

(A) family, tribal, territorial, immigration, employment, administrative agency, housing matters, campus administrative or protection or stay away order proceedings, and other similar matters; and

(B) criminal justice investigations, prosecutions and post-trial matters (including sentencing, parole, and probation) that impact the victim's safety and privacy.

(17) Linguistically and culturally specific services. The term "linguistically and culturally specific services" means community-based services that offer full linguistic access and culturally specific services and resources, includ-

ing outreach, collaboration, and support mechanisms primarily directed toward underserved communities.

(18) Personally identifying information or personal information. The term "personally identifying information" or "personal information" means individually identifying information for or about an individual including information likely to disclose the location of a victim of domestic violence, dating violence, sexual assault, or stalking, including—

(A) a first and last name;

(B) a home or other physical address;

(C) contact information (including a postal, e-mail or Internet protocol address, or telephone or facsimile number);

(D) a social security number; and

(E) any other information, including date of birth, racial or ethnic background, or religious affiliation, that, in combination with any of subparagraphs (A) through (D), would serve to identify any individual.

(19) Prosecution. The term "prosecution" means any public agency charged with direct responsibility for prosecuting criminal offenders, including such agency's component bureaus (such as governmental victim services programs).

(20) Protection order or restraining order. The term "protection order" or "restraining order" includes—

(A) any injunction, restraining order, or any other order issued by a civil or criminal court for the purpose of preventing violent or threatening acts or harassment against, sexual violence or contact or communication with or physical proximity to, another person, including any temporary or final orders issued by civil or criminal courts whether obtained by filing an independent action or as a pendente lite order in another proceeding so long as any civil order was issued in response to a complaint, petition, or motion filed by or on behalf of a person seeking protection; and

(B) any support, child custody or visitation provisions, orders, remedies, or relief issued as part of a protection order, restraining order, or stay away injunction pursuant to State, tribal, territorial, or local law authorizing the issuance of protection orders, restraining orders, or injunctions for the protection of victims of domestic violence, dating violence, sexual assault, or stalking.

(21) Rural area and rural community. The term "rural area" and "rural community" mean—

(A) any area or community, respectively, no part of which is within an area designated as a standard metropolitan statistical area by the Office of Management and Budget; or

(B) any area or community, respectively, that is—

(i) within an area designated as a metropolitan statistical area or considered as part of a metropolitan statistical area; and

(ii) located in a rural census tract.

(22) Rural State. The term "rural State" means a State that has a population density of 52 or fewer persons per square mile or a State in which the

largest county has fewer than 150,000 people, based on the most recent decennial census.

(23) Sexual assault. The term "sexual assault" means any conduct proscribed by chapter 109A of title 18, United States Code [18 USCS §§ 2241 et seq.], whether or not the conduct occurs in the special maritime and territorial jurisdiction of the United States or in a Federal prison and includes both assaults committed by offenders who are strangers to the victim and assaults committed by offenders who are known or related by blood or marriage to the victim.

(24) Stalking. The term "stalking" means engaging in a course of conduct directed at a specific person that would cause a reasonable person to—

   (A) fear for his or her safety or the safety of others; or

   (B) suffer substantial emotional distress.

(25) State. The term "State" means each of the several States and the District of Columbia, and except as otherwise provided, the Commonwealth of Puerto Rico, Guam, American Samoa, the Virgin Islands, and the Northern Mariana Islands.

(26) State domestic violence coalition. The term "State domestic violence coalition" means a program determined by the Administration for Children and Families under sections 302 and 311 of the Family Violence Prevention and Services Act [42 USCS §§ 10402 and 10411].

(27) State sexual assault coalition. The term "State sexual assault coalition" means a program determined by the Center for Injury Prevention and Control of the Centers for Disease Control and Prevention under the Public Health Service Act (42 U.S.C. 280b et seq.).

(28) Territorial domestic violence or sexual assault coalition. The term "territorial domestic violence or sexual assault coalition" means a program addressing domestic or sexual violence that is—

   (A) an established nonprofit, nongovernmental territorial coalition addressing domestic violence or sexual assault within the territory; or

   (B) a nongovernmental organization with a demonstrated history of addressing domestic violence or sexual assault within the territory that proposes to incorporate as a nonprofit, nongovernmental territorial coalition.

(29) Tribal coalition. The term "tribal coalition" means—

   (A) an established nonprofit, nongovernmental tribal coalition addressing domestic violence and sexual assault against American Indian or Alaskan Native women; or

   (B) individuals or organizations that propose to incorporate as nonprofit, nongovernmental tribal coalitions to address domestic violence and sexual assault against American Indian or Alaska Native women.

(30) Tribal government. The term "tribal government" means—

   (A) the governing body of an Indian tribe; or

   (B) a tribe, band, pueblo, nation, or other organized group or community of Indians, including any Alaska Native village or regional or village corporation (as defined in, or established pursuant to, the Alaska Native

Claims Settlement Act (43 U.S.C. 1601 et seq.)), that is recognized as eligible for the special programs and services provided by the United States to Indians because of their status as Indians.

(31) Tribal nonprofit organization. The term "tribal nonprofit organization" means—

(A) a victim services provider that has as its primary purpose to assist Native victims of domestic violence, dating violence, sexual assault, or stalking; and

(B) staff and leadership of the organization must include persons with a demonstrated history of assisting American Indian or Alaska Native victims of domestic violence, dating violence, sexual assault, or stalking.

(32) Tribal organization. The term "tribal organization" means—

(A) the governing body of any Indian tribe;

(B) any legally established organization of Indians which is controlled, sanctioned, or chartered by such governing body of a tribe or tribes to be served, or which is democratically elected by the adult members of the Indian community to be served by such organization and which includes the maximum participation of Indians in all phases of its activities; or

(C) any tribal nonprofit organization.

(33) Underserved populations. The term "underserved populations" includes populations underserved because of geographic location, underserved racial and ethnic populations, populations underserved because of special needs (such as language barriers, disabilities, alienage status, or age), and any other population determined to be underserved by the Attorney General or by the Secretary of Health and Human Services, as appropriate.

(34) Victim advocate. The term "victim advocate" means a person, whether paid or serving as a volunteer, who provides services to victims of domestic violence, sexual assault, stalking, or dating violence under the auspices or supervision of a victim services program.

(35) Victim assistant. The term "victim assistant" means a person, whether paid or serving as a volunteer, who provides services to victims of domestic violence, sexual assault, stalking, or dating violence under the auspices or supervision of a court or a law enforcement or prosecution agency.

(36) Victim services or victim service provider. The term "victim services" or "victim service provider" means a nonprofit, nongovernmental organization that assists domestic violence, dating violence, sexual assault, or stalking victims, including rape crisis centers, domestic violence shelters, faith-based organizations, and other organizations, with a documented history of effective work concerning domestic violence, dating violence, sexual assault, or stalking.

(37) Youth. The term "youth" means teen and young adult victims of domestic violence, dating violence, sexual assault, or stalking.

(b) **Grant conditions.** (1) Match. No matching funds shall be required for any grant or subgrant made under this Act for—

(A) any tribe, territory, or victim service provider; or

(B) any other entity, including a State, that—

(i) petitions for a waiver of any match condition imposed by the Attorney General or the Secretaries of Health and Human Services or Housing and Urban Development; and

(ii) whose petition for waiver is determined by the Attorney General or the Secretaries of Health and Human Services or Housing and Urban Development to have adequately demonstrated the financial need of the petitioning entity.

(2) Nondisclosure of confidential or private information. (A) In general. In order to ensure the safety of adult, youth, and child victims of domestic violence, dating violence, sexual assault, or stalking, and their families, grantees and subgrantees under this title shall protect the confidentiality and privacy of persons receiving services.

(B) Nondisclosure. Subject to subparagraphs (C) and (D), grantees and subgrantees shall not—

(i) disclose any personally identifying information or individual information collected in connection with services requested, utilized, or denied through grantees' and subgrantees' programs; or

(ii) reveal individual client information without the informed, written, reasonably time-limited consent of the person (or in the case of an unemancipated minor, the minor and the parent or guardian or in the case of persons with disabilities, the guardian) about whom information is sought, whether for this program or any other Federal, State, tribal, or territorial grant program, except that consent for release may not be given by the abuser of the minor, person with disabilities, or the abuser of the other parent of the minor.

(C) Release. If release of information described in subparagraph (B) is compelled by statutory or court mandate—

(i) grantees and subgrantees shall make reasonable attempts to provide notice to victims affected by the disclosure of information; and

(ii) grantees and subgrantees shall take steps necessary to protect the privacy and safety of the persons affected by the release of the information.

(D) Information sharing. Grantees and subgrantees may share—

(i) nonpersonally identifying data in the aggregate regarding services to their clients and nonpersonally identifying demographic information in order to comply with Federal, State, tribal, or territorial reporting, evaluation, or data collection requirements;

(ii) court-generated information and law-enforcement generated information contained in secure, governmental registries for protection order enforcement purposes; and

(iii) law enforcement- and prosecution-generated information necessary for law enforcement and prosecution purposes.

(E) Oversight. Nothing in this paragraph shall prevent the Attorney General from disclosing grant activities authorized in this Act to the chairman and ranking members of the Committee on the Judiciary of the House of Representatives and the Committee on the Judiciary of the Senate exercising Congressional oversight authority. All disclosures shall protect confidentiality and omit personally identifying information, including location information about individuals.

(3) Approved activities. In carrying out the activities under this title, grantees and subgrantees may collaborate with and provide information to Federal, State, local, tribal, and territorial public officials and agencies to develop and implement policies to reduce or eliminate domestic violence, dating violence, sexual assault, and stalking.

(4) Non-supplantation. Any Federal funds received under this title shall be used to supplement, not supplant, non-Federal funds that would otherwise be available for activities under this title.

(5) Use of funds. Funds authorized and appropriated under this title may be used only for the specific purposes described in this title and shall remain available until expended.

(6) Reports. An entity receiving a grant under this title shall submit to the disbursing agency a report detailing the activities undertaken with the grant funds, including and providing additional information as the agency shall require.

(7) Evaluation. Federal agencies disbursing funds under this title shall set aside up to 3 percent of such funds in order to conduct—

(A) evaluations of specific programs or projects funded by the disbursing agency under this title or related research; or

(B) evaluations of promising practices or problems emerging in the field or related research, in order to inform the agency or agencies as to which programs or projects are likely to be effective or responsive to needs in the field.

(8) Nonexclusivity. Nothing in this title shall be construed to prohibit male victims of domestic violence, dating violence, sexual assault, and stalking from receiving benefits and services under this title.

(9) Prohibition on tort litigation. Funds appropriated for the grant program under this title may not be used to fund civil representation in a lawsuit based on a tort claim. This paragraph should not be construed as a prohibition on providing assistance to obtain restitution in a protection order or criminal case.

(10) Prohibition on lobbying. Any funds appropriated for the grant program shall be subject to the prohibition in section 1913 of title 18, United States Code, relating to lobbying with appropriated moneys.

(11) Technical assistance. Of the total amounts appropriated under this title, not less than 3 percent and up to 8 percent, unless otherwise noted, shall be available for providing training and technical assistance relating to the purposes of this title to improve the capacity of the grantees, subgrantees, and other entities. If there is a demonstrated history that the Office on Violence Against Women has previously set aside amounts greater than 8 percent for technical assistance and training relating to grant programs authorized under this title, the Office has the authority to continue setting aside amounts greater than 8 percent.

(Sept. 13, 1994, P. L. 103-322, Title IV, § 40002, as added Jan. 5, 2006, P. L.

109-162, § 3, 119 Stat. 2964; Aug. 12, 2006, P. L. 109-271, §§ 1(d)–(f), 2(e), 120 Stat. 751, 752; Dec. 20, 2010, P. L. 111-320, Title II, § 202(d), 124 Stat. 3509.)

HISTORY; ANCILLARY LAWS AND DIRECTIVES

References in text:
"This Act", referred to in this section, is Act Sept. 13, 1994, P. L. 103-322, which is popularly known as the Violent Crime Control and Law Enforcement Act of 1994. For full classification of such Act, consult USCS Tables volumes.

"This title", referred to in this section, is Title IV of Act Sept. 13, 1994, P. L. 103-322, which appears generally as 42 USCS §§ 13925 et seq. For full classification of such Title, consult USCS Tables volumes.

Amendments:
2006. Act Aug. 12, 2006, in subsec. (a), in para. (1), substituted "Alaska Native" for "Alaskan", in para. (23), substituted "proscribed" for "prescribed", redesignated paras. (31)–(36) as paras. (32)–(37), respectively, and inserted new para. (31); and, in subsec. (b), substituted para. (1) for one which read: "(1) Match. No matching funds shall be required for a grant or subgrant made under this title for any tribe, territory, victim service provider, or any entity that the Attorney General determines has adequately demonstrated financial need.", and, in para. (11), inserted the sentence beginning "Of the total amounts . . . .".

2010. Act Dec. 20, 2010, in subsec. (a)(26), substituted "under sections 302 and 311 of the Family Violence Prevention and Services Act" for "under the Family Violence Prevention and Services Act (42 U.S.C. 10410(b))".

Other provisions:
Improving services for victims of domestic violence, dating violence, sexual assault, and stalking; findings. Act Jan. 5, 2006, P. L. 109-162, Title II, § 201, 119 Stat. 2993, provides:

"Congress finds the following:

"(1) Nearly ⅓ of American women report physical or sexual abuse by a husband or boyfriend at some point in their lives.

"(2) According to the National Crime Victimization Survey, 248,000 Americans 12 years of age and older were raped or sexually assaulted in 2002.

"(3) Rape and sexual assault in the United States is estimated to cost $127,000,000,000 per year, including—

"(A) lost productivity;

"(B) medical and mental health care;

"(C) police and fire services;

"(D) social services;

"(E) loss of and damage to property; and

"(F) reduced quality of life.

"(4) Nonreporting of sexual assault in rural areas is a particular problem because of the high rate of nonstranger sexual assault.

"(5) Geographic isolation often compounds the problems facing sexual assault victims. The lack of anonymity and accessible support services can limit opportunities for justice for victims.

"(6) Domestic elder abuse is primarily family abuse. The National Elder Abuse Incidence Study found that the perpetrator was a family member in 90 percent of cases.

"(7) Barriers for older victims leaving abusive relationships include—

"(A) the inability to support themselves;

"(B) poor health that increases their dependence on the abuser;

"(C) fear of being placed in a nursing home; and

"(D) ineffective responses by domestic abuse programs and law enforcement.

"(8) Disabled women comprise another vulnerable population with unmet needs. Women with disabilities are more likely to be the victims of abuse and violence than women without disabilities because of their increased physical, economic, social, or psychological dependence on others.

"(9) Many women with disabilities also fail to report the abuse, since they are dependent on their abusers and fear being abandoned or institutionalized.

"(10) Of the 598 battered women's programs surveyed—

"(A) only 35 percent of these programs offered disability awareness training for their staff; and

"(B) only 16 percent dedicated a staff member to provide services to women with disabilities.

"(11) Problems of domestic violence are exacerbated for immigrants when spouses control the immigration status of their family members, and abusers use threats of refusal to file immigration papers and threats to deport spouses and children as powerful tools to prevent battered immigrant women from seeking help, trapping battered immigrant women in violent homes because of fear of deportation.

"(12) Battered immigrant women who attempt to flee abusive relationships may not have access to bilingual shelters or bilingual professionals, and face restrictions on public or financial assistance. They may also lack assistance of a certified interpreter in court, when reporting complaints to the police or a 9-1-1 operator, or even in acquiring information about their rights and the legal system.

"(13) More than 500 men and women call the National Domestic Violence Hotline every day to get immediate, informed, and confidential assistance to help deal with family violence.

"(14) The National Domestic Violence Hotline service is available, toll-free, 24 hours a day and 7 days a week, with bilingual staff, access to translators in 150 languages, and a TTY line for the hearing-impaired.

"(15) With access to over 5,000 shelters and service providers across the United States, Puerto Rico, and the United States Virgin Islands, the National Domestic Violence Hotline provides crisis intervention and immediately connects callers with sources of help in their local community.

"(16) Approximately 60 percent of the callers indicate that calling the Hotline is their first attempt to address a domestic violence situation and that they have not called the police or any other support services.

"(17) Between 2000 and 2003, there was a 27 percent increase in call volume at the National Domestic Violence Hotline.

"(18) Improving technology infrastructure at the National Domestic

Violence Hotline and training advocates, volunteers, and other staff on upgraded technology will drastically increase the Hotline's ability to answer more calls quickly and effectively.''.

Services, protection, and justice for young victims of violence; findings. Act Jan. 5, 2006, P. L. 109-162, Title III, § 301, 119 Stat. 3003, provides: ''Congress finds the following:

''(1) Youth, under the age of 18, account for 67 percent of all sexual assault victimizations reported to law enforcement officials.

''(2) The Department of Justice consistently finds that young women between the ages of 16 and 24 experience the highest rate of non-fatal intimate partner violence.

''(3) In 1 year, over 4,000 incidents of rape or sexual assault occurred in public schools across the country.

''(4) Young people experience particular obstacles to seeking help. They often do not have access to money, transportation, or shelter services. They must overcome issues such as distrust of adults, lack of knowledge about available resources, or pressure from peers and parents.

''(5) A needs assessment on teen relationship abuse for the State of California, funded by the California Department of Health Services, identified a desire for confidentiality and confusion about the law as 2 of the most significant barriers to young victims of domestic and dating violence seeking help.

''(6) Only one State specifically allows for minors to petition the court for protection orders.

''(7) Many youth are involved in dating relationships, and these relationships can include the same kind of domestic violence and dating violence seen in the adult population. In fact, more than 40 percent of all incidents of domestic violence involve people who are not married.

''(8) 40 percent of girls ages 14 to 17 report knowing someone their age who has been hit or beaten by a boyfriend, and 13 percent of college women report being stalked.

''(9) Of college women who said they had been the victims of rape or attempted rape, 12.8 percent of completed rapes, 35 percent of attempted rapes, and 22.9 percent of threatened rapes took place on a date. Almost 60 percent of the completed rapes that occurred on campus took place in the victim's residence.

''(10) According to a 3-year study of student-athletes at 10 Division I universities, male athletes made up only 3.3 percent of the general male university population, but they accounted for 19 percent of the students reported for sexual assault and 35 percent of domestic violence perpetrators.''.

CROSS REFERENCES

This section is referred to in 42 USCS §§ 1437d, 1437f, 3796gg-2, 3796gg-6, 3796hh-4, 14045, 14045a, 14045b.

RESEARCH GUIDE

Law Review Articles:

Hafemeister. If All You Have Is a Hammer: Society's Ineffective Response to Intimate Partner Violence. 60 Cath UL Rev 919, Fall, 2011.

Rachmilovitz. Bringing Down the Bedroom Walls: Emphasizing Substance

Over Form in Personalized Abuse. 14 Wm & Mary J of Women & L 495, Spring, 2008.

SAFE STREETS FOR WOMEN

Safety for Women in Public Transit

§ 13931. Grants for capital improvements to prevent crime in public transportation

(a) General purpose. There is authorized to be appropriated not to exceed $10,000,000, for the Secretary of Transportation (referred to in this section as the "Secretary") to make capital grants for the prevention of crime and to increase security in existing and future public transportation systems. None of the provisions of this Act may be construed to prohibit the financing of projects under this section where law enforcement responsibilities are vested in a local public body other than the grant applicant.

(b) Grants for lighting, camera surveillance, and security phones. (1) From the sums authorized for expenditure under this section for crime prevention, the Secretary is authorized to make grants and loans to States and local public bodies or agencies for the purpose of increasing the safety of public transportation by—

(A) increasing lighting within or adjacent to public transportation systems, including bus stops, subway stations, parking lots, or garages;

(B) increasing camera surveillance of areas within and adjacent to public transportation systems, including bus stops, subway stations, parking lots, or garages;

(C) providing emergency phone lines to contact law enforcement or security personnel in areas within or adjacent to public transportation systems, including bus stops, subway stations, parking lots, or garages; or

(D) any other project intended to increase the security and safety of existing or planned public transportation systems.

(2) From the sums authorized under this section, at least 75 percent shall be expended on projects of the type described in subsection (b)(1) (A) and (B).

(c) Reporting. All grants under this section are contingent upon the filing of a report with the Secretary and the Department of Justice, Office of Victims of Crime, showing crime rates in or adjacent to public transportation before, and for a 1-year period after, the capital improvement. Statistics shall be compiled on the basis of the type of crime, sex, race, ethnicity, language, and relationship of victim to the offender.

(d) Increased Federal share. Notwithstanding any other provision of law, the Federal share under this section for each capital improvement project that enhances the safety and security of public transportation systems and that is not required by law (including any other provision of this Act) shall be 90 percent of the net project cost of the project.

(e) Special grants for projects to study increasing security for women. From the sums authorized under this section, the Secretary shall provide grants and loans for the purpose of studying ways to reduce violent crimes against women in public transit through better design or operation of public transit systems.

(f) General requirements. All grants or loans provided under this section shall be subject to the same terms, conditions, requirements, and provisions applicable to grants and loans as specified in section 5321 of title 49, United States Code.

(Sept. 13, 1994, P. L. 103-322, Title IV, Subtitle A, Ch 3, § 40131, 108 Stat. 1916.)

HISTORY; ANCILLARY LAWS AND DIRECTIVES

References in text:
"This Act", referred to in this section, is Act Sept. 13, 1994, P. L. 103-322, 108 Stat. 1796, popularly known as the Violent Crime Control and Law Enforcement Act of 1994. For full classification of this Act, consult USCS Tables volumes.

CODE OF FEDERAL REGULATIONS

Department of Justice—Grants for correctional facilities, 28 CFR 91.1 et seq.

RESEARCH GUIDE

Am Jur Trials:
92 Am Jur Trials, Criminal Defense: Assault and Battery Cases, p. 1.

Assistance to Victims of Sexual Assault

§ 13941. Training programs

(a) In general. The Attorney General, after consultation with victim advocates and individuals who have expertise in treating sex offenders, shall establish criteria and develop training programs to assist probation and parole officers and other personnel who work with released sex offenders in the areas of—

(1) case management;

(2) supervision; and

(3) relapse prevention.

(b) Training programs. The Attorney General shall ensure, to the extent practicable, that training programs developed under subsection (a) are available in geographically diverse locations throughout the country.

(c) Authorization of appropriations. There are authorized to be appropriated to carry out this section $5,000,000 for each of fiscal years 2007 through 2011.
(Sept. 13, 1994, P. L. 103-322, Title IV, Subtitle A, Ch 5, § 40152, 108 Stat. 1920; Jan. 5, 2006, P. L. 109-162, Title I, § 108, Title XI, Subtitle B, Ch. 5, § 1167, 119 Stat. 2984, 3121; Aug. 12, 2006, P. L. 109-271, § 2(a), (b), 120 Stat. 751.)

HISTORY; ANCILLARY LAWS AND DIRECTIVES
Amendments:
2006. Act Jan. 5, 2006, § 108, was repealed by § 2(a) of Act Aug. 12, 2006. Such § 108 substituted subsec. (c) for one which read:

"(c) Authorization of appropriations. There are authorized to be appropriated to carry out this section—
    "(1) $1,000,000 for fiscal year 1996; and
    "(2) $1,000,000 for fiscal year 1997.".
Section 1167 of such Act, as amended by § 2(b) of Act Aug. 12, 2006, substituted subsec. (c) for one which read: "(c) There are authorized to be appropriated to carry out this section $3,000,000 for each of fiscal years 2007 through 2011.".
Act Aug. 12, 2006, amended Act Jan. 5, 2006, by repealing § 108 and amending § 1167, both of which amended this section.

CROSS REFERENCES
This section is referred to in 42 USCS §§ 14071, 14214.

§ 13942. Confidentiality of communications between sexual assault or domestic violence victims and their counselors

(a) Study and development of model legislation. The Attorney General shall—
    (1) study and evaluate the manner in which the States have taken measures to protect the confidentiality of communications between sexual assault or domestic violence victims and their therapists or trained counselors;
    (2) develop model legislation that will provide the maximum protection possible for the confidentiality of such communications, within any applicable constitutional limits, taking into account the following factors:
        (A) the danger that counseling programs for victims of sexual assault and domestic violence will be unable to achieve their goal of helping victims recover from the trauma associated with these crimes if there is no assurance that the records of the counseling sessions will be kept confidential;
        (B) consideration of the appropriateness of an absolute privilege for communications between victims of sexual assault or domestic violence and their therapists or trained counselors, in light of the likelihood that such an absolute privilege will provide the maximum guarantee of confidentiality but also in light of the possibility that such an absolute privilege may be held to violate the rights of criminal defendants under the Federal or State constitutions by denying them the opportunity to obtain exculpatory evidence and present it at trial; and
        (C) consideration of what limitations on the disclosure of confidential communications between victims of these crimes and their counselors, short of an absolute privilege, are most likely to ensure that the counseling programs will not be undermined, and specifically whether no such disclosure should be allowed unless, at a minimum, there has been a particularized showing by a criminal defendant of a compelling need for records of such communications, and adequate procedural safeguards are in place to prevent unnecessary or damaging disclosures; and
    (3) prepare and disseminate to State authorities the findings made and model legislation developed as a result of the study and evaluation.
(b) Report and recommendations. Not later than the date that is 1 year after

the date of enactment of this Act [enacted Sept. 13, 1994], the Attorney General shall report to the Congress—

(1) the findings of the study and the model legislation required by this section; and

(2) recommendations based on the findings on the need for and appropriateness of further action by the Federal Government.

(c) Review of Federal evidentiary rules. The Judicial Conference of the United States shall evaluate and report to Congress its views on whether the Federal Rules of Evidence should be amended, and if so, how they should be amended, to guarantee that the confidentiality of communications between sexual assault victims and their therapists or trained counselors will be adequately protected in Federal court proceedings.

(Sept. 13, 1994, P. L. 103-322, Title IV, Subtitle A, Ch 5, § 40153, 108 Stat. 1921.)

§ 13943. Information programs

The Attorney General shall compile information regarding sex offender treatment programs and ensure that information regarding community treatment programs in the community into which a convicted sex offender is released is made available to each person serving a sentence of imprisonment in a Federal penal or correctional institution for a commission of an offense under chapter 109A of title 18, United States Code [18 USCS §§ 2241 et seq.], or for the commission of a similar offense, including halfway houses and psychiatric institutions.

(Sept. 13, 1994, P. L. 103-322, Title IV, Subtitle A, Ch 5, § 40154, 108 Stat. 1922.)

SAFE HOMES FOR WOMEN

Confidentiality for Abused Persons

§ 13951. Confidentiality of abused person's address

(a) Regulations. Not later than 90 days after the date of enactment of this Act [enacted Sept. 13, 1994], the United States Postal Service shall promulgate regulations to secure the confidentiality of domestic violence shelters and abused persons' addresses.

(b) Requirements. The regulations under subsection (a) shall require—

(1) in the case of an individual, the presentation to an appropriate postal official of a valid, outstanding protection order; and

(2) in the case of a domestic violence shelter, the presentation to an appropriate postal authority of proof from a State domestic violence coalition that meets the requirements of section 311 of the Family Violence Prevention and Services Act (42 U.S.C. 10410)) verifying that the organization is a domestic violence shelter.

(c) Disclosure for certain purposes. The regulations under subsection (a) shall not prohibit the disclosure of addresses to State or Federal agencies for legitimate law enforcement or other governmental purposes.

(d) Existing compilations. Compilations of addresses existing at the time at which order is presented to an appropriate postal official shall be excluded from the scope of the regulations under subsection (a).

(Sept. 13, 1994, P. L. 103-322, Title IV, Subtitle B, Ch 8, § 40281, 108 Stat. 1938.)

HISTORY; ANCILLARY LAWS AND DIRECTIVES

References in text:

42 USCS § 10410, referred to in subsec. (b)(2), was generally amended by Act Dec. 20, 2010, P. L. 111-320, Title II, § 201, 124 Stat. 3497, and, as so amended, no longer contains provisions relating to grants for State domestic violence coalitions. See 42 USCS § 10411.

CROSS REFERENCES

This section is referred to in 42 USCS § 1395u.

RESEARCH GUIDE

Am Jur Trials:

92 Am Jur Trials, Criminal Defense: Assault and Battery Cases, p. 1.

Data and Research

§ 13961.   Research agenda

(a) Request for contract. The Attorney General shall request the National Academy of Sciences, through its National Research Council, to enter into a contract to develop a research agenda to increase the understanding and control of violence against women, including rape and domestic violence. In further-ance of the contract, the National Academy shall convene a panel of nationally recognized experts on violence against women, in the fields of law, medicine, criminal justice, and direct services to victims and experts on domestic violence in diverse, ethnic, social, and language minority communities and the social sciences. In setting the agenda, the Academy shall focus primarily on preven-tive, educative, social, and legal strategies, including addressing the needs of underserved populations.

(b) Declination of request. If the National Academy of Sciences declines to conduct the study and develop a research agenda, it shall recommend a nonprofit private entity that is qualified to conduct such a study. In that case, the Attorney General shall carry out subsection (a) through the nonprofit private entity recommended by the Academy. In either case, whether the study is conducted by the National Academy of Sciences or by the nonprofit group it recommends, the funds for the contract shall be made available from sums ap-propriated for the conduct of research by the National Institute of Justice.

(c) Report. The Attorney General shall ensure that no later than 1 year after the date of enactment of this Act [enacted Sept. 13, 1994], the study required under subsection (a) is completed and a report describing the findings made is submitted to the Committee on the Judiciary of the Senate and the Committee on the Judiciary of the House of Representatives.

(Sept. 13, 1994, P. L. 103-322, Title IV, Subtitle B, Ch 9, § 40291, 108 Stat. 1939.)

HISTORY; ANCILLARY LAWS AND DIRECTIVES

Other provisions:

Development of research agenda. Act Oct. 28, 2000, P. L. 106-386, Div B, Title IV, § 1404, 114 Stat. 1514, provides:

"(a) In general. The Attorney General shall—

"(1) direct the National Institute of Justice, in consultation and coordination with the Bureau of Justice Statistics and the National Academy of Sciences, through its National Research Council, to develop a research agenda based on the recommendations contained in the report entitled 'Understanding Violence Against Women' of the National Academy of Sciences; and

"(2) not later than 1 year after the date of the enactment of this Act, in consultation with the Secretary of the Department of Health and Human Services, submit to Congress a report which shall include—

"(A) a description of the research agenda developed under paragraph (1) and a plan to implement that agenda; and

"(B) recommendations for priorities in carrying out that agenda to most effectively advance knowledge about and means by which to prevent or reduce violence against women.

"(b) Authorization of appropriations. There are authorized to be appropriated such sums as may be necessary to carry out this section.".

RESEARCH GUIDE

Am Jur Trials:

92 Am Jur Trials, Criminal Defense: Assault and Battery Cases, p. 1.

§ 13962. State databases

(a) **In general.** The Attorney General shall study and report to the States and to Congress on how the States may collect centralized databases on the incidence of sexual and domestic violence offenses within a State.

(b) **Consultation.** In conducting its study, the Attorney General shall consult persons expert in the collection of criminal justice data, State statistical administrators, law enforcement personnel, and nonprofit nongovernmental agencies that provide direct services to victims of domestic violence. The final report shall set forth the views of the persons consulted on the recommendations.

(c) **Report.** The Attorney General shall ensure that no later than 1 year after the date of enactment of this Act [enacted Sept. 13, 1994], the study required under subsection (a) is completed and a report describing the findings made is submitted to the Committees on the Judiciary of the Senate and the House of Representatives.

(d) **Authorization of appropriations.** There are authorized to be appropriated to carry out this section $200,000 for fiscal year 1996.

(Sept. 13, 1994, P. L. 103-322, Title IV, Subtitle B, Ch 9, § 40292, 108 Stat. 1939.)

CROSS REFERENCES
This section is referred to in 42 USCS § 14214.

§ 13963. Number and cost of injuries

(a) **Study.** The Secretary of Health and Human Services, acting through the Centers for Disease Control [Centers for Disease Control and Prevention] Injury Control Division, shall conduct a study to obtain a national projection of the incidence of injuries resulting from domestic violence, the cost of injuries to health care facilities, and recommend health care strategies for reducing the incidence and cost of such injuries.

(b) **Authorization of appropriations.** There are authorized to be appropriated to carry out this section—$100,000 for fiscal year 1996.
(Sept. 13, 1994, P. L. 103-322, Title IV, Subtitle B, Ch 9, § 40293, 108 Stat. 1940.)

HISTORY; ANCILLARY LAWS AND DIRECTIVES

Explanatory notes:
The bracketed words "Centers for Disease Control and Prevention" have been inserted in subsec. (a) on the authority of Act Oct. 27, 1992, P. L. 102-531, § 312, 106 Stat. 3504, which provided that the name of the Centers for Disease Control be changed to the Centers for Disease Control and Prevention.

CROSS REFERENCES
This section is referred to in 42 USCS § 14214.

Rural Domestic Violence and Child Abuse Enforcement

§ 13971. Rural domestic violence, dating violence, sexual assault, stalking, and child abuse enforcement assistance

(a) **Purposes.** The purposes of this section are—
(1) to identify, assess, and appropriately respond to child, youth, and adult victims of domestic violence, sexual assault, dating violence, and stalking in rural communities, by encouraging collaboration among—
(A) domestic violence, dating violence, sexual assault, and stalking victim service providers;
(B) law enforcement agencies;
(C) prosecutors;
(D) courts;
(E) other criminal justice service providers;
(F) human and community service providers;
(G) educational institutions; and
(H) health care providers;
(2) to establish and expand nonprofit, nongovernmental, State, tribal, territorial, and local government victim services in rural communities to child, youth, and adult victims; and

(3) to increase the safety and well-being of women and children in rural communities, by—

(A) dealing directly and immediately with domestic violence, sexual assault, dating violence, and stalking occurring in rural communities; and

(B) creating and implementing strategies to increase awareness and prevent domestic violence, sexual assault, dating violence, and stalking.

(b) Grants authorized. The Attorney General, acting through the Director of the Office on Violence Against Women (referred to in this section as the "Director"), may award grants to States, Indian tribes, local governments, and nonprofit, public or private entities, including tribal nonprofit organizations, to carry out programs serving rural areas or rural communities that address domestic violence, dating violence, sexual assault, and stalking by—

(1) implementing, expanding, and establishing cooperative efforts and projects among law enforcement officers, prosecutors, victim advocacy groups, and other related parties to investigate and prosecute incidents of domestic violence, dating violence, sexual assault, and stalking;

(2) providing treatment, counseling, advocacy, and other long- and short-term assistance to adult and minor victims of domestic violence, dating violence, sexual assault, and stalking in rural communities, including assistance in immigration matters; and

(3) working in cooperation with the community to develop education and prevention strategies directed toward such issues.

(c) Use of funds. Funds appropriated pursuant to this section shall be used only for specific programs and activities expressly described in subsection (a).

(d) Allotments and priorities. (1) Allotment for Indian tribes.

(A) In general. Not less than 10 percent of the total amount available under this section for each fiscal year shall be available for grants under the program authorized by section 2015 of the Omnibus Crime Control and Safe Streets Act of 1968 (42 U.S.C. 3796gg-10).

(B) Applicability of part [section]. The requirements of this section shall not apply to funds allocated for the program described in subparagraph (A).

(2) Allotment for sexual assault. (A) In general. Not less than 25 percent of the total amount appropriated in a fiscal year under this section shall fund services that meaningfully address sexual assault in rural communities, however at such time as the amounts appropriated reach the amount of $45,000,000, the percentage allocated shall rise to 30 percent of the total amount appropriated, at such time as the amounts appropriated reach the amount of $50,000,000, the percentage allocated shall rise to 35 percent of the total amount appropriated, and at such time as the amounts appropriated reach the amount of $55,000,000, the percentage allocated shall rise to 40 percent of the amounts appropriated.

(B) Multiple purpose applications. Nothing in this section shall prohibit any applicant from applying for funding to address sexual assault, domestic violence, stalking, or dating violence in the same application.

(3) Allotment for technical assistance. Of the amounts appropriated for each

fiscal year to carry out this section, not more than 8 percent may be used by the Director for technical assistance costs. Of the amounts appropriated in this subsection, no less than 25 percent of such amounts shall be available to a nonprofit, nongovernmental organization or organizations whose focus and expertise is in addressing sexual assault to provide technical assistance to sexual assault grantees.

(4) Underserved populations. In awarding grants under this section, the Director shall give priority to the needs of underserved populations.

(5) Allocation of funds for rural States. Not less than 75 percent of the total amount made available for each fiscal year to carry out this section shall be allocated to eligible entities located in rural States.

(e) Authorization of appropriations. (1) In general. There are authorized to be appropriated $55,000,000 for each of the fiscal years 2007 through 2011 to carry out this section.

(2) Additional funding. In addition to funds received through a grant under subsection (b), a law enforcement agency may use funds received through a grant under part Q of title I of the Omnibus Crime Control and Safe Streets Act of 1968 (42 U.S.C. 3796dd et seq.) to accomplish the objectives of this section.

(Sept. 13, 1994, P. L. 103-322, Title IV, Subtitle B, Ch 10, § 40295, 108 Stat. 1940; Oct. 28, 2000, P. L. 106-386, Div B, Title I, §§ 1105, 1109(d), Title V, § 1512(c), 114 Stat. 1497, 1503, 1533; Jan. 5, 2006, P. L. 109-162, Title II, § 203, Title IX, § 906(d), 119 Stat. 2998, 3081; Aug. 12, 2006, P. L. 109-271, § 7(b)(1), (2)(A), 120 Stat. 764.)

HISTORY; ANCILLARY LAWS AND DIRECTIVES

Explanatory notes:
The bracketed word "section" has been inserted in subsec. (d)(1)(B) to indicate the word probably intended by Congress.

Amendments:
2000. Act Oct. 28, 2000, in subsec. (a), in paras. (1) and (2), inserted "and dating violence (as defined in section 2003 of title I of the Omnibus Crime Control and Safe Streets Act of 1968 (42 U.S.C. 3996gg-2))"; and, in subsec. (c), substituted para. (1) for one which read:

> "(1) In general. There are authorized to be appropriated to carry out this section—
> "(A) $7,000,000 for fiscal year 1996;
> "(B) $8,000,000 for fiscal year 1997; and
> "(C) $15,000,000 for fiscal year 1998.",

and added para. (3).

Such Act further, in subsec. (a), substituted para. (2) for one which read:
"(2) to provide treatment and counseling to victims of domestic violence and dating violence (as defined in section 2003 of title I of the Omnibus Crime Control and Safe Streets Act of 1968 (42 U.S.C. 3996gg-2)) and child abuse; and".

2006. Act Jan. 5, 2006, § 203 (effective 10/1/2006, pursuant to § 4 of such Act, which appears as 42 USCS § 3793 note), substituted this section for one which read:

"Rural domestic violence and child abuse enforcement assistance

"(a) Grants. The Attorney General may make grants to States, Indian tribal governments, and local governments of rural States, and to other public or private entities of rural States—

"(1) to implement, expand, and establish cooperative efforts and projects between law enforcement officers, prosecutors, victim advocacy groups, and other related parties to investigate and prosecute incidents of domestic violence and dating violence (as defined in section 2003 of title I of the Omnibus Crime Control and Safe Streets Act of 1968 (42 U.S.C. 3996gg-2)) and child abuse;

"(2) to provide treatment, counseling, and assistance to victims of domestic violence and child abuse, including in immigration matters; and

"(3) to work in cooperation with the community to develop education and prevention strategies directed toward such issues.

"(b) Definitions. In this section—

" 'Indian tribe' means a tribe, band, pueblo, nation, or other organized group or community of Indians, including an Alaska Native village (as defined in or established under the Alaska Native Claims Settlement Act (43 U.S.C. 1601 et seq.)), that is recognized as eligible for the special programs and services provided by the United States to Indians because of their status as Indians.

" 'rural State' has the meaning stated in section 1501(b) of title I of the Omnibus Crime Control and Safe Streets Act of 1968 (42 U.S.C. 3796bb(B)).

"(c) Authorization of appropriations. (1) In general. There is authorized to be appropriated to carry out this section $40,000,000 for each of fiscal years 2001 through 2005.

"(2) Additional funding. In addition to funds received under a grant under subsection (a), a law enforcement agency may use funds received under a grant under section 103 to accomplish the objectives of this section.

"(3) Allotment for Indian tribes. Not less than 5 percent of the total amount made available to carry out this section for each fiscal year shall be available for grants to Indian tribal governments.".

Section 906(d) of such Act (repealed by Act Aug. 12, 2006) purported to amend subsec. (c) by striking para. (3) and inserting the following: "(3) Not less than 10 percent of the total amount available under this section for each fiscal year shall be available for grants under the program authorized in section 2007 of the Omnibus Crime Control and Safe Streets Act of 1968. The requirements of this paragraph shall not apply to funds allocated for such program."; however, because of prior amendments, this amendment could not be executed.

Act Aug. 12, 2006, in subsec. (d), substituted para. (1) for one which read: "(1) Allotment for Indian tribes. Not less than 10 percent of the total amount made available for each fiscal year to carry out this section shall be allocated for grants to Indian tribes or tribal organizations.".

Such Act further repealed § 906(d) of Act Jan. 5, 2006, which amended this section.

CROSS REFERENCES

This section is referred to in 42 USCS §§ 14214, 14045a.

RESEARCH GUIDE
Am Jur Trials:
92 Am Jur Trials, Criminal Defense: Assault and Battery Cases, p. 1.
Other Treatises:
Cohen's Handbook of Federal Indian Law (Matthew Bender), ch 22, Government Services for Indians § 22.07.

Research on Effective Interventions to Address Violence Against Women

§ 13973. Research on effective interventions in the health care setting

(a) **Purpose.** The Secretary, acting through the Director of the Centers for Disease Control and Prevention and the Director of the Agency for Healthcare Research and Quality, shall award grants and contracts to fund research on effective interventions in the health care setting that prevent domestic violence, dating violence, and sexual assault across the lifespan and that prevent the health effects of such violence and improve the safety and health of individuals who are currently being victimized.

(b) **Use of funds.** Research conducted with amounts received under a grant or contract under this section shall include the following:

(1) With respect to the authority of the Centers for Disease Control and Prevention—

(A) research on the effects of domestic violence, dating violence, sexual assault, and childhood exposure to domestic, dating, or sexual violence, on health behaviors, health conditions, and the health status of individuals, families, and populations;

(B) research and testing of best messages and strategies to mobilize public and health care provider action concerning the prevention of domestic, dating, or sexual violence; and

(C) measure the comparative effectiveness and outcomes of efforts under this Act to reduce violence and increase women's safety.

(2) With respect to the authority of the Agency for Healthcare Research and Quality—

(A) research on the impact on the health care system, health care utilization, health care costs, and health status of domestic violence, dating violence, and childhood exposure to domestic and dating violence, sexual violence and stalking and childhood exposure; and

(B) research on effective interventions within primary care and emergency health care settings and with health care settings that include clinical partnerships within community domestic violence providers for adults and children exposed to domestic or dating violence.

(c) **Use of data.** Research funded under this section shall be utilized by eligible entities under section 399O of the Public Health Service Act.

(d) **Authorization of appropriations.** There is authorized to be appropriated to carry out this section, $5,000,000 for each of fiscal years 2007 through 2011.
(Sept. 13, 1994, P. L. 103-322, Title IV, Subtitle B, Ch. 11, § 40297, as added Jan. 5, 2006, P. L. 109-162, Title V, § 505, 119 Stat. 3028.)

HISTORY; ANCILLARY LAWS AND DIRECTIVES

References in text:

Regarding the reference in subsec. (c) to "section 3990 of the Public Health Service Act", such Act contains two sections designated "3990", which are classified to 42 USCS §§ 280g-3 and 280g-4. Congress probably intended to refer to the section that appears as 42 USCS § 280g-4.

Explanatory notes:

Another Chapter 11 of Subtitle B of Title IV of Act Sept. 13, 1994, P. L. 103-322, appears as 42 USCS § 13975.

Transitional Housing Assistance Grants for Child Victims of Domestic Violence, Stalking, or Sexual Assault

§ 13975. Transitional housing assistance grants for child victims of domestic violence, stalking, or sexual assault

(a) In general. The Attorney General, acting in consultation with the Director of the Violence Against Women Office of the Department of Justice, the Department of Housing and Urban Development, and the Department of Health and Human Services, shall award grants under this section to States, units of local government, Indian tribes, and other organizations, including domestic violence and sexual assault victim service providers, domestic violence and sexual assault coalitions, other nonprofit, nongovernmental organizations, or community-based and culturally specific organizations, that have a documented history of effective work concerning domestic violence, dating violence, sexual assault, or stalking (referred to in this section as the "recipient") to carry out programs to provide assistance to minors, adults, and their dependents—

(1) who are homeless, or in need of transitional housing or other housing assistance, as a result of fleeing a situation of domestic violence, dating violence, sexual assault, or stalking; and

(2) for whom emergency shelter services or other crisis intervention services are unavailable or insufficient.

(b) Grants. Grants awarded under this section may be used for programs that provide—

(1) transitional housing, including funding for the operating expenses of newly developed or existing transitional housing.[;]

(2) short-term housing assistance, including rental or utilities payments assistance and assistance with related expenses such as payment of security deposits and other costs incidental to relocation to transitional housing for persons described in subsection (a); and

(3) support services designed to enable a minor, an adult, or a dependent of such minor or adult, who is fleeing a situation of domestic violence, dating violence, sexual assault, or stalking to—

(A) locate and secure permanent housing; and

(B) integrate into a community by providing that minor, adult, or dependent with services, such as transportation, counseling, child care services, case management, employment counseling, and other assistance. Participation in the support services shall be voluntary. Receipt of the benefits of the housing assistance described in paragraph (2) shall not be conditioned upon the participation of the youth, adults, or their dependents in any or all of the support services offered them.

(c) Duration. (1) In general. Except as provided in paragraph (2), a minor, an adult, or a dependent, who receives assistance under this section shall receive that assistance for not more than 24 months.

(2) Waiver. The recipient of a grant under this section may waive the restriction under paragraph (1) for not more than an additional 6 month period with respect to any minor, adult, or dependent, who—

(A) has made a good-faith effort to acquire permanent housing; and

(B) has been unable to acquire permanent housing.

(d) Application. (1) In general. Each eligible entity desiring a grant under this section shall submit an application to the Attorney General at such time, in such manner, and accompanied by such information as the Attorney General may reasonably require.

(2) Contents. Each application submitted pursuant to paragraph (1) shall—

(A) describe the activities for which assistance under this section is sought;

(B) provide assurances that any supportive services offered to participants in programs developed under subsection (b)(3) are voluntary and that refusal to receive such services shall not be grounds for termination from the program or eviction from the victim's housing; and

(C) provide such additional assurances as the Attorney General determines to be essential to ensure compliance with the requirements of this section.

(3) Application. Nothing in this subsection shall be construed to require—

(A) victims to participate in the criminal justice system in order to receive services; or

(B) domestic violence advocates to breach client confidentiality.

(e) Report to the Attorney General. (1) In general. A recipient of a grant under this section shall annually prepare and submit to the Attorney General a report describing—

(A) the number of minors, adults, and dependents assisted under this section; and

(B) the types of housing assistance and support services provided under this section.

(2) Contents. Each report prepared and submitted pursuant to paragraph (1) shall include information regarding—

(A) the purpose and amount of housing assistance provided to each minor, adult, or dependent, assisted under this section and the reason for that assistance;

(B) the number of months each minor, adult, or dependent, received assistance under this section;

(C) the number of minors, adults, and dependents who—

(i) were eligible to receive assistance under this section; and

(ii) were not provided with assistance under this section solely due to a lack of available housing;

(D) the type of support services provided to each minor, adult, or dependent, assisted under this section; and

(E) the client population served and the number of individuals requesting services that the transitional housing program is unable to serve as a result of a lack of resources.

(f) Report to Congress. (1) Reporting requirement. The Attorney General, with the Director of the Violence Against Women Office, shall prepare and submit to the Committee on the Judiciary of the House of Representatives and the Committee on the Judiciary of the Senate a report that contains a compilation of the information contained in the report submitted under subsection (e) of this section not later than 1 month after the end of each even-numbered fiscal year.

(2) Availability of report. In order to coordinate efforts to assist the victims of domestic violence, the Attorney General, in coordination with the Director of the Violence Against Women Office, shall transmit a copy of the report submitted under paragraph (1) to—

(A) the Office of Community Planning and Develop ment at the United States Department of Housing and Urban Development; and

(B) the Office of Women's Health at the United States Department of Health and Human Services.

(g) Authorization of appropriations. (1) In general. There are authorized to be appropriated to carry out this section $40,000,000 for each of the fiscal years 2007 through 2011.

(2) Limitations. Of the amount made available to carry out this section in any fiscal year, up to 5 percent may be used by the Attorney General for evaluation, monitoring, technical assistance, salaries and administrative expenses.

(3) Minimum amount. (A) In general. Except as provided in subparagraph (B), unless all eligible applications submitted by any States, units of local government, Indian tribes, or organizations within a State for a grant under this section have been funded, that State, together with the grantees within the State (other than Indian tribes), shall be allocated in each fiscal year, not less than 0.75 percent of the total amount appropriated in the fiscal year for grants pursuant to this section.

(B) Exception. The United States Virgin Islands, American Samoa, Guam, and the Northern Mariana Islands shall each be allocated not less than 0.25 percent of the total amount appropriated in the fiscal year for grants pursuant to this section.

(C) Underserved populations. (i) Indian tribes.

(I) In general. Not less than 10 percent of the total amount available under this section for each fiscal year shall be available for grants under the program authorized by section 2015 of the Omnibus Crime Control and Safe Streets Act of 1968 (42 U.S.C. 3796gg-10).

(II) Applicability of part [section]. The requirements of this section shall not apply to funds allocated for the program described in subclause (I).

(ii) Priority shall be given to projects developed under subsection (b) that primarily serve underserved populations.

(Sept. 13, 1994, P. L. 103-322, Title IV, Subtitle B, Ch. 11, § 40299, as added April 30, 2003, P. L. 108-21, Title VI, § 611, 117 Stat. 693; Jan. 5, 2006, P. L. 109-162, § 3(b)(4), Title VI, § 602, Title IX, § 906(e) [906(f)], Title XI, Subtitle B, Ch. 3, § 1135(e), 119 Stat. 2971, 3038, 3081, 3109; Aug. 12, 2006, P. L. 109-271, §§ 2(d), 7(b)(2)(B), (c)(1), (8)(b), 120 Stat. 752, 764, 765, 766.)

HISTORY; ANCILLARY LAWS AND DIRECTIVES

Explanatory notes:

The bracketed semicolon has been inserted in subsec. (b)(1) to indicate the punctuation probably intended by Congress.

The bracketed word "section" has been inserted in subsec. (g)(3)(C)(i)(II) to indicate the word probably intended by Congress.

Another Chapter 11 of Subtitle B of Title IV of Act Sept. 13, 1994, P. L. 103-322, appears as 42 USCS § 13973.

Amendments:

2006. Act Jan. 5, 2006 (effective 10/1/2006, pursuant to § 4 of such Act, which appears as 42 USCS § 3793 note), in subsec. (a), in the introductory matter, inserted "the Department of Housing and Urban Development, and the Department of Health and Human Services," and ", including domestic violence and sexual assault victim service providers, domestic violence and sexual assault coalitions, other nonprofit, nongovernmental organizations, or community-based and culturally specific organizations, that have a documented history of effective work concerning domestic violence, dating violence, sexual assault, or stalking", and, in para. (1), inserted ", dating violence, sexual assault, or stalking"; in subsec. (b), redesignated paras. (1) and (2) as paras. (2) and (3), respectively, inserted new para. (1), and, in para. (3) as redesignated, in the introductory matter, inserted ", dating violence, sexual assault, or stalking", and, in subpara. (B), added the sentences beginning "Participation . . ." and "Receipt of the benefits . . ."; in subsec. (c)(1), substituted "24 months" for "18 months"; in subsec. (d)(2), in subpara. (A), deleted "and" following the concluding semicolon, redesignated subpara. (B) as subpara. (C), and inserted new subpara. (B); in subsec. (e)(2), in subpara. (A), inserted "purpose and", in subpara. (C)(ii), deleted "and" following the concluding semicolon, in subpara. (D), substituted "; and" for a concluding period, and added subpara. (E); and, in subsec. (g), in para. (1), substituted "$40,000,000" for "$30,000,000", substituted "2007" for "2004", and substituted "2011" for "2008", in para. (2), substituted "up to 5 percent" for "not more than 3 percent" and inserted "evaluation, monitoring, technical assistance,", and, in para. (3), added subpara. (C).

Section 906(f) of such Act (effective as above) added subsec. (g)(4).

Section 3(b)(4) of such Act purported to amend subsec. (f) by substituting "shall prepare and submit to the Committee on the Judiciary of the House of Representatives and the Committee on the Judiciary of the Senate a report that contains a compilation of the information contained in the report submitted under subsection (e) of this section not later than one month after the end of each even-numbered fiscal year." for "shall annually prepare and submit to the Committee on the Judiciary of the House of Representatives and the Committee on the Judiciary of the Senate a report that contains a compilation of the information contained in the report submitted under subsection (e) of this section.''; however, the substitution was made in subsec. (f)(1) for ''shall annually prepare and submit to the Committee on the Judiciary of the House of Representatives and the Committee on the Judiciary of the Senate a report that contains a compilation of the information contained in the report submitted under subsection (e).'' in order to effectuate the probable intent of Congress.

Section 1135(e) of such Act (repealed by Act Aug. 12, 2006) purported to make an amendment substantially identical to the amendment made by § 3(b)(4).

Act Aug. 12, 2006, repealed § 1135 of Act Jan. 5, 2006, and the amendments made by such section; and, in subsec. (g), in para. (3)(C), substituted cl. (i) for one which read: ''(i) A minimum of 7 percent of the total amount appropriated in any fiscal year shall be allocated to tribal organizations serving adult and youth victims of domestic violence, dating violence, sexual assault, or stalking, and their dependents.'', and deleted para. (4), which read: ''(4) Tribal program. Not less than 10 percent of the total amount available under this section for each fiscal year shall be available for grants under the program authorized in section 2007 of the Omnibus Crime Control and Safe Streets Act of 1968. The requirements of this paragraph shall not apply to funds allocated for such program.''.

Redesignation:

Section 906(f) of Act Jan. 5, 2006, which amended this section, was redesignated § 906(e) of such Act by Act Aug. 12, 2006, P. L. 109-271, § 7(b)(2)(B), 120 Stat. 764.

Transfer of functions:

Functions of the Office on Women's Health of the Public Health Service exercised prior to March 23, 2010, were transferred to the Office on Women's Health established under 42 USCS § 237a. See § 3509(a)(2) of Act March 23, 2010, P. L. 111-148, which appears as 42 USCS § 237a note.

CIVIL RIGHTS FOR WOMEN

§ 13981.   Civil rights [Caution: The Supreme Court held in United States v Morrison (2000) 529 US 598, 146 L Ed 2d 658, 120 S Ct 1740, that neither the Commerce Clause nor § 5 of the Fourteenth Amendment gave Congress the authority to enact this section.]

(a) Purpose. Pursuant to the affirmative power of Congress to enact this subtitle under section 5 of the Fourteenth Amendment to the Constitution, as well as under section 8 of Article I of the Constitution, it is the purpose of this subtitle to protect the civil rights of victims of gender motivated violence and to promote public safety, health, and activities affecting interstate commerce by establishing a Federal civil rights cause of action for victims of crimes of violence motivated by gender.

(b) Right to be free from crimes of violence. All persons within the United States shall have the right to be free from crimes of violence motivated by gender (as defined in subsection (d)).

(c) Cause of action. A person (including a person who acts under color of any statute, ordinance, regulation, custom, or usage of any State) who commits a crime of violence motivated by gender and thus deprives another of the right declared in subsection (b) shall be liable to the party injured, in an action for the recovery of compensatory and punitive damages, injunctive and declaratory relief, and such other relief as a court may deem appropriate.

(d) Definitions. For purposes of this section—

(1) the term "crime of violence motivated by gender" means a crime of violence committed because of gender or on the basis of gender, and due, at least in part, to an animus based on the victim's gender; and

(2) the term "crime of violence" [means]—

(A) [means] an act or series of acts that would constitute a felony against the person or that would constitute a felony against property if the conduct presents a serious risk of physical injury to another, and that would come within the meaning of State or Federal offenses described in section 16 of title 18, United States Code, whether or not those acts have actually resulted in criminal charges, prosecution, or conviction and whether or not those acts were committed in the special maritime, territorial, or prison jurisdiction of the United States; and

(B) includes an act or series of acts that would constitute a felony described in subparagraph (A) but for the relationship between the person who takes such action and the individual against whom such action is taken.

(e) Limitation and procedures. (1) Limitation. Nothing in this section entitles a person to a cause of action under subsection (c) for random acts of violence unrelated to gender or for acts that cannot be demonstrated, by a preponderance of the evidence, to be motivated by gender (within the meaning of subsection (d)).

(2) No prior criminal action. Nothing in this section requires a prior criminal complaint, prosecution, or conviction to establish the elements of a cause of action under subsection (c).

(3) Concurrent jurisdiction. The Federal and State courts shall have concurrent jurisdiction over actions brought pursuant to this subtitle.

(4) Supplemental jurisdiction. Neither section 1367 of title 28, United States Code, nor subsection (c) of this section shall be construed, by reason of a claim arising under such subsection, to confer on the courts of the United States jurisdiction over any State law claim seeking the establishment of a divorce, alimony, equitable distribution of marital property, or child custody decree.

(Sept. 13, 1994, P. L. 103-322, Title IV, Subtitle C, § 40302, 108 Stat. 1941.)

HISTORY; ANCILLARY LAWS AND DIRECTIVES

References in text:

"This subtitle", referred to in this section, is Subtitle C of Title IV of Act Sept. 13, 1994, P. L. 103-322, 108 Stat. 1941, which enacted this section, among other things. For full classification of this Subtitle, consult USCS Tables volumes.

Explanatory notes:

The word "means" has been enclosed in brackets in the introductory matter of subsec. (d)(2), and the same word has been inserted in brackets in subsec. (d)(2)(A) to indicate the probable intent of Congress that the word should appear in the second location.

Subsec. (e)(5), which has been omitted, amended 28 USCS § 1445.

CROSS REFERENCES

This section is referred to in 28 USCS § 1445; 42 USCS § 1988.

RESEARCH GUIDE

Federal Procedure:

16 Moore's Federal Practice (Matthew Bender 3d ed.), ch 106, Supplemental Jurisdiction § 106.05.

16 Moore's Federal Practice (Matthew Bender 3d ed.), ch 107, Removal § 107.17.

17A Moore's Federal Practice (Matthew Bender 3d ed.), ch 123, Access to Courts: Eleventh Amendment and State Sovereign Immunity § 123.42.

Am Jur:

7 Am Jur 2d, Attorneys at Law § 239.

32A Am Jur 2d, Federal Courts § 1375.

45C Am Jur 2d, Job Discrimination § 2680.

Am Jur Trials:

92 Am Jur Trials, Criminal Defense: Assault and Battery Cases, p. 1.

Am Jur Proof of Facts:

42 Am Jur Proof of Facts 3d, Claims Under the Gender Motivated Violence Against Women Act, p. 85.

Annotations:

Validity, Construction, and Application of 18 U.S.C.A. § 922(g)(9) [18 USCS § 922(g)(9)], Prohibiting Possession of Firearm by Persons Convicted of Misdemeanor Crime of Domestic Violence. 50 ALR Fed 2d 31.

Intentional Infliction of Distress in Marital Context. 110 ALR5th 371.

Other Treatises:

12 Banking Law (Matthew Bender), ch 230, Judicial Proceedings and the Law Applicable to Credits, Guarantees, and Bonds § 230.02.

4 Rapp, Education Law (Matthew Bender), ch 10, Educational Opportunities and Equality § 10.10.

Law Review Articles:

Zietlow. "John Bingham and the Meaning of the Fourteenth Amendment": Congressional Enforcement of Civil Rights and John Bingham's Theory of Citizenship. 36 Akron L Rev 717, 2003.

Rotunda. Garrett, Disability Policy, and Federalism: A Symposium on Board of Trustees of the University of Alabama v Garrett [(2001)148 L Ed 2d 866]: The Eleventh Amendment, Garrett, and Protection for Civil Rights. 53 Ala L Rev 1183, Summer 2002.

Woodbury. Pursuing civil rights claims under the Violence Against Women Act. 14 Am J Fam L 108, Summer 2000.

Howard. Current Events: United States v Morrison 529 U.S. 598 (2000). 9 Am UJ Gender Soc Pol'y & L 461, 2001.

Goldfarb. Symposium: Applying the Discrimination Model to Violence Against Women: Some Reflections on Theory and Practice. 11 Am UJ Gender Soc Pol'y & L 251, 2003.

Goldfarb. Applying the Discrimination Model to Violence Against Women: Some Reflections on Theory and Practice. 11 Am UJ Gender Soc Pol'y & L 251, 2003.

Goldscheid. The Second Circuit Addresses Genderbased Violence: A Review of Violence Against Women Act Cases. 66 Brooklyn L Rev 457, Summer/Fall 2000.

Weissman. Gender-Based Violence as Judicial Anomaly: Between "The Truly National and the Truly Local". 42 BC L Rev 1081, September 2001.

Wells; Motley. Reinforcing the Myth of the Crazed Rapist: A Feminist Critique of Recent Rape Legislation. 81 BUL Rev 127, February 2001.

Tiefenbrun. The Cultural, Political, and Legal Climate Behind the Fight to Stop Trafficking in Women: William J. Clinton's Legacy to Women's Rights. 12 Cardozo JL & Gender 855, Summer 2006.

Goldscheid; Kraham. The Civil Rights Remedy of The Violence Against Women Act. 29 Clearinghouse Rev 505, August/September 1995.

Rotunda. The Commerce Clause, the Political Question Doctrine, and Morrison. 18 Const Commentary 319, Summer 2001.

Goldscheid. United States v Morrison [120 S Ct 1740 (2000)] and the Civil Rights Remedy of the Violence Against Women Act: a Civil Rights Law Struck Down in the Name of Federalism. 86 Cornell L Rev 109, 2000.

Bryant; Simeone. Remanding to Congress: The Supreme Court's New "On the Record" Constitutional Review of Federal Statutes. 86 Cornell L Rev 328, January 2001.

Goldscheid. Elusive Equality in Domestic and Sexual Violence Law Reform. 34 Fla St UL Rev 731, Spring, 2007.

Romaine. Fourth Annual Review of Gender and Sexuality Law: Constitutional Law Chapter: Hate Crimes. 4 Geo J Gender & L 115, Fall 2002.

Crais. Sixth Annual Review of Gender and Sexuality Law: II. Criminal Law Chapter: Domestic Violence and the Federal Government. 6 Geo J Gender & L 405, 2005.

Lopez. Forty Yeas and Five Nays—The Nays Have it: Morrison's Blurred Political Accountability and the Defeat of the Civil Rights Provision of the Violence Against Women Act. 69 Geo Wash L Rev 251, February 2001.

Biden. The Civil Rights Remedy of the Violence Against Women Act: A Defense. 37 Harv J on Legis 1, 2000.

Dimino. Recent Developments the United States Supreme Court, 1999 Term: Yes, Virginia (Tech), Our Government is one of Limited Powers: United States v Morrison, (2000). 24 Harv JL & Pub Pol'y 895, Summer 2001.

Siegel. She the People: the Nineteenth Amendment, Sex Equality, Federalism, and the Family. 115 Harv L Rev 947, February 2002.

Saylor. Federalism and the Family After Morrison [United States v Morrison (2000) 146 L Ed 2d 658]: An Examination of the Child Support Recovery Act, the Freedom of Access to Clinic Entrances Act, and a Federal Law Outlawing Gun Possession by Domestic Violence Abusers. 25 Harv Women's LJ 57, Spring 2002.

Snyder; Morgan. Domestic Violence Ten Years Later. 19 J Am Acad Matrimonial Law 33, 2004.

Bono. Judicial Limitations on Congressional Power Under United States v Morrison [United States v Morrison (2000) 146 L Ed 2d 658]. 2 Loy J Pub Int L 229, Spring 2001.

Davis; Levey; Medina. Domestic Violence—A Proper Subject of National Legislation? United States v Morrison [United States v Morrison (2000) 146 L Ed 2d 658] and the Violence Against Women Act: a Mock Debate. 47 Loy L Rev 535, Spring 2001.

Young. The Significance of Border Crossings: Lopez [United States v Lopez (1995) 131 L Ed 2d 626], Morrison [United States v Morrison (2000) 146 L Ed 2d 658] and the Fate of Congressional Power to Regulate Goods, and Transactions Connected With Them, Based on Prior Passage Through Interstate Commerce. 61 Md L Rev 177, 2002.

Merico-Stephens. Of Federalism, Human Rights, and the Holland Caveat: Congressional Power to Implement Treaties. 25 Mich J Int'l L 265, Winter 2004.

Goldscheid; Kaufman. Seeking Redress for Gender-Based Bias Crimes—Charting New Ground in Familiar Legal Territory. 6 Mich J Race & L 265, Spring 2001.

Colker; Brudney. Dissing Congress. 100 Mich L Rev 80, October 2001.

Jennings; Razook. United States v Morrison [(2000) 146 L Ed 2d 658]: Where the Commerce Clause Meets Civil Rights and Reasonable Minds Part Ways: A Point and Counterpoint from a Constitutional and Social Perspective. 35 New EngL Rev 23, Fall 2000.

Goldfarb. Violence Against Women and the Persistence of Privacy. 61 Ohio St LJ 1, 2000.

Resnik. The Programmatic Judiciary: Lobbying, Judging, and Invalidating the Violence Against Women Act. 74 S Cal L Rev 269, November 2000.

Wriggins. Domestic Violence Torts. 75 S Cal L Rev 121, 2001.

Duffy. Article I § 8 & Section 5 of the Fourteenth Amendment -Commerce and Enforcement Clauses—Congress lacks the Authority to Enact a Statute Awarding a Civil Remedy to Victims of Gender-Motivated Crimes Due to the Lack of Effect of Such Violence on Interstate Commerce—United States v Morrison, 529 U.S. 598 (2000). 11 Seton Hall Const LJ 569, Spring 2001.

Estreicher; Lemos. The Section 5 Mystique, Morrison [United States v Morrison (2000) 146 L Ed 2d 658], and the Future of Federal Antidiscrimination Law. 2000 Sup Ct Rev 109, 2000.

Wildman. Vision and Revision: Exploring the History, Evolution, and Future of the Fourteenth Amendment: Privilege, Gender, and the Fourteenth Amendment: Reclaiming Equal Protection of the Laws. 13 Temp Pol & Civ Rts L Rev 707, Spring 2004.

Law. William Howard Taft Lecture: in the Name of Federalism: The Supreme Court's Assault on Democracy and Civil Rights. 70 U Cin L Rev 367, Winter, 2002.

Brown. Constitutionalizing the Federal Criminal Law Debate: Morrison [United States v Morrison (2000) 146 L Ed 2d 658], Jones [Jones v United States (2000) 146 L Ed 2d 902], and the ABA. 2001 U Ill L Rev 983, 2001.

Virelli; Leibowitz. "Federalism Whether They Want It or Not": The New Commerce Clause Doctrine and the Future of Federal Civil Rights Legislation After United States v Morrison [(2000) 146 L Ed 2d 658]:. 3 U Pa J Const L 926, May 2001.

Hopkins. Rescripting Relationships: Towards a Nuanced Theory of Intimate Violence as Sex Discrimination. 9 Va J Soc Pol'y & L 411, 2001.

Anderson. New Voices on the New Federalism Women Do Not Report the Violence They Suffer: Violence Against Women and the State Action Doctrine. 46 Vill L Rev 907, 2001.

Goldfarb. "No Civilized System of Justice": The Fate of the Violence Against Women Act. 102 W Va L Rev 499, Spring 2000.

Chemerinsky. Does Federalism Advance Liberty? 47 Wayne L Rev 911, Fall 2001.

Claeys. The Living Commerce Clause: Federalism in Progressive Political Theory and the Commerce Clause after Lopez and Morrison. 11 Wm & Mary Bill of Rts J 403, December 2002.

Resnik. Feminist Justice, at Home and Abroad: Reconstructing Equality: of Justice, Justicia, and the Gender of Jurisdiction. 14 Yale JL & Feminism 393, 2002.

Siegel. "The rule of love": wife beating as prerogative and privacy. 105 Yale LJ 2117, June 1996.

Resnik. Categorical Federalism: Jurisdiction, Gender, and the Globe 111 Yale LJ 619, December 2001.

SHEPARD'S® Citations Service. For further research of authorities referenced here, use SHEPARD'S to be sure your case or statute is still good law and to find additional authorities that support your position. SHEPARD'S is available exclusively from LexisNexis®.

INTERPRETIVE NOTES AND DECISIONS

1. Constitutionality
2. —Commerce clause
3. Construction
4. Miscellaneous

1. Constitutionality

Congress has no authority to enact 42 USCS § 13981 under either Commerce Clause (Art I, § 8, cl 3) or § 5 of the Fourteenth Amendment. United States v Morrison (2000) 529 US 598, 120 S Ct 1740, 146 L Ed 2d 658, 2000 CDOS 3788, 2000 Daily Journal DAR 5061, 82 BNA FEP Cas 1313, 77 CCH EPD ¶ 46376, 2000 Colo J C A R 2583, 13 FLW Fed S 287 (criticized in Cazarez-Gutierrez v Ashcroft (2004, CA9 Cal) 356 F3d 1015) and (criticized in United States v Shivers (2005, ND Fla) 390 F Supp 2d 1067) and (criticized in United States v Cramer (2005, MD Pa) 2005 US Dist LEXIS 31761).

Prophylactic legislation under § 5 of Constitution's Fourteenth Amendment must have congruence and proportionality between injury to be prevented or remedied and means adopted to that end; under this test, civil remedy provided by 42 USCS § 13981 for victims of gender-motivated violence is not corrective in character, that is, remedy is not adapted to

counteract and redress operation of such prohibited state laws or proceedings of state officers; moreover, for such purposes, § 13981 is not aimed at proscribing discrimination by officials which Fourteenth Amendment might not itself proscribe, for § 13981 is directed at individuals who have committed criminal acts motivated by gender bias, rather than at any state or state actor. United States v Morrison (2000) 529 US 598, 120 S Ct 1740, 146 L Ed 2d 658, 2000 CDOS 3788, 2000 Daily Journal DAR 5061, 82 BNA FEP Cas 1313, 77 CCH EPD ¶ 46376, 2000 Colo J C A R 2583, 13 FLW Fed S 287 (criticized in Cazarez-Gutierrez v Ashcroft (2004, CA9 Cal) 356 F3d 1015) and (criticized in United States v Shivers (2005, ND Fla) 390 F Supp 2d 1067) and (criticized in United States v Cramer (2005, MD Pa) 2005 US Dist LEXIS 31761).

Private cause of action under Violence Against Women Act (42 USCS § 13981) must be dismissed, despite arguments that violence against women is widespread social problem with ultimate effects on national economy, and that bias and discrimination against women in state criminal justice systems often deny legal redress to victims of gender-motivated crimes of violence, because § 13981 is excessive congressional exercise under both Commerce Clause and Fourteenth Amendment Enforcement Clause. Santiago v Alonso (2000, DC Puerto Rico) 96 F Supp 2d 58.

Claim for relief for gender-motivated violence under 42 USCS § 13981 is dismissed, even though remaining claims for sexual harassment, negligent hiring, false imprisonment, outrageous conduct, invasion of privacy, and intrusion upon seclusion may proceed, because Supreme Court has now held that Congress lacked authority to enact civil remedies provision of § 13981. Blair v All Stars Sports Cabaret (2000, DC Colo) 98 F Supp 2d 1223.

2. —Commerce clause

United States v Lopez (1995) 514 US 549, 131 L Ed 2d 626, 115 S Ct 1624—which held that Gun-Free School Zones Act of 1990 (18 USCS § 922(q)(1)(A)), making it federal crime to knowingly possess firearm in school zone, exceeded Congress' authority under Constitution's commerce clause (Art I, § 8, cl 3)—(1) provides proper framework for conducting required commerce clause analysis of 42 USCS § 13981, which provides federal civil remedy for victims of gender-motivated violence; and (2) demonstrates that while Supreme Court need not adopt categorical rule in order to decide § 13981 question, in those cases where Supreme Court has sustained federal regulation of intrastate activity based upon activity's substantial effects on interstate commerce, activity in question has been some sort of economic endeavor. United States v Morrison (2000) 529 US 598, 120 S Ct 1740, 146 L Ed 2d 658, 2000 CDOS 3788, 2000 Daily Journal DAR 5061, 82 BNA FEP Cas 1313, 77 CCH EPD ¶ 46376, 2000 Colo J C A R 2583, 13 FLW Fed S 287 (criticized in Cazarez-Gutierrez v Ashcroft (2004, CA9 Cal) 356 F3d 1015) and (criticized in United States v Shivers (2005, ND Fla) 390 F Supp 2d 1067) and (criticized in United States v Cramer (2005, MD Pa) 2005 US Dist LEXIS 31761).

Like Gun-Free School Zones Act of 1990 (18 USCS § 922(q)(1)(A)) at issue in United States v Lopez (1995) 514 US 549, 131 L Ed 2d 626, 115 S Ct 1624—holding that federal crime of knowingly possessing firearm in school zone exceeded Congress' authority under Constitution's commerce clause (Art I, § 8, cl 3)—42 USCS § 13981, which provides federal civil remedy for victims of gender-motivated violence, contains no jurisdictional element establishing that federal cause of action is in pursuance of Congress' power to regulate interstate commerce, as Congress instead elected to cast § 13981's remedy over wider, and more purely intrastate, body of violent crime. United States v Morrison (2000) 529 US 598, 120 S Ct 1740, 146 L Ed 2d 658, 2000 CDOS 3788, 2000 Daily Journal DAR 5061, 82 BNA FEP Cas 1313, 77 CCH EPD ¶ 46376, 2000 Colo J C A R 2583, 13 FLW Fed S 287 (criticized in Cazarez-Gutierrez v Ashcroft (2004,

CA9 Cal) 356 F3d 1015) and (criticized in United States v Shivers (2005, ND Fla) 390 F Supp 2d 1067) and (criticized in United States v Cramer (2005, MD Pa) 2005 US Dist LEXIS 31761).

Although 42 USCS § 13981, which provides federal civil remedy for victims of gender-motivated violence, is supported by numerous findings regarding serious impact that gender-motivated violence has on victims and families of victims, existence of congressional findings is not sufficient, by itself, to sustain constitutionality of legislation under Constitution's commerce clause (Art I, § 8, cl 3); whether particular operations affect interstate commerce sufficiently to come under constitutional power of Congress to regulate those operations (1) is ultimately judicial rather than legislative question, and (2) can be settled finally only by Supreme Court. United States v Morrison (2000) 529 US 598, 120 S Ct 1740, 146 L Ed 2d 658, 2000 CDOS 3788, 2000 Daily Journal DAR 5061, 82 BNA FEP Cas 1313, 77 CCH EPD ¶ 46376, 2000 Colo J C A R 2583, 13 FLW Fed S 287 (criticized in Cazarez-Gutierrez v Ashcroft (2004, CA9 Cal) 356 F3d 1015) and (criticized in United States v Shivers (2005, ND Fla) 390 F Supp 2d 1067) and (criticized in United States v Cramer (2005, MD Pa) 2005 US Dist LEXIS 31761).

3. Construction

Action on behalf of female middle school student is dismissed as to school officials, to extent it asserts claim under 42 USCS § 13981(c) for school custodian's alleged rape of student, because complaint does not address any action officials have taken which would support theory of recovery under agency theory or based upon status as employer under § 13981. Sherman ex rel. v Helms (2000, MD Ga) 80 F Supp 2d 1365.

Employee's claim against union organizer under Violence Against Women Act (42 USCS §§ 13981 et seq.) must fail, even though she alleges organizer stalked and threatened her, and may have "egged" her car, where she admits he never threatened her with physical harm and never touched her in any way, because it is clear that parties did not like each other due to their respective positions regarding unions, not because of gender. Harris v Franklin-Williamson Human Servs. (2000, SD Ill) 97 F Supp 2d 892, 46 FR Serv 3d 1167.

4. Miscellaneous

Claim against car dealership under Violence Against Women Act (42 USCS § 13981) is dismissed, even though nothing in language or legislative history of statute precludes extension of liability to corporations as "persons" under § 13981(c), because, in order to hold corporation accountable for alleged sexual assault of sales consultant by her supervisor, it must be shown that supervisor had final policymaking authority with respect to sexual harassment or that final policymaker ratified or was deliberately indifferent to supervisor's conduct.

Grace v Thomason Nissan (1999, DC Or) 76 F Supp 2d 1083.

EQUAL JUSTICE FOR WOMEN IN COURTS

Education and Training for Judges and Court Personnel in State Courts

§ 13991. Grants authorized

The State Justice Institute may award grants for the purpose of developing, testing, presenting, and disseminating model programs to be used by States (as defined in section 202 of the State Justice Institute Act of 1984 (42 U.S.C. 10701)) in training judges and court personnel in the laws of the States and by Indian tribes in training tribal judges and court personnel in the laws of the tribes on rape, sexual assault, domestic violence, dating violence, and other crimes of violence motivated by the victim's gender. Nothing shall preclude the attendance of tribal judges and court personnel at programs funded under this section for States to train judges and court personnel on the laws of the States. (Sept. 13, 1994, P. L. 103-322, Title IV, Subtitle D, Ch 1, § 40411, 108 Stat. 1942; Oct. 28, 2000, P. L. 106-386, Div B, Title IV, § 1406(c)(2), (d)(1), 114 Stat. 1516, 1517.)

HISTORY; ANCILLARY LAWS AND DIRECTIVES
Amendments:
2000. Act Oct. 28, 2000, inserted "dating violence," and added the sentence beginning "Nothing shall preclude . . .".

CROSS REFERENCES
This section is referred to in 42 USCS § 14214.

RESEARCH GUIDE
Am Jur Trials:
92 Am Jur Trials, Criminal Defense: Assault and Battery Cases, p. 1.

§ 13992. Training provided by grants

Training provided pursuant to grants made under this subtitle [42 USCS §§ 13991 et seq.] may include current information, existing studies, or current data on—

(1) the nature and incidence of rape and sexual assault by strangers and nonstrangers, marital rape, and incest;

(2) the underreporting of rape, sexual assault, and child sexual abuse;

(3) the physical, psychological, and economic impact of rape and sexual assault on the victim, the costs to society, and the implications for sentencing;

(4) the psychology of sex offenders, their high rate of recidivism, and the implications for sentencing;

(5) the historical evolution of laws and attitudes on rape and sexual assault;

(6) sex stereotyping of female and male victims of rape and sexual assault, racial stereotyping of rape victims and defendants, and the impact of such stereotypes on credibility of witnesses, sentencing, and other aspects of the administration of justice;

(7) application of rape shield laws and other limits on introduction of evidence that may subject victims to improper sex stereotyping and harassment in both rape and nonrape cases, including the need for sua sponte judicial intervention in inappropriate cross-examination;

(8) the use of expert witness testimony on rape trauma syndrome, child sexual abuse accommodation syndrome, post-traumatic stress syndrome, and similar issues;

(9) the legitimate reasons why victims of rape, sexual assault, and incest may refuse to testify against a defendant;

(10) the nature and incidence of domestic violence and dating violence (as defined in section 2003 of title I of the Omnibus Crime Control and Safe Streets Act of 1968 (42 U.S.C. 3996gg-2));

(11) the physical, psychological, and economic impact of domestic violence and dating violence on the victim, the costs to society, and the implications for court procedures and sentencing;

(12) the psychology and self-presentation of batterers and victims and the implications for court proceedings and credibility of witnesses;

(13) sex stereotyping of female and male victims of domestic violence and dating violence, myths about presence or absence of domestic violence and dating violence in certain racial, ethnic, religious, or socioeconomic groups, and their impact on the administration of justice;

(14) historical evolution of laws and attitudes on domestic violence;

(15) proper and improper interpretations of the defenses of self-defense and provocation, and the use of expert witness testimony on battered woman syndrome;

(16) the likelihood of retaliation, recidivism, and escalation of violence by batterers, and the potential impact of incarceration and other meaningful sanctions for acts of domestic violence including violations of orders of protection;

(17) economic, psychological, social and institutional reasons for victims' inability to leave the batterer, to report domestic violence or dating violence or to follow through on complaints, including the influence of lack of support from police, judges, and court personnel, and the legitimate reasons why victims of domestic violence or dating violence may refuse to testify against a defendant;

(18) the need for orders of protection, and the implications of mutual orders of protection, dual arrest policies, and mediation in domestic violence and dating violence cases;

(19) recognition of and response to gender-motivated crimes of violence other than rape, sexual assault and domestic violence, such as mass or serial murder motivated by the gender of the victims;

(20) the issues raised by domestic violence in determining custody and visitation, including how to protect the safety of the child and of a parent who is not a predominant aggressor of domestic violence, the legitimate reasons parents may report domestic violence, the ways domestic violence may relate to an abuser's desire to seek custody, and evaluating expert

testimony in custody and visitation determinations involving domestic violence;

(21) the issues raised by child sexual assault in determining custody and visitation, including how to protect the safety of the child, the legitimate reasons parents may report child sexual assault, and evaluating expert testimony in custody and visitation determinations involving child sexual assault, including the current scientifically-accepted and empirically valid research on child sexual assault; [and]

(22) the extent to which addressing domestic violence and victim safety contributes to the efficient administration of justice;[.]

(Sept. 13, 1994, P. L. 103-322, Title IV, Subtitle D, Ch 1, § 40412, 108 Stat. 1943; Oct. 28, 2000, P. L. 106-386, Div B, Title IV, § 1406(a)(1), (d)(2), 114 Stat. 1515, 1517.)

HISTORY; ANCILLARY LAWS AND DIRECTIVES

References in text:
42 USCS § 3796gg-2, referred to in para. (10), was subsequently repealed and a new § 3796gg-2 enacted which does not define the terms "domestic violence" or "dating violence". However, such terms are defined in 42 USCS § 13925.

Explanatory notes:
The word "and" has been inserted in brackets at the end of para. (21) to indicate the probable intent of Congress to include such word.
The concluding period has been inserted in brackets at the end of para. (22) to indicate the probable intent of Congress to include such punctuation.

Amendments:
2000. Act Oct. 28, 2000, in para. (10), inserted "and dating violence (as defined in section 2003 of title I of the Omnibus Crime Control and Safe Streets Act of 1968 (42 U.S.C. 3996gg-2))", in para. (11), inserted "and dating violence", in para. (13), inserted "and dating violence" in two places, in para. (17), inserted "or dating violence" in two places, in para. (18), inserted "and dating violence" and deleted "and" following the concluding semicolon, in para. (19), substituted the concluding semicolon for a period, and added paras. (20)–(22).

CROSS REFERENCES

This section is referred to in 42 USCS §§ 14001, 14214.

§ 13993. Cooperation in developing programs in making grants under this title [42 USCS §§ 13991 et seq.]

The State Justice Institute shall ensure that model programs carried out pursuant to grants made under this subtitle [42 USCS §§ 13991 et seq.] are developed with the participation of law enforcement officials, public and private nonprofit victim advocates, including national, State, tribal, and local domestic violence and sexual assault programs and coalitions, legal experts, prosecutors, defense attorneys, and recognized experts on gender bias in the courts.

(Sept. 13, 1994, P. L. 103-322, Title IV, Subtitle D, Ch 1, § 40413, 108 Stat.

1944; Oct. 28, 2000, P. L. 106-386, Div B, Title IV, § 1406(c)(1), 114 Stat. 1516.)

HISTORY; ANCILLARY LAWS AND DIRECTIVES
Amendments:
2000. Act Oct. 28, 2000, inserted ", including national, State, tribal, and local domestic violence and sexual assault programs and coalitions".

CROSS REFERENCES
This section is referred to in 42 USCS § 14214.

§ 13994. Authorization of appropriations

(a) In general. There are authorized to be appropriated to carry out this chapter [42 USCS §§ 13991 et seq.] $600,000 for fiscal year 1996 and $1,500,000 for each of the fiscal years 2001 through 2005.

(b) Model programs. Of amounts appropriated under this section, the State Justice Institute shall expend not less than 40 percent on model programs regarding domestic violence and not less than 40 percent on model programs regarding rape and sexual assault.

(c) State Justice Institute. The State Justice Institute may use up to 5 percent of the funds appropriated under this section for annually compiling and broadly disseminating (including through electronic publication) information about the use of funds and about the projects funded under this section, including any evaluations of the projects and information to enable the replication and adoption of the projects.
(Sept. 13, 1994, P. L. 103-322, Title IV, Subtitle D, Ch 1, § 40414, 108 Stat. 1944; Oct. 28, 2000, P. L. 106-386, Div B, Title IV, § 1406(a)(2), (c)(3), 114 Stat. 1516.)

HISTORY; ANCILLARY LAWS AND DIRECTIVES
Amendments:
2000. Act Oct. 28, 2000, in subsec. (a), inserted "and $1,500,000 for each of the fiscal years 2001 through 2005"; and added subsec. (c).

CROSS REFERENCES
This section is referred to in 42 USCS § 14214.

Education and Training for Judges and Court Personnel in Federal Courts

§ 14001. Authorizations of circuit studies; education and training grants

(a) Studies. In order to gain a better understanding of the nature and the extent of gender bias in the Federal courts, the circuit judicial councils are encouraged to conduct studies of the instances, if any, of gender bias in their respective circuits and to implement recommended reforms.

(b) Matters for examination. The studies under subsection (a) may include an examination of the effects of gender on—

(1) the treatment of litigants, witnesses, attorneys, jurors, and judges in the courts, including before magistrate and bankruptcy judges;

(2) the interpretation and application of the law, both civil and criminal;

(3) treatment of defendants in criminal cases;

(4) treatment of victims of violent crimes in judicial proceedings;

(5) sentencing;

(6) sentencing alternatives and the nature of supervision of probation and parole;

(7) appointments to committees of the Judicial Conference and the courts;

(8) case management and court sponsored alternative dispute resolution programs;

(9) the selection, retention, promotion, and treatment of employees;

(10) appointment of arbitrators, experts, and special masters;

(11) the admissibility of the victim's past sexual history in civil and criminal cases; and

(12) the aspects of the topics listed in section 40412 [42 USCS § 13992] that pertain to issues within the jurisdiction of the Federal courts.

(c) Clearinghouse. The Administrative Office of the United States Courts shall act as a clearinghouse to disseminate any reports and materials issued by the gender bias task forces under subsection (a) and to respond to requests for such reports and materials. The gender bias task forces shall provide the Administrative Office of the Courts of the United States [Administrative Office of the United States Courts] with their reports and related material.

(d) Continuing education and training programs. The Federal Judicial Center, in carrying out section 620(b)(3) of title 28, United States Code, shall include in the educational programs it prepares, including the training programs for newly appointed judges, information on the aspects of the topics listed in section 40412 [42 USCS § 13992] that pertain to issues within the jurisdiction of the Federal courts, and shall prepare materials necessary to implement this subsection.

(Sept. 13, 1994, P. L. 103-322, Title IV, Subtitle D, Ch 2, § 40421, 108 Stat. 1944; Oct. 28, 2000, P. L. 106-386, Div B, Title IV, § 1406(b)(1), 114 Stat. 1516.)

HISTORY; ANCILLARY LAWS AND DIRECTIVES

Explanatory notes:

"Administrative Office of the United States Courts" has been inserted in brackets in subsec. (c) as the entity probably intended by Congress.

Amendments:

2000. Act Oct. 28, 2000, substituted subsec. (d) for one which read:

"(d) Model programs. The Federal Judicial Center, in carrying out section 620(b)(3) of title 28, United States Code, may—

"(1) include in the educational programs it presents and prepares, including the training programs for newly appointed judges, information on issues related to gender bias in the courts including such areas as are listed in subsection (a) along with such other topics as the Federal Judicial Center deems appropriate;

"(2) prepare materials necessary to implement this subsection; and

"(3) take into consideration the findings and recommendations of the studies conducted pursuant to subsection (a), and to consult with individuals and groups with relevant expertise in gender bias issues as it prepares or revises such materials.".

CROSS REFERENCES
This section is referred to in 42 USCS §§ 14002, 14214.

§ 14002. Authorization of appropriations

There are authorized to be appropriated—

(1) to the Salaries and Expenses Account of the Courts of Appeals, District Courts, and other Judicial Services to carry out section 40421(a) [42 USCS § 14001(a)] $500,000 for fiscal year 1996;

(2) to the Federal Judicial Center to carry out section 40421(d) [42 USCS § 14001(d)] $100,000 for fiscal year 1996 and $500,000 for each of the fiscal years 2001 through 2005; and

(3) to the Administrative Office of the United States Courts to carry out section 40421(c) [42 USCS § 14001(c)] $100,000 for fiscal year 1996.

(Sept. 13, 1994, P. L. 103-322, Title IV, Subtitle D, Ch 2, § 40422, 108 Stat. 1945; Oct. 28, 2000, P. L. 106-386, Div B, Title IV, § 1406(b)(2), 114 Stat. 1516.)

HISTORY; ANCILLARY LAWS AND DIRECTIVES
Amendments:
2000. Act Oct. 28, 2000, in para. (2), inserted "and $500,000 for each of the fiscal years 2001 through 2005".

CROSS REFERENCES
This section is referred to in 42 USCS § 14214.

VIOLENCE AGAINST WOMEN ACT IMPROVEMENTS

§ 14011. Payment of cost of testing for sexually transmitted diseases

(a) [Omitted]

(b) **Limited testing of defendants.** (1) Court order. The victim of an offense of the type referred to in subsection (a) may obtain an order in the district court of the United States for the district in which charges are brought against the defendant charged with the offense, after notice to the defendant and an opportunity to be heard, requiring that the defendant be tested for the presence of the etiologic agent for acquired immune deficiency syndrome, and that the results of the test be communicated to the victim and the defendant. Any test result of the defendant given to the victim or the defendant must be accompanied by appropriate counseling.

(2) Showing required. To obtain an order under paragraph (1), the victim must demonstrate that—

(A) the defendant has been charged with the offense in a State or Federal court, and if the defendant has been arrested without a warrant, a probable cause determination has been made;

(B) the test for the etiologic agent for acquired immune deficiency syndrome is requested by the victim after appropriate counseling; and

(C) the test would provide information necessary for the health of the victim of the alleged offense and the court determines that the alleged conduct of the defendant created a risk of transmission, as determined by the Centers for Disease Control [Centers for Disease Control and Prevention], of the etiologic agent for acquired immune deficiency syndrome to the victim.

(3) Follow-up testing. The court may order follow-up tests and counseling under paragraph (1) if the initial test was negative. Such follow-up tests and counseling shall be performed at the request of the victim on dates that occur six months and twelve months following the initial test.

(4) Termination of testing requirements. An order for follow-up testing under paragraph (3) shall be terminated if the person obtains an acquittal on, or dismissal of, all charges of the type referred to in subsection (a).

(5) Confidentiality of test. The results of any test ordered under this subsection shall be disclosed only to the victim or, where the court deems appropriate, to the parent or legal guardian of the victim, and to the person tested. The victim may disclose the test results only to any medical professional, counselor, family member or sexual partner(s) the victim may have had since the attack. Any such individual to whom the test results are disclosed by the victim shall maintain the confidentiality of such information.

(6) Disclosure of test results. The court shall issue an order to prohibit the disclosure by the victim of the results of any test performed under this subsection to anyone other than those mentioned in paragraph (5). The contents of the court proceedings and test results pursuant to this section shall be sealed. The results of such test performed on the defendant under this section shall not be used as evidence in any criminal trial.

(7) Contempt for disclosure. Any person who discloses the results of a test in violation of this subsection may be held in contempt of court.

(c) Penalties for intentional transmission of HIV. Not later than 6 months after the date of enactment of this Act [enacted Sept. 13, 1994], the United States Sentencing Commission shall conduct a study and prepare and submit to the committees [Committees] on the Judiciary of the Senate and the House of Representatives a report concerning recommendations for the revision of sentencing guidelines that relate to offenses in which an HIV infected individual engages in sexual activity if the individual knows that he or she is infected with HIV and intends, through such sexual activity, to expose another to HIV.

(Sept. 13, 1994, P. L. 103-322, Title IV, Subtitle E, § 40503, 108 Stat. 1946; Oct. 11, 1996, P. L. 104-294, Title VI, § 604(b)(1), 110 Stat. 3506.)

HISTORY; ANCILLARY LAWS AND DIRECTIVES

Explanatory notes:

The bracketed words "Centers for Disease Control and Prevention" have been inserted in subsec. (a) on the authority of Act Oct. 27, 1992, P. L. 102-531, § 312, 106 Stat. 3504, which provided that the name of the Centers for Disease Control be changed to the Centers for Disease Control and Prevention.

The bracketed word "Committees" has been inserted in subsec. (c) as the capitalization probably intended by Congress.

Subsec. (a) of § 40503 of Act Sept. 13, 1994, P. L. 103-322, which has been omitted from this section, amended 42 USCS § 10607.

Amendments:

1996. Act Oct. 11, 1996 (effective on 9/13/94, pursuant to § 604(d) of such Act, which appears as 18 USCS § 13 note), in subsec. (b)(3), substituted "paragraph (1)" for "paragraph (b)(1)".

RESEARCH GUIDE

Am Jur Trials:

92 Am Jur Trials, Criminal Defense: Assault and Battery Cases, p. 1.

Annotations:

Validity, and Propriety under Circumstances, of Court-Ordered HIV Testing. 87 ALR5th 631.

§ 14012. National baseline study on campus sexual assault

(a) Study. The Attorney General, in consultation with the Secretary of Education, shall provide for a national baseline study to examine the scope of the problem of campus sexual assaults and the effectiveness of institutional and legal policies in addressing such crimes and protecting victims. The Attorney General may utilize the Bureau of Justice Statistics, the National Institute of Justice, and the Office for Victims of Crime in carrying out this section.

(b) Report. Based on the study required by subsection (a) and data collected under the Student Right-To-Know and Campus Security Act (20 U.S.C. 1001 note; Public Law 101-542) and amendments made by that Act, the Attorney General shall prepare a report including an analysis of—

(1) the number of reported allegations and estimated number of unreported allegations of campus sexual assaults, and to whom the allegations are reported (including authorities of the educational institution, sexual assault victim service entities, and local criminal authorities);

(2) the number of campus sexual assault allegations reported to authorities of educational institutions which are reported to criminal authorities;

(3) the number of campus sexual assault allegations that result in criminal prosecution in comparison with the number of non-campus sexual assault allegations that result in criminal prosecution;

(4) Federal and State laws or regulations pertaining specifically to campus sexual assaults;

(5) the adequacy of policies and practices of educational institutions in addressing campus sexual assaults and protecting victims, including consideration of—

(A) the security measures in effect at educational institutions, such as utilization of campus police and security guards, control over access to grounds and buildings, supervision of student activities and student living arrangements, control over the consumption of alcohol by students, lighting, and the availability of escort services;

(B) the articulation and communication to students of the institution's policies concerning sexual assaults;

(C) policies and practices that may prevent or discourage the reporting of campus sexual assaults to local criminal authorities, or that may otherwise obstruct justice or interfere with the prosecution of perpetrators of campus sexual assaults;

(D) the nature and availability of victim services for victims of campus sexual assaults;

(E) the ability of educational institutions' disciplinary processes to address allegations of sexual assault adequately and fairly;

(F) measures that are taken to ensure that victims are free of unwanted contact with alleged assailants, and disciplinary sanctions that are imposed when a sexual assault is determined to have occurred; and

(G) the grounds on which educational institutions are subject to lawsuits based on campus sexual assaults, the resolution of these cases, and measures that can be taken to avoid the likelihood of lawsuits and civil liability;

(6) in conjunction with the report produced by the Department of Education in coordination with institutions of education under the Student Right-To-Know and Campus Security Act (20 U.S.C. 1001 note; Public Law 101-542) and amendments made by that Act, an assessment of the policies and practices of educational institutions that are of greatest effectiveness in addressing campus sexual assaults and protecting victims, including policies and practices relating to the particular issues described in paragraph (5); and

(7) any recommendations the Attorney General may have for reforms to address campus sexual assaults and protect victims more effectively, and any other matters that the Attorney General deems relevant to the subject of the study and report required by this section.

(c) Submission of report. The report required by subsection (b) shall be submitted to the Congress no later than September 1, 1996.

(d) "Campus sexual assaults" defined. For purposes of this section, "campus sexual assaults" includes sexual assaults occurring at institutions of postsecondary education and sexual assaults committed against or by students or employees of such institutions.

(e) Authorization of appropriations. There are authorized to be appropriated to carry out the study required by this section—$200,000 for fiscal year 1996.
(Sept. 13, 1994, P. L. 103-322, Title IV, Subtitle E, § 40506, 108 Stat. 1948.)

HISTORY; ANCILLARY LAWS AND DIRECTIVES

References in text:
The "Student Right-To-Know and Campus Security Act", referred to in this section, is Act Nov. 8, 1990, P. L. 101-542, 104 Stat. 2381. For full classification of this Act, consult USCS Tables volumes.

CROSS REFERENCES
This section is referred to in 42 USCS § 14214.

§ 14013. Report on battered women's syndrome

(a) Report. Not less than 1 year after the date of enactment of this Act [enacted Sept. 13, 1994], the Attorney General and the Secretary of Health and Human Services shall transmit to the House Committee on Energy and Commerce, the Senate Committee on Labor and Human Resources, and the Committees on the Judiciary of the Senate and the House of Representatives a report on the medical and psychological basis of "battered women's syndrome" and on the extent to which evidence of the syndrome has been considered in criminal trials.

(b) Components. The report under subsection (a) shall include—
(1) medical and psychological testimony on the validity of battered women's syndrome as a psychological condition;
(2) a compilation of State, tribal, and Federal court cases in which evidence of battered women's syndrome was offered in criminal trials; and
(3) an assessment by State, tribal, and Federal judges, prosecutors, and defense attorneys of the effects that evidence of battered women's syndrome may have in criminal trials.
(Sept. 13, 1994, P. L. 103-322, Title IV, Subtitle E, § 40507, 108 Stat. 1949.)

HISTORY; ANCILLARY LAWS AND DIRECTIVES

References in text:
With respect to the Committee on Energy and Commerce of the House of Representatives, referred to in this section, § 1(a)(4), (c)(1) of Act June 3, 1995, P. L. 104-14, which appears as a note preceding 2 USCS § 21, provides that any reference to such Committee in any provision of law enacted before January 4, 1995, shall be treated as referring to the Committee on Commerce of the House of Representatives, except that it shall be treated as referring to (A) the Committee on Agriculture of the House of Representatives, in the case of a provision of law relating to inspection of seafood or seafood products, (B) the Committee on Banking and Financial Services of the House of Representatives, in the case of a provision of law relating to bank capital markets activities generally or to depository institution securities activities generally, and (C) the Committee on Transportation and Infrastructure of the House of Representatives, in the case of a provision of law relating to railroads, railway labor, or railroad retirement and unemployment (except revenue measures related thereto). The Committee on Commerce of the House of Representatives was renamed the Committee on Energy and Commerce of the House of Representatives and jurisdiction over matters relating to securities and exchanges and insurance generally was transferred to the Committee on Financial Service of the House of representatives by H. Res. No. 5 of Jan. 3, 2001.
The "Senate Committee on Labor and Human Resources", referred to in subsec. (a), was renamed the Committee on Health, Education, Labor, and Pensions of the Senate by S. Res. No. 20, Jan. 19, 1999, One Hundred Sixth Congress.

§ 14014. Report on confidentiality of addresses for victims of domestic violence

(a) Report. The Attorney General shall conduct a study of the means by which abusive spouses may obtain information concerning the addresses or locations of estranged or former spouses, notwithstanding the desire of the victims to have such information withheld to avoid further exposure to abuse. Based on the study, the Attorney General shall transmit a report to Congress including—

(1) the findings of the study concerning the means by which information concerning the addresses or locations of abused spouses may be obtained by abusers; and

(2) analysis of the feasibility of creating effective means of protecting the confidentiality of information concerning the addresses and locations of abused spouses to protect such persons from exposure to further abuse while preserving access to such information for legitimate purposes.

(b) Use of components. The Attorney General may use the National Institute of Justice and the Office for Victims of Crime in carrying out this section.

(Sept. 13, 1994, P. L. 103-322, Title IV, Subtitle E, § 40508, 108 Stat. 1950.)

§ 14015. Report on recordkeeping relating to domestic violence

Not later than 1 year after the date of enactment of this Act [enacted Sept. 13, 1994], the Attorney General shall complete a study of, and shall submit to Congress a report and recommendations on, problems of recordkeeping of criminal complaints involving domestic violence. The study and report shall examine—

(1) the efforts that have been made by the Department of Justice, including the Federal Bureau of Investigation, to collect statistics on domestic violence; and

(2) the feasibility of requiring that the relationship between an offender and victim be reported in Federal records of crimes of aggravated assault, rape, and other violent crimes.

(Sept. 13, 1994, P. L. 103-322, Title IV, Subtitle E, § 40509, 108 Stat. 1950.)

§ 14016. Enforcement of statutory rape laws

(a) Sense of the Senate. It is the sense of the Senate that States and local jurisdictions should aggressively enforce statutory rape laws.

(b) Justice Department program on statutory rape. Not later than January 1, 1997, the Attorney General shall establish and implement a program that—

(1) studies the linkage between statutory rape and teenage pregnancy, particularly by predatory older men committing repeat offenses; and

(2) educates State and local criminal law enforcement officials on the prevention and prosecution of statutory rape, focusing in particular on the commission of statutory rape by predatory older men committing repeat offenses, and any links to teenage pregnancy.

(c) Violence Against Women initiative. The Attorney General shall ensure

that the Department of Justice's Violence Against Women initiative addresses the issue of statutory rape, particularly the commission of statutory rape by predatory older men committing repeat offenses.
(Aug. 22, 1996, P. L. 104-193, Title IX, § 906, 110 Stat. 2349.)

HISTORY; ANCILLARY LAWS AND DIRECTIVES

Explanatory notes:
This section was enacted as part of Act Aug. 22, 1996, P. L. 104-193, and not as part of Act Sept. 13, 1994, P. L. 103-322, which generally comprises this chapter.

NATIONAL STALKER AND DOMESTIC VIOLENCE REDUCTION

§ 14031. Grant program

(a) In general. The Attorney General is authorized to provide grants to States and units of local government to improve and implement processes for entering data regarding stalking and domestic violence into local, State, and national crime information databases.

(b) Eligibility. To be eligible to receive a grant under subsection (a), a State or unit of local government shall certify that it has or intends to establish a program that enters into the National Crime Information Center records of—

(1) warrants for the arrest of persons violating protection orders intended to protect victims from stalking or domestic violence;

(2) arrests or convictions of persons violating protection [orders intended to protect victims from stalking] or domestic violence; and

(3) protection orders for the protection of persons from stalking or domestic violence.

(Sept. 13, 1994, P. L. 103-322, Title IV, Subtitle F, § 40602, 108 Stat. 1951; Oct. 28, 2000, P. L. 106-386, Div B, Title I, § 1106(b), 114 Stat. 1497.)

HISTORY; ANCILLARY LAWS AND DIRECTIVES

Explanatory notes:
The bracketed phrase "orders intended to protect victims from stalking" has been inserted in subsec. (b)(2) to indicate the probable intent of Congress to include such language.

Amendments:
2000. Act Oct. 28, 2000, in subsec. (a), inserted "and implement".

CROSS REFERENCES
This section is referred to in 42 USCS § 14214.

RESEARCH GUIDE
Am Jur Trials:
92 Am Jur Trials, Criminal Defense: Assault and Battery Cases, p. 1.

§ 14032. Authorization of appropriations

There is authorized to be appropriated to carry out this subtitle $3,000,000 for each of fiscal years 2007 through 2011.

(Sept. 13, 1994, P. L. 103-322, Title IV, Subtitle F, § 40603, 108 Stat. 1951; Oct. 28, 2000, P. L. 106-386, Div B, Title I, § 1106(a), 114 Stat. 1497; Jan 5, 2006, P. L. 109-162, Title I, § 109, 119 Stat. 2984.)

HISTORY; ANCILLARY LAWS AND DIRECTIVES

References in text:

"This subtitle", referred to in this section, is Subtitle F of Title IV of Act Sept. 13, 1994, P. L. 103-322, which appears generally as 42 USCS §§ 14031 et seq. For full classification of such Subtitle, consult USCS Tables volumes.

Amendments:

2000. Act Oct. 28, 2000, substituted this section for one which read:
"Authorization of appropriations

"There are authorized to be appropriated to carry out this subtitle—

"(1) $1,500,000 for fiscal year 1996;

"(2) $1,750,000 for fiscal year 1997; and

"(3) $2,750,000 for fiscal year 1998.".

2006. Act Jan. 5, 2006, substituted "2007" for "2001". Such Act further directed that "2011" be substituted for "2006"; however, since "2006" did not appear in the section, "2011" has instead been substituted for "2005" to reflect the probable intent of Congress.

CROSS REFERENCES

This section is referred to in 42 USCS § 14214.

§ 14033. Application requirements

An application for a grant under this subtitle shall be submitted in such form and manner, and contain such information, as the Attorney General may prescribe. In addition, applications shall include documentation showing—

(1) the need for grant funds and that State or local funding, as the case may be, does not already cover these operations;

(2) intended use of the grant funds, including a plan of action to increase record input; and

(3) an estimate of expected results from the use of the grant funds.

(Sept. 13, 1994, P. L. 103-322, Title IV, Subtitle F, § 40604, 108 Stat. 1951.)

HISTORY; ANCILLARY LAWS AND DIRECTIVES

References in text:

"This subtitle", referred to in this section, is Subtitle F of Title IV of Act Sept. 13, 1994, P. L. 103-322, which appears generally as 42 USCS §§ 14031 et seq. For full classification of this Subtitle, consult USCS Tables volumes.

CROSS REFERENCES

This section is referred to in 42 USCS § 14214.

§ 14034. Disbursement

Not later than 90 days after the receipt of an application under this subtitle, the

Attorney General shall either provide grant funds or shall inform the applicant why grant funds are not being provided.
(Sept. 13, 1994, P. L. 103-322, Title IV, Subtitle F, § 40605, 108 Stat. 1952.)

HISTORY; ANCILLARY LAWS AND DIRECTIVES

References in text:
"This subtitle", referred to in this section, is Subtitle F of Title IV of Act Sept. 13, 1994, P. L. 103-322, which appears generally as 42 USCS §§ 14031 et seq. For full classification of this Subtitle, consult USCS Tables volumes.

CROSS REFERENCES
This section is referred to in 42 USCS § 14214.

§ 14035.   Technical assistance, training, and evaluations

The Attorney General may provide technical assistance and training in furtherance of the purposes of this subtitle, and may provide for the evaluation of programs that receive funds under this subtitle, in addition to any evaluation requirements that the Attorney General may prescribe for grantees. The technical assistance, training, and evaluations authorized by this section may be carried out directly by the Attorney General, or through contracts or other arrangements with other entities.
(Sept. 13, 1994, P. L. 103-322, Title IV, Subtitle F, § 40606, 108 Stat. 1952.)

HISTORY; ANCILLARY LAWS AND DIRECTIVES

References in text:
"This subtitle", referred to in this section, is Subtitle F of Title IV of Act Sept. 13, 1994, P. L. 103-322, which appears generally as 42 USCS §§ 14031 et seq. For full classification of this Subtitle, consult USCS Tables volumes.

CROSS REFERENCES
This section is referred to in 42 USCS § 14214.

§ 14036.   Training programs for judges

The State Justice Institute, after consultation with nationally recognized nonprofit organizations with expertise in stalking and domestic violence cases, shall conduct training programs for State (as defined in section 202 of the State Justice Institute [Authorization] Act of 1984 (42 U.S.C. 10701)) and Indian tribal judges to ensure that a judge issuing an order in a stalking or domestic violence case has all available criminal history and other information, whether from State or Federal sources.
(Sept. 13, 1994, P. L. 103-322, Title IV, Subtitle F, § 40607, 108 Stat. 1952.)

HISTORY; ANCILLARY LAWS AND DIRECTIVES

Explanatory notes:
The word "Authorization" has been enclosed in brackets to indicate the probable intent of Congress to delete it.

CROSS REFERENCES
This section is referred to in 42 USCS § 14214.

§ 14037.   Recommendations on intrastate communication

The State Justice Institute, after consultation with nationally recognized non-profit associations with expertise in data sharing among criminal justice agencies and familiarity with the issues raised in stalking and domestic violence cases, shall recommend proposals regarding how State courts may increase intrastate communication between civil and criminal courts.
(Sept. 13, 1994, P. L. 103-322, Title IV, Subtitle F, § 40608, 108 Stat. 1952.)

CROSS REFERENCES
This section is referred to in 42 USCS § 14214.

§ 14038.   Inclusion in national incident-based reporting system

Not later than 2 years after the date of enactment of this Act [enacted Sept. 13, 1994], the Attorney General, in accordance with the States, shall compile data regarding domestic violence and intimidation (including stalking) as part of the National Incident-Based Reporting System (NIBRS).
(Sept. 13, 1994, P. L. 103-322, Title IV, Subtitle F, § 40609, 108 Stat. 1952.)

CROSS REFERENCES
This section is referred to in 42 USCS § 14214.

§ 14039.   Report to Congress

Each even-numbered fiscal year, the Attorney General shall submit to the Congress a biennial report that provides information concerning the incidence of stalking and domestic violence, and evaluates the effectiveness of State antistalking efforts and legislation.
(Sept. 13, 1994, P. L. 103-322, Title IV, Subtitle F, § 40610, 108 Stat. 1952; Jan. 5, 2006, P. L. 109-162, § 3(b)(1), Title XI, Subtitle B, Ch. 3, § 1135(a), 119 Stat. 2971, 3108; Aug. 12, 2006, P. L. 109-271, §§ 2(d), 8(b), 120 Stat. 752, 766.)

HISTORY; ANCILLARY LAWS AND DIRECTIVES
Amendments:
2006. Act Jan. 5, 2006, § 3(b)(1), substituted "Each even-numbered fiscal year, the Attorney General shall submit to the Congress a biennial report that provides" for "The Attorney General shall submit to the Congress an annual report, beginning one year after the date of the enactment of this Act, that provides".
Section 1135(a) of such Act (repealed by Act Aug. 12, 2006) purported to make the same amendment as § 3(b)(1).
Act Aug. 12, 2006, repealed § 1135 of Act Jan. 5, 2006, and the amendments made by such section.

Other provisions:
State laws and penalties for stalking crimes against children. Act Nov.

26, 1997, P. L. 105-119, Title I, § 115(b)(2), 111 Stat. 2467 (effective as provided by § 115(c) of such Act, which appears as 42 USCS § 14071 note), provides: "The Attorney General shall include in an annual report under section 40610 of the Violent Crime Control and Law Enforcement Act of 1994 (42 U.S.C. 14039) information concerning existing or proposed State laws and penalties for stalking crimes against children.".

CROSS REFERENCES
This section is referred to in 42 USCS § 14214.

§ 14040. Definitions
As used in this subtitle—

(1) the term "national crime information databases" refers to the National Crime Information Center and its incorporated criminal history databases, including the Interstate Identification Index; and

(2) the term "protection order" includes an injunction or any other order issued for the purpose of preventing violent or threatening acts or harassment against, or contact or communication with or physical proximity to, another person, including temporary and final orders issued by civil or criminal courts (other than support or child custody orders) whether obtained by filing an independent action or as a pendente lite order in another proceeding so long as any civil order was issued in response to a complaint, petition, or motion filed by or on behalf of a person seeking protection.

(Sept. 13, 1994, P. L. 103-322, Title IV, Subtitle F, § 40611, 108 Stat. 1952.)

HISTORY; ANCILLARY LAWS AND DIRECTIVES
References in text:
"This subtitle", referred to in this section, is Subtitle F of Title IV of Act Sept. 13, 1994, P. L. 103-322, which appears generally as 42 USCS §§ 14031 et seq. For full classification of this Subtitle, consult USCS Tables volumes.

CROSS REFERENCES
This section is referred to in 42 USCS § 14214.

ELDER ABUSE, NEGLECT, AND EXPLOITATION, INCLUDING DOMESTIC VIOLENCE AND SEXUAL ASSAULT AGAINST OLDER OR DISABLED INDIVIDUALS

§ 14041. Definitions
In this subtitle [42 USCS §§ 14041 et seq.]:

(1) In general. The terms "elder abuse, neglect, and exploitation", and "older individual" have the meanings given the terms in section 102 of the Older Americans Act of 1965 (42 U.S.C. 3002).

(2) Domestic violence. The term "domestic violence" has the meaning given such term by section 2003 of title I of the Omnibus Crime Control and Safe Streets Act of 1968 (42 U.S.C. 3796gg-2).

(3) Sexual assault. The term "sexual assault" has the meaning given the

term in section 2003 of title I of the Omnibus Crime Control and Safe Streets Act of 1968 (42 U.S.C. 3796gg-2).

(Sept. 13, 1994, P. L. 103-322, Title IV, Subtitle H, § 40801, as added Oct. 28, 2000, P. L. 106-386, Div B, Title II, § 1209(a), 114 Stat. 1508.)

HISTORY; ANCILLARY LAWS AND DIRECTIVES

References in text:

42 USCS § 3796gg-2, referred to in paras. (2) and (3), was subsequently repealed and a new § 3796gg-2 enacted which does not define the terms "domestic violence" or "sexual assault". However, such terms are defined in 42 USCS § 13925.

CODE OF FEDERAL REGULATIONS

Department of Justice—Grants for correctional facilities, 28 CFR 91.1 et seq.

RESEARCH GUIDE

Am Jur Trials:

92 Am Jur Trials, Criminal Defense: Assault and Battery Cases, p. 1.

§ 14041a. Enhanced training and services to end violence against and abuse of women later in life

(a) **Grants authorized.** The Attorney General, through the Director of the Office on Violence Against Women, may award grants, which may be used for—

(1) training programs to assist law enforcement, prosecutors, governmental agencies, victim assistants, and relevant officers of Federal, State, tribal, territorial, and local courts in recognizing, addressing, investigating, and prosecuting instances of elder abuse, neglect, and exploitation, including domestic violence, dating violence, sexual assault, or stalking against victims who are 50 years of age or older;

(2) providing or enhancing services for victims of elder abuse, neglect, and exploitation, including domestic violence, dating violence, sexual assault, or stalking, who are 50 years of age or older;

(3) creating or supporting multidisciplinary collaborative community responses to victims of elder abuse, neglect, and exploitation, including domestic violence, dating violence, sexual assault, and stalking, who are 50 years of age or older; and

(4) conducting cross-training for victim service organizations, governmental agencies, courts, law enforcement, and nonprofit, nongovernmental organizations serving victims of elder abuse, neglect, and exploitation, including domestic violence, dating violence, sexual assault, and stalking, who are 50 years of age or older.

(b) **Eligible entities.** An entity shall be eligible to receive a grant under this section if the entity is—

(1) a State;

(2) a unit of local government;

(3) an Indian tribal government or tribal organization; or

(4) a nonprofit and nongovernmental victim services organization with

demonstrated experience in assisting elderly women or demonstrated experience in addressing domestic violence, dating violence, sexual assault, and stalking.

(c) Underserved populations. In awarding grants under this section, the Director shall ensure that services are culturally and linguistically relevant and that the needs of underserved populations are being addressed.

(Sept. 13, 1994, P. L. 103-322, Title IV, Subtitle H, § 40802, as added Oct. 28, 2000, P. L. 106-386, Div B, Title II, § 1209(a), 114 Stat. 1509; Jan. 5, 2006, P. L. 109-162, Title II, § 205(a), 119 Stat. 3002.)

HISTORY; ANCILLARY LAWS AND DIRECTIVES
Amendments:
2006. Act Jan. 5, 2006 (effective 10/1/2006, pursuant to § 4 of such Act, which appears as 42 USCS § 3793 note), substituted this section for one which read:

"Training programs for law enforcement officers

"The Attorney General may make grants for training programs to assist law enforcement officers, prosecutors, and relevant officers of Federal, State, tribal, and local courts in recognizing, addressing, investigating, and prosecuting instances of elder abuse, neglect, and exploitation and violence against individuals with disabilities, including domestic violence and sexual assault, against older or disabled individuals.".

§ 14041b.   Authorization of appropriations

There are authorized to be appropriated to carry out this subtitle [42 USCS §§ 14041 et seq.] $10,000,000 for each of fiscal years 2007 through 2011.

(Sept. 13, 1994, P. L. 103-322, Title IV, Subtitle H, § 40803, as added Oct. 28, 2000, P. L. 106-386, Div B, Title II, § 1209(a), 114 Stat. 1509; Jan. 5, 2006, P. L. 109-162, Title II, § 205(b), 119 Stat. 3002.)

HISTORY; ANCILLARY LAWS AND DIRECTIVES
Amendments:
2006. Act Jan. 5, 2006 (effective 10/1/2006, pursuant to § 4 of such Act, which appears as 42 USCS § 3793 note), substituted "$10,000,000 for each of fiscal years 2007 through 2011" for "$5,000,000 for each of fiscal years 2001 through 2005".

DOMESTIC VIOLENCE TASK FORCE

§ 14042.   Task force

(a) Establish. The Attorney General, in consultation with national nonprofit, nongovernmental organizations whose primary expertise is in domestic violence, shall establish a task force to coordinate research on domestic violence and to report to Congress on any overlapping or duplication of efforts on domestic violence issues. The task force shall be comprised of representatives from all Federal agencies that fund such research.

(b) Uses of funds. Funds appropriated under this section shall be used to—

(1) develop a coordinated strategy to strengthen research focused on domestic violence education, prevention, and intervention strategies;

(2) track and report all Federal research and expenditures on domestic violence; and

(3) identify gaps and duplication of efforts in domestic violence research and governmental expenditures on domestic violence issues.

(c) Report. The Task Force shall report to Congress annually on its work under subsection (b).

(d) Definition. For purposes of this section, the term "domestic violence" has the meaning given such term by section 2003 of title I of the Omnibus Crime Control and Safe Streets Act of 1968 (42 U.S.C. 3796gg-2(1)).

(e) Authorization of appropriations. There is authorized to be appropriated to carry out this section $500,000 for each of fiscal years 2001 through 2004.

(Sept. 13, 1994, P. L. 103-322, Title IV, Subtitle I, § 40901, as added Oct. 28, 2000, P. L. 106-386, Div B, Title IV, § 1407, 114 Stat. 1517.)

HISTORY; ANCILLARY LAWS AND DIRECTIVES

References in text:

42 USCS § 3796gg-2, referred to in subsec. (d), was subsequently repealed and a new § 3796gg-2 enacted which does not define "domestic violence". However, such term is defined in 42 USCS § 13925.

Other provisions:

Study of State laws regarding insurance discrimination against victims of violence against women. Act Oct. 28, 2000, P. L. 106-386, Div B, Title II, § 1206, 114 Stat. 1507, provides:

"(a) In general. The Attorney General shall conduct a national study to identify State laws that address discrimination against victims of domestic violence and sexual assault related to issuance or administration of insurance policies.

"(b) Report. Not later than 1 year after the date of the enactment of this Act, the Attorney General shall submit to Congress a report on the findings and recommendations of the study required by subsection (a).".

Study of workplace effects from violence against women. Act Oct. 28, 2000, P. L. 106-386, Div B, Title II, § 1207, 114 Stat. 1507, provides:

"The Attorney General shall—

"(1) conduct a national survey of plans, programs, and practices developed to assist employers and employees on appropriate responses in the workplace related to victims of domestic violence, stalking, or sexual assault; and

"(2) not later than 18 months after the date of the enactment of this Act, submit to Congress a report describing the results of that survey, which report shall include the recommendations of the Attorney General to assist employers and employees affected in the workplace by incidents of domestic violence, stalking, and sexual assault.".

Study of unemployment compensation for victims of violence against women. Act Oct. 28, 2000, P. L. 106-386, Div B, Title II, § 1208, 114 Stat. 1508, provides:

"The Secretary of Labor, in consultation with the Attorney General, shall—

"(1) conduct a national study to identify State laws that address the separation from employment of an employee due to circumstances directly resulting from the experience of domestic violence by the employee and circumstances governing that receipt (or nonreceipt) by the employee of unemployment compensation based on such separation; and

"(2) not later than 1 year after the date of the enactment of this Act, submit to Congress a report describing the results of that study, together with any recommendations based on that study.".

CODE OF FEDERAL REGULATIONS

Department of Justice—Grants for correctional facilities, 28 CFR 91.1 et seq.

RESEARCH GUIDE

Am Jur Trials:

92 Am Jur Trials, Criminal Defense: Assault and Battery Cases, p. 1.

VIOLENCE AGAINST WOMEN ACT COURT TRAINING AND IMPROVEMENTS

§ 14043. Purpose

The purpose of this subtitle [42 USCS §§ 14043 et seq.] is to enable the Attorney General, though [through] the Director of the Office on Violence Against Women, to award grants to improve court responses to adult and youth domestic violence, dating violence, sexual assault, and stalking to be used for—

(1) improved internal civil and criminal court functions, responses, practices, and procedures;

(2) education for court-based and court-related personnel on issues relating to victims' needs, including safety, security, privacy, confidentiality, and economic independence, as well as information about perpetrator behavior and best practices for holding perpetrators accountable;

(3) collaboration and training with Federal, State, tribal, territorial, and local public agencies and officials and nonprofit, nongovernmental organizations to improve implementation and enforcement of relevant Federal, State, tribal, territorial, and local law;

(4) enabling courts or court-based or court-related programs to develop new or enhance current—

(A) court infrastructure (such as specialized courts, dockets, intake centers, or interpreter services);

(B) community-based initiatives within the court system (such as court watch programs, victim assistants, or community-based supplementary services);

(C) offender management, monitoring, and accountability programs;

(D) safe and confidential information-storage and -sharing databases within and between court systems;

(E) education and outreach programs to improve community access, including enhanced access for underserved populations; and

(F) other projects likely to improve court responses to domestic violence, dating violence, sexual assault, and stalking; and

(5) providing technical assistance to Federal, State, tribal, territorial, or local courts wishing to improve their practices and procedures or to develop new programs.

(Sept. 13, 1994, P. L. 103-322, Title IV, Subtitle J, § 41002, as added Jan. 5, 2006, P. L. 109-162, Title I, § 105(a), 119 Stat. 2979.)

HISTORY; ANCILLARY LAWS AND DIRECTIVES

Explanatory notes:
The bracketed word "through" has been inserted in the introductory matter to indicate the word probably intended by Congress.

§ 14043a. Grant requirements

Grants awarded under this subtitle [42 USCS §§ 14043 et seq.] shall be subject to the following conditions:

(1) Eligible grantees. Eligible grantees may include—
(A) Federal, State, tribal, territorial, or local courts or court-based programs; and
(B) national, State, tribal, territorial, or local private, nonprofit organizations with demonstrated expertise in developing and providing judicial education about domestic violence, dating violence, sexual assault, or stalking.

(2) Conditions of eligibility. To be eligible for a grant under this section, applicants shall certify in writing that—
(A) any courts or court-based personnel working directly with or making decisions about adult or youth parties experiencing domestic violence, dating violence, sexual assault, and stalking have completed or will complete education about domestic violence, dating violence, sexual assault, and stalking;
(B) any education program developed under section 41002 [42 USCS § 14043] has been or will be developed with significant input from and in collaboration with a national, tribal, State, territorial, or local victim services provider or coalition; and
(C) the grantee's internal organizational policies, procedures, or rules do not require mediation or counseling between offenders and victims physically together in cases where domestic violence, dating violence, sexual assault, or stalking is an issue.

(Sept. 13, 1994, P. L. 103-322, Title IV, Subtitle J, § 41003, as added Jan. 5, 2006, P. L. 109-162, Title I, § 105(a), 119 Stat. 2980.)

§ 14043a-1. National education curricula

(a) In general. The Attorney General, through the Director of the Office on Violence Against Women, shall fund efforts to develop a national education curriculum for use by State and national judicial educators to ensure that all courts and court personnel have access to information about relevant Federal, State, territorial, or local law, promising practices, procedures, and policies regarding court responses to adult and youth domestic violence, dating violence, sexual assault, and stalking.

(b) Eligible entities. Any curricula developed under this section—

(1) shall be developed by an entity or entities having demonstrated expertise in developing judicial education curricula on issues relating to domestic violence, dating violence, sexual assault, and stalking; or

(2) if the primary grantee does not have demonstrated expertise with such issues, shall be developed by the primary grantee in partnership with an organization having such expertise.

(Sept. 13, 1994, P. L. 103-322, Title IV, Subtitle J, § 41004, as added Jan. 5, 2006, P. L. 109-162, Title I, § 105(a), 119 Stat. 2980.)

§ 14043a-2. Tribal curricula

(a) In general. The Attorney General, through the Office on Violence Against Women, shall fund efforts to develop education curricula for tribal court judges to ensure that all tribal courts have relevant information about promising practices, procedures, policies, and law regarding tribal court responses to adult and youth domestic violence, dating violence, sexual assault, and stalking.

(b) Eligible entities. Any curricula developed under this section—

(1) shall be developed by a tribal organization having demonstrated expertise in developing judicial education curricula on issues relating to domestic violence, dating violence, sexual assault, and stalking; or

(2) if the primary grantee does not have such expertise, the curricula shall be developed by the primary grantee through partnership with organizations having such expertise.

(Sept. 13, 1994, P. L. 103-322, Title IV, Subtitle J, § 41005, as added Jan. 5, 2006, P. L. 109-162, Title I, § 105(a), 119 Stat. 2981.)

§ 14043a-3. Authorization of appropriations

(a) In general. There is authorized to be appropriated to carry out this subtitle [42 USCS §§ 14043 et seq.] $5,000,000 for each of fiscal years 2007 to 2011.

(b) Availability. Funds appropriated under this section shall remain available until expended and may only be used for the specific programs and activities described in this subtitle.

(c) Set aside. (1) In general. Not less than 10 percent of the total amount available under this section for each fiscal year shall be available for grants under the program authorized by section 2015 of the Omnibus Crime Control and Safe Streets Act of 1968 (42 U.S.C. 3796gg-10).

(2) Applicability of part [section]. The requirements of this section shall not apply to funds allocated for the program described in paragraph (1).

(Sept. 13, 1994, P. L. 103-322, Title IV, Subtitle J, § 41006, as added Jan. 5, 2006, P. L. 109-162, Title I, § 105(a), 119 Stat. 2981; Aug. 12, 2006, P. L. 109-271, § 7(c)(2), 120 Stat. 765.)

HISTORY; ANCILLARY LAWS AND DIRECTIVES

Explanatory notes:
The bracketed word "section" has been inserted in subsec. (c)(2) to indicate the word probably intended by Congress.

Amendments:
2006. Act Aug. 12, 2006, substituted subsec. (c) for one which read: "(c) Set aside. Of the amounts made available under this subsection in each fiscal year, not less than 10 percent shall be used for grants for tribal courts, tribal court-related programs, and tribal nonprofits.".

PRIVACY PROTECTIONS FOR VICTIMS OF DOMESTIC VIOLENCE, DATING VIOLENCE, SEXUAL VIOLENCE, AND STALKING

§ 14043b. Grants to protect the privacy and confidentiality of victims of domestic violence, dating violence, sexual assault, and stalking

The Attorney General, through the Director of the Office on Violence Against Women, may award grants under this subtitle [42 USCS §§ 14043b et seq.] to States, Indian tribes, territories, or local agencies or nonprofit, nongovernmental organizations to ensure that personally identifying information of adult, youth, and child victims of domestic violence, sexual violence, stalking, and dating violence shall not be released or disclosed to the detriment of such victimized persons.

(Sept. 13, 1994, P. L. 103-322, Title IV, Subtitle K, § 41101, as added Jan. 5, 2006, P. L. 109-162, Title I, § 107, 119 Stat. 2983.)

§ 14043b-1. Purpose areas

Grants made under this subtitle [42 USCS §§ 14043b et seq.] may be used—

(1) to develop or improve protocols, procedures, and policies for the purpose of preventing the release of personally identifying information of victims (such as developing alternative identifiers);

(2) to defray the costs of modifying or improving existing databases, registries, and victim notification systems to ensure that personally identifying information of victims is protected from release, unauthorized information sharing and disclosure;

(3) to develop confidential opt out systems that will enable victims of violence to make a single request to keep personally identifying information out of multiple databases, victim notification systems, and registries; or

(4) to develop safe uses of technology (such as notice requirements regarding electronic surveillance by government entities), to protect against abuses of technology (such as electronic or GPS stalking), or providing training for law enforcement on high tech electronic crimes of domestic violence, dating violence, sexual assault, and stalking.

(Sept. 13, 1994, P. L. 103-322, Title IV, Subtitle K, § 41102, as added Jan. 5, 2006, P. L. 109-162, Title I, § 107, 119 Stat. 2983.)

§ 14043b-2. Eligible entities

Entities eligible for grants under this subtitle [42 USCS §§ 14043b et seq.] include—

(1) jurisdictions or agencies within jurisdictions having authority or responsibility for developing or maintaining public databases, registries or victim notification systems;

(2) nonprofit nongovernmental victim advocacy organizations having expertise regarding confidentiality, privacy, and information technology and how these issues are likely to impact the safety of victims;

(3) States or State agencies;

(4) local governments or agencies;

(5) Indian tribal governments or tribal organizations;

(6) territorial governments, agencies, or organizations; or

(7) nonprofit nongovernmental victim advocacy organizations, including statewide domestic violence and sexual assault coalitions.

(Sept. 13, 1994, P. L. 103-322, Title IV, Subtitle K, § 41103, as added Jan. 5, 2006, P. L. 109-162, Title I, § 107, 119 Stat. 2983.)

§ 14043b-3. Grant conditions

Applicants described in paragraph (1) and paragraphs (3) through (6) shall demonstrate that they have entered into a significant partnership with a State, tribal, territorial, or local victim service or advocacy organization or condition in order to develop safe, confidential, and effective protocols, procedures, policies, and systems for protecting personally identifying information of victims.

(Sept. 13, 1994, P. L. 103-322, Title IV, Subtitle K, § 41104, as added Jan. 5, 2006, P. L. 109-162, Title I, § 107, 119 Stat. 2984.)

§ 14043b-4. Authorization of appropriations

(a) **In general.** There is authorized to be appropriated to carry out this subtitle [42 USCS §§ 14043b et seq.] $5,000,000 for each of fiscal years 2007 through 2011.

(b) **Tribal allocation.** Of the amount made available under this section in each fiscal year, 10 percent shall be used for grants to Indian tribes for programs that assist victims of domestic violence, dating violence, stalking, and sexual assault.

(c) **Technical assistance and training.** Of the amount made available under this section in each fiscal year, not less than 5 percent shall be used for grants to organizations that have expertise in confidentiality, privacy, and technology issues impacting victims of domestic violence, dating violence, sexual assault, and stalking to provide technical assistance and training to grantees and non-grantees on how to improve safety, privacy, confidentiality, and technology to protect victimized persons.

(Sept. 13, 1994, P. L. 103-322, Title IV, Subtitle K, § 41105, as added Jan. 5, 2006, P. L. 109-162, Title I, § 107, 119 Stat. 2984.)

SERVICES, EDUCATION, PROTECTION AND JUSTICE FOR YOUNG
VICTIMS OF VIOLENCE

§ 14043c. Services to advocate for and respond to youth

(a) Grants authorized. The Attorney General, in consultation with the Department of Health and Human Services, shall award grants to eligible entities to conduct programs to serve youth victims of domestic violence, dating violence, sexual assault, and stalking. Amounts appropriated under this section may only be used for programs and activities described under subsection (c).

(b) Eligible grantees. To be eligible to receive a grant under this section, an entity shall be—

(1) a nonprofit, nongovernmental entity, the primary purpose of which is to provide services to teen and young adult victims of domestic violence, dating violence, sexual assault, or stalking;

(2) a community-based organization specializing in intervention or violence prevention services for youth;

(3) an Indian Tribe or tribal organization providing services primarily to tribal youth or tribal victims of domestic violence, dating violence, sexual assault or stalking; or

(4) a nonprofit, nongovernmental entity providing services for runaway or homeless youth affected by domestic or sexual abuse.

(c) Use of funds. (1) In general. An entity that receives a grant under this section shall use amounts provided under the grant to design or replicate, and implement, programs and services, using domestic violence, dating violence, sexual assault, and stalking intervention models to respond to the needs of youth who are victims of domestic violence, dating violence, sexual assault or stalking.

(2) Types of programs. Such a program—

(A) shall provide direct counseling and advocacy for youth and young adults, who have experienced domestic violence, dating violence, sexual assault or stalking;

(B) shall include linguistically, culturally, and community relevant services for underserved populations or linkages to existing services in the community tailored to the needs of underserved populations;

(C) may include mental health services for youth and young adults who have experienced domestic violence, dating violence, sexual assault, or stalking;

(D) may include legal advocacy efforts on behalf of youth and young adults with respect to domestic violence, dating violence, sexual assault or stalking;

(E) may work with public officials and agencies to develop and implement policies, rules, and procedures in order to reduce or eliminate domestic violence, dating violence, sexual assault, and stalking against youth and young adults; and

(F) may use not more than 25 percent of the grant funds to provide additional services and resources for youth, including childcare, transportation, educational support, and respite care.

(d) Awards basis. (1) Grants to Indian tribes. Not less than 7 percent of funds appropriated under this section in any year shall be available for grants to Indian Tribes or tribal organizations.

(2) Administration. The Attorney General shall not use more than 2.5 percent of funds appropriated under this section in any year for administration, monitoring, and evaluation of grants made available under this section.

(3) Technical assistance. Not less than 5 percent of funds appropriated under this section in any year shall be available to provide technical assistance for programs funded under this section.

(e) Term. The Attorney General shall make the grants under this section for a period of 3 fiscal years.

(f) Authorization of appropriations. There is authorized to be appropriated to carry out this section, $15,000,000 for each of fiscal years 2007 through 2011. (Sept. 13, 1994, P. L. 103-322, Title IV, Subtitle L, § 41201, as added Jan. 5, 2006, P. L. 109-162, Title III, § 303, 119 Stat. 3004.)

§ 14043c-1. Access to justice for youth

(a) Purpose. It is the purpose of this section to encourage cross training and collaboration between the courts, domestic violence and sexual assault service providers, youth organizations and service providers, violence prevention programs, and law enforcement agencies, so that communities can establish and implement policies, procedures, and practices to protect and more comprehensively and effectively serve young victims of dating violence, domestic violence, sexual assault, and stalking who are between the ages of 12 and 24, and to engage, where necessary, other entities addressing the safety, health, mental health, social service, housing, and economic needs of young victims of domestic violence, dating violence, sexual assault, and stalking, including community-based supports such as schools, local health centers, community action groups, and neighborhood coalitions.

(b) Grant authority. (1) In general. The Attorney General, through the Director of the Office on Violence Against Women (in this section referred to as the "Director"), shall make grants to eligible entities to carry out the purposes of this section.

(2) Grant periods. Grants shall be awarded under this section for a period of 2 fiscal years.

(3) Eligible entities. To be eligible for a grant under this section, a grant applicant shall establish a collaboration that—

   (A) shall include a victim service provider that has a documented history of effective work concerning domestic violence, dating violence, sexual assault, or stalking and the effect that those forms of abuse have on young people;

   (B) shall include a court or law enforcement agency partner; and

   (C) may include—

(i) batterer intervention programs or sex offender treatment programs with specialized knowledge and experience working with youth offenders;

(ii) community-based youth organizations that deal specifically with the concerns and problems faced by youth, including programs that target teen parents and underserved communities;

(iii) schools or school-based programs designed to provide prevention or intervention services to youth experiencing problems;

(iv) faith-based entities that deal with the concerns and problems faced by youth;

(v) healthcare entities eligible for reimbursement under title XVIII of the Social Security Act [42 USCS §§ 1395 et seq.], including providers that target the special needs of youth;

(vi) education programs on HIV and other sexually transmitted diseases that are designed to target teens;

(vii) Indian Health Service, tribal child protective services, the Bureau of Indian Affairs, or the Federal Bureau of Investigations [Investigation]; or

(viii) law enforcement agencies of the Bureau of Indian Affairs providing tribal law enforcement.

(c) Uses of funds. An entity that receives a grant under this section shall use the funds made available through the grant for cross-training and collaborative efforts—

(1) addressing domestic violence, dating violence, sexual assault, and stalking, assessing and analyzing currently available services for youth and young adult victims, determining relevant barriers to such services in a particular locality, and developing a community protocol to address such problems collaboratively;

(2) to establish and enhance linkages and collaboration between—

(A) domestic violence and sexual assault service providers; and

(B) where applicable, law enforcement agencies, courts, Federal agencies, and other entities addressing the safety, health, mental health, social service, housing, and economic needs of young victims of abuse, including community-based supports such as schools, local health centers, community action groups, and neighborhood coalitions—

(i) to respond effectively and comprehensively to the varying needs of young victims of abuse;

(ii) to include linguistically, culturally, and community relevant services for underserved populations or linkages to existing services in the community tailored to the needs of underserved populations; and

(iii) to include where appropriate legal assistance, referral services, and parental support;

(3) to educate the staff of courts, domestic violence and sexual assault service providers, and, as applicable, the staff of law enforcement agencies, Indian child welfare agencies, youth organizations, schools, healthcare providers, and other community prevention and intervention programs to responsibly

address youth victims and perpetrators of domestic violence, dating violence, sexual assault, and stalking;

(4) to identify, assess, and respond appropriately to dating violence, domestic violence, sexual assault, or stalking against teens and young adults and meet the needs of young victims of violence; and

(5) to provide appropriate resources in juvenile court matters to respond to dating violence, domestic violence, sexual assault, and stalking and ensure necessary services dealing with the health and mental health of victims are available.

(d) Grant applications. To be eligible for a grant under this section, the entities that are members of the applicant collaboration described in subsection (b)(3) shall jointly submit an application to the Director at such time, in such manner, and containing such information as the Director may require.

(e) Priority. In awarding grants under this section, the Director shall give priority to entities that have submitted applications in partnership with community organizations and service providers that work primarily with youth, especially teens, and who have demonstrated a commitment to coalition building and cooperative problem solving in dealing with problems of dating violence, domestic violence, sexual assault, and stalking in teen populations.

(f) Distribution. In awarding grants under this section—

(1) not less than 10 percent of funds appropriated under this section in any year shall be available to Indian tribal governments to establish and maintain collaborations involving the appropriate tribal justice and social services departments or domestic violence or sexual assault service providers, the purpose of which is to provide culturally appropriate services to American Indian women or youth;

(2) the Director shall not use more than 2.5 percent of funds appropriated under this section in any year for monitoring and evaluation of grants made available under this section;

(3) the Attorney General of the United States shall not use more than 2.5 percent of funds appropriated under this section in any year for administration of grants made available under this section; and

(4) up to 8 percent of funds appropriated under this section in any year shall be available to provide technical assistance for programs funded under this section.

(g) Dissemination of information. Not later than 12 months after the end of the grant period under this section, the Director shall prepare, submit to Congress, and make widely available, including through electronic means, summaries that contain information on—

(1) the activities implemented by the recipients of the grants awarded under this section; and

(2) related initiatives undertaken by the Director to promote attention to dating violence, domestic violence, sexual assault, and stalking and their impact on young victims by—

(A) the staffs of courts;

(B) domestic violence, dating violence, sexual assault, and stalking victim service providers; and

(C) law enforcement agencies and community organizations.

(h) Authorization of appropriations. There are authorized to be appropriated to carry out this section, $5,000,000 in each of fiscal years 2007 through 2011. (Sept. 13, 1994, P. L. 103-322, Title IV, Subtitle L, § 41202, as added Jan. 5, 2006, P. L. 109-162, Title III, § 303, 119 Stat. 3005.)

HISTORY; ANCILLARY LAWS AND DIRECTIVES

Explanatory notes:

The bracketed word "Investigation" has been inserted in subsec. (b)(3)(C)(vii) to indicate the word probably intended by Congress.

§ 14043c-2. Grants for training and collaboration on the intersection between domestic violence and child maltreatment

(a) Purpose. The purpose of this section is to support efforts by child welfare agencies, domestic violence or dating violence victim services providers, courts, law enforcement, and other related professionals and community organizations to develop collaborative responses and services and provide cross-training to enhance community responses to families where there is both child maltreatment and domestic violence.

(b) Grants authorized. The Secretary of the Department of Health and Human Services (in this section referred to as the "Secretary"), through the Family and Youth Services Bureau, and in consultation with the Office on Violence Against Women, shall award grants on a competitive basis to eligible entities for the purposes and in the manner described in this section.

(c) Authorization of appropriations. There are authorized to be appropriated to carry out this section $5,000,000 for each of fiscal years 2007 through 2011. Funds appropriated under this section shall remain available until expended. Of the amounts appropriated to carry out this section for each fiscal year, the Secretary shall—

(1) use not more than 3 percent for evaluation, monitoring, site visits, grantee conferences, and other administrative costs associated with conducting activities under this section;

(2) set aside not more than 7 percent for grants to Indian tribes to develop programs addressing child maltreatment and domestic violence or dating violence that are operated by, or in partnership with, a tribal organization; and

(3) set aside up to 8 percent for technical assistance and training to be provided by organizations having demonstrated expertise in developing collaborative community and system responses to families in which there is both child maltreatment and domestic violence or dating violence, which technical assistance and training may be offered to jurisdictions in the process of developing community responses to families in which children are exposed to child maltreatment and domestic violence or dating violence, whether or not they are receiving funds under this section.

(d) Underserved populations. In awarding grants under this section, the Secretary shall consider the needs of underserved populations.

(e) Grant awards. The Secretary shall award grants under this section for periods of not more than 2 fiscal years.

(f) Uses of funds. Entities receiving grants under this section shall use amounts provided to develop collaborative responses and services and provide cross-training to enhance community responses to families where there is both child maltreatment and domestic violence or dating violence. Amounts distributed under this section may only be used for programs and activities described in subsection (g).

(g) Programs and activities. The programs and activities developed under this section shall—

(1) encourage cross training, education, service development, and collaboration among child welfare agencies, domestic violence victim service providers, and courts, law enforcement agencies, community-based programs, and other entities, in order to ensure that such entities have the capacity to and will identify, assess, and respond appropriately to—

(A) domestic violence or dating violence in homes where children are present and may be exposed to the violence;

(B) domestic violence or dating violence in child protection cases; and

(C) the needs of both the child and nonabusing parent;

(2) establish and implement policies, procedures, programs, and practices for child welfare agencies, domestic violence victim service providers, courts, law enforcement agencies, and other entities, that are consistent with the principles of protecting and increasing the immediate and long-term safety and well being of children and non-abusing parents and caretakers;

(3) increase cooperation and enhance linkages between child welfare agencies, domestic violence victim service providers, courts, law enforcement agencies, and other entities to provide more comprehensive community-based services (including health, mental health, social service, housing, and neighborhood resources) to protect and to serve both child and adult victims;

(4) identify, assess, and respond appropriately to domestic violence or dating violence in child protection cases and to child maltreatment when it co-occurs with domestic violence or dating violence;

(5) analyze and change policies, procedures, and protocols that contribute to overrepresentation of certain populations in the court and child welfare system; and

(6) provide appropriate referrals to community-based programs and resources, such as health and mental health services, shelter and housing assistance for adult and youth victims and their children, legal assistance and advocacy for adult and youth victims, assistance for parents to help their children cope with the impact of exposure to domestic violence or dating violence and child maltreatment, appropriate intervention and treatment for adult perpetrators of domestic violence or dating violence whose children are the subjects of child protection cases, programs providing support and assistance to underserved populations, and other necessary supportive services.

(h) Grantee requirements. (1) Applications. Under this section, an entity shall prepare and submit to the Secretary an application at such time, in such manner, and containing such information as the Secretary may require, consistent with the requirements described herein. The application shall—

(A) ensure that communities impacted by these systems or organizations are adequately represented in the development of the application, the programs and activities to be undertaken, and that they have a significant role in evaluating the success of the project;

(B) describe how the training and collaboration activities will enhance or ensure the safety and economic security of families where both child maltreatment and domestic violence or dating violence occurs by providing appropriate resources, protection, and support to the victimized parents of such children and to the children themselves; and

(C) outline methods and means participating entities will use to ensure that all services are provided in a developmentally, linguistically and culturally competent manner and will utilize community-based supports and resources.

(2) Eligible entities. To be eligible for a grant under this section, an entity shall be a collaboration that—

(A) shall include a State or local child welfare agency or Indian Tribe;

(B) shall include a domestic violence or dating violence victim service provider;

(C) shall include a law enforcement agency or Bureau of Indian Affairs providing tribal law enforcement;

(D) may include a court; and

(E) may include any other such agencies or private nonprofit organizations and faith-based organizations, including community-based organizations, with the capacity to provide effective help to the child and adult victims served by the collaboration.

(Sept. 13, 1994, P. L. 103-322, Title IV, Subtitle L, § 41203, as added Jan. 5, 2006, P. L. 109-162, Title III, § 303, 119 Stat. 3008.)

§ 14043c-3. Grants to combat domestic violence, dating violence, sexual assault, and stalking in middle and high schools

(a) Short title. This section may be cited as the "Supporting Teens through Education and Protection Act of 2005" or the "STEP Act".

(b) Grants authorized. The Attorney General, through the Director of the Office on Violence Against Women, is authorized to award grants to middle schools and high schools that work with domestic violence and sexual assault experts to enable the schools—

(1) to provide training to school administrators, faculty, counselors, coaches, healthcare providers, security personnel, and other staff on the needs and concerns of students who experience domestic violence, dating violence, sexual assault, or stalking, and the impact of such violence on students;

(2) to develop and implement policies in middle and high schools regarding

appropriate, safe responses to, and identification and referral procedures for, students who are experiencing or perpetrating domestic violence, dating violence, sexual assault, or stalking, including procedures for handling the requirements of court protective orders issued to or against students or school personnel, in a manner that ensures the safety of the victim and holds the perpetrator accountable;

(3) to provide support services for students and school personnel, such as a resource person who is either on-site or on-call, and who is an expert described in subsections (i)(2) and (i)(3), for the purpose of developing and strengthening effective prevention and intervention strategies for students and school personnel experiencing domestic violence, dating violence, sexual assault or stalking;

(4) to provide developmentally appropriate educational programming to students regarding domestic violence, dating violence, sexual assault, and stalking, and the impact of experiencing domestic violence, dating violence, sexual assault, and stalking on children and youth by adapting existing curricula activities to the relevant student population;

(5) to work with existing mentoring programs and develop strong mentoring programs for students, including student athletes, to help them understand and recognize violence and violent behavior, how to prevent it and how to appropriately address their feelings; and

(6) to conduct evaluations to assess the impact of programs and policies assisted under this section in order to enhance the development of the programs.

(c) Award basis. The Director shall award grants and contracts under this section on a competitive basis.

(d) Policy dissemination. The Director shall disseminate to middle and high schools any existing Department of Justice, Department of Health and Human Services, and Department of Education policy guidance and curricula regarding the prevention of domestic violence, dating violence, sexual assault, and stalking, and the impact of the violence on children and youth.

(e) Nondisclosure of confidential or private information. In order to ensure the safety of adult, youth, and minor victims of domestic violence, dating violence, sexual assault, or stalking and their families, grantees and subgrantees shall protect the confidentiality and privacy of persons receiving services. Grantees and subgrantees pursuant to this section shall not disclose any personally identifying information or individual information collected in connection with services requested, utilized, or denied through grantees' and subgrantees' programs. Grantees and subgrantees shall not reveal individual client information without the informed, written, reasonably time-limited consent of the person (or in the case of unemancipated minor, the minor and the parent or guardian, except that consent for release may not be given by the abuser of the minor or of the other parent of the minor) about whom information is sought, whether for this program or any other Tribal, Federal, State or Territorial grant program. If release of such information is compelled by statutory or court mandate, grantees and subgrantees shall make reasonable attempts to provide notice to victims affected by the disclosure of information. If such personally identifying information is or will be revealed, grantees and subgrantees shall take steps necessary to protect the privacy and safety of the persons affected by the release of the information. Grantees may share non-personally identifying data in the aggregate regarding services to their clients and non-personally identifying demographic information in order to comply with Tribal, Federal, State or Territorial reporting, evaluation, or data collection requirements. Grantees and subgrantees may share court-generated information contained in secure, governmental registries for protection order enforcement purposes.

(f) Grant term and allocation. (1) Term. The Director shall make the grants under this section for a period of 3 fiscal years.

(2) Allocation. Not more than 15 percent of the funds available to a grantee in a given year shall be used for the purposes described in subsection (b)(4), (b)(5), and (b)(6).

(g) Distribution. (1) In general. Not less than 5 percent of funds appropriated under subsection (l) in any year shall be available for grants to tribal schools, schools on tribal lands or schools whose student population is more than 25 percent Native American.

(2) Administration. The Director shall not use more than 5 percent of funds appropriated under subsection (l) in any year for administration, monitoring and evaluation of grants made available under this section.

(3) Training, technical assistance, and data collection. Not less than 5 percent of funds appropriated under subsection (l) in any year shall be available to provide training, technical assistance, and data collection for programs funded under this section.

(h) Application. To be eligible to be awarded a grant or contract under this section for any fiscal year, a middle or secondary school, in consultation with an expert as described in subsections (i)(2) and (i)(3), shall submit an application to the Director at such time and in such manner as the Director shall prescribe.

(i) Eligible entities. To be eligible to receive a grant under this section, an entity shall be a partnership that—

(1) shall include a public, charter, tribal, or nationally accredited private middle or high school, a school administered by the Department of Defense under 10 U.S.C. 2164 or 20 U.S.C. 921, a group of schools, or a school district;

(2) shall include a domestic violence victim service provider that has a history of working on domestic violence and the impact that domestic violence and dating violence have on children and youth;

(3) shall include a sexual assault victim service provider, such as a rape crisis center, program serving tribal victims of sexual assault, or coalition or other nonprofit nongovernmental organization carrying out a community-based sexual assault program, that has a history of effective work concerning sexual assault and the impact that sexual assault has on children and youth; and

(4) may include a law enforcement agency, the State, Tribal, Territorial or

local court, nonprofit nongovernmental organizations and service providers addressing sexual harassment, bullying or gang-related violence in schools, and any other such agencies or nonprofit nongovernmental organizations with the capacity to provide effective assistance to the adult, youth, and minor victims served by the partnership.

(j) Priority. In awarding grants under this section, the Director shall give priority to entities that have submitted applications in partnership with relevant courts or law enforcement agencies.

(k) Reporting and dissemination of information. (1) Reporting. Each of the entities that are members of the applicant partnership described in subsection (i), that receive a grant under this section shall jointly prepare and submit to the Director every 18 months a report detailing the activities that the entities have undertaken under the grant and such additional information as the Director shall require.

(2) Dissemination of information. Within 9 months of the completion of the first full grant cycle, the Director shall publicly disseminate, including through electronic means, model policies and procedures developed and implemented in middle and high schools by the grantees, including information on the impact the policies have had on their respective schools and communities.

(l) Authorization of appropriations. (1) In general. There is authorized to be appropriated to carry out this section, $5,000,000 for each of fiscal years 2007 through 2011.

(2) Availability. Funds appropriated under paragraph (1) shall remain available until expended.

(Sept. 13, 1994, P. L. 103-322, Title IV, Subtitle L, § 41204, as added Jan. 5, 2006, P. L. 109-162, Title III, § 303, 119 Stat. 3010; Aug. 12, 2006, P. L. 109-271, § 4(a), 120 Stat. 758.)

HISTORY; ANCILLARY LAWS AND DIRECTIVES
Amendments:
2006. Act Aug. 12, 2006, in subsec. (f)(2), substituted ''(b)(4)'' for ''(b)(4)(D)''.

STRENGTHENING AMERICA'S FAMILIES BY PREVENTING VIOLENCE AGAINST WOMEN AND CHILDREN

§ 14043d. Findings

Congress finds that—

(1) the former United States Advisory Board on Child Abuse suggests that domestic violence may be the single major precursor to child abuse and neglect fatalities in this country;

(2) studies suggest that as many as 10,000,000 children witness domestic violence every year;

(3) studies suggest that among children and teenagers, recent exposure to violence in the home was a significant factor in predicting a child's violent behavior;

(4) a study by the Nurse-Family Partnership found that children whose parents did not participate in home visitation programs that provided coaching in parenting skills, advice and support, were almost 5 times more likely to be abused in their first 2 years of life;

(5) a child's exposure to domestic violence seems to pose the greatest independent risk for being the victim of any act of partner violence as an adult;

(6) children exposed to domestic violence are more likely to believe that using violence is an effective means of getting one's needs met and managing conflict in close relationships;

(7) children exposed to abusive parenting, harsh or erratic discipline, or domestic violence are at increased risk for juvenile crime; and

(8) in a national survey of more than 6,000 American families, 50 percent of men who frequently assaulted their wives also frequently abused their children.

(Sept. 13, 1994, P. L. 103-322, Title IV, Subtitle M, § 41301, as added Jan. 5, 2006, P. L. 109-162, Title IV, § 401, 119 Stat. 3017.)

§ 14043d-1. Purpose

The purpose of this subtitle [42 USCS §§ 14043d et seq.] is to—

(1) prevent crimes involving violence against women, children, and youth;

(2) increase the resources and services available to prevent violence against women, children, and youth;

(3) reduce the impact of exposure to violence in the lives of children and youth so that the intergenerational cycle of violence is interrupted;

(4) develop and implement education and services programs to prevent children in vulnerable families from becoming victims or perpetrators of domestic violence, dating violence, sexual assault, or stalking;

(5) promote programs to ensure that children and youth receive the assistance they need to end the cycle of violence and develop mutually respectful, nonviolent relationships; and

(6) encourage collaboration among community-based organizations and governmental agencies serving children and youth, providers of health and mental health services and providers of domestic violence, dating violence, sexual assault, and stalking victim services to prevent violence against women and children.

(Sept. 13, 1994, P. L. 103-322, Title IV, Subtitle M, § 41302, as added Jan. 5, 2006, P. L. 109-162, Title IV, § 401, 119 Stat. 3018.)

§ 14043d-2. Grants to assist children and youth exposed to violence

(a) Grants authorized. (1) In general. The Attorney General, acting through the Director of the Office on Violence Against Women, and in collaboration with the Department of Health and Human Services, is authorized to award grants on a competitive basis to eligible entities for the purpose of mitigating the effects of domestic violence, dating violence, sexual assault, and stalking on children exposed to such violence, and reducing the risk of future victimization or perpetration of domestic violence, dating violence, sexual assault, and stalking.

(2) Term. The Director shall make grants under this section for a period of 2 fiscal years.

(3) Award basis. The Director shall award grants—

    (A) considering the needs of underserved populations;

    (B) awarding not less than 10 percent of such amounts to Indian tribes for the funding of tribal projects from the amounts made available under this section for a fiscal year;

    (C) awarding up to 8 percent for the funding of technical assistance programs from the amounts made available under this section for a fiscal year; and

    (D) awarding not less than 66 percent to programs described in subsection (c)(1) from the amounts made available under this section for a fiscal year.

(b) Authorization of appropriations. There is authorized to be appropriated to carry out this section $20,000,000 for each of fiscal years 2007 through 2011.

(c) Use of funds. The funds appropriated under this section shall be used for—

(1) programs that provide services for children exposed to domestic violence, dating violence, sexual assault, or stalking, which may include direct counseling, advocacy, or mentoring, and must include support for the nonabusing parent or the child's caretaker; or

(2) training, coordination, and advocacy for programs that serve children and youth (such as Head Start, child care, and after-school programs) on how to safely and confidentially identify children and families experiencing domestic violence and properly refer them to programs that can provide direct services to the family and children, and coordination with other domestic violence or other programs serving children exposed to domestic violence, dating violence, sexual assault, or stalking that can provide the training and direct services referenced in this subsection.

(d) Eligible entities. To be eligible to receive a grant under this section, an entity shall be [a]—

(1) a victim service provider, tribal nonprofit organization or community-based organization that has a documented history of effective work concerning children or youth exposed to domestic violence, dating violence, sexual assault, or stalking, including programs that provide culturally specific services, Head Start, childcare, faith-based organizations, after school programs, and health and mental health providers; or

(2) a State, territorial, or tribal, or local unit of government agency that is partnered with an organization described in paragraph (1).

(e) Grantee requirements. Under this section, an entity shall—

(1) prepare and submit to the Director an application at such time, in such manner, and containing such information as the Director may require; and

(2) at a minimum, describe in the application the policies and procedures that the entity has or will adopt to—

(A) enhance or ensure the safety and security of children who have been or are being exposed to violence and their nonabusing parent, enhance or ensure the safety and security of children and their nonabusing parent in homes already experiencing domestic violence, dating violence, sexual assault, or stalking; and

(B) ensure linguistically, culturally, and community relevant services for underserved communities.

(Sept. 13, 1994, P. L. 103-322, Title IV, Subtitle M, § 41303, as added Jan. 5, 2006, P. L. 109-162, Title IV, § 401, 119 Stat. 3018.)

HISTORY; ANCILLARY LAWS AND DIRECTIVES

Explanatory notes:
The word "a" has been enclosed in brackets in the introductory matter of subsec. (d) to indicate the probable intent of Congress to delete it.

§ 14043d-3. Development of curricula and pilot programs for home visitation projects

(a) **Grants authorized.** (1) In general. The Attorney General, acting through the Director of the Office on Violence Against Women, and in collaboration with the Department of Health and Human Services, shall award grants on a competitive basis to home visitation programs, in collaboration with victim service providers, for the purposes of developing and implementing model policies and procedures to train home visitation service providers on addressing domestic violence, dating violence, sexual assault, and stalking in families experiencing violence, or at risk of violence, to reduce the impact of that violence on children, maintain safety, improve parenting skills, and break intergenerational cycles of violence.

(2) Term. The Director shall make the grants under this section for a period of 2 fiscal years.

(3) Award basis. The Director shall—

(A) consider the needs of underserved populations;

(B) award not less than 7 percent of such amounts for the funding of tribal projects from the amounts made available under this section for a fiscal year; and

(C) award up to 8 percent for the funding of technical assistance programs from the amounts made available under this section for a fiscal year.

(b) **Authorization of appropriations.** There is authorized to be appropriated to carry out this section $7,000,000 for each of fiscal years 2007 through 2011.

(c) **Eligible entities.** To be eligible to receive a grant under this section, an entity shall be a national, Federal, State, local, territorial, or tribal—

(1) home visitation program that provides services to pregnant women and to young children and their parent or primary caregiver that are provided in the permanent or temporary residence or in other familiar surroundings of the individual or family receiving such services; or

(2) victim services organization or agency in collaboration with an organization or organizations listed in paragraph (1).

(d) Grantee requirements. Under this section, an entity shall—

(1) prepare and submit to the Director an application at such time, in such manner, and containing such information as the Director may require; and

(2) describe in the application the policies and procedures that the entity has or will adopt to—

(A) enhance or ensure the safety and security of children and their nonabusing parent in homes already experiencing domestic violence, dating violence, sexual assault, or stalking;

(B) ensure linguistically, culturally, and community relevant services for underserved communities;

(C) ensure the adequate training by domestic violence, dating violence, sexual assault or stalking victim service providers of home visitation grantee program staff to—

(i) safely screen for and/or recognize domestic violence, dating violence, sexual assault, and stalking;

(ii) understand the impact of domestic violence or sexual assault on children and protective actions taken by a nonabusing parent or caretaker in response to violence against anyone in the household; and

(iii) link new parents with existing community resources in communities where resources exist; and

(D) ensure that relevant State and local domestic violence, dating violence, sexual assault, and stalking victim service providers and coalitions are aware of the efforts of organizations receiving grants under this section, and are included as training partners, where possible.

(Sept. 13, 1994, P. L. 103-322, Title IV, Subtitle M, § 41304, as added Jan. 5, 2006, P. L. 109-162, Title IV, § 401, 119 Stat. 3020.)

§ 14043d-4. Engaging men and youth in preventing domestic violence, dating violence, sexual assault, and stalking

(a) Grants authorized. (1) In general. The Attorney General, acting through the Director of the Office on Violence Against Women, and in collaboration with the Department of Health and Human Services, shall award grants on a competitive basis to eligible entities for the purpose of developing or enhancing programs related to engaging men and youth in preventing domestic violence, dating violence, sexual assault, and stalking by helping them to develop mutually respectful, nonviolent relationships.

(2) Term. The Director shall make grants under this section for a period of 2 fiscal years.

(3) Award basis. The Director shall award grants—

(A) considering the needs of underserved populations;

(B) awarding not less than 10 percent of such amounts for the funding of Indian tribes from the amounts made available under this section for a fiscal year; and

(C) awarding up to 8 percent for the funding of technical assistance for grantees and non-grantees working in this area from the amounts made available under this section for a fiscal year.

(b) Authorization of appropriations. There is authorized to be appropriated to carry out this section $10,000,000 for each of fiscal years 2007 through 2011.

(c) Use of funds. (1) Programs. The funds appropriated under this section shall be used by eligible entities—

(A) to develop or enhance community-based programs, including gender-specific programs in accordance with applicable laws that—

(i) encourage children and youth to pursue nonviolent relationships and reduce their risk of becoming victims or perpetrators of domestic violence, dating violence, sexual assault, or stalking; and

(ii) [that] include at a minimum—

(I) information on domestic violence, dating violence, sexual assault, stalking, or child sexual abuse and how they affect children and youth; and

(II) strategies to help participants be as safe as possible; or

(B) to create public education campaigns and community organizing to encourage men and boys to work as allies with women and girls to prevent violence against women and girls conducted by entities that have experience in conducting public education campaigns that address domestic violence, dating violence, sexual assault, or stalking.

(2) Media limits. No more than 40 percent of funds received by a grantee under this section may be used to create and distribute media materials.

(d) Eligible entities. (1) Relationships. Eligible entities under subsection (c)(1)(A) are—

(A) nonprofit, nongovernmental domestic violence, dating violence, sexual assault, or stalking victim service providers or coalitions;

(B) community-based child or youth services organizations with demonstrated experience and expertise in addressing the needs and concerns of young people;

(C) a State, territorial, tribal, or unit of local governmental entity that is partnered with an organization described in subparagraph (A) or (B); or

(D) a program that provides culturally specific services.

(2) Awareness campaign. Eligible entities under subsection (c)(1)(B) are—

(A) nonprofit, nongovernmental organizations or coalitions that have a documented history of creating and administering effective public education campaigns addressing the prevention of domestic violence, dating violence, sexual assault or stalking; or

(B) a State, territorial, tribal, or unit of local governmental entity that is partnered with an organization described in subparagraph (A).

(e) Grantee requirements. Under this section, an entity shall—

(1) prepare and submit to the Director an application at such time, in such manner, and containing such information as the Director may require; and

(2) eligible entities pursuant to subsection (c)(1)(A) shall describe in the application the policies and procedures that the entity has or will adopt to—

(A) enhance or ensure the safety and security of children and youth already experiencing domestic violence, dating violence, sexual assault, or stalking in their lives;

(B) ensure linguistically, culturally, and community relevant services for underserved communities;

(C) inform participants about laws, services, and resources in the community, and make referrals as appropriate; and

(D) ensure that State and local domestic violence, dating violence, sexual assault, and stalking victim service providers and coalitions are aware of the efforts of organizations receiving grants under this section.

(Sept. 13, 1994, P. L. 103-322, Title IV, Subtitle M, § 41305, as added Jan. 5, 2006, P. L. 109-162, Title IV, § 401, 119 Stat. 3021.)

HISTORY; ANCILLARY LAWS AND DIRECTIVES

Explanatory notes:
The word "that" has been enclosed in brackets in subsec. (c)(1)(A)(ii) to indicate the probable intent of Congress to delete it.

ADDRESSING THE HOUSING NEEDS OF VICTIMS OF DOMESTIC VIOLENCE, DATING VIOLENCE, SEXUAL ASSAULT, AND STALKING

§ 14043e.   Findings

Congress finds that:

(1) There is a strong link between domestic violence and homelessness. Among cities surveyed, 44 percent identified domestic violence as a primary cause of homelessness.

(2) Ninety-two percent of homeless women have experienced severe physical or sexual abuse at some point in their lives. Of all homeless women and children, 60 percent had been abused by age 12, and 63 percent have been victims of intimate partner violence as adults.

(3) Women and families across the country are being discriminated against, denied access to, and even evicted from public and subsidized housing because of their status as victims of domestic violence.

(4) A recent survey of legal service providers around the country found that these providers have responded to almost 150 documented eviction cases in the last year alone where the tenant was evicted because of the domestic violence crimes committed against her. In addition, nearly 100 clients were denied housing because of their status as victims of domestic violence.

(5) Women who leave their abusers frequently lack adequate emergency shelter options. The lack of adequate emergency options for victims presents a serious threat to their safety and the safety of their children. Requests for emergency shelter by homeless women with children increased by 78 percent of United States cities surveyed in 2004. In the same year, 32 percent of the requests for shelter by homeless families went unmet due to the lack of available emergency shelter beds.

(6) The average stay at an emergency shelter is 60 days, while the average length of time it takes a homeless family to secure housing is 6 to 10 months.

(7) Victims of domestic violence often return to abusive partners because they cannot find long-term housing.

(8) There are not enough Federal housing rent vouchers available to accom-

modate the number of people in need of long-term housing. Some people remain on the waiting list for Federal housing rent vouchers for years, while some lists are closed.

(9) Transitional housing resources and services provide an essential continuum between emergency shelter provision and independent living. A majority of women in transitional housing programs stated that had these programs not existed, they would have likely gone back to abusive partners.

(10) Because abusers frequently manipulate finances in an effort to control their partners, victims often lack steady income, credit history, landlord references, and a current address, all of which are necessary to obtain long-term permanent housing.

(11) Victims of domestic violence in rural areas face additional barriers, challenges, and unique circumstances, such as geographical isolation, poverty, lack of public transportation systems, shortages of health care providers, under-insurance or lack of health insurance, difficulty ensuring confidentiality in small communities, and decreased access to many resources (such as advanced education, job opportunities, and adequate childcare).

(12) Congress and the Secretary of Housing and Urban Development have recognized in recent years that families experiencing domestic violence have unique needs that should be addressed by those administering the Federal housing programs.

(Sept. 13, 1994, P. L. 103-322, Title IV, Subtitle N, § 41401, as added Jan. 5, 2006, P. L. 109-162, Title VI, § 601, 119 Stat. 3030.)

§ 14043e-1. Purpose

The purpose of this subtitle [42 USCS §§ 14043e et seq.] is to reduce domestic violence, dating violence, sexual assault, and stalking, and to prevent homelessness by—

(1) protecting the safety of victims of domestic violence, dating violence, sexual assault, and stalking who reside in homeless shelters, public housing, assisted housing, tribally designated housing, or other emergency, transitional, permanent, or affordable housing, and ensuring that such victims have meaningful access to the criminal justice system without jeopardizing such housing;

(2) creating long-term housing solutions that develop communities and provide sustainable living solutions for victims of domestic violence, dating violence, sexual assault, and stalking;

(3) building collaborations among victim service providers, homeless service providers, housing providers, and housing agencies to provide appropriate services, interventions, and training to address the housing needs of victims of domestic violence, dating violence, sexual assault, and stalking; and

(4) enabling public and assisted housing agencies, tribally designated housing entities, private landlords, property management companies, and other housing providers and agencies to respond appropriately to domestic violence, dating violence, sexual assault, and stalking, while maintaining a safe environment for all housing residents.

(Sept. 13, 1994, P. L. 103-322, Title IV, Subtitle N, § 41402, as added Jan. 5, 2006, P. L. 109-162, Title VI, § 601, 119 Stat. 3031.)

§ 14043e-2. Definitions

For purposes of this subtitle [42 USCS §§ 14043e et seq.]—
  (1) the term "assisted housing" means housing assisted—
    (A) under sections [section] 213, 220, 221(d)(3), 221(d)(4), 223(e), 231, or 236 of the National Housing Act (12 U.S.C. 1715l(d)(3), (d)(4), or 1715z-1);
    (B) under section 101 of the Housing and Urban Development Act of 1965 (12 U.S.C. 1701s);
    (C) under section 202 of the Housing Act of 1959 (12 U.S.C. 1701q);
    (D) under section 811 of the Cranston-Gonzales [Cranston-Gonzalez] National Affordable Housing Act (42 U.S.C. 8013);
    (E) under title II of the Cranston-Gonzales [Cranston-Gonzalez] National Affordable Housing Act (42 U.S.C. 12701 et seq.);
    (F) under subtitle D of title VIII of the Cranston-Gonzalez National Affordable Housing Act (42 U.S.C. 12901 et seq.);
    (G) under title I of the Housing and Community Development Act of 1974 (42 U.S.C. 5301 et seq.); or
    (H) under section 8 of the United States Housing Act of 1937 (42 U.S.C. 1437f);
  (2) the term "continuum of care" means a community plan developed to organize and deliver housing and services to meet the specific needs of people who are homeless as they move to stable housing and achieve maximum self-sufficiency;
  (3) the term "low-income housing assistance voucher" means housing assistance described in section 8 of the United States Housing Act of 1937 (42 U.S.C. 1437f);
  (4) the term "public housing" means housing described in section 3(b)(1) of the United States Housing Act of 1937 (42 U.S.C. 1437a(b)(1));
  (5) the term "public housing agency" means an agency described in section 3(b)(6) of the United States Housing Act of 1937 (42 U.S.C. 1437a(b)(6));
  (6) the terms "homeless", "homeless individual", and "homeless person"—
    (A) mean an individual who lacks a fixed, regular, and adequate nighttime residence; and
    (B) includes—
      (i) an individual who—
        (I) is sharing the housing of other persons due to loss of housing, economic hardship, or a similar reason;
        (II) is living in a motel, hotel, trailer park, or campground due to the lack of alternative adequate accommodations;
        (III) is living in an emergency or transitional shelter;
        (IV) is abandoned in a hospital; or

(V) is awaiting foster care placement;

(ii) an individual who has a primary nighttime residence that is a public or private place not designed for or ordinarily used as a regular sleeping accommodation for human beings; or

(iii) migratory children (as defined in section 1309 of the Elementary and Secondary Education Act of 1965; 20 U.S.C. 6399) who qualify as homeless under this section because the children are living in circumstances described in this paragraph;

(7) the term "homeless service provider" means a nonprofit, nongovernmental homeless service provider, such as a homeless shelter, a homeless service or advocacy program, a tribal organization serving homeless individuals, or coalition or other nonprofit, nongovernmental organization carrying out a community-based homeless or housing program that has a documented history of effective work concerning homelessness;

(8) the term "tribally designated housing" means housing assistance described in the Native American Housing Assistance and Self-Determination Act of 1996 (25 U.S.C. 4101 et seq.); and

(9) the term "tribally designated housing entity" means a housing entity described in the Native American Housing Assistance and Self-Determination Act of 1996 (25 U.S.C. 4103(21)); [.]

(Sept. 13, 1994, P. L. 103-322, Title IV, Subtitle N, § 41403, as added Jan. 5, 2006, P. L. 109-162, Title VI, § 601, 119 Stat. 3031.)

HISTORY; ANCILLARY LAWS AND DIRECTIVES

Explanatory notes:

The bracketed word "section" has been inserted in para. (1)(A) to indicate the word probably intended by Congress.

In para. (1)(D) and (E), "Cranston-Gonzalez" has been inserted in brackets to indicate the spelling probably intended by Congress.

The bracketed period has been inserted at the end of para. (9) to indicate the punctuation probably intended by Congress.

§ 14043e-3. Collaborative grants to increase the long-term stability of victims

(a) **Grants authorized.** (1) In general. The Secretary of Health and Human Services, acting through the Administration for Children and Families, in partnership with the Secretary of Housing and Urban Development, shall award grants, contracts, or cooperative agreements for a period of not less than 2 years to eligible entities to develop long-term sustainability and self-sufficiency options for adult and youth victims of domestic violence, dating violence, sexual assault, and stalking who are currently homeless or at risk for becoming homeless.

(2) Amount. The Secretary of Health and Human Services shall award funds in amounts—

(A) not less than $25,000 per year; and

(B) not more than $1,000,000 per year.

(b) Eligible entities. To be eligible to receive funds under this section, an entity shall demonstrate that it is a coalition or partnership, applying jointly, that—

(1) shall include a domestic violence victim service provider;

(2) shall include—

(A) a homeless service provider;

(B) a nonprofit, nongovernmental community housing development organization or a Department of Agriculture rural housing service program; or

(C) in the absence of a homeless service provider on tribal lands or nonprofit, nongovernmental community housing development organization on tribal lands, a tribally designated housing entity or tribal housing consortium;

(3) may include a dating violence, sexual assault, or stalking victim service provider;

(4) may include housing developers, housing corporations, State housing finance agencies, other housing agencies, and associations representing landlords;

(5) may include a public housing agency or tribally designated housing entity;

(6) may include tenant organizations in public or tribally designated housing, as well as nonprofit, nongovernmental tenant organizations;

(7) may include other nonprofit, nongovernmental organizations participating in the Department of Housing and Urban Development's Continuum of Care process;

(8) may include a State, tribal, territorial, or local government or government agency; and

(9) may include any other agencies or nonprofit, nongovernmental organizations with the capacity to provide effective help to adult and youth victims of domestic violence, dating violence, sexual assault, or stalking.

(c) Application. Each eligible entity seeking funds under this section shall submit an application to the Secretary of Health and Human Services at such time, in such manner, and containing such information as the Secretary of Health and Human Services may require.

(d) Use of funds. Funds awarded to eligible entities under subsection (a) shall be used to design or replicate and implement new activities, services, and programs to increase the stability and self-sufficiency of, and create partnerships to develop long-term housing options for adult and youth victims of domestic violence, dating violence, sexual assault, or stalking, and their dependents, who are currently homeless or at risk of becoming homeless. Such activities, services, or programs—

(1) shall develop sustainable long-term living solutions in the community by—

(A) coordinating efforts and resources among the various groups and organizations comprised in the entity to access existing private and public funding;

(B) assisting with the placement of individuals and families in long-term housing; and

(C) providing services to help individuals or families find and maintain long-term housing, including financial assistance and support services;

(2) may develop partnerships with individuals, organizations, corporations, or other entities that provide capital costs for the purchase, preconstruction, construction, renovation, repair, or conversion of affordable housing units;

(3) may use funds for the administrative expenses related to the continuing operation, upkeep, maintenance, and use of housing described in paragraph (2); and

(4) may provide to the community information about housing and housing programs, and the process to locate and obtain long-term housing.

(e) Limitation. Funds provided under paragraph [subsection] (a) shall not be used for construction, modernization or renovation.

(f) Underserved populations and priorities. In awarding grants under this section, the Secretary of Health and Human Services shall—

(1) give priority to linguistically and culturally specific services;

(2) give priority to applications from entities that include a sexual assault service provider as described in subsection (b)(3); and

(3) award a minimum of 15 percent of the funds appropriated under this section in any fiscal year to tribal organizations.

(g) Definitions. For purposes of this section:

(1) Affordable housing. The term "affordable housing" means housing that complies with the conditions set forth in section 215 of the Cranston-Gonzalez National Affordable Housing Act (42 U.S.C. 12745).

(2) Long-term housing. The term "long-term housing" means housing that is sustainable, accessible, affordable, and safe for the foreseeable future and is—

(A) rented or owned by the individual;

(B) subsidized by a voucher or other program which is not time-limited and is available for as long as the individual meets the eligibility requirements for the voucher or program; or

(C) provided directly by a program, agency, or organization and is not time-limited and is available for as long as the individual meets the eligibility requirements for the program, agency, or organization.

(h) Evaluation, monitoring, administration, and technical assistance. For purposes of this section—

(1) up to 5 percent of the funds appropriated under subsection (i) for each fiscal year may be used by the Secretary of Health and Human Services for evaluation, monitoring, and administration costs under this section; and

(2) up to 8 percent of the funds appropriated under subsection (i) for each fiscal year may be used to provide technical assistance to grantees under this section.

(i) Authorization of appropriations. There are authorized to be appropriated $10,000,000 for each of fiscal years 2007 through 2011 to carry out the provisions of this section.

(Sept. 13, 1994, P. L. 103-322, Title IV, Subtitle N, § 41404, as added Jan. 5,

2006, P. L. 109-162, Title VI, § 601, 119 Stat. 3033; Aug. 12, 2006, P. L. 109-271, § 5(a), 120 Stat. 759.)

HISTORY; ANCILLARY LAWS AND DIRECTIVES

Explanatory notes:

The bracketed word "subsection" has been inserted in subsec. (e) to indicate the word probably intended by Congress.

Amendments:

2006. Act Aug. 12, 2006, in subsec. (a)(1), substituted "for Children" for "of Children"; and, in subsec. (d), redesignated para. (1) as the introductory matter of the subsection, deleted "In general." preceding "Funds", and added "Such activities, services, or programs—", redesignated paras. (2)–(5) as paras. (1)–(4), respectively, in para. (1) as redesignated, deleted "Activities, services, programs. Such activities, services, or programs described in paragraph (1)" preceding "shall develop", and, in para. (3) as redesignated, substituted "paragraph (2)" for "paragraph (3)".

§ 14043e-4. Grants to combat violence against women in public and assisted housing

(a) Purpose. It is the purpose of this section to assist eligible grantees in responding appropriately to domestic violence, dating violence, sexual assault, and stalking so that the status of being a victim of such a crime is not a reason for the denial or loss of housing. Such assistance shall be accomplished through—

(1) education and training of eligible entities;

(2) development and implementation of appropriate housing policies and practices;

(3) enhancement of collaboration with victim service providers and tenant organizations; and

(4) reduction of the number of victims of such crimes who are evicted or denied housing because of crimes and lease violations committed or directly caused by the perpetrators of such crimes.

(b) Grants authorized. (1) In general. The Attorney General, acting through the Director of the Violence Against Women Office of the Department of Justice ("Director"), and in consultation with the Secretary of Housing and Urban Development ("Secretary"), and the Secretary of Health and Human Services, acting through the Administration for Children, Youth and Families ("ACYF"), shall award grants and contracts for not less than 2 years to eligible grantees to promote the full and equal access to and use of housing by adult and youth victims of domestic violence, dating violence, sexual assault, and stalking.

(2) Amounts. Not less than 15 percent of the funds appropriated to carry out this section shall be available for grants to tribally designated housing entities.

(3) Award basis. The Attorney General shall award grants and contracts under this section on a competitive basis.

(4) Limitation. Appropriated funds may only be used for the purposes described in subsection (f).

(c) Eligible grantees. (1) In general. Eligible grantees are—

(A) public housing agencies;

(B) principally managed public housing resident management corporations, as determined by the Secretary;

(C) public housing projects owned by public housing agencies;

(D) tribally designated housing entities; and

(E) private, for-profit, and nonprofit owners or managers of assisted housing.

(2) Submission required for all grantees. To receive assistance under this section, an eligible grantee shall certify that—

(A) its policies and practices do not prohibit or limit a resident's right to summon police or other emergency assistance in response to domestic violence, dating violence, sexual assault, or stalking;

(B) programs and services are developed that give a preference in admission to adult and youth victims of such violence, consistent with local housing needs, and applicable law and the Secretary's instructions;

(C) it does not discriminate against any person—

(i) because that person is or is perceived to be, or has a family or household member who is or is perceived to be, a victim of such violence; or

(ii) because of the actions or threatened actions of the individual who the victim, as certified in subsection (e), states has committed or threatened to commit acts of such violence against the victim, or against the victim's family or household member;

(D) plans are developed that establish meaningful consultation and coordination with local victim service providers, tenant organizations, linguistically and culturally specific service providers, State domestic violence and sexual assault coalitions, and, where they exist, tribal domestic violence and sexual assault coalitions; and

(E) its policies and practices will be in compliance with those described in this paragraph within the later of 1 year or a period selected by the Attorney General in consultation with the Secretary and ACYF.

(d) Application. Each eligible entity seeking a grant under this section shall submit an application to the Attorney General at such a time, in such a manner, and containing such information as the Attorney General may require.

(e) Certification. (1) In general. A public housing agency, tribally designated housing entity, or assisted housing provider receiving funds under this section may request that an individual claiming relief under this section certify that the individual is a victim of domestic violence, dating violence, sexual assault, or stalking. The individual shall provide a copy of such certification to the public housing agency, tribally designated housing entity, or assisted housing provider within a reasonable period of time after the agency or authority requests such certification.

(2) Contents. An individual may satisfy the certification requirement of paragraph (1) by—

(A) providing the public housing agency, tribally designated housing entity, or assisted housing provider with documentation, signed by an employee, agent, or volunteer of a victim service provider, an attorney, a member of the clergy, a medical professional, or any other professional from whom the victim has sought assistance in addressing domestic violence, dating violence, sexual assault, or stalking, or the effects of abuse; or

(B) producing a Federal, State, tribal, territorial, or local police or court record.

(3) Limitation. Nothing in this subsection shall be construed to require any housing agency, assisted housing provider, tribally designated housing entity, owner, or manager to demand that an individual produce official documentation or physical proof of the individual's status as a victim of domestic violence, dating violence, sexual assault, or stalking, in order to receive any of the benefits provided in this section. A housing agency, assisted housing provider, tribally designated housing entity, owner, or manager may provide benefits to an individual based solely on the individual's statement or other corroborating evidence.

(4) Confidentiality. (A) In general. All information provided to any housing agency, assisted housing provider, tribally designated housing entity, owner, or manager pursuant to paragraph (1), including the fact that an individual is a victim of domestic violence, dating violence, sexual assault, or stalking, shall be retained in confidence by such agency, and shall neither be entered into any shared database, nor provided to any related housing agency, assisted housing provider, tribally designated housing entity, owner, or manager, except to the extent that disclosure is—

(i) requested or consented to by the individual in writing; or

(ii) otherwise required by applicable law.

(B) Notification. Public housing agencies must provide notice to tenants of their rights under this section, including their right to confidentiality and the limits thereof, and to owners and managers of their rights and obligations under this section.

(f) Use of funds. Grants and contracts awarded pursuant to subsection (a) shall provide to eligible entities personnel, training, and technical assistance to develop and implement policies, practices, and procedures, making physical improvements or changes, and developing or enhancing collaborations for the purposes of—

(1) enabling victims of domestic violence, dating violence, sexual assault, and stalking with otherwise disqualifying rental, credit, or criminal histories to be eligible to obtain housing or housing assistance, if such victims would otherwise qualify for housing or housing assistance and can provide documented evidence that demonstrates the causal connection between such violence or abuse and the victims' negative histories;

(2) permitting applicants for housing or housing assistance to provide

incomplete rental and employment histories, otherwise required as a condition of admission or assistance, if the victim believes that providing such rental and employment history would endanger the victim's or the victim children's safety;

(3) protecting victims' confidentiality, including protection of victims' personally identifying information, address, or rental history;

(4) assisting victims who need to leave a public housing, tribally designated housing, or assisted housing unit quickly to protect their safety, including those who are seeking transfer to a new public housing unit, tribally designated housing unit, or assisted housing unit, whether in the same or a different neighborhood or jurisdiction;

(5) enabling the public housing agency, tribally designated housing entity, or assisted housing provider, or the victim, to remove, consistent with applicable State law, the perpetrator of domestic violence, dating violence, sexual assault, or stalking without evicting, removing, or otherwise penalizing the victim;

(6) enabling the public housing agency, tribally designated housing entity, or assisted housing provider, when notified, to honor court orders addressing rights of access to or control of the property, including civil protection orders issued to protect the victim and issued to address the distribution or possession of property among the household members in cases where a family breaks up;

(7) developing and implementing more effective security policies, protocols, and services;

(8) allotting not more than 15 percent of funds awarded under the grant to make modest physical improvements to enhance safety;

(9) training personnel to more effectively identify and respond to victims of domestic violence, dating violence, sexual assault, and stalking; and

(10) effectively providing notice to applicants and residents of the above housing policies, practices, and procedures.

(g) Authorization of appropriations. There are authorized to be appropriated $10,000,000 for each of fiscal years 2007 through 2011 to carry out the provisions of this section.

(h) Technical assistance. Up to 12 percent of the amount appropriated under subsection (g) for each fiscal year shall be used by the Attorney General for technical assistance costs under this section.

(Sept. 13, 1994, P. L. 103-322, Title IV, Subtitle N, § 41405, as added Jan. 5, 2006, P. L. 109-162, Title VI, § 601, 119 Stat. 3035.)

NATIONAL RESOURCE CENTER

§ 14043f. Grant for national resource center on workplace responses to assist victims of domestic and sexual violence

(a) Authority. The Attorney General, acting through the Director of the Office on Violence Against Women, may award a grant to an eligible nonprofit nongovernmental entity or tribal organization, in order to provide for the establishment and operation of a national resource center on workplace responses to assist victims of domestic and sexual violence. The resource center shall provide information and assistance to employers and labor organizations to aid in their efforts to develop and implement responses to such violence.

(b) Applications. To be eligible to receive a grant under this section, an entity or organization shall submit an application to the Attorney General at such time, in such manner, and containing such information as the Attorney General may require, including—

(1) information that demonstrates that the entity or organization has nationally recognized expertise in the area of domestic or sexual violence;

(2) a plan to maximize, to the extent practicable, outreach to employers (including private companies and public entities such as public institutions of higher education and State and local governments) and labor organizations described in subsection (a) concerning developing and implementing workplace responses to assist victims of domestic or sexual violence; and

(3) a plan for developing materials and training for materials for employers that address the needs of employees in cases of domestic violence, dating violence, sexual assault, and stalking impacting the workplace, including the needs of underserved communities.

(c) Use of grant amount. (1) In general. An entity or organization that receives a grant under this section may use the funds made available through the grant for staff salaries, travel expenses, equipment, printing, and other reasonable expenses necessary to develop, maintain, and disseminate to employers and labor organizations described in subsection (a), information and assistance concerning workplace responses to assist victims of domestic or sexual violence.

(2) Responses. Responses referred to in paragraph (1) may include—

(A) providing training to promote a better understanding of workplace assistance to victims of domestic or sexual violence;

(B) providing conferences and other educational opportunities; and

(C) developing protocols and model workplace policies.

(d) Liability. The compliance or noncompliance of any employer or labor organization with any protocol or policy developed by an entity or organization under this section shall not serve as a basis for liability in tort, express or implied contract, or by any other means. No protocol or policy developed by an entity or organization under this section shall be referenced or enforced as a workplace safety standard by any Federal, State, or other governmental agency.

(e) Authorization of appropriations. There is authorized to be appropriated to carry out this section $1,000,000 for each of fiscal years 2007 through 2011.

(f) Availability of grant funds. Funds appropriated under this section shall remain available until expended.
(Sept. 13, 1994, P. L. 103-322, Title IV, Subtitle O, § 41501, as added Jan. 5, 2006, P. L. 109-162, Title VII, § 701, 119 Stat. 3052.)

SEXUAL ASSAULT SERVICES

§ 14043g.   Sexual assault services program

(a) Purposes. The purposes of this section are—

(1) to assist States, Indian tribes, and territories in providing intervention, advocacy, accompaniment, support services, and related assistance for—

(A) adult, youth, and child victims of sexual assault;

(B) family and household members of such victims; and

(C) those collaterally affected by the victimization, except for the perpetrator of such victimization; and

(2) to provide for technical assistance and training relating to sexual assault to—

(A) Federal, State, tribal, territorial and local governments, law enforcement agencies, and courts;

(B) professionals working in legal, social service, and health care settings;

(C) nonprofit organizations;

(D) faith-based organizations; and

(E) other individuals and organizations seeking such assistance.

(b) Grants to States and territories. (1) Grants authorized. The Attorney General shall award grants to States and territories to support the establishment, maintenance, and expansion of rape crisis centers and other programs and projects to assist those victimized by sexual assault.

(2) Allocation and use of funds. (A) Administrative costs. Not more than 5 percent of the grant funds received by a State or territory governmental agency under this subsection for any fiscal year may be used for administrative costs.

(B) Grant funds. Any funds received by a State or territory under this subsection that are not used for administrative costs shall be used to provide grants to rape crisis centers and other nonprofit, nongovernmental organizations for programs and activities within such State or territory that provide direct intervention and related assistance.

(C) Intervention and related assistance. Intervention and related assistance under subparagraph (B) may include—

(i) 24-hour hotline services providing crisis intervention services and referral;

(ii) accompaniment and advocacy through medical, criminal justice, and social support systems, including medical facilities, police, and court proceedings;

(iii) crisis intervention, short-term individual and group support services, and comprehensive service coordination and supervision to assist sexual assault victims and family or household members;

(iv) information and referral to assist the sexual assault victim and family or household members;

(v) community-based, linguistically and culturally specific services and support mechanisms, including outreach activities for underserved communities; and

(vi) the development and distribution of materials on issues related to the services described in clauses (i) through (v).

(3) Application. (A) In general. Each eligible entity desiring a grant under this subsection shall submit an application to the Attorney General at such time and in such manner as the Attorney General may reasonably require.

 (B) Contents. Each application submitted under subparagraph (A) shall—

  (i) set forth procedures designed to ensure meaningful involvement of the State or territorial sexual assault coalition and representatives from underserved communities in the development of the application and the implementation of the plans;

  (ii) set forth procedures designed to ensure an equitable distribution of grants and grant funds within the State or territory and between urban and rural areas within such State or territory;

  (iii) identify the State or territorial agency that is responsible for the administration of programs and activities; and

  (iv) meet other such requirements as the Attorney General reasonably determines are necessary to carry out the purposes and provisions of this section.

(4) Minimum amount. The Attorney General shall allocate to each State not less than 1.50 percent of the total amount appropriated in a fiscal year for grants under this section, except that the United States Virgin Islands, American Samoa, Guam, the District of Columbia, Puerto Rico, and the Commonwealth of the Northern Mariana Islands shall each be allocated 0.125 percent of the total appropriations. The remaining funds shall be allotted to each State and each territory in an amount that bears the same ratio to such remaining funds as the population of such State and such territory bears to the population of all the States and the territories. The District of Columbia shall be treated as a territory for purposes of calculating its allocation under the preceding formula.

(c) **Grants for culturally specific programs addressing sexual assault.** (1) Grants authorized. The Attorney General shall award grants to eligible entities to support the establishment, maintenance, and expansion of culturally specific intervention and related assistance for victims of sexual assault.

(2) Eligible entities. To be eligible to receive a grant under this section, an entity shall—

 (A) be a private nonprofit organization that focuses primarily on culturally specific communities;

 (B) must have documented organizational experience in the area of sexual assault intervention or have entered into a partnership with an organization having such expertise;

 (C) have expertise in the development of community-based, linguistically and culturally specific outreach and intervention services relevant for the specific communities to whom assistance would be provided or have the capacity to link to existing services in the community tailored to the needs of culturally specific populations; and

 (D) have an advisory board or steering committee and staffing which is reflective of the targeted culturally specific community.

(3) Award basis. The Attorney General shall award grants under this section on a competitive basis.

(4) Distribution. (A) The Attorney General shall not use more than 2.5 percent of funds appropriated under this subsection in any year for administration, monitoring, and evaluation of grants made available under this subsection.

(B) Up to 5 percent of funds appropriated under this subsection in any year shall be available for technical assistance by a national, nonprofit, nongovernmental organization or organizations whose primary focus and expertise is in addressing sexual assault within underserved culturally specific populations.

(5) Term. The Attorney General shall make grants under this section for a period of no less than 2 fiscal years.

(6) Reporting. Each entity receiving a grant under this subsection shall submit a report to the Attorney General that describes the activities carried out with such grant funds.

(d) **Grants to State, territorial, and tribal sexual assault coalitions.** (1) Grants authorized. (A) In general. The Attorney General shall award grants to State, territorial, and tribal sexual assault coalitions to assist in supporting the establishment, maintenance, and expansion of such coalitions.

(B) Minimum amount. Not less than 10 percent of the total amount appropriated to carry out this section shall be used for grants under subparagraph (A).

(C) Eligible applicants. Each of the State, territorial, and tribal sexual assault coalitions.

(2) Use of funds. Grant funds received under this subsection may be used to—

(A) work with local sexual assault programs and other providers of direct services to encourage appropriate responses to sexual assault within the State, territory, or tribe;

(B) work with judicial and law enforcement agencies to encourage appropriate responses to sexual assault cases;

(C) work with courts, child protective services agencies, and children's advocates to develop appropriate responses to child custody and visitation issues when sexual assault has been determined to be a factor;

(D) design and conduct public education campaigns;

(E) plan and monitor the distribution of grants and grant funds to their State, territory, or tribe; or

(F) collaborate with and inform Federal, State, or local public officials and agencies to develop and implement policies to reduce or eliminate sexual assault.

(3) Allocation and use of funds. From amounts appropriated for grants under this subsection for each fiscal year—

(A) not less than 10 percent of the funds shall be available for grants to tribal sexual assault coalitions; and

(B) the remaining funds shall be available for grants to State and territorial coalitions, and the Attorney General shall allocate an amount equal to $1/56$ of the amounts so appropriated to each of those State and territorial coalitions.

(4) Application. Each eligible entity desiring a grant under this subsection shall submit an application to the Attorney General at such time, in such manner, and containing such information as the Attorney General determines to be essential to carry out the purposes of this section.

(5) First-time applicants. No entity shall be prohibited from submitting an application under this subsection during any fiscal year for which funds are available under this subsection because such entity has not previously applied or received funding under this subsection.

(e) **Grants to tribes.** (1) Grants authorized. The Attorney General may award grants to Indian tribes, tribal organizations, and nonprofit tribal organizations for the operation of sexual assault programs or projects in Indian tribal lands and Alaska Native villages to support the establishment, maintenance, and expansion of programs and projects to assist those victimized by sexual assault.

(2) Allocation and use of funds. (A) Administrative costs. Not more than 5 percent of the grant funds received by an Indian tribe, tribal organization, and nonprofit tribal organization under this subsection for any fiscal year may be used for administrative costs.

(B) Grant funds. Any funds received under this subsection that are not used for administrative costs shall be used to provide grants to tribal organizations and nonprofit tribal organizations for programs and activities within Indian country and Alaskan native villages that provide direct intervention and related assistance.

(f) **Authorization of appropriations.** (1) In general. There are authorized to be appropriated $50,000,000 to remain available until expended for each of the fiscal years 2007 through 2011 to carry out the provisions of this section.

(2) Allocations. Of the total amounts appropriated for each fiscal year to carry out this section—

(A) not more than 2.5 percent shall be used by the Attorney General for evaluation, monitoring, and other administrative costs under this section;

(B) not more than 2.5 percent shall be used for the provision of technical assistance to grantees and subgrantees under this section;

(C) not less than 65 percent shall be used for grants to States and territories under subsection (b);

(D) not less than 10 percent shall be used for making grants to State, territorial, and tribal sexual assault coalitions under subsection (d);

(E) not less than 10 percent shall be used for grants to tribes under subsection (e); and

(F) not less than 10 percent shall be used for grants for culturally specific programs addressing sexual assault under subsection (c).

(Sept. 13, 1994, P. L. 103-322, Title IV, Subtitle P, § 41601, as added Aug. 12, 2006, P. L. 109-271, § 3(b), 120 Stat. 754.)

COMBATTING DOMESTIC TRAFFICKING IN PERSONS

§ 14044. Prevention of domestic trafficking in persons

(a) Program to reduce trafficking in persons and demand for commercial sex acts in the United States. (1) Comprehensive research and statistical review and analysis of incidents of trafficking in persons and commercial sex acts. (A) In general. The Attorney General shall use available data from State and local authorities as well as research data to carry out a biennial comprehensive research and statistical review and analysis of severe forms of trafficking in persons, and a biennial comprehensive research and statistical review and analysis of sex trafficking and unlawful commercial sex acts in the United States, and shall submit to Congress separate biennial reports on the findings.

(B) Contents. The research and statistical review and analysis under this paragraph shall consist of two separate studies, utilizing the same statistical data where appropriate, as follows:

(i) The first study shall address severe forms of trafficking in persons in the United States and shall include, but need not be limited to—

(I) the estimated number and demographic characteristics of persons engaged in acts of severe forms of trafficking in persons; and

(II) the number of investigations, arrests, prosecutions, and incarcerations of persons engaged in acts of severe forms of trafficking in persons by States and their political subdivisions.

(ii) The second study shall address sex trafficking and unlawful commercial sex acts in the United States and shall include, but need not be limited to—

(I) the estimated number and demographic characteristics of persons engaged in sex trafficking and commercial sex acts, including purchasers of commercial sex acts;

(II) the estimated value in dollars of the commercial sex economy, including the estimated average annual personal income derived from acts of sex trafficking;

(III) the number of investigations, arrests, prosecutions, and incarcerations of persons engaged in sex trafficking and unlawful commercial sex acts, including purchasers of commercial sex acts, by States and their political subdivisions; and

(IV) a description of the differences in the enforcement of laws relating to unlawful commercial sex acts across the United States.

(2) Trafficking conference. (A) In general. The Attorney General, in consultation and cooperation with the Secretary of Health and Human Services, shall conduct an annual conference in each of the fiscal years 2006, 2007, and 2008, and thereafter conduct a biennial conference, addressing severe forms of trafficking in persons and commercial sex acts that occur, in whole or in part, within the territorial jurisdiction of the United States. At each such conference, the Attorney General, or his designee, shall—

(i) announce and evaluate the findings contained in the research and statistical reviews carried out under paragraph (1);

(ii) disseminate best methods and practices for enforcement of laws prohibiting acts of severe forms of trafficking in persons and other laws related to acts of trafficking in persons, including, but not limited to, best methods and practices for training State and local law enforcement personnel on the enforcement of such laws;

(iii) disseminate best methods and practices for training State and local law enforcement personnel on the enforcement of laws prohibiting sex trafficking and commercial sex acts, including, but not limited to, best methods for investigating and prosecuting exploiters and persons who solicit or purchase an unlawful commercial sex act; and

(iv) disseminate best methods and practices for training State and local law enforcement personnel on collaborating with social service providers and relevant nongovernmental organizations and establishing trust of persons subjected to commercial sex acts or severe forms of trafficking in persons.

(B) Participation. Each annual conference conducted under this paragraph shall involve the participation of persons with expertise or professional responsibilities with relevance to trafficking in persons, including, but not limited to—

(i) Federal Government officials, including law enforcement and prosecutorial officials;

(ii) State and local government officials, including law enforcement and prosecutorial officials;

(iii) persons who have been subjected to severe forms of trafficking in persons or commercial sex acts;

(iv) medical personnel;

(v) social service providers and relevant nongovernmental organizations; and

(vi) academic experts.

(C) Reports. The Attorney General and the Secretary of Health and Human Services shall prepare and post on the respective Internet Web sites of the Department of Justice and the Department of Health and Human Services reports on the findings and best practices identified and disseminated at the conference described in this paragraph.

(b) [Omitted]

(c) **Authorization of appropriations.** There are authorized to be appropriated—

(1) $1,500,000 for each of the fiscal years 2008 through 2011 to carry out the activities described in subsection (a)(1)(B)(i) and $1,500,000 for each of the fiscal years 2008 through 2011 to carry out the activities described in subsection (a)(1)(B)(ii); and

(2) $1,000,000 for each of the fiscal years 2008 through 2011 to carry out the activities described in subsection (a)(2).

(Jan. 10, 2006, P. L. 109-164, Title II, § 201, 119 Stat. 3567; Dec. 23, 2008, P. L. 110-457, Title III, § 302(2), 122 Stat. 5087.)

HISTORY; ANCILLARY LAWS AND DIRECTIVES

Explanatory notes:
Subsec. (b) of this section, which has been omitted, amended 22 USCS § 7104(g).
This section was enacted as part of Act Jan. 10, 2006, P. L. 109-164, and not as part of Act Sept. 13, 1994, P. L. 103-322, which generally comprises this chapter.

Amendments:
2008. Act Dec. 23, 2008, in subsec. (c), in para. (1), substituted "$1,500,000 for each of the fiscal years 2008 through 2011" for "$2,500,000 for each of the fiscal years 2006 and 2007" in two places, and in para. (2), substituted "2008 through 2011" for "2006 and 2007".

Other provisions:
Coordination of Federal agencies. Act July 29, 2010, P. L. 111-211, Title II, Subtitle F, § 264, 124 Stat. 2300, provides: "Any report of the Secretary of Health and Human Services to Congress on the development of Indian victim services and victim advocate training programs shall include any recommendations that the Secretary determines to be necessary to prevent the sex trafficking of Indian women.".

RESEARCH GUIDE

Law Review Articles:
Chuang. Rescuing Trafficking From Ideological Capture: Prostitution Reform and Anti-Trafficking Law and Policy. 158 U Pa L Rev 1655, 2010.
Hughes. Combating Sex Trafficking: a Perpetrator-Focused Approach. 6 U St Thomas LJ 28, Fall, 2008.

§ 14044a.   Establishment of grant program to develop, expand, and strengthen assistance programs for certain persons subject to trafficking

(a) **Grant program.** The Secretary of Health and Human Services may make grants to States, Indian tribes, units of local government, and nonprofit, nongovernmental victims' service organizations to establish, develop, expand, and strengthen assistance programs for United States citizens or aliens admitted for permanent residence who are the subject of sex trafficking or severe forms of trafficking in persons that occurs, in whole or in part, within the territorial jurisdiction of the United States.

(b) **Selection factor.** In selecting among applicants for grants under subsection (a), the Secretary shall give priority to applicants with experience in the delivery of services to persons who have been subjected to sexual abuse or commercial sexual exploitation and to applicants who would employ survivors of sexual abuse or commercial sexual exploitation as a part of their proposed project.

(c) **Limitation on Federal share.** The Federal share of a grant made under this section may not exceed 75 percent of the total costs of the projects described in the application submitted.

(d) **Authorization of appropriations.** There are authorized to be appropriated

$8,000,000 for each of the fiscal years 2008 through 2011 to carry out the activities described in this section.

(Jan. 10, 2006, P. L. 109-164, Title II, § 202, 119 Stat. 3569; Dec. 23, 2008, P. L. 110-457, Title III, § 302(3), 122 Stat. 5087.)

HISTORY; ANCILLARY LAWS AND DIRECTIVES

Explanatory notes:

This section was enacted as part of Act Jan. 10, 2006, P. L. 109-164, and not as part of Act Sept. 13, 1994, P. L. 103-322, which generally comprises this chapter.

Amendments:

2008. Act Dec. 23, 2008, in subsec. (d), substituted "$8,000,000 for each of the fiscal years 2008 through 2011" for "$10,000,000 for each of the fiscal years 2006 and 2007".

CROSS REFERENCES

This section is referred to in 22 USCS § 7103.

§ 14044b.   Protection of juvenile victims of trafficking in persons

(a) Establishment of pilot program. Not later than 180 days after the date of the enactment of this Act [enacted Jan. 10, 2006], the Secretary of Health and Human Services shall establish and carry out a pilot program to establish residential treatment facilities in the United States for juveniles subjected to trafficking.

(b) Purposes. The purposes of the pilot program established pursuant to subsection (a) are to—

(1) provide benefits and services to juveniles subjected to trafficking, including shelter, psychological counseling, and assistance in developing independent living skills;

(2) assess the benefits of providing residential treatment facilities for juveniles subjected to trafficking, as well as the most efficient and cost-effective means of providing such facilities; and

(3) assess the need for and feasibility of establishing additional residential treatment facilities for juveniles subjected to trafficking.

(c) Selection of sites. The Secretary of Health and Human Services shall select three sites at which to operate the pilot program established pursuant to subsection (a).

(d) Form of assistance. In order to carry out the responsibilities of this section, the Secretary of Health and Human Services shall enter into contracts with, or make grants to, organizations that—

(1) have relevant expertise in the delivery of services to juveniles who have been subjected to sexual abuse or commercial sexual exploitation; or

(2) have entered into partnerships with organizations that have expertise as described in paragraph (1) for the purpose of implementing the contracts or grants.

(e) Report. Not later than one year after the date on which the first pilot program is established pursuant to subsection (a), the Secretary of Health and Human Services shall submit to Congress a report on the implementation of this section.

(f) Definition. In this section, the term "juvenile subjected to trafficking" means a United States citizen, or alien admitted for permanent residence, who is the subject of sex trafficking or severe forms of trafficking in persons that occurs, in whole or in part, within the territorial jurisdiction of the United States and who has not attained 18 years of age at the time the person is identified as having been the subject of sex trafficking or severe forms of trafficking in persons.

(g) Authorization of appropriations. There are authorized to be appropriated to the Secretary of Health and Human Services to carry out this section $5,000,000 for each of the fiscal years 2008 through 2011.

(Jan. 10, 2006, P. L. 109-164, Title II, § 203, 119 Stat. 3570; Dec. 23, 2008, P. L. 110-457, Title III, § 302(4), 122 Stat. 5087.)

HISTORY; ANCILLARY LAWS AND DIRECTIVES

Explanatory notes:
This section was enacted as part of Act Jan. 10, 2006, P. L. 109-164, and not as part of Act Sept. 13, 1994, P. L. 103-322, which generally comprises this chapter.

Amendments:
2008. Act Dec. 23, 2008, in subsec. (g), substituted "2008 through 2011" for "2006 and 2007".

§ 14044c. Enhancing State and local efforts to combat trafficking in persons

(a) Establishment of grant program for law enforcement. (1) In general. The Attorney General may make grants to States and local law enforcement agencies to establish, develop, expand, or strengthen programs—

(A) to investigate and prosecute acts of severe forms of trafficking in persons, and related offenses, which involve United States citizens, or aliens admitted for permanent residence, and that occur, in whole or in part, within the territorial jurisdiction of the United States;

(B) to investigate and prosecute persons who engage in the purchase of commercial sex acts;

(C) to educate persons charged with, or convicted of, purchasing or attempting to purchase commercial sex acts; and

(D) to educate and train law enforcement personnel in how to establish trust of persons subjected to trafficking and encourage cooperation with prosecution efforts.

(2) Definition. In this subsection, the term "related offenses" includes violations of tax laws, transacting in illegally derived proceeds, money laundering, racketeering, and other violations of criminal laws committed in connection with an act of sex trafficking or a severe form of trafficking in persons.

(b) Multi-disciplinary approach required. Grants under subsection (a) may be made only for programs in which the State or local law enforcement agency works collaboratively with social service providers and relevant nongovernmental organizations, including organizations with experience in the delivery of services to persons who are the subject of trafficking in persons.

(c) Limitation on Federal share. The Federal share of a grant made under this section may not exceed 75 percent of the total costs of the projects described in the application submitted.

(d) Authorization of appropriations. There are authorized to be appropriated to the Attorney General to carry out this section $20,000,000 for each of the fiscal years 2008 through 2011.
(Jan. 10, 2006, P. L. 109-164, Title II, § 204, 119 Stat. 3571; Dec. 23, 2008, P. L. 110-457, Title III, § 302(5), 122 Stat. 5087.)

HISTORY; ANCILLARY LAWS AND DIRECTIVES

Explanatory notes:
This section was enacted as part of Act Jan. 10, 2006, P. L. 109-164, and not as part of Act Sept. 13, 1994, P. L. 103-322, which generally comprises this chapter.

Amendments:
2008. Act Dec. 23, 2008, in subsec. (d), substituted "$20,000,000 for each of the fiscal years 2008 through 2011" for "$25,000,000 for each of the fiscal years 2006 and 2007".

CROSS REFERENCES
This section is referred to in 22 USCS § 7103.

§ 14044d.   Senior Policy Operating Group

Each Federal department or agency involved in grant activities related to combatting trafficking or providing services to persons subjected to trafficking inside the United States shall apprise the Senior Policy Operating Group established by section 105(f) of the Victims of Trafficking and Violence Protection Act of 2000 (22 U.S.C. 7103(f)), under the procedures established by the Senior Policy Operating Group, of such activities of the department or agency to ensure that the activities are consistent with the purposes of the Trafficking Victims Protection Act of 2000 (22 U.S.C. 7101 et seq.).
(Jan. 10, 2006, P. L. 109-164, Title II, § 206, 119 Stat. 3571; Dec. 23, 2008, P. L. 110-457, Title II, Subtitle D, § 233, 122 Stat. 5074.)

HISTORY; ANCILLARY LAWS AND DIRECTIVES

Explanatory notes:
This section was enacted as part of Act Jan. 10, 2006, P. L. 109-164, and not as part of Act Sept. 13, 1994, P. L. 103-322, which generally comprises this chapter.

Amendments:
2008. Act Dec. 23, 2008, deleted ", as the department or agency determines appropriate," preceding "apprise".

§ 14044e. Definitions

In this title:

(1) Severe forms of trafficking in persons. The term "severe forms of trafficking in persons" has the meaning given the term in section 103(8) of the Trafficking Victims Protection Act of 2000 (22 U.S.C. 7102(8)).

(2) Sex trafficking. The term "sex trafficking" has the meaning given the term in section 103(9) of the Trafficking Victims Protection Act of 2000 (22 U.S.C. 7102(9)).

(3) Commercial sex act. The term "commercial sex act" has the meaning given the term in section 103(3) of the Trafficking Victims Protection Act of 2000 (22 U.S.C. 7102(3)).

(Jan. 10, 2006, P. L. 109-164, Title II, § 207, 119 Stat. 3572.)

HISTORY; ANCILLARY LAWS AND DIRECTIVES

References in text:

"This title", referred to in this section, is Title II of Act Jan. 10, 2006, P. L. 109-164, which appears as 42 USCS §§ 14044 et seq., except for § 205 of such Title, which amended 22 USCS § 7103(d)(7).

Explanatory notes:

This section was enacted as part of Act Jan. 10, 2006, P. L. 109-164, and not as part of Act Sept. 13, 1994, P. L. 103-322, which generally comprises this chapter.

§ 14044f. Grants for law enforcement training programs

(a) **Definitions.** In this section:

(1) Act of trafficking. The term "act of trafficking" means an act or practice described in paragraph (8) of section 103 of the Trafficking Victims Protection Act of 2000 (22 U.S.C. 7102).

(2) Eligible entity. The term "eligible entity" means a State or a local government.

(3) State. The term "State" means any State of the United States, the District of Columbia, the Commonwealth of Puerto Rico, Guam, the United States Virgin Islands, the Commonwealth of the Northern Mariana Islands, American Samoa, and any other territory or possession of the United States.

(4) Victim of trafficking. The term "victim of trafficking" means a person subjected to an act of trafficking.

(b) **Grants authorized.** The Attorney General may award grants to eligible entities to provide training to State and local law enforcement personnel to identify and protect victims of trafficking.

(c) **Use of funds.** A grant awarded under this section shall be used to—

(1) train law enforcement personnel to identify and protect victims of trafficking, including training such personnel to utilize Federal, State, or local resources to assist victims of trafficking;

(2) train law enforcement or State or local prosecutors to identify, investigate, or prosecute acts of trafficking; or

(3) train law enforcement or State or local prosecutors to utilize laws that prohibit acts of trafficking and to assist in the development of State and local laws to prohibit acts of trafficking.

(d) Restrictions. (1) Administrative expenses. An eligible entity that receives a grant under this section may use not more than 5 percent of the total amount of such grant for administrative expenses.

(2) Nonexclusivity. Nothing in this section may be construed to restrict the ability of an eligible entity to apply for or obtain funding from any other source to carry out the training described in subsection (c).

(e) Authorization of appropriations. There are authorized to be appropriated $10,000,000 for each of the fiscal years 2007 through 2011 to carry out the provisions of this section.
(Jan. 5, 2006, P. L. 109-162, Title I, § 111, 119 Stat. 2984.)

HISTORY; ANCILLARY LAWS AND DIRECTIVES

Explanatory notes:
This section was enacted as part of Act Jan. 5, 2006, P. L. 109-162, and not as part of Act Sept. 13, 1994, P. L. 103-322, which generally comprises this chapter.

MISCELLANEOUS AUTHORITIES

§ 14045. Grants for outreach to underserved populations

(a) Grants authorized. (1) In general. From amounts made available to carry out this section, the Attorney General, acting through the Director of the Office on Violence Against Women, shall award grants to eligible entities described in subsection (b) to carry out local, regional, or national public information campaigns focused on addressing adult, youth, or minor domestic violence, dating violence, sexual assault, stalking, or trafficking within tribal and underserved populations and immigrant communities, including information on services available to victims and ways to prevent or reduce domestic violence, dating violence, sexual assault, and stalking.

(2) Term. The Attorney General shall award grants under this section for a period of 1 fiscal year.

(b) Eligible entities. Eligible entities under this section are—
(1) nonprofit, nongovernmental organizations or coalitions that represent the targeted tribal and underserved populations or immigrant community that—
(A) have a documented history of creating and administering effective public awareness campaigns addressing domestic violence, dating violence, sexual assault, and stalking; or
(B) work in partnership with an organization that has a documented history of creating and administering effective public awareness campaigns addressing domestic violence, dating violence, sexual assault, and stalking; or
(2) a governmental entity that demonstrates a partnership with organizations described in paragraph (1).

(c) **Allocation of funds.** Of the amounts appropriated for grants under this section—

(1) not more than 20 percent shall be used for national model campaign materials targeted to specific tribal and underserved populations or immigrant community, including American Indian tribes and Alaskan native villages for the purposes of research, testing, message development, and preparation of materials; and

(2) the balance shall be used for not less than 10 State, regional, territorial, tribal, or local campaigns targeting specific communities with information and materials developed through the national campaign or, if appropriate, new materials to reach an underserved population or a particularly isolated community.

(d) **Use of funds.** Funds appropriated under this section shall be used to conduct a public information campaign and build the capacity and develop leadership of racial, ethnic populations, or immigrant community members to address domestic violence, dating violence, sexual assault, and stalking.

(e) **Application.** An eligible entity desiring a grant under this section shall submit an application to the Director of the Office on Violence Against Women at such time, in such form, and in such manner as the Director may prescribe.

(f) **Criteria.** In awarding grants under this section, the Attorney General shall ensure—

(1) reasonable distribution among eligible grantees representing various underserved and immigrant communities;

(2) reasonable distribution among State, regional, territorial, tribal, and local campaigns; and

(3) that not more than 8 percent of the total amount appropriated under this section for each fiscal year is set aside for training, technical assistance, and data collection.

(g) **Reports.** Each eligible entity receiving a grant under this section shall submit to the Director of the Office of Violence Against Women a report that describes the activities carried out with grant funds.

(h) **Authorization of appropriations.** There are authorized to be appropriated to carry out this section $2,000,000 for each of fiscal years 2007 through 2011.

(i) **Definitions and grant conditions.** In this section the definitions and grant conditions in section 40002 of the Violence Against Women Act of 1994 [42 USCS § 13925] shall apply.

(Jan. 5, 2006, P. L. 109-162, Title I, § 120, 119 Stat. 2990; Aug. 12, 2006, P. L. 109-271, §§ 1(c)(2), 2(h), 120 Stat. 750, 752.)

HISTORY; ANCILLARY LAWS AND DIRECTIVES

Explanatory notes:

This section was enacted as part of Act Jan. 5, 2006, P. L. 109-162, and not as part of Act Sept. 13, 1994, P. L. 103-322, which generally comprises this chapter.

Amendments:

2006. Act Aug. 12, 2006, in subsec. (g), deleted ", every 18 months," preceding "a report"; and added subsec. (i).

§ 14045a. Enhancing culturally and linguistically specific services for victims of domestic violence, dating violence, sexual assault, and stalking

(a) **Establishment.** (1) In general. Of the amounts appropriated under certain grant programs identified in paragraph (a)(2) of this Section, the Attorney General, through the Director of the Violence Against Women Office (referred to in this section as the "Director"), shall take 5 percent of such appropriated amounts and combine them to establish a new grant program to enhance culturally and linguistically specific services for victims of domestic violence, dating violence, sexual assault, and stalking. Grants made under this new program shall be administered by the Director. The requirements of the grant programs identified in paragraph (2) shall not apply to this new grant program.

(2) Programs covered. The programs covered by paragraph (1) are the programs carried out under the following provisions:

   (A) Section 2101 [of the Omnibus Crime Control and Safe Streets Act of 1968] (42 U.S.C. 3796hh), Grants to Encourage Arrest Policies.

   (B) Section 1201 of the Violence Against Women Act of 2000 (42 U.S.C. 3796gg-6), Legal Assistance for Victims.

   (C) Section 40295 of the Violence Against Women Act of 1994 (42 U.S.C. 13971), Rural Domestic Violence and Child Abuser Enforcement Assistance.

   (D) Section ___ of the Violence Against Women Act of 1994 (42 U.S.C. ___), Older Battered Women.

   (E) Section ___ of the Violence Against Women Act of 2000 (42 U.S.C. ___), Disabled Women Program.

(b) **Purpose of program and grants.** (1) General program purpose. The purpose of the program required by this section is to promote:

   (A) The maintenance and replication of existing successful services in domestic violence, dating violence, sexual assault, and stalking community-based programs providing culturally and linguistically specific services and other resources.

   (B) The development of innovative culturally and linguistically specific strategies and projects to enhance access to services and resources for victims of domestic violence, dating violence, sexual assault, and stalking who face obstacles to using more traditional services and resources.

(2) Purposes for which grants may be used. The Director shall make grants to community-based programs for the purpose of enhancing culturally and linguistically specific services for victims of domestic violence, dating violence, sexual assault, and stalking. Grants under the program shall support community-based efforts to address distinctive cultural and linguistic responses to domestic violence, dating violence, sexual assault, and stalking, including—

   (A) working with State and local governments and social service agencies to develop and enhance effective strategies to provide culturally and linguistically specific services to victims of domestic violence, dating violence, sexual assault, and stalking;

(B) increasing communities' capacity to provide culturally and linguistically specific resources and support for victims of domestic violence, dating violence, sexual assault, and stalking crimes and their families;

(C) strengthening criminal justice interventions, by providing training for law enforcement, prosecution, courts, probation, and correctional facilities on culturally and linguistically specific responses to domestic violence, dating violence, sexual assault, and stalking;

(D) enhancing traditional services to victims of domestic violence, dating violence, sexual assault, and stalking through the leadership of culturally and linguistically specific programs offering services to victims of domestic violence, dating violence, sexual assault, and stalking;

(E) working in cooperation with the community to develop education and prevention strategies highlighting culturally and linguistically specific issues and resources regarding victims of domestic violence, dating violence, sexual assault, and stalking;

(F) providing culturally and linguistically specific programs for children exposed to domestic violence, dating violence, sexual assault, and stalking;

(G) providing culturally and linguistically specific resources and services that address the safety, economic, housing, and workplace needs of victims of domestic violence, dating violence, sexual assault, or stalking, including emergency assistance; or

(H) examining the dynamics of culture and its impact on victimization and healing.

(3) Technical assistance and training. The Director shall provide technical assistance and training to grantees of this and other programs under this Act regarding the development and provision of effective culturally and linguistically specific community-based services by entering into cooperative agreements or contracts with an organization or organizations having a demonstrated expertise in and whose primary purpose is addressing the development and provision of culturally and linguistically specific community-based services to victims of domestic violence, dating violence, sexual assault, and stalking.

(c) **Eligible entities.** Eligible entities for grants under this Section include—

(1) community-based programs whose primary purpose is providing culturally and linguistically specific services to victims of domestic violence, dating violence, sexual assault, and stalking; and

(2) community-based programs whose primary purpose is providing culturally and linguistically specific services who can partner with a program having demonstrated expertise in serving victims of domestic violence, dating violence, sexual assault, and stalking.

(d) **Reporting.** The Director shall issue a biennial report on the distribution of funding under this section, the progress made in replicating and supporting increased services to victims of domestic violence, dating violence, sexual assault, and stalking who face obstacles to using more traditional services and resources, and the types of culturally and linguistically accessible programs, strategies, technical assistance, and training developed or enhanced through this program.

(e) Grant period. The Director shall award grants for a 2-year period, with a possible extension of another 2 years to implement projects under the grant.

(f) Evaluation. The Director shall award a contract or cooperative agreement to evaluate programs under this section to an entity with the demonstrated expertise in and primary goal of providing enhanced cultural and linguistic access to services and resources for victims of domestic violence, dating violence, sexual assault, and stalking who face obstacles to using more traditional services and resources.

(g) Non-exclusivity. Nothing in this Section shall be interpreted to exclude linguistic and culturally specific community-based programs from applying to other grant programs authorized under this Act.

(h) Definitions and grant conditions. In this section the definitions and grant conditions in section 40002 of the Violence Against Women Act of 1994 [42 USCS § 13925] shall apply.
(Jan. 5, 2006, P. L. 109-162, Title I, § 121, 119 Stat. 2991; Aug. 12, 2006, P. L. 109-271, §§ 1(c)(3), 2(k), 120 Stat. 751, 753.)

HISTORY; ANCILLARY LAWS AND DIRECTIVES

References in text:
"This Act", referred to in this section, is Act Jan. 5, 2006, P. L. 109-162. For full classification of such Act, consult USCS Tables volumes.
"Section ___ of the Violence Against Women Act of 1994 (42 U.S.C. ___), Older Battered Women", as used in this section, may refer to § 40802 of Title IV of Act Sept. 13, 1994, P. L. 103-322, which appears as 42 USCS § 14041a.
"Section ___ of the Violence Against Women Act of 2000 (42 U.S.C. ___), Disabled Women Program", as used in this section, may refer to § 1402 of Div B of Act Oct. 28, 2000, P. L. 106-386, which appears as 42 USCS § 3796gg-7.

Explanatory notes:
The bracketed words "of the Omnibus Crime Control and Safe Streets Act of 1968" have been inserted in subsec. (a)(2)(A) to indicate the probable intent of Congress to include them.
This section was enacted as part of Act Jan. 5, 2006, P. L. 109-162, and not as part of Act Sept. 13, 1994, P. L. 103-322, which generally comprises this chapter.

Effective date of section:
This section takes effect on Oct. 1, 2006, pursuant to § 4 of Act Jan. 5, 2006, P. L. 109-162, which appears as 42 USCS § 3793 note.

Amendments:
2006. Act Aug. 12, 2006, in subsec. (a)(1), added the sentence beginning "The requirements . . ."; in subsec. (b)(2), substituted ", including—" for a concluding period and added subparas. (A)–(H); and added subsec. (h).

§ 14045b. Grants to combat violent crimes on campuses

(a) Grants authorized. (1) In general. The Attorney General is authorized to make grants to institutions of higher education, for use by such institutions or consortia consisting of campus personnel, student organizations, campus administrators, security personnel, and regional crisis centers affiliated with the institution, to develop and strengthen effective security and investigation strategies to combat domestic violence, dating violence, sexual assault, and stalking on campuses, and to develop and strengthen victim services in cases involving such crimes against women on campuses, which may include partnerships with local criminal justice authorities and community-based victim services agencies.

(2) Award basis. The Attorney General shall award grants and contracts under this section on a competitive basis for a period of 3 years. The Attorney General, through the Director of the Office on Violence Against Women, shall award the grants in amounts of not more than $500,000 for individual institutions of higher education and not more than $1,000,000 for consortia of such institutions.

(3) Equitable participation. The Attorney General shall make every effort to ensure—

(A) the equitable participation of private and public institutions of higher education in the activities assisted under this section;

(B) the equitable geographic distribution of grants under this section among the various regions of the United States; and

(C) the equitable distribution of grants under this section to tribal colleges and universities and traditionally black colleges and universities.

(b) Use of grant funds. Grant funds awarded under this section may be used for the following purposes:

(1) To provide personnel, training, technical assistance, data collection, and other equipment with respect to the increased apprehension, investigation, and adjudication of persons committing domestic violence, dating violence, sexual assault, and stalking on campus.

(2) To develop and implement campus policies, protocols, and services that more effectively identify and respond to the crimes of domestic violence, dating violence, sexual assault and stalking, and to train campus administrators, campus security personnel, and personnel serving on campus disciplinary or judicial boards on such policies, protocols, and services. Within 90 days after the date of enactment of this Act [enacted Jan. 5, 2006], the Attorney General shall issue and make available minimum standards of training relating to domestic violence, dating violence, sexual assault, and stalking on campus, for all campus security personnel and personnel serving on campus disciplinary or judicial boards.

(3) To implement and operate education programs for the prevention of domestic violence, dating violence, sexual assault, and stalking.

(4) To develop, enlarge, or strengthen victim services programs on the campuses of the institutions involved, including programs providing legal, medical, or psychological counseling, for victims of domestic violence, dat-

ing violence, sexual assault, and stalking, and to improve delivery of victim assistance on campus. To the extent practicable, such an institution shall collaborate with any entities carrying out nonprofit and other victim services programs, including domestic violence, dating violence, sexual assault, and stalking victim services programs in the community in which the institution is located. If appropriate victim services programs are not available in the community or are not accessible to students, the institution shall, to the extent practicable, provide a victim services program on campus or create a victim services program in collaboration with a community-based organization. The institution shall use not less than 20 percent of the funds made available through the grant for a victim services program provided in accordance with this paragraph.

(5) To create, disseminate, or otherwise provide assistance and information about victims' options on and off campus to bring disciplinary or other legal action, including assistance to victims in immigration matters.

(6) To develop, install, or expand data collection and communication systems, including computerized systems, linking campus security to the local law enforcement for the purpose of identifying and tracking arrests, protection orders, violations of protection orders, prosecutions, and convictions with respect to the crimes of domestic violence, dating violence, sexual assault, and stalking on campus.

(7) To provide capital improvements (including improved lighting and communications facilities but not including the construction of buildings) on campuses to address the crimes of domestic violence, dating violence, sexual assault, and stalking.

(8) To support improved coordination among campus administrators, campus security personnel, and local law enforcement to reduce domestic violence, dating violence, sexual assault, and stalking on campus.

(c) **Applications.** (1) In general. In order to be eligible to be awarded a grant under this section for any fiscal year, an institution of higher education shall submit an application to the Attorney General at such time and in such manner as the Attorney General shall prescribe.

(2) Contents. Each application submitted under paragraph (1) shall—

(A) describe the need for grant funds and the plan for implementation for any of the purposes described in subsection (b);

(B) include proof that the institution of higher education collaborated with any non-profit, nongovernmental entities carrying out other victim services programs, including domestic violence, dating violence, sexual assault, and stalking victim services programs in the community in which the institution is located;

(C) describe the characteristics of the population being served, including type of campus, demographics of the population, and number of students;

(D) provide measurable goals and expected results from the use of the grant funds;

(E) provide assurances that the Federal funds made available under this section shall be used to supplement and, to the extent practical, increase the level of funds that would, in the absence of Federal funds, be made available by the institution for the purposes described in subsection (b); and

(F) include such other information and assurances as the Attorney General reasonably determines to be necessary.

(3) Compliance with campus crime reporting required. No institution of higher education shall be eligible for a grant under this section unless such institution is in compliance with the requirements of section 485(f) of the Higher Education Act of 1965 (20 U.S.C. 1092(f)). Up to $200,000 of the total amount of grant funds appropriated under this section for fiscal years 2007 through 2011 may be used to provide technical assistance in complying with the mandatory reporting requirements of section 485(f) of such Act.

(d) **General terms and conditions.** (1) Nonmonetary assistance. In addition to the assistance provided under this section, the Attorney General may request any Federal agency to use the agency's authorities and the resources granted to the agency under Federal law (including personnel, equipment, supplies, facilities, and managerial, technical, and advisory services) in support of campus security, and investigation and victim service efforts.

(2) Grantee reporting. (A) Annual report. Each institution of higher education receiving a grant under this section shall submit a performance report to the Attorney General. The Attorney General shall suspend funding under this section for an institution of higher education if the institution fails to submit such a report.

(B) Final report. Upon completion of the grant period under this section, the institution shall file a performance report with the Attorney General and the Secretary of Education explaining the activities carried out under this section together with an assessment of the effectiveness of those activities in achieving the purposes described in subsection (b).

(3) Report to Congress. Not later than 180 days after the end of the fiscal year for which grants are awarded under this section, the Attorney General shall submit to Congress a report that includes—

(A) the number of grants, and the amount of funds, distributed under this section;

(B) a summary of the purposes for which the grants were provided and an evaluation of the progress made under the grant;

(C) a statistical summary of the persons served, detailing the nature of victimization, and providing data on age, sex, race, ethnicity, language, disability, relationship to offender, geographic distribution, and type of campus; and

(D) an evaluation of the effectiveness of programs funded under this part.

(e) **Authorization of appropriations.** For the purpose of carrying out this section, there are authorized to be appropriated $12,000,000 for fiscal year 2007 and $15,000,000 for each of fiscal years 2008 through 2011.

(f) [Omitted]

(g) **Definitions and grant conditions.** In this section the definitions and grant conditions in section 40002 of the Violence Against Women Act of 1994 [42 USCS § 13925] shall apply.

(Jan. 5, 2006, P. L. 109-162, Title III, § 304, 119 Stat. 3013; Aug. 12, 2006, P. L. 109-271, §§ 1(c)(1), 4(b), (d), 120 Stat. 750, 758.)

HISTORY; ANCILLARY LAWS AND DIRECTIVES

References in text:

As used in subsec. (d)(3)(D), the meaning of "this part" is not clear. Congress may have intended a reference to "this section".

Explanatory notes:

Subsec. (f) of this section, which is omitted, repealed 20 USCS § 1152.

This section was enacted as part of Act Jan. 5, 2006, P. L. 109-162, and not as part of Act Sept. 13, 1994, P. L. 103-322, which generally comprises this chapter.

Effective date of section:

This section takes effect Oct. 1, 2006, pursuant to § 4 of Act Jan. 5, 2006, P. L. 109-162, which appears as 42 USCS § 3793 note.

Amendments:

2006. Act Aug. 12, 2006, in subsec. (b)(2), substituted the sentence beginning "To develop and implement . . ." for "To train campus administrators, campus security personnel, and personnel serving on campus disciplinary or judicial boards to develop and implement campus policies, protocols, and services that more effectively identify and respond to the crimes of domestic violence, dating violence, sexual assault, and stalking."; in subsec. (d)(2)(A), deleted "biennial" preceding "performance report"; and added subsec. (g).

§ 14045c. Public awareness campaign

(a) In general. The Attorney General, acting through the Office on Violence Against Women], shall make grants to States for carrying out a campaign to increase public awareness of issues regarding domestic violence against pregnant women.

(b) Authorization of appropriations. For the purpose of carrying out this section, there are authorized to be appropriated such sums as may be necessary for each of the fiscal years 2006 through 2010.

(Jan. 5, 2006, P. L. 109-162, Title IV, § 403, 119 Stat. 3023.)

HISTORY; ANCILLARY LAWS AND DIRECTIVES

Explanatory notes:

The bracket following "Women" in subsec. (a) is in the original but probably should not appear.

This section was enacted as part of Act Jan. 5, 2006, P. L. 109-162, and not as part of Act Sept. 13, 1994, P. L. 103-322, which generally comprises this chapter.

§ 14045d. Consultation

(a) In general. The Attorney General shall conduct annual consultations with

Indian tribal governments concerning the Federal administration of tribal funds and programs established under this Act, the Violence Against Women Act of 1994 (title IV of Public Law 103-322; 108 Stat. 1902) and the Violence Against Women Act of 2000 (division B of Public Law 106-386; 114 Stat. 1491).

(b) Recommendations. During consultations under subsection (a), the Secretary of the Department of Health and Human Services and the Attorney General shall solicit recommendations from Indian tribes concerning—

(1) administering tribal funds and programs;

(2) enhancing the safety of Indian women from domestic violence, dating violence, sexual assault, and stalking; and

(3) strengthening the Federal response to such violent crimes.

(Jan. 5, 2006, P. L. 109-162, Title IX, § 903, 119 Stat. 3078.)

HISTORY; ANCILLARY LAWS AND DIRECTIVES

References in text:
"This Act", referred to in this section, is Act Jan. 5, 2006, P. L. 109-162, popularly known as the Violence Against Women and Department of Justice Reauthorization Act of 2005. For full classification of such Act, consult USCS Tables volumes.

The "Violence Against Women Act of 1994", referred to in this section, is Title IV of Act Sept. 13, 1994, P. L. 103-322. For full classification of such Title, consult USCS Tables volumes.

The "Violence Against Women Act of 2000", referred to in this section, is Division B of Act Oct. 27, 2000, P. L. 106-386. For full classification of such Division, consult USCS Tables volumes.

Explanatory notes:
This section was enacted as part of Act Jan. 5, 2006, P. L. 109-162, and not as part of Act Sept. 13, 1994, P. L. 103-322, which generally comprises this chapter.

DRUG CONTROL

§ 14051.   Increased penalties for drug-dealing in "drug-free" zones

Pursuant to its authority under section 994 of title 28, United States Code, the United States Sentencing Commission shall amend its sentencing guidelines to provide an appropriate enhancement for a defendant convicted of violating section 419 of the Controlled Substances Act (21 U.S.C. 860).

(Sept. 13, 1994, P. L. 103-322, Title IX, Subtitle A, § 90102, 108 Stat. 1987.)

CODE OF FEDERAL REGULATIONS

Department of Justice—Grants for correctional facilities, 28 CFR 91.1 et seq.

RESEARCH GUIDE

Am Jur:
25 Am Jur 2d, Drugs and Controlled Substances § 174.

§ 14052.   Enhanced penalties for illegal drug use in federal prisons and for smuggling drugs into Federal prisons

(a) Declaration of policy. It is the policy of the Federal Government that the use or distribution of illegal drugs in the Nation's Federal prisons will not be tolerated and that such crimes shall be prosecuted to the fullest extent of the law.

(b) Sentencing guidelines. Pursuant to its authority under section 994 of title 28, United States Code, the United States Sentencing Commission shall amend its sentencing guidelines to appropriately enhance the penalty for a person convicted of an offense—

(1) under section 404 of the Controlled Substances Act [21 USCS § 844] involving simple possession of a controlled substance within a Federal prison or other Federal detention facility; or

(2) under section 401(b) of the Controlled Substances Act [21 USCS § 841(b)] involving the smuggling of a controlled substance into a Federal prison or other Federal detention facility or the distribution or intended distribution of a controlled substance within a Federal prison or other Federal detention facility.

(c) No probation. Notwithstanding any other law, the court shall not sentence a person convicted of an offense described in subsection (b) to probation.

(Sept. 13, 1994, P. L. 103-322, Title IX, Subtitle A, § 90103, 108 Stat. 1987.)

RESEARCH GUIDE

Am Jur:
25 Am Jur 2d, Drugs and Controlled Substances §§ 141, 150.

§ 14053.   Violent crime and drug emergency areas

(a) Definitions. In this section—

"major violent crime or drug-related emergency" means an occasion or instance in which violent crime, drug smuggling, drug trafficking, or drug abuse violence reaches such levels, as determined by the President, that Federal assistance is needed to supplement State and local efforts and capabilities to save lives, and to protect property and public health and safety.

"State" means a State, the District of Columbia, the Commonwealth of Puerto Rico, the United States Virgin Islands, American Samoa, Guam, and the Northern Mariana Islands.

(b) Declaration of violent crime and drug emergency areas. If a major violent crime or drug-related emergency exists throughout a State or a part of a State, the President may declare the State or part of a State to be a violent crime or drug emergency area and may take appropriate actions authorized by this section.

(c) Procedure. (1) In general. A request for a declaration designating an area to be a violent crime or drug emergency area shall be made, in writing, by the chief executive officer of a State or local government, respectively (or in the case of the District of Columbia, the mayor), and shall be forwarded to the Attorney General in such form as the Attorney General may by regulation require. One or more cities, counties, States, or the District of Columbia may submit a joint request for designation as a major violent crime or drug emergency area under this subsection.

(2) Finding. A request made under paragraph (1) shall be based on a written finding that the major violent crime or drug-related emergency is of such severity and magnitude that Federal assistance is necessary to ensure an effective response to save lives and to protect property and public health and safety.

(d) Irrelevancy of population density. The President shall not limit declarations made under this section to highly populated centers of violent crime or drug trafficking, drug smuggling, or drug use, but shall also consider applications from governments of less populated areas where the magnitude and severity of such activities is beyond the capability of the State or local government to respond.

(e) Requirements. As part of a request for a declaration under this section, and as a prerequisite to Federal violent crime or drug emergency assistance under this section, the chief executive officer of a State or local government shall—

(1) take appropriate action under State or local law and furnish information on the nature and amount of State and local resources that have been or will be committed to alleviating the major violent crime- or drug-related emergency;

(2) submit a detailed plan outlining that government's short- and long-term plans to respond to the violent crime or drug emergency, specifying the types and levels of Federal assistance requested and including explicit goals (including quantitative goals) and timetables; and

(3) specify how Federal assistance provided under this section is intended to achieve those goals.

(f) Review period. The Attorney General shall review a request submitted pursuant to this section, and the President shall decide whether to declare a violent crime or drug emergency area, within 30 days after receiving the request.

(g) Federal assistance. The President may—

(1) direct any Federal agency, with or without reimbursement, to utilize its authorities and the resources granted to it under Federal law (including personnel, equipment, supplies, facilities, financial assistance, and managerial, technical, and advisory services) in support of State and local assistance efforts; and

(2) provide technical and advisory assistance, including communications support and law enforcement-related intelligence information.

(h) Duration of Federal assistance. (1) In general. Federal assistance under this section shall not be provided to a violent crime or drug emergency area for more than 1 year.

(2) Extension. The chief executive officer of a jurisdiction may apply to the President for an extension of assistance beyond 1 year. The President may extend the provision of Federal assistance for not more than an additional 180 days.

(i) Regulations. Not later than 120 days after the date of enactment of this Act [enacted Sept. 13, 1994], the Attorney General shall issue regulations to implement this section.

(j) No effect on existing authority. Nothing in this section shall diminish or detract from existing authority possessed by the President or Attorney General. (Sept. 13, 1994, P. L. 103-322, Title IX, Subtitle A, § 90107, 108 Stat. 1988.)

RESEARCH GUIDE
Am Jur:
25 Am Jur 2d, Drugs and Controlled Substances § 190.

CRIMINAL STREET GANGS

§ 14061. Juvenile anti-drug and anti-gang grants in federally assisted low-income housing

Grants authorized in this Act to reduce or prevent juvenile drug and gang-related activity in "public housing" may be used for such purposes in federally assisted, low-income housing.
(Sept. 13, 1994, P. L. 103-322, Title XV, § 150007, 108 Stat. 2035.)

HISTORY; ANCILLARY LAWS AND DIRECTIVES
References in text:
"This Act", referred to in this section, is Act Sept. 13, 1994, P. L. 103-322, 108 Stat. 1796. For full classification of this Act, consult USCS Tables volumes.

CODE OF FEDERAL REGULATIONS
Department of Justice—Grants for correctional facilities, 28 CFR 91.1 et seq.

§ 14062. Gang investigation coordination and information collection

(a) Coordination. The Attorney General (or the Attorney General's designee), in consultation with the Secretary of the Treasury (or the Secretary's designee), shall develop a national strategy to coordinate gang-related investigations by Federal law enforcement agencies.

(b) Data collection. The Director of the Federal Bureau of Investigation shall acquire and collect information on incidents of gang violence for inclusion in an annual uniform crime report.

(c) Report. The Attorney General shall prepare a report on national gang violence outlining the strategy developed under subsection (a) to be submitted to the President and Congress by January 1, 1996.

(d) Authorization of appropriations. There are authorized to be appropriated to carry out this section $1,000,000 for fiscal year 1996.
(Sept. 13, 1994, P. L. 103-322, Title XV, § 150008, 108 Stat. 2036.)

CROSS REFERENCES
This section is referred to in 42 USCS § 14214.

CRIMES AGAINST CHILDREN

§ 14071. [Repealed]

HISTORY; ANCILLARY LAWS AND DIRECTIVES

Explanatory notes:
This section (Act Sept. 13, 1994, P. L. 103-322, Title XVII, Subtitle A, § 170101, 108 Stat. 2038; May 17, 1996, P. L. 104-145, § 2, 110 Stat. 1345; Oct. 3, 1996, P. L. 104-236, §§ 3–7, 110 Stat. 3096; Nov. 26, 1997, P. L. 105-119, Title I, § 115(a)(1)–(5), 111 Stat. 2461; Oct 30, 1998, P. L. 105-314, Title VI, § 607(a), 112 Stat. 2985; Oct. 28, 2000, P. L. 106-386, Div B, Title VI, § 1601(b)(1), 114 Stat. 1537; April 30, 2003, P. L. 108-21, Title VI, §§ 604(a), 605(a), 606, 117 Stat. 688; Jan. 5, 2006, P. L. 109-162, Title XI, Subtitle B, Ch. 5, § 1153(b), 119 Stat. 3113) was repealed by § 129(a) of Act July 27, 2006, P. L. 109-248, effective 7/27/2009, as provided by § 129(b) of such Act, which appears as a note to this section. Such section provided for the Jacob Wetterling crimes against children and sexually violent offender registration program.

Other provisions:
Effective date of repeal. Act July 27, 2006, P. L. 109-248, Title I, Subtitle A, § 129(b), 120 Stat. 601, provides: "Notwithstanding any other provision of this Act, this section [repealing 42 USCS §§ 14071–14073] shall take effect on the date of the deadline determined in accordance with section 124(a) [42 USCS § 16924(a)].".

§ 14072. [Repealed]

HISTORY; ANCILLARY LAWS AND DIRECTIVES

Explanatory notes:
This section (Act Sept. 13, 1994, P. L. 103-322, Title XVII, Subtitle A, § 170102, as added Oct. 3, 1996, P. L. 104-236, § 2(a), 110 Stat. 3093; Nov. 26, 1997, P. L. 105-119, Title I, § 115(a)(6), 111 Stat. 2463; Oct. 21, 1998, P. L. 105-277, Div A, § 101(b) [Title I, § 123], 112 Stat. 2681-72) was repealed by § 129(a) of Act July 27, 2006, P. L. 109-248, effective 7/27/2009, as provided by § 129(b) of such Act, which appears as 42 USCS § 14071 note. Such section provided for establishment of a national FBI database to track sexual offenders.

§ 14073. [Repealed]

HISTORY; ANCILLARY LAWS AND DIRECTIVES

Explanatory notes:
This section (Oct. 3, 1996, P. L. 104-236, § 8, 110 Stat. 3097) was repealed by § 129(a) of Act July 27, 2006, P. L. 109-248, effective 7/27/2009, as provided by § 129(b) of such Act, which appears as 42 USCS § 14071 note. Such section provided for immunity for certain agencies from liability for good faith conduct under former 42 USCS § 14072.

RURAL CRIME

§ 14081. Rural Crime and Drug Enforcement Task Forces

(a) Establishment. The Attorney General, in consultation with the Governors, mayors, and chief executive officers of State and local law enforcement agencies, may establish a Rural Crime and Drug Enforcement Task Force in judicial districts that encompass significant rural lands. Assets seized as a result of investigations initiated by a Rural Crime and Drug Enforcement Task Force and forfeited under Federal law shall be used, consistent with the guidelines on equitable sharing established by the Attorney General and of the Secretary of the Treasury, primarily to enhance the operations of the task force and its participating State and local law enforcement agencies.

(b) Task force membership. The Task Forces [task forces] established under subsection (a) shall be carried out under policies and procedures established by the Attorney General. The Attorney General may deputize State and local law enforcement officers and may cross-designate up to 100 Federal law enforcement officers, when necessary to undertake investigations pursuant to section 503(a) of the Controlled Substances Act (21 U.S.C. 873(a)) or offenses punishable by a term of imprisonment of 10 years or more under title 18, United States Code. The task forces—

(1) shall include representatives from—

(A) State and local law enforcement agencies;

(B) the office of the United States Attorney for the judicial district; and

(C) the Federal Bureau of Investigation, the Drug Enforcement Administration, the Immigration and Naturalization Service, and the United States Marshals Service; and

(2) may include representatives of other Federal law enforcement agencies, such as the United States Customs Service, United States Park Police, United States Forest Service, Bureau of Alcohol, Tobacco, and Firearms, and Bureau of Land Management.

(Sept. 13, 1994, P. L. 103-322, Title XVIII, Subtitle A, § 180102, 108 Stat. 2045.)

HISTORY; ANCILLARY LAWS AND DIRECTIVES

Explanatory notes:

The bracketed words "task forces" have been inserted in subsec. (b) to indicate the capitalization probably intended by Congress.

Transfer of functions:

For transfer of functions, personnel, assets, and liabilities of the United States Customs Service of the Department of the Treasury, including the functions of the Secretary of the Treasury relating thereto, to the Secretary of Homeland Security, and for treatment of related references, see 6 USCS §§ 203(1), 551(d), 552(d), 557, and the Department of Homeland Security Reorganization Plan of Nov. 25, 2002, which appears as 6 USCS § 542 note.

For transfer of authorities, functions, personnel, and assets of the Bureau of

Alcohol, Tobacco and Firearms, including the related functions of the Secretary of the Treasury, to the Department of Justice, see section 6 USCS § 531(c).

For abolition of the Immigration and Naturalization Service, transfer of functions, and treatment of related references, see transfer of functions note under 8 USCS § 1551.

CODE OF FEDERAL REGULATIONS

Department of Justice—Grants for correctional facilities, 28 CFR 91.1 et seq.

RESEARCH GUIDE

Am Jur:
25 Am Jur 2d, Drugs and Controlled Substances § 190.

§ 14082. Rural drug enforcement training

(a) Specialized training for rural officers. The Director of the Federal Law Enforcement Training Center shall develop a specialized course of instruction devoted to training law enforcement officers from rural agencies in the investigation of drug trafficking and related crimes.

(b) Authorization of appropriations. There are authorized to be appropriated to carry out subsection (a)—

(1) $1,000,000 for fiscal year 1996;

(2) $1,000,000 for fiscal year 1997;

(3) $1,000,000 for fiscal year 1998;

(4) $1,000,000 for fiscal year 1999; and

(5) $1,000,000 for fiscal year 2000.

(Sept. 13, 1994, P. L. 103-322, Title XVIII, Subtitle A, § 180103, 108 Stat. 2046.)

HISTORY; ANCILLARY LAWS AND DIRECTIVES
Transfer of functions:
For transfer of functions, personnel, assets, and liabilities of the Federal Law Enforcement Training Center of the Department of the Treasury to the Secretary of Homeland Security, and for treatment of related references, see 6 USCS §§ 203(4), 551(d), 552(d), and 557, and the Department of Homeland Security Reorganization Plan of November 25, 2002, as modified, which appears as 6 USCS § 542 note.

CROSS REFERENCES
This section is referred to in 42 USCS § 14214.

RESEARCH GUIDE
Am Jur:
25 Am Jur 2d, Drugs and Controlled Substances § 190.

§ 14083. More agents for the Drug Enforcement Administration

There are authorized to be appropriated for the hiring of additional Drug Enforcement Administration agents—

(1) $12,000,000 for fiscal year 1996;
(2) $20,000,000 for fiscal year 1997;
(3) $30,000,000 for fiscal year 1998;
(4) $40,000,000 for fiscal year 1999; and
(5) $48,000,000 for fiscal year 2000.

(Sept. 13, 1994, P. L. 103-322, Title XVIII, Subtitle A, § 180104, 108 Stat. 2046.)

CROSS REFERENCES
This section is referred to in 42 USCS § 14214.

POLICE CORPS AND LAW ENFORCEMENT OFFICERS TRAINING AND EDUCATION
POLICE CORPS

§ 14091.   Purposes
The purposes of this subtitle [42 USCS §§ 14091 et seq.] are to—
(1) address violent crime by increasing the number of police with advanced education and training on community patrol; and
(2) provide educational assistance to law enforcement personnel and to students who possess a sincere interest in public service in the form of law enforcement.

(Sept. 13, 1994, P. L. 103-322, Title XX, Subtitle A, § 200102, 108 Stat. 2049.)

CODE OF FEDERAL REGULATIONS
Department of Justice—Grants for correctional facilities, 28 CFR 91.1 et seq.
Department of Justice—Office of Community Oriented Policing Services (COPS), 28 CFR 92.1 et seq.

§ 14092.   Definitions
In this subtitle [42 USCS §§ 14091 et seq.]—
"academic year" means a traditional academic year beginning in August or September and ending in the following May or June.
"dependent child" means a natural or adopted child or stepchild of a law enforcement officer who at the time of the officer's death—
(A) was no more than 21 years old; or
(B) if older than 21 years, was in fact dependent on the child's parents for at least one-half of the child's support (excluding educational expenses), as determined by the Director.
"Director" means the Director of the Office of the Police Corps and Law Enforcement Education appointed under section 200104.
"educational expenses" means expenses that are directly attributable to a course of education leading to the award of either a baccalaureate or graduate degree in a course of study which, in the judgment of the State or local police force to which the participant will be assigned, includes appropriate

preparation for police service including the cost of tuition, fees, books, supplies, transportation, room and board and miscellaneous expenses.

"institution of higher education" has the meaning stated in the first sentence of section 101 of the Higher Education Act of 1965 [20 USCS § 1001].

"participant" means a participant in the Police Corps program selected pursuant to section 200106 [section 200107].

"State" means a State of the United States, the District of Columbia, the Commonwealth of Puerto Rico, the Virgin Islands, American Samoa, Guam, and the Commonwealth of the Northern Mariana Islands.

"State Police Corps program" means a State police corps program that meets the requirements of section 200110 [42 USCS § 14099].

(Sept. 13, 1994, P. L. 103-322, Title XX, Subtitle A, § 200103, 108 Stat. 2049; April 26, 1996, P. L. 104-134, Title I, § 121, 110 Stat. 1321-22; May 2, 1996, P. L. 104-140, § 1(a), 110 Stat. 1327; Oct. 7, 1998, P. L. 105-244, Title I, § 102(a)(13)(O), 112 Stat. 1621.)

HISTORY; ANCILLARY LAWS AND DIRECTIVES

References in text:

"Section 200104", referred to in the paragraph defining "Director", is § 200104 of Act Sept. 13, 1994, P. L. 103-322, which appears as 42 USCS § 14093. Such section, however, does not provide for the appointment of a Director.

Explanatory notes:

The bracketed reference "section 200107" has been inserted in the paragraph defining "participant" to indicate the reference probably intended by Congress. Section 200107 of Act Sept. 13, 1994, P. L. 103-322, is classified to 42 USCS § 14096.

Act May 2, 1996, P. L. 104-140, § 1(a), 110 Stat. 1327, inserted the heading "TITLE I—OMNIBUS APPROPRIATIONS" after the enacting clause of Act April 26, 1996, P. L. 104-134.

Amendments:

1996. Act April 26, 1996 substituted the definition of "educational expenses" for one which read:

" 'educational expenses' means expenses that are directly attributable to—

"(A) a course of education leading to the award of the baccalaureate degree in legal- or criminal justice-related studies; or

"(B) a course of graduate study legal or criminal justice studies following award of a baccalaureate degree,

including the cost of tuition, fees, books, supplies, transportation, room and board and miscellaneous expenses.".

1998. Act Oct. 7, 1998 (effective on 10/1/98, as provided by § 3 of such Act, which appears as 20 USCS § 1001 note), in the definition of "institution of higher education", substituted "101" for "1201(a)" and deleted "(20 U.S.C. 1141(a))" following "1965".

§ 14093. Establishment of Office of the Police Corps and Law Enforcement Education

There is established in the Department of Justice, under the general authority of the Attorney General, an Office of the Police Corps and Law Enforcement Education.

(Sept. 13, 1994, P. L. 103-322, Title XX, Subtitle A, § 200104, 108 Stat. 2050.)

CROSS REFERENCES

This section is referred to in 42 USCS §§ 14092, 14111.

§ 14094. Designation of lead agency and submission of state plan

(a) Lead agency. A State that desires to participate in the Police Corps program under this subtitle [42 USCS §§ 14091 et seq.] shall designate a lead agency that will be responsible for—

(1) submitting to the Director a State plan described in subsection (b); and

(2) administering the program in the State.

(b) State plans. A State plan shall—

(1) contain assurances that the lead agency shall work in cooperation with the local law enforcement liaisons, representatives of police labor organizations and police management organizations, and other appropriate State and local agencies to develop and implement interagency agreements designed to carry out the program;

(2) contain assurances that the State shall advertise the assistance available under this subtitle [42 USCS §§ 14091 et seq.];

(3) contain assurances that the State shall screen and select law enforcement personnel for participation in the program; and

(4) meet the requirements of section 200110 [42 USCS § 14099].

(Sept. 13, 1994, P. L. 103-322, Title XX, Subtitle A, § 200105, 108 Stat. 2050.)

§ 14095. Scholarship assistance

(a) Scholarships authorized. (1) The Director may award scholarships to participants who agree to work in a State or local police force in accordance with agreements entered into pursuant to subsection (d).

(2)(A) Except as provided in subparagraph (B), each scholarship payment made under this section for each academic year shall not exceed—

(i) $10,000; or

(ii) the cost of the educational expenses related to attending an institution of higher education.

(B) In the case of a participant who is pursuing a course of educational study during substantially an entire calendar year, the amount of scholarship payments made during such year shall not exceed $13,333.

(C) The total amount of scholarship assistance received by any one student under this section shall not exceed $40,000.

(3) Recipients of scholarship assistance under this section shall continue to receive such scholarship payments only during such periods as the Director finds that the recipient is maintaining satisfactory progress as determined by the institution of higher education the recipient is attending.

(4)(A) The Director shall make scholarship payments under this section directly to the institution of higher education that the student is attending.

(B) Each institution of higher education receiving a payment on behalf of a participant pursuant to subparagraph (A) shall remit to such student any funds in excess of the costs of tuition, fees, and room and board payable to the institution.

(b) Reimbursement authorized. (1) The Director may make payments to a participant to reimburse such participant for the costs of educational expenses if the student agrees to work in a State or local police force in accordance with the agreement entered into pursuant to subsection (d).

(2)(A) Each payment made pursuant to paragraph (1) for each academic year of study shall not exceed—

(i) $10,000; or

(ii) the cost of educational expenses related to attending an institution of higher education.

(B) In the case of a participant who is pursuing a course of educational study during substantially an entire calendar year, the amount of scholarship payments made during such year shall not exceed $13,333.

(C) The total amount of payments made pursuant to subparagraph (A) to any 1 student shall not exceed $40,000.

(c) Use of scholarship. Scholarships awarded under this subsection [section] shall only be used to attend a 4-year institution of higher education, except that—

(1) scholarships may be used for graduate and professional study; and

(2) if a participant has enrolled in the program upon or after transfer to a 4-year institution of higher education, the Director may reimburse the participant for the participant's prior educational expenses.

(d) Agreement. (1)(A) Each participant receiving a scholarship or a payment under this section shall enter into an agreement with the Director.

(B) An agreement under subparagraph (A) shall contain assurances that the participant shall—

(i) after successful completion of a baccalaureate program and training as prescribed in section 200108 [42 USCS § 14097], work for 4 years in a State or local police force without there having arisen sufficient cause for the participant's dismissal under the rules applicable to members of the police force of which the participant is a member;

(ii) complete satisfactorily—

(I) an educational course of study and receipt of a baccalaureate degree (in the case of undergraduate study) or the reward of credit to the participant for having completed one or more graduate courses (in the case of graduate study); and

(II) Police Corps training and certification by the Director that the participant has met such performance standards as may be established pursuant to section 200108 [42 USCS § 14097]; and

(iii) repay all of the scholarship or payment received plus interest at the rate of 10 percent if the conditions of clauses (i) and (ii) are not complied with.

(2)(A) A recipient of a scholarship or payment under this section shall not be considered to be in violation of the agreement entered into pursuant to paragraph (1) if the recipient—

(i) dies; or

(ii) becomes permanently and totally disabled as established by the sworn affidavit of a qualified physician.

(B) If a scholarship recipient is unable to comply with the repayment provision set forth in paragraph (1)(B)(ii) [paragraph (1)(B)(iii)] because of a physical or emotional disability or for good cause as determined by the Director, the Director may substitute community service in a form prescribed by the Director for the required repayment.

(C) The Director shall expeditiously seek repayment from a participant who violates an agreement described in paragraph (1).

(e) Dependent child. A dependent child of a law enforcement officer—

(1) who is a member of a State or local police force or is a Federal criminal investigator or uniformed police officer,

(2) who is not a participant in the Police Corps program, but

(3) who serves in a State for which the Director has approved a Police Corps plan, and

(4) who is killed in the course of performing police duties,

shall be entitled to the scholarship assistance authorized in this section for any course of study in any accredited institution of higher education. Such dependent child shall not incur any repayment obligation in exchange for the scholarship assistance provided in this section.

(f) Application. Each participant desiring a scholarship or payment under this section shall submit an application as prescribed by the Director in such manner and accompanied by such information as the Director may reasonably require.

(Sept. 13, 1994, P. L. 103-322, Title XX, Subtitle A, § 200106, 108 Stat. 2050; Nov. 2, 2002, P. L. 107-273, Div C, Title I, Subtitle A, § 11006(1), 116 Stat. 1817.)

HISTORY; ANCILLARY LAWS AND DIRECTIVES

Explanatory notes:

The bracketed word "section" has been inserted in the introductory matter of subsec. (c) to indicate the probable intent of Congress to include such word.

The bracketed reference "paragraph (1)(B)(iii)" has been inserted in subsec. (d)(2)(B) to indicate the reference probably intended by Congress.

Amendments:

2002. Act Nov. 2, 2002, in subsecs. (a)(2) and (b)(2), in subpara. (A)(i), substituted "$10,000" for "$7,500", in subpara. (B), substituted "$13,333" for "$10,000", and, in subpara. (C), substituted "$40,000" for "$30,000".

CROSS REFERENCES

This section is referred to in 42 USCS § 14098.

§ 14096.   Selection of participants

(a) In general. Participants in State Police Corps programs shall be selected on a competitive basis by each State under regulations prescribed by the Director.

(b) Selection criteria and qualifications. (1) In order to participate in a State Police Corps program, a participant shall—

(A) be a citizen of the United States or an alien lawfully admitted for permanent residence in the United States;

(B) meet the requirements for admission as a trainee of the State or local police force to which the participant will be assigned pursuant to section 200110(5) [42 USCS § 14099(5)], including achievement of satisfactory scores on any applicable examination, except that failure to meet the age requirement for a trainee of the State or local police shall not disqualify the applicant if the applicant will be of sufficient age upon completing an undergraduate course of study;

(C) possess the necessary mental and physical capabilities and emotional characteristics to discharge effectively the duties of a law enforcement officer;

(D) be of good character and demonstrate sincere motivation and dedication to law enforcement and public service;

(E) in the case of an undergraduate, agree in writing that the participant will complete an educational course of study leading to the award of a baccalaureate degree and will then accept an appointment and complete 4 years of service as an officer in the State police or in a local police department within the State;

(F) in the case of a participant desiring to undertake or continue graduate study, agree in writing that the participant will accept an appointment and complete 4 years of service as an officer in the State police or in a local police department within the State before undertaking or continuing graduate study;

(G) contract, with the consent of the participant's parent or guardian if the participant is a minor, to serve for 4 years as an officer in the State police or in a local police department, if an appointment is offered; and

(H) except as provided in paragraph (2), be without previous law enforcement experience.

(2)(A) Until the date that is 5 years after the date of enactment of this Act [enacted Sept. 13, 1994], up to 10 percent of the applicants accepted into the Police Corps program may be persons who—

(i) have had some law enforcement experience; and

(ii) have demonstrated special leadership potential and dedication to law enforcement.

(B)(i) The prior period of law enforcement of a participant selected pursuant to subparagraph (A) shall not be counted toward satisfaction of the participant's 4-year service obligation under section 200109 [42 USCS § 14098], and such a participant shall be subject to the same benefits and obligations under this subtitle [42 USCS §§ 14091 et seq.] as other participants, including those stated in section [subsection] (b)(1) (E) and (F).

(ii) Clause (i) shall not be construed to preclude counting a participant's previous period of law enforcement experience for purposes other than satisfaction of the requirements of section 200109, such as for purposes of determining such a participant's pay and other benefits, rank, and tenure.

(3) It is the intent of this subtitle [42 USCS §§ 14091 et seq.] that there shall be no more than 20,000 participants in each graduating class. The Director shall approve State plans providing in the aggregate for such enrollment of applicants as shall assure, as nearly as possible, annual graduating classes of 20,000. In a year in which applications are received in a number greater than that which will produce, in the judgment of the Director, a graduating class of more than 20,000, the Director shall, in deciding which applications to grant, give preference to those who will be participating in State plans that provide law enforcement personnel to areas of greatest need.

(c) Recruitment of minorities. Each State participating in the Police Corps program shall make special efforts to seek and recruit applicants from among members of all racial, ethnic or gender groups. This subsection does not authorize an exception from the competitive standards for admission established pursuant to subsections (a) and (b).

(d) Enrollment of applicant. (1) An applicant shall be accepted into a State Police Corps program on the condition that the applicant will be matriculated in, or accepted for admission at, a 4-year institution of higher education—

(A) as a full-time student in an undergraduate program; or

(B) for purposes of taking a graduate course.

(2) If the applicant is not matriculated or accepted as set forth in paragraph (1), the applicant's acceptance in the program shall be revoked.

(e) Leave of absence. (1) A participant in a State Police Corps program who requests a leave of absence from educational study, training or service for a period not to exceed 1 year (or 18 months in the aggregate in the event of multiple requests) due to temporary physical or emotional disability shall be granted such leave of absence by the State.

(2) A participant who requests a leave of absence from educational study, training or service for a period not to exceed 1 year (or 18 months in the aggregate in the event of multiple requests) for any reason other than those listed in paragraph (1) may be granted such leave of absence by the State.

(3) A participant who requests a leave of absence from educational study or training for a period not to exceed 30 months to serve on an official church mission may be granted such leave of absence.

(f) Admission of applicants. An applicant may be admitted into a State Police Corps program either before commencement of or during the applicant's course of educational study.

(Sept. 13, 1994, P. L. 103-322, Title XX, Subtitle A, § 200107, 108 Stat. 2052.)

HISTORY; ANCILLARY LAWS AND DIRECTIVES

Explanatory notes:

The bracketed word "subsection" has been inserted in subsec. (b)(2)(B)(i) as the word probably intended by Congress.

CROSS REFERENCES
This section is referred to in 42 USCS §§ 14092, 14099.

§ 14097. Police Corps training

(a) In general. (1) The Director shall establish programs of training for Police Corps participants. Such programs may be carried out at up to 3 training centers established for this purpose and administered by the Director, or by contracting with existing State training facilities. The Director shall contract with a State training facility upon request of such facility if the Director determines that such facility offers a course of training substantially equivalent to the Police Corps training program described in this subtitle [42 USCS §§ 14091 et seq.].

(2) The Director may enter into contracts with individuals, institutions of learning, and government agencies (including State and local police forces) to obtain the services of persons qualified to participate in and contribute to the training process.

(3) The Director may enter into agreements with agencies of the Federal Government to utilize on a reimbursable basis space in Federal buildings and other resources.

(4) The Director may authorize such expenditures as are necessary for the effective maintenance of the training centers, including purchases of supplies, uniforms, and educational materials, and the provision of subsistence, quarters, and medical care to participants.

(b) Training sessions. A participant in a State Police Corps program shall attend up to 24 weeks, but no less than 16 weeks, of training at a training center. The Director may approve training conducted in not more than 3 separate sessions.

(c) Further training. The Police Corps training authorized in this section is intended to serve as basic law enforcement training but not to exclude further training of participants by the State and local authorities to which they will be assigned. Each State plan approved by the Director under section 10 shall include assurances that following completion of a participant's course of education each participant shall receive appropriate additional training by the State or local authority to which the participant is assigned. The time spent by a participant in such additional training, but not the time spent in Police Corps training, shall be counted toward fulfillment of the participant's 4-year service obligation.

(d) Course of training. The training sessions at training centers established under this section shall be designed to provide basic law enforcement training, including vigorous physical and mental training to teach participants self-discipline and organizational loyalty and to impart knowledge and understanding of legal processes and law enforcement.

(e) Evaluation of participants. A participant shall be evaluated during training for mental, physical, and emotional fitness, and shall be required to meet performance standards prescribed by the Director at the conclusion of each training session in order to remain in the Police Corps program.

(f) Stipend. The Director shall pay participants in training sessions a stipend of $400 a week during training.

(Sept. 13, 1994, P. L. 103-322, Title XX, Subtitle A, § 200108, 108 Stat. 2054; Oct. 21, 1998, P. L. 105-277, Div C, Title I, § 138(a), 112 Stat. 2681-597; Nov. 2, 2002, P. L. 107-273, Div C, Title I, Subtitle A, § 11006(2), 116 Stat. 1817.)

HISTORY; ANCILLARY LAWS AND DIRECTIVES

References in text:
"Section 10", as used in subsec. (c), probably refers to § 200110 of Act Sept. 13, 1994, P. L. 103-322, which appears as 42 USCS § 14099.

Amendments:
1998. Act Oct. 21, 1998, substituted subsec. (b) for one which read: "(b) Training sessions. A participant in a State Police Corps program shall attend two 8-week training sessions at a training center, one during the summer following completion of sophomore year and one during the summer following completion of junior year. If a participant enters the program after sophomore year, the participant shall complete 16 weeks of training at times determined by the Director."; and, in subsec. (c), deleted "16 weeks of" preceding "Police Corps training authorized".

2002. Act Nov. 2, 2002, in subsec. (f), substituted "$400" for "$250".

CROSS REFERENCES
This section is referred to in 42 USCS §§ 14095, 14098.

§ 14098. Service obligation

(a) Swearing in. Upon satisfactory completion of the participant's course of education and training program established in section 200108 [42 USCS § 14097] and meeting the requirements of the police force to which the participant is assigned, a participant shall be sworn in as a member of the police force to which the participant is assigned pursuant to the State Police Corps plan, and shall serve for 4 years as a member of that police force.

(b) Rights and responsibilities. A participant shall have all of the rights and responsibilities of and shall be subject to all rules and regulations applicable to other members of the police force of which the participant is a member, including those contained in applicable agreements with labor organizations and those provided by State and local law.

(c) Discipline. If the police force of which the participant is a member subjects the participant to discipline such as would preclude the participant's completing 4 years of service, and result in denial of educational assistance under section 200106 [42 USCS § 14095], the Director may, upon a showing of good cause, permit the participant to complete the service obligation in an equivalent alternative law enforcement service and, if such service is satisfactorily completed, section 200106(d)(1)(B)(iii) [42 USCS § 14095(d)(1)(B)(iii)] shall not apply.

(d) Layoffs. If the police force of which the participant is a member lays off the participant such as would preclude the participant's completing 4 years of

service, and result in denial of educational assistance under section 200106 [42 USCS § 14095], the Director may permit the participant to complete the service obligation in an equivalent alternative law enforcement service and, if such service is satisfactorily completed, section 200106(d)(1)(B)(iii) [42 USCS § 14095(d)(1)(B)(iii)] shall not apply.
(Sept. 13, 1994, P. L. 103-322, Title XX, Subtitle A, § 200109, 108 Stat. 2055.)

CROSS REFERENCES

This section is referred to in 42 USCS § 14096.

§ 14099.   State plan requirements

A State Police Corps plan shall—

(1) provide for the screening and selection of participants in accordance with the criteria set out in section 200107 [42 USCS § 14096];

(2) state procedures governing the assignment of participants in the Police Corps program to State and local police forces (except with permission of the Director, no more than 25 percent of all the participants assigned in each year by each State to be assigned to a statewide police force or forces);

(3) provide that participants shall be assigned to those geographic areas in which—

(A) there is the greatest need for additional law enforcement personnel; and

(B) the participants will be used most effectively;

(4) provide that to the extent consistent with paragraph (3), a participant shall be assigned to an area near the participant's home or such other place as the participant may request;

(5) provide that to the extent feasible, a participant's assignment shall be made at the time the participant is accepted into the program, subject to change—

(A) prior to commencement of a participant's fourth year of undergraduate study, under such circumstances as the plan may specify; and

(B) from commencement of a participant's fourth year of undergraduate study until completion of 4 years of police service by participant, only for compelling reasons or to meet the needs of the State Police Corps program and only with the consent of the participant;

(6) provide that no participant shall be assigned to serve with a local police force—

(A) whose size has declined by more than 5 percent since June 21, 1989; or

(B) which has members who have been laid off but not retired;

(7) provide that participants shall be placed and to the extent feasible kept on community and preventive patrol;

(8) ensure that participants will receive effective training and leadership;

(9) provide that the State may decline to offer a participant an appointment following completion of Federal training, or may remove a participant from the Police Corps program at any time, only for good cause (including failure

to make satisfactory progress in a course of educational study) and after following reasonable review procedures stated in the plan; and

(10) provide that a participant shall, while serving as a member of a police force, be compensated at the same rate of pay and benefits and enjoy the same rights under applicable agreements with labor organizations and under State and local law as other police officers of the same rank and tenure in the police force of which the participant is a member.

(Sept. 13, 1994, P. L. 103-322, Title XX, Subtitle A, § 200110, 108 Stat. 2056; Nov. 2, 2002, P. L. 107-273, Div C, Title I, Subtitle A, § 11006(3), 116 Stat. 1817.)

HISTORY; ANCILLARY LAWS AND DIRECTIVES
Amendments:
2002. Act Nov. 2, 2002, in para. (2), substituted "except with permission of the Director, no more than 25 percent" for "no more than 10 percent".

CROSS REFERENCES
This section is referred to in 42 USCS §§ 14092, 14094, 14096.

§ 14100. [Repealed]

HISTORY; ANCILLARY LAWS AND DIRECTIVES
This section (Act Sept. 13, 1994, P. L. 103-322, Title XX, Subtitle A, § 200111, 108 Stat. 2056) was repealed by Act Nov. 2, 2002, P. L. 107-273, Div C, Title I, Subtitle A, § 11006(4), 116 Stat. 1817. It provided for assistance to States and localities employing Police Corps officers.

§ 14101. Authorization of appropriations

There are authorized to be appropriated to carry out this subtitle [42 USCS §§ 14091 et seq.] $50,000,000 for fiscal year 1999, $70,000,000 for fiscal year 2000, $90,000,000 for fiscal year 2001, and $90,000,000 for each of fiscal years 2002 through 2005.

(Sept. 13, 1994, P. L. 103-322, Title XX, Subtitle A, § 200112, 108 Stat. 2057; Oct. 21, 1998, P. L. 105-277, Div C, Title I, § 138(b), 112 Stat. 2681-597; Nov. 2, 2002, P. L. 107-273, Div C, Title I, Subtitle A, § 11006(5), 116 Stat. 1817.)

HISTORY; ANCILLARY LAWS AND DIRECTIVES
Amendments:
1998. Act Oct. 21, 1998, substituted "$50,000,000 for fiscal year 1999, $70,000,000 for fiscal year 2000, $90,000,000 for fiscal year 2001, and $90,000,000 for fiscal year 2002" for "$20,000 for each of the fiscal years 1996 through 2000".
2002. Act Nov. 2, 2002, substituted "each of fiscal years 2002 through 2005" for "fiscal year 2002".

§ 14102. Reports to Congress

(a) In general. Not later than April 1 of each year, the Director shall submit a report to the Attorney General, the President, the Speaker of the House of Representatives, and the President of the Senate.

(b) Contents. A report under subsection (a) shall—

(1) state the number of current and past participants in the Police Corps program, broken down according to the levels of educational study in which they are engaged and years of service they have served on police forces (including service following completion of the 4-year service obligation);

(2) describe the geographic, racial, and gender dispersion of participants in the Police Corps program; and

(3) describe the progress of the Police Corps program and make recommendations for changes in the program.

(Sept. 13, 1994, P. L. 103-322, Title XX, Subtitle A, § 200113, 108 Stat. 2057.)

LAW ENFORCEMENT SCHOLARSHIP PROGRAM

§ 14111. Definitions

In this subtitle [42 USCS §§ 14111 et seq.]—

"Director" means the Director of the Office of the Police Corps and Law Enforcement Education appointed under section 200104.

"educational expenses" means expenses that are directly attributable to—

(A) a course of education leading to the award of an associate degree;

(B) a course of education leading to the award of a baccalaureate degree; or

(C) a course of graduate study following award of a baccalaureate degree, including the cost of tuition, fees, books, supplies, and related expenses.

"institution of higher education" has the meaning stated in the first sentence of section 101 of the Higher Education Act of 1965 [20 USCS § 1001].

"law enforcement position" means employment as an officer in a State or local police force, or correctional institution.

"State" means a State of the United States, the District of Columbia, the Commonwealth of Puerto Rico, the Virgin Islands of the United States, American Samoa, Guam, and the Commonwealth of the Northern Mariana Islands.

(Sept. 13, 1994, P. L. 103-322, Title XX, Subtitle B, § 200202, 108 Stat. 2057; Oct. 7, 1998, P. L. 105-244, Title I, § 102(a)(13)(P), 112 Stat. 1621.)

HISTORY; ANCILLARY LAWS AND DIRECTIVES

References in text:

"Section 200104", referred to in the paragraph defining "Director", is § 200104 of Act Sept. 13, 1994, P. L. 103-322, which appears as 42 USCS § 14093. Such section, however, does not provide for the appointment of a Director.

Amendments:

1998. Act Oct. 7, 1998 (effective on 10/1/98, as provided by § 3 of such Act, which appears as 20 USCS § 1001 note), in the definition of "institution of higher education", substituted "101" for "1201(a)" and deleted "(20 U.S.C. 1141(a))" following "1965".

§ 14112. Allotment

From amounts appropriated under section 200210 [42 USCS § 14119], the Director shall allot—

(1) 80 percent of such amounts to States on the basis of the number of law enforcement officers in each State compared to the number of law enforcement officers in all States; and

(2) 20 percent of such amounts to States on the basis of the shortage of law enforcement personnel and the need for assistance under this subtitle [42 USCS §§ 14111 et seq.] in the State compared to the shortage of law enforcement personnel and the need for assistance under this subtitle [42 USCS §§ 14111 et seq.] in all States.

(Sept. 13, 1994, P. L. 103-322, Title XX, Subtitle B, § 200203, 108 Stat. 2058.)

CROSS REFERENCES

This section is referred to in 42 USCS §§ 14113, 14116.

§ 14113. Establishment of program

(a) Use of allotment. (1) In general. A State that receives an allotment pursuant to section 200203 [42 USCS § 14112] shall use the allotment to pay the Federal share of the costs of—

(A) awarding scholarships to in-service law enforcement personnel to enable such personnel to seek further education; and

(B) providing—

(i) full-time employment in summer; or

(ii) part-time (not to exceed 20 hours per week) employment for a period not to exceed 1 year.

(2) Employment. The employment described in paragraph (1)(B)—

(A) shall be provided by State and local law enforcement agencies for students who are juniors or seniors in high school or are enrolled in an institution of higher education and who demonstrate an interest in undertaking a career in law enforcement;

(B) shall not be in a law enforcement position; and

(C) shall consist of performing meaningful tasks that inform students of the nature of the tasks performed by law enforcement agencies.

(b) Payments; Federal share; non-Federal share. (1) Payments. Subject to the availability of appropriations, the Director shall pay to each State that receives an allotment under section 200203 [42 USCS § 14112] the Federal share of the cost of the activities described in the application submitted pursuant to section 200203 [section 200207].

(2) Federal share. The Federal share shall not exceed 60 percent.

(3) Non-Federal share. The non-Federal share of the cost of scholarships and student employment provided under this subtitle [42 USCS §§ 14111 et seq.] shall be supplied from sources other than the Federal Government.

(c) Responsibilities of Director. The Director shall be responsible for the administration of the programs conducted pursuant to this subtitle [42 USCS

§§ 14111 et seq.] and shall, in consultation with the Assistant Secretary for Postsecondary Education, issue rules to implement this subtitle [42 USCS §§ 14111 et seq.].

(d) Administrative expenses. A State that receives an allotment under section 200203 [42 USCS § 14112] may reserve not more than 8 percent of the allotment for administrative expenses.

(e) Special rule. A State that receives an allotment under section 200203 [42 USCS § 14112] shall ensure that each scholarship recipient under this subtitle [42 USCS §§ 14111 et seq.] be compensated at the same rate of pay and benefits and enjoy the same rights under applicable agreements with labor organizations and under State and local law as other law enforcement personnel of the same rank and tenure in the office of which the scholarship recipient is a member.

(f) Supplementation of funding. Funds received under this subtitle [42 USCS §§ 14111 et seq.] shall only be used to supplement, and not to supplant, Federal, State, or local efforts for recruitment and education of law enforcement personnel.

(Sept. 13, 1994, P. L. 103-322, Title XX, Subtitle B, § 200204, 108 Stat. 2058.)

HISTORY; ANCILLARY LAWS AND DIRECTIVES

Explanatory notes:
The bracketed reference "section 200207" has been inserted in subsec. (b)(1) to indicate the reference probably intended by Congress. Section 200207 of Act Sept. 13, 1994, P. L. 103-322 is classified to 42 USCS § 14116.

CROSS REFERENCES
This section is referred to in 42 USCS § 14119.

§ 14114. Scholarships

(a) Period of award. Scholarships awarded under this subtitle [42 USCS §§ 14111 et seq.] shall be for a period of 1 academic year.

(b) Use of scholarships. Each individual awarded a scholarship under this subtitle [42 USCS §§ 14111 et seq.] may use the scholarship for educational expenses at an institution of higher education.

(Sept. 13, 1994, P. L. 103-322, Title XX, Subtitle B, § 200205, 108 Stat. 2059.)

§ 14115. Eligibility

(a) Scholarships. A person shall be eligible to receive a scholarship under this subtitle [42 USCS §§ 14111 et seq.] if the person has been employed in law enforcement for the 2-year period immediately preceding the date on which assistance is sought.

(b) Ineligibility for student employment. A person who has been employed as a law enforcement officer is ineligible to participate in a student employment program carried out under this subtitle [42 USCS §§ 14111 et seq.].

(Sept. 13, 1994, P. L. 103-322, Title XX, Subtitle B, § 200206, 108 Stat. 2059.)

§ 14116. State application

(a) In general. Each State desiring an allotment under section 200203 [42 USCS § 14112] shall submit an application to the Director at such time, in such manner, and accompanied by such information as the Director may reasonably require.

(b) Contents. An application under subsection (a) shall—

(1) describe the scholarship program and the student employment program for which assistance under this subtitle [42 USCS §§ 14111 et seq.] is sought;

(2) contain assurances that the lead agency will work in cooperation with the local law enforcement liaisons, representatives of police labor organizations and police management organizations, and other appropriate State and local agencies to develop and implement interagency agreements designed to carry out this subtitle [42 USCS §§ 14111 et seq.];

(3) contain assurances that the State will advertise the scholarship assistance and student employment it will provide under this subtitle [42 USCS §§ 14111 et seq.] and that the State will use such programs to enhance recruitment efforts;

(4) contain assurances that the State will screen and select law enforcement personnel for participation in the scholarship program under this subtitle [42 USCS §§ 14111 et seq.];

(5) contain assurances that under such student employment program the State will screen and select, for participation in such program, students who have an interest in undertaking a career in law enforcement;

(6) contain assurances that under such scholarship program the State will make scholarship payments to institutions of higher education on behalf of persons who receive scholarships under this subtitle [42 USCS §§ 14111 et seq.];

(7) with respect to such student employment program, identify—

(A) the employment tasks that students will be assigned to perform;

(B) the compensation that students will be paid to perform such tasks; and

(C) the training that students will receive as part of their participation in the program;

(8) identify model curriculum and existing programs designed to meet the educational and professional needs of law enforcement personnel; and

(9) contain assurances that the State will promote cooperative agreements with educational and law enforcement agencies to enhance law enforcement personnel recruitment efforts in institutions of higher education.

(Sept. 13, 1994, P. L. 103-322, Title XX, Subtitle B, § 200207, 108 Stat. 2059.)

§ 14117. Local application

(a) In general. A person who desires a scholarship or employment under this subtitle [42 USCS §§ 14111 et seq.] shall submit an application to the State at such time, in such manner, and accompanied by such information as the State may reasonably require.

(b) Contents. An application under subsection (a) shall describe—

(1) the academic courses for which a scholarship is sought; or

(2) the location and duration of employment that is sought.

(c) Priority. In awarding scholarships and providing student employment under this subtitle [42 USCS §§ 14111 et seq.], each State shall give priority to applications from persons who are—

(1) members of racial, ethnic, or gender groups whose representation in the law enforcement agencies within the State is substantially less than in the population eligible for employment in law enforcement in the State;

(2) pursuing an undergraduate degree; and

(3) not receiving financial assistance under the Higher Education Act of 1965 [20 USCS §§ 1001 et seq.].

(Sept. 13, 1994, P. L. 103-322, Title XX, Subtitle B, § 200208, 108 Stat. 2060.)

§ 14118. Scholarship agreement

(a) In general. A person who receives a scholarship under this subtitle [42 USCS §§ 14111 et seq.] shall enter into an agreement with the Director.

(b) Contents. An agreement described in subsection (a) shall—

(1) provide assurances that the scholarship recipient will work in a law enforcement position in the State that awarded the scholarship in accordance with the service obligation described in subsection (c) after completion of the scholarship recipient's academic courses leading to an associate, bachelor, or graduate degree;

(2) provide assurances that the scholarship recipient will repay the entire scholarship in accordance with such terms and conditions as the Director shall prescribe if the requirements of the agreement are not complied with, unless the scholarship recipient—

(A) dies;

(B) becomes physically or emotionally disabled, as established by the sworn affidavit of a qualified physician; or

(C) has been discharged in bankruptcy; and

(3) set forth the terms and conditions under which the scholarship recipient may seek employment in the field of law enforcement in a State other than the State that awarded the scholarship.

(c) Service obligation. (1) In general. Except as provided in paragraph (2), a person who receives a scholarship under this subtitle [42 USCS §§ 14111 et seq.] shall work in a law enforcement position in the State that awarded the scholarship for a period of 1 month for each credit hour for which funds are received under the scholarship.

(2) Special rule. For purposes of satisfying the requirement of paragraph (1), a scholarship recipient shall work in a law enforcement position in the State that awarded the scholarship for not less than 6 months but shall not be required to work in such a position for more than 2 years.

(Sept. 13, 1994, P. L. 103-322, Title XX, Subtitle B, § 200209, 108 Stat. 2060.)

§ 14119. Authorization of appropriations

(a) General authorization of appropriations. There are authorized to be appropriated to carry out this subtitle [42 USCS §§ 14111 et seq.]—

(1) $20,000,000 for fiscal year 1996;

(2) $20,000,000 for fiscal year 1997;

(3) $20,000,000 for fiscal year 1998;

(4) $20,000,000 for fiscal year 1999; and

(5) $20,000,000 for fiscal year 2000.

(b) Uses of funds. Of the funds appropriated under subsection (a) for a fiscal year—

(1) 80 percent shall be available to provide scholarships described in section 200204(a)(1)(A) [42 USCS § 14113(a)(1)(A)]; and

(2) 20 percent shall be available to provide employment described in sections 200204(a)(1)(B) and 200204(a)(2) [42 USCS § 14113(a)(1)(B) and (a)(2)].

(Sept. 13, 1994, P. L. 103-322, Title XX, Subtitle B, § 200210, 108 Stat. 2061.)

CROSS REFERENCES

This section is referred to in 42 USCS § 14112.

STATE AND LOCAL LAW ENFORCEMENT

DNA IDENTIFICATION

§ 14131. Quality assurance and proficiency testing standards

(a) Publication of quality assurance and proficiency testing standards.
(1)(A) Not later than 180 days after the date of enactment of this Act [enacted Sept. 13, 1994], the Director of the Federal Bureau of Investigation shall appoint an advisory board on DNA quality assurance methods from among nominations proposed by the head of the National Academy of Sciences and professional societies of crime laboratory officials.

(B) The advisory board shall include as members scientists from State, local, and private forensic laboratories, molecular geneticists and population geneticists not affiliated with a forensic laboratory, and a representative from the National Institute of Standards and Technology.

(C) The advisory board shall develop, and if appropriate, periodically revise, recommended standards for quality assurance, including standards for testing the proficiency of forensic laboratories, and forensic analysts, in conducting analyses of DNA.

(2) The Director of the Federal Bureau of Investigation, after taking into consideration such recommended standards, shall issue (and revise from time to time) standards for quality assurance, including standards for testing the proficiency of forensic laboratories, and forensic analysts, in conducting analyses of DNA.

(3) The standards described in paragraphs (1) and (2) shall specify criteria for quality assurance and proficiency tests to be applied to the various types of DNA analyses used by forensic laboratories. The standards shall also include a system for grading proficiency testing performance to determine whether a laboratory is performing acceptably.

(4) Until such time as the advisory board has made recommendations to the Director of the Federal Bureau of Investigation and the Director has acted upon those recommendations, the quality assurance guidelines adopted by the technical working group on DNA analysis methods shall be deemed the Director's standards for purposes of this section.

(b) Administration of the advisory board. (1) For administrative purposes, the advisory board appointed under subsection (a) shall be considered an advisory board to the Director of the Federal Bureau of Investigation.

(2) Section 14 of the Federal Advisory Committee Act (5 U.S.C. App.) shall not apply with respect to the advisory board appointed under subsection (a).

(3) The DNA advisory board established under this section shall be separate and distinct from any other advisory board administered by the FBI, and is to be administered separately.

(4) The board shall cease to exist on the date 5 years after the initial appointments are made to the board, unless the existence of the board is extended by the Director of the Federal Bureau of Investigation.

(c) Proficiency testing program. (1) Not later than 1 year after the effective date of this Act, the Director of the National Institute of Justice shall certify to the Committees on the Judiciary of the House and Senate that—

(A) the Institute has entered into a contract with, or made a grant to, an appropriate entity for establishing, or has taken other appropriate action to ensure that there is established, not later than 2 years after the date of enactment of this Act [enacted Sept. 13, 1994], a blind external proficiency testing program for DNA analyses, which shall be available to public and private laboratories performing forensic DNA analyses;

(B) a blind external proficiency testing program for DNA analyses is already readily available to public and private laboratories performing forensic DNA analyses; or

(C) it is not feasible to have blind external testing for DNA forensic analyses.

(2) As used in this subsection, the term "blind external proficiency test" means a test that is presented to a forensic laboratory through a second agency and appears to the analysts to involve routine evidence.

(3) Notwithstanding any other provision of law, the Attorney General shall make available to the Director of the National Institute of Justice during the first fiscal year in which funds are distributed under this subtitle up to $250,000 from the funds available under part X of Title I of the Omnibus Crime Control and Safe Streets Act of 1968 [42 USCS §§ 3796kk et seq.] to carry out this subsection.

(Sept. 13, 1994, P. L. 103-322, Title XXI, Subtitle C, § 210303, 108 Stat. 2068.)

HISTORY; ANCILLARY LAWS AND DIRECTIVES

References in text:

"This subtitle", referred to in this section, is Subtitle C of Title XXI of Act Sept. 13, 1994, P. L. 103-322, which appears generally as 42 USCS §§ 14131 et seq. For full classification of such Subtitle, consult USCS Tables volumes.

The "effective date of this Act", referred to in subsec. (c)(1), is probably the date of enactment of Act Sept. 13, 1994, P. L. 103-322.

CODE OF FEDERAL REGULATIONS

Department of Justice—Grants for correctional facilities, 28 CFR 91.1 et seq.

CROSS REFERENCES

This section is referred to in 42 USCS §§ 3796kk-2, 14132, 14133, 14134, 14214.

RESEARCH GUIDE

Law Review Articles:

Giannelli. Science For Judges VII: Evaluating Evidence of Causation & Forensic Laboratories: Current Issues & Standards: Regulating Crime Laboratories: The Impact of DNA Evidence. 15 JL & Pol'y 59, 2007.

Giannelli. Wrongful Convictions and Forensic Science: the Need to Regulate Crime Labs. 86 NCL Rev 163, 2007.

INTERPRETIVE NOTES AND DECISIONS

In violation of Administrative Procedures Act (APA), 5 USCS § 706, FBI acted arbitrarily in refusing convicted murderer's request, which was accompanied by state court's order, to run manual keyboard search comparing DNA found on victim against FBI's nationwide databank of DNA samples; nothing in DNA Identification Act, 42 USCS §§ 14131 et seq., restricted such searches to federal court orders or required certain accreditation standards for labs running profiles on DNA submitted for comparison, as opposed to labs that provided DNA profiles submitted into FBI's index of samples. Rivera v Mueller (2009, ND Ill) 596 F Supp 2d 1163.

§ 14132. Index to facilitate law enforcement exchange of DNA identification information

(a) Establishment of index. The Director of the Federal Bureau of Investigation may establish an index of—

  (1) DNA identification records of—

    (A) persons convicted of crimes;

    (B) persons who have been charged in an indictment or information with a crime; and

    (C) other persons whose DNA samples are collected under applicable legal authorities, provided that DNA samples that are voluntarily submitted solely for elimination purposes shall not be included in the National DNA Index System;

  (2) analyses of DNA samples recovered from crime scenes;

  (3) analyses of DNA samples recovered from unidentified human remains; and

  (4) analyses of DNA samples voluntarily contributed from relatives of missing persons.

(b) Information. The index described in subsection (a) shall include only information on DNA identification records and DNA analyses that are—

(1) based on analyses performed by or on behalf of a criminal justice agency (or the Secretary of Defense in accordance with section 1565 of title 10, United States Code) in accordance with publicly available standards that satisfy or exceed the guidelines for a quality assurance program for DNA analysis, issued by the Director of the Federal Bureau of Investigation under section 210303 [42 USCS § 14131];

(2) prepared by laboratories that—

(A) not later than 2 years after the date of enactment of the DNA Sexual Assault Justice Act of 2004 [enacted Oct. 30, 2004], have been accredited by a nonprofit professional association of persons actively involved in forensic science that is nationally recognized within the forensic science community; and

(B) undergo external audits, not less than once every 2 years, that demonstrate compliance with standards established by the Director of the Federal Bureau of Investigation; and

(3) maintained by Federal, State, and local criminal justice agencies (or the Secretary of Defense in accordance with section 1565 of title 10, United States Code) pursuant to rules that allow disclosure of stored DNA samples and DNA analyses only—

(A) to criminal justice agencies for law enforcement identification purposes;

(B) in judicial proceedings, if otherwise admissible pursuant to applicable statutes or rules;

(C) for criminal defense purposes, to a defendant, who shall have access to samples and analyses performed in connection with the case in which such defendant is charged; or

(D) if personally identifiable information is removed, for a population statistics database, for identification research and protocol development purposes, or for quality control purposes.

(c) Failure to comply. Access to the index established by this section is subject to cancellation if the quality control and privacy requirements described in subsection (b) are not met.

(d) Expungement of records. (1) By Director. (A) The Director of the Federal Bureau of Investigation shall promptly expunge from the index described in subsection (a) the DNA analysis of a person included in the index—

(i) on the basis of conviction for a qualifying Federal offense or a qualifying District of Columbia offense (as determined under sections 3 and 4 of the DNA Analysis Backlog Elimination Act of 2000 (42 U.S.C. 14135a, 14135b), respectively), if the Director receives, for each conviction of the person of a qualifying offense, a certified copy of a final court order establishing that such conviction has been overturned; or

(ii) on the basis of an arrest under the authority of the United States, if the Attorney General receives, for each charge against the person on the basis of which the analysis was or could have been included in the index, a certified copy of a final court order establishing that such charge has been dismissed or has resulted in an acquittal or that no charge was filed within the applicable time period.

(B) For purposes of subparagraph (A), the term "qualifying offense" means any of the following offenses:

(i) A qualifying Federal offense, as determined under section 3 of the DNA Analysis Backlog Elimination Act of 2000 [42 USCS § 14135a].

(ii) A qualifying District of Columbia offense, as determined under section 4 of the DNA Analysis Backlog Elimination Act of 2000 [42 USCS § 14135b].

(iii) A qualifying military offense, as determined under section 1565 of title 10, United States Code.

(C) For purposes of subparagraph (A), a court order is not "final" if time remains for an appeal or application for discretionary review with respect to the order.

(2) By States. (A) As a condition of access to the index described in subsection (a), a State shall promptly expunge from that index the DNA analysis of a person included in the index by that State if—

(i) the responsible agency or official of that State receives, for each conviction of the person of an offense on the basis of which that analysis was or could have been included in the index, a certified copy of a final court order establishing that such conviction has been overturned; or

(ii) the person has not been convicted of an offense on the basis of which that analysis was or could have been included in the index, and the responsible agency or official of that State receives, for each charge against the person on the basis of which the analysis was or could have been included in the index, a certified copy of a final court order establishing that such charge has been dismissed or has resulted in an acquittal or that no charge was filed within the applicable time period.

(B) For purposes of subparagraph (A), a court order is not "final" if time remains for an appeal or application for discretionary review with respect to the order.

(Sept. 13, 1994, P. L. 103-322, Title XXI, Subtitle C, § 210304, 108 Stat. 2069; Nov. 29, 1999, P. L. 106-113, Div B, § 1000(a)(1), 113 Stat. 1535; Dec. 19, 2000, P. L. 106-546, § 6(b), 114 Stat. 2733; Oct. 30, 2004, P. L. 108-405, Title II, § 203(a), (d), Title III, § 302, 118 Stat. 2269, 2270, 2272; Jan. 5, 2006, P. L. 109-162, Title X, § 1002, 119 Stat. 3084.)

HISTORY; ANCILLARY LAWS AND DIRECTIVES

Explanatory notes:

The amendment made by § 1000(a)(1) of Act Nov. 29, 1999, P. L. 106-113, is based on § 120 of Title I of H.R. 3421 (113 Stat. 1501A-23), as introduced on Nov. 17, 1999, which was enacted into law by such § 1000(a)(1).

Amendments:

1999. Act Nov. 29, 1999, in subsec. (a), in para. (2), deleted "and" after the concluding semicolon, in para. (3), substituted ''; and'' for a concluding period, and added para. (4).

2000. Act Dec. 19, 2000, in subsec. (b), in para. (1), inserted ''(or the Secretary of Defense in accordance with section 1565 of title 10, United States Code)'', in para. (2), substituted ''semiannual'' for '', at regular intervals of not to exceed 180 days,'', and, in para. (3), inserted ''(or the Secretary of Defense in accordance with section 1565 of title 10, United States Code)''; and added subsec. (d).

2004. Act Oct. 30, 2004, in subsec. (a)(1), substituted ''of—'' and subparas. (A)–(C) for ''of persons convicted of crimes;''; in subsec. (b), substituted para. (2) for one which read: ''(2) prepared by laboratories, and DNA analysts, that undergo semiannual external proficiency testing by a DNA proficiency testing program meeting the standards issued under section 210303; and''; in subsec. (d)(2)(A), substituted ''if—

''(i) the responsible agency''

for ''if the responsible agency'', substituted ''; or'' for a concluding period, and added cl. (ii); and added subsec. (e).

2006. Act Jan. 5, 2006, in subsec. (a)(1)(C), deleted ''DNA profiles from arrestees who have not been charged in an indictment or information with a crime, and'' following ''provided that''; in subsec. (d), in para. (1), substituted subpara. (A) for one which read: ''(A) The Director of the Federal Bureau of Investigation shall promptly expunge from the index described in subsection (a) the DNA analysis of a person included in the index on the basis of a qualifying Federal offense or a qualifying District of Columbia offense (as determined under sections 3 and 4 of the DNA Analysis Backlog Elimination Act of 2000, respectively) if the Director receives, for each conviction of the person of a qualifying offense, a certified copy of a final court order establishing that such conviction has been overturned.'', and, in para. (2)(A)(ii), substituted ''the responsible agency or official of that State receives, for each charge against the person on the basis of which the analysis was or could have been included in the index, a certified copy of a final court order establishing that such charge has been dismissed or has resulted in an acquittal or that no charge was filed within the applicable time period.'' for ''all charges for which the analysis was or could have been included in the index have been dismissed or resulted in acquittal.''; and deleted subsec. (e), which read:

''(e) Authority for keyboard searches. (1) In general. The Director shall ensure that any person who is authorized to access the index described in subsection (a) for purposes of including information on DNA identification records or DNA analyses in that index may also access that index for purposes of carrying out a one-time keyboard search on information obtained from any DNA sample lawfully collected for a criminal justice purpose except for a DNA sample voluntarily submitted solely for elimination purposes.

''(2) Definition. For purposes of paragraph (1), the term 'keyboard search' means a search under which information obtained from a DNA sample is compared with information in the index without resulting in the information obtained from a DNA sample being included in the index.

''(3) No preemption. This subsection shall not be construed to preempt State law.''.

CODE OF FEDERAL REGULATIONS
Department of Justice—DNA identification system, 28 CFR 28.1 et seq.

CROSS REFERENCES
This section is referred to in 10 USCS § 1565; 42 USCS §§ 14134, 14135, 14135e, 14214.

RESEARCH GUIDE
Law Review Articles:

Tracy; Morgan. Criminology: Big Brother and His Science Kit: Dna Databases For 21st Century Crime Control?. 90 J Crim L & Criminology 635, Winter, 2000.

Murphy. Relative Doubt: Familial Searches of DNA Databases. 109 Mich L Rev 291, 2010.

Joh. Reclaiming "Abandoned" DNA: the Fourth Amendment and Genetic Privacy. 100 Nw UL Rev 857, Winter, 2006.

Giannelli. Wrongful Convictions and Forensic Science: the Need to Regulate Crime Labs. 86 NCL Rev 163, 2007.

Giannelli. Forensic Science: Under the Microscope. 34 Ohio NUL Rev 315, 2008.

INTERPRETIVE NOTES AND DECISIONS

1. Constitutionality
2. Expungement of records
3. Miscellaneous

1. Constitutionality

District court properly modified conditions of federal probationer's probation to require him to have his DNA collected as directed by his probation officer pursuant to DNA Analysis Backlog Elimination Act of 2000; under totality of circumstances, collection of DNA under 42 USCS § 14135a(a)(2) for inclusion in Combined DNA Index System database under 42 USCS § 14132 did not constitute unreasonable search and seizure in violation of Fourth Amendment, given probationers' diminished privacy rights, minimal intrusion involved in obtaining DNA samples, and legitimate governmental interest in using DNA as crime investigating tool. United States v Kraklio (2006, CA8 Iowa) 451 F3d 922, reh den, reh, en banc, den (2006, CA8) 2006 US App LEXIS 20456 and cert den (2006) 549 US 1044, 127 S Ct 611, 166 L Ed 2d 453 and (criticized in State v Martin (2008) 184 Vt 23, 2008 VT 53, 955 A2d 1144).

Collection of DNA samples pursuant to DNA Analysis Backlog Elimination Act of 2000, Pub. L. No. 106-546, 114 Stat. 2726, codified as amended in part at 18 USCS § 3563 and 42 USCS §§ 14132, 14135a, 14135e, did not violate Fourth Amendment as to probationers in light of U.S. Court of Appeals for First Circuit's holding in U.S. v. Weikert, 504 F.3d 1 (1st Cir. 2007); though defendants pled guilty to non-violent, property-related crimes pursuant to

18 USCS §§ 641 and 473, their argument that new balancing test should be applied to them as result stemmed from flawed assumption that DNA evidence was only useful for solving-and thereby deterring-violent crimes; moreover, they did not have greater expectation of privacy than did supervised releasees as both probation, pursuant to 18 USCS §§ 3561, 3563, and supervised release, pursuant to 18 USCS § 3583, were forms of conditional release. United States v Stewart (2008, CA1 Mass) 532 F3d 32.

During probation, plaintiff probationer had diminished expectation of privacy and DNA Analysis Backlog Elimination Act of 2000 and D.C. Code Ann. § 22-4151 furthered compelling public interest under totality of circumstances analysis as to reasonableness, so that taking of probationer's DNA sample by defendant probation officers did not violate Fourth Amendment, and further, 42 USCS § 14132(b)(3) limited use of DNA profiles to, inter alia, criminal justice agencies for law enforcement purposes and in judicial proceedings and 42 USCS § 14135e(c) prescribed criminal penalties for improper acquisition, use, or disclosure of DNA or of DNA sample results. Johnson v Quander (2005, DC Dist Col) 370 F Supp 2d 79, affd (2006, App DC) 370 US App DC 167, 440 F3d 489, cert den (2006) 549 US 945, 127 S Ct 103, 166 L Ed 2d 255 and (criticized in United States v Stewart (2007, DC Mass) 468 F Supp 2d 261) and (criticized in State v Martin (2008) 184 Vt 23, 2008 VT 53, 955 A2d 1144).

2. Expungement of records

Where, 11 years after her guilty plea, defendant filed motion in her original criminal case to expunge her conviction alleging that there was inadequate basis for her Alford plea, that her attorney had conflict of interest, and that her plea rested on search and seizure that was later declared unlawful in co-defendant's matter, defendant's claims were solely "equitable" and, thus, to obtain expungement, defendant was required to first obtain judgment that her conviction was unlawful; defendant had not first sought relief under any statute such as 18 USCS §§ 921(a)(20), (33)(B)(ii), 3607(b), (c), 5010(a) (repealed 1984), 21 USCS § 844a(j), 38 USCS § 7462(d)(1), 10 USCS § 1565(e), 42 USCS § 14132(d), 28 USCS § 2255, or All Writs Act, 28 USCS § 1651, or under theory stemming from pardon under U.S. Const. art. II, § 2, cl. 1. United States v Crowell (2004, CA9 Or) 374 F3d 790, cert den (2005) 543 US 1070, 125 S Ct 911, 160 L Ed 2d 806.

Under 42 USCS § 14132(d), part of DNA Analysis Backlog Elimination Act of 2000, if conviction for predicate offense was later overturned or reversed on appeal, individual's DNA information could be removed from Combined DNA Index System (CODIS) database and thus, prospect that innocent individual's DNA would be erroneously included in CODIS database was minimal; if there was question as to whether offense was "qualifying offense," person could always bring challenge in court of competent jurisdiction, and since 42 USCS § 14135b(b) explicitly limited how DNA samples could be used, and 42 USCS § 14135b(c)(2) provided that such analysis was only conducted to determine "identification information in bodily sample," risk of erroneous deprivation of liberty interest in plaintiff probationer's DNA was remote. Johnson v Quander (2005, DC Dist Col) 370 F Supp 2d 79, affd (2006, App DC) 370 US App DC 167, 440 F3d 489, cert den (2006) 549 US 945, 127 S Ct 103, 166 L Ed 2d 255 and (criticized in United States v Stewart (2007, DC Mass) 468 F Supp 2d 261) and (criticized in State v Martin (2008) 184 Vt 23, 2008 VT 53, 955 A2d 1144).

3. Miscellaneous

DNA Analysis Backlog Elimination Act of 2000, Pub. L. No. 106-546 (codified as amended in scattered sections of 10 USCS, 18 USCS, and 42 USCS), included safeguards to protect privacy interests of supervised releasee who was required to provide sample; 42 USCS § 14132(b)(3) strictly limited use

of information, which was stored in centralized database. 42 USCS § 14135e(c) provided penalties for misuse of DNA samples; moreover, DNA Act included no discretionary component, given explicit directive set forth in 42 USCS § 14135a(a)(2). United States v Weikert (2007, CA1 Mass) 504 F3d 1, reh den, reh, en banc, den (2007, CA1) 504 F3d 20 and (criticized in State v Martin (2008) 184 Vt 23, 2008 VT 53, 955 A2d 1144) and (criticized in Boroian v Mueller (2010, CA1 Mass) 616 F3d 60).

While plaintiff former probationer challenged retaining and matching of his DNA profile, as provided for in 42 USCS § 14135a given stringent restrictions on uses of DNA profiles, as set forth in 42 USCS § 14132(b)(3), 14135e(c), possible future extraction of other information beyond identification did not significantly augment current privacy interest which was lacking. Boroian v Mueller (2010, CA1 Mass) 616 F3d 60.

Where defendant's DNA was extracted from clothing that had been seized as evidence in connection with shooting in which defendant was victim and defendant was excluded as source of DNA sample from unrelated homicide, Maryland and federal DNA indexing statutes supported conclusion that defendant retained significant privacy interest in his DNA profile because 42 USCS § 14132(d) and Md. Code Ann., Pub. Safety § 2-511 suggested that victims' DNA was not intended to be included in DNA databases, defendant's clothing was not tested promptly within meaning of Md. Code Ann., Pub. Safety § 2-504(a)(3)(iii), and defendant's DNA would have been subject to expungement under Md. Code Ann., Pub. Safety § 2-505(a)(1)(i); because generalized interest in crime control did not overcome defendant's continuing privacy interest in his DNA profile, inclusion of defendant's DNA profile in local law enforcement database was not reasonable under Fourth Amendment. United States v Davis (2009, DC Md) 657 F Supp 2d 630.

Plaintiff was precluded from obtaining records from National DNA Information System through Freedom of Information Act request, in part, because plaintiff could not show that he was criminal defendant before court. Moore v Nat'l DNA Index Sys. (2009, DC Dist Col) 662 F Supp 2d 136.

Where pro se plaintiff sought disclosure of his DNA profile that was incorporated into National DNA Identification System under DNA Identification Act of 1994, because of his status as sex offender, proper jurisdiction lay in district court. Doe v United States (2006) 74 Fed Cl 794.

§ 14133. Federal Bureau of Investigation

(a) **Proficiency testing requirements.** (1) **Generally.** (A) Personnel at the Federal Bureau of Investigation who perform DNA analyses shall undergo semiannual external proficiency testing by a DNA proficiency testing program meeting the standards issued under section 210303 [42 USCS § 14131].

(B) Within 1 year after the date of enactment of this Act [enacted Sept. 13, 1994], the Director of the Federal Bureau of Investigation shall arrange for periodic blind external tests to determine the proficiency of DNA analysis performed at the Federal Bureau of Investigation laboratory.

(C) In this paragraph, "blind external test" means a test that is presented to the laboratory through a second agency and appears to the analysts to involve routine evidence.

(2) Report. For 5 years after the date of enactment of this Act [enacted Sept. 13, 1994], the Director of the Federal Bureau of Investigation shall submit to the Committees on the Judiciary of the House and Senate an annual report on the results of each of the tests described in paragraph (1).

(b) Privacy protection standards. (1) Generally. Except as provided in paragraph (2), the results of DNA tests performed for a Federal law enforcement agency for law enforcement purposes may be disclosed only—

(A) to criminal justice agencies for law enforcement identification purposes;

(B) in judicial proceedings, if otherwise admissible pursuant to applicable statues [statutes] or rules; and

(C) for criminal defense purposes, to a defendant, who shall have access to samples and analyses performed in connection with the case in which such defendant is charged.

(2) Exception. If personally identifiable information is removed, test results may be disclosed for a population statistics database, for identification research and protocol development purposes, or for quality control purposes.

(c) Criminal penalty. (1) A person who—

(A) by virtue of employment or official position, has possession of, or access to, individually identifiable DNA information indexed in a database created or maintained by any Federal law enforcement agency; and

(B) knowingly discloses such information in any manner to any person or agency not authorized to receive it,

shall be fined not more than $100,000.

(2) A person who, without authorization, knowingly obtains DNA samples or individually identifiable DNA information indexed in a database created or maintained by any Federal law enforcement agency shall be fined not more than $250,000, or imprisoned for a period of not more than one year, or both.

(Sept. 13, 1994, P. L. 103-322, Title XXI, Subtitle C, § 210305, 108 Stat. 2070; Dec. 19, 2000, P. L. 106-546, § 8(c), 114 Stat. 2735; Oct. 30, 2004, P. L. 108-405, Title II, § 203(e)(1), 118 Stat. 2270.)

HISTORY; ANCILLARY LAWS AND DIRECTIVES

Explanatory notes:
The bracketed word "statutes" has been inserted in subsec. (b)(1)(B) as the word probably intended by Congress.

Amendments:

2000. Act Dec. 19, 2000, in subsec. (a)(1)(A), substituted "semiannual" for ", at regular intervals of not to exceed 180 days,".

2004. Act Oct. 30, 2004, in subsec. (c)(2), substituted "$250,000, or imprisoned for a period of not more than one year, or both" for "$100,000".

CROSS REFERENCES

This section is referred to in 42 USCS §§ 14134, 14214.

§ 14134. Authorization of appropriations

There are authorized to be appropriated to the Federal Bureau of Investigation to carry out sections 210303, 210304, and 210305 [42 USCS §§ 14131, 14132, 14133]—

(1) $5,500,000 for fiscal year 1996;

(2) $8,000,000 for fiscal year 1997;

(3) $8,000,000 for fiscal year 1998;

(4) $2,500,000 for fiscal year 1999; and

(5) $1,000,000 for fiscal year 2000.

(Sept. 13, 1994, P. L. 103-322, Title XXI, Subtitle C, § 210306, 108 Stat. 2071.)

CROSS REFERENCES

This section is referred to in 42 USCS § 14214.

§ 14135. The Debbie Smith DNA Backlog Grant Program

(a) Authorization of grants. The Attorney General may make grants to eligible States or units of local government for use by the State or unit of local government for the following purposes:

(1) To carry out, for inclusion in the Combined DNA Index System of the Federal Bureau of Investigation, DNA analyses of samples collected under applicable legal authority.

(2) To carry out, for inclusion in such Combined DNA Index System, DNA analyses of samples from crime scenes, including samples from rape kits, samples from other sexual assault evidence, and samples taken in cases without an identified suspect.

(3) To increase the capacity of laboratories owned by the State or by units of local government to carry out DNA analyses of samples specified in paragraph (1) or (2).

(4) To collect DNA samples specified in paragraph (1).

(5) To ensure that DNA testing and analysis of samples from crimes, including sexual assault and other serious violent crimes, are carried out in a timely manner.

(b) Eligibility. For a State or unit of local government to be eligible to receive a grant under this section, the chief executive officer of the State or unit of local government shall submit to the Attorney General an application in such form and containing such information as the Attorney General may require. The application shall, as required by the Attorney General—

    (1) provide assurances that the State or unit of local government has implemented, or will implement not later than 120 days after the date of such application, a comprehensive plan for the expeditious DNA analysis of samples in accordance with this section;

    (2) include a certification that each DNA analysis carried out under the plan shall be maintained pursuant to the privacy requirements described in section 210304(b)(3) of the Violent Crime Control and Law Enforcement Act of 1994 (42 U.S.C. 14132(b)(3));

    (3) include a certification that the State or unit of local government has determined, by statute, rule, or regulation, those offenses under State law that shall be treated for purposes of this section as qualifying State offenses;

    (4) specify the allocation that the State or unit of local government shall make, in using grant amounts to carry out DNA analyses of samples, as between samples specified in subsection (a)(1) and samples specified in subsection (a)(2);

    (5) specify that portion of grant amounts that the State or unit of local government shall use for the purpose specified in subsection (a)(3);

    (6) if submitted by a unit of local government, certify that the unit of local government has taken, or is taking, all necessary steps to ensure that it is eligible to include, directly or through a State law enforcement agency, all analyses of samples for which it has requested funding in the Combined DNA Index System; and

    (7) specify that portion of grant amounts that the State or unit of local government shall use for the purpose specified in subsection (a)(4).

(c) Formula for distribution of grants. (1) In general. The Attorney General shall distribute grant amounts, and establish appropriate grant conditions under this section, in conformity with a formula or formulas that are designed to effectuate a distribution of funds among eligible States and units of local government that—

    (A) maximizes the effective utilization of DNA technology to solve crimes and protect public safety; and

    (B) allocates grants among eligible entities fairly and efficiently to address jurisdictions in which significant backlogs exist, by considering—

        (i) the number of offender and casework samples awaiting DNA analysis in a jurisdiction;

        (ii) the population in the jurisdiction; and

        (iii) the number of part 1 violent crimes in the jurisdiction.

(2) Minimum amount. The Attorney General shall allocate to each State not less than 0.50 percent of the total amount appropriated in a fiscal year for grants under this section, except that the United States Virgin Islands, American Samoa, Guam, and the Northern Mariana Islands shall each be allocated 0.125 percent of the total appropriation.

(3) Limitation. Grant amounts distributed under paragraph (1) shall be awarded to conduct DNA analyses of samples from casework or from

victims of crime under subsection (a)(2) in accordance with the following limitations:

(A) For fiscal year 2009, not less than 40 percent of the grant amounts shall be awarded for purposes under subsection (a)(2).

(B) For each of the fiscal years 2010 through 2014, not less than 40 percent of the grant amounts shall be awarded for purposes under subsection (a)(2).

(d) **Analysis of samples.** (1) In general. A plan pursuant to subsection (b)(1) shall require that, except as provided in paragraph (3), each DNA analysis be carried out in a laboratory that satisfies quality assurance standards and is—

(A) operated by the State or a unit of local government; or

(B) operated by a private entity pursuant to a contract with the State or a unit of local government.

(2) Quality assurance standards. (A) The Director of the Federal Bureau of Investigation shall maintain and make available to States and units of local government a description of quality assurance protocols and practices that the Director considers adequate to assure the quality of a forensic laboratory.

(B) For purposes of this section, a laboratory satisfies quality assurance standards if the laboratory satisfies the quality control requirements described in paragraphs (1) and (2) of section 210304(b) of the Violent Crime Control and Law Enforcement Act of 1994 (42 U.S.C. 14132(b)).

(3) Use of vouchers or contracts for certain purposes. (A) In general. A grant for the purposes specified in paragraph (1), (2), or (5) of subsection (a) may be made in the form of a voucher or contract for laboratory services, even if the laboratory makes a reasonable profit for the services.

(B) Redemption. A voucher or contract under subparagraph (A) may be redeemed at a laboratory operated on a nonprofit or for-profit basis, by a private entity that satisfies quality assurance standards and has been approved by the Attorney General.

(C) Payments. The Attorney General may use amounts authorized under subsection (j) to make payments to a laboratory described under subparagraph (B).

(e) **Restrictions on use of funds.** (1) Nonsupplanting. Funds made available pursuant to this section shall not be used to supplant State or local government funds, but shall be used to increase the amount of funds that would, in the absence of Federal funds, be made available from State or local government sources for the purposes of this Act.

(2) Administrative costs. A State or unit of local government may not use more than 3 percent of the funds it receives from this section for administrative expenses.

(f) **Reports to the Attorney General.** Each State or unit of local government which receives a grant under this section shall submit to the Attorney General, for each year in which funds from a grant received under this section is expended, a report at such time and in such manner as the Attorney General may reasonably require, which contains—

(1) a summary of the activities carried out under the grant and an assessment of whether such activities are meeting the needs identified in the application; and

(2) such other information as the Attorney General may require.

(g) Reports to Congress. Not later than 90 days after the end of each fiscal year for which grants are made under this section, the Attorney General shall submit to the Congress a report that includes—

(1) the aggregate amount of grants made under this section to each State or unit of local government for such fiscal year;

(2) a summary of the information provided by States or units of local government receiving grants under this section; and

(3) a description of the priorities and plan for awarding grants among eligible States and units of local government, and how such plan will ensure the effective use of DNA technology to solve crimes and protect public safety.

(h) Expenditure records. (1) In general. Each State or unit of local government which receives a grant under this section shall keep records as the Attorney General may require to facilitate an effective audit of the receipt and use of grant funds received under this section.

(2) Access. Each State or unit of local government which receives a grant under this section shall make available, for the purpose of audit and examination, such records as are related to the receipt or use of any such grant.

(i) Definition. For purposes of this section, the term "State" means a State of the United States, the District of Columbia, the Commonwealth of Puerto Rico, the United States Virgin Islands, American Samoa, Guam, and the Northern Mariana Islands.

(j) Authorization of appropriations. There are authorized to be appropriated to the Attorney General for grants under subsection (a) $151,000,000 for each of fiscal years 2009 through 2014.

(k) Use of funds for accreditation and audits. The Attorney General may distribute not more than 1 percent of the grant amounts under subsection (j)—

(1) to States or units of local government to defray the costs incurred by laboratories operated by each such State or unit of local government in preparing for accreditation or reaccreditation;

(2) in the form of additional grants to States, units of local government, or nonprofit professional organizations of persons actively involved in forensic science and nationally recognized within the forensic science community—

(A) to defray the costs of external audits of laboratories operated by such State or unit of local government, which participates in the National DNA Index System, to determine whether the laboratory is in compliance with quality assurance standards;

(B) to assess compliance with any plans submitted to the National Institute of Justice, which detail the use of funds received by States or units of local government under this Act; and

(C) to support future capacity building efforts; and

(3) in the form of additional grants to nonprofit professional associations actively involved in forensic science and nationally recognized within the forensic science community to defray the costs of training persons who conduct external audits of laboratories operated by States and units of local government and which participate in the National DNA Index System.

(l) Use of funds for other forensic sciences. The Attorney General may award a grant under this section to a State or unit of local government to alleviate a backlog of cases with respect to a forensic science other than DNA analysis if the State or unit of local government—

(1) certifies to the Attorney General that in such State or unit—

(A) all of the purposes set forth in subsection (a) have been met;

(B) a significant backlog of casework is not waiting for DNA analysis; and

(C) there is no need for significant laboratory equipment, supplies, or additional personnel for timely DNA processing of casework or offender samples; and

(2) demonstrates to the Attorney General that such State or unit requires assistance in alleviating a backlog of cases involving a forensic science other than DNA analysis.

(m) External audits and remedial efforts. In the event that a laboratory operated by a State or unit of local government which has received funds under this Act has undergone an external audit conducted to determine whether the laboratory is in compliance with standards established by the Director of the Federal Bureau of Investigation, and, as a result of such audit, identifies measures to remedy deficiencies with respect to the compliance by the laboratory with such standards, the State or unit of local government shall implement any such remediation as soon as practicable.

(Dec. 19, 2000, P. L. 106-546, § 2, 114 Stat. 2726; Oct. 30, 2004, P. L. 108-405, Title II, §§ 202, 206, 118 Stat. 2266, 2272; Jan. 5, 2006, P. L. 109-162, Title X, § 1003, 119 Stat. 3085; Oct. 8, 2008, P. L. 110-360, § 2, 122 Stat. 4008.)

HISTORY; ANCILLARY LAWS AND DIRECTIVES

References in text:

"This Act", referred to in this section, is Act Dec. 19, 2000, P. L. 106-546, which is classified in part to 42 USCS §§ 14135 et seq. For full classification of such Act, consult USCS Tables volumes.

Explanatory notes:

This section was enacted as part of Act Dec. 19, 2000, P. L. 106-546, and not as part of Act Sept. 13, 1994, P. L. 103-322, which generally comprises this chapter.

Amendments:

2004. Act Oct. 30, 2004, substituted the section heading for one which read: "Authorization of grants"; in subsec. (a), in the introductory matter, inserted "or units of local government" and "or unit of local government", in para. (2), inserted ", including samples from rape kits, samples from

other sexual assault evidence, and samples taken in cases without an identified suspect", in para. (3), deleted "within the State" following "government" and inserted "(1) or", and added paras. (4) and (5); in subsec. (b),
in the introductory matter, inserted "or unit of local government" in two
places, and inserted ", as required by the Attorney General", in paras. (1)
and (3), inserted "or unit of local government", in para. (4), inserted "or
unit of local government" and deleted "and" following the concluding
semicolon, in para. (5), inserted "or unit of local government" and
substituted the concluding semicolon for a period, and added paras. (6) and
(7); substituted subsec. (c) for one which read: "(c) Crimes without
suspects. A State that proposes to allocate grant amounts under paragraph
(4) or (5) of subsection (b) for the purposes specified in paragraph (2) or
(3) of subsection (a) shall use such allocated amounts to conduct or
facilitate DNA analyses of those samples that relate to crimes in connection with which there are no suspects."; in subsec. (d), in para. (1), in the
introductory matter, substituted "A plan pursuant to subsection (b)(1)" for
"The plan", and, in subparas. (A) and (B), deleted "within the State" following "government", in para. (2)(A), inserted "and units of local government", and substituted para. (3) for one which read: "(3) Use of vouchers
for certain purposes. A grant for the purposes specified in paragraph (1) or
(2) of subsection (a) may be made in the form of a voucher for laboratory
services, which may be redeemed at a laboratory operated by a private
entity approved by the Attorney General that satisfies quality assurance
standards. The Attorney General may make payment to such a laboratory
for the analysis of DNA samples using amounts authorized for those
purposes under subsection (j)."; in subsec. (e), in para. (1), inserted "or
local government" in two places, and, in para. (2), inserted "or units of
local government"; in subsec. (f), in the introductory matter, inserted "or
unit of local government"; in subsec. (g), in para. (1), inserted "or unit of
local government" and deleted "and" following the concluding semicolon,
in para. (2), inserted "or units of local government" and substituted
"; and" for a concluding period, and added para. (3); in subsec. (h), in
paras. (1) and (2), inserted "or unit of local government"; in subsec. (j),
substituted paras. (1)–(5) for former paras. (1) and (2), which read:

"(1) For grants for the purposes specified in paragraph (1) of such
subsection—

"(A) $15,000,000 for fiscal year 2001;

"(B) $15,000,000 for fiscal year 2002; and

"(C) $15,000,000 for fiscal year 2003.

"(2) For grants for the purposes specified in paragraphs (2) and (3) of
such subsection—

"(A) $25,000,000 for fiscal year 2001;

"(B) $50,000,000 for fiscal year 2002;

"(C) $25,000,000 for fiscal year 2003; and

"(D) $25,000,000 for fiscal year 2004.";

and added subsecs. (k)–(m).

2006. Act Jan. 5, 2006, in subsec. (a)(1), substituted "collected under applicable legal authority" for "taken from individuals convicted of a
qualifying State offense (as determined under subsection (b)(3))".

2008. Act Oct. 8, 2008, in subsec. (c)(3), deleted subparas. (A)–(D) which
read:

"(A) For fiscal year 2005, not less than 50 percent of the grant amounts shall be awarded for purposes under subsection (a)(2).

"(B) For fiscal year 2006, not less than 50 percent of the grant amounts shall be awarded for purposes under subsection (a)(2).

"(C) For fiscal year 2007, not less than 45 percent of the grant amounts shall be awarded for purposes under subsection (a)(2).

"(D) For fiscal year 2008, not less than 40 percent of the grant amounts shall be awarded for purposes under subsection (a)(2).";

and substituted subsec. (j) for one which read:

"(j) Authorization of appropriations. Amounts are authorized to be appropriated to the Attorney General for grants under subsection (a) as follows:

"(1) $151,000,000 for fiscal year 2005;

"(2) $151,000,000 for fiscal year 2006;

"(3) $151,000,000 for fiscal year 2007;

"(4) $151,000,000 for fiscal year 2008; and

"(5) $151,000,000 for fiscal year 2009.".

Such Act further, in subsec. (c)(3), directed the amendment of subsec. (c)(3) "by redesignating subparagraph (E) and subparagraph (A)"; however, subpara. (E) was redesignated as subpara. (A) in order to effectuate the probable intent of Congress.

Such Act further, in subsec. (c)(3), added subpara. (B).

Other provisions:

Sense of Congress regarding obligation of grantee States to ensure access to post-conviction DNA testing and competent counsel in capital cases. Acts Dec. 19, 2000, P. L. 106-546, § 11, 114 Stat. 2735, and Dec. 21, 2000, P. L. 106-561, § 4, 114 Stat. 2791, provide:

"(a) Findings. Congress finds that—

"(1) over the past decade, deoxyribonucleic acid testing (referred to in this section as 'DNA testing') has emerged as the most reliable forensic technique for identifying criminals when biological material is left at a crime scene;

"(2) because of its scientific precision, DNA testing can, in some cases, conclusively establish the guilt or innocence of a criminal defendant;

"(3) in other cases, DNA testing may not conclusively establish guilt or innocence, but may have significant probative value to a finder of fact;

"(4) DNA testing was not widely available in cases tried prior to 1994;

"(5) new forensic DNA testing procedures have made it possible to get results from minute samples that could not previously be tested, and to obtain more informative and accurate results than earlier forms of forensic DNA testing could produce, resulting in some cases of convicted inmates being exonerated by new DNA tests after earlier tests had failed to produce definitive results;

"(6) DNA testing can and has resulted in the post-conviction exoneration of more than 75 innocent men and women, including some under sentence of death;

"(7) in more than a dozen cases, post-conviction DNA testing that has exonerated an innocent person has also enhanced public safety by providing evidence that led to the apprehension of the actual perpetrator;

"(8) experience has shown that it is not unduly burdensome to make DNA testing available to inmates in appropriate cases;

"(9) under current Federal and State law, it is difficult to obtain post-conviction DNA testing because of time limits on introducing newly discovered evidence;

"(10) the National Commission on the Future of DNA Evidence, a Federal panel established by the Department of Justice and comprised of law enforcement, judicial, and scientific experts, has urged that post-conviction DNA testing be permitted in the relatively small number of cases in which it is appropriate, notwithstanding procedural rules that could be invoked to preclude such testing, and notwithstanding the inability of an inmate to pay for the testing;

"(11) only a few States have adopted post-conviction DNA testing procedures;

"(12) States have received millions of dollars in DNA-related grants, and more funding is needed to improve State forensic facilities and to reduce the nationwide backlog of DNA samples from convicted offenders and crime scenes that need to be tested or retested using upgraded methods;

"(13) States that accept such financial assistance should not deny the promise of truth and justice for both sides of our adversarial system that DNA testing offers;

"(14) post-conviction DNA testing and other post-conviction investigative techniques have shown that innocent people have been sentenced to death in this country;

"(15) a constitutional error in capital cases is incompetent defense lawyers who fail to present important evidence that the defendant may have been innocent or does not deserve to be sentenced to death; and

"(16) providing quality representation to defendants facing loss of liberty or life is essential to fundamental due process and the speedy final resolution of judicial proceedings.

"(b) Sense of Congress. It is the sense of Congress that—

"(1) Congress should condition forensic science-related grants to a State or State forensic facility on the State's agreement to ensure post-conviction DNA testing in appropriate cases; and

"(2) Congress should work with the States to improve the quality of legal representation in capital cases through the establishment of standards that will assure the timely appointment of competent counsel with adequate resources to represent defendants in capital cases at each stage of the proceedings.".

CODE OF FEDERAL REGULATIONS

Department of Justice—DNA identification system, 28 CFR 28.1 et seq.

CROSS REFERENCES

This section is referred to in 42 USCS § 14135e.

RESEARCH GUIDE

Am Jur:

68 Am Jur 2d, Searches and Seizures § 52.

Federal Taxation:

1 Tax Controversies: Audits, Investigations, Trials (Matthew Bender), ch 10, Fifth Amendment Right Against Self-Incrimination § 10.04.

Annotations:
Validity, Construction, and Application of DNA Analysis Backlog Elimination Act of 2000, 42 U.S.C.A. §§ 14135 et seq. [42 USCS §§ 14135 et seq.] and 10 U.S.C.A. § 1565 [10 USCS § 1565]. 187 ALR Fed 373.

INTERPRETIVE NOTES AND DECISIONS

1. Generally
2. Constitutionality
3. Miscellaneous

1. Generally

Because Congress expressly delegated interpretive authority to Attorney General, under DNA Analysis Backlog Elimination Act of 2000, 42 USCS §§ 14135 et seq., and Attorney General's interpretation has been expressed through rule-making process under Administrative Procedure Act, 5 USCS §§ 500 et seq., Attorney General's construction of statute is entitled to substantial deference and must be sustained if reasonable. United States v Henderson (2004, CA7 Wis) 376 F3d 730.

2. Constitutionality

Dismissal of inmates' complaint, which challenged collection of DNA samples pursuant to DNA Analysis Backlog Elimination Act of 2000, 42 USCS §§ 14135–14135e, was affirmed because collection of samples was reasonable in light of inmates' diminished privacy rights, minimal intrusion involved, and legitimate government interest in using DNA to fight crime. Groceman v United States DOJ (2004, CA5 Tex) 354 F3d 411 (criticized in United States v Weikert (2006, DC Mass) 421 F Supp 2d 259) and (criticized in State v O'Hagen (2007) 189 NJ 140, 914 A2d 267) and (criticized in United States v Amerson (2007, CA2 NY) 483 F3d 73) and (criticized in State v Martin (2008) 184 Vt 23, 2008 VT 53, 955 A2d 1144).

Given diminished privacy rights of non-violent felons on parole, supervised release, or probation, minimal intrusion involved in obtaining deoxyribonucleic acid (DNA) sample, and restrictive provisions of DNA Analysis Backlog Elimination Act of 2000, 42 USCS § 14135, as amended by USA PATRIOT Act of 2001, Pub. L. No. 107-56, 115 Stat. 272, as amended by Justice For All Act of 2004, Pub. L. No. 108-405, 118 Stat. 2260, and given legitimate governmental interests in accurately identifying offenders, solving past and future crimes, and combating recidivism, Tenth Circuit holds that collecting and profiling DNA of such felons, as authorized and regulated by DNA Analysis Backlog Elimination Act of 2000, as amended, does not violate Fourth Amendment. Banks v United States (2007, CA10 Okla) 490 F3d 1178.

Every court of appeals that has considered issue has concluded that DNA Analysis Backlog Elimination Act of 2000 is constitutional. Johnson v Quander (2006, App DC) 370 US App DC 167, 440 F3d 489, cert den (2006) 549 US 945, 127 S Ct 103, 166 L Ed 2d 255 and (criticized in United States v Stewart (2007, DC Mass) 468 F Supp 2d 261) and (criticized in State v Martin (2008) 184 Vt 23, 2008 VT 53, 955 A2d 1144).

In case in which federal inmate alleged that DNA Analysis Backlog Elimination Act of 2000 (DNA Act), 42 USCS §§ 14135–14135e, violated his rights under Religious Freedom Restoration Act, 42 USCS §§ 2000bb–2000bb-4, and First, Fourth, and Fifth Amendments of U.S. Constitution, district court incorrectly dismissed case for failure to exhaust administrative remedies under Prison Litigation Reform Act (PLRA), 42 USCS § 1997e; case was rare instance in which there was no administrative process to exhaust because U.S. Bureau of Prisons lacked authority to provide inmate any relief or to take any action whatsoever in response to his complaint because of mandatory language in DNA Act. Kaemmerling v Lappin (2008, App DC) 384 US App DC 240, 553 F3d 669.

DNA testing of convicted inmate pursuant to DNA Analysis Backlog Elimination Act of 2000, 42 USCS §§ 14135(a)–14135(e), was constitutional where Government's significant interest in filling CODIS database, increasing accuracy of criminal justice system, and providing means to solve future crimes, outweighed minimal intrusion upon inmate's person. Vore v United States DOJ (2003, DC Ariz) 281 F Supp 2d 1129 (criticized in United States v Kincade (2004, CA9 Cal) 379 F3d 813) and (criticized in Polston v State (2005) 360 Ark 317, 201 SW3d 406) and (criticized in State v Transou (2005, Tenn Crim) 2005 Tenn Crim App LEXIS 463) and (criticized in State v Scarborough (2005, Tenn Crim) 2005 Tenn Crim App LEXIS 544).

3. Miscellaneous

28 C.F.R. § 28.2 states that any offense under 18 USCS § 2113 constitutes "qualifying offense," under DNA Analysis Backlog Elimination Act of 2000, 42 USCS §§ 14135 et seq., and given that larceny falls under one of enumerated code sections contained within 18 USCS § 2113, 28 C.F.R. § 28.2 does not contradict, but rather is consistent with, legislative intent of Congress in DNA Act. United States v Henderson (2004, CA7 Wis) 376 F3d 730.

§ 14135a. Collection and use of DNA identification information from certain Federal offenders

(a) Collection of DNA samples. (1) From individuals in custody. (A) The Attorney General may, as prescribed by the Attorney General in regulation, collect DNA samples from individuals who are arrested, facing charges, or convicted or from non-United States persons who are detained under the authority of the United States. The Attorney General may delegate this function within the Department of Justice as provided in section 510 of title 28, United States Code, and may also authorize and direct any other agency of the United States that arrests or detains individuals or supervises individuals facing charges to carry out any function and exercise any power of the Attorney General under this section.

(B) The Director of the Bureau of Prisons shall collect a DNA sample from each individual in the custody of the Bureau of Prisons who is, or has been, convicted of a qualifying Federal offense (as determined under subsection (d)) or a qualifying military offense, as determined under section 1565 of title 10, United States Code.

(2) From individuals on release, parole, or probation. The probation office responsible for the supervision under Federal law of an individual on probation, parole, or supervised release shall collect a DNA sample from each such individual who is, or has been, convicted of a qualifying Federal offense (as determined under subsection (d)) or a qualifying military offense, as determined under section 1565 of title 10, United States Code.

(3) Individuals already in CODIS. For each individual described in paragraph (1) or (2), if the Combined DNA Index System (in this section referred to as "CODIS") of the Federal Bureau of Investigation contains a DNA analysis with respect to that individual, or if a DNA sample has been collected from that individual under section 1565 of title 10, United States Code, the Attorney General, the Director of the Bureau of Prisons, or the probation office responsible (as applicable) may (but need not) collect a DNA sample from that individual.

(4) Collection procedures. (A) The Attorney General, the Director of the Bureau of Prisons, or the probation office responsible (as applicable) may use or authorize the use of such means as are reasonably necessary to detain, restrain, and collect a DNA sample from an individual who refuses to cooperate in the collection of the sample.

(B) The Attorney General, the Director of the Bureau of Prisons, or the probation office, as appropriate, may enter into agreements with units of State or local government or with private entities to provide for the collection of the samples described in paragraph (1) or (2).

(5) Criminal penalty. An individual from whom the collection of a DNA sample is authorized under this subsection who fails to cooperate in the collection of that sample shall be—

(A) guilty of a class A misdemeanor; and

(B) punished in accordance with title 18, United States Code.

(b) Analysis and use of samples. The Attorney General, the Director of the

Bureau of Prisons, or the probation office responsible (as applicable) shall furnish each DNA sample collected under subsection (a) to the Director of the Federal Bureau of Investigation, who shall carry out a DNA analysis on each such DNA sample and include the results in CODIS.

(c) Definitions. In this section:

(1) The term "DNA sample" means a tissue, fluid, or other bodily sample of an individual on which a DNA analysis can be carried out.

(2) The term "DNA analysis" means analysis of the deoxyribonucleic acid (DNA) identification information in a bodily sample.

(d) Qualifying Federal offenses. The offenses that shall be treated for purposes of this section as qualifying Federal offenses are the following offenses, as determined by the Attorney General:

(1) Any felony.

(2) Any offense under chapter 109A of title 18, United States Code [18 USCS §§ 2241 et seq.].

(3) Any crime of violence (as that term is defined in section 16 of title 18, United States Code).

(4) Any attempt or conspiracy to commit any of the offenses in paragraphs (1) through (3).

(e) Regulations. (1) In general. Except as provided in paragraph (2), this section shall be carried out under regulations prescribed by the Attorney General.

(2) Probation officers. The Director of the Administrative Office of the United States Courts shall make available model procedures for the activities of probation officers in carrying out this section.

(f) Commencement of collection. Collection of DNA samples under subsection (a) shall, subject to the availability of appropriations, commence not later than the date that is 180 days after the date of the enactment of this Act [enacted Dec. 19, 2000].

(Dec. 19, 2000, P. L. 106-546, § 3, 114 Stat. 2728; Oct. 26, 2001, P. L. 107-56, Title V, § 503, 115 Stat. 364; Oct. 30, 2004, P. L. 108-405, Title II, § 203(b), 118 Stat. 2270; Jan. 5, 2006, P. L. 109-162, Title X, § 1004(a), 119 Stat. 3085; July 27, 2006, P. L. 109-248, Title I, Subtitle C, § 155, 120 Stat. 611.)

HISTORY; ANCILLARY LAWS AND DIRECTIVES

Explanatory notes:

This section was enacted as part of Act Dec. 19, 2000, P. L. 106-546, and not as part of Act Sept. 13, 1994, P. L. 103-322, which generally comprises this chapter.

Amendments:

2001. Act Oct. 26, 2001, in subsec. (d), substituted para. (2) for one which read: "(2) The initial determination of qualifying Federal offenses shall be made not later than 120 days after the date of the enactment of this Act.".

2004. Act Oct. 30, 2004, substituted subsec. (d) for one which read:

"(d) Qualifying Federal offenses. (1) The offenses that shall be treated for purposes of this section as qualifying Federal offenses are the following offenses under title 18, United States Code, as determined by the Attorney General:

"(A) Murder (as described in section 1111 of such title), voluntary manslaughter (as described in section 1112 of such title), or other offense relating to homicide (as described in chapter 51 of such title, sections 1113, 1114, 1116, 1118, 1119, 1120, and 1121).

"(B) An offense relating to sexual abuse (as described in chapter 109A of such title, sections 2241 through 2245), to sexual exploitation or other abuse of children (as described in chapter 110 of such title, sections 2251 through 2252), or to transportation for illegal sexual activity (as described in chapter 117 of such title, sections 2421, 2422, 2423, and 2425).

"(C) An offense relating to peonage and slavery (as described in chapter 77 of such title).

"(D) Kidnapping (as defined in section 3559(c)(2)(E) of such title).

"(E) An offense involving robbery or burglary (as described in chapter 103 of such title, sections 2111 through 2114, 2116, and 2118 through 2119).

"(F) Any violation of section 1153 involving murder, manslaughter, kidnapping, maiming, a felony offense relating to sexual abuse (as described in chapter 109A), incest, arson, burglary, or robbery.

"(G) Any attempt or conspiracy to commit any of the above offenses.

"(2) In addition to the offenses described in paragraph (1), the following offenses shall be treated for purposes of this section as qualifying Federal offenses, as determined by the Attorney General:

"(A) Any offense listed in section 2332b(g)(5)(B) of title 18, United States Code.

"(B) Any crime of violence (as defined in section 16 of title 18, United States Code).

"(C) Any attempt or conspiracy to commit any of the above offenses.".

2006. Act Jan. 5, 2006, in subsec. (a), in para. (1), designated the existing provisions as subpara. (B) and inserted subpara. (A), and, in paras. (3) and (4), substituted "Attorney General, the Director of the Bureau of Prisons," for "Director of the Bureau of Prisons" wherever appearing; and, in subsec. (b), substituted "Attorney General, the Director of the Bureau of Prisons," for "Director of the Bureau of Prisons".

Act July 27, 2006, in subsec. (a)(1)(A), inserted ", facing charges, or convicted".

CODE OF FEDERAL REGULATIONS

Department of Justice—DNA identification system, 28 CFR 28.1 et seq.

CROSS REFERENCES

This section is referred to in 10 USCS § 1565; 18 USCS §§ 3142, 3563, 3583; 42 USCS §§ 14132, 14135c, 14135e.

RESEARCH GUIDE

Federal Procedure:

27 Moore's Federal Practice (Matthew Bender 3d ed.), ch 641, Search and Seizure § 641.183.

Federal Taxation:

1 Tax Controversies: Audits, Investigations, Trials (Matthew Bender), ch 10, Fifth Amendment Right Against Self-Incrimination § 10.04.

Annotations:

Validity, Construction, and Application of DNA Analysis Backlog Elimination Act of 2000, 42 U.S.C.A. §§ 14135 et seq. [42 USCS §§ 14135 et seq.] and 10 U.S.C.A. § 1565 [10 USCS § 1565]. 187 ALR Fed 373.

Law Review Articles:

Nevin; Scott. The USA Patriot Act: Time To Speak Up [Discussion of T. Derden, One Year Under the Patriot Act]. 46 Advoc (Boise) 19, December 2003.

Brandt; Van Valkenburgh. The USA Patriot Act: The Devil is in the Details [Discussion of T. Derden, One Year Under the Patriot Act]. 46 Advoc (Boise) 24, December 2003.

Chemerinsky. Litigation alerts in the USA Patriot Act. 23 Cal Law 29, April 2003.

Rosenszweig. Civil Liberty and the Response to Terrorism. 42 Duq L Rev 663, Summer 2004.

Sproule. The Effect of the USA Patriot Act on Workplace Privacy. 49 Prac Law 35, February 2003.

SHEPARD'S® Citations Service. For further research of authorities referenced here, use SHEPARD'S to be sure your case or statute is still good law and to find additional authorities that support your position. SHEPARD'S is available exclusively from LexisNexis®.

INTERPRETIVE NOTES AND DECISIONS

1. Generally
2. Constitutionality
3. —Ex post facto clause
4. —Fourth amendment
5. — —Individuals facing charges
6. — —Inmates
7. — —Probationers
8. — —Individuals on supervised release
9. — —Parolees
10. —Fifth amendment
11. —Eighth amendment
12. Qualifying federal offense
13. —Bank larceny
14. Miscellaneous

1. Generally

In appealing from their sentences under 18 USCS § 3742, defendants could not challenge constitutionality of 42 USCS § 14135a(a)(1), part of DNA Analysis Backlog Elimination Act of 2000, because requirement that Bureau of Prisons take DNA samples from defendants during their term of imprisonment was not part of defendants' sentences; instead, requirement was condition of confinement that

could only be challenged in separate civil suit following exhaustion of administrative remedies. United States v Carmichael (2003, CA5 Tex) 343 F3d 756, cert den (2004) 540 US 1136, 157 L Ed 2d 943, 124 S Ct 1116.

In Carmichael decision, Court of Appeals interpreted DNA Analysis Backlog Elimination Act of 2000 (DNA Act) as giving Bureau of Prisons (BOP) power to take samples, as well as authority to determine who is eligible for deoxyribonucleic acid (DNA) sampling; DNA Act's provision for BOP's collection of federal offenders' DNA during incarceration is not part of sentence, but is rather prison condition that must be challenged through separate civil action after exhaustion of administrative remedies. United States v Riascos-Cuenu (2005, CA5 Tex) 428 F3d 1100, vacated, remanded, motion gr on other grounds (2006) 549 US 1093, 127 S Ct 827, 166 L Ed 2d 661, on remand, dismd on other grounds (2007, CA5 Tex) 225 Fed Appx 287, cert den (2008) 552 US 1179, 128 S Ct 1216, 170 L Ed 2d 58 and (Abrogated as stated in United States v Ruiz-Carmona (2007, CA5 Tex) 214 Fed Appx 483).

Purpose of DNA Act, 42 USCS § 14135a, was to

have national registry of information regarding those covered by statute and to deter future criminal conduct; such administrative intent and corresponding blood test and retention of information was not punitive, was not bill of attainder, and did not violate Ex Post Facto Clause, U.S. Const. art. I, § 9, cl. 3. United States v Hook (2006, CA7 Ill) 471 F3d 766, cert den (2007) 549 US 1343, 127 S Ct 2081, 167 L Ed 2d 771 and (criticized in United States v Weikert (2007, CA1 Mass) 504 F3d 1) and (criticized in United States v Kriesel (2007, CA9 Wash) 508 F3d 941) and (criticized in Wilson v Collins (2008, CA6 Ohio) 517 F3d 421, 2008 FED App 88P) and (criticized in State v Bartylla (2008, Minn) 755 NW2d 8) and (criticized in State v Hutchinson (2009) 2009 ME 44, 969 A2d 923) and (criticized in United States v Pool (2009, ED Cal) 645 F Supp 2d 903) and (criticized in United States v Davis (2009, DC Md) 657 F Supp 2d 630) and (criticized in United States v Mitchell (2011, CA3 Pa) 652 F3d 387).

Requiring supervised releasee to provide DNA sample, as called for by DNA Analysis Backlog Elimination Act of 2000, Pub. L. No. 106-546 (codified as amended in scattered sections of 10 USCS, 18 USCS, and 42 USCS), did not violate his rights under Fourth Amendment because, under totality of circumstances, supervised releasee's expectation of privacy was outweighed by Government's interests, such as monitoring and rehabilitating supervised releasees and solving crimes; based on totality of circumstances, neither blood draw nor creation of DNA profile and entry of that profile into centralized database constituted unreasonable search or seizure. United States v Weikert (2007, CA1 Mass) 504 F3d 1, reh den, reh, en banc, den (2007, CA1) 504 F3d 20 and (criticized in State v Martin (2008) 184 Vt 23, 2008 VT 53, 955 A2d 1144) and (criticized in Boroian v Mueller (2010, CA1 Mass) 616 F3d 60).

Question of whether requiring individual on supervised release to provide blood sample for purposes of creating DNA profile and entering it into centralized database violates Fourth Amendment's prohibition against unreasonable searches and seizures is properly analyzed using "totality of circumstances" approach, rather than "special needs" analysis. United States v Weikert (2007, CA1 Mass) 504 F3d 1, reh den, reh, en banc, den (2007, CA1) 504 F3d 20 and (criticized in State v Martin (2008) 184 Vt 23, 2008 VT 53, 955 A2d 1144) and (criticized in Boroian v Mueller (2010, CA1 Mass) 616 F3d 60).

DNA Analysis Backlog Elimination Act of 2000 (DNA Act), 42 USCS §§ 14135–14135e, which authorizes U.S. Probation Office to collect DNA sample from individual on supervised release by operation of 42 USCS § 14135a(a)(2), does not constitute suspicionless search in violation of Fourth Amendment, as Ninth Circuit has upheld compulsory DNA collection based on "totality of circum-

stances" analysis. United States v Lujan (2007, CA9 Or) 504 F3d 1003.

DNA Analysis Backlog Elimination Act of 2000 (DNA Act), 42 USCS §§ 14135–14135e, which authorizes U.S. Probation Office to collect DNA sample from individual on supervised release by operation of 42 USCS § 14135a(a)(2), is not unconstitutional bill of attainder on ground that DNA Act imposes punishment on disfavored class without judicial involvement because DNA Act was not enacted for punitive reasons. United States v Lujan (2007, CA9 Or) 504 F3d 1003.

2. Constitutionality

DNA Analysis Backlog Elimination Act of 2000 (DNA Act), 42 USCS §§ 14135–14135e, which authorizes U.S. Probation Office to collect DNA sample from individual on supervised release by operation of 42 USCS § 14135a(a)(2), does not violate separation of powers doctrine on ground that DNA Act allows probation officers, who work for judicial branch, to exercise executive branch functions by detaining, restraining, and collecting DNA sample from uncooperative defendant. Congress may delegate to judicial branch non-adjudicatory functions that do not trench upon prerogatives of another branch and that are appropriate to central mission of judiciary, and DNA Act is legitimate delegation of congressional authority because DNA Act does not encroach on prerogatives of executive branch and purpose of DNA Act is consistent with mission of judiciary. United States v Lujan (2007, CA9 Or) 504 F3d 1003.

DNA Analysis Backlog Elimination Act of 2000 (DNA Act), 42 USCS §§ 14135–14135e, which authorizes U.S. Probation Office to collect DNA sample from individual on supervised release by operation of 42 USCS § 14135a(a)(2), does not constitute suspicionless search in violation of Fourth Amendment, as Ninth Circuit has upheld DNA collection based on "special needs" doctrine. United States v Lujan (2007, CA9 Or) 504 F3d 1003.

When terms of defendant's supervised release did not include requirement that she submit to DNA sample, but DNA Analysis Backlog Elimination Act of 2000 (DNA Act), 42 USCS §§ 14135–14135e, went into effect after her sentence was imposed such that defendant was required to provide DNA sample to U.S. Probation Office pursuant to 42 USCS § 14135a(a)(2) or risk possible revocation hearing, DNA Act did not impose new condition on her supervised release in violation of Ex Post Facto Clause because DNA Act did not have punitive effect. United States v Lujan (2007, CA9 Or) 504 F3d 1003.

DNA Analysis Backlog Elimination Act of 2000 (DNA Act), 42 USCS §§ 14135–14135e, which authorizes U.S. Probation Office to collect DNA sample from individual on supervised release by operation of 42 USCS § 14135a(a)(2), is not unconstitutional bill of attainder on ground that DNA Act imposes punishment on disfavored class without judicial involvement because (i) neither blood nor DNA collection has been historically viewed as punishment and (ii) disability imposed by DNA Act is minimal and DNA Act was reasonable means by which Congress could achieve and regulate non-punitive goal. United States v Lujan (2007, CA9 Or) 504 F3d 1003.

In case in which pro se federal inmate alleged DNA Analysis Backlog Elimination Act of 2000 (DNA Act), 42 USCS §§ 14135–14135e, violated his rights under First Amendment because mandatory collection and analysis of his deoxyribonucleic acid (DNA) under DNA Act burdened free exercise of his religious belief that DNA sampling, collection and storage defiled God's temple, that argument failed; right of free exercise protected by First Amendment did not relieve individual of obligation to comply with valid and neutral law of general applicability on ground that law proscribed or prescribed conduct that his religion prescribed or proscribed. Kaemmerling v Lappin (2008, App DC) 384 US App DC 240, 553 F3d 669.

Parolee's request to enjoin U.S. Parole Commission from obtaining his DNA sample in compliance with U.S. Patriot Act was denied where Act was found not to violate his due process, ex post facto or Fourth Amendment rights. Miller v United States Parole Comm'n (2003, DC Kan) 259 F Supp 2d 1166 (criticized in United States v Kincade (2003, CA9 Cal) 345 F3d 1095, 2003 CDOS 8835, 2003 Daily Journal DAR 11144) and (criticized in United States v Kincade (2004, CA9 Cal) 379 F3d 813) and (criticized in Polston v State (2005) 360 Ark 317, 201 SW3d 406) and (criticized in State v Transou (2005, Tenn Crim) 2005 Tenn Crim App LEXIS 463).

2004 amendments to 42 USCS § 14135a, which extended reach of Act to nonviolent and nonsexual felonies, is constitutional because minimal intrusions occasioned by blood draw or cheek swab and retention of genetic information is outweighed by legitimate government interests of identification for purposes of crime solving and supervision of parolees and probationers, and combating recidivism. Banks v Gonzales (2006, ND Okla) 415 F Supp 2d 1248 (criticized in United States v Amerson (2007, CA2 NY) 483 F3d 73) and affd (2007, CA10 Okla) 490 F3d 1178.

3. —Ex post facto clause

Purpose of DNA Act, 42 USCS § 14135a, was to have national registry of information regarding those covered by statute and to deter future criminal conduct; such administrative intent and corresponding blood test and retention of information was not punitive, was not bill of attainder, and did not violate Ex Post Facto Clause, U.S. Const. art. I, § 9, cl. 3. United States v Hook (2006, CA7 Ill) 471 F3d 766,

cert den (2007) 549 US 1343, 127 S Ct 2081, 167 L Ed 2d 771 and (criticized in United States v Weikert (2007, CA1 Mass) 504 F3d 1) and (criticized in United States v Kriesel (2007, CA9 Wash) 508 F3d 941) and (criticized in Wilson v Collins (2008, CA6 Ohio) 517 F3d 421, 2008 FED App 88P) and (criticized in State v Bartylla (2008, Minn) 755 NW2d 8) and (criticized in State v Hutchinson (2009) 2009 ME 44, 969 A2d 923) and (criticized in United States v Pool (2009, ED Cal) 645 F Supp 2d 903) and (criticized in United States v Davis (2009, DC Md) 657 F Supp 2d 630) and (criticized in United States v Mitchell (2011, CA3 Pa) 652 F3d 387).

DNA Analysis Backlog Elimination Act of 2000, Pub. L. No. 106-546 (codified as amended in scattered sections of 10 USCS, 18 USCS, and 42 USCS), included safeguards to protect privacy interests of supervised releasee who was required to provide sample; 42 USCS § 14132(b)(3) strictly limited use of information, which was stored in centralized database. 42 USCS § 14135e(c) provided penalties for misuse of DNA samples; moreover, DNA Act included no discretionary component, given explicit directive set forth in 42 USCS § 14135a(a)(2). United States v Weikert (2007, CA1 Mass) 504 F3d 1, reh den, reh, en banc, den (2007, CA1) 504 F3d 20 and (criticized in State v Martin (2008) 184 Vt 23, 2008 VT 53, 955 A2d 1144) and (criticized in Boroian v Mueller (2010, CA1 Mass) 616 F3d 60).

While defendant was not subject to DNA Analysis Backlog Elimination Act of 2000 when originally convicted, applying 42 USCS § 14135a(d) retroactively under 42 USCS § 14135a(a)(2) upon finding violation of supervised release was affirmed as not violating Ex Post Facto Clause since Congress intended regulatory scheme, not punitive purpose. United States v Coccia (2010, CA6 Mich) 598 F3d 293, 2010 FED App 77P.

U.S.A. Patriot Act, P. L. 107-56, 115 Stat. 272 (2001), did not implicate ex post facto clause as applied to paroled prisoner seeking to avoid collection of his DNA where it was well settled that conditions of parole could be changed at any time such that condition mandating giving of DNA sample, was not itself penal in nature and could not be ex post facto; further, mere fact of failure to comply with this condition subjected parolee to revocation, and did not implicate ex post facto clause. Miller v United States Parole Comm'n (2003, DC Kan) 259 F Supp 2d 1166 (criticized in United States v Kincade (2003, CA9 Cal) 345 F3d 1095, 2003 CDOS 8835, 2003 Daily Journal DAR 11144) and (criticized in United States v Kincade (2004, CA9 Cal) 379 F3d 813) and (criticized in Polston v State (2005) 360 Ark 317, 201 SW3d 406) and (criticized in State v Transou (2005, Tenn Crim) 2005 Tenn Crim App LEXIS 463).

U.S.A. Patriot Act, in requiring parolee to provide DNA sample, did not violate ex post facto clause,

U.S. Const. art. I, § 10, cl. 1, by creating new criminal offense because while prior conviction for qualifying offense was element of new crime of failing to give DNA sample, conduct of failing to give sample triggered new charge and punishment; thus, it could not be said that Patriot Act as applied under these circumstances violated ex post facto principles. Miller v United States Parole Comm'n (2003, DC Kan) 259 F Supp 2d 1166 (criticized in United States v Kincade (2003, CA9 Cal) 345 F3d 1095, 2003 CDOS 8835, 2003 Daily Journal DAR 11144) and (criticized in United States v Kincade (2004, CA9 Cal) 379 F3d 813) and (criticized in Polston v State (2005) 360 Ark 317, 201 SW3d 406) and (criticized in State v Transou (2005, Tenn Crim) 2005 Tenn Crim App LEXIS 463).

Requiring defendant to provide blood sample after he began serving term of supervised release did not violate Ex Post Facto Clause, U.S. Const. art. I, § 10, cl. 1, where potential revocation of defendant's supervised release did not increase his punishment for firearms conviction and potential misdemeanor conviction for violating DNA Analysis Backlog Elimination Act of 2000, 42 USCS §§ 14135 et seq., was new act, not increase in punishment for firearms conviction. United States v Stegman (2003, DC Md) 295 F Supp 2d 542.

Under 42 USCS § 14135a(a)(1)–(2), part of DNA Analysis Backlog Elimination Act of 2000, individuals were required to submit only one DNA sample and no further action by individual was required; therefore, under analysis in connection with plaintiff probationer's Ex Post Facto Clauses of U.S. Const. art. 1, §§ 9, 10, challenges, "Affirmative disability or restraint" was minimal. Johnson v Quander (2005, DC Dist Col) 370 F Supp 2d 79, affd (2006, App DC) 370 US App DC 167, 440 F3d 489, cert den (2006) 549 US 945, 127 S Ct 103, 166 L Ed 2d 255 and (criticized in State v Martin (2008) 184 Vt 23, 2008 VT 53, 955 A2d 1144).

Under 42 USCS § 14135a(a)(5)(A)–(B), individual's failure to comply with requirement to provide sample is punishable under DNA Analysis Backlog Elimination Act of 2000 as separate offense—class A misdemeanor—as opposed to enhancing sentence previously imposed for qualifying offense, and legislative history of Act indicates that there is nonpunitive, alternative purpose underlying its enactment—eliminating prospect that innocent individuals will be wrongly held for crimes they did not commit, and thus, Act did not violate Ex Post Facto Clauses of U.S. Const. art. 1, §§ 9, 10. Johnson v Quander (2005, DC Dist Col) 370 F Supp 2d 79, affd (2006, App DC) 370 US App DC 167, 440 F3d 489, cert den (2006) 549 US 945, 127 S Ct 103, 166 L Ed 2d 255 and (criticized in State v Martin (2008) 184 Vt 23, 2008 VT 53, 955 A2d 1144).

4. —Fourth amendment

In light of conditional releasees' substantially di-

minished expectations of privacy, minimal intrusion occasioned by blood sampling, and overwhelming societal interests that were so clearly furthered by collection of deoxyribonucleic acid (DNA) information from convicted offenders, compulsory DNA profiling of qualified federal offenders is reasonable under totality of circumstances; therefore, DNA Analysis Backlog Elimination Act of 2000, Pub. L. No. 106-546, 114 Stat. 2726, satisfies requirements of Fourth Amendment. United States v Kincade (2004, CA9 Cal) 379 F3d 813, cert den (2005) 544 US 924, 125 S Ct 1638, 161 L Ed 2d 483 and (criticized in Nicholas v Goord (2005, CA2 NY) 430 F3d 652) and (criticized in United States v Weikert (2006, DC Mass) 421 F Supp 2d 259) and (criticized in State v O'Hagen (2007) 189 NJ 140, 914 A2d 267) and (criticized in United States v Amerson (2007, CA2 NY) 483 F3d 73) and (criticized in State v Martin (2008) 184 Vt 23, 2008 VT 53, 955 A2d 1144).

Defendant's conviction and sentence for involuntary manslaughter, in violation of 18 USCS §§ 1153 and 1112, were affirmed because, even though jury instructions were in error, they did not affect defendant's substantial rights under plain error rule or result in violation of defendant's Fifth Amendment rights with regard to indictments, and special condition of providing DNA sample was minimal intrusion into defendant's right to privacy and did not violate Fourth Amendment. United States v Hugs (2004, CA9 Mont) 384 F3d 762, cert den (2005) 544 US 933, 125 S Ct 1680, 161 L Ed 2d 500.

Because DNA testing of supervised releasees was ultimately for law enforcement goal, it fit within special needs analysis United States Supreme Court had developed for drug testing and searches of probationers' homes, since it was not undertaken for investigation of specific crime; DNA Act, 42 USCS § 14135a, did not violate Fourth Amendment. United States v Hook (2006, CA7 Ill) 471 F3d 766, cert den (2007) 549 US 1343, 127 S Ct 2081, 167 L Ed 2d 771 and (criticized in United States v Weikert (2007, CA1 Mass) 504 F3d 1) and (criticized in United States v Kriesel (2007, CA9 Wash) 508 F3d 941) and (criticized in Wilson v Collins (2008, CA6 Ohio) 517 F3d 421, 2008 FED App 88P) and (criticized in State v Bartylla (2008, Minn) 755 NW2d 8) and (criticized in State v Hutchinson (2009) 2009 ME 44, 969 A2d 923) and (criticized in United States v Pool (2009, ED Cal) 645 F Supp 2d 903) and (criticized in United States v Davis (2009, DC Md) 657 F Supp 2d 630) and (criticized in United States v Mitchell (2011, CA3 Pa) 652 F3d 387).

5. —— —Individuals facing charges

Required DNA testing under 42 USCS § 14135a after issuance of felony criminal charges did not violate Fourth Amendment because test was minimally invasive, it served vital law enforcement interest, and law provided privacy protection of test results. United States v Pool (2009, ED Cal) 645 F Supp 2d 903 (criticized in United States v Mitchell (2009, WD Pa) 681 F Supp 2d 597) and affd (2010, CA9 Cal) 621 F3d 1213, vacated, remanded, app dismd, as moot on other grounds (2011, CA9 Cal) 659 F3d 761 and (Vacatur noted in United States v Fricosu (2012, DC Colo) 2012 US Dist LEXIS 22654) and (Vacatur noted in Haskell v Harris (2012, CA9 Cal) 669 F3d 1049).

6. — —Inmates

In case in which pro se federal inmate argued that DNA Analysis Backlog Elimination Act of 2000 (DNA Act), 42 USCS §§ 14135–14135e, violated his Fourth Amendment right to be free from unreasonable searches and seizures because statute unconstitutionally authorized blanket, suspicionless search for general law enforcement purposes, that argument failed; Fourth Amendment certainly permitted collection of blood sample for deoxyribonucleic acid analysis from convicted felon while he was still on probation, much less from currently incarcerated felon; Fourth Amendment did not require additional finding of individualized suspicion before blood could be taken from incarcerated felons for purpose of identifying them. Kaemmerling v Lappin (2008, App DC) 384 US App DC 240, 553 F3d 669.

DNA testing of convicted inmate pursuant to DNA Analysis Backlog Elimination Act of 2000, 42 USCS §§ 14135(a)-14135(e), was constitutional where Government's significant interest in filling CODIS database, increasing accuracy of criminal justice system, and providing means to solve future crimes, outweighed minimal intrusion upon inmate's person. Vore v United States DOJ (2003, DC Ariz) 281 F Supp 2d 1129 (criticized in United States v Kincade (2004, CA9 Cal) 379 F3d 813) and (criticized in Polston v State (2005) 360 Ark 317, 201 SW3d 406) and (criticized in State v Transou (2005, Tenn Crim) 2005 Tenn Crim App LEXIS 463) and (criticized in State v Scarborough (2005, Tenn Crim) 2005 Tenn Crim App LEXIS 544).

7. — —Probationers

District court properly modified conditions of federal probationer's probation to require him to have his DNA collected as directed by his probation officer pursuant to DNA Analysis Backlog Elimination Act of 2000; under totality of circumstances, collection of DNA under 42 USCS § 14135a(a)(2) for inclusion in Combined DNA Index System database under 42 USCS § 14132 did not constitute unreasonable search and seizure in violation of Fourth Amendment, given probationers' diminished privacy rights, minimal intrusion involved in obtaining DNA samples, and legitimate governmental interest in using DNA as crime investigating tool. United States v Kraklio (2006, CA8 Iowa) 451 F3d 922, reh den, reh, en banc, den (2006, CA8) 2006 US App LEXIS 20456 and cert den (2006) 549 US 1044, 127 S Ct

611, 166 L Ed 2d 453 and (criticized in State v Martin (2008) 184 Vt 23, 2008 VT 53, 955 A2d 1144).

Taking and storing samples of DNA under restrictions of Justice For All Act of 2004, Pub. L. No. 108-405, 118 Stat. 2260, fulfilled many important governmental interests, only some of which were limited to criminal history of subjects of DNA testing; invasion of privacy, both immediate, and long term, from DNA testing of convicted felons—even those convicted of non-violent crimes and sentenced only to probation—was, given safeguards of Act, relatively small; accordingly Act, as applied to defendants—probationers convicted of non-violent crimes—did not constitute unreasonable search or seizure and hence did not violate Fourth Amendment. United States v Amerson (2007, CA2 NY) 483 F3d 73 (criticized in United States v Weikert (2007, CA1 Mass) 504 F3d 1) and cert den (2007) 552 US 1042, 128 S Ct 646, 169 L Ed 2d 515 and (criticized in United States v Kriesel (2007, CA9 Wash) 508 F3d 941) and (criticized in Wilson v Collins (2008, CA6 Ohio) 517 F3d 421, 2008 FED App 88P) and (criticized in State v Bartylla (2008, Minn) 755 NW2d 8) and (criticized in State v Hutchinson (2009) 2009 ME 44, 969 A2d 923) and (criticized in United States v Pool (2009, ED Cal) 645 F Supp 2d 903) and (criticized in United States v Davis (2009, DC Md) 657 F Supp 2d 630) and (criticized in United States v Thomas (2011, WD NY) 2011 US Dist LEXIS 45333) and (criticized in United States v Mitchell (2011, CA3 Pa) 652 F3d 387).

Convicted defendant who was asked to give DNA sample pursuant to 42 USCS § 14135a, did not have actionable claim for Fourth Amendment violation because defendant did not have Fourth Amendment argument when defendant had not finished serving period of probation. United States v Zimmerman (2007, CA9 Cal) 514 F3d 851, appeal after remand, decision reached on appeal by (2009, CA9 Cal) 2009 US App LEXIS 22689.

Collection of DNA samples pursuant to DNA Analysis Backlog Elimination Act of 2000, Pub. L. No. 106-546, 114 Stat. 2726, codified as amended in part at 18 USCS § 3563 and 42 USCS §§ 14132, 14135a, 14135e, did not violate Fourth Amendment as to probationers in light of U.S. Court of Appeals for First Circuit's holding in U.S. v. Weikert, 504 F.3d 1 (1st Cir. 2007); though defendants pled guilty to non-violent, property-related crimes pursuant to 18 USCS §§ 641 and 473, their argument that new balancing test should be applied to them as result stemmed from flawed assumption that DNA evidence was only useful for solving-and thereby deterring-violent crimes; moreover, they did not have greater expectation of privacy than did supervised releasees as both probation, pursuant to 18 USCS §§ 3561, 3563, and supervised release, pursuant to 18 USCS § 3583, were forms of conditional release. United States v Stewart (2008, CA1 Mass) 532 F3d 32.

Retaining and matching plaintiff former probationer's DNA profile, as provided for in 42 USCS § 14135a was not separate search under Fourth Amendment; thus, probationer's challenge to Act, asserted against defendant federal officials, failed to state claim. Boroian v Mueller (2010, CA1 Mass) 616 F3d 60.

8. — —Individuals on supervised release

Collecting DNA from nonviolent felons as authorized by DNA Analysis Backlog Elimination Act of 2000 does not violate Fourth Amendment; 2004 amendments to DNA Analysis Backlog Elimination Act of 2000, Pub. L. No. 108-405, § 203(b), 118 Stat. 2260, 2270, did not violate Fourth Amendment rights of defendant on supervised release because government's significant interests in identifying supervised releasees, preventing recidivism, and solving past crimes outweighed diminished privacy interests that could be advanced by convicted felon serving term of supervised release. United States v Kriesel (2007, CA9 Wash) 508 F3d 941.

Application of DNA Analysis Backlog Elimination Act of 2000, 42 USCS §§ 14135 et seq., to defendant serving term of supervised release for firearms conviction did not violate Fourth Amendment because applicable judicial precedent from Court of Appeals for Fourth Circuit held that additional finding of individualized suspicion was not required before blood could be taken from incarcerated felons and there was no reason to distinguish persons on supervised release. United States v Stegman (2003, DC Md) 295 F Supp 2d 542.

Compulsory DNA profiling of all felons as required by 42 USCS § 14135a(a)(2) was reasonable under Fourth Amendment because blood sample was minimally intrusive, conditional releasees had diminished expectation of privacy, and government had compelling interest in ensuring compliance with release terms, deterring past offenders from future crimes, and potentially contributing to solution of past crimes. United States v Kriesel (2006, WD Wash) 416 F Supp 2d 1037, affd (2007, CA9 Wash) 508 F3d 941.

9. — —Parolees

Taking of DNA sample from parolee pursuant to Patriot Act, P. L. 107-56, 115 Stat. 272 (2001), did not violate his right to privacy under Fourth Amendment where as parolee he enjoyed lesser right to personal privacy and remained under jurisdiction and supervision of U.S. Parole Commission. Miller v United States Parole Comm'n (2003, DC Kan) 259 F Supp 2d 1166 (criticized in United States v Kincade (2003, CA9 Cal) 345 F3d 1095, 2003 CDOS 8835, 2003 Daily Journal DAR 11144) and (criticized in United States v Kincade (2004, CA9 Cal) 379 F3d 813) and (criticized in Polston v State (2005) 360 Ark 317, 201 SW3d 406) and (criticized in State v Transou (2005, Tenn Crim) 2005 Tenn Crim App LEXIS 463).

10. — Fifth amendment

Because taking of blood samples or fingerprints is not testimonial evidence and as such is not protected by Fifth Amendment and Fifth Amendment also does not protect photographing or requiring individual to speak for identification purposes, accordingly, DNA collection done by means of non-testimonial blood draw pursuant to DNA Act, 42 USCS § 14135a, is not protected by Fifth Amendment. United States v Hook (2006, CA7 Ill) 471 F3d 766, cert den (2007) 549 US 1343, 127 S Ct 2081, 167 L Ed 2d 771 and (criticized in United States v Weikert (2007, CA1 Mass) 504 F3d 1) and (criticized in United States v Kriesel (2007, CA9 Wash) 508 F3d 941) and (criticized in Wilson v Collins (2008, CA6 Ohio) 517 F3d 421, 2008 FED App 88P) and (criticized in State v Bartylla (2008, Minn) 755 NW2d 8) and (criticized in State v Hutchinson (2009) 2009 ME 44, 969 A2d 923) and (criticized in United States v Pool (2009, ED Cal) 645 F Supp 2d 903) and (criticized in United States v Davis (2009, DC Md) 657 F Supp 2d 630) and (criticized in United States v Mitchell (2011, CA3 Pa) 652 F3d 387).

Extraction of DNA pursuant to 42 USCS § 14135a did not violate defendant's privilege against self-incrimination because DNA samples are physical evidence and not testimonial evidence. United States v Zimmerman (2007, CA9 Cal) 514 F3d 851, appeal after remand, decision reached on appeal by (2009, CA9 Cal) 2009 US App LEXIS 22689.

In case in which pro se federal inmate argued that DNA Analysis Backlog Elimination Act of 2000 (DNA Act), 42 USCS §§ 14135–14135e, violated equal protection component of Due Process Clause because it required collection of deoxyribonucleic acid (DNA) from felons who were incarcerated or on supervised release but did not mandate collection of DNA from free felons, who were no longer under supervision of U.S. Bureau of Prisons (BOP), that argument failed; DNA Act passed rationale basis test; BOP exerted measure of control over incarcerated felons and felons on supervised release that it did not exert over felons who were now out of prison system, making it significantly easier for BOP to collect DNA samples from incarcerated and supervised felons than from free felons. Kaemmerling v Lappin (2008, App DC) 384 US App DC 240, 553 F3d 669.

In case in which pro se federal inmate argued that DNA Analysis Backlog Elimination Act of 2000 (DNA Act), 42 USCS §§ 14135–14135e, violated privilege against compelled self-incrimination, that argument failed; Fifth Amendment privilege barred only compelling testimonial communications from accused, not making accused source of physical evidence. Kaemmerling v Lappin (2008, App DC) 384 US App DC 240, 553 F3d 669.

Parolee's request to enjoin U.S. Parole Commission from obtaining his DNA sample as required under 42 USCS § 14135a, was denied where, inter alia, his providing DNA sample was not unconstitutional taking without due process, because parolee did not have liberty interest in parole. Miller v United States Parole Comm'n (2003, DC Kan) 259 F Supp 2d 1166 (criticized in United States v Kincade (2003, CA9 Cal) 345 F3d 1095, 2003 CDOS 8835, 2003 Daily Journal DAR 11144) and (criticized in United States v Kincade (2004, CA9 Cal) 379 F3d 813) and (criticized in Polston v State (2005) 360 Ark 317, 201 SW3d 406) and (criticized in State v Transou (2005, Tenn Crim) 2005 Tenn Crim App LEXIS 463).

11. —Eighth amendment

Because blood draws were considered routine, and government's desire for identifying information along with minimal pain and discomfort accompanying blood draw took DNA Act, 42 USCS § 14135a, outside of ambit of cruel and unusual punishment; DNA collection did not constitute cruel and unusual punishment. United States v Hook (2006, CA7 Ill) 471 F3d 766, cert den (2007) 549 US 1343, 127 S Ct 2081, 167 L Ed 2d 771 and (criticized in United States v Weikert (2007, CA1 Mass) 504 F3d 1) and (criticized in United States v Kriesel (2007, CA9 Wash) 508 F3d 941) and (criticized in Wilson v Collins (2008, CA6 Ohio) 517 F3d 421, 2008 FED App 88P) and (criticized in State v Bartylla (2008, Minn) 755 NW2d 8) and (criticized in State v Hutchinson (2009) 2009 ME 44, 969 A2d 923) and (criticized in United States v Pool (2009, ED Cal) 645 F Supp 2d 903) and (criticized in United States v Davis (2009, DC Md) 657 F Supp 2d 630) and (criticized in United States v Mitchell (2011, CA3 Pa) 652 F3d 387).

12. Qualifying federal offense

Trial court did not err by ordering defendant, who was convicted of receiving or distributing, by computer, images of minors engaged in sexually explicit conduct; possession of images; and distribution of images, to cooperate in collection of DNA sample as condition of his supervised release following his prison sentence as defendant's conduct amounted to sexual exploitation and abuse of children. United States v Kimler (2003, CA10 Kan) 335 F3d 1132, 61 Fed Rules Evid Serv 1024, 7 ALR Fed 2d 583 (criticized in United States v Kincade (2003, CA9 Cal) 345 F3d 1095, 2003 CDOS 8835, 2003 Daily Journal DAR 11144) and cert den (2003) 540 US 1083, 124 S Ct 945, 157 L Ed 2d 759 and (criticized in United States v Kincade (2004, CA9 Cal) 379 F3d 813) and post-conviction relief den (2004, CA10) 119 Fed Appx 213 and (criticized in Polston v State (2005) 360 Ark 317, 201 SW3d 406) and (criticized in State v Cremeans (2005, Montgomery Co) 160 Ohio App 3d 1, 2005 Ohio 928, 825 NE2d 1124) and (criticized in United States v Bracy (2005, SD Iowa) 2005 US Dist LEXIS 6468) and (criticized in

State v Transou (2005, Tenn Crim) 2005 Tenn Crim App LEXIS 463) and (criticized in State v Scarborough (2005, Tenn Crim) 2005 Tenn Crim App LEXIS 544) and (criticized in United States v Kraklio (2006, SD Iowa) 2006 US Dist LEXIS 1982) and (criticized in Banks v Gonzales (2006, ND Okla) 415 F Supp 2d 1248) and (criticized in United States v Weikert (2006, DC Mass) 421 F Supp 2d 259) and (criticized in United States v Kraklio (2006, CA8 Iowa) 451 F3d 922) and (criticized in Banks v United States (2007, CA10 Okla) 490 F3d 1178) and (criticized in United States v Weikert (2007, CA1 Mass) 504 F3d 1) and (criticized in United States v Davis (2009, DC Md) 657 F Supp 2d 630).

To extent that language of DNA Analysis Backlog Elimination Act of 2000 (DNA Act), 42 USCS §§ 14135 et seq., describing, in 42 USCS § 14135a(d), "qualifying federal offenses," for purposes of DNA Act, is ambiguous, court may not substitute its own construction of statute for reasonable interpretation made by Attorney General, and in determining whether Attorney General's statutory construction is permissible one, reviewing court should give that construction "controlling weight," unless construction is manifestly contrary to statute. United States v Henderson (2004, CA7 Wis) 376 F3d 730.

13. —Bank larceny

When defendant pled guilty to bank larceny, under 18 USCS § 2113(B), 42 USCS § 14135a(d)(E) was ambiguous as to whether bank larceny was qualifying offense under DNA Analysis Backlog Elimination Act of 2000 (DNA Act), 42 USCS §§ 14135 et seq., because it was unclear whether Congress intended bank larceny to be qualifying offense; interpretation of Attorney General, as set forth in 28 C.F.R. § 28.2(a), was therefore given deference because it did not contradict but was consistent with legislative intent of Congress in DNA Act, and defendant had to provide DNA sample as condition of probation. United States v Henderson (2004, CA7 Wis) 376 F3d 730.

Because DNA Analysis Backlog Elimination Act of 2000, 42 USCS § 14135a, did not require defendant convicted of bank larceny to submit DNA sample, defendant did not violate Act or conditions of his probation. United States v Peterson (2005, CA2 NY) 394 F3d 98.

District court's order for defendant to submit DNA sample to her probation officer was reversed because DNA Analysis Backlog Elimination Act of 2000, 42 USCS § 14135a, appertained to violent crimes and it was illogical to construe 42 USCS § 14135a(d)(1) to include for which defendant was convicted—possession of stolen bank funds pursuant to 18 USCS § 2113(c). United States v Cooper (2005, CA3 Pa) 396 F3d 308.

Defendant was not required to provide DNA sample as probation condition where defendant was convicted of bank larceny, which was not qualifying federal offense. United States v Curtis (2003, WD NY) 245 F Supp 2d 512.

Defendant, who was convicted by guilty plea of misdemeanor bank larceny under 18 USCS § 2113(b), was not required to provide DNA sample under DNA Analysis Backlog Elimination Act of 2000 as misdemeanor bank larceny was not "qualifying federal offense" listed under 42 USCS § 14135a(d)(1). United States v Curtis (2003, WD NY) 245 F Supp 2d 512.

14. Miscellaneous

Matter was remanded to district court so that district court could properly analyze whether or not taking of DNA sample from defendant pursuant to 42 USCS § 14135a violated defendant's rights under Religious Freedom Restoration Act, 42 USCS § 2000bb-1, because it was error to conclude that defendant's beliefs were not religious, without first determining precise scope of defendant's beliefs; after determining precise scope of defendant's beliefs, district court needed to consider whether or not beliefs were religious, whether beliefs were sincerely held, whether defendant's exercise of religion would be substantially burdened by giving DNA sample, and whether or not giving up sample was nonetheless permissible to serve compelling government

interest. United States v Zimmerman (2007, CA9 Cal) 514 F3d 851, appeal after remand, decision reached on appeal by (2009, CA9 Cal) 2009 US App LEXIS 22689.

In case in which pro se federal inmate alleged DNA Analysis Backlog Elimination Act of 2000 (DNA Act), 42 USCS §§ 14135–14135e, violated his rights under Religious Freedom Restoration Act, 42 USCS §§ 2000bb–2000bb-4, he did not allege facts sufficient to state substantial burden on his religious exercise because he could not identify any exercise which was subject of burden to which he objected; inmate's objection to deoxyribonucleic acid (DNA) sampling and collection was not objection to U.S. Bureau of Prisons collecting any bodily specimen that contains DNA material such as blood, saliva, skin, or hair, but rather objection to government extracting DNA information from specimen. Kaemmerling v Lappin (2008, App DC) 384 US App DC 240, 553 F3d 669.

Federal Bureau of Prisons (BOP), contractor that operated prison, and employees of BOP or contractor had authority to take DNA sample from inmate for inclusion in federal prison index system because inmate had been convicted of felony. Jackson v Fed. Bureau of Prisons (2009, DC Dist Col) 657 F Supp 2d 176.

§ 14135b. Collection and use of DNA identification information from certain District of Columbia offenders

(a) **Collection of DNA samples.** (1) From individuals in custody. The Director of the Bureau of Prisons shall collect a DNA sample from each individual in the custody of the Bureau of Prisons who is, or has been, convicted of a qualifying District of Columbia offense (as determined under subsection (d)).

(2) From individuals on release, parole, or probation. The Director of the Court Services and Offender Supervision Agency for the District of Columbia shall collect a DNA sample from each individual under the supervision of the Agency who is on supervised release, parole, or probation who is, or has been, convicted of a qualifying District of Columbia offense (as determined under subsection (d)).

(3) Individuals already in CODIS. For each individual described in paragraph (1) or (2), if the Combined DNA Index System (in this section referred to as "CODIS") of the Federal Bureau of Investigation contains a DNA analysis with respect to that individual, the Director of the Bureau of Prisons or Agency (as applicable) may (but need not) collect a DNA sample from that individual.

(4) Collection procedures. (A) The Director of the Bureau of Prisons or Agency (as applicable) may use or authorize the use of such means as are reasonably necessary to detain, restrain, and collect a DNA sample from an individual who refuses to cooperate in the collection of the sample.

(B) The Director of the Bureau of Prisons or Agency, as appropriate, may enter into agreements with units of State or local government or with private entities to provide for the collection of the samples described in paragraph (1) or (2).

(5) Criminal penalty. An individual from whom the collection of a DNA sample is authorized under this subsection who fails to cooperate in the collection of that sample shall be—

(A) guilty of a class A misdemeanor; and

(B) punished in accordance with title 18, United States Code.

(b) Analysis and use of samples. The Director of the Bureau of Prisons or Agency (as applicable) shall furnish each DNA sample collected under subsection (a) to the Director of the Federal Bureau of Investigation, who shall carry out a DNA analysis on each such DNA sample and include the results in CODIS.

(c) Definitions. In this section:

(1) The term "DNA sample" means a tissue, fluid, or other bodily sample of an individual on which a DNA analysis can be carried out.

(2) The term "DNA analysis" means analysis of the deoxyribonucleic acid (DNA) identification information in a bodily sample.

(d) Qualifying District of Columbia offenses. The government of the District of Columbia may determine those offenses under the District of Columbia Code that shall be treated for purposes of this section as qualifying District of Columbia offenses.

(e) Commencement of collection. Collection of DNA samples under subsection (a) shall, subject to the availability of appropriations, commence not later than the date that is 180 days after the date of the enactment of this Act [enacted Dec. 19, 2000].

(f) Authorization of appropriations. There are authorized to be appropriated to the Court Services and Offender Supervision Agency for the District of Columbia to carry out this section such sums as may be necessary for each of fiscal years 2001 through 2005.

(Dec. 19, 2000, P. L. 106-546, § 4, 114 Stat. 2730.)

HISTORY; ANCILLARY LAWS AND DIRECTIVES

Explanatory notes:

This section was enacted as part of Act Dec. 19, 2000, P. L. 106-546, and not as part of Act Sept. 13, 1994, P. L. 103-322, which generally comprises this chapter.

CODE OF FEDERAL REGULATIONS

Department of Justice—DNA identification system, 28 CFR 28.1 et seq.

CROSS REFERENCES

This section is referred to in 10 USCS § 1565; 42 USCS §§ 14132, 14135c, 14135e.

RESEARCH GUIDE

Annotations:

Validity, Construction, and Application of DNA Analysis Backlog Elimination Act of 2000, 42 U.S.C.A. §§ 14135 et seq. [42 USCS §§ 14135 et seq.] and 10 U.S.C.A. § 1565 [10 USCS § 1565]. 187 ALR Fed 373.

INTERPRETIVE NOTES AND DECISIONS

1. Generally
2. Constitutionality

1. Generally

Pursuant to U.S. Court of Appeals for District of Columbia, neither DNA Analysis Backlog Elimination Act of 2000 nor D.C. Code § 22-4151 is punitive in either purpose or effect. Johnson v Quander (2006, App DC) 370 US App DC 167, 440 F3d 489, cert den (2006) 549 US 945, 127 S Ct 103, 166 L Ed 2d 255 and (criticized in United States v Stewart (2007, DC Mass) 468 F Supp 2d 261) and (criticized in State v Martin (2008) 184 Vt 23, 2008 VT 53, 955 A2d 1144).

Under 42 USCS § 14132(d), part of DNA Analysis Backlog Elimination Act of 2000, if conviction for predicate offense was later overturned or reversed on appeal, individual's DNA information could be removed from Combined DNA Index System (CODIS) database and thus, prospect that innocent individual's DNA would be erroneously included in CODIS database was minimal; if there was question as to whether offense was "qualifying offense," person could always bring challenge in court of competent jurisdiction, and since 42 USCS § 14135b(b) explicitly limited how DNA samples could be used, and 42 USCS § 14135b(c)(2) provided that such analysis was only conducted to determine "identification information in bodily sample," risk of erroneous deprivation of liberty interest in plaintiff probationer's DNA was remote. Johnson v Quander (2005, DC Dist Col) 370 F Supp 2d 79, affd (2006, App DC) 370 US App DC 167, 440 F3d 489, cert den (2006) 549 US 945, 127 S Ct 103, 166 L Ed 2d 255 and (criticized in United States

v Stewart (2007, DC Mass) 468 F Supp 2d 261) and (criticized in State v Martin (2008) 184 Vt 23, 2008 VT 53, 955 A2d 1144).

2. Constitutionality

During probation, plaintiff probationer had diminished expectation of privacy and DNA Analysis Backlog Elimination Act of 2000 and D.C. Code Ann. § 22-4151 furthered compelling public interest under totality of circumstances analysis as to reasonableness, so that taking of probationer's DNA sample by defendant probation officers did not violate Fourth Amendment. Johnson v Quander (2005, DC Dist Col) 370 F Supp 2d 79, affd (2006, App DC) 370 US App DC 167, 440 F3d 489, cert den (2006) 549 US 945, 127 S Ct 103, 166 L Ed 2d 255 and (criticized in United States v Stewart (2007, DC Mass) 468 F Supp 2d 261) and (criticized in State v Martin (2008) 184 Vt 23, 2008 VT 53, 955 A2d 1144).

Court dismissed complaint by plaintiff against Probation Department, alleging that DNA Analysis Backlog Elimination Act of 2000 (Act), 42 USCS § 14135b, which penalized his failure to provide DNA sample, violated Fourth Amendment and Ex Post Facto Clause, U.S. Const. art. 1, § 9 because (1) government's interests furthered by Act outweighed plaintiff's substantially decreased expectations of privacy, and minimal intrusion of blood sample was reasonable, and (2) penalty for Act's violation was based on failure to comply with its terms and was not increased punishment for plaintiff's prior firearms conviction. Word v United States Prob. Dep't (2006, DC SC) 439 F Supp 2d 497.

§ 14135c.   Conditions of release generally

If the collection of a DNA sample from an individual on probation, parole, or supervised release is authorized pursuant to section 3 or 4 of this Act [42 USCS § 14135a or 14135b] or section 1565 of title 10, United States Code, the individual shall cooperate in the collection of a DNA sample as a condition of that probation, parole, or supervised release.

(Dec. 19, 2000, P. L. 106-546, § 7(d), 114 Stat. 2734.)

HISTORY; ANCILLARY LAWS AND DIRECTIVES

Explanatory notes:

This section was enacted as part of Act Dec. 19, 2000, P. L. 106-546, and not as part of Act Sept. 13, 1994, P. L. 103-322, which generally comprises this chapter.

RESEARCH GUIDE

Annotations:

Validity, Construction, and Application of DNA Analysis Backlog Elimination Act of 2000, 42 U.S.C.A. §§ 14135 et seq. [42 USCS §§ 14135 et seq.] and 10 U.S.C.A. § 1565 [10 USCS § 1565]. 187 ALR Fed 373.

INTERPRETIVE NOTES AND DECISIONS

District court lacked jurisdiction to hear defendant's challenge to constitutionality of DNA Analysis Backlog Elimination Act of 2002, 42 USCS §§ 14135–14135e, because finding that collection of DNA was unconstitutional as condition of defendant's future probation would necessarily implicate defendant's current parole; thus, issue fell squarely within jurisdiction of Parole Commission. United States v Fazzini (2005, CA7 Ill) 414 F3d 695, reh den (2005, CA7 Ill) 2005 US App LEXIS 15484 and cert den (2006) 547 US 1034, 126 S Ct 1604, 164 L Ed 2d 325 and habeas corpus proceeding, remanded (2006, CA6 Ohio) 473 F3d 229, 2006 FED App 472P.

§ 14135d. Authorization of appropriations

There are authorized to be appropriated to the Attorney General to carry out this Act (including to reimburse the Federal judiciary for any reasonable costs incurred in implementing such Act, as determined by the Attorney General) such sums as may be necessary.

(Dec. 19, 2000, P. L. 106-546, § 9, 114 Stat. 2753.)

HISTORY; ANCILLARY LAWS AND DIRECTIVES

References in text:

"This Act", referred to in this section, is Act Dec. 19, 2000, P. L. 106-546, which is classified in part to 42 USCS §§ 14135 et seq. For full classification of such Act, consult USCS Tables volumes.

Explanatory notes:

This section was enacted as part of Act Dec. 19, 2000, P. L. 106-546, and not as part of Act Sept. 13, 1994, P. L. 103-322, which generally comprises this chapter.

CODE OF FEDERAL REGULATIONS

Department of Justice—DNA identification system, 28 CFR 28.1 et seq.

RESEARCH GUIDE

Annotations:

Validity, Construction, and Application of DNA Analysis Backlog Elimination Act of 2000, 42 U.S.C.A. §§ 14135 et seq. [42 USCS §§ 14135 et seq.] and 10 U.S.C.A. § 1565 [10 USCS § 1565]. 187 ALR Fed 373.

§ 14135e. Privacy protection standards

(a) In general. Except as provided in subsection (b), any sample collected under, or any result of any analysis carried out under, section 2, 3, or 4 [42 USCS § 14135, 14135a, or 14135b] may be used only for a purpose specified in such section.

(b) Permissive uses. A sample or result described in subsection (a) may be disclosed under the circumstances under which disclosure of information included in the Combined DNA Index System is allowed, as specified in subparagraphs (A) through (D) of section 210304(b)(3) of the Violent Crime Control and Law Enforcement Act of 1994 (42 U.S.C. 14132(b)(3)).

(c) Criminal penalty. A person who knowingly discloses a sample or result described in subsection (a) in any manner to any person not authorized to receive it, or obtains or uses, without authorization, such sample or result, shall be fined not more than $250,000, or imprisoned for a period of not more than one year. Each instance of disclosure, obtaining, or use shall constitute a separate offense under this subsection.

(Dec. 19, 2000, P. L. 106-546, § 10, 114 Stat. 2735; Oct. 30, 2004, P. L. 108-405, Title II, § 203(e)(2), Title III, § 309, 118 Stat. 2271, 2275.)

HISTORY; ANCILLARY LAWS AND DIRECTIVES

Explanatory notes:
This section was enacted as part of Act Dec. 19, 2000, P. L. 106-546, and not as part of Act Sept. 13, 1994, P. L. 103-322, which generally comprises this chapter.

Amendments:
2004. Act Oct. 30, 2004, in subsec. (c)(2), substituted "$250,000, or imprisoned for a period of not more than one year, or both" for "$100,000".

Such Act further substituted a new subsec. (c) for subsec. (c) as amended, which read:

"(c) Criminal penalty. A person who knowingly—

"(1) discloses a sample or result described in subsection (a) in any manner to any person not authorized to receive it; or

"(2) obtains, without authorization, a sample or result described in subsection (a), shall be fined not more than $250,000, or imprisoned for a period of not more than one year, or both.".

CODE OF FEDERAL REGULATIONS

Department of Justice—DNA identification system, 28 CFR 28.1 et seq.

RESEARCH GUIDE

Annotations:
Validity, Construction, and Application of DNA Analysis Backlog Elimination Act of 2000, 42 U.S.C.A. §§ 14135 et seq. [42 USCS §§ 14135 et seq.] and 10 U.S.C.A. § 1565 [10 USCS § 1565]. 187 ALR Fed 373.

INTERPRETIVE NOTES AND DECISIONS

1. Generally
2. Constitutionality

1. Generally
DNA Analysis Backlog Elimination Act of 2000, Pub. L. No. 106-546 (codified as amended in scattered sections of 10 USCS, 18 USCS, and 42 USCS), included safeguards to protect privacy interests of supervised releasee who was required to provide sample; 42 USCS § 14132(b)(3) strictly limited use

of information, which was stored in centralized database. 42 USCS § 14135e(c) provided penalties for misuse of DNA samples; moreover, DNA Act included no discretionary component, given explicit directive set forth in 42 USCS § 14135a(a)(2). United States v Weikert (2007, CA1 Mass) 504 F3d 1, reh den, reh, en banc, den (2007, CA1) 504 F3d 20 and (criticized in State v Martin (2008) 184 Vt 23, 2008 VT 53, 955 A2d 1144) and (criticized in Boroian v Mueller (2010, CA1 Mass) 616 F3d 60).

While plaintiff former probationer challenged retaining and matching of his DNA profile, as provided for in 42 USCS § 14135a, given stringent restrictions on uses of DNA profiles, as set forth in 42 USCS § 14132(b)(3), 14135e(c), possible future extraction of other information beyond identification did not significantly augment current privacy interest which was lacking. Boroian v Mueller (2010, CA1 Mass) 616 F3d 60.

2. Constitutionality

Collection of DNA samples pursuant to DNA Analysis Backlog Elimination Act of 2000, Pub. L. No. 106-546, 114 Stat. 2726, codified as amended in part at 18 USCS § 3563 and 42 USCS §§ 14132, 14135a, 14135e, did not violate Fourth Amendment as to probationers in light of U.S. Court of Appeals for First Circuit's holding in U.S. v. Weikert, 504 F.3d 1 (1st Cir. 2007); though defendants pled guilty to non-violent, property-related crimes pursuant to 18 USCS §§ 641 and 473, their argument that new balancing test should be applied to them as result stemmed from flawed assumption that DNA evidence was only useful for solving-and thereby deterring-violent crimes; moreover, they did not have greater expectation of privacy than did supervised releasees as both probation, pursuant to 18

USCS §§ 3561, 3563, and supervised release, pursuant to 18 USCS § 3583, were forms of conditional release. United States v Stewart (2008, CA1 Mass) 532 F3d 32.

During probation, plaintiff probationer had diminished expectation of privacy and DNA Analysis Backlog Elimination Act of 2000 and D.C. Code Ann. § 22-4151 furthered compelling public interest under totality of circumstances analysis as to reasonableness, so that taking of probationer's DNA sample by defendant probation officers did not violate Fourth Amendment, and further, 42 USCS § 14132(b)(3) limited use of DNA profiles to, inter alia, criminal justice agencies for law enforcement purposes and in judicial proceedings and 42 USCS § 14135e(c) prescribed criminal penalties for improper acquisition, use, or disclosure of DNA or of DNA sample results. Johnson v Quander (2005, DC Dist Col) 370 F Supp 2d 79, aff'd (2006, App DC) 370 US App DC 167, 440 F3d 489, cert den (2006) 549 US 945, 127 S Ct 103, 166 L Ed 2d 255 and (criticized in United States v Stewart (2007, DC Mass) 468 F Supp 2d 261) and (criticized in State v Martin (2008) 184 Vt 23, 2008 VT 53, 955 A2d 1144).

§ 14136. DNA training and education for law enforcement, correctional personnel, and court officers

(a) In general. The Attorney General shall make grants to provide training, technical assistance, education, and information relating to the identification, collection, preservation, analysis, and use of DNA samples and DNA evidence by—

    (1) law enforcement personnel, including police officers and other first responders, evidence technicians, investigators, and others who collect or examine evidence of crime;

    (2) court officers, including State and local prosecutors, defense lawyers, and judges;

    (3) forensic science professionals; and

    (4) corrections personnel, including prison and jail personnel, and probation, parole, and other officers involved in supervision.

(b) Authorization of appropriations. There are authorized to be appropriated $12,500,000 for each of fiscal years 2009 through 2014 to carry out this section.

(Oct. 30, 2004, P. L. 108-405, Title III, § 303, 118 Stat. 2273; Oct. 8, 2008, P. L. 110-360, § 3, 122 Stat. 4008.)

HISTORY; ANCILLARY LAWS AND DIRECTIVES

Explanatory notes:

This section was enacted as part of Oct. 30, 2004, P. L. 108-405, and not as part of Act Sept. 13, 1994, P. L. 103-322, which generally comprises this chapter.

Amendments:

2008. Act Oct. 8, 2008, in subsec. (b), substituted "2009 through 2014" for "2005 through 2009".

Other provisions:

Incentive grants to States to ensure consideration of claims of actual innocence. Act Oct. 30, 2004, P. L. 108-405, Title IV, § 413, 118 Stat. 2285, provides:

"For each of fiscal years 2005 through 2009, all funds appropriated to carry out sections 303, 305, 308, and 412 [42 USCS §§ 14136, 14136b, 14136d, 14136e] shall be reserved for grants to eligible entities that—

"(1) meet the requirements under section 303, 305, 308, or 412 [42 USCS § 14136, 14136b, 14136d, or 14136e], as appropriate; and

"(2) demonstrate that the State in which the eligible entity operates—

"(A) provides post-conviction DNA testing of specified evidence—

"(i) under a State statute enacted before the date of enactment of this Act (or extended or renewed after such date), to persons convicted after trial and under a sentence of imprisonment or death for a State felony offense, in a manner that ensures a reasonable process for resolving claims of actual innocence; or

"(ii) under a State statute enacted after the date of enactment of this Act, or under a State rule, regulation, or practice, to persons under a sentence of imprisonment or death for a State felony offense, in a manner comparable to section 3600(a) of title 18, United States Code (provided that the State statute, rule, regulation, or practice may make post-conviction DNA testing available in cases in which such testing is not required by such section), and if the results of such testing exclude the applicant, permits the applicant to apply for post-conviction relief, notwithstanding any provision of law that would otherwise bar such application as untimely; and

"(B) preserves biological evidence secured in relation to the investigation or prosecution of a State offense—

"(i) under a State statute or a State or local rule, regulation, or practice, enacted or adopted before the date of enactment of this Act (or extended or renewed after such date), in a manner that ensures that reasonable measures are taken by all jurisdictions within the State to preserve such evidence; or

"(ii) under a State statute or a State or local rule, regulation, or practice, enacted or adopted after the date of enactment of this Act, in a manner comparable to section 3600A of title 18, United States Code, if—

"(I) all jurisdictions within the State comply with this requirement; and

"(II) such jurisdictions may preserve such evidence for longer than the period of time that such evidence would be required to be preserved under such section 3600A.".

§ 14136a. Sexual assault forensic exam program grants

(a) **In general.** The Attorney General shall make grants to eligible entities to provide training, technical assistance, education, equipment, and information relating to the identification, collection, preservation, analysis, and use of DNA samples and DNA evidence by medical personnel and other personnel, including doctors, medical examiners, coroners, nurses, victim service providers, and other professionals involved in treating victims of sexual assault and sexual assault examination programs, including SANE (Sexual Assault Nurse Examiner), SAFE (Sexual Assault Forensic Examiner), and SART (Sexual Assault Response Team).

(b) Eligible entity. For purposes of this section, the term "eligible entity" includes—

    (1) States;

    (2) units of local government; and

    (3) sexual assault examination programs, including—

        (A) sexual assault nurse examiner (SANE) programs;

        (B) sexual assault forensic examiner (SAFE) programs;

        (C) sexual assault response team (SART) programs;

        (D) State sexual assault coalitions;

        (E) medical personnel, including doctors, medical examiners, coroners, and nurses, involved in treating victims of sexual assault; and

        (F) victim service providers involved in treating victims of sexual assault.

(c) Authorization of appropriations. There are authorized to be appropriated $30,000,000 for each of fiscal years 2009 through 2014 to carry out this section.

(Oct. 30, 2004, P. L. 108-405, Title III, § 304, 118 Stat. 2273; Oct. 8, 2008, P. L. 110-360, § 4, 122 Stat. 4009.)

HISTORY; ANCILLARY LAWS AND DIRECTIVES

Explanatory notes:

This section was enacted as part of Oct. 30, 2004, P. L. 108-405, and not as part of Act Sept. 13, 1994, P. L. 103-322, which generally comprises this chapter.

Amendments:

2008. Act Oct. 8, 2008, in subsec. (c), substituted "2009 through 2014" for "2005 through 2009".

§ 14136b.   DNA research and development

(a) Improving DNA technology. The Attorney General shall make grants for research and development to improve forensic DNA technology, including increasing the identification accuracy and efficiency of DNA analysis, decreasing time and expense, and increasing portability.

(b) Demonstration projects. The Attorney General shall make grants to appropriate entities under which research is carried out through demonstration projects involving coordinated training and commitment of resources to law enforcement agencies and key criminal justice participants to demonstrate and evaluate the use of forensic DNA technology in conjunction with other forensic tools. The demonstration projects shall include scientific evaluation of the public safety benefits, improvements to law enforcement operations, and cost-effectiveness of increased collection and use of DNA evidence.

(c) Authorization of appropriations. There are authorized to be appropriated $15,000,000 for each of fiscal years 2005 through 2009 to carry out this section.

(Oct. 30, 2004, P. L. 108-405, Title III, § 305, 118 Stat. 2273.)

HISTORY; ANCILLARY LAWS AND DIRECTIVES

Explanatory notes:
This section was enacted as part of Oct. 30, 2004, P. L. 108-405, and not as part of Act Sept. 13, 1994, P. L. 103-322, which generally comprises this chapter.

§ 14136c.   National Forensic Science Commission

(a) Appointment. The Attorney General shall appoint a National Forensic Science Commission (in this section referred to as the "Commission"), composed of persons experienced in criminal justice issues, including persons from the forensic science and criminal justice communities, to carry out the responsibilities under subsection (b).

(b) Responsibilities. The Commission shall—

(1) assess the present and future resource needs of the forensic science community;

(2) make recommendations to the Attorney General for maximizing the use of forensic technologies and techniques to solve crimes and protect the public;

(3) identify potential scientific advances that may assist law enforcement in using forensic technologies and techniques to protect the public;

(4) make recommendations to the Attorney General for programs that will increase the number of qualified forensic scientists available to work in public crime laboratories;

(5) disseminate, through the National Institute of Justice, best practices concerning the collection and analyses of forensic evidence to help ensure quality and consistency in the use of forensic technologies and techniques to solve crimes and protect the public;

(6) examine additional issues pertaining to forensic science as requested by the Attorney General;

(7) examine Federal, State, and local privacy protection statutes, regulations, and practices relating to access to, or use of, stored DNA samples or DNA analyses, to determine whether such protections are sufficient;

(8) make specific recommendations to the Attorney General, as necessary, to enhance the protections described in paragraph (7) to ensure—

(A) the appropriate use and dissemination of DNA information;

(B) the accuracy, security, and confidentiality of DNA information;

(C) the timely removal and destruction of obsolete, expunged, or inaccurate DNA information; and

(D) that any other necessary measures are taken to protect privacy; and

(9) provide a forum for the exchange and dissemination of ideas and information in furtherance of the objectives described in paragraphs (1) through (8).

(c) Personnel; procedures. The Attorney General shall—

(1) designate the Chair of the Commission from among its members;

(2) designate any necessary staff to assist in carrying out the functions of the Commission; and

(3) establish procedures and guidelines for the operations of the Commission.

(d) Authorization of appropriations. There are authorized to be appropriated $500,000 for each of fiscal years 2005 through 2009 to carry out this section. (Oct. 30, 2004, P. L. 108-405, Title III, § 306, 118 Stat. 2274.)

HISTORY; ANCILLARY LAWS AND DIRECTIVES

Explanatory notes:

This section was enacted as part of Oct. 30, 2004, P. L. 108-405, and not as part of Act Sept. 13, 1994, P. L. 103-322, which generally comprises this chapter.

§ 14136d.   DNA identification of missing persons

(a) In general. The Attorney General shall make grants to promote the use of forensic DNA technology to identify missing persons and unidentified human remains.

(b) Requirement. Each State or unit of local government that receives funding under this section shall be required to submit the DNA profiles of such missing persons and unidentified human remains to the National Missing Persons DNA Database of the Federal Bureau of Investigation.

(c) Authorization of appropriations. There are authorized to be appropriated $2,000,000 for each of fiscal years 2005 through 2009 to carry out this section. (Oct. 30, 2004, P. L. 108-405, Title III, § 308, 118 Stat. 2275.)

HISTORY; ANCILLARY LAWS AND DIRECTIVES

Explanatory notes:

This section was enacted as part of Oct. 30, 2004, P. L. 108-405, and not as part of Act Sept. 13, 1994, P. L. 103-322, which generally comprises this chapter.

§ 14136e.   Kirk Bloodsworth Post-Conviction DNA Testing Grant Program

(a) In general. The Attorney General shall establish the Kirk Bloodsworth Post-Conviction DNA Testing Grant Program to award grants to States to help defray the costs of post-conviction DNA testing.

(b) Authorization of appropriations. There are authorized to be appropriated $5,000,000 for each of fiscal years 2005 through 2009 to carry out this section.

(c) **State defined.** For purposes of this section, the term "State" means a State of the United States, the District of Columbia, the Commonwealth of Puerto Rico, the United States Virgin Islands, American Samoa, Guam, and the Northern Mariana Islands.

(Oct. 30, 2004, P. L. 108-405, Title IV, § 412, 118 Stat. 2284.)

HISTORY; ANCILLARY LAWS AND DIRECTIVES

Explanatory notes:
This section was enacted as part of Oct. 30, 2004, P. L. 108-405, and not as part of Act Sept. 13, 1994, P. L. 103-322, which generally comprises this chapter.

POLICE PATTERN OR PRACTICE

§ 14141.   Cause of action

(a) **Unlawful conduct.** It shall be unlawful for any governmental authority, or any agent thereof, or any person acting on behalf of a governmental authority, to engage in a pattern or practice of conduct by law enforcement officers or by officials or employees of any governmental agency with responsibility for the administration of juvenile justice or the incarceration of juveniles that deprives persons of rights, privileges, or immunities secured or protected by the Constitution or laws of the United States.

(b) **Civil action by Attorney General.** Whenever the attorney General has reasonable cause to believe that a violation of paragraph (1) [subsection (a) of this section] has occurred, the Attorney General, for or in the name of the United States, may in a civil action obtain appropriate equitable and declaratory relief to eliminate the pattern or practice.

(Sept. 13, 1994, P. L. 103-322, Title XXI, Subtitle D, § 210401, 108 Stat. 2071.)

HISTORY; ANCILLARY LAWS AND DIRECTIVES

Explanatory notes:
The bracketed phrase "subsection (a) of this section" has been inserted in subsec. (b) as the phrase probably intended by Congress.

RESEARCH GUIDE

Law Review Articles:
Simmons. Cooperative Federalism and Police Reform: Using Congressional Spending Power to Promote Police Accountability. 62 Ala L Rev 351, 2011.

Simmons. New Governance and the "New Paradigm" of Police Accountability: a Democratic Approach to Police Reform. 59 Cath UL Rev 373, Winter, 2010.

Armacost. Organizational Culture and Police Misconduct. 72 Geo Wash L Rev 453, 2004.

Harmon. Promoting Civil Rights Through Proactive Policing Reform. 62 Stan L Rev 1, 2009.

Fan. The Police Gamesmanship Dilemma in Criminal Procedure. 44 UC Davis L Rev 1407, 2011.

Jacobi. Prosecuting Police Misconduct. 2000 Wis L Rev 789, 2000.

INTERPRETIVE NOTES AND DECISIONS

Possible future injury to members of police fraternal organization resulting from enforcement of 42 USCS § 14141 was not imminent, and, thus, members lacked standing to bring action against U.S. and Attorney General challenging constitutionality of statute, even if defendants had committed past wrongs in use of consent decrees to enforce statute, where chain of events needed to occur to cause injury to members was too conjectural and hypothetical to be real and immediate threat to individual members. Grand Lodge of the Fraternal Order of Police v Ashcroft (2001, DC Dist Col) 185 F Supp 2d 9.

Police organization lacked standing to bring its suit, which challenged constitutionality of 42 USCS § 14141 and sought to enjoin government from applying § 14141 in form of consent decrees, because alleged injuries were not imminent. Grand Lodge of the Fraternal Order of Police v Ashcroft (2001, DC Dist Col) 185 F Supp 2d 9.

Complaint filed by pro se plaintiff in U.S. Court of Federal Claims was dismissed for lack of jurisdiction because plaintiff was not entitled to prosecute claim under 42 USCS § 14141, which provided civil cause of action that was only available to Attorney General of United States. Adams v United States (2008) 82 Fed Cl 558.

§ 14142. Data on use of excessive force

(a) Attorney General to collect. The Attorney General shall, through appropriate means, acquire data about the use of excessive force by law enforcement officers.

(b) Limitation on use of data. Data acquired under this section shall be used only for research or statistical purposes and may not contain any information that may reveal the identity of the victim or any law enforcement officer.

(c) Annual summary. The Attorney General shall publish an annual summary of the data acquired under this section.
(Sept. 13, 1994, P. L. 103-322, Title XXI, Subtitle D, § 210402, 108 Stat. 2071.)

§ 14151. [Repealed]

HISTORY; ANCILLARY LAWS AND DIRECTIVES
This section (Act Sept. 13, 1994, P. L. 103-322, Title XXI, Subtitle E, § 210501, 108 Stat. 2072) was repealed by Act Jan. 5, 2006, P. L. 109-162, Title XI, Subtitle B, Ch. 5, § 1154(b)(3), 119 Stat. 3113. It provided for improved training and technical automation.

§ 14161. [Repealed]

HISTORY; ANCILLARY LAWS AND DIRECTIVES
This section (Act Sept. 13, 1994, P. L. 103-322, Title XXI, Subtitle F, § 210602, 108 Stat. 2073) was repealed by Act Jan. 5, 2006, P. L. 109-162, Title XI, Subtitle B, Ch. 5, § 1154(b)(4), 119 Stat. 3113. It provided for Federal assistance to ease the increased burdens on State court systems resulting from the enactment of the Violent Crime Control and Law Enforcement Act of 1994 (Act Sept. 13, 1994, P. L. 103-322).

IMPROVING THE QUALITY OF REPRESENTATION IN STATE CAPITAL
CASES

§ 14163. Capital representation improvement grants

(a) In general. The Attorney General shall award grants to States for the purpose of improving the quality of legal representation provided to indigent defendants in State capital cases.

(b) Defined term. In this section, the term "legal representation" means legal counsel and investigative, expert, and other services necessary for competent representation.

(c) Use of funds. Grants awarded under subsection (a)—

(1) shall be used to establish, implement, or improve an effective system for providing competent legal representation to—

(A) indigents charged with an offense subject to capital punishment;

(B) indigents who have been sentenced to death and who seek appellate or collateral relief in State court; and

(C) indigents who have been sentenced to death and who seek review in the Supreme Court of the United States; and

(2) shall not be used to fund, directly or indirectly, representation in specific capital cases.

(d) Apportionment of funds. (1) In general. Of the funds awarded under subsection (a)—

(A) not less than 75 percent shall be used to carry out the purpose described in subsection (c)(1)(A); and

(B) not more than 25 percent shall be used to carry out the purpose described in subsection (c)(1)(B).

(2) Waiver. The Attorney General may waive the requirement under this subsection for good cause shown.

(e) Effective system. As used in subsection (c)(1), an effective system for providing competent legal representation is a system that—

(1) invests the responsibility for appointing qualified attorneys to represent indigents in capital cases—

(A) in a public defender program that relies on staff attorneys, members of the private bar, or both, to provide representation in capital cases;

(B) in an entity established by statute or by the highest State court with jurisdiction in criminal cases, which is composed of individuals with demonstrated knowledge and expertise in capital cases, except for individuals currently employed as prosecutors; or

(C) pursuant to a statutory procedure enacted before the date of the enactment of this Act [enacted Oct. 30, 2004] under which the trial judge is required to appoint qualified attorneys from a roster maintained by a State or regional selection committee or similar entity; and

(2) requires the program described in paragraph (1)(A), the entity described in paragraph (1)(B), or an appropriate entity designated pursuant to the statutory procedure described in paragraph (1)(C), as applicable, to—

(A) establish qualifications for attorneys who may be appointed to represent indigents in capital cases;

(B) establish and maintain a roster of qualified attorneys;

(C) except in the case of a selection committee or similar entity described in paragraph (1)(C), assign 2 attorneys from the roster to represent an indigent in a capital case, or provide the trial judge a list of not more than 2 pairs of attorneys from the roster, from which 1 pair shall be assigned, provided that, in any case in which the State elects not to seek the death penalty, a court may find, subject to any requirement of State law, that a second attorney need not remain assigned to represent the indigent to ensure competent representation;

(D) conduct, sponsor, or approve specialized training programs for attorneys representing defendants in capital cases;

(E)(i) monitor the performance of attorneys who are appointed and their attendance at training programs; and

(ii) remove from the roster attorneys who—

(I) fail to deliver effective representation or engage in unethical conduct;

(II) fail to comply with such requirements as such program, entity, or selection committee or similar entity may establish regarding participation in training programs; or

(III) during the past 5 years, have been sanctioned by a bar association or court for ethical misconduct relating to the attorney's conduct as defense counsel in a criminal case in Federal or State court; and

(F) ensure funding for the cost of competent legal representation by the defense team and outside experts selected by counsel, who shall be compensated—

(i) in the case of a State that employs a statutory procedure described in paragraph (1)(C), in accordance with the requirements of that statutory procedure; and

(ii) in all other cases, as follows:

(I) Attorneys employed by a public defender program shall be compensated according to a salary scale that is commensurate with the salary scale of the prosecutor's office in the jurisdiction.

(II) Appointed attorneys shall be compensated for actual time and service, computed on an hourly basis and at a reasonable hourly rate in light of the qualifications and experience of the attorney and the local market for legal representation in cases reflecting the complexity and responsibility of capital cases.

(III) Non-attorney members of the defense team, including investigators, mitigation specialists, and experts, shall be compensated at a rate that reflects the specialized skills needed by those who assist counsel with the litigation of death penalty cases.

(IV) Attorney and non-attorney members of the defense team shall be reimbursed for reasonable incidental expenses.

(Oct. 30, 2004, P. L. 108-405, Title IV, Subtitle B, § 421, 118 Stat. 2286.)

HISTORY; ANCILLARY LAWS AND DIRECTIVES

Explanatory notes:
This section was enacted as part of Oct. 30, 2004, P. L. 108-405, and not
as part of Act Sept. 13, 1994, P. L. 103-322, which generally comprises this
chapter.

CROSS REFERENCES
This section is referred to in 42 USCS §§ 14163c, 14163d, 14163e.

§ 14163a. Capital prosecution improvement grants

(a) In general. The Attorney General shall award grants to States for the
purpose of enhancing the ability of prosecutors to effectively represent the
public in State capital cases.

(b) Use of funds. (1) Permitted uses. Grants awarded under subsection (a) shall
be used for one or more of the following:

(A) To design and implement training programs for State and local
prosecutors to ensure effective representation in State capital cases.

(B) To develop and implement appropriate standards and qualifications
for State and local prosecutors who litigate State capital cases.

(C) To assess the performance of State and local prosecutors who litigate
State capital cases, provided that such assessment shall not include
participation by the assessor in the trial of any specific capital case.

(D) To identify and implement any potential legal reforms that may be
appropriate to minimize the potential for error in the trial of capital cases.

(E) To establish a program under which State and local prosecutors
conduct a systematic review of cases in which a death sentence was
imposed in order to identify cases in which post-conviction DNA testing
may be appropriate.

(F) To provide support and assistance to the families of murder victims.

(2) Prohibited use. Grants awarded under subsection (a) shall not be used to
fund, directly or indirectly, the prosecution of specific capital cases.

(Oct. 30, 2004, P. L. 108-405, Title IV, Subtitle B, § 422, 118 Stat. 2288.)

HISTORY; ANCILLARY LAWS AND DIRECTIVES

Explanatory notes:
This section was enacted as part of Oct. 30, 2004, P. L. 108-405, and not
as part of Act Sept. 13, 1994, P. L. 103-322, which generally comprises this
chapter.

CROSS REFERENCES
This section is referred to in 42 USCS §§ 14163c, 14163d, 14163e.

§ 14163b. Applications

(a) In general. The Attorney General shall establish a process through which
a State may apply for a grant under this subtitle [42 USCS §§ 14163 et seq.].

(b) Application. (1) In general. A State desiring a grant under this subtitle [42

USCS §§ 14163 et seq.] shall submit an application to the Attorney General at such time, in such manner, and containing such information as the Attorney General may reasonably require.

(2) Contents. Each application submitted under paragraph (1) shall contain—

(A) a certification by an appropriate officer of the State that the State authorizes capital punishment under its laws and conducts, or will conduct, prosecutions in which capital punishment is sought;

(B) a description of the communities to be served by the grant, including the nature of existing capital defender services and capital prosecution programs within such communities;

(C) a long-term statewide strategy and detailed implementation plan that—

(i) reflects consultation with the judiciary, the organized bar, and State and local prosecutor and defender organizations; and

(ii) establishes as a priority improvement in the quality of trial-level representation of indigents charged with capital crimes and trial-level prosecution of capital crimes;

(D) in the case of a State that employs a statutory procedure described in section 421(e)(1)(C) [42 USCS § 14163(e)(1)(C)], a certification by an appropriate officer of the State that the State is in substantial compliance with the requirements of the applicable State statute; and

(E) assurances that Federal funds received under this subtitle [42 USCS §§ 14163 et seq.] shall be—

(i) used to supplement and not supplant non-Federal funds that would otherwise be available for activities funded under this subtitle [42 USCS §§ 14163 et seq.]; and

(ii) allocated in accordance with section 426(b) [42 USCS § 14163e(b)].

(Oct. 30, 2004, P. L. 108-405, Title IV, Subtitle B, § 423, 118 Stat. 2288.)

HISTORY; ANCILLARY LAWS AND DIRECTIVES

Explanatory notes:
This section was enacted as part of Oct. 30, 2004, P. L. 108-405, and not as part of Act Sept. 13, 1994, P. L. 103-322, which generally comprises this chapter.

§ 14163c. State reports

(a) **In general.** Each State receiving funds under this subtitle [42 USCS §§ 14163 et seq.] shall submit an annual report to the Attorney General that—

(1) identifies the activities carried out with such funds; and

(2) explains how each activity complies with the terms and conditions of the grant.

(b) **Capital representation improvement grants.** With respect to the funds provided under section 421 [42 USCS § 14163], a report under subsection (a) shall include—

(1) an accounting of all amounts expended;

(2) an explanation of the means by which the State—

(A) invests the responsibility for identifying and appointing qualified attorneys to represent indigents in capital cases in a program described in section 421(e)(1)(A) [42 USCS § 14163(e)(1)(A)], an entity described in section 421(e)(1)(B) [42 USCS § 14163(e)(1)(B)], or a selection committee or similar entity described in section 421(e)(1)(C) [42 USCS § 14163(e)(1)(C)]; and

(B) requires such program, entity, or selection committee or similar entity, or other appropriate entity designated pursuant to the statutory procedure described in section 421(e)(1)(C) [42 USCS § 14163(e)(1)(C)], to—

(i) establish qualifications for attorneys who may be appointed to represent indigents in capital cases in accordance with section 421(e)(2)(A) [42 USCS § 14163(e)(2)(A)];

(ii) establish and maintain a roster of qualified attorneys in accordance with section 421(e)(2)(B) [42 USCS § 14163(e)(2)(B)];

(iii) assign attorneys from the roster in accordance with section 421(e)(2)(C) [42 USCS § 14163(e)(2)(C)];

(iv) conduct, sponsor, or approve specialized training programs for attorneys representing defendants in capital cases in accordance with section 421(e)(2)(D) [42 USCS § 14163(e)(2)(D)];

(v) monitor the performance and training program attendance of appointed attorneys, and remove from the roster attorneys who fail to deliver effective representation or fail to comply with such requirements as such program, entity, or selection committee or similar entity may establish regarding participation in training programs, in accordance with section 421(e)(2)(E) [42 USCS § 14163(e)(2)(E)]; and

(vi) ensure funding for the cost of competent legal representation by the defense team and outside experts selected by counsel, in accordance with section 421(e)(2)(F) [42 USCS § 14163(e)(2)(F)], including a statement setting forth—

(I) if the State employs a public defender program under section 421(e)(1)(A) [42 USCS § 14163(e)(1)(A)], the salaries received by the attorneys employed by such program and the salaries received by attorneys in the prosecutor's office in the jurisdiction;

(II) if the State employs appointed attorneys under section 421(e)(1)(B) [42 USCS § 14163(e)(1)(B)], the hourly fees received by such attorneys for actual time and service and the basis on which the hourly rate was calculated;

(III) the amounts paid to non-attorney members of the defense team, and the basis on which such amounts were determined; and

(IV) the amounts for which attorney and non-attorney members of the defense team were reimbursed for reasonable incidental expenses;

(3) in the case of a State that employs a statutory procedure described in section 421(e)(1)(C) [42 USCS § 14163(e)(1)(C)], an assessment of the extent to which the State is in compliance with the requirements of the applicable State statute; and

(4) a statement confirming that the funds have not been used to fund representation in specific capital cases or to supplant non-Federal funds.

(c) Capital prosecution improvement grants. With respect to the funds provided under section 422 [42 USCS § 14163a], a report under subsection (a) shall include—

(1) an accounting of all amounts expended;

(2) a description of the means by which the State has—

(A) designed and established training programs for State and local prosecutors to ensure effective representation in State capital cases in accordance with section 422(b)(1)(A) [42 USCS § 14163a(b)(1)(A)];

(B) developed and implemented appropriate standards and qualifications for State and local prosecutors who litigate State capital cases in accordance with section 422(b)(1)(B) [42 USCS § 14163a(b)(1)(B)];

(C) assessed the performance of State and local prosecutors who litigate State capital cases in accordance with section 422(b)(1)(C) [42 USCS § 14163a(b)(1)(C)];

(D) identified and implemented any potential legal reforms that may be appropriate to minimize the potential for error in the trial of capital cases in accordance with section 422(b)(1)(D) [42 USCS § 14163a(b)(1)(D)];

(E) established a program under which State and local prosecutors conduct a systematic review of cases in which a death sentence was imposed in order to identify cases in which post-conviction DNA testing may be appropriate in accordance with section 422(b)(1)(E) [42 USCS § 14163a(b)(1)(E)]; and

(F) provided support and assistance to the families of murder victims; and

(3) a statement confirming that the funds have not been used to fund the prosecution of specific capital cases or to supplant non-Federal funds.

(d) Public disclosure of annual State reports. The annual reports to the Attorney General submitted by any State under this section shall be made available to the public.

(Oct. 30, 2004, P. L. 108-405, Title IV, Subtitle B, § 424, 118 Stat. 2289.)

HISTORY; ANCILLARY LAWS AND DIRECTIVES

Explanatory notes:
This section was enacted as part of Oct. 30, 2004, P. L. 108-405, and not as part of Act Sept. 13, 1994, P. L. 103-322, which generally comprises this chapter.

CROSS REFERENCES
This section is referred to in 42 USCS § 14163d.

§ 14163d. Evaluations by Inspector General and administrative remedies

(a) Evaluation by Inspector General. (1) In general. As soon as practicable after the end of the first fiscal year for which a State receives funds under a grant made under this subtitle [42 USCS §§ 14163 et seq.], the Inspector General of the Department of Justice (in this section referred to as the "Inspector General") shall—

(A) submit to the Committee on the Judiciary of the House of Representatives and the Committee on the Judiciary of the Senate a report evaluating the compliance by the State with the terms and conditions of the grant; and

(B) if the Inspector General concludes that the State is not in compliance with the terms and conditions of the grant, specify any deficiencies and make recommendations to the Attorney General for corrective action.

(2) Priority. In conducting evaluations under this subsection, the Inspector General shall give priority to States that the Inspector General determines, based on information submitted by the State and other comments provided by any other person, to be at the highest risk of noncompliance.

(3) Determination for statutory procedure States. For each State that employs a statutory procedure described in section 421(e)(1)(C) [42 USCS § 14163(e)(1)(C)], the Inspector General shall submit to the Committee on the Judiciary of the House of Representatives and the Committee on the Judiciary of the Senate, not later than the end of the first fiscal year for which such State receives funds, a determination as to whether the State is in substantial compliance with the requirements of the applicable State statute.

(4) Comments from public. The Inspector General shall receive and consider comments from any member of the public regarding any State's compliance with the terms and conditions of a grant made under this subtitle [42 USCS §§ 14163 et seq.]. To facilitate the receipt of such comments, the Inspector General shall maintain on its website a form that any member of the public may submit, either electronically or otherwise, providing comments. The Inspector General shall give appropriate consideration to all such public comments in reviewing reports submitted under section 424 [42 USCS § 14163c] or in establishing the priority for conducting evaluations under this section.

(b) **Administrative review.** (1) Comment. Upon the submission of a report under subsection (a)(1) or a determination under subsection (a)(3), the Attorney General shall provide the State with an opportunity to comment regarding the findings and conclusions of the report or the determination.

(2) Corrective action plan. If the Attorney General, after reviewing a report under subsection (a)(1) or a determination under subsection (a)(3), determines that a State is not in compliance with the terms and conditions of the grant, the Attorney General shall consult with the appropriate State authorities to enter into a plan for corrective action. If the State does not agree to a plan for corrective action that has been approved by the Attorney General within 90 days after the submission of the report under subsection (a)(1) or the determination under subsection (a)(3), the Attorney General shall, within 30 days, issue guidance to the State regarding corrective action to bring the State into compliance.

(3) Report to Congress. Not later than 90 days after the earlier of the

implementation of a corrective action plan or the issuance of guidance under paragraph (2), the Attorney General shall submit a report to the Committee on the Judiciary of the House of Representatives and the Committee on the Judiciary of the Senate as to whether the State has taken corrective action and is in compliance with the terms and conditions of the grant.

(c) Penalties for noncompliance. If the State fails to take the prescribed corrective action under subsection (b) and is not in compliance with the terms and conditions of the grant, the Attorney General shall discontinue all further funding under sections 421 and 422 [42 USCS §§ 14163 and 14163a] and require the State to return the funds granted under such sections for that fiscal year. Nothing in this paragraph shall prevent a State which has been subject to penalties for noncompliance from reapplying for a grant under this subtitle [42 USCS §§ 14163 et seq.] in another fiscal year.

(d) Periodic reports. During the grant period, the Inspector General shall periodically review the compliance of each State with the terms and conditions of the grant.

(e) Administrative costs. Not less than 2.5 percent of the funds appropriated to carry out this subtitle [42 USCS §§ 14163 et seq.] for each of fiscal years 2005 through 2009 shall be made available to the Inspector General for purposes of carrying out this section. Such sums shall remain available until expended.

(f) Special rule for "statutory procedure" States not in substantial compliance with statutory procedures. (1) In general. In the case of a State that employs a statutory procedure described in section 421(e)(1)(C) [42 USCS § 14163(e)(1)(C)], if the Inspector General submits a determination under subsection (a)(3) that the State is not in substantial compliance with the requirements of the applicable State statute, then for the period beginning with the date on which that determination was submitted and ending on the date on which the Inspector General determines that the State is in substantial compliance with the requirements of that statute, the funds awarded under this subtitle [42 USCS §§ 14163 et seq.] shall be allocated solely for the uses described in section 421 [42 USCS § 14163].

(2) Rule of construction. The requirements of this subsection apply in addition to, and not instead of, the other requirements of this section.

(Oct. 30, 2004, P. L. 108-405, Title IV, Subtitle B, § 425, 118 Stat. 2291.)

HISTORY; ANCILLARY LAWS AND DIRECTIVES

Explanatory notes:
This section was enacted as part of Oct. 30, 2004, P. L. 108-405, and not as part of Act Sept. 13, 1994, P. L. 103-322, which generally comprises this chapter.

CROSS REFERENCES
This section is referred to in 42 USCS § 14163e.

§ 14163e. Authorization of appropriations

(a) Authorization for grants. There are authorized to be appropriated

$75,000,000 for each of fiscal years 2005 through 2009 to carry out this subtitle [42 USCS §§ 14163 et seq.].

(b) Restriction on use of funds to ensure equal allocation. Each State receiving a grant under this subtitle [42 USCS §§ 14163 et seq.] shall allocate the funds equally between the uses described in section 421 [42 USCS § 14163] and the uses described in section 422 [42 USCS § 14163a], except as provided in section 425(f) [42 USCS § 14163d(f)].
(Oct. 30, 2004, P. L. 108-405, Title IV, Subtitle B, § 426, 118 Stat. 2292.)

HISTORY; ANCILLARY LAWS AND DIRECTIVES

Explanatory notes:
This section was enacted as part of Oct. 30, 2004, P. L. 108-405, and not as part of Act Sept. 13, 1994, P. L. 103-322, which generally comprises this chapter.

CROSS REFERENCES
This section is referred to in 42 USCS § 14163b.

MOTOR VEHICLE THEFT PREVENTION

§ 14171. Motor vehicle theft prevention program

(a) In general. Not later than 180 days after the date of enactment of this section [enacted Sept. 13, 1994], the Attorney General shall develop, in cooperation with the States, a national voluntary motor vehicle theft prevention program (in this section referred to as the "program") under which—

(1) the owner of a motor vehicle may voluntarily sign a consent form with a participating State or locality in which the motor vehicle owner—
   (A) states that the vehicle is not normally operated under certain specified conditions; and
   (B) agrees to—
      (i) display program decals or devices on the owner's vehicle; and
      (ii) permit law enforcement officials in any State to stop the motor vehicle and take reasonable steps to determine whether the vehicle is being operated by or with the permission of the owner, if the vehicle is being operated under the specified conditions; and
(2) participating States and localities authorize law enforcement officials in the State or locality to stop motor vehicles displaying program decals or devices under specified conditions and take reasonable steps to determine whether the vehicle is being operated by or with the permission of the owner.

(b) Uniform decal or device designs. (1) In general. The motor vehicle theft prevention program developed pursuant to this section shall include a uniform design or designs for decals or other devices to be displayed by motor vehicles participating in the program.
(2) Type of design. The uniform design shall—
   (A) be highly visible; and
   (B) explicitly state that the motor vehicle to which it is affixed may be

stopped under the specified conditions without additional grounds for establishing a reasonable suspicion that the vehicle is being operated unlawfully.

(c) Voluntary consent form. The voluntary consent form used to enroll in the program shall—

(1) clearly state that participation in the program is voluntary;

(2) clearly explain that participation in the program means that, if the participating vehicle is being operated under the specified conditions, law enforcement officials may stop the vehicle and take reasonable steps to determine whether it is being operated by or with the consent of the owner, even if the law enforcement officials have no other basis for believing that the vehicle is being operated unlawfully;

(3) include an express statement that the vehicle is not normally operated under the specified conditions and that the operation of the vehicle under those conditions would provide sufficient grounds for a prudent law enforcement officer to reasonably believe that the vehicle was not being operated by or with the consent of the owner; and

(4) include any additional information that the Attorney General may reasonably require.

(d) Specified conditions under which stops may be authorized. (1) In general. The Attorney General shall promulgate rules establishing the conditions under which participating motor vehicles may be authorized to be stopped under this section. These conditions may not be based on race, creed, color, national origin, gender, or age. These conditions may include—

(A) the operation of the vehicle during certain hours of the day; or

(B) the operation of the vehicle under other circumstances that would provide a sufficient basis for establishing a reasonable suspicion that the vehicle was not being operated by the owner, or with the consent of the owner.

(2) More than one set of conditions. The Attorney General may establish more than one set of conditions under which participating motor vehicles may be stopped. If more than one set of conditions is established, a separate consent form and a separate design for program decals or devices shall be established for each set of conditions. The Attorney General may choose to satisfy the requirement of a separate design for program decals or devices under this paragraph by the use of a design color that is clearly distinguishable from other design colors.

(3) No new conditions without consent. After the program has begun, the conditions under which a vehicle may be stopped if affixed with a certain decal or device design may not be expanded without the consent of the owner.

(4) Limited participation by states and localities. A State or locality need not authorize the stopping of motor vehicles under all sets of conditions specified under the program in order to participate in the program.

(e) Motor vehicles for hire. (1) Notification to lessees. Any person who is in the business of renting or leasing motor vehicles and who rents or leases a motor vehicle on which a program decal or device is affixed shall, prior to transferring possession of the vehicle, notify the person to whom the motor vehicle is rented or leased about the program.

(2) Type of notice. The notice required by this subsection shall—

(A) be in writing;

(B) be in a prominent format to be determined by the Attorney General; and

(C) explain the possibility that if the motor vehicle is operated under the specified conditions, the vehicle may be stopped by law enforcement officials even if the officials have no other basis for believing that the vehicle is being operated unlawfully.

(3) Fine for failure to provide notice. Failure to provide proper notice under this subsection shall be punishable by a fine not to exceed $5,000.

(f) **Notification of police.** As a condition of participating in the program, a State or locality must agree to take reasonable steps to ensure that law enforcement officials throughout the State or locality are familiar with the program, and with the conditions under which motor vehicles may be stopped under the program.

(g) **Regulations.** The Attorney General shall promulgate regulations to implement this section.

(h) **Authorization of appropriations.** There are authorized to carry out this section.[—]

(1) $1,500,000 for fiscal year 1996;

(2) $1,700,000 for fiscal year 1997; and

(3) $1,800,000 for fiscal year 1998.

(Sept. 13, 1994, P. L. 103-322, Title XXII, § 220002, 108 Stat. 2074.)

HISTORY; ANCILLARY LAWS AND DIRECTIVES

Explanatory notes:
The bracketed dash has been inserted in subsec. (h) as the punctuation probably intended by Congress.

CODE OF FEDERAL REGULATIONS

Department of Justice—Motor Vehicle Theft Prevention Act regulations, 28 CFR 29.1 et seq.
Department of Justice—Grants for correctional facilities, 28 CFR 91.1 et seq.

CROSS REFERENCES

This section is referred to in 42 USCS § 14214.

RESEARCH GUIDE

Am Jur:
7A Am Jur 2d, Automobiles and Highway Traffic § 388.

PROTECTIONS FOR THE ELDERLY

§ 14181. Missing Alzheimer's Disease Patient Alert Program

(a) **Grant.** The Attorney General shall, subject to the availability of appropriations, award a grant to an eligible organization to assist the organization in paying for the costs of planning, designing, establishing, and operating a Missing Alzheimer's Disease Patient Alert Program, which shall be a locally based, proactive program to protect and locate missing patients with Alzheimer's disease and related dementias.

(b) Application. To be eligible to receive a grant under subsection (a), an organization shall submit an application to the Attorney General at such time, in such manner, and containing such information as the Attorney General may require, including, at a minimum, an assurance that the organization will obtain and use assistance from private nonprofit organizations to support the program.

(c) Eligible organization. The Attorney General shall award the grant described in subsection (a) to a national voluntary organization that has a direct link to patients, and families of patients, with Alzheimer's disease and related dementias.

(d) Authorization of appropriations. There are authorized to be appropriated to carry out this section—

    (1) $900,000 for fiscal year 1996;

    (2) $900,000 for fiscal year 1997; and

    (3) $900,000 for fiscal year 1998.

(Sept. 13, 1994, P. L. 103-322, Title XXIV, § 240001, 108 Stat. 2080.)

CODE OF FEDERAL REGULATIONS

Department of Justice—Grants for correctional facilities, 28 CFR 91.1 et seq.

CROSS REFERENCES

This section is referred to in 42 USCS § 14214.

PRESIDENTIAL SUMMIT ON VIOLENCE AND NATIONAL COMMISSION ON CRIME PREVENTION AND CONTROL

§ 14191. Presidential summit

Congress calls on the President to convene a national summit on violence in America prior to convening the Commission established under this title [42 USCS §§ 14191 et seq.].

(Sept. 13, 1994, P. L. 103-322, Title XXVII, § 270001, 108 Stat. 2089.)

CODE OF FEDERAL REGULATIONS

Department of Justice—Grants for correctional facilities, 28 CFR 91.1 et seq.

CROSS REFERENCES

This section is referred to in 42 USCS § 14198.

§ 14192. Establishment; committees and task forces; representation

(a) Establishment and appointment of members. There is established a commission to be known as the "National Commission on Crime Control and Prevention". The Commission shall be composed of 28 members appointed as follows:

(1) 10 persons by the President, not more than 6 of whom shall be of the same major political party.

(2) 9 persons by the President pro tempore of the Senate, 5 of whom shall be appointed on the recommendation of the Majority Leader of the Senate and the chairman of the Committee on the Judiciary of the Senate, and 4 of whom shall be appointed on the recommendation of the Minority Leader of the Senate and the ranking minority member of the Committee on the Judiciary of the Senate.

(3) 9 persons appointed by the Speaker of the House of Representatives, in consultation with the chairman of the Committee on the Judiciary of the House of Representatives, and 4 of whom shall be appointed on the recommendation of the Minority Leader of the House of Representatives, in consultation with the ranking member of the Committee on the Judiciary.

(b) Committees and task forces. The Commission shall establish committees or task forces from among its members for the examination of specific subject areas and the carrying out of other functions or responsibilities of the Commission, including committees or task forces for the examination of the subject areas of crime and violence generally, the causes of the demand for drugs, violence in schools, and violence against women, as described in subsections (b) through (e) of section 270004 [42 USCS § 14194(b)–(e)].

(c) Representation. (1) At least 1 member of the Commission appointed by the President, at least 2 members of the Commission appointed by the President pro tempore of the Senate, and at least 2 members of the Commission appointed by the Speaker of the House of Representatives shall be persons well-qualified to participate in the Commission's examination of the subject area of crime and violence generally, with education, training, expertise, or experience in such areas as law enforcement, law, sociology, psychology, social work, and ethnography and urban poverty (including health care, housing, education, and employment).

(2) At least 1 member of the Commission appointed by the President, at least 2 members of the Commission appointed by the President pro tempore of the Senate, and at least 2 members of the Commission appointed by the Speaker of the House of Representatives shall be persons well-qualified to participate in the Commission's examination of the subject area of the causes of the demand for drugs, with education, training, expertise, or experience in such areas as addiction, biomedicine, sociology, psychology, law, and ethnography and urban poverty (including health care, housing, education, and employment).

(3) At least 1 member of the Commission appointed by the President, at least 2 members of the Commission appointed by the President pro tempore of the Senate, and at least 2 members of the Commission appointed by the Speaker of the House of Representatives shall be persons well-qualified to participate in the Commission's examination of the subject area of violence in schools,

with education, training, expertise, or experience in such areas as law enforcement, education, school governance policy and teaching, law, sociology, psychology, and ethnography and urban poverty (including health care, housing, education, and employment).

(4) At least 1 member of the Commission appointed by the President, at least 2 members of the Commission appointed by the President pro tempore of the Senate, and at least 2 members of the Commission appointed by the Speaker of the House of Representatives shall be persons well-qualified to participate in the Commission's examination of the subject area of violence against women, as survivors of violence, or as persons with education, training, expertise, or experience in such areas as law enforcement, law, judicial administration, prosecution, defense, victim services or advocacy in sexual assault or domestic violence cases (including medical services and counseling), and protection of victims' rights.

(Sept. 13, 1994, P. L. 103-322, Title XXVII, § 270002, 108 Stat. 2089.)

§ 14193. Purposes

The purposes of the Commission are as follows:

(1) To develop a comprehensive proposal for preventing and controlling crime and violence in the United States, including cost estimates for implementing any recommendations made by the Commission.

(2) To bring attention to successful models and programs in crime prevention and crime control.

(3) To reach out beyond the traditional criminal justice community for ideas for controlling and preventing crime.

(4) To recommend improvements in the coordination of local, State, Federal, and international crime control and prevention efforts, including efforts relating to crime near international borders.

(5) To make a comprehensive study of the economic and social factors leading to or contributing to crime and violence, including the causes of illicit drug use and other substance abuse, and to develop specific proposals for legislative and administrative actions to reduce crime and violence and the factors that contribute to it.

(6) To recommend means of utilizing criminal justice resources as effectively as possible, including targeting finite correctional facility space to the most serious and violent offenders, and considering increased use of intermediate sanctions for offenders who can be dealt with adequately by such means.

(7) To examine distinctive crime problems and the impact of crime on members of minority groups, Indians living on reservations, and other groups defined by race, ethnicity, religion, age, disability, or other characteristics, and to recommend specific responses to the distinctive crime problems of such groups.

(8) To examine the problem of sexual assaults, domestic violence, and other criminal and unlawful acts that particularly affect women, and to recommend Federal, State, and local strategies for more effectively preventing and punishing such crimes and acts.

(9) To examine the treatment of victims in Federal, State, and local criminal justice systems, and to develop recommendations to enhance and protect the rights of victims.

(10) To examine the ability of Federal, State, and local criminal justice systems to administer criminal law and criminal sanctions impartially without discrimination on the basis of race, ethnicity, religion, gender, or other legally proscribed grounds, and to make recommendations for correcting any deficiencies in the impartial administration of justice on these grounds.

(11) To examine the nature, scope, causes, and complexities of violence in schools and to recommend a comprehensive response to that problem.

(Sept. 13, 1994, P. L. 103-322, Title XXVII, § 270003, 108 Stat. 2091.)

CROSS REFERENCES

This section is referred to in 42 USCS § 14194.

§ 14194. Responsibilities of the Commission

(a) **In general.** The responsibilities of the Commission shall include such study and consultation as may be necessary or appropriate to carry out the purposes set forth in section 270003 [42 USCS § 14193], including the specific measures described in subsections (b) through (e) in relation to the subject areas addressed in those subsections.

(b) **Crime and violence generally.** In addressing the subject of crime and violence generally, the activities of the Commission shall include the following:

(1) Reviewing the effectiveness of traditional criminal justice approaches in preventing and controlling crime and violence.

(2) Examining the impact that changes in Federal and State law have had in controlling crime and violence.

(3) Examining the impact of changes in Federal immigration laws and policies and increased development and growth along United States international borders on crime and violence in the United States, particularly among the Nation's youth.

(4) Examining the problem of youth gangs and providing recommendations as to how to reduce youth involvement in violent crime.

(5) Examining the extent to which the use of dangerous weapons in the commission of crime has contributed to violence and murder in the United States.

(6) Convening field hearings in various regions of the country to receive testimony from a cross section of criminal justice professionals, business leaders, elected officials, medical doctors, and other persons who wish to participate.

(7) Reviewing all segments of the Nation's criminal justice systems, including the law enforcement, prosecution, defense, judicial, and corrections components in developing the crime control and prevention proposal.

(c) **Causes of the demand for drugs.** In addressing the subject of the causes of the demand for drugs, the activities of the Commission shall include the following:

(1) Examining the root causes of illicit drug use and abuse in the United States, including by compiling existing research regarding those root causes, and including consideration of the following factors:

(A) The characteristics of potential illicit drug users and abusers or drug traffickers, including age and social, economic, and educational backgrounds.

(B) Environmental factors that contribute to illicit drug use and abuse, including the correlation between unemployment, poverty, and homelessness and drug experimentation and abuse.

(C) The effects of substance use and abuse by a relative or friend in contributing to the likelihood and desire of an individual to experiment with illicit drugs.

(D) Aspects of, and changes in cultural values, attitudes and traditions that contribute to illicit drug use and abuse.

(E) The physiological and psychological factors that contribute to the desire for illicit drugs.

(2) Evaluating Federal, State, and local laws and policies on the prevention of drug abuse, control of unlawful production, distribution and use of controlled substances, and the efficacy of sentencing policies with regard to those laws.

(3) Analyzing the allocation of resources among interdiction of controlled substances entering the United States, enforcement of Federal laws relating to the unlawful production, distribution, and use of controlled substances, education with regard to and the prevention of the unlawful use of controlled substances, and treatment and rehabilitation of drug abusers.

(4) Analyzing current treatment and rehabilitation methods and making recommendations for improvements.

(5) Identifying any existing gaps in drug abuse policy that result from the lack of attention to the root causes of drug abuse.

(6) Assessing the needs of government at all levels for resources and policies for reducing the overall desire of individuals to experiment with and abuse illicit drugs.

(7) Making recommendations regarding necessary improvements in policies for reducing the use of illicit drugs in the United States.

(d) Violence in schools. In addressing the subject of violence in schools, the activities of the Commission shall include the following:

(1) Defining the causes of violence in schools.

(2) Defining the scope of the national problem of violence in schools.

(3) Providing statistics and data on the problem of violence in schools on a State-by-State basis.

(4) Investigating the problem of youth gangs and their relation to violence in schools and providing recommendations on how to reduce youth involvement in violent crime in schools.

(5) Examining the extent to which dangerous weapons have contributed to violence and murder in schools.

(6) Exploring the extent to which the school environment has contributed to violence in schools.

(7) Reviewing the effectiveness of current approaches in preventing violence in schools.

(e) Violence against women. In addressing the subject of sexual assault, domestic violence, and other criminal and unlawful acts that particularly affect women, the activities of the Commission shall include the following:

(1) Evaluating the adequacy of, and making recommendations regarding, current law enforcement efforts at the Federal, State, and local levels to reduce the incidence of such crimes and acts, and to punish those responsible for such crimes and acts.

(2) Evaluating the adequacy of, and making recommendations regarding, the responsiveness of prosecutors and courts to such crimes and acts.

(3) Evaluating the adequacy of rules of evidence, practice, and procedure to ensure the effective prosecution and conviction of perpetrators of such crimes and acts and to protect victims of such crimes and acts from abuse in legal proceedings, making recommendations, where necessary, to improve those rules.

(4) Evaluating the adequacy of pretrial release, sentencing, incarceration, and post-conviction release in relation to such crimes and acts.

(5) Evaluating the adequacy of, and making recommendations regarding, the adequacy of Federal and State laws on sexual assault and the need for a more uniform statutory response to sex offenses, including sexual assaults and other sex offenses committed by offenders who are known or related by blood or marriage to the victim.

(6) Evaluating the adequacy of, and making recommendations regarding, the adequacy of Federal and State laws on domestic violence and the need for a more uniform statutory response to domestic violence.

(7) Evaluating the adequacy of, and making recommendations regarding, the adequacy of current education, prevention, and protective services for victims of such crimes and acts.

(8) Assessing the issuance, formulation, and enforcement of protective orders, whether or not related to a criminal proceeding, and making recommendations for their more effective use in domestic violence and stalking cases.

(9) Assessing the problem of stalking and recommending effective means of response to the problem.

(10) Evaluating the adequacy of, and making recommendations regarding, programs for public awareness and public dissemination of information to prevent such crimes and acts.

(11) Evaluating the treatment of victims of such crimes and acts in Federal, State, and local criminal justice systems, and making recommendations designed to improve such treatment.

(Sept. 13, 1994, P. L. 103-322, Title XXVII, § 270004, 108 Stat. 2092.)

CROSS REFERENCES

This section is referred to in 42 USCS § 14192.

§ 14195. Administrative matters

(a) Chair. The President shall designate a member of the Commission to chair the Commission.

(b) No additional pay or benefits; per diem. Members of the Commission shall receive no pay or benefits by reason of their service on the Commission, but shall receive travel expenses, including per diem in lieu of subsistence, at rates authorized for employees of agencies under sections 5702 and 5703 of title 5, United States Code.

(c) Vacancies. Vacancies on the Commission shall be filled in the same manner as initial appointments.

(d) Meetings open to the public. The Commission shall be considered to be an agency for the purposes of section 552b of title 5, United States Code, relating to the requirement that meetings of Federal agencies be open to the public. (Sept. 13, 1994, P. L. 103-322, Title XXVII, § 270005, 108 Stat. 2094.)

§ 14196. Staff and support services

(a) Director. With the approval of the Commission, the chairperson shall appoint a staff director for the Commission.

(b) Staff. With the approval of the Commission, the staff director may appoint and fix the compensation of staff personnel for the Commission.

(c) Civil service laws. The staff of the Commission shall be appointed without regard to the provisions of title 5, United States Code, governing appointments in the competitive service. Staff compensation may be set without regard to the provisions of chapter 51 and subchapter III of chapter 53 of that title [5 USCS §§ 5101 et seq., 5331 et seq.] relating to classification and General Schedule pay rates, but in no event shall any such personnel be compensated at a rate greater than the rate of basic pay for level ES-4 of the Senior Executive Service Schedule under section 5382 of that title. The staff director shall be paid at a rate not to exceed the rate of basic pay for level V of the Executive Schedule.

(d) Consultants. With the approval of the Commission, the staff director may procure temporary and intermittent services under section 3109(b) of title 5, United States Code.

(e) Staff of Federal agencies. Upon the request of the Commission, the head of any Federal agency may detail, on a reimbursable basis, personnel of that agency to the Commission to assist in carrying out its duties.

(f) Physical facilities. The Administrator of the General Service Administration shall provide suitable office space for the operation of the Commission. The facilities shall serve as the headquarters of the Commission and shall include all necessary equipment and incidentals required for proper functioning. (Sept. 13, 1994, P. L. 103-322, Title XXVII, § 270006, 108 Stat. 2094.)

HISTORY; ANCILLARY LAWS AND DIRECTIVES

References in text:
The "civil service laws", referred to in this section, are generally located in Title 5, USCS; see particularly 5 USCS §§ 1101 et seq.

The "provisions of title 5, United States Code, governing appointments in the competitive service", referred to in this section, appear generally as 5 USCS §§ 3301 et seq.

"Level V of the Executive Schedule", referred to in this section, is contained in 5 USCS § 5316.

§ 14197. Powers

(a) Hearings. For the purposes of carrying out this title [42 USCS §§ 14191 et seq.], the Commission may conduct such hearings, sit and act at such times and places, take such testimony, and receive such evidence, as the Commission considers appropriate. The Commission may administer oaths before the Commission.

(b) Delegation. Any committee, task force, member, or agent, of the Commission may, if authorized by the Commission, take any action that the Commission is authorized to take under this title [42 USCS §§ 14191 et seq.].

(c) Access to information. The Commission may request directly from any Federal agency or entity in the executive or legislative branch such information as is needed to carry out its functions.

(d) Mail. The Commission may use the United States mails in the same manner and under the same conditions as other Federal agencies.

(Sept. 13, 1994, P. L. 103-322, Title XXVII, § 270007, 108 Stat. 2095.)

§ 14198. Report; termination

Not later than 2 years after the date on which the Commission is fully constituted under section 270001 [42 USCS § 14191], the Commission shall submit a detailed report to the Congress and the President containing its findings and recommendations. The Commission shall terminate 30 days after the submission of its report.

(Sept. 13, 1994, P. L. 103-322, Title XXVII, § 270008, 108 Stat. 2095.)

§ 14199. Authorization of appropriations

There are authorized to be appropriated to carry out this title [42 USCS §§ 14191 et seq.]—

[(1)] $1,000,000 for fiscal year 1996.

(Sept. 13, 1994, P. L. 103-322, Title XXVII, § 270009, 108 Stat. 2095.)

HISTORY; ANCILLARY LAWS AND DIRECTIVES

Explanatory notes:
The paragraph designator (1) has been enclosed in brackets since the section was enacted without paragraph (2).

CROSS REFERENCES
This section is referred to in 42 USCS § 14214.

VIOLENT CRIME REDUCTION TRUST FUND

§ 14211. Creation of Violent Crime Reduction Trust Fund

(a) Violent Crime Reduction Trust Fund. There is established a separate account in the Treasury, known as the "Violent Crime Reduction Trust Fund" (referred to in this section as the "Fund") into which shall be transferred, in accordance with subsection (b), savings realized from implementation of section 5 of the Federal Workforce Restructuring Act of 1994 (5 U.S.C. 3101 note; Public Law 103-226).

(b) Transfers into the Fund. On the first day of the following fiscal years (or as soon thereafter as possible for fiscal year 1995), the following amounts shall be transferred from the general fund to the Fund—

(1) for fiscal year 1995, $2,423,000,000;
(2) for fiscal year 1996, $4,287,000,000;
(3) for fiscal year 1997, $5,000,000,000;
(4) for fiscal year 1998, $5,500,000,000;
(5) for fiscal year 1999, $6,500,000,000; and
(6) for fiscal year 2000, $6,500,000,000.

(c) Appropriations from the Fund. (1) Amounts in the Fund may be appropriated exclusively for the purposes authorized in this Act and for those expenses authorized by any Act enacted before this Act [enacted Sept. 13, 1994] that are expressly qualified for expenditure from the Fund.

(2) Amounts appropriated under paragraph (1) and outlays flowing from such appropriations shall not be taken into account for purposes of any budget enforcement procedures under the Balanced Budget and Emergency Deficit Control Act of 1985 except section 251A of that Act as added by subsection (g) [2 USCS § 901a], or for purposes of section 605(b) of the Congressional Budget Act of 1974. Amounts of new budget authority and outlays under paragraph (1) that are included in concurrent resolutions on the budget shall not be taken into account for purposes of sections 601(b), 606(b), and 606(c) of the Congressional Budget Act of 1974, or for purposes of section 24 of House Concurrent Resolution 218 (One Hundred Third Congress).
(Sept. 13, 1994, P. L. 103-322, Title XXXI, § 310001(a)–(c), 108 Stat. 2102.)

HISTORY; ANCILLARY LAWS AND DIRECTIVES

References in text:
"This section", referred to in subsec. (a), is § 31001 of Act Sept. 13, 1994, P. L. 103-322. For full classification of such section, consult USCS Tables volumes.
"This Act", referred to in this section, is Act Sept. 13, 1994, P. L. 103-322. For full classification of such Act, consult USCS Tables volumes.
The "Balanced Budget and Emergency Deficit Control Act of 1985", referred to in this section, is Act Dec. 12, 1985, P. L. 99-177, 99 Stat. 1037. For full classification of this Act, consult USCS Tables volumes.
"Section 605(b) of the Congressional Budget Act of 1974" and "sections 601(b), 606(b), and 606(c) of the Congressional Budget Act of 1974", referred to in subsec. (c)(2), are §§ 605(b), 601(b), 606(b), and 606(c) of Act July 12, 1974, P. L. 93-344, which appeared as 2 USCS §§ 665d(b), 665(b), 665e(b), and 665e(c), prior to their repeal by Act Aug. 5, 1997, P. L. 105-33, Title X, § 10118(a), 111 Stat. 695.

CODE OF FEDERAL REGULATIONS
Department of Justice—Grants for correctional facilities, 28 CFR 91.1 et seq.

§ 14212. [Repealed]

HISTORY; ANCILLARY LAWS AND DIRECTIVES

This section (Act Sept. 13, 1994, P. L. 103-322, Title XXXI, § 310002, 108 Stat. 2105) was repealed by Act Aug. 5, 1997, P. L. 105-33, Title X, Subtitle B, § 10204(b), 111 Stat. 702. It provided for a conforming reduction in discretionary spending limits.

§ 14213. Extension of authorizations of appropriations for fiscal years for which the full amount authorized is not appropriated

If, in making an appropriation under any provision of this Act or amendment made by this Act that authorizes the making of an appropriation for a certain purpose for a certain fiscal year in a certain amount, the Congress makes an appropriation for that purpose for that fiscal year in a lesser amount, that provision or amendment shall be considered to authorize the making of appropriations for that purpose for later fiscal years in an amount equal to the difference between the amount authorized to be appropriated and the amount that has been appropriated.

(Sept. 13, 1994, P. L. 103-322, Title XXXI, § 310003, 108 Stat. 2105.)

HISTORY; ANCILLARY LAWS AND DIRECTIVES

References in text:

"This Act", referred to in this section, is Act Sept. 13, 1994, P. L. 103-322, 108 Stat. 1796. For full classification of this Act, consult USCS Tables volumes.

§ 14214. Flexibility in making of appropriations

(a) **Federal law enforcement.** In the making of appropriations under any provision of this Act or amendment made by this Act that authorizes the making of an appropriation for a Federal law enforcement program for a certain fiscal year in a certain amount out of the Violent Crime Reduction Trust Fund, not to exceed 10 percent of that amount is authorized to be appropriated for that fiscal year for any other Federal law enforcement program for which appropriations are authorized by any other Federal law enforcement provision of this Act or amendment made by this Act. The aggregate reduction in the authorization for any particular Federal law enforcement program may not exceed 10 percent of the total amount authorized to be appropriated from the Violent Crime Reduction Trust Fund for that program in this Act or amendment made by this Act.

(b) **State and local law enforcement.** In the making of appropriations under any provision of this Act or amendment made by this Act that authorizes the making of an appropriation for a State and local law enforcement program for a certain fiscal year in a certain amount out of the Violent Crime Reduction Trust Fund, not to exceed 10 percent of that amount is authorized to be appropriated for that fiscal year for any other State and local law enforcement program for which appropriations are authorized by any other State and local law enforcement provision of this Act or amendment made by this Act. The aggregate reduction in the authorization for any particular State and local law enforcement program may not exceed 10 percent of the total amount authorized to be appropriated from the Violent Crime Reduction Trust Fund for that program in this Act or amendment made by this Act.

(c) **Prevention.** In the making of appropriations under any provision of this Act or amendment made by this Act that authorizes the making of an appropriation for a prevention program for a certain fiscal year in a certain amount out of the Violent Crime Reduction Trust Fund, not to exceed 10 percent of that amount is authorized to be appropriated for that fiscal year for any other prevention program for which appropriations are authorized by any other prevention provision of this Act or amendment made by this Act. The aggregate reduction in the authorization for any particular prevention program may not exceed 10 percent of the total amount authorized to be appropriated from the Violent Crime Reduction Trust Fund for that program in this Act or amendment made by this Act.

(d) **Definitions.** In this section—"Federal law enforcement program" means a program authorized in any of the following sections:

(1) section 190001(a) [unclassified];
(2) section 190001(b) [unclassified];
(3) section 190001(c) [unclassified];
(4) section 190001(d) [unclassified];
(5) section 190001(e) [unclassified];
(6) section 320925;
(7) section 150008 [42 USCS § 14062];
(8) section 220002 [42 USCS § 14171];
(9) section 130002 [8 USCS § 1252 note];
(10) section 130005 [8 USCS § 1158 note];
(11) section 130006 [8 USCS § 1101 note];
(12) section 130007 [8 USCS § 1252 note];
(13) section 250005 [unclassified];
(14) sections 210303–210306 [42 USCS §§ 14131–14134];
(15) section 180104 [42 USCS § 14083]; and
(16) section 270009 [42 USCS § 14199].

"State and local law enforcement program" means a program authorized in any of the following sections:

(1) sections 10001–10003;
(2) section 210201;
(3) section 210603 [18 USCS § 922 notes];
(4) section 180101 [amending 42 USCS §§ 3793(a)(9) and 3796bb(a), (b)]
(5) section 180103 [42 USCS § 14082];
(6) sections 31701–31708 [42 USCS §§ 13861–13868];
(7) section 210602;
(8) sections 308017–30802 [42 USCS §§ 13811, 13812];

(9) section 210302;

(10) section 210501;

(11) section 210101 [unclassified];

(12) section 320930;

(13) sections 20101–20109 [42 USCS §§ 13701–13709];

(14) section 20301 [8 USCS § 1252(j) and notes];

(15) section 32201 [42 USCS § 13911]; and

(16) section 20201.

"prevention program" means a program authorized in any of the following sections:

(1) section 50001;

(2) sections 30101–30104 [42 USCS §§ 13741–13744];

(3) sections 30201–30208;

(4) sections 30301–30307 [42 USCS §§ 13771–13777]

(5) sections 30401–30403;

(6) sections 30701–30702;

(7) sections 31001–31002 [31 USCS §§ 6701–6720];

(8) sections 31101–31133 [42 USCS § 13701 note and §§ 13821–13853];

(9) sections 31501–31505;

(10) sections 31901–31922 [42 USCS § 13701 note and §§ 13881–13902];

(11) section 32001 [amending 18 USCS § 3621];

(12) section 32101;

(13) section 32401 [42 USCS § 13921];

(14) section 40114 [unclassified];

(15) section 40121;

(16) section 40151;

(17) section 40152 [42 USCS § 13941];

(18) section 40155;

(19) section 40156;

(20) section 313 of the Family Violence Prevention and Services Act (relating to a hotline) [42 USCS § 10413];

(21) section 40231;

(22) sections 301 through 312 of the Family Violence Prevention and Services Act [42 USCS §§ 10401–10412]

(23) section 40251;

(24) section 314 of the Family Violence Prevention and Services Act (relating to community projects to prevent family violence, domestic violence, and dating violence) [42 USCS § 10414];

(25) section 40292 [42 USCS § 13962];

(26) section 40293 [42 USCS § 13963];

(27) section 40295 [42 USCS § 13971];

(28) sections 40411–40414 [42 USCS §§ 13991–13994];

(29) sections 40421–40422 [42 USCS §§ 14001, 14002];

(30) section 40506 [42 USCS § 14012];

(31) sections 40601–40611; and

(32) section 24001.

(Sept. 13, 1994, P. L. 103-322, Title XXXI, § 310004, 108 Stat. 2106; Dec. 20, 2010, P. L. 111-320, Title II, § 202(e), 124 Stat. 3509.)

HISTORY; ANCILLARY LAWS AND DIRECTIVES

References in text:

"This Act", referred to in this section, is Act Sept. 13, 1994, P. L. 103-322, 108 Stat. 1796. For full classification of this Act, consult USCS Tables volumes.

The meaning of "section 320925", referred to in subsec. (d), is unclear, since Act Sept. 13, 1994, P. L. 103-322, has no section 320925.

"Sections 10001–10003", referred in this section, are §§ 10001–10003 of Act Sept. 13, 1994, P. L. 103-322, which appear generally as 42 USCS §§ 3796dd et seq.; for full classification, consult USCS Tables volumes.

"Section 210201", referred to in this section, is § 210201 of Act Sept. 13, 1994, P. L. 103-322, which appears generally as 42 USCS §§ 3796jj et seq.; for full classification, consult USCS Tables volumes.

"Section 210602", referred to in this section, is § 210602 of Act Sept. 13, 1994, P. L. 103-322, which formerly appeared as 42 USCS § 14161, prior to its repeal by Act Jan. 5, 2006, P. L. 109-162, Title XI, Subtitle B, Ch. 5, § 1154(b)(4), 119 Stat. 113.

"Section 210302", referred to in this section, is § 210302 of Act Sept. 13, 1994, P. L. 103-322, which appears generally as 42 USCS §§ 3796kk et seq.; for full classification, consult USCS Tables volumes.

"Section 210501", referred to in this section, is § 210501 of Act Sept. 13, 1994, P. L. 103-322, which formerly appeared as 42 USCS § 14151, prior to its repeal by Act Jan. 5, 2006, P. L. 109-162, Title XI, Subtitle B, Ch. 5, § 1154(b)(3), 119 Stat. 113.

The meaning of "section 320930", referred to in subsec. (d), is unclear, since Act Sept. 13, 1994, P. L. 103-322, has no section 320930.

"Section 20201", referred to in this section, is § 20201 of Act Sept. 13, 1994, P. L. 103-322, which appears generally as 42 USCS §§ 3796ee et seq.; for full classification, consult USCS Tables volumes.

"Section 50001", referred to in this section, is § 50001 of Act Sept. 13, 1994, P. L. 103-322, which appears generally as 42 USCS §§ 3796ii et seq.; for full classification, consult USCS Tables volumes.

"Sections 30201–30208", referred to in this section, are §§ 30201–30208 of Act Sept. 13, 1994, P. L. 103-322, which formerly appeared as 42 USCS §§ 13751–13758, prior to their repeal by Act Jan. 5, 2006, P. L. 109-162, Title XI, Subtitle B, Ch. 5, § 1154(b)(1), 119 Stat. 113.

"Sections 30401–30403", referred to in this section, are §§ 30401–30403 of Act Sept. 13, 1994, P. L. 103-322. Sections 30401 and 30403 appear as 42 USCS §§ 13791 and 13793, respectively; § 30402 formerly appeared as 42 USCS § 13792 prior to its repeal by Act Oct. 21, 1998, P. L. 105-277, Div A [101(f) [Title VIII, Subtitle III, § 301(d)], 112 Stat. 2681-410.

"Sections 30701–30702", referred to in this section are § 30701 and 30702 of Act Sept. 13, 1994, P. L. 103-322, which formerly appeared as 42 USCS §§ 13801 and 13802 prior to their repeal by Act Jan. 5, 2006, P. L. 109-162, Title XI, Subtitle B, Ch. 5, § 1154(b)(2), 119 Stat. 113.

"Sections 31501–31505", referred to in this section, are §§ 31501–31505 of Act Sept. 13, 1994, P. L. 103-322; for full classification, consult USCS Tables volumes.

"Section 32101", referred to in this section, is § 332101 of Act Sept. 13, 1994, P. L. 103-322, which appears generally as 42 USCS §§ 3796ff et seq.; for full classification, consult USCS Tables volumes.

"Section 40121", referred to in this section, is § 40121 of Act Sept. 13, 1994, P. L. 103-322, which appears generally as 42 USCS §§ 3796gg et seq.; for full classification, consult USCS Tables volumes.

"Section 40151", referred to in this section, is § 40151 of Act Sept. 13, 1994, P. L. 103-322, which formerly appeared as 42 USCS § 300w-10 prior to its repeal by Act Oct. 28, 2000, P. L. 106-386, Div B, Title IV, § 1401(b), 114 Stat. 1513.

"Section 40155", referred to in this section, is § 40155 of Act Sept. 13, 1994, P. L. 103-322, which formerly appeared as 42 USCS § 5712d prior to its repeal by Act Jan. 5, 2006, P. L. 109-162, Title XI, Subtitle C, § 1172(b), 119 Stat. 3123.

"Section 40156", referred to in this section, is § 40156 of Act Sept. 13, 1994, P. L. 103-322; for full classification, consult USCS Tables volumes.

"Section 40231", referred to in this section, is § 40231 of Act Sept. 13, 1994, P. L. 103-322, which appears generally as 42 USCS §§ 3796hh et seq.; for full classification, consult USCS Tables volumes.

"Section 40251", referred to in this section is § 40251 of Act Sept. 13, 1994, P. L. 103-322, which formerly appeared as 42 USCS § 10417 prior to its repeal by Act June 25, 2003, P. L. 108-36, Title IV, § 412, 117 Stat. 829.

"Sections 40601–40611", referred to in this section, are §§ 40601–40611 of Act Sept. 13, 1994, P. L. 103-322, which appear generally as 42 USCS §§ 14031 et seq; for full classification, consult USCS Tables volumes.

"Section 24001", referred to in this section, probably means § 240001 of Act Sept. 13, 1994, P. L. 103-322, which appears as 42 USCS § 14181.

Amendments:

2010. Act Dec. 20, 2010, in subsec. (d), in the part relating to the definition of "prevention program", in para. (20), substituted "section 313 of the Family Violence Prevention and Services Act (relating to a hotline)" for "section 40211", in para. (22), substituted "sections 301 through 312 of the Family Violence Prevention and Services Act" for "section 40241", and in para. (24), substituted "section 314 of the Family Violence Prevention and Services Act (relating to community projects to prevent family violence, domestic violence, and dating violence)" for "section 40261".

MISCELLANEOUS

§ 14221. Task force relating to the introduction of nonindigenous species

(1) In general. The Attorney General is authorized to convene a law enforcement task force in Hawaii to facilitate the prosecution of violations of Federal laws, and laws of the State of Hawaii, relating to the wrongful conveyance, sale, or introduction of nonindigenous plant and animal species.

(2) Membership. (A) The task force shall be composed of representatives of—

    (i) the Office of the United States Attorney for the District of Hawaii;

    (ii) the United States Customs Service;

    (iii) the Animal and Plant Health Inspection Service;

    (iv) the Fish and Wildlife Service;

    (v) the National Park Service;

    (vi) the United States Forest Service;

    (vii) the Military Customs Inspection Office of the Department of Defense;

    (viii) the United States Postal Service;

    (ix) the office of the Attorney General of the State of Hawaii;

    (x) the Hawaii Department of Agriculture;

    (xi) the Hawaii Department of Land and Natural Resources; and

    (xii) such other individuals as the Attorney General deems appropriate.

(B) The Attorney General shall, to the extent practicable, select individuals to serve on the task force who have experience with the enforcement of laws relating to the wrongful conveyance, sale, or introduction of nonindigenous plant and animal species.

(3) Duties. The task force shall—

(A) facilitate the prosecution of violations of Federal and State laws relating to the conveyance, sale, or introduction of nonindigenous plant and animal species into Hawaii; and

(B) make recommendations on ways to strengthen Federal and State laws and law enforcement strategies designed to prevent the introduction of nonindigenous plant and animal species.

(4) Report. The task force shall report to the Attorney General, the Secretary of Agriculture, the Secretary of the Interior, and to the Committee on the Judiciary and Committee on Agriculture, Nutrition, and Forestry of the Senate and the Committee on the Judiciary, Committee on Agriculture, and Committee on Merchant Marine and Fisheries of the House of Representatives on—

(A) the progress of its enforcement efforts; and

(B) the adequacy of existing Federal laws and laws of the State of Hawaii that relate to the introduction of nonindigenous plant and animal species.

Thereafter, the task force shall make such reports as the task force deems appropriate.

(5) Consultation. The task force shall consult with Hawaii agricultural interests and representatives of Hawaii conservation organizations about methods of preventing the wrongful conveyance, sale, or introduction of nonindigenous plant and animal species into Hawaii.

(Sept. 13, 1994, P. L. 103-322, Title XXXII, Subtitle A, § 320108(a), 108 Stat. 2111.)

HISTORY; ANCILLARY LAWS AND DIRECTIVES

References in text:

With respect to the Committee on Merchant Marine and Fisheries of the

House of Representatives, referred to in this section, § 1(b)(3) of Act June 3, 1995, P. L. 104-14, which appears as a note preceding 2 USCS § 21, provides that any reference to such Committee in any provision of law enacted before January 4, 1995, shall be treated as referring to (A) the Committee on Agriculture of the House of Representatives, in the case of a provision of law relating to inspection of seafood or seafood products, (B) the Committee on National Security of the House of Representatives, in the case of a provision of law relating to interoceanic canals, the Merchant Marine Academy and State Maritime Academies, or national security aspects of merchant marine, (C) the Committee on Resources of the House of Representatives, in the case of a provision of law relating to fisheries, wildlife, international fishing agreements, marine affairs (including coastal zone management) except for measures relating to oil and other pollution of navigable waters, or oceanography, (D) the Committee on Science of the House of Representatives, in the case of a provision of law relating to marine research, and (E) the Committee on Transportation and Infrastructure of the House of Representatives, in the case of a provision of law relating to a matter other than a matter described in any of subparagraphs (A) through (D).

Transfer of functions:

For transfer of functions, personnel, assets, and liabilities of the United States Customs Service of the Department of the Treasury, including the functions of the Secretary of the Treasury relating thereto, to the Secretary of Homeland Security, and for treatment of related references, see 6 USCS §§ 203(1), 551(d), 552(d), 557, and the Department of Homeland Security Reorganization Plan of Nov. 25, 2002, which appears as 6 USCS § 542 note.

CODE OF FEDERAL REGULATIONS

Department of Justice—Grants for correctional facilities, 28 CFR 91.1 et seq.

§ 14222. Coordination of substance abuse treatment and prevention programs

The Attorney General shall consult with the Secretary of the Department of Health and Human Services in establishing and carrying out the substance abuse treatment and prevention components of the programs authorized under this Act, to assure coordination of programs, eliminate duplication of efforts and enhance the effectiveness of such services.

(Sept. 13, 1994, P. L. 103-322, Title XXXII, Subtitle D, § 320401, 108 Stat. 2114.)

HISTORY; ANCILLARY LAWS AND DIRECTIVES

References in text:

"This Act", referred to in this section, is Act Sept. 13, 1994, P. L. 103-322, 108 Stat. 1796. For full classification of this Act, consult USCS Tables volumes.

§ 14223. Edward Byrne Memorial Formula Grant Program

Nothing in this Act shall be construed to prohibit or exclude the expenditure

of appropriations to grant recipients that would have been or are eligible to receive grants under subpart 1 of part E [of Title I] of the Omnibus Crime Control and Safe Streets Act of 1968 [42 USCS §§ 3751 et seq.].
(Sept. 13, 1994, P. L. 103-322, Title XXXII, § 320919, 108 Stat. 2130.)

HISTORY; ANCILLARY LAWS AND DIRECTIVES

References in text:
"This Act", referred to in this section, is Act Sept. 13, 1994, P. L. 103-322, 108 Stat. 1796. For full classification of this Act, consult USCS Tables volumes.

Explanatory notes:
The bracketed words "of Title I" have been inserted in this section to indicate the probable intent of Congress to include them.

CHAPTER 137. MANAGEMENT OF RECHARGEABLE BATTERIES AND BATTERIES CONTAINING MERCURY

GENERALLY

GENERALLY

§ 14301. Findings

The Congress finds that—

(1) it is in the public interest to—

(A) phase out the use of mercury in batteries and provide for the efficient and cost-effective collection and recycling or proper disposal of used nickel cadmium batteries, small sealed lead-acid batteries, and other regulated batteries; and

(B) educate the public concerning the collection, recycling, and proper disposal of such batteries;

(2) uniform national labeling requirements for regulated batteries, rechargeable consumer products, and product packaging will significantly benefit programs for regulated battery collection and recycling or proper disposal; and

(3) it is in the public interest to encourage persons who use rechargeable batteries to participate in collection for recycling of used nickel-cadmium, small sealed lead-acid, and other regulated batteries.

(May 13, 1996, P. L. 104-142, § 2, 110 Stat. 1329.)

HISTORY; ANCILLARY LAWS AND DIRECTIVES

Short title:

Act May 13, 1996, P. L. 104-142, § 1, 110 Stat. 1329, provides: "This Act [42 USCS §§ 14301 et seq.] may be cited as the 'Mercury-Containing and Rechargeable Battery Management Act'.".

Act May 13, 1996, P. L. 104-142, Title I, § 101, 110 Stat. 1332, provides: "This title [42 USCS §§ 14321 et seq.] may be cited as the 'Rechargeable Battery Recycling Act'.".

Act May 13, 1996, P. L. 104-142, Title II, § 201, 110 Stat. 1336, provides: "This title [42 USCS §§ 14331 et seq.] may be cited as the 'Mercury-Containing Battery Management Act'.".

RESEARCH GUIDE

Other Treatises:

4A Environmental Law Practice Guide (Matthew Bender), ch 29, Hazardous Waste Management § 29.02.

§ 14302. Definitions

For purposes of this Act [42 USCS §§ 14301 et seq.]:

(1) Administrator. The term "Administrator" means the Administrator of the Environmental Protection Agency.

(2) Button cell. The term "button cell" means a button- or coin-shaped battery.

(3) Easily removable. The term "easily removable", with respect to a battery, means detachable or removable at the end of the life of the battery—

(A) from a consumer product by a consumer with the use of common household tools; or

(B) by a retailer of replacements for a battery used as the principal electrical power source for a vehicle.

(4) Mercuric-oxide battery. The term "mercuric-oxide battery" means a battery that uses a mercuric-oxide electrode.

(5) Rechargeable battery. The term "rechargeable battery"—

(A) means 1 or more voltaic or galvanic cells, electrically connected to produce electric energy, that is designed to be recharged for repeated uses; and

(B) includes any type of enclosed device or sealed container consisting of 1 or more such cells, including what is commonly called a battery pack (and in the case of a battery pack, for the purposes of the requirements of easy removability and labeling under section 103 [42 USCS § 14322], means the battery pack as a whole rather than each component individually); but

(C) does not include—

(i) a lead-acid battery used to start an internal combustion engine or as the principal electrical power source for a vehicle, such as an automobile, a truck, construction equipment, a motorcycle, a garden tractor, a golf cart, a wheelchair, or a boat;

(ii) a lead-acid battery used for load leveling or for storage of electricity generated by an alternative energy source, such as a solar cell or wind-driven generator;

(iii) a battery used as a backup power source for memory or program instruction storage, timekeeping, or any similar purpose that requires uninterrupted electrical power in order to function if the primary energy supply fails or fluctuates momentarily; or

(iv) a rechargeable alkaline battery.

(6) Rechargeable consumer product. The term "rechargeable consumer product"—

(A) means a product that, when sold at retail, includes a regulated battery as a primary energy supply, and that is primarily intended for personal or household use; but

(B) does not include a product that only uses a battery solely as a source of backup power for memory or program instruction storage, timekeeping, or any similar purpose that requires uninterrupted electrical power in order to function if the primary energy supply fails or fluctuates momentarily.

(7) Regulated battery. The term "regulated battery" means a rechargeable battery that—

(A) contains a cadmium or a lead electrode or any combination of cadmium and lead electrodes; or

(B) contains other electrode chemistries and is the subject of a determination by the Administrator under section 103(d) [42 USCS § 14322(d)].

(8) Remanufactured product. The term "remanufactured product" means a rechargeable consumer product that has been altered by the replacement of parts, repackaged, or repaired after initial sale by the original manufacturer.

(May 13, 1996, P. L. 104-142, § 3, 110 Stat. 1329.)

CROSS REFERENCES

This section is referred to in 42 USCS § 14323.

§ 14303. Information dissemination

The Administrator shall, in consultation with representatives of rechargeable

battery manufacturers, rechargeable consumer product manufacturers, and retailers, establish a program to provide information to the public concerning the proper handling and disposal of used regulated batteries and rechargeable consumer products with nonremovable batteries.
(May 13, 1996, P. L. 104-142, § 4, 110 Stat. 1330.)

§ 14304. Enforcement

(a) **Civil penalty.** When on the basis of any information the Administrator determines that a person has violated, or is in violation of, any requirement of this Act [42 USCS §§ 14301 et seq.] (except a requirement of section 104 [42 USCS § 14323]) the Administrator—

(1) in the case of any violation, may issue an order assessing a civil penalty of not more than $10,000 for each violation, or requiring compliance immediately or within a reasonable specified time period, or both; or

(2) in the case of any violation or failure to comply with an order issued under this section, may commence a civil action in the United States district court in the district in which the violation occurred or in the district in which the violator resides for appropriate relief, including a temporary or permanent injunction.

(b) **Contents of order.** An order under subsection (a)(1) shall state with reasonable specificity the nature of the violation.

(c) **Considerations.** In assessing a civil penalty under subsection (a)(1), the Administrator shall take into account the seriousness of the violation and any good faith efforts to comply with applicable requirements.

(d) **Finality of order; request for hearing.** An order under subsection (a)(1) shall become final unless, not later than 30 days after the order is served, a person named in the order requests a hearing on the record.

(e) **Hearing.** On receiving a request under subsection (d), the Administrator shall promptly conduct a hearing on the record.

(f) **Subpoena power.** In connection with any hearing on the record under this section, the Administrator may issue subpoenas for the attendance and testimony of witnesses and for the production of relevant papers, books, and documents.

(g) **Continued violation after expiration of period for compliance.** If a violator fails to take corrective action within the time specified in an order under subsection (a)(1), the Administrator may assess a civil penalty of not more than $10,000 for the continued noncompliance with the order.

(h) **Savings provision.** The Administrator may not take any enforcement action against a person for selling, offering for sale, or offering for promotional purposes to the ultimate consumer a battery or product covered by this Act [42 USCS §§ 14301 et seq.] that was—

(1) purchased ready for sale to the ultimate consumer; and

(2) sold, offered for sale, or offered for promotional purposes without modification.

The preceding sentence shall not apply to a person—
  (A) who is the importer of a battery covered by this Act [42 USCS §§ 14301 et seq.], and
  (B) who has knowledge of the chemical contents of the battery

when such chemical contents make the sale, offering for sale, or offering for promotional purposes of such battery unlawful under title II of this Act [42 USCS §§ 14331 et seq.].
(May 13, 1996, P. L. 104-142, § 5, 110 Stat. 1331.)

RESEARCH GUIDE
Am Jur:
61B Am Jur 2d, Pollution Control § 12.

§ 14305. Information gathering and access

(a) Records and reports. A person who is required to carry out the objectives of this Act [42 USCS §§ 14301 et seq.], including—
  (1) a regulated battery manufacturer;
  (2) a rechargeable consumer product manufacturer;
  (3) a mercury-containing battery manufacturer; and
  (4) an authorized agent of a person described in paragraph (1), (2), or (3),

shall establish and maintain such records and report such information as the Administrator may by regulation reasonably require to carry out the objectives of this Act [42 USCS §§ 14301 et seq.].

(b) Access and copying. The Administrator or the Administrator's authorized representative, on presentation of credentials of the Administrator, may at reasonable times have access to and copy any records required to be maintained under subsection (a).

(c) Confidentiality. The Administrator shall maintain the confidentiality of documents and records that contain proprietary information.
(May 13, 1996, P. L. 104-142, § 6, 110 Stat. 1332.)

§ 14306. State authority

Nothing in this Act [42 USCS §§ 14301 et seq.] shall be construed to prohibit a State from enacting and enforcing a standard or requirement that is identical to a standard or requirement established or promulgated under this Act [42 USCS §§ 14301 et seq.]. Except as provided in sections 103(e) and 104 [42 USCS §§ 14322(e), 14323], nothing in this Act [42 USCS §§ 14301 et seq.] shall be construed to prohibit a State from enacting and enforcing a standard or requirement that is more stringent than a standard or requirement established or promulgated under this Act [42 USCS §§ 14301 et seq.].
(May 13, 1996, P. L. 104-142, § 7, 110 Stat. 1332.)

§ 14307. Authorization of appropriations

There are authorized to be appropriated such sums as are necessary to carry out this Act [42 USCS §§ 14301 et seq.].

(May 13, 1996, P. L. 104-142, § 8, 110 Stat. 1332.)

RECYCLING OF RECHARGEABLE BATTERIES

§ 14321. Purpose

The purpose of this title [42 USCS §§ 14321 et seq.] is to facilitate the efficient recycling or proper disposal of used nickel-cadmium rechargeable batteries, used small sealed lead-acid rechargeable batteries, other regulated batteries, and such rechargeable batteries in used consumer products, by—

(1) providing for uniform labeling requirements and streamlined regulatory requirements for regulated battery collection programs; and

(2) encouraging voluntary industry programs by eliminating barriers to funding the collection and recycling or proper disposal of used rechargeable batteries.

(May 13, 1996, P. L. 104-142, Title I, § 102, 110 Stat. 1332.)

§ 14322. Rechargeable consumer products and labeling

(a) Prohibition. (1) In general. No person shall sell for use in the United States a regulated battery that is ready for retail sale or a rechargeable consumer product that is ready for retail sale, if such battery or product was manufactured on or after the date 12 months after the date of enactment of this Act [enacted May 13, 1996], unless the labeling requirements of subsection (b) are met and, in the case of a regulated battery, the regulated battery—

(A) is easily removable from the rechargeable consumer product; or

(B) is sold separately.

(2) Application. Paragraph (1) does not apply to any of the following:

(A) The sale of a remanufactured product unit unless paragraph (1) applied to the sale of the unit when originally manufactured.

(B) The sale of a product unit intended for export purposes only.

(b) Labeling. Each regulated battery or rechargeable consumer product without an easily removable battery manufactured on or after the date that is 1 year after the date of enactment of this Act [enacted May 13, 1996], whether produced domestically or imported shall bear the following labels:

(1) 3 chasing arrows or a comparable recycling symbol.

(2)(A) On each regulated battery which is a nickel-cadmium battery, the chemical name or the abbreviation "Ni-Cd" and the phrase "BATTERY MUST BE RECYCLED OR DISPOSED OF PROPERLY.".

(B) On each regulated battery which is a lead-acid battery, "Pb" or the words "LEAD", "RETURN", and "RECYCLE" and if the regulated battery is sealed, the phrase "BATTERY MUST BE RECYCLED.".

(3) On each rechargeable consumer product containing a regulated battery that is not easily removable, the phrase "CONTAINS NICKEL-CADMIUM BATTERY. BATTERY MUST BE RECYCLED OR DISPOSED OF PROPERLY." or "CONTAINS SEALED LEAD BATTERY. BATTERY MUST BE RECYCLED.", as applicable.

(4) On the packaging of each rechargeable consumer product, and the packaging of each regulated battery sold separately from such a product, unless the required label is clearly visible through the packaging, the phrase "CONTAINS NICKEL-CADMIUM BATTERY. BATTERY MUST BE RECYCLED OR DISPOSED OF PROPERLY." or "CONTAINS SEALED LEAD BATTERY. BATTERY MUST BE RECYCLED.", as applicable.

(c) Existing or alternative labeling. (1) Initial period. For a period of 2 years after the date of enactment of this Act [enacted May 13, 1996], regulated batteries, rechargeable consumer products containing regulated batteries, and rechargeable consumer product packages that are labeled in substantial compliance with subsection (b) shall be deemed to comply with the labeling requirements of subsection (b).

(2) Certification. (A) In general. On application by persons subject to the labeling requirements of subsection (b) or the labeling requirements promulgated by the Administrator under subsection (d), the Administrator shall certify that a different label meets the requirements of subsection (b) or (d), respectively, if the different label—

(i) conveys the same information as the label required under subsection (b) or (d), respectively; or

(ii) conforms with a recognized international standard that is consistent with the overall purposes of this title [42 USCS §§ 14321 et seq.].

(B) Constructive certification. Failure of the Administrator to object to an application under subparagraph (A) on the ground that a different label does not meet either of the conditions described in subparagraph (A) (i) or (ii) within 120 days after the date on which the application is made shall constitute certification for the purposes of this Act [42 USCS §§ 14301 et seq.].

(d) Rulemaking authority of the Administrator. (1) In general. If the Administrator determines that other rechargeable batteries having electrode chemistries different from regulated batteries are toxic and may cause substantial harm to human health and the environment if discarded into the solid waste stream for land disposal or incineration, the Administrator may, with the advice and counsel of State regulatory authorities and manufacturers of rechargeable batteries and rechargeable consumer products, and after public comment—

(A) promulgate labeling requirements for the batteries with different electrode chemistries, rechargeable consumer products containing such batteries that are not easily removable batteries, and packaging for the batteries and products; and

(B) promulgate requirements for easy removability of regulated batteries from rechargeable consumer products designed to contain such batteries.

(2) Substantial similarity. The regulations promulgated under paragraph (1) shall be substantially similar to the requirements set forth in subsections (a) and (b).

(e) Uniformity. After the effective dates of a requirement set forth in subsection (a), (b), or (c) or a regulation promulgated by the Administrator under subsection (d), no Federal agency, State, or political subdivision of a State may enforce any easy removability or environmental labeling requirement for a rechargeable battery or rechargeable consumer product that is not identical to the requirement or regulation.

(f) Exemptions. (1) In general. With respect to any rechargeable consumer product, any person may submit an application to the Administrator for an exemption from the requirements of subsection (a) in accordance with the procedures under paragraph (2). The application shall include the following information:

  (A) A statement of the specific basis for the request for the exemption.

  (B) The name, business address, and telephone number of the applicant.

(2) Granting of exemption. Not later than 60 days after receipt of an application under paragraph (1), the Administrator shall approve or deny the application. On approval of the application the Administrator shall grant an exemption to the applicant. The exemption shall be issued for a period of time that the Administrator determines to be appropriate, except that the period shall not exceed 2 years. The Administrator shall grant an exemption on the basis of evidence supplied to the Administrator that the manufacturer has been unable to commence manufacturing the rechargeable consumer product in compliance with the requirements of this section and with an equivalent level of product performance without the product—

  (A) posing a threat to human health, safety, or the environment; or

  (B) violating requirements for approvals from governmental agencies or widely recognized private standard-setting organizations (including Underwriters Laboratories).

(3) Renewal of exemption. A person granted an exemption under paragraph (2) may apply for a renewal of the exemption in accordance with the requirements and procedures described in paragraphs (1) and (2). The Administrator may grant a renewal of such an exemption for a period of not more than 2 years after the date of the granting of the renewal.

(May 13, 1996, P. L. 104-142, Title I, § 103, 110 Stat. 1332.)

CROSS REFERENCES

This section is referred to in 42 USCS §§ 14302, 14306.

§ 14323. Requirements

(a) Batteries subject to certain regulations. The collection, storage, or transportation of used rechargeable batteries, batteries described in section 3(5)(C) or in title II [42 USCS § 14302(5)(C) or §§ 14331 et seq.], and used rechargeable consumer products containing rechargeable batteries that are not easily removable rechargeable batteries, shall, notwithstanding any law of a State or political subdivision thereof governing such collection, storage, or transportation, be regulated under applicable provisions of the regulations promulgated by the Environmental Protection Agency at 60 Fed. Reg. 25492 (May 11, 1995), as effective on May 11, 1995, except as provided in paragraph (2) of subsection (b) and except that—

(1) the requirements of 40 CFR 260.20, 260.40, and 260.41 and the equivalent requirements of an approved State program shall not apply, and
(2) this section shall not apply to any lead acid battery managed under 40 CFR 266 subpart G or the equivalent requirements of an approved State program.

(b) Enforcement under Solid Waste Disposal Act. (1) Any person who fails to comply with the requirements imposed by subsection (a) of this section may be subject to enforcement under applicable provisions of the Solid Waste Disposal Act [42 USCS §§ 6901 et seq.].
(2) States may implement and enforce the requirements of subsection (a) if the Administrator finds that—

(A) the State has adopted requirements that are identical to those referred to in subsection (a) governing the collection, storage, or transportation of batteries referred to in subsection (a); and

(B) the State provides for enforcement of such requirements.
(May 13, 1996, P. L. 104-142, Title I, § 104, 110 Stat. 1335.)

CROSS REFERENCES
This section is referred to in 42 USCS §§ 14304, 14306.

MANAGEMENT OF BATTERIES CONTAINING MERCURY

CROSS REFERENCES
This title (42 USCS §§ 14331 et seq.) is referred to in 42 USCS §§ 14304, 14323.

§ 14331.   Purpose

The purpose of this title [42 USCS §§ 14331 et seq.] is to phase out the use of batteries containing mercury.
(May 13, 1996, P. L. 104-142, Title II, § 202, 110 Stat. 1336.)

§ 14332.   Limitations on sale of alkaline-manganese batteries containing mercury.

No person shall sell, offer for sale, or offer for promotional purposes any alkaline-manganese battery manufactured on or after the date of enactment of this Act [enacted May 13, 1996], with a mercury content that was intentionally introduced (as distinguished from mercury that may be incidentally present in other materials), except that the limitation on mercury content in alkaline-manganese button cells shall be 25 milligrams of mercury per button cell.
(May 13, 1996, P. L. 104-142, Title II, § 203, 110 Stat. 1336.)

CROSS REFERENCES
This section is referred to in 42 USCS § 14333.

§ 14333.   Limitations on sale of zinc-carbon batteries containing mercury

No person shall sell, offer for sale, or offer for promotional purposes any zinc-carbon battery manufactured on or after the date of enactment of this Act [enacted May 13, 1996], that contains mercury that was intentionally introduced as described in section 203 [42 USCS § 14332].

(May 13, 1996, P. L. 104-142, Title II § 204, 110 Stat. 1336.)

§ 14334. Limitations on sale of button cell mercuric-oxide batteries

No person shall sell, offer for sale, or offer for promotional purposes any button cell mercuric-oxide battery for use in the United States on or after the date of enactment of this Act [enacted May 13, 1996].

(May 13, 1996, P. L. 104-142, Title II, § 205, 110 Stat. 1336.)

§ 14335. Limitations on sale of other mercuric-oxide batteries

(a) Prohibition. On or after the date of enactment of this Act [enacted May 13, 1996], no person shall sell, offer for sale, or offer for promotional purposes a mercuric-oxide battery for use in the United States unless the battery manufacturer, or the importer of such a battery—

(1) identifies a collection site in the United States that has all required Federal, State, and local government approvals, to which persons may send used mercuric-oxide batteries for recycling or proper disposal;

(2) informs each of its purchasers of mercuric-oxide batteries of the collection site identified under paragraph (1); and

(3) informs each of its purchasers of mercuric-oxide batteries of a telephone number that the purchaser may call to get information about sending mercuric-oxide batteries for recycling or proper disposal.

(b) Application of section. This section does not apply to a sale or offer of a mercuric-oxide button cell battery.

(May 13, 1996, P. L. 104-142, Title II, § 206, 110 Stat. 1336.)

§ 14336. New product or use

On petition of a person that proposes a new use for a battery technology described in this title [42 USCS §§ 14331 et seq.] or the use of a battery described in this title [42 USCS §§ 14331 et seq. in a new product, the Administrator may exempt from this title [42 USCS §§ 14331 et seq.] the new use of the technology or the use of such a battery in the new product on the condition, if appropriate, that there exist reasonable safeguards to ensure that the resulting battery or product without an easily removable battery will not be disposed of in an incinerator, composting facility, or landfill (other than a facility regulated under subtitle C of the Solid Waste Disposal Act (42 U.S.C. 6921 et seq.)).

(May 13, 1996, P. L. 104-142, Title II, § 207, 110 Stat. 1336.)

CHAPTER 138.   ASSISTED SUICIDE FUNDING RESTRICTION

CROSS REFERENCES

This Act (42 USCS §§ 14401 et seq.) is referred to in 5 USCS § 8902; 10 USCS § 1073; 18 USCS § 4005; 22 USCS § 2504; 25 USCS § 1621x; 38 USCS § 1707; 42 USCS §§ 2380, 701, 1395y, 1396b, 1397d, 2996f.

§ 14401.   Findings and purpose

(a) Findings. Congress finds the following:

(1) The Federal Government provides financial support for the provision of and payment for health care services, as well as for advocacy activities to protect the rights of individuals.

(2) Assisted suicide, euthanasia, and mercy killing have been criminal offenses throughout the United States and, under current law, it would be unlawful to provide services in support of such illegal activities.

(3) Because of recent legal developments, it may become lawful in areas of the United States to furnish services in support of such activities.

(4) Congress is not providing Federal financial assistance in support of assisted suicide, euthanasia, and mercy killing and intends that Federal funds not be used to promote such activities.

(b) Purpose. It is the principal purpose of this Act to continue current Federal policy by providing explicitly that Federal funds may not be used to pay for items and services (including assistance) the purpose of which is to cause (or assist in causing) the suicide, euthanasia, or mercy killing of any individual.
(April 30, 1997, P. L. 105-12, § 2, 111 Stat. 23.)

HISTORY; ANCILLARY LAWS AND DIRECTIVES

References in text:

"This Act", referred to in this section, is Act April 30, 1997, P. L. 105-

12, 111 Stat. 23, which appears generally as 42 USCS §§ 14401 et seq. For full classification of such Act, consult USCS Tables volumes.

Effective date of section:
This section took effect upon enactment, pursuant to § 11 of Act April 30, 1997, P. L. 105-12, which appears as a note to this section.

Short title:
Act April 30, 1997, P. L. 105-12, § 1(a), 111 Stat. 23, provides: "This Act may be cited as the 'Assisted Suicide Funding Restriction Act of 1997'.". For full classification of such Act, consult USCS Tables volumes.

Other provisions:
Construction of conforming amendments. Act April 30, 1997, P. L. 105-12, § 9(p), 111 Stat. 29, provides: "The fact that a law is not amended under this section [for full classification, consult USCS Tables volumes] shall not be construed as indicating that the provisions of this Act do not apply to such a law.".

Effective date and applicability of Act April 30, 1997. Act April 30, 1997, P. L. 105-12, § 11, 111 Stat. 29, provides:

"(a) In general. The provisions of this Act (and the amendments made by this Act) [for full classification, consult USCS Tables volumes] take effect upon its enactment and apply, subject to subsection (b), to Federal payments made pursuant to obligations incurred after the date of the enactment of this Act for items and services provided on or after such date.

"(b) Application to contracts. Such provisions shall apply with respect to contracts entered into, renewed, or extended after the date of the enactment of this Act and shall also apply to a contract entered into before such date to the extent permitted under such contract.".

RESEARCH GUIDE
Am Jur:
22A Am Jur 2d, Death § 571.

§ 14402. Restriction on use of Federal funds under health care programs

(a) Restriction on Federal funding of health care services. Subject to subsection (b), no funds appropriated by Congress for the purpose of paying (directly or indirectly) for the provision of health care services may be used—

(1) to provide any health care item or service furnished for the purpose of causing, or for the purpose of assisting in causing, the death of any individual, such as by assisted suicide, euthanasia, or mercy killing;

(2) to pay (directly, through payment of Federal financial participation or other matching payment, or otherwise) for such an item or service, including payment of expenses relating to such an item or service; or

(3) to pay (in whole or in part) for health benefit coverage that includes any coverage of such an item or service or of any expenses relating to such an item or service.

(b) Construction and treatment of certain services. Nothing in subsection (a), or in any other provision of this Act (or in any amendment made by this Act), shall be construed to apply to or to affect any limitation relating to—

(1) the withholding or withdrawing of medical treatment or medical care;

(2) the withholding or withdrawing of nutrition or hydration;

(3) abortion; or

(4) the use of an item, good, benefit, or service furnished for the purpose of alleviating pain or discomfort, even if such use may increase the risk of death, so long as such item, good, benefit, or service is not also furnished for the purpose of causing, or the purpose of assisting in causing, death, for any reason.

(c) Limitation on Federal facilities and employees. Subject to subsection (b), with respect to health care items and services furnished—

(1) by or in a health care facility owned or operated by the Federal government, or

(2) by any physician or other individual employed by the Federal government to provide health care services within the scope of the physician's or individual's employment,

no such item or service may be furnished for the purpose of causing, or for the purpose of assisting in causing, the death of any individual, such as by assisted suicide, euthanasia, or mercy killing.

(d) List of programs to which restrictions apply. (1) Federal health care funding programs. Subsection (a) applies to funds appropriated under or to carry out the following:

(A) Medicare program. Title XVIII of the Social Security Act [42 USCS §§ 1395 et seq.].

(B) Medicaid program. Title XIX of the Social Security Act [42 USCS §§ 1396 et seq.].

(C) Title XX social services block grant. Title XX of the Social Security Act [42 USCS §§ 1397 et seq.].

(D) Maternal and child health block grant program. Title V of the Social Security Act [42 USCS §§ 701 et seq.].

(E) Public Health Service Act. The Public Health Service Act.

(F) Indian Health Care Improvement Act. The Indian Health Care Improvement Act [25 USCS §§ 1601 et seq.].

(G) Federal employees health benefits program. Chapter 89 of title 5, United States Code [5 USCS §§ 8901 et seq.].

(H) Military health care system (including TRICARE and CHAMPUS programs). Chapter 55 of title 10, United States Code [10 USCS §§ 1071 et seq.].

(I) Veterans medical care. Chapter 17 of title 38, United States Code [38 USCS §§ 1701 et seq.].

(J) Health services for Peace Corps volunteers. Section 5(e) of the Peace Corps Act (22 U.S.C. 2504(e)).

(K) Medical services for Federal prisoners. Section 4005(a) of title 18, United States Code.

(2) Federal facilities and personnel. The provisions of subsection (c) apply to facilities and personnel of the following:

(A) Military health care system. The Department of Defense operating under chapter 55 of title 10, United States Code [10 USCS §§ 1071 et seq.].

(B) Veterans medical care. The Veterans Health Administration of the Department of Veterans Affairs.

(C) Public health service. The Public Health Service.

(3) Nonexclusive list. Nothing in this subsection shall be construed as limiting the application of subsection (a) to the programs specified in paragraph (1) or the application of subsection (c) to the facilities and personnel specified in paragraph (2).

(April 30, 1997, P. L. 105-12, § 3, 111 Stat. 23.)

HISTORY; ANCILLARY LAWS AND DIRECTIVES

References in text:
The "Public Health Service Act", referred to in this section, is Act July 1, 1944, ch 373, 58 Stat. 582, which appears generally as 42 USCS §§ 201 et seq. For full classification of such Act, consult USCS Tables volumes.

Effective date of section:
This section took effect upon enactment, pursuant to § 11 of Act April 30, 1997, P. L. 105-12, which appears as 42 USCS § 14401 note.

Other provisions:
Applicability of section. For applicability of this section, see § 11 of Act April 30, 1997, P. L. 105-12, which appears as 42 USCS § 14401 note.

CROSS REFERENCES
This section is referred to in 42 USCS §§ 14403, 14404, 14405, 14406.

§ 14403. Restriction on use of Federal funds under certain grant programs

Subject to section 3(b) [42 USCS § 14402(b)] (relating to construction and treatment of certain services), no funds appropriated by Congress to carry out subtitle B, D, or E [of title I] of the Developmental Disabilities Assistance and Bill of Rights Act of 2000 [42 USCS §§ 15021 et seq., 15061 et seq., or 15081 et seq.] may be used to support or fund any program or service which has a purpose of assisting in procuring any item, benefit, or service furnished for the purpose of causing, or the purpose of assisting in causing, the death of any individual, such as by assisted suicide, euthanasia, or mercy killing.

(April 30, 1997, P. L. 105-12, § 4, 111 Stat. 25; Oct. 30, 2000, P. L. 106-402, Title IV, § 401(b)(15)(A), 114 Stat. 1740.)

HISTORY; ANCILLARY LAWS AND DIRECTIVES

Explanatory notes:
The words "of title I" have been inserted in brackets to indicate the probable intent of Congress to include such language.

Effective date of section:
This section took effect upon enactment, pursuant to § 11 of Act April 30, 1997, P. L. 105-12, which appears as 42 USCS § 14401 note.

Amendments:

2000. Act Oct. 30, 2000, substituted the section heading for one which read: "Restriction on use of Federal funds under certain grant programs under the Developmental Disabilities Assistance and Bill of Rights Act" and, in the text, substituted "subtitle B, D, or E of the Developmental Disabilities Assistance and Bill of Rights Act of 2000" for "part B, D, or E of the Developmental Disabilities Assistance and Bill of Rights Act".

Other provisions:

Applicability of section. For applicability of this section, see § 11 of Act April 30, 1997, P. L. 105-12, which appears as 42 USCS § 14401 note.

CROSS REFERENCES

This section is referred to in 42 USCS § 14405.

§ 14404. Restriction on use of Federal funds by advocacy programs

(a) In general. Subject to section 3(b) [42 USCS § 14402(b)] (relating to construction and treatment of certain services), no funds appropriated by Congress may be used to assist in, to support, or to fund any activity or service which has a purpose of assisting in, or to bring suit or provide any other form of legal assistance for the purpose of—

(1) securing or funding any item, benefit, program, or service furnished for the purpose of causing, or the purpose of assisting in causing, the suicide, euthanasia, or mercy killing of any individual;

(2) compelling any person, institution, [or] governmental entity to provide or fund any item, benefit, program, or service for such purpose; or

(3) asserting or advocating a legal right to cause, or to assist in causing, the suicide, euthanasia, or mercy killing of any individual.

(b) List of programs to which restrictions apply. (1) In general. Subsection (a) applies to funds appropriated under or to carry out the following:

(A) Protection and advocacy systems under the Developmental Disabilities Assistance and Bill of Rights Act of 2000. Subtitle C [of title I] of the Developmental Disabilities Assistance and Bill of Rights Act of 2000 [42 USCS §§ 15041 et seq.].

(B) Protection and advocacy systems under the Protection and Advocacy for Mentally Ill Individuals Act. The Protection and Advocacy for Mentally Ill Individuals Act of 1986 [42 USCS §§ 10801 et seq.].

(C) Protection and advocacy systems under the Rehabilitation Act of 1973. Section 509 of the Rehabilitation Act of 1973 (29 U.S.C. 794e).

(D) Ombudsman programs under the Older Americans Act of 1965. Ombudsman programs under the Older Americans Act of 1965.

(E) Legal assistance. Legal assistance programs under the Legal Services Corporation Act [42 USCS §§ 2996 et seq.].

(2) Nonexclusive list. Nothing in this subsection shall be construed as limiting the application of subsection (a) to the programs specified in paragraph (1).

(April 30, 1997, P. L. 105-12, § 5, 111 Stat. 25; Oct. 30, 2000, P. L. 106-402, Title IV, § 401(b)(15)(B), 114 Stat. 1740.)

HISTORY; ANCILLARY LAWS AND DIRECTIVES

References in text:
The "Older Americans Act of 1965", referred to in this section, is Act July 14, 1965, P. L. 89-73, 79 Stat. 218, which appears generally as 42 USCS §§ 3001 et seq. For full classification of such Act, consult USCS Tables volumes.

Explanatory notes:
The bracketed word "or" has been inserted in subsec. (a)(2) to indicate the probable intent of Congress to include such word.
The words "of title I" have been inserted in brackets in subsec. (b)(1)(A) to indicate the probable intent of Congress to include such language.

Effective date of section:
This section took effect upon enactment, pursuant to § 11 of Act April 30, 1997, P. L. 105-12, which appears as 42 USCS § 14401 note.

Amendments:
2000. Act Oct. 30, in subsec. (b)(1), substituted subpara. (A) for one which read: "(A) Protection and advocacy systems under the Developmental Disabilities Assistance and Bill of Rights Act. Part C of the Developmental Disabilities Assistance and Bill of Rights Act.".

Other provisions:
Applicability of section. For applicability of this section, see § 11 of Act April 30, 1997, P. L. 105-12, which appears as 42 USCS § 14401 note.

CROSS REFERENCES
This section is referred to in 42 USCS §§ 10805, 14405, 15044.

§ 14405. Restriction on use of other Federal funds

(a) In general. Subject to section 3(b) [42 USCS § 14402(b)] (relating to construction and treatment of certain services) and subsection (b) of this section, no funds appropriated by the Congress shall be used to provide, procure, furnish, or fund any item, good, benefit, activity, or service, furnished or performed for the purpose of causing, or assisting in causing, the suicide, euthanasia, or mercy killing of any individual.

(b) Nonduplication. Subsection (a) shall not apply to funds to which section 3, 4, or 5 [42 USCS § 14402, 14403, or 14404] applies, except that subsection (a), rather than section 3 [42 USCS § 14402], shall apply to funds appropriated to carry out title 10, United States Code (other than chapter 55 [10 USCS §§ 1071 et seq.]), title 18, United States Code (other than section 4005(a)), and chapter 37 of title 28, United States Code [28 USCS §§ 561 et seq.].
(April 30, 1997, P. L. 105-12, § 6, 111 Stat. 25.)

HISTORY; ANCILLARY LAWS AND DIRECTIVES

Effective date of section:
This section took effect upon enactment, pursuant to § 11 of Act April 30, 1997, P. L. 105-12, which appears as 42 USCS § 14401 note.

Other provisions:
Applicability of section. For applicability of this section, see § 11 of Act April 30, 1997, P. L. 105-12, which appears as 42 USCS § 14401 note.

§ 14406. Clarification with respect to advance directives

Subject to section 3(b) [42 USCS § 14402(b)] (relating to construction and treatment of certain services), sections 1866(f) and 1902(w) of the Social Security Act [42 USCS §§ 1395cc(f), 1396a(w)] shall not be construed—

(1) to require any provider or organization, or any employee of such a provider or organization, to inform or counsel any individual regarding any right to obtain an item or service furnished for the purpose of causing, or the purpose of assisting in causing, the death of the individual, such as by assisted suicide, euthanasia, or mercy killing; or

(2) to apply to or to affect any requirement with respect to a portion of an advance directive that directs the purposeful causing of, or the purposeful assisting in causing, the death of any individual, such as by assisted suicide, euthanasia, or mercy killing.

(April 30, 1997, P. L. 105-12, § 7, 111 Stat. 26.)

HISTORY; ANCILLARY LAWS AND DIRECTIVES

Effective date of section:

This section took effect upon enactment, pursuant to § 11 of Act April 30, 1997, P. L. 105-12, which appears as 42 USCS § 14401 note.

Other provisions:

Applicability of section. For applicability of this section, see § 11 of Act April 30, 1997, P. L. 105-12, which appears as 42 USCS § 14401 note.

CROSS REFERENCES

This section is referred to in 42 USCS §§ 1395cc, 1396a.

§ 14407. Application to District of Columbia

For purposes of this Act, the term "funds appropriated by Congress" includes funds appropriated to the District of Columbia pursuant to an authorization of appropriations under title V of the District of Columbia Self-Government and Governmental Reorganization Act [District of Columbia Home Rule Act] and the term "Federal government" includes the government of the District of Columbia.

(April 30, 1997, P. L. 105-12, § 8, 111 Stat. 26.)

HISTORY; ANCILLARY LAWS AND DIRECTIVES

References in text:

"Title V of the District of Columbia Self-Government and Governmental Reorganization Act", referred to in this section, is Title V of Act Dec. 24, 1973, P. L. 93-198, 97 Stat. 779, which is not classified to the Code.

"This Act", referred to in this section, is Act April 30, 1997, P. L. 105-12, 111 Stat. 23, which appears generally as 42 USCS §§ 14401 et seq. For full classification of such Act, consult USCS Tables volumes.

Explanatory notes:

The bracketed words "District of Columbia Home Rule Act" have been inserted in this section on the authority of Act Aug. 5, 1997, P. L. 105-33, Title XI, Subtitle C, Ch 2, § 11717(b), 111 Stat. 786, which provides that any reference in law or regulation to the District of Columbia Self-Government and Governmental Reorganization Act shall be deemed to be a reference to the District of Columbia Home Rule Act.

Effective date of section:
This section took effect upon enactment, pursuant to § 11 of Act April 30, 1997, P. L. 105-12, which appears as 42 USCS § 14401 note.

Other provisions:
Applicability of section. For applicability of this section, see § 11 of Act April 30, 1997, P. L. 105-12, which appears as 42 USCS § 14401 note.

§ 14408. Relation to other laws

The provisions of this Act supersede other Federal laws (including laws enacted after the date of the enactment of this Act [enacted April 30, 1997]) except to the extent such laws specifically supersede the provisions of this Act.
(April 30, 1997, P. L. 105-12, § 10, 111 Stat. 29.)

HISTORY; ANCILLARY LAWS AND DIRECTIVES

References in text:
"This Act", referred to in this section, is Act April 30, 1997, P. L. 105-12, 111 Stat. 23, which appears generally as 42 USCS §§ 14401 et seq. For full classification of such Act, consult USCS Tables volumes.

Effective date of section:
This section took effect upon enactment, pursuant to § 11 of Act April 30, 1997, P. L. 105-12, which appears as 42 USCS § 14401 note.

Other provisions:
Applicability of section. For applicability of this section, see § 11 of Act April 30, 1997, P. L. 105-12, which appears as 42 USCS § 14401 note.

CHAPTER 139. VOLUNTEER PROTECTION

CROSS REFERENCES

This Act (42 USCS §§ 14501 et seq.) is referred to in 50 USCS § 441j-2.

§ 14501. Findings and purpose

(a) Findings. The Congress finds and declares that—

(1) the willingness of volunteers to offer their services is deterred by the potential for liability actions against them;

(2) as a result, many nonprofit public and private organizations and governmental entities, including voluntary associations, social service agencies, educational institutions, and other civic programs, have been adversely affected by the withdrawal of volunteers from boards of directors and service in other capacities;

(3) the contribution of these programs to their communities is thereby diminished, resulting in fewer and higher cost programs than would be obtainable if volunteers were participating;

(4) because Federal funds are expended on useful and cost-effective social service programs, many of which are national in scope, depend heavily on volunteer participation, and represent some of the most successful public-private partnerships, protection of volunteerism through clarification and limitation of the personal liability risks assumed by the volunteer in connection with such participation is an appropriate subject for Federal legislation;

(5) services and goods provided by volunteers and nonprofit organizations would often otherwise be provided by private entities that operate in interstate commerce;

(6) due to high liability costs and unwarranted litigation costs, volunteers and nonprofit organizations face higher costs in purchasing insurance, through interstate insurance markets, to cover their activities; and

(7) clarifying and limiting the liability risk assumed by volunteers is an appropriate subject for Federal legislation because—

(A) of the national scope of the problems created by the legitimate fears of volunteers about frivolous, arbitrary, or capricious lawsuits;

(B) the citizens of the United States depend on, and the Federal Government expends funds on, and provides tax exemptions and other consideration to, numerous social programs that depend on the services of volunteers;

(C) it is in the interest of the Federal Government to encourage the continued operation of volunteer service organizations and contributions of volunteers because the Federal Government lacks the capacity to carry out all of the services provided by such organizations and volunteers; and

(D)(i) liability reform for volunteers, will promote the free flow of goods and services, lessen burdens on interstate commerce and uphold constitutionally protected due process rights; and

(ii) therefore, liability reform is an appropriate use of the powers contained in article 1, section 8, clause 3 of the United States Constitution, and the fourteenth amendment to the United States Constitution.

(b) Purpose. The purpose of this Act [42 USCS §§ 14501 et seq.] is to promote the interests of social service program beneficiaries and taxpayers and to sustain the availability of programs, nonprofit organizations, and governmental entities that depend on volunteer contributions by reforming the laws to provide certain protections from liability abuses related to volunteers serving nonprofit organizations and governmental entities.

(June 18, 1997, P. L. 105-19, § 2, 111 Stat. 218.)

HISTORY; ANCILLARY LAWS AND DIRECTIVES

Effective date of section:
This section took effect 90 days after enactment pursuant to § 7 of Act June 18, 1997, P. L. 105-19, which appears as a note to this section.

Short title:
Act June 18, 1997, P. L. 105-19, § 1, 111 Stat. 218, provides: "This Act [42 USCS §§ 14501 et seq.] may be cited as the 'Volunteer Protection Act of 1997'.".

Other provisions:
Effective date and application of 42 USCS §§ 14501 et seq. Act June 18, 1997, P. L. 105-19, § 7, 111 Stat. 223, provides:
"(a) In general. This Act [42 USCS §§ 14501 et seq.] shall take effect 90 days after the date of enactment of this Act.
"(b) Application. This Act [42 USCS §§ 14501 et seq.] applies to any claim for harm caused by an act or omission of a volunteer where that claim is filed on or after the effective date of this Act but only if the harm that is the subject of the claim or the conduct that caused such harm occurred after such effective date.".

RESEARCH GUIDE
Am Jur:
15 Am Jur 2d, Charities § 188.

Corporate and Business Law:
1 Liability of Corporate Officers and Directors (Matthew Bender), ch 12, Nonprofitable and Charitable Organizations § 12.01.

Other Treatises:
5 Rapp, Education Law (Matthew Bender), ch 12, General Liabilities and Litigation § 12.07.

Law Review Articles:
Apelbaum; Ryder. The Third Wave of Federal Tort Reform: Protecting the Public or Pushing the Constitutional Envelope? 8 Cornell J L & Pub Pol'y 591, Spring 1999.

Hoffman. Responders' Responsibility: Liability and Immunity in Public Health Emergencies. 96 Geo LJ 1913, 2008.

Popper. A One-Term Tort Reform Tale: Victimizing the Vulnerable. 35 Harv J on Legis 123, Winter 1998.

Paulsen. Does No Good Deed Really Go Unpunished?: Malpractice Myths and Realities in Pro Bono Representation. 44 Houston Lawyer 10, 2007.

Mowrey; Epstein. The Little Act That Could: The Volunteer Protection Act of 1997. 13 J Legal Aspects of Sport 289, Fall 2003.

Mowrey; Epstein. General Aspects of Recreation Law: The Little Act That Could: The Volunteer Protection Act of 1997. 13 J Legal Aspects of Sport 289, Fall, 2003.

Stern. Toward a Coherent Approach to Tort Immunity in Judicially Mandated Family Court Services. 92 Ky LJ 373, Winter 2003/2004.

Light. Conscripting State Law to Protect Volunteers: The Odd Formulation of Federalism in "Opt-Out" Preemption. 10 Seton Hall J Sports L 9, 2000.

Biedzynski. The Federal Volunteer Protection Act: Does Congress Want to Play Ball? 23 Seton Hall Legis J 319, 1999.

Baez. Volunteers, Victims, and Vicarious Liability: Why Tort Law Should Recognize Altruism. 48 U Louisville L Rev 221, Winter, 2009.

§ 14502. Preemption and election of State nonapplicability

(a) **Preemption.** This Act [42 USCS §§ 14501 et seq.] preempts the laws of any State to the extent that such laws are inconsistent with this Act [42 USCS §§ 14501 et seq.], except that this Act [42 USCS §§ 14501 et seq.] shall not preempt any State law that provides additional protection from liability relating to volunteers or to any category of volunteers in the performance of services for a nonprofit organization or governmental entity.

(b) **Election of State regarding nonapplicability.** This Act [42 USCS §§ 14501 et seq.] shall not apply to any civil action in a State court against a volunteer in which all parties are citizens of the State if such State enacts a statute in accordance with State requirements for enacting legislation—

(1) citing the authority of this subsection;

(2) declaring the election of such State that this Act [42 USCS §§ 14501 et seq.] shall not apply, as of a date certain, to such civil action in the State; and

(3) containing no other provisions.

(June 18, 1997, P. L. 105-19, § 3, 111 Stat. 219.)

HISTORY; ANCILLARY LAWS AND DIRECTIVES
Effective date of section:
This section took effect 90 days after enactment, pursuant to § 7 of Act
June 18, 1997, P. L. 105-19, which appears as 42 USCS § 14501 note.

RESEARCH GUIDE
Other Treatises:
5 Rapp, Education Law (Matthew Bender), ch 12, General Liabilities and
Litigation § 12.07.

Law Review Articles:
Apelbaum; Ryder. The Third Wave of Federal Tort Reform: Protecting the
Public or Pushing the Constitutional Envelope? 8 Cornell J L & Pub Pol'y
591, Spring 1999.

Popper. A One-Term Tort Reform Tale: Victimizing the Vulnerable. 35
Harv J on Legis 123, Winter 1998.

Mowrey; Epstein. The Little Act That Could: The Volunteer Protection Act
of 1997. 13 J Legal Aspects of Sport 289, Fall 2003.

Stern. Toward a Coherent Approach to Tort Immunity in Judicially
Mandated Family Court Services. 92 Ky LJ 373, Winter 2003/2004.

Light. Conscripting State Law to Protect Volunteers: The Odd Formulation
of Federalism in "Opt-Out" Preemption. 10 Seton Hall J Sports L 9, 2000.

Biedzynski. The Federal Volunteer Protection Act: Does Congress Want to
Play Ball? 23 Seton Hall Legis J 319, 1999.

§ 14503.   Limitation on liability for volunteers

(a) Liability protection for volunteers. Except as provided in subsections (b)
and (d), no volunteer of a nonprofit organization or governmental entity shall
be liable for harm caused by an act or omission of the volunteer on behalf of
the organization or entity if—

(1) the volunteer was acting within the scope of the volunteer's responsibilities in the nonprofit organization or governmental entity at the time of the
act or omission;

(2) if appropriate or required, the volunteer was properly licensed, certified,
or authorized by the appropriate authorities for the activities or practice in
the State in which the harm occurred, where the activities were or practice
was undertaken within the scope of the volunteer's responsibilities in the
nonprofit organization or governmental entity;

(3) the harm was not caused by willful or criminal misconduct, gross
negligence, reckless misconduct, or a conscious, flagrant indifference to the
rights or safety of the individual harmed by the volunteer; and

(4) the harm was not caused by the volunteer operating a motor vehicle,
vessel, aircraft, or other vehicle for which the State requires the operator or
the owner of the vehicle, craft, or vessel to—

(A) possess an operator's license; or

(B) maintain insurance.

(b) Concerning responsibility of volunteers to organizations and entities.
Nothing in this section shall be construed to affect any civil action brought by

any nonprofit organization or any governmental entity against any volunteer of such organization or entity.

(c) No effect on liability of organization or entity. Nothing in this section shall be construed to affect the liability of any nonprofit organization or governmental entity with respect to harm caused to any person.

(d) Exceptions to volunteer liability protection. If the laws of a State limit volunteer liability subject to one or more of the following conditions, such conditions shall not be construed as inconsistent with this section:

(1) A State law that requires a nonprofit organization or governmental entity to adhere to risk management procedures, including mandatory training of volunteers.

(2) A State law that makes the organization or entity liable for the acts or omissions of its volunteers to the same extent as an employer is liable for the acts or omissions of its employees.

(3) A State law that makes a limitation of liability inapplicable if the civil action was brought by an officer of a State or local government pursuant to State or local law.

(4) A State law that makes a limitation of liability applicable only if the nonprofit organization or governmental entity provides a financially secure source of recovery for individuals who suffer harm as a result of actions taken by a volunteer on behalf of the organization or entity. A financially secure source of recovery may be an insurance policy within specified limits, comparable coverage from a risk pooling mechanism, equivalent assets, or alternative arrangements that satisfy the State that the organization or entity will be able to pay for losses up to a specified amount. Separate standards for different types of liability exposure may be specified.

(e) Limitation on punitive damages based on the actions of volunteers. (1) General rule. Punitive damages may not be awarded against a volunteer in an action brought for harm based on the action of a volunteer acting within the scope of the volunteer's responsibilities to a nonprofit organization or governmental entity unless the claimant establishes by clear and convincing evidence that the harm was proximately caused by an action of such volunteer which constitutes willful or criminal misconduct, or a conscious, flagrant indifference to the rights or safety of the individual harmed.

(2) Construction. Paragraph (1) does not create a cause of action for punitive damages and does not preempt or supersede any Federal or State law to the extent that such law would further limit the award of punitive damages.

(f) Exceptions to limitations on liability. (1) In general. The limitations on the liability of a volunteer under this Act [42 USCS §§ 14501 et seq.] shall not apply to any misconduct that—

(A) constitutes a crime of violence (as that term is defined in section 16 of title 18, United States Code) or act of international terrorism (as that term is defined in section 2331 of title 18) for which the defendant has been convicted in any court;

(B) constitutes a hate crime (as that term is used in the Hate Crime Statistics Act (28 U.S.C. 534 note));

(C) involves a sexual offense, as defined by applicable State law, for which the defendant has been convicted in any court;

(D) involves misconduct for which the defendant has been found to have violated a Federal or State civil rights law; or

(E) where the defendant was under the influence (as determined pursuant to applicable State law) of intoxicating alcohol or any drug at the time of the misconduct.

(2) Rule of construction. Nothing in this subsection shall be construed to effect subsection (a)(3) or (e).

(June 18, 1997, P. L. 105-19, § 4, 111 Stat. 219.)

HISTORY; ANCILLARY LAWS AND DIRECTIVES

Effective date of section:

This section took effect 90 days after enactment, pursuant to § 7 of Act June 18, 1997, P. L. 105-19, which appears as 42 USCS § 14501 note.

CROSS REFERENCES

This section is referred to in 50 USCS § 441j-2.

RESEARCH GUIDE

Corporate and Business Law:

1 Liability of Corporate Officers and Directors (Matthew Bender), ch 12, Nonprofitable and Charitable Organizations § 12.01.

Other Treatises:

5 Rapp, Education Law (Matthew Bender), ch 12, General Liabilities and Litigation § 12.07.

Law Review Articles:

Apelbaum; Ryder. The Third Wave of Federal Tort Reform: Protecting the Public or Pushing the Constitutional Envelope? 8 Cornell J L & Pub Pol'y 591, Spring 1999.

Popper. A One-Term Tort Reform Tale: Victimizing the Vulnerable. 35 Harv J on Legis 123, Winter 1998.

Mowrey; Epstein. The Little Act That Could: The Volunteer Protection Act of 1997. 13 J Legal Aspects of Sport 289, Fall 2003.

Stern. Toward a Coherent Approach to Tort Immunity in Judicially Mandated Family Court Services. 92 Ky LJ 373, Winter 2003/2004.

Light. Conscripting State Law to Protect Volunteers: The Odd Formulation of Federalism in "Opt-Out" Preemption. 10 Seton Hall J Sports L 9, 2000.

Biedzynski. The Federal Volunteer Protection Act: Does Congress Want to Play Ball? 23 Seton Hall Legis J 319, 1999.

INTERPRETIVE NOTES AND DECISIONS

Individual volunteer members of nonprofit's board of directors were entitled to protection under Volunteer Protection Act of 1997, 42 USCS §§ 14501 et seq., from wage claim brought by former employee of nonprofit under Fair Labor Standards Act (FLSA), 29 USCS § 201, and their motion to dismiss for failure to state claim for relief under Fed. R. Civ. P. 12(b)(6) was granted. Armendarez v Glendale Youth Ctr., Inc. (2003, DC Ariz) 265 F Supp 2d 1136, 8 BNA WH Cas 2d 1356.

§ 14504. Liability for noneconomic loss

(a) General rule. In any civil action against a volunteer, based on an action of a volunteer acting within the scope of the volunteer's responsibilities to a nonprofit organization or governmental entity, the liability of the volunteer for noneconomic loss shall be determined in accordance with subsection (b).

(b) Amount of liability. (1) In general. Each defendant who is a volunteer, shall be liable only for the amount of noneconomic loss allocated to that defendant in direct proportion to the percentage of responsibility of that defendant (determined in accordance with paragraph (2)) for the harm to the claimant with respect to which that defendant is liable. The court shall render a separate judgment against each defendant in an amount determined pursuant to the preceding sentence.

(2) Percentage of responsibility. For purposes of determining the amount of noneconomic loss allocated to a defendant who is a volunteer under this section, the trier of fact shall determine the percentage of responsibility of that defendant for the claimant's harm.

(June 18, 1997, P. L. 105-19, § 5, 111 Stat. 221.)

HISTORY; ANCILLARY LAWS AND DIRECTIVES
Effective date of section:
This section took effect 90 days after enactment, pursuant to § 7 of Act June 18, 1997, P. L. 105-19, which appears as 42 USCS § 14501 note.

RESEARCH GUIDE
Other Treatises:
5 Rapp, Education Law (Matthew Bender), ch 12, General Liabilities and Litigation § 12.07.

Law Review Articles:
Apelbaum; Ryder. The Third Wave of Federal Tort Reform: Protecting the Public or Pushing the Constitutional Envelope? 8 Cornell J L & Pub Pol'y 591, Spring 1999.

Popper. A One-Term Tort Reform Tale: Victimizing the Vulnerable. 35 Harv J on Legis 123, Winter 1998.

Mowrey; Epstein. The Little Act That Could: The Volunteer Protection Act of 1997. 13 J Legal Aspects of Sport 289, Fall 2003.

Stern. Toward a Coherent Approach to Tort Immunity in Judicially Mandated Family Court Services. 92 Ky LJ 373, Winter 2003/2004.

Light. Conscripting State Law to Protect Volunteers: The Odd Formulation of Federalism in "Opt-Out" Preemption. 10 Seton Hall J Sports L 9, 2000.

Biedzynski. The Federal Volunteer Protection Act: Does Congress Want to Play Ball? 23 Seton Hall Legis J 319, 1999.

§ 14505. Definitions

For purposes of this Act [42 USCS §§ 14501 et seq.]:
(1) Economic loss. The term "economic loss" means any pecuniary loss resulting from harm (including the loss of earnings or other benefits related to employment, medical expense loss, replacement services loss, loss due to

death, burial costs, and loss of business or employment opportunities) to the extent recovery for such loss is allowed under applicable State law.

(2) Harm. The term "harm" includes physical, nonphysical, economic, and noneconomic losses.

(3) Noneconomic losses. The term "noneconomic losses" means losses for physical and emotional pain, suffering, inconvenience, physical impairment, mental anguish, disfigurement, loss of enjoyment of life, loss of society and companionship, loss of consortium (other than loss of domestic service), hedonic damages, injury to reputation and all other nonpecuniary losses of any kind or nature.

(4) Nonprofit organization. The term "nonprofit organization" means—

    (A) any organization which is described in section 501(c)(3) of the Internal Revenue Code of 1986 [26 USCS § 501(c)(3)] and exempt from tax under section 501(a) of such Code [26 USCS § 501(a)] and which does not practice any action which constitutes a hate crime referred to in subsection (b)(1) of the first section of the Hate Crime Statistics Act (28 U.S.C. 534 note); or

    (B) any not-for-profit organization which is organized and conducted for public benefit and operated primarily for charitable, civic, educational, religious, welfare, or health purposes and which does not practice any action which constitutes a hate crime referred to in subsection (b)(1) of the first section of the Hate Crime Statistics Act (28 U.S.C. 534 note).

(5) State. The term "State" means each of the several States, the District of Columbia, the Commonwealth of Puerto Rico, the Virgin Islands, Guam, American Samoa, the Northern Mariana Islands, any other territory or possession of the United States, or any political subdivision of any such State, territory, or possession.

(6) Volunteer. The term "volunteer" means an individual performing services for a nonprofit organization or a governmental entity who does not receive—

    (A) compensation (other than reasonable reimbursement or allowance for expenses actually incurred); or

    (B) any other thing of value in lieu of compensation,

in excess of $500 per year, and such term includes a volunteer serving as a director, officer, trustee, or direct service volunteer.
(June 18, 1997, P. L. 105-19, § 6, 111 Stat. 221.)

HISTORY; ANCILLARY LAWS AND DIRECTIVES
Effective date of section:
This section took effect 90 days after enactment, pursuant to § 7 of Act June 18, 1997, P. L. 105-19, which appears as 42 USCS § 14501 note.

RESEARCH GUIDE
Law Review Articles:
Apelbaum; Ryder. The Third Wave of Federal Tort Reform: Protecting the Public or Pushing the Constitutional Envelope? 8 Cornell J L & Pub Pol'y 591, Spring 1999.

Popper. A One-Term Tort Reform Tale: Victimizing the Vulnerable. 35 Harv J on Legis 123, Winter 1998.

Mowrey; Epstein. The Little Act That Could: The Volunteer Protection Act of 1997. 13 J Legal Aspects of Sport 289, Fall 2003.

Stern. Toward a Coherent Approach to Tort Immunity in Judicially Mandated Family Court Services. 92 Ky LJ 373, Winter 2003/2004.

Light. Conscripting State Law to Protect Volunteers: The Odd Formulation of Federalism in "Opt-Out" Preemption. 10 Seton Hall J Sports L 9, 2000.

Biedzynski. The Federal Volunteer Protection Act: Does Congress Want to Play Ball? 23 Seton Hall Legis J 319, 1999.

CHAPTER 140. CRIMINAL JUSTICE IDENTIFICATION, INFORMATION, AND COMMUNICATION

CRIME IDENTIFICATION TECHNOLOGY

CRIME IDENTIFICATION TECHNOLOGY

§ 14601. State grant program for criminal justice identification, information, and communication.

(a) **In general.** Subject to the availability of amounts provided in advance in appropriations Acts, the Office of Justice Programs relying principally on the expertise of the Bureau of Justice Statistics shall make a grant to each State, in a manner consistent with the national criminal history improvement program, which shall be used by the State, in conjunction with units of local government, State and local courts, other States, or combinations thereof, to establish or upgrade an integrated approach to develop information and identification technologies and systems to—

    (1) upgrade criminal history and criminal justice record systems, including systems operated by law enforcement agencies and courts;

    (2) improve criminal justice identification;

    (3) promote compatibility and integration of national, State, and local systems for—

(A) criminal justice purposes;

(B) firearms eligibility determinations;

(C) identification of sexual offenders;

(D) identification of domestic violence offenders; and

(E) background checks for other authorized purposes unrelated to criminal justice; and

(4) capture information for statistical and research purposes to improve the administration of criminal justice.

(b) Use of grant amounts. Grants under this section may be used for programs to establish, develop, update, or upgrade—

(1) State centralized, automated, adult and juvenile criminal history record information systems, including arrest and disposition reporting;

(2) automated fingerprint identification systems that are compatible with standards established by the National Institute of Standards and Technology and interoperable with the Integrated Automated Fingerprint Identification System (IAFIS) of the Federal Bureau of Investigation;

(3) finger imaging, live scan, and other automated systems to digitize fingerprints and to communicate prints in a manner that is compatible with standards established by the National Institute of Standards and Technology and interoperable with systems operated by States and by the Federal Bureau of Investigation;

(4) programs and systems to facilitate full participation in the Interstate Identification Index of the National Crime Information Center;

(5) systems to facilitate full participation in any compact relating to the Interstate Identification Index of the National Crime Information Center;

(6) systems to facilitate full participation in the national instant criminal background check system established under section 103(b) of the Brady Handgun Violence Prevention Act (18 U.S.C. 922 note) for firearms eligibility determinations;

(7) integrated criminal justice information systems to manage and communicate criminal justice information among law enforcement agencies, courts, prosecutors, and corrections agencies;

(8) noncriminal history record information systems relevant to firearms eligibility determinations for availability and accessibility to the national instant criminal background check system established under section 103(b) of the Brady Handgun Violence Prevention Act (18 U.S.C. 922 note);

(9) court-based criminal justice information systems that promote—

(A) reporting of dispositions to central State repositories and to the Federal Bureau of Investigation; and

(B) compatibility with, and integration of, court systems with other criminal justice information systems;

(10) ballistics identification and information programs that are compatible and integrated with the National Integrated Ballistics Network (NIBN);

(11) the capabilities of forensic science programs and medical examiner programs related to the administration of criminal justice, including programs leading to accreditation or certification of individuals or departments,

agencies, or laboratories, and programs relating to the identification and analysis of deoxyribonucleic acid;

(12) sexual offender identification and registration systems;

(13) domestic violence offender identification and information systems;

(14) programs for fingerprint-supported background checks capability for noncriminal justice purposes, including youth service employees and volunteers and other individuals in positions of responsibility, if authorized by Federal or State law and administered by a government agency;

(15) criminal justice information systems with a capacity to provide statistical and research products including incident-based reporting systems that are compatible with the National Incident-Based Reporting System (NIBRS) and uniform crime reports;

(16) multiagency, multijurisdictional communications systems among the States to share routine and emergency information among Federal, State, and local law enforcement agencies;

(17) the capability of the criminal justice system to deliver timely, accurate, and complete criminal history record information to child welfare agencies, organizations, and programs that are engaged in the assessment of risk and other activities related to the protection of children, including protection against child sexual abuse, and placement of children in foster care; and

(18) notwithstanding subsection (c), antiterrorism purposes as they relate to any other uses under this section or for other antiterrorism programs.

(c) **Assurances.** (1) In general. To be eligible to receive a grant under this section, a State shall provide assurances to the Attorney General that the State has the capability to contribute pertinent information to the national instant criminal background check system established under section 103(b) of the Brady Handgun Violence Prevention Act (18 U.S.C. 922 note).

(2) Information sharing. Such assurances shall include a provision that ensures that a statewide strategy for information sharing systems is underway, or will be initiated, to improve the functioning of the criminal justice system, with an emphasis on integration of all criminal justice components, law enforcement, courts, prosecution, corrections, and probation and parole. The strategy shall be prepared after consultation with State and local officials with emphasis on the recommendation of officials whose duty it is to oversee, plan, and implement integrated information technology systems, and shall contain—

  (A) a definition and analysis of "integration" in the State and localities developing integrated information sharing systems;

  (B) an assessment of the criminal justice resources being devoted to information technology;

  (C) Federal, State, regional, and local information technology coordination requirements;

  (D) an assurance that the individuals who developed the grant application took into consideration the needs of all branches of the State Government and specifically sought the advice of the chief of the highest court of the State with respect to the application;

(E) State and local resource needs;

(F) the establishment of statewide priorities for planning and implementation of information technology systems; and

(G) a plan for coordinating the programs funded under this title with other federally funded information technology programs, including directly funded local programs such as the Edward Byrne Justice Assistance Grant Program and the M.O.R.E. program established pursuant to part Q of title I of the Omnibus Crime Control and Safe Streets Act of 1968 [42 USCS §§ 3796dd et seq.].

(d) Matching funds. The Federal share of a grant received under this title [this section] may not exceed 90 percent of the costs of a program or proposal funded under this title [this section] unless the Attorney General waives, wholly or in part, the requirements of this subsection.

(e) Authorization of appropriations. (1) In general. There is authorized to be appropriated to carry out this section $250,000,000 for each of fiscal years 2002 through 2007.

(2) Limitations. Of the amount made available to carry out this section in any fiscal year—

(A) not more than 3 percent may be used by the Attorney General for salaries and administrative expenses;

(B) not more than 5 percent may be used for technical assistance, training and evaluations, and studies commissioned by Bureau of Justice Statistics of the Department of Justice (through discretionary grants or otherwise) in furtherance of the purposes of this section; and

(C) the Attorney General shall ensure the amounts are distributed on an equitable geographic basis.

(f) Grants to Indian tribes. Notwithstanding any other provision of this section, the Attorney General may use amounts made available under this section to make grants to Indian tribes for use in accordance with this section.

(Oct. 9, 1998, P. L. 105-251, Title I, § 102, 112 Stat. 1871; March 10, 2000, P. L. 106-177, Title I, § 102, 114 Stat. 35; Dec. 21, 2000, P. L. 106-561, § 2(c)(4), 114 Stat. 2791; Oct. 26, 2001, P. L. 107-56, Title X, § 1015, 115 Stat. 400; Jan. 5, 2006, P. L. 109-162, Title XI, Subtitle B, Ch. 1, § 1111(c)(1), 119 Stat. 3101.)

HISTORY; ANCILLARY LAWS AND DIRECTIVES
Amendments:

2000. Act March 10, 2000, in subsec. (b), in para. (15), deleted "and" after the concluding semicolon, in para. (16), substituted "; and" for a concluding period, and added para. (17).

Act Dec. 21, 2000, in subsec. (e), in para. (2), in subpara. (B), added "and" following the concluding semicolon, deleted subpara. (C) which read: "(C) not less than 20 percent shall be used by the Attorney General for the purposes described in paragraph (11) of subsection (b); and", and redesignated subpara. (D) as subpara. (C).

2001. Act Oct. 26, 2001, in subsec. (b), in para. (16), deleted "and" following the concluding semicolon, in para. (17), substituted "; and" for a concluding period, and added para. (18); and, in subsec. (e)(1), substituted "this section $250,000,000 for each of fiscal years 1999 through 2003." for "this section $250,000,000 for each of fiscal years 1999 through 2003."

2006. Act Jan. 5, 2006 (applicable with respect to the first fiscal year beginning after enactment and each fiscal year thereafter, as provided by § 1111(d) of such Act, which appears as 42 USCS § 3750 note), in subsec. (c)(2)(G), substituted "such as the Edward Byrne Justice Assistance Grant Program and the M.O.R.E. program" for "such as the Local Law Enforcement Block Grant program (described under the heading 'Violent Crime Reduction Programs, State and Local Law Enforcement Assistance' of the Departments of Commerce, Justice, and State, the Judiciary, and Related Agencies Appropriations Act, 1998 (Public Law 105-119)) and the M.O.R.E. program".

Short title:
Act Oct. 9, 1998, P. L. 105-251, Title I, § 101, 112 Stat. 1871, provides: "This title [42 USCS § 14601] may be cited as the 'Crime Identification Technology Act of 1998'.".

Act Oct. 9, 1998, P. L. 105-251, Title II, § 201, 112 Stat. 1874, provides: "This title [appearing in part as 42 USCS §§ 14611 et seq. and amending 42 USCS §§ 5119a and 5119b] may be cited as the 'National Criminal History Access and Child Protection Act'.".

Act Oct. 9, 1998, P. L. 105-251, Title II, Subtitle A, § 211, 112 Stat. 1874, provides: "This subtitle [42 USCS §§ 14611 et seq.] may be cited as the 'National Crime Prevention and Privacy Compact Act of 1998'.".

RESEARCH GUIDE

Law Review Articles:
Nevin; Scott. The USA Patriot Act: Time To Speak Up [Discussion of T. Derden, One Year Under the Patriot Act]. 46 Advoc (Boise) 19, December 2003.

Brandt; Van Valkenburgh. The USA Patriot Act: The Devil is in the Details [Discussion of T. Derden, One Year Under the Patriot Act]. 46 Advoc (Boise) 24, December 2003.

Chemerinsky. Litigation alerts in the USA Patriot Act. 23 Cal Law 29, April 2003.

Rosenszweig. Civil Liberty and the Response to Terrorism. 42 Duq L Rev 663, Summer 2004.

Sproule. The Effect of the USA Patriot Act on Workplace Privacy. 49 Prac Law 35, February 2003.

EXCHANGE OF CRIMINAL HISTORY RECORDS FOR NONCRIMINAL JUSTICE PURPOSES

§ 14611. Findings

Congress finds that—

(1) both the Federal Bureau of Investigation and State criminal history record repositories maintain fingerprint-based criminal history records;

(2) these criminal history records are shared and exchanged for criminal justice purposes through a Federal-State program known as the Interstate Identification Index System;

(3) although these records are also exchanged for legally authorized, noncriminal justice uses, such as governmental licensing and employment background checks, the purposes for and procedures by which they are exchanged vary widely from State to State;

(4) an interstate and Federal-State compact is necessary to facilitate authorized interstate criminal history record exchanges for noncriminal justice purposes on a uniform basis, while permitting each State to effectuate its own dissemination policy within its own borders; and

(5) such a compact will allow Federal and State records to be provided expeditiously to governmental and nongovernmental agencies that use such records in accordance with pertinent Federal and State law, while simultaneously enhancing the accuracy of the records and safeguarding the information contained therein from unauthorized disclosure or use.

(Oct. 9, 1998, P. L. 105-251, § 212, 112 Stat. 1874.)

RESEARCH GUIDE

Am Jur:

51 Am Jur 2d, Licenses and Permits § 54.

§ 14612.   Definitions

In this subtitle [42 USCS §§ 14611 et seq.]:

(1) Attorney general. The term "Attorney General" means the Attorney General of the United States.

(2) Compact. The term "Compact" means the National Crime Prevention and Privacy Compact set forth in section 217 [42 USCS § 14616].

(3) Council. The term "Council" means the Compact Council established under Article VI of the Compact.

(4) FBI. The term "FBI" means the Federal Bureau of Investigation.

(5) Party State. The term "Party State" means a State that has ratified the Compact.

(6) State. The term "State" means any State, territory, or possession of the United States, the District of Columbia, and the Commonwealth of Puerto Rico.

(Oct. 9, 1998, P. L. 105-251, § 213, 112 Stat. 1874.)

§ 14613.   Enactment and consent of the United States

The National Crime Prevention and Privacy Compact, as set forth in section 217 [42 USCS § 14616], is enacted into law and entered into by the Federal Government. The consent of Congress is given to States to enter into the Compact.

(Oct. 9, 1998, P. L. 105-251, § 214, 112 Stat. 1875.)

§ 14614.   Effect on other laws

(a) Privacy Act of 1974. Nothing in the Compact shall affect the obligations and responsibilities of the FBI under section 552a of title 5, United States Code (commonly known as the "Privacy Act of 1974").

(b) Access to certain records not affected. Nothing in the Compact shall interfere in any manner with—

(1) access, direct or otherwise, to records pursuant to—

(A) section 9101 of title 5, United States Code;

(B) the National Child Protection Act;

(C) the Brady Handgun Violence Prevention Act (Public Law 103-159; 107 Stat. 1536);

(D) the Violent Crime Control and Law Enforcement Act of 1994 (Public Law 103-322; 108 Stat. 2074) or any amendment made by that Act;

(E) the United States Housing Act of 1937 (42 U.S.C. 1437 et seq.); or

(F) the Native American Housing Assistance and Self-Determination Act of 1996 (25 U.S.C. 4101 et seq.); or

(2) any direct access to Federal criminal history records authorized by law.

(c) Authority of FBI under Departments of State, Justice, and Commerce, the Judiciary, and Related Agencies Appropriation Act, 1973. Nothing in the Compact shall be construed to affect the authority of the FBI under the Departments of State, Justice, and Commerce, the Judiciary, and Related Agencies Appropriation Act, 1973 (Public Law 92-544 (86 Stat. 1115)).

(d) Federal Advisory Committee Act. The Council shall not be considered to be a Federal advisory committee for purposes of the Federal Advisory Committee Act (5 U.S.C. App.).

(e) Members of Council not Federal officers or employees. Members of the Council (other than a member from the FBI or any at-large member who may be a Federal official or employee) shall not, by virtue of such membership, be deemed—

(1) to be, for any purpose other than to effect the Compact, officers or employees of the United States (as defined in sections 2104 and 2105 of title 5, United States Code); or

(2) to become entitled by reason of Council membership to any compensation or benefit payable or made available by the Federal Government to its officers or employees.

(Oct. 9, 1998, P. L. 105-251, § 215, 112 Stat. 1875.)

HISTORY; ANCILLARY LAWS AND DIRECTIVES

References in text:
The "Brady Handgun Violence Prevention Act", referred to in this section, is Title I of Act Nov. 30, 1993, P. L. 103-159. For full classification of such Title, consult USCS Tables volumes.

The "Departments of State, Justice, and Commerce, the Judiciary, and Related Agencies Appropriation Act, 1973", referred to in this section, is Act Oct. 25, 1972, P. L. 92-544. For full classification of such Act, consult USCS Tables volumes.

The "National Child Protection Act of 1993", referred to in this section, is Act Dec. 20, 1993, P. L. 103-209, which appears generally as 42 USCS §§ 5119 et seq. For full classification of such Act, consult USCS Tables volumes.

The "Violent Crime Control and Law Enforcement Act of 1994", referred to in this section, is Act Sept. 13, 1994, P. L. 103-322. For full classification of such Act, consult USCS Tables volumes.

§ 14615. Enforcement and implementation

All departments, agencies, officers, and employees of the United States shall enforce the Compact and cooperate with one another and with all Party States in enforcing the Compact and effectuating its purposes. For the Federal Government, the Attorney General shall make such rules, prescribe such instructions, and take such other actions as may be necessary to carry out the Compact and this subtitle [42 USCS §§ 14611 et seq.].
(Oct. 9, 1998, P. L. 105-251, § 216, 112 Stat. 1875.)

§ 14616. National Crime Prevention and Privacy Compact

The Contracting Parties agree to the following:

OVERVIEW

(a) In general. This Compact organizes an electronic information sharing system among the Federal Government and the States to exchange criminal history records for noncriminal justice purposes authorized by Federal or State law, such as background checks for governmental licensing and employment.

(b) Obligations of Parties. Under this Compact, the FBI and the Party States agree to maintain detailed databases of their respective criminal history records, including arrests and dispositions, and to make them available to the Federal Government and to Party States for authorized purposes. The FBI shall also manage the Federal data facilities that provide a significant part of the infrastructure for the system.

ARTICLE I—DEFINITIONS

In this Compact:

(1) Attorney General. The term "Attorney General" means the Attorney General of the United States.

(2) Compact officer. The term "Compact officer" means—

(A) with respect to the Federal Government, an official so designated by the Director of the FBI; and

(B) with respect to a Party State, the chief administrator of the State's criminal history record repository or a designee of the chief administrator who is a regular full-time employee of the repository.

(3) Council. The term "Council" means the Compact Council established under Article VI.

(4) Criminal history records. The term "criminal history records"—

(A) means information collected by criminal justice agencies on individuals consisting of identifiable descriptions and notations of arrests, detentions, indictments, or other formal criminal charges, and any disposition arising therefrom, including acquittal, sentencing, correctional supervision, or release; and

(B) does not include identification information such as fingerprint records if such information does not indicate involvement of the individual with the criminal justice system.

(5) Criminal history record repository. The term "criminal history record repository" means the State agency designated by the Governor or other appropriate executive official or the legislature of a State to perform centralized recordkeeping functions for criminal history records and services in the State.

(6) Criminal justice. The term "criminal justice" includes activities relating to the detection, apprehension, detention, pretrial release, post-trial release, prosecution, adjudication, correctional supervision, or rehabilitation of accused persons or criminal offenders. The administration of criminal justice includes criminal identification activities and the collection, storage, and dissemination of criminal history records.

(7) Criminal justice agency. The term "criminal justice agency"—

(A) means—

(i) courts; and

(ii) a governmental agency or any subunit thereof that—

(I) performs the administration of criminal justice pursuant to a statute or Executive order; and

(II) allocates a substantial part of its annual budget to the administration of criminal justice; and

(B) includes Federal and State inspectors general offices.

(8) Criminal justice services. The term "criminal justice services" means services provided by the FBI to criminal justice agencies in response to a request for information about a particular individual or as an update to information previously provided for criminal justice purposes.

(9) Criterion offense. The term "criterion offense" means any felony or misdemeanor offense not included on the list of nonserious offenses published periodically by the FBI.

(10) Direct access. The term "direct access" means access to the National Identification Index by computer terminal or other automated means not requiring the assistance of or intervention by any other party or agency.

(11) Executive order. The term "Executive order" means an order of the President of the United States or the chief executive officer of a State that has the force of law and that is promulgated in accordance with applicable law.

(12) FBI. The term "FBI" means the Federal Bureau of Investigation.

(13) Interstate identification system. The term "Interstate Identification Index System" or "III System"—

(A) means the cooperative Federal-State system for the exchange of criminal history records; and

(B) includes the National Identification Index, the National Fingerprint File and, to the extent of their participation in such system, the criminal history record repositories of the States and the FBI.

(14) National fingerprint file. The term "National Fingerprint File" means a

database of fingerprints, or other uniquely personal identifying information, relating to an arrested or charged individual maintained by the FBI to provide positive identification of record subjects indexed in the III System.

(15) National Identification Index. The term "National Identification Index" means an index maintained by the FBI consisting of names, identifying numbers, and other descriptive information relating to record subjects about whom there are criminal history records in the III System.

(16) National indices. The term "National indices" means the National Identification Index and the National Fingerprint File.

(17) Nonparty State. The term "Nonparty State" means a State that has not ratified this Compact.

(18) Noncriminal justice purposes. The term "noncriminal justice purposes" means uses of criminal history records for purposes authorized by Federal or State law other than purposes relating to criminal justice activities, including employment suitability, licensing determinations, immigration and naturalization matters, and national security clearances.

(19) Party State. The term "Party State" means a State that has ratified this Compact.

(20) Positive identification. The term "positive identification" means a determination, based upon a comparison of fingerprints or other equally reliable biometric identification techniques, that the subject of a record search is the same person as the subject of a criminal history record or records indexed in the III System. Identifications based solely upon a comparison of subjects' names or other nonunique identification characteristics or numbers, or combinations thereof, shall not constitute positive identification.

(21) Sealed record information. The term "sealed record information" means—

    (A) with respect to adults, that portion of a record that is—

        (i) not available for criminal justice uses;

        (ii) not supported by fingerprints or other accepted means of positive identification; or

        (iii) subject to restrictions on dissemination for noncriminal justice purposes pursuant to a court order related to a particular subject or pursuant to a Federal or State statute that requires action on a sealing petition filed by a particular record subject; and

    (B) with respect to juveniles, whatever each State determines is a sealed record under its own law and procedure.

(22) State. The term "State" means any State, territory, or possession of the United States, the District of Columbia, and the Commonwealth of Puerto Rico.

ARTICLE II—PURPOSES

The purposes of this Compact are to—

(1) provide a legal framework for the establishment of a cooperative Federal-State system for the interstate and Federal-State exchange of criminal history records for noncriminal justice uses;

(2) require the FBI to permit use of the National Identification Index and the National Fingerprint File by each Party State, and to provide, in a timely fashion, Federal and State criminal history records to requesting States, in accordance with the terms of this Compact and with rules, procedures, and standards established by the Council under Article VI;

(3) require Party States to provide information and records for the National Identification Index and the National Fingerprint File and to provide criminal history records, in a timely fashion, to criminal history record repositories of other States and the Federal Government for noncriminal justice purposes, in accordance with the terms of this Compact and with rules, procedures, and standards established by the Council under Article VI;

(4) provide for the establishment of a Council to monitor III System operations and to prescribe system rules and procedures for the effective and proper operation of the III System for noncriminal justice purposes; and

(5) require the FBI and each Party State to adhere to III System standards concerning record dissemination and use, response times, system security, data quality, and other duly established standards, including those that enhance the accuracy and privacy of such records.

ARTICLE III—RESPONSIBILITIES OF COMPACT PARTIES

(a) FBI responsibilities. The Director of the FBI shall—

(1) appoint an FBI Compact officer who shall—

(A) administer this Compact within the Department of Justice and among Federal agencies and other agencies and organizations that submit search requests to the FBI pursuant to Article V(c);

(B) ensure that Compact provisions and rules, procedures, and standards prescribed by the Council under Article VI are complied with by the Department of Justice and the Federal agencies and other agencies and organizations referred to in Article III(1)(A); and

(C) regulate the use of records received by means of the III System from Party States when such records are supplied by the FBI directly to other Federal agencies;

(2) provide to Federal agencies and to State criminal history record repositories, criminal history records maintained in its database for the noncriminal justice purposes described in Article IV, including—

(A) information from Nonparty States; and

(B) information from Party States that is available from the FBI through the III System, but is not available from the Party State through the III System;

(3) provide a telecommunications network and maintain centralized facilities for the exchange of criminal history records for both criminal justice purposes and the noncriminal justice purposes described in Article IV, and ensure that the exchange of such records for criminal justice purposes has priority over exchange for noncriminal justice purposes; and

(4) modify or enter into user agreements with Nonparty State criminal history record repositories to require them to establish record request procedures conforming to those prescribed in Article V.

(b) State responsibilities. Each Party State shall—

    (1) appoint a Compact officer who shall—

        (A) administer this Compact within that State;

        (B) ensure that Compact provisions and rules, procedures, and standards established by the Council under Article VI are complied with in the State; and

        (C) regulate the in-State use of records received by means of the III System from the FBI or from other Party States;

    (2) establish and maintain a criminal history record repository, which shall provide—

        (A) information and records for the National Identification Index and the National Fingerprint File; and

        (B) the State's III System-indexed criminal history records for noncriminal justice purposes described in Article IV;

    (3) participate in the National Fingerprint File; and

    (4) provide and maintain telecommunications links and related equipment necessary to support the services set forth in this Compact.

(c) Compliance with III System standards. In carrying out their responsibilities under this Compact, the FBI and each Party State shall comply with III System rules, procedures, and standards duly established by the Council concerning record dissemination and use, response times, data quality, system security, accuracy, privacy protection, and other aspects of III System operation.

(d) Maintenance of record services. (1) Use of the III System for noncriminal justice purposes authorized in this Compact shall be managed so as not to diminish the level of services provided in support of criminal justice purposes.

    (2) Administration of Compact provisions shall not reduce the level of service available to authorized noncriminal justice users on the effective date of this Compact.

ARTICLE IV—AUTHORIZED RECORD DISCLOSURES

(a) State criminal history record repositories. To the extent authorized by section 552a of title 5, United States Code (commonly known as the "Privacy Act of 1974"), the FBI shall provide on request criminal history records (excluding sealed records) to State criminal history record repositories for noncriminal justice purposes allowed by Federal statute, Federal Executive order, or a State statute that has been approved by the Attorney General and that authorizes national indices checks.

(b) Criminal justice agencies and other governmental or nongovernmental agencies. The FBI, to the extent authorized by section 552a of title 5, United States Code (commonly known as the "Privacy Act of 1974"), and State criminal history record repositories shall provide criminal history records (excluding sealed records) to criminal justice agencies and other governmental or nongovernmental agencies for noncriminal justice purposes allowed by

Federal statute, Federal Executive order, or a State statute that has been approved by the Attorney General, that authorizes national indices checks.

(c) **Procedures.** Any record obtained under this Compact may be used only for the official purposes for which the record was requested. Each Compact officer shall establish procedures, consistent with this Compact, and with rules, procedures, and standards established by the Council under Article VI, which procedures shall protect the accuracy and privacy of the records, and shall—

(1) ensure that records obtained under this Compact are used only by authorized officials for authorized purposes;

(2) require that subsequent record checks are requested to obtain current information whenever a new need arises; and

(3) ensure that record entries that may not legally be used for a particular noncriminal justice purpose are deleted from the response and, if no information authorized for release remains, an appropriate "no record" response is communicated to the requesting official.

ARTICLE V—RECORD REQUEST PROCEDURES

(a) **Positive identification.** Subject fingerprints or other approved forms of positive identification shall be submitted with all requests for criminal history record checks for noncriminal justice purposes.

(b) **Submission of State requests.** Each request for a criminal history record check utilizing the national indices made under any approved State statute shall be submitted through that State's criminal history record repository. A State criminal history record repository shall process an interstate request for noncriminal justice purposes through the national indices only if such request is transmitted through another State criminal history record repository or the FBI.

(c) **Submission of Federal requests.** Each request for criminal history record checks utilizing the national indices made under Federal authority shall be submitted through the FBI or, if the State criminal history record repository consents to process fingerprint submissions, through the criminal history record repository in the State in which such request originated. Direct access to the National Identification Index by entities other than the FBI and State criminal history records repositories shall not be permitted for noncriminal justice purposes.

(d) **Fees.** A State criminal history record repository or the FBI—

(1) may charge a fee, in accordance with applicable law, for handling a request involving fingerprint processing for noncriminal justice purposes; and

(2) may not charge a fee for providing criminal history records in response to an electronic request for a record that does not involve a request to process fingerprints.

(e) **Additional search.** (1) If a State criminal history record repository cannot positively identify the subject of a record request made for noncriminal justice purposes, the request, together with fingerprints or other approved identifying information, shall be forwarded to the FBI for a search of the national indices.

(2) If, with respect to a request forwarded by a State criminal history record repository under paragraph (1), the FBI positively identifies the subject as having a III System-indexed record or records—

(A) the FBI shall so advise the State criminal history record repository; and

(B) the State criminal history record repository shall be entitled to obtain the additional criminal history record information from the FBI or other State criminal history record repositories.

ARTICLE VI—ESTABLISHMENT OF COMPACT COUNCIL

(a) Establishment. (1) In general. There is established a council to be known as the "Compact Council", which shall have the authority to promulgate rules and procedures governing the use of the III System for noncriminal justice purposes, not to conflict with FBI administration of the III System for criminal justice purposes.

(2) Organization. The Council shall—

(A) continue in existence as long as this Compact remains in effect;

(B) be located, for administrative purposes, within the FBI; and

(C) be organized and hold its first meeting as soon as practicable after the effective date of this Compact.

(b) Membership. The Council shall be composed of 15 members, each of whom shall be appointed by the Attorney General, as follows:

(1) Nine members, each of whom shall serve a 2-year term, who shall be selected from among the Compact officers of Party States based on the recommendation of the Compact officers of all Party States, except that, in the absence of the requisite number of Compact officers available to serve, the chief administrators of the criminal history record repositories of Nonparty States shall be eligible to serve on an interim basis.

(2) Two at-large members, nominated by the Director of the FBI, each of whom shall serve a 3-year term, of whom—

(A) 1 shall be a representative of the criminal justice agencies of the Federal Government and may not be an employee of the FBI; and

(B) 1 shall be a representative of the noncriminal justice agencies of the Federal Government.

(3) Two at-large members, nominated by the Chairman of the Council, once the Chairman is elected pursuant to Article VI(c), each of whom shall serve a 3-year term, of whom—

(A) 1 shall be a representative of State or local criminal justice agencies; and

(B) 1 shall be a representative of State or local noncriminal justice agencies.

(4) One member, who shall serve a 3-year term, and who shall simultaneously be a member of the FBI's advisory policy board on criminal justice information services, nominated by the membership of that policy board.

(5) One member, nominated by the Director of the FBI, who shall serve a 3-year term, and who shall be an employee of the FBI.

(c) Chairman and Vice Chairman. (1) In general. From its membership, the Council shall elect a Chairman and a Vice Chairman of the Council, respectively. Both the Chairman and Vice Chairman of the Council—

(A) shall be a Compact officer, unless there is no Compact officer on the Council who is willing to serve, in which case the Chairman may be an at-large member; and

(B) shall serve a 2-year term and may be reelected to only 1 additional 2-year term.

(2) Duties of Vice Chairman. The Vice Chairman of the Council shall serve as the Chairman of the Council in the absence of the Chairman.

(d) Meetings. (1) In general. The Council shall meet at least once each year at the call of the Chairman. Each meeting of the Council shall be open to the public. The Council shall provide prior public notice in the Federal Register of each meeting of the Council, including the matters to be addressed at such meeting.

(2) Quorum. A majority of the Council or any committee of the Council shall constitute a quorum of the Council or of such committee, respectively, for the conduct of business. A lesser number may meet to hold hearings, take testimony, or conduct any business not requiring a vote.

(e) Rules, procedures, and standards. The Council shall make available for public inspection and copying at the Council office within the FBI, and shall publish in the Federal Register, any rules, procedures, or standards established by the Council.

(f) Assistance from FBI. The Council may request from the FBI such reports, studies, statistics, or other information or materials as the Council determines to be necessary to enable the Council to perform its duties under this Compact. The FBI, to the extent authorized by law, may provide such assistance or information upon such a request.

(g) Committees. The Chairman may establish committees as necessary to carry out this Compact and may prescribe their membership, responsibilities, and duration.

ARTICLE VII—RATIFICATION OF COMPACT

This Compact shall take effect upon being entered into by 2 or more States as between those States and the Federal Government. Upon subsequent entering into this Compact by additional States, it shall become effective among those States and the Federal Government and each Party State that has previously ratified it. When ratified, this Compact shall have the full force and effect of law within the ratifying jurisdictions. The form of ratification shall be in accordance with the laws of the executing State.

ARTICLE VIII—MISCELLANEOUS PROVISIONS

(a) Relation of Compact to certain FBI activities. Administration of this

Compact shall not interfere with the management and control of the Director of the FBI over the FBI's collection and dissemination of criminal history records and the advisory function of the FBI's advisory policy board chartered under the Federal Advisory Committee Act (5 U.S.C. App.) for all purposes other than noncriminal justice.

(b) No authority for nonappropriated expenditures. Nothing in this Compact shall require the FBI to obligate or expend funds beyond those appropriated to the FBI.

(c) Relating to Public Law 92-544. Nothing in this Compact shall diminish or lessen the obligations, responsibilities, and authorities of any State, whether a Party State or a Nonparty State, or of any criminal history record repository or other subdivision or component thereof, under the Departments of State, Justice, and Commerce, the Judiciary, and Related Agencies Appropriation Act, 1973 (Public Law 92-544), or regulations and guidelines promulgated thereunder, including the rules and procedures promulgated by the Council under Article VI(a), regarding the use and dissemination of criminal history records and information.

ARTICLE IX—RENUNCIATION

(a) In general. This Compact shall bind each Party State until renounced by the Party State.

(b) Effect. Any renunciation of this Compact by a Party State shall—
   (1) be effected in the same manner by which the Party State ratified this Compact; and
   (2) become effective 180 days after written notice of renunciation is provided by the Party State to each other Party State and to the Federal Government.

ARTICLE X—SEVERABILITY

The provisions of this Compact shall be severable, and if any phrase, clause, sentence, or provision of this Compact is declared to be contrary to the constitution of any participating State, or to the Constitution of the United States, or the applicability thereof to any government, agency, person, or circumstance is held invalid, the validity of the remainder of this Compact and the applicability thereof to any government, agency, person, or circumstance shall not be affected thereby. If a portion of this Compact is held contrary to the constitution of any Party State, all other portions of this Compact shall remain in full force and effect as to the remaining Party States and in full force and effect as to the Party State affected, as to all other provisions.

ARTICLE XI—ADJUDICATION OF DISPUTES

(a) In general. The Council shall—
   (1) have initial authority to make determinations with respect to any dispute regarding—
      (A) interpretation of this Compact;
      (B) any rule or standard established by the Council pursuant to Article V; and

(C) any dispute or controversy between any parties to this Compact; and (2) hold a hearing concerning any dispute described in paragraph (1) at a regularly scheduled meeting of the Council and only render a decision based upon a majority vote of the members of the Council. Such decision shall be published pursuant to the requirements of Article VI(e).

(b) Duties of FBI. The FBI shall exercise immediate and necessary action to preserve the integrity of the III System, maintain system policy and standards, protect the accuracy and privacy of records, and to prevent abuses, until the Council holds a hearing on such matters.

(c) Right of appeal. The FBI or a Party State may appeal any decision of the Council to the Attorney General, and thereafter may file suit in the appropriate district court of the United States, which shall have original jurisdiction of all cases or controversies arising under this Compact. Any suit arising under this Compact and initiated in a State court shall be removed to the appropriate district court of the United States in the manner provided by section 1446 of title 28, United States Code, or other statutory authority.
(Oct. 9, 1998, P. L. 105-251, § 217, 112 Stat. 1876.)

HISTORY; ANCILLARY LAWS AND DIRECTIVES

References in text:
The "Departments of State, Justice, and Commerce, the Judiciary, and Related Agencies Appropriation Act, 1973", referred to in this section, is Act Oct. 25, 1972, P. L. 92-544. For full classification of such Act, consult USCS Tables volumes.

CODE OF FEDERAL REGULATIONS

National Crime Prevention and Privacy Compact Council—Fingerprint submission requirements, 28 CFR 901.1 et seq.

National Crime Prevention and Privacy Compact Council—Dispute adjudication procedures, 28 CFR 902.1 et seq.

National Crime Prevention and Privacy Compact Council—National Fingerprint File (NFF) Program qualification requirements, 28 CFR 905.1 et seq.

National Crime Prevention and Privacy Compact Council—Outsourcing of non-criminal justice administrative functions, 28 CFR 906.1 et seq.

National Crime Prevention and Privacy Compact Council—Compact Council procedures for compliant conduct and responsible use of the Interstate Identification Index (III) system for noncriminal justice purposes, 28 CFR 907.1 et seq.

CROSS REFERENCES

This section is referred to in 42 USCS §§ 14612, 14613.

RESEARCH GUIDE

Am Jur:
51 Am Jur 2d, Licenses and Permits § 54.
58 Am Jur 2d, Occupations, Trades, and Professions § 6.

CHAPTER 140A.   JENNIFER'S LAW

§ 14661.   Program authorized

The Attorney General is authorized to provide grant awards to States to enable States to improve the reporting of unidentified and missing persons.
(March 10, 2000, P. L. 106-177, Title II, § 202, 114 Stat. 36.)

HISTORY; ANCILLARY LAWS AND DIRECTIVES

Short title:
Act March 10, 2000, P. L. 106-177, Title II, § 201, 114 Stat. 36, provides: "This title [42 USCS §§ 14661 et seq.] may be cited as 'Jennifer's Law'.".
Act Nov. 9, 2000, P. L. 106-468, § 1, 114 Stat. 2027, provides: "This Act [42 USCS § 14665 and note to such section] may be cited as 'Kristen's Act'.".

RESEARCH GUIDE

Am Jur:
1 Am Jur 2d, Absentees § 4.

§ 14662.   Eligibility

(a) Application. To be eligible to receive a grant award under this title [42 USCS §§ 14661 et seq.], a State shall submit an application at such time and in such form as the Attorney General may reasonably require.

(b) Contents. Each such application shall include assurances that the State shall, to the greatest extent possible—

(1) report to the National Crime Information Center and when possible, to law enforcement authorities throughout the State regarding every deceased unidentified person, regardless of age, found in the State's jurisdiction;

(2) enter a complete profile of such unidentified person in compliance with the guidelines established by the Department of Justice for the National Crime Information Center Missing and Unidentified Persons File, including dental records, DNA records, x-rays, and fingerprints, if available;

(3) enter the National Crime Information Center number or other appropriate number assigned to the unidentified person on the death certificate of each such unidentified person; and

(4) retain all such records pertaining to unidentified persons until a person is identified.

(March 10, 2000, P. L. 106-177, Title II, § 203, 114 Stat. 36.)

CROSS REFERENCES

This section is referred to in 42 USCS § 14663.

§ 14663. Uses of funds

A State that receives a grant award under this title [42 USCS §§ 14661 et seq.] may use such funds received to establish or expand programs developed to improve the reporting of unidentified persons in accordance with the assurances provided in the application submitted pursuant to section 203(b) [42 USCS § 14662(b)].

(March 10, 2000, P. L. 106-177, Title II, § 204, 114 Stat. 36.)

§ 14664. Authorization of appropriations

There are authorized to be appropriated to carry out this title [42 USCS §§ 14661 et seq.] $2,000,000 for each of fiscal years 2000, 2001, and 2002.

(March 10, 2000, P. L. 106-177, Title II, § 205, 114 Stat. 36.)

§ 14665. Grants for the assistance of organizations to find missing adults

(a) **In general.** The Attorney General may make grants to public agencies or nonprofit private organizations, or combinations thereof, for programs—

(1) to assist law enforcement and families in locating missing adults;

(2) to maintain a national, interconnected database for the purpose of tracking missing adults who are determined by law enforcement to be endangered due to age, diminished mental capacity, or the circumstances of disappearance, when foul play is suspected or circumstances are unknown;

(3) to maintain statistical information of adults reported as missing;

(4) to provide informational resources and referrals to families of missing adults;

(5) to assist in public notification and victim advocacy related to missing adults; and

(6) to establish and maintain a national clearinghouse for missing adults.

(b) **Regulations.** The Attorney General may make such rules and regulations as may be necessary to carry out this Act.

(Nov. 9, 2000, P. L. 106-468, § 2, 114 Stat. 2027.)

HISTORY; ANCILLARY LAWS AND DIRECTIVES

References in text:

"This Act", referred to in this section, is Act Nov. 9, 2000, P. L. 106-468, popularly known as Kristen's Act, which appears as 42 USCS § 14665 and note.

Explanatory notes:

This section was enacted as part of Act Nov. 9, 2000, P. L. 106-468, and not as part of Title II of Act March 10, 2000, P. L. 106-177, which generally comprises this chapter.

Other provisions:

Authorization of appropriations. Act Nov. 9, 2000, P. L. 106-468, § 3, 114 Stat. 2028, provides: "There are authorized to be appropriated to carry out this Act [this section] $1,000,000 each year for fiscal years 2001 through 2004.".

RESEARCH GUIDE

Am Jur:

1 Am Jur 2d, Absentees § 4.

CHAPTER 141. COMMERCIAL SPACE OPPORTUNITIES AND TRANSPORTATION SERVICES

§ 14701.   [Repealed]

HISTORY; ANCILLARY LAWS AND DIRECTIVES

This section (Act Oct. 28, 1998, P. L. 105-303, § 2, 112 Stat. 2843) was repealed by Act Dec. 18, 2010, P. L. 111-314, § 6, 124 Stat. 3444, except with respect to rights and duties that matured, penalties that were incurred, or proceedings that were begun before enactment, as provided by § 6 of such Act, which appears as a note preceding 51 USCS § 10101. It provided definitions. For similar provisions, see 51 USCS § 50101.

PROMOTION OF COMMERCIAL SPACE OPPORTUNITIES

§ 14711.   [Repealed]

HISTORY; ANCILLARY LAWS AND DIRECTIVES

This section (Act Oct. 28, 1998, P. L. 105-303, Title I, § 101, 112 Stat. 2845) was repealed by Act Dec. 18, 2010, P. L. 111-314, § 6, 124 Stat. 3444, except with respect to rights and duties that matured, penalties that were incurred, or proceedings that were begun before enactment, as provided by § 6 of such Act, which appears as a note preceding 51 USCS § 10101. It related to commercialization of the Space Station. For provisions similar to subsec. (a) of this section, see 51 USCS § 50111(a).

§ 14712.   [Repealed and transferred]

HISTORY; ANCILLARY LAWS AND DIRECTIVES

Subsec. (b) of this section (Act Oct. 28, 1998, P. L. 105-303, Title I, § 104,

112 Stat. 2852) was repealed by Act Dec. 18, 2010, P. L. 111-314, § 6, 124 Stat. 3444, except with respect to rights and duties that matured, penalties that were incurred, or proceedings that were begun before enactment, as provided by § 6 of such Act, which appears as a note preceding 51 USCS § 10101. It related to the promotion of United States Global Positioning System standards. Subsection (a), setting out congressional findings, was transferred to 51 USCS § 50112 note by the compilers of the official United States Code. For provisions similar to subsec. (b) of this section, see 51 USCS § 50112.

§ 14713. [Repealed]

HISTORY; ANCILLARY LAWS AND DIRECTIVES
This section (Act Oct. 28, 1998, P. L. 105-303, Title I, § 105, 112 Stat. 2852) was repealed by Act Dec. 18, 2010, P. L. 111-314, § 6, 124 Stat. 3444, except with respect to rights and duties that matured, penalties that were incurred, or proceedings that were begun before enactment, as provided by § 6 of such Act, which appears as a note preceding 51 USCS § 10101. It related to the acquisition of space science data. For similar provisions, see 51 USCS § 50113.

§ 14714. [Repealed]

HISTORY; ANCILLARY LAWS AND DIRECTIVES
This section (Act Oct. 28, 1998, P. L. 105-303, Title I, § 106, 112 Stat. 2853) was repealed by Act Dec. 18, 2010, P. L. 111-314, § 6, 124 Stat. 3444, except with respect to rights and duties that matured, penalties that were incurred, or proceedings that were begun before enactment, as provided by § 6 of such Act, which appears as a note preceding 51 USCS § 10101. It related to the administration of commercial space centers. For similar provisions, see 51 USCS § 50114.

§ 14715. [Repealed]

HISTORY; ANCILLARY LAWS AND DIRECTIVES
This section (Act Oct. 28, 1998, P. L. 105-303, Title I, § 107, 112 Stat. 2853) was repealed by Act Dec. 18, 2010, P. L. 111-314, § 6, 124 Stat. 3444, except with respect to rights and duties that matured, penalties that were incurred, or proceedings that were begun before enactment, as provided by § 6 of such Act, which appears as a note preceding 51 USCS § 10101. It related to sources of Earth Science data. For provisions similar to subsecs. (a), (b), (d), and (e) of this section, see 51 USCS § 50115.

FEDERAL ACQUISITION OF SPACE TRANSPORTATION SERVICES

§ 14731. [Repealed]

HISTORY; ANCILLARY LAWS AND DIRECTIVES
This section (Act Oct. 28, 1998, P. L. 105-303, Title II, § 201, 112 Stat. 2854) was repealed by Act Dec. 18, 2010, P. L. 111-314, § 6, 124 Stat.

3444, except with respect to rights and duties that matured, penalties that were incurred, or proceedings that were begun before enactment, as provided by § 6 of such Act, which appears as a note preceding 51 USCS § 10101. It related to a requirement to procure commercial space transportation services. For similar provisions, see 51 USCS § 50131.

§ 14732. [Repealed]

HISTORY; ANCILLARY LAWS AND DIRECTIVES
This section (Act Oct. 28, 1998, P. L. 105-303, Title II, § 202, 112 Stat. 2854) was repealed by Act Dec. 18, 2010, P. L. 111-314, § 6, 124 Stat. 3444, except with respect to rights and duties that matured, penalties that were incurred, or proceedings that were begun before enactment, as provided by § 6 of such Act, which appears as a note preceding 51 USCS § 10101. It related to the acquisition of commercial space transportation services. For similar provisions, see 51 USCS § 50132.

§ 14733. [Repealed]

HISTORY; ANCILLARY LAWS AND DIRECTIVES
This section (Act Oct. 28, 1998, P. L. 105-303, Title II, § 204, 112 Stat. 2856) was repealed by Act Dec. 18, 2010, P. L. 111-314, § 6, 124 Stat. 3444, except with respect to rights and duties that matured, penalties that were incurred, or proceedings that were begun before enactment, as provided by § 6 of such Act, which appears as a note preceding 51 USCS § 10101. It related to shuttle privatization. For provisions similar to subsec. (a) of this section, see 51 USCS § 50133.

§ 14734. [Repealed]

HISTORY; ANCILLARY LAWS AND DIRECTIVES
This section (Act Oct. 28, 1998, P. L. 105-303, Title II, § 205, 112 Stat. 2857; Oct. 5, 1999, P. L. 106-65, Div A, Title X, Subtitle G, § 1067(21), 113 Stat. 775) was repealed by Act Dec. 18, 2010, P. L. 111-314, § 6, 124 Stat. 3444, except with respect to rights and duties that matured, penalties that were incurred, or proceedings that were begun before enactment, as provided by § 6 of such Act, which appears as a note preceding 51 USCS § 10101. It related to the use of excess intercontinental ballistic missiles. For similar provisions, see 51 USCS § 50134.

§ 14735. [Repealed]

HISTORY; ANCILLARY LAWS AND DIRECTIVES
This section (Act Oct. 28, 1998, P. L. 105-303, Title II, § 206, 112 Stat. 2857) was repealed by Act Dec. 18, 2010, P. L. 111-314, § 6, 124 Stat. 3444, except with respect to rights and duties that matured, penalties that were incurred, or proceedings that were begun before enactment, as provided by § 6 of such Act, which appears as a note preceding 51 USCS § 10101. It related to a national launch capability study.

COMMERCIAL REUSABLE IN-SPACE TRANSPORTATION

§ 14751.   [Transferred]

HISTORY; ANCILLARY LAWS AND DIRECTIVES

This section, setting out congressional findings on commercial reusable in-space transportation, was transferred to 51 USCS § 50301 note by the compilers of the official United States Code.

§ 14752.   [Repealed]

HISTORY; ANCILLARY LAWS AND DIRECTIVES

This section (Act Oct. 23, 2002, P. L. 107-248, Title IX, § 903, 116 Stat. 1574) was repealed by Act Dec. 18, 2010, P. L. 111-314, § 6, 124 Stat. 3444, except with respect to rights and duties that matured, penalties that were incurred, or proceedings that were begun before enactment, as provided by § 6 of such Act, which appears as a note preceding 51 USCS § 10101. It related to loan guarantees for production of commercial reusable in-space transportation. For similar provisions, see 51 USCS § 50302.

§ 14753.   [Repealed]

HISTORY; ANCILLARY LAWS AND DIRECTIVES

This section (Act Oct. 23, 2002, P. L. 107-248, Title IX, § 904, 116 Stat. 1576) was repealed by Act Dec. 18, 2010, P. L. 111-314, § 6, 124 Stat. 3444, except with respect to rights and duties that matured, penalties that were incurred, or proceedings that were begun before enactment, as provided by § 6 of such Act, which appears as a note preceding 51 USCS § 10101. It provided definitions. For similar provisions, see 51 USCS § 50301.

CHAPTER 142. POISON CONTROL CENTER ENHANCEMENT AND AWARENESS [REPEALED]

Section
14801. [Repealed]
14802. [Repealed]
14803. [Repealed]
14804. [Repealed]
14805. [Repealed]

§ 14801.   [Repealed]

HISTORY; ANCILLARY LAWS AND DIRECTIVES

This section (Act Feb. 25, 2000, P. L. 106-174, § 2, 114 Stat. 18) was repealed by Act Dec. 19, 2003, P. L. 108-194, § 4, 117 Stat. 2891. It related to congressional findings regarding poison control centers. For similar provisions, see 42 USCS § 300d-71 note.

Short title:

Act Feb. 25, 2000, P. L. 106-174, § 1, 114 Stat. 18, which formerly appeared as a note to this section, was repealed by Act Dec. 19, 2003, P. L. 108-194, § 4, 117 Stat. 2891. Such note provided for citation of former 42 USCS §§ 14801 et seq. as the "Poison Control Center Enhancement and Awareness Act".

§ 14802.   [Repealed]

HISTORY; ANCILLARY LAWS AND DIRECTIVES

This section (Act Feb. 25, 2000, P. L. 106-174, § 3, 114 Stat. 18) was repealed by Act Dec. 19, 2003, P. L. 108-194, § 4, 117 Stat. 2891. It defined "Secretary".

§ 14803.   [Repealed]

HISTORY; ANCILLARY LAWS AND DIRECTIVES

This section (Act Feb. 25, 2000, P. L. 106-174, § 4, 114 Stat. 18) was repealed by Act Dec. 19, 2003, P. L. 108-194, § 4, 117 Stat. 2891. It established a national toll-free number to be used to access regional poison control centers. For similar provisions, see 42 USCS § 300d-71.

§ 14804.   [Repealed]

HISTORY; ANCILLARY LAWS AND DIRECTIVES

This section (Act Feb. 25, 2000, P. L. 106-174, § 5, 114 Stat. 19) was repealed by Act Dec. 19, 2003, P. L. 108-194, § 4, 117 Stat. 2891. It established a nationwide media campaign to educate the public and health care providers about poison prevention and the availability of poison control resources in local communities. For similar provisions, see 42 USCS § 300d-72.

§ 14805.   [Repealed]

HISTORY; ANCILLARY LAWS AND DIRECTIVES

This section (Act Feb. 25, 2000, P. L. 106-174, § 6, 114 Stat. 19) was repealed by Act Dec. 19, 2003, P. L. 108-194, § 4, 117 Stat. 2891. It related to the award of grants to certified regional poison control centers. For similar provisions, see 42 USCS § 300d-73.

CHAPTER 143. INTERCOUNTRY ADOPTIONS

CROSS REFERENCES

Hague Convention on Protection of Children and Co-operation in Respect of Intercountry Adoption, USCS Hague Intercountry.

§ 14901. Findings and purposes

(a) Findings. Congress recognizes—

(1) the international character of the Convention on Protection of Children and Co-operation in Respect of Intercountry Adoption (done at The Hague on May 29, 1993); and

(2) the need for uniform interpretation and implementation of the Convention in the United States and abroad,

and therefore finds that enactment of a Federal law governing adoptions and prospective adoptions subject to the Convention involving United States residents is essential.

(b) Purposes. The purposes of this Act are—
(1) to provide for implementation by the United States of the Convention;
(2) to protect the rights of, and prevent abuses against, children, birth families, and adoptive parents involved in adoptions (or prospective adoptions) subject to the Convention, and to ensure that such adoptions are in the children's best interests; and
(3) to improve the ability of the Federal Government to assist United States citizens seeking to adopt children from abroad and residents of other countries party to the Convention seeking to adopt children from the United States.
(Oct. 6, 2000, P. L. 106-279, § 2, 114 Stat. 825.)

HISTORY; ANCILLARY LAWS AND DIRECTIVES

References in text:
"This Act", referred to in this section, is Act Oct. 6, 2000, P. L. 106-279, popularly known as the Intercountry Adoption Act of 2000, which appears generally as 42 USCS §§ 14901 et seq. For full classification of such Act, consult USCS Tables volumes.

Effective date of section:
This section took effect on October 6, 2000, pursuant to § 505 of Act Oct. 6, 2000, P. L. 106-279, which appears as a note to this section.

Short title:
Act Oct. 6, 2000, P. L. 106-279, § 1(a), 114 Stat. 825, provides: "This Act [42 USCS §§ 14901 et seq. generally; for full classification, consult USCS Tables volumes] may be cited as the 'Intercountry Adoption Act of 2000'.".

Other provisions:
Intercountry Adoption Act of 2000; effective dates; transition rule. Act Oct. 6, 2000, P. L. 106-279, Title V, § 505, 114 Stat. 844, provides:

"(a) Effective dates. (1) Provisions effective upon enactment. Sections 2, 3, 101 through 103, 202 through 205, 401(a), 403, 503, and 505(a) [42 USCS §§ 14901, 14902, 14911–14913, 14922–14924, 14941(a), 14943, 14953, subsec. (a) of this note, and amendment of 42 USCS § 622] shall take effect on the date of the enactment of this Act.

"(2) Provisions effective upon the entry into force of the Convention. Subject to subsection (b), the provisions of this Act not specified in paragraph (1) [42 USCS §§ 14914, 14921, 14931, 14932, 14941(b), (c), 14942, 14944, 14951, 14952, 14954, subsec. (b) of this note, and amendments of 8 USCS §§ 1101 and 1154] shall take effect upon the entry into force of the Convention [the Hague Convention on Protection of Children and Co-operation in Respect of Intercountry Adoption] for the United States [April 1, 2008] pursuant to Article 46(2)(a) of the Convention.

"(b) Transition rule. The Convention and this Act [42 USCS §§ 14901 et seq. generally; for full classification, consult USCS Tables volumes] shall not apply—
  "(1) in the case of a child immigrating to the United States, if the application for advance processing of an orphan petition or petition to clas-

sify an orphan as an immediate relative for the child is filed before the effective date described in subsection (a)(2); or

"(2) in the case of a child emigrating from the United States, if the prospective adoptive parents of the child initiated the adoption process in their country of residence with the filing of an appropriate application before the effective date described in subsection (a)(2).".

CODE OF FEDERAL REGULATIONS

Department of State—Accreditation of agencies and approval of persons under the Intercountry Adoption Act of 2000 (IAA), 22 CFR 96.1 et seq.

Department of State—Issuance of adoption certificates and custody declarations in Hague Convention adoption cases, 22 CFR 97.1 et seq.

Department of State—Intercountry adoption—Convention record preservation, 22 CFR 98.1 et seq.

Department of State—Reporting on Convention and non-Convention adoptions of emigrating children, 22 CFR 99.1 et seq.

RESEARCH GUIDE

Am Jur:

2 Am Jur 2d, Adoption § 46.

Other Treatises:

2 Adoption Law and Practice (Matthew Bender), ch 11, Intercountry Adoption: Legal Requirements and Practical Considerations §§ 11.03, 11.07.

2 Adoption Law and Practice (Matthew Bender), ch 16, Liability of Adoption Agencies and Attorneys for Misconduct in the Disclosure of Health-Related Information § 16.03A.

Law Review Articles:

Smolin. Child Laundering: How the Intercountry Adoption System Legitimizes and Incentivizes the Practices of Buying, Trafficking, Kidnaping, and Stealing Children. 52 Wayne L Rev 113, Spring, 2006.

§ 14902. Definitions

As used in this Act:

(1) Accredited agency. The term "accredited agency" means an agency accredited under title II to provide adoption services in the United States in cases subject to the Convention.

(2) Accrediting entity. The term "accrediting entity" means an entity designated under section 202(a) [42 USCS § 14922(a)] to accredit agencies and approve persons under title II.

(3) Adoption service. The term "adoption service" means—

(A) identifying a child for adoption and arranging an adoption;

(B) securing necessary consent to termination of parental rights and to adoption;

(C) performing a background study on a child or a home study on a prospective adoptive parent, and reporting on such a study;

(D) making determinations of the best interests of a child and the appropriateness of adoptive placement for the child;

(E) post-placement monitoring of a case until final adoption; and

(F) where made necessary by disruption before final adoption, assuming custody and providing child care or any other social service pending an alternative placement.

The term "providing", with respect to an adoption service, includes facilitating the provision of the service.

(4) Agency. The term "agency" means any person other than an individual.

(5) Approved person. The term "approved person" means a person approved under title II to provide adoption services in the United States in cases subject to the Convention.

(6) Attorney General. Except as used in section 404 [42 USCS § 14944], the term "Attorney General" means the Attorney General, acting through the Commissioner of Immigration and Naturalization.

(7) Central authority. The term "central authority" means the entity designated as such by any Convention country under Article 6(1) of the Convention.

(8) Central authority function. The term "central authority function" means any duty required to be carried out by a central authority under the Convention.

(9) Convention. The term "Convention" means the Convention on Protection of Children and Co-operation in Respect of Intercountry Adoption, done at The Hague on May 29, 1993.

(10) Convention adoption. The term "Convention adoption" means an adoption of a child resident in a foreign country party to the Convention by a United States citizen, or an adoption of a child resident in the United States by an individual residing in another Convention country.

(11) Convention record. The term "Convention record" means any item, collection, or grouping of information contained in an electronic or physical document, an electronic collection of data, a photograph, an audio or video tape, or any other information storage medium of any type whatever that contains information about a specific past, current, or prospective Convention adoption (regardless of whether the adoption was made final) that has been preserved in accordance with section 401(a) [42 USCS § 14941(a)] by the Secretary of State or the Attorney General.

(12) Convention country. The term "Convention country" means a country party to the Convention.

(13) Other Convention country. The term "other Convention country" means a Convention country other than the United States.

(14) Person. The term "person" shall have the meaning provided in section 1 of title 1, United States Code, and shall not include any agency of government or tribal government entity.

(15) Person with an ownership or control interest. The term "person with an ownership or control interest" has the meaning given such term in section 1124(a)(3) of the Social Security Act (42 U.S.C. 1320a-3).

(16) Secretary. The term "Secretary" means the Secretary of State.

(17) State. The term "State" means the 50 States, the District of Columbia,

the Commonwealth of Puerto Rico, the Commonwealth of the Northern Mariana Islands, Guam, and the Virgin Islands.
(Oct. 6, 2000, P. L. 106-279, § 3, 114 Stat. 826.)

HISTORY; ANCILLARY LAWS AND DIRECTIVES

References in text:
"This Act", referred to in this section, is Act Oct. 6, 2000, P. L. 106-279, popularly known as the Intercountry Adoption Act of 2000, which appears generally as 42 USCS §§ 14901 et seq. For full classification of such Act, consult USCS Tables volumes.
"Title II", referred to in this section, is Title II of Act Oct. 6, 2000, P. L. 106-279, which appears generally as 42 USCS §§ 14921 et seq. For full classification of such Title, consult USCS Tables volumes.

Effective date of section:
This section took effect on October 6, 2000, pursuant to § 505 of Act Oct. 6, 2000, P. L. 106-279, which appears as 42 USCS § 14901 note.

Transfer of functions:
For abolition of the Immigration and Naturalization Service, transfer of functions, and treatment of related references, see transfer of functions note under 8 USCS § 1551.

RESEARCH GUIDE

Am Jur:
2 Am Jur 2d, Adoption § 46.

Other Treatises:
2 Adoption Law and Practice (Matthew Bender), ch 11, Intercountry Adoption: Legal Requirements and Practical Considerations § 11.07.
2 Adoption Law and Practice (Matthew Bender), ch 16, Liability of Adoption Agencies and Attorneys for Misconduct in the Disclosure of Health-Related Information § 16.03A.

UNITED STATES CENTRAL AUTHORITY

§ 14911. Designation of central authority

(a) In general. For purposes of the Convention and this Act—
(1) the Department of State shall serve as the central authority of the United States; and
(2) the Secretary shall serve as the head of the central authority of the United States.

(b) Performance of central authority functions. (1) Except as otherwise provided in this Act, the Secretary shall be responsible for the performance of all central authority functions for the United States under the Convention and this Act.
(2) All personnel of the Department of State performing core central authority functions in a professional capacity in the Office of Children's Issues shall have a strong background in consular affairs, personal experience in

international adoptions, or professional experience in international adoptions or child services.

(c) Authority to issue regulations. Except as otherwise provided in this Act, the Secretary may prescribe such regulations as may be necessary to carry out central authority functions on behalf of the United States.
(Oct. 6, 2000, P. L. 106-279, Title I, § 101, 114 Stat. 827.)

HISTORY; ANCILLARY LAWS AND DIRECTIVES

References in text:
"This Act", referred to in this section, is Act Oct. 6, 2000, P. L. 106-279, popularly known as the Intercountry Adoption Act of 2000, which appears generally as 42 USCS §§ 14901 et seq. For full classification of such Act, consult USCS Tables volumes.

Effective date of section:
This section took effect on October 6, 2000, pursuant to § 505 of Act Oct. 6, 2000, P. L. 106-279, which appears as 42 USCS § 14901 note.

CODE OF FEDERAL REGULATIONS

Department of State—Accreditation of agencies and approval of persons under the Intercountry Adoption Act of 2000 (IAA), 22 CFR 96.1 et seq.

Department of State—Issuance of adoption certificates and custody declarations in Hague Convention adoption cases, 22 CFR 97.1 et seq.

Department of State—Intercountry adoption—Convention record preservation, 22 CFR 98.1 et seq.

Department of State—Reporting on Convention and non-Convention adoptions of emigrating children, 22 CFR 99.1 et seq.

RESEARCH GUIDE

Am Jur:
2 Am Jur 2d, Adoption § 46.

Other Treatises:
2 Adoption Law and Practice (Matthew Bender), ch 16, Liability of Adoption Agencies and Attorneys for Misconduct in the Disclosure of Health-Related Information § 16.03A.

§ 14912. Responsibilities of the Secretary of State

(a) Liaison responsibilities. The Secretary shall have responsibility for—
(1) liaison with the central authorities of other Convention countries; and
(2) the coordination of activities under the Convention by persons subject to the jurisdiction of the United States.

(b) Information exchange. The Secretary shall be responsible for—
(1) providing the central authorities of other Convention countries with information concerning—
(A) accredited agencies and approved persons, agencies and persons whose accreditation or approval has been suspended or canceled, and agencies and persons who have been temporarily or permanently debarred from accreditation or approval;

(B) Federal and State laws relevant to implementing the Convention; and

(C) any other matters necessary and appropriate for implementation of the Convention;

(2) not later than the date of the entry into force of the Convention for the United States (pursuant to Article 46(2)(a) of the Convention) and at least once during each subsequent calendar year, providing to the central authority of all other Convention countries a notice requesting the central authority of each such country to specify any requirements of such country regarding adoption, including restrictions on the eligibility of persons to adopt, with respect to which information on the prospective adoptive parent or parents in the United States would be relevant;

(3) making responses to notices under paragraph (2) available to—

(A) accredited agencies and approved persons; and

(B) other persons or entities performing home studies under section 201(b)(1) [42 USCS § 14921(b)(1)];

(4) ensuring the provision of a background report (home study) on prospective adoptive parent or parents (pursuant to the requirements of section 203(b)(1)(A)(ii) [42 USCS § 14923(b)(1)(A)(ii)]), through the central authority of each child's country of origin, to the court having jurisdiction over the adoption (or, in the case of a child emigrating to the United States for the purpose of adoption, to the competent authority in the child's country of origin with responsibility for approving the child's emigration) in adequate time to be considered prior to the granting of such adoption or approval;

(5) providing Federal agencies, State courts, and accredited agencies and approved persons with an identification of Convention countries and persons authorized to perform functions under the Convention in each such country; and

(6) facilitating the transmittal of other appropriate information to, and among, central authorities, Federal and State agencies (including State courts), and accredited agencies and approved persons.

(c) Accreditation and approval responsibilities. The Secretary shall carry out the functions prescribed by the Convention with respect to the accreditation of agencies and the approval of persons to provide adoption services in the United States in cases subject to the Convention as provided in title II. Such functions may not be delegated to any other Federal agency.

(d) Additional responsibilities. The Secretary—

(1) shall monitor individual Convention adoption cases involving United States citizens; and

(2) may facilitate interactions between such citizens and officials of other Convention countries on matters relating to the Convention in any case in which an accredited agency or approved person is unwilling or unable to provide such facilitation.

(e) Establishment of registry. The Secretary and the Attorney General shall jointly establish a case registry of all adoptions involving immigration of children into the United States and emigration of children from the United States, regardless of whether the adoption occurs under the Convention. Such registry shall permit tracking of pending cases and retrieval of information on both pending and closed cases.

(f) Methods of performing responsibilities. The Secretary may—

(1) authorize public or private entities to perform appropriate central authority functions for which the Secretary is responsible, pursuant to regulations or under agreements published in the Federal Register; and

(2) carry out central authority functions through grants to, or contracts with, any individual or public or private entity, except as may be otherwise specifically provided in this Act.

(Oct. 6, 2000, P. L. 106-279, Title I, § 102, 114 Stat. 828.)

HISTORY; ANCILLARY LAWS AND DIRECTIVES

References in text:

"This Act", referred to in this section, is Act Oct. 6, 2000, P. L. 106-279, popularly known as the Intercountry Adoption Act of 2000, which appears generally as 42 USCS §§ 14901 et seq. For full classification of such Act, consult USCS Tables volumes.

"Title II", referred to in this section, is Title II of Act Oct. 6, 2000, P. L. 106-279, which appears generally as 42 USCS §§ 14921 et seq. For full classification of such Title, consult USCS Tables volumes.

Effective date of section:

This section took effect on October 6, 2000, pursuant to § 505 of Act Oct. 6, 2000, P. L. 106-279, which appears as 42 USCS § 14901 note.

CROSS REFERENCES

This section is referred to in 42 USCS §§ 14923, 14932.

RESEARCH GUIDE

Am Jur:

2 Am Jur 2d, Adoption § 46.

Other Treatises:

2 Adoption Law and Practice (Matthew Bender), ch 11, Intercountry Adoption: Legal Requirements and Practical Considerations § 11.07.

§ 14913. Responsibilities of the Attorney General

In addition to such other responsibilities as are specifically conferred upon the Attorney General by this Act, the central authority functions specified in Article 14 of the Convention (relating to the filing of applications by prospective adoptive parents to the central authority of their country of residence) shall be performed by the Attorney General.

(Oct. 6, 2000, P. L. 106-279, Title I, § 103, 114 Stat. 829.)

HISTORY; ANCILLARY LAWS AND DIRECTIVES

References in text:

"This Act", referred to in this section, is Act Oct. 6, 2000, P. L. 106-279, popularly known as the Intercountry Adoption Act of 2000, which appears generally as 42 USCS §§ 14901 et seq. For full classification of such Act, consult USCS Tables volumes.

Effective date of section:
This section took effect on October 6, 2000, pursuant to § 505 of Act Oct. 6, 2000, P. L. 106-279, which appears as 42 USCS § 14901 note.

RESEARCH GUIDE
Am Jur:
2 Am Jur 2d, Adoption § 46.

§ 14914. Annual report on intercountry adoptions

(a) Reports required. Beginning 1 year after the date of the entry into force of the Convention for the United States and each year thereafter, the Secretary, in consultation with the Attorney General and other appropriate agencies, shall submit a report describing the activities of the central authority of the United States under this Act during the preceding year to the Committee on International Relations [Committee on Foreign Affairs], the Committee on Ways and Means, and the Committee on the Judiciary of the House of Representatives and the Committee on Foreign Relations, the Committee on Finance, and the Committee on the Judiciary of the Senate.

(b) Report elements. Each report under subsection (a) shall set forth with respect to the year concerned, the following:

(1) The number of intercountry adoptions involving immigration to the United States, regardless of whether the adoption occurred under the Convention, including the country from which each child emigrated, the State to which each child immigrated, and the country in which the adoption was finalized.

(2) The number of intercountry adoptions involving emigration from the United States, regardless of whether the adoption occurred under the Convention, including the country to which each child immigrated and the State from which each child emigrated.

(3) The number of Convention placements for adoption in the United States that were disrupted, including the country from which the child emigrated, the age of the child, the date of the placement for adoption, the reasons for the disruption, the resolution of the disruption, the agencies that handled the placement for adoption, and the plans for the child, and in addition, any information regarding disruption or dissolution of adoptions of children from other countries received pursuant to section 422(b)(12) of the Social Security Act [42 USCS § 622(b)(12)].

(4) The average time required for completion of a Convention adoption, set forth by country from which the child emigrated.

(5) The current list of agencies accredited and persons approved under this Act to provide adoption services.

(6) The names of the agencies and persons temporarily or permanently debarred under this Act, and the reasons for the debarment.

(7) The range of adoption fees charged in connection with Convention adoptions involving immigration to the United States and the median of such fees set forth by the country of origin.

(8) The range of fees charged for accreditation of agencies and the approval

of persons in the United States engaged in providing adoption services under the Convention.

(Oct. 6, 2000, P. L. 106-279, Title I, § 104, 114 Stat. 829; Sept. 28, 2006, P. L. 109-288, § 6(f)((9), 120 Stat. 1248.)

HISTORY; ANCILLARY LAWS AND DIRECTIVES

References in text:
"This Act", referred to in this section, is Act Oct. 6, 2000, P. L. 106-279, popularly known as the Intercountry Adoption Act of 2000, which appears generally as 42 USCS §§ 14901 et seq. For full classification of such Act, consult USCS Tables volumes.

Explanatory notes:
"Committee on Foreign Affairs" has been inserted in brackets in subsec. (a) because the Committee on International Relations of the House of Representatives was renamed the Committee on Foreign Affairs of the House of Representatives by House Resolution No. 6, One Hundred Tenth Congress, Jan. 5, 2007.

Effective date of section:
Pursuant to § 505 of Act Oct. 6, 2000, P. L. 106-279, which appears as 42 USCS § 14901 note, this section takes effect upon the entry into force for the United States of the Hague Convention on Protection of Children and Co-operation in Respect of Intercountry Adoption [April 1, 2008].

Amendments:
2006. Act Sept. 28, 2006 (effective 10/1/2006 and applicable as provided by § 12(a) of such Act, which appears as 42 USCS § 621 note), in subsec. (b)(3), substituted "422(b)(12) of the Social Security Act" for "section 422(b)(14) of the Social Security Act, as amended by section 205 of this Act".

CROSS REFERENCES

This section is referred to in 42 USCS §§ 14923, 14953.

RESEARCH GUIDE

Am Jur:
2 Am Jur 2d, Adoption § 46.

PROVISIONS RELATING TO ACCREDITATION AND APPROVAL

CROSS REFERENCES

This title (42 USCS §§ 14921 et seq.) is referred to in 42 USCS §§ 14902, 14912, 14944.

§ 14921. Accreditation or approval required in order to provide adoption services in cases subject to the Convention

(a) In general. Except as otherwise provided in this title, no person may offer or provide adoption services in connection with a Convention adoption in the United States unless that person—

(1) is accredited or approved in accordance with this title; or

(2) is providing such services through or under the supervision and responsibility of an accredited agency or approved person.

(b) Exceptions. Subsection (a) shall not apply to the following:

(1) Background studies and home studies. The performance of a background study on a child or a home study on a prospective adoptive parent, or any report on any such study by a social work professional or organization who is not providing any other adoption service in the case, if the background or home study is approved by an accredited agency.

(2) Child welfare services. The provision of a child welfare service by a person who is not providing any other adoption service in the case.

(3) Legal services. The provision of legal services by a person who is not providing any adoption service in the case.

(4) Prospective adoptive parents acting on own behalf. The conduct of a prospective adoptive parent on his or her own behalf in the case, to the extent not prohibited by the law of the State in which the prospective adoptive parent resides.

(Oct. 6, 2000, P. L. 106-279, Title II, § 201, 114 Stat. 830.)

HISTORY; ANCILLARY LAWS AND DIRECTIVES

References in text:

"This title", referred to in this section, is Title II of Act Oct. 6, 2000, P. L. 106-279, which appears generally as 42 USCS §§ 14921 et seq. For full classification of such Title, consult USCS Tables volumes.

Effective date of section:

Pursuant to § 505 of Act Oct. 6, 2000, P. L. 106-279, which appears as 42 USCS § 14901 note, this section takes effect upon the entry into force for the United States of the Hague Convention on Protection of Children and Co-operation in Respect of Intercountry Adoption [April 1, 2008].

CODE OF FEDERAL REGULATIONS

Department of State—Accreditation of agencies and approval of persons under the Intercountry Adoption Act of 2000 (IAA), 22 CFR 96.1 et seq.

Department of State—Issuance of adoption certificates and custody declarations in Hague Convention adoption cases, 22 CFR 97.1 et seq.

Department of State—Intercountry adoption—Convention record preservation, 22 CFR 98.1 et seq.

Department of State—Reporting on Convention and non-Convention adoptions of emigrating children, 22 CFR 99.1 et seq.

CROSS REFERENCES

This section is referred to in 42 USCS §§ 14912, 14944.

RESEARCH GUIDE

Am Jur:

2 Am Jur 2d, Adoption § 46.

Other Treatises:

2 Adoption Law and Practice (Matthew Bender), ch 11, Intercountry Adoption: Legal Requirements and Practical Considerations § 11.07.

2 Adoption Law and Practice (Matthew Bender), ch 16, Liability of Adoption Agencies and Attorneys for Misconduct in the Disclosure of Health-Related Information § 16.03A.

§ 14922. Process for accreditation and approval; role of accrediting entities

(a) **Designation of accrediting entities.** (1) In general. The Secretary shall enter into agreements with one or more qualified entities under which such entities will perform the duties described in subsection (b) in accordance with the Convention, this title, and the regulations prescribed under section 203 [42 USCS § 14923], and upon entering into each such agreement shall designate the qualified entity as an accrediting entity.

(2) Qualified entities. In paragraph (1), the term "qualified entity" means—

(A) a nonprofit private entity that has expertise in developing and administering standards for entities providing child welfare services and that meets such other criteria as the Secretary may by regulation establish; or

(B) a public entity (other than a Federal entity), including an agency or instrumentality of State government having responsibility for licensing adoption agencies, that—

(i) has expertise in developing and administering standards for entities providing child welfare services;

(ii) accredits only agencies located in the State in which the public entity is located; and

(iii) meets such other criteria as the Secretary may by regulation establish.

(b) **Duties of accrediting entities.** The duties described in this subsection are the following:

(1) Accreditation and approval. Accreditation of agencies, and approval of persons, to provide adoption services in the United States in cases subject to the Convention.

(2) Oversight. Ongoing monitoring of the compliance of accredited agencies and approved persons with applicable requirements, including review of complaints against such agencies and persons in accordance with procedures established by the accrediting entity and approved by the Secretary.

(3) Enforcement. Taking of adverse actions (including requiring corrective action, imposing sanctions, and refusing to renew, suspending, or canceling accreditation or approval) for noncompliance with applicable requirements, and notifying the agency or person against whom adverse actions are taken of the deficiencies necessitating the adverse action.

(4) Data, records, and reports. Collection of data, maintenance of records, and reporting to the Secretary, the United States central authority, State courts, and other entities (including on persons and agencies granted or denied approval or accreditation), to the extent and in the manner that the Secretary requires.

(c) **Remedies for adverse action by accrediting entity.** (1) Correction of deficiency. An agency or person who is the subject of an adverse action by an accrediting entity may re-apply for accreditation or approval (or petition for termination of the adverse action) on demonstrating to the satisfaction of the accrediting entity that the deficiencies necessitating the adverse action have been corrected.

(2) No other administrative review. An adverse action by an accrediting entity shall not be subject to administrative review.

(3) Judicial review. An agency or person who is the subject of an adverse action by an accrediting entity may petition the United States district court in the judicial district in which the agency is located or the person resides to set aside the adverse action. The court shall review the adverse action in accordance with section 706 of title 5, United States Code, and for purposes of such review the accrediting entity shall be considered an agency within the meaning of section 701 of such title.

(d) Fees. The amount of fees assessed by accrediting entities for the costs of accreditation shall be subject to approval by the Secretary. Such fees may not exceed the costs of accreditation. In reviewing the level of such fees, the Secretary shall consider the relative size of, the geographic location of, and the number of Convention adoption cases managed by the agencies or persons subject to accreditation or approval by the accrediting entity.
(Oct. 6, 2000, P. L. 106-279, Title II, § 202, 114 Stat. 831.)

HISTORY; ANCILLARY LAWS AND DIRECTIVES

References in text:
"This title", referred to in this section, is Title II of Act Oct. 6, 2000, P. L. 106-279, which appears generally as 42 USCS §§ 14921 et seq. For full classification of such Title, consult USCS Tables volumes.

Effective date of section:
This section took effect on October 6, 2000, pursuant to § 505 of Act Oct. 6, 2000, P. L. 106-279, which appears as 42 USCS § 14901 note.

CROSS REFERENCES
This section is referred to in 42 USCS §§ 14902, 14924, 14953.

RESEARCH GUIDE
Am Jur:
2 Am Jur 2d, Adoption § 46.

Other Treatises:
2 Adoption Law and Practice (Matthew Bender), ch 11, Intercountry Adoption: Legal Requirements and Practical Considerations § 11.07.
2 Adoption Law and Practice (Matthew Bender), ch 16, Liability of Adoption Agencies and Attorneys for Misconduct in the Disclosure of Health-Related Information § 16.03A.

§ 14923. Standards and procedures for providing accreditation or approval

(a) In general. (1) Promulgation of regulations. The Secretary, shall, by regulation, prescribe the standards and procedures to be used by accrediting entities for the accreditation of agencies and the approval of persons to provide adoption services in the United States in cases subject to the Convention.

(2) Consideration of views. In developing such regulations, the Secretary shall consider any standards or procedures developed or proposed by, and the views of, individuals and entities with interest and expertise in international adoptions and family social services, including public and private entities with experience in licensing and accrediting adoption agencies.

(3) Applicability of notice and comment rules. Subsections (b), (c), and (d) of section 553 of title 5, United States Code, shall apply in the development and issuance of regulations under this section.

(b) Minimum requirements. (1) Accreditation. The standards prescribed under subsection (a) shall include the requirement that accreditation of an agency may not be provided or continued under this title unless the agency meets the following requirements:

    (A) Specific requirements. (i) The agency provides prospective adoptive parents of a child in a prospective Convention adoption a copy of the medical records of the child (which, to the fullest extent practicable, shall include an English-language translation of such records) on a date which is not later than the earlier of the date that is 2 weeks before: (I) the adoption; or (II) the date on which the prospective parents travel to a foreign country to complete all procedures in such country relating to the adoption.

    (ii) The agency ensures that a thorough background report (home study) on the prospective adoptive parent or parents has been completed in accordance with the Convention and with applicable Federal and State requirements and transmitted to the Attorney General with respect to each Convention adoption. Each such report shall include a criminal background check and a full and complete statement of all facts relevant to the eligibility of the prospective adopting parent or parents to adopt a child under any requirements specified by the central authority of the child's country of origin under section 102(b)(3) [42 USCS § 14912(b)(3)], including, in the case of a child emigrating to the United States for the purpose of adoption, the requirements of the child's country of origin applicable to adoptions taking place in such country. For purposes of this clause, the term "background report (home study)" includes any supplemental statement submitted by the agency to the Attorney General for the purpose of providing information relevant to any requirements specified by the child's country of origin.

    (iii) The agency provides prospective adoptive parents with a training program that includes counseling and guidance for the purpose of promoting a successful intercountry adoption before such parents travel to adopt the child or the child is placed with such parents for adoption.

    (iv) The agency employs personnel providing intercountry adoption services on a fee for service basis rather than on a contingent fee basis.

    (v) The agency discloses fully its policies and practices, the disruption rates of its placements for intercountry adoption, and all fees charged by such agency for intercountry adoption.

(B) Capacity to provide adoption services. The agency has, directly or through arrangements with other persons, a sufficient number of appropriately trained and qualified personnel, sufficient financial resources, appropriate organizational structure, and appropriate procedures to enable the agency to provide, in accordance with this Act, all adoption services in cases subject to the Convention.

(C) Use of social service professionals. The agency has established procedures designed to ensure that social service functions requiring the application of clinical skills and judgment are performed only by professionals with appropriate qualifications and credentials.

(D) Records, reports, and information matters. The agency is capable of—

(i) maintaining such records and making such reports as may be required by the Secretary, the United States central authority, and the accrediting entity that accredits the agency;

(ii) cooperating with reviews, inspections, and audits;

(iii) safeguarding sensitive individual information; and

(iv) complying with other requirements concerning information management necessary to ensure compliance with the Convention, this Act, and any other applicable law.

(E) Liability insurance. The agency agrees to have in force adequate liability insurance for professional negligence and any other insurance that the Secretary considers appropriate.

(F) Compliance with applicable rules. The agency has established adequate measures to comply (and to ensure compliance of their agents and clients) with the Convention, this Act, and any other applicable law.

(G) Nonprofit organization with State license to provide adoption services. The agency is a private nonprofit organization licensed to provide adoption services in at least one State.

(2) Approval. The standards prescribed under subsection (a) shall include the requirement that a person shall not be approved under this title unless the person is a private for-profit entity that meets the requirements of subparagraphs (A) through (F) of paragraph (1) of this subsection.

(3) Renewal of accreditation or approval. The standards prescribed under subsection (a) shall provide that the accreditation of an agency or approval of a person under this title shall be for a period of not less than 3 years and not more than 5 years, and may be renewed on a showing that the agency or person meets the requirements applicable to original accreditation or approval under this title.

(c) **Temporary registration of community based agencies.** (1) One-year registration period for medium community based agencies. For a 1-year period after the entry into force of the Convention and notwithstanding subsection (b), the Secretary may provide, in regulations issued pursuant to subsection (a), that an agency may register with the Secretary and be accredited to provide adoption services in the United States in cases subject to the Convention during such period if the agency has provided adoption services in fewer than 100 intercountry adoptions in the preceding calendar year and meets the criteria described in paragraph (3).

(2) Two-year registration period for small community-based agencies. For a 2-year period after the entry into force of the Convention and notwithstanding subsection (b), the Secretary may provide, in regulations issued pursuant to subsection (a), that an agency may register with the Secretary and be accredited to provide adoption services in the United States in cases subject to the Convention during such period if the agency has provided adoption services in fewer than 50 intercountry adoptions in the preceding calendar year and meets the criteria described in paragraph (3).

(3) Criteria for registration. Agencies registered under this subsection shall meet the following criteria:

(A) The agency is licensed in the State in which it is located and is a nonprofit agency.

(B) The agency has been providing adoption services in connection with intercountry adoptions for at least 3 years.

(C) The agency has demonstrated that it will be able to provide the United States Government with all information related to the elements described in section 104(b) [42 USCS § 14914(b)] and provides such information.

(D) The agency has initiated the process of becoming accredited under the provisions of this Act and is actively taking steps to become an accredited agency.

(E) The agency has not been found to be involved in any improper conduct relating to intercountry adoptions.

(Oct. 6, 2000, P. L. 106-279, Title II, § 203, 114 Stat. 832.)

HISTORY; ANCILLARY LAWS AND DIRECTIVES

References in text:

"This Act", referred to in this section, is Act Oct. 6, 2000, P. L. 106-279, popularly known as the Intercountry Adoption Act of 2000, which appears generally as 42 USCS §§ 14901 et seq. For full classification of such Act, consult USCS Tables volumes.

"This title", referred to in this section, is Title II of Act Oct. 6, 2000, P. L. 106-279, which appears generally as 42 USCS §§ 14921 et seq. For full classification of such Title, consult USCS Tables volumes.

Effective date of section:

This section took effect on October 6, 2000, pursuant to § 505 of Act Oct. 6, 2000, P. L. 106-279, which appears as 42 USCS § 14901 note.

CROSS REFERENCES

This section is referred to in 42 USCS §§ 14912, 14922, 14924.

RESEARCH GUIDE

Am Jur:

2 Am Jur 2d, Adoption §§ 46, 47.

Other Treatises:

2 Adoption Law and Practice (Matthew Bender), ch 11, Intercountry Adoption: Legal Requirements and Practical Considerations § 11.07.

2 Adoption Law and Practice (Matthew Bender), ch 16, Liability of Adoption Agencies and Attorneys for Misconduct in the Disclosure of Health-Related Information § 16.03A.

§ 14924. Secretarial oversight of accreditation and approval

(a) Oversight of accrediting entities. The Secretary shall—

(1) monitor the performance by each accrediting entity of its duties under section 202 [42 USCS § 14922] and its compliance with the requirements of the Convention, this Act, other applicable laws, and implementing regulations under this Act; and

(2) suspend or cancel the designation of an accrediting entity found to be substantially out of compliance with the Convention, this Act, other applicable laws, or implementing regulations under this Act.

(b) Suspension or cancellation of accreditation or approval. (1) Secretary's authority. The Secretary shall suspend or cancel the accreditation or approval granted by an accrediting entity to an agency or person pursuant to section 202 [42 USCS § 14922] when the Secretary finds that—

(A) the agency or person is substantially out of compliance with applicable requirements; and

(B) the accrediting entity has failed or refused, after consultation with the Secretary, to take appropriate enforcement action.

(2) Correction of deficiency. At any time when the Secretary is satisfied that the deficiencies on the basis of which an adverse action is taken under paragraph (1) have been corrected, the Secretary shall—

(A) notify the accrediting entity that the deficiencies have been corrected; and

(B)(i) in the case of a suspension, terminate the suspension; or

(ii) in the case of a cancellation, notify the agency or person that the agency or person may re-apply to the accrediting entity for accreditation or approval.

(c) Debarment. (1) Secretary's authority. On the initiative of the Secretary, or on request of an accrediting entity, the Secretary may temporarily or permanently debar an agency from accreditation or a person from approval under this title, but only if—

(A) there is substantial evidence that the agency or person is out of compliance with applicable requirements; and

(B) there has been a pattern of serious, willful, or grossly negligent failures to comply or other aggravating circumstances indicating that continued accreditation or approval would not be in the best interests of the children and families concerned.

(2) Period of debarment. The Secretary's debarment order shall state whether the debarment is temporary or permanent. If the debarment is temporary, the Secretary shall specify a date, not earlier than 3 years after the date of the order, on or after which the agency or person may apply to the Secretary for withdrawal of the debarment.

(3) Effect of debarment. An accrediting entity may take into account the

circumstances of the debarment of an agency or person that has been debarred pursuant to this subsection in considering any subsequent application of the agency or person, or of any other entity in which the agency or person has an ownership or control interest, for accreditation or approval under this title.

(d) Judicial review. A person (other than a prospective adoptive parent), an agency, or an accrediting entity who is the subject of a final action of suspension, cancellation, or debarment by the Secretary under this title may petition the United States District Court for the District of Columbia or the United States district court in the judicial district in which the person resides or the agency or accrediting entity is located to set aside the action. The court shall review the action in accordance with section 706 of title 5, United States Code.

(e) Failure to ensure a full and complete home study. (1) In general. Willful, grossly negligent, or repeated failure to ensure the completion and transmission of a background report (home study) that fully complies with the requirements of section 203(b)(1)(A)(ii) [42 USCS § 14923(b)(1)(A)(ii)] shall constitute substantial noncompliance with applicable requirements.

(2) Regulations. Regulations promulgated under section 203 [42 USCS § 14923] shall provide for—

(A) frequent and careful monitoring of compliance by agencies and approved persons with the requirements of section 203(b)[(1)](A)(ii) [42 USCS § 14923(b)(1)(A)(ii)]; and

(B) consultation between the Secretary and the accrediting entity where an agency or person has engaged in substantial noncompliance with the requirements of section 203(b)[(1)](A)(ii) [42 USCS § 14923(b)(1)(A)(ii)], unless the accrediting entity has taken appropriate corrective action and the noncompliance has not recurred.

(3) Repeated failures to comply. Repeated serious, willful, or grossly negligent failures to comply with the requirements of section 203(b)(1)(A)(ii) [42 USCS § 14923(b)(1)(A)(ii)] by an agency or person after consultation between Secretary and the accrediting entity with respect to previous noncompliance by such agency or person shall constitute a pattern of serious, willful, or grossly negligent failures to comply under subsection (c)(1)(B).

(4) Failure to comply with certain requirements. A failure to comply with the requirements of section 203(b)(1)(A)(ii) [42 USCS § 14923(b)(1)(A)(ii)] shall constitute a serious failure to comply under subsection (c)(1)(B) unless it is shown by clear and convincing evidence that such noncompliance had neither the purpose nor the effect of determining the outcome of a decision or proceeding by a court or other competent authority in the United States or the child's country of origin.

(Oct. 6, 2000, P. L. 106-279, Title II, § 204, 114 Stat. 835.)

HISTORY; ANCILLARY LAWS AND DIRECTIVES

References in text:

"This Act", referred to in this section, is Act Oct. 6, 2000, P. L. 106-279, popularly known as the Intercountry Adoption Act of 2000, which appears generally as 42 USCS §§ 14901 et seq. For full classification of such Act, consult USCS Tables volumes.

"This title", referred to in this section, is Title II of Act Oct. 6, 2000, P. L. 106-279, which appears generally as 42 USCS §§ 14921 et seq. For full classification of such Title, consult USCS Tables volumes.

Explanatory notes:

The paragraph designator "(1)" has been inserted in brackets in subparas. (A) and (B) of subsec. (e)(2) to indicate the probable intent of Congress to include such designator.

Effective date of section:

This section took effect on October 6, 2000, pursuant to § 505 of Act Oct. 6, 2000, P. L. 106-279, which appears as 42 USCS § 14901 note.

RESEARCH GUIDE

Am Jur:

2 Am Jur 2d, Adoption § 46.

Other Treatises:

2 Adoption Law and Practice (Matthew Bender), ch 11, Intercountry Adoption: Legal Requirements and Practical Considerations § 11.07.

2 Adoption Law and Practice (Matthew Bender), ch 16, Liability of Adoption Agencies and Attorneys for Misconduct in the Disclosure of Health-Related Information § 16.03A.

RECOGNITION OF CONVENTION ADOPTIONS IN THE UNITED STATES

§ 14931. Adoptions of children immigrating to the United States

(a) **Legal effect of certificates issued by the Secretary of State.** (1) Issuance of certificates by the Secretary of State. The Secretary of State shall, with respect to each Convention adoption, issue a certificate to the adoptive citizen parent domiciled in the United States that the adoption has been granted or, in the case of a prospective adoptive citizen parent, that legal custody of the child has been granted to the citizen parent for purposes of emigration and adoption, pursuant to the Convention and this Act, if the Secretary of State—

   (A) receives appropriate notification from the central authority of such child's country of origin; and

   (B) has verified that the requirements of the Convention and this Act have been met with respect to the adoption.

(2) Legal effect of certificates. If appended to an original adoption decree, the certificate described in paragraph (1) shall be treated by Federal and State agencies, courts, and other public and private persons and entities as conclusive evidence of the facts certified therein and shall constitute the certification required by section 204(d)(2) of the Immigration and Nationality Act [8 USCS § 1154(d)], as amended by this Act.

(b) **Legal effect of Convention adoption finalized in another Convention**

country. A final adoption in another Convention country, certified by the Secretary of State pursuant to subsection (a) of this section or section 303(c) [42 USCS § 14932(c)], shall be recognized as a final valid adoption for purposes of all Federal, State, and local laws of the United States.

(c) Condition on finalization of Convention adoption by State court. In the case of a child who has entered the United States from another Convention country for the purpose of adoption, an order declaring the adoption final shall not be entered unless the Secretary of State has issued the certificate provided for in subsection (a) with respect to the adoption.
(Oct. 6, 2000, P. L. 106-279, Title III, § 301, 114 Stat. 837.)

HISTORY; ANCILLARY LAWS AND DIRECTIVES

References in text:
"This Act", referred to in this section, is Act Oct. 6, 2000, P. L. 106-279, popularly known as the Intercountry Adoption Act of 2000, which appears generally as 42 USCS §§ 14901 et seq. For full classification of such Act, consult USCS Tables volumes.

Effective date of section:
Pursuant to § 505 of Act Oct. 6, 2000, P. L. 106-279, which appears as 42 USCS § 14901 note, this section takes effect upon the entry into force for the United States of the Hague Convention on Protection of Children and Co-operation in Respect of Intercountry Adoption [April 1, 2008].

CODE OF FEDERAL REGULATIONS

Department of State—Accreditation of agencies and approval of persons under the Intercountry Adoption Act of 2000 (IAA), 22 CFR 96.1 et seq.

Department of State—Issuance of adoption certificates and custody declarations in Hague Convention adoption cases, 22 CFR 97.1 et seq.

Department of State—Intercountry adoption—Convention record preservation, 22 CFR 98.1 et seq.

Department of State—Reporting on Convention and non-Convention adoptions of emigrating children, 22 CFR 99.1 et seq.

RESEARCH GUIDE

Am Jur:
2 Am Jur 2d, Adoption § 48.

Other Treatises:
2 Adoption Law and Practice (Matthew Bender), ch 11, Intercountry Adoption: Legal Requirements and Practical Considerations § 11.07.
2 Adoption Law and Practice (Matthew Bender), ch 16, Liability of Adoption Agencies and Attorneys for Misconduct in the Disclosure of Health-Related Information § 16.03A.

§ 14932. Adoptions of children emigrating from the United States

(a) Duties of accredited agency or approved person. In the case of a Convention adoption involving the emigration of a child residing in the United States to a foreign country, the accredited agency or approved person providing adoption services, or the prospective adoptive parent or parents acting on their own behalf (if permitted by the laws of such other Convention country in which they reside and the laws of the State in which the child resides), shall do the following:

(1) Ensure that, in accordance with the Convention—

(A) a background study on the child is completed;

(B) the accredited agency or approved person—

(i) has made reasonable efforts to actively recruit and make a diligent search for prospective adoptive parents to adopt the child in the United States; and

(ii) despite such efforts, has not been able to place the child for adoption in the United States in a timely manner; and

(C) a determination is made that placement with the prospective adoptive parent or parents is in the best interests of the child.

(2) Furnish to the State court with jurisdiction over the case—

(A) documentation of the matters described in paragraph (1);

(B) a background report (home study) on the prospective adoptive parent or parents (including a criminal background check) prepared in accordance with the laws of the receiving country; and

(C) a declaration by the central authority (or other competent authority) of such other Convention country—

(i) that the child will be permitted to enter and reside permanently, or on the same basis as the adopting parent, in the receiving country; and

(ii) that the central authority (or other competent authority) of such other Convention country consents to the adoption, if such consent is necessary under the laws of such country for the adoption to become final.

(3) Furnish to the United States central authority—

(A) official copies of State court orders certifying the final adoption or grant of custody for the purpose of adoption;

(B) the information and documents described in paragraph (2), to the extent required by the United States central authority; and

(C) any other information concerning the case required by the United States central authority to perform the functions specified in subsection (c) or otherwise to carry out the duties of the United States central authority under the Convention.

(b) Conditions on State court orders. An order declaring an adoption to be final or granting custody for the purpose of adoption in a case described in subsection (a) shall not be entered unless the court—

(1) has received and verified to the extent the court may find necessary—

(A) the material described in subsection (a)(2); and

(B) satisfactory evidence that the requirements of Articles 4 and 15 through 21 of the Convention have been met; and

(2) has determined that the adoptive placement is in the best interests of the child.

(c) Duties of the Secretary of State. In a case described in subsection (a), the Secretary, on receipt and verification as necessary of the material and information described in subsection (a)(3), shall issue, as applicable, an official certification that the child has been adopted or a declaration that custody for purposes of adoption has been granted, in accordance with the Convention and this Act.

(d) Filing with registry regarding non-Convention adoptions. Accredited agencies, approved persons, and other persons, including governmental authorities, providing adoption services in an intercountry adoption not subject to the Convention that involves the emigration of a child from the United States shall file information required by regulations jointly issued by the Attorney General and the Secretary of State for purposes of implementing section 102(e) [42 USCS § 14912(e)].

(Oct. 6, 2000, P. L. 106-279, Title III, § 303, 114 Stat. 839.)

HISTORY; ANCILLARY LAWS AND DIRECTIVES

References in text:
"This Act", referred to in this section, is Act Oct. 6, 2000, P. L. 106-279, popularly known as the Intercountry Adoption Act of 2000, which appears generally as 42 USCS §§ 14901 et seq. For full classification of such Act, consult USCS Tables volumes.

Effective date of section:
Pursuant to § 505 of Act Oct. 6, 2000, P. L. 106-279, which appears as 42 USCS § 14901 note, this section takes effect upon the entry into force for the United States of the Hague Convention on Protection of Children and Co-operation in Respect of Intercountry Adoption [April 1, 2008].

CROSS REFERENCES
This section is referred to in 42 USCS §§ 14931, 14953.

RESEARCH GUIDE
Am Jur:
2 Am Jur 2d, Adoption § 48.

Other Treatises:
2 Adoption Law and Practice (Matthew Bender), ch 11, Intercountry Adoption: Legal Requirements and Practical Considerations § 11.07.

ADMINISTRATION AND ENFORCEMENT

§ 14941. Access to Convention records

(a) Preservation of Convention records. (1) In general. Not later than 180 days after the date of the enactment of this Act [enacted Oct. 6, 2000], the Secretary, in consultation with the Attorney General, shall issue regulations that establish procedures and requirements in accordance with the Convention and this section for the preservation of Convention records.

(2) Applicability of notice and comment rules. Subsections (b), (c), and (d) of section 553 of title 5, United States Code, shall apply in the development and issuance of regulations under this section.

(b) Access to Convention records. (1) Prohibition. Except as provided in paragraph (2), the Secretary or the Attorney General may disclose a Convention record, and access to such a record may be provided in whole or in part, only if such record is maintained under the authority of the and disclosure of, or access to, such record is permitted or required by applicable Federal law.

(2) Exception for administration of the convention. A Convention record may be disclosed, and access to such a record may be provided, in whole or in part, among the Secretary, the Attorney General, central authorities, accredited agencies, and approved persons, only to the extent necessary to administer the Convention or this Act.

(3) Penalties for unlawful disclosure. Unlawful disclosure of all or part of a Convention record shall be punishable in accordance with applicable Federal law.

(c) Access to non-Convention records. Disclosure of, access to, and penalties for unlawful disclosure of, adoption records that are not Convention records, including records of adoption proceedings conducted in the United States, shall be governed by applicable State law.

(Oct. 6, 2000, P. L. 106-279, Title IV, § 401, 114 Stat. 841.)

HISTORY; ANCILLARY LAWS AND DIRECTIVES

References in text:

"This Act", referred to in this section, is Act Oct. 6, 2000, P. L. 106-279, popularly known as the Intercountry Adoption Act of 2000, which appears generally as 42 USCS §§ 14901 et seq. For full classification of such Act, consult USCS Tables volumes.

The "Immigration and Nationality Act", referred to in this section, is Act June 27, 1952, ch 477, which appears generally as 8 USCS §§ 1101 et seq. For full classification of such Act, consult USCS Tables volumes.

Effective date of section:

Pursuant to § 505 of Act Oct. 6, 2000, P. L. 106-279, which appears as 42 USCS § 14901 note, subsec. (a) of this section took effect on October 6, 2000, and subsecs. (b) and (c) of this section take effect upon the entry into force for the United States of the Hague Convention on Protection of Children and Co-operation in Respect of Intercountry Adoption [April 1, 2008].

CODE OF FEDERAL REGULATIONS

Department of State—Accreditation of agencies and approval of persons under the Intercountry Adoption Act of 2000 (IAA), 22 CFR 96.1 et seq.

Department of State—Issuance of adoption certificates and custody declarations in Hague Convention adoption cases, 22 CFR 97.1 et seq.

Department of State—Intercountry adoption—Convention record preservation, 22 CFR 98.1 et seq.

Department of State—Reporting on Convention and non-Convention adoptions of emigrating children, 22 CFR 99.1 et seq.

CROSS REFERENCES

This section is referred to in 42 USCS § 14902.

RESEARCH GUIDE
Other Treatises:
2 Adoption Law and Practice (Matthew Bender), ch 16, Liability of Adoption Agencies and Attorneys for Misconduct in the Disclosure of Health-Related Information § 16.03A.

§ 14942. Documents of other Convention countries

Documents originating in any other Convention country and related to a Convention adoption case shall require no authentication in order to be admissible in any Federal, State, or local court in the United States, unless a specific and supported claim is made that the documents are false, have been altered, or are otherwise unreliable.

(Oct. 6, 2000, P. L. 106-279, Title IV, § 402, 114 Stat. 841.)

HISTORY; ANCILLARY LAWS AND DIRECTIVES
Effective date of section:
Pursuant to § 505 of Act Oct. 6, 2000, P. L. 106-279, which appears as 42 USCS § 14901 note, this section takes effect upon the entry into force for the United States of the Hague Convention on Protection of Children and Co-operation in Respect of Intercountry Adoption [April 1, 2008].

§ 14943. Authorization of appropriations; collection of fees

(a) **Authorization of appropriations.** (1) In general. There are authorized to be appropriated such sums as may be necessary to agencies of the Federal Government implementing the Convention and the provisions of this Act.

(2) Availability of funds. Amounts appropriated pursuant to paragraph (1) are authorized to remain available until expended.

(b) **Assessment of fees.** (1) The Secretary may charge a fee for new or enhanced services that will be undertaken by the Department of State to meet the requirements of this Act with respect to intercountry adoptions under the Convention and comparable services with respect to other intercountry adoptions. Such fee shall be prescribed by regulation and shall not exceed the cost of such services.

(2) Fees collected under paragraph (1) shall be retained and deposited as an offsetting collection to any Department of State appropriation to recover the costs of providing such services. Such fees shall remain available for obligation until expended.

(c) **Restriction.** No funds collected under the authority of this section may be made available to an accrediting entity to carry out the purposes of this Act.

(Oct. 6, 2000, P. L. 106-279, Title IV, § 403, 114 Stat. 841; Sept. 30, 2002, P. L. 107-228, Div A, Title II, Subtitle A, § 211(a), 116 Stat. 1365.)

HISTORY; ANCILLARY LAWS AND DIRECTIVES

References in text:
"This Act", referred to in this section, is Act Oct. 6, 2000, P. L. 106-279, popularly known as the Intercountry Adoption Act of 2000, which appears

generally as 42 USCS §§ 14901 et seq. For full classification of such Act, consult USCS Tables volumes.

Effective date of section:
This section took effect on October 6, 2000, pursuant to § 505 of Act Oct. 6, 2000, P. L. 106-279, which appears as 42 USCS § 14901 note.

Amendments:
2002. Act Sept. 30, 2002, in subsec. (b), in para. (2), added the sentence beginning "Such fees . . .", and deleted para. (3), which read: "(3) Fees authorized under this section shall be available for obligation only to the extent and in the amount provided in advance in appropriations Acts.".

§ 14944. Enforcement

(a) Civil penalties. Any person who—

(1) violates section 201 [42 USCS § 14921];

(2) makes a false or fraudulent statement, or misrepresentation, with respect to a material fact, or offers, gives, solicits, or accepts inducement by way of compensation, intended to influence or affect in the United States or a foreign country—

(A) a decision by an accrediting entity with respect to the accreditation of an agency or approval of a person under title II;

(B) the relinquishment of parental rights or the giving of parental consent relating to the adoption of a child in a case subject to the Convention; or

(C) a decision or action of any entity performing a central authority function; or

(3) engages another person as an agent, whether in the United States or in a foreign country, who in the course of that agency takes any of the actions described in paragraph (1) or (2),

shall be subject, in addition to any other penalty that may be prescribed by law, to a civil money penalty of not more than $50,000 for a first violation, and not more than $100,000 for each succeeding violation.

(b) Civil enforcement. (1) Authority of Attorney General. The Attorney General may bring a civil action to enforce subsection (a) against any person in any United States district court.

(2) Factors to be considered in imposing penalties. In imposing penalties the court shall consider the gravity of the violation, the degree of culpability of the defendant, and any history of prior violations by the defendant.

(c) Criminal penalties. Whoever knowingly and willfully violates paragraph (1) or (2) of subsection (a) shall be subject to a fine of not more than $250,000, imprisonment for not more than 5 years, or both.

(Oct. 6, 2000, P. L. 106-279, Title IV, § 404, 114 Stat. 842.)

HISTORY; ANCILLARY LAWS AND DIRECTIVES

References in text:
"Title II", referred to in this section, is Title II of Act Oct. 6, 2000, P. L. 106-279, which appears generally as 42 USCS §§ 14921 et seq. For full classification of such Title, consult USCS Tables volumes.

Effective date of section:
Pursuant to § 505 of Act Oct. 6, 2000, P. L. 106-279, which appears as 42 USCS § 14901 note, this section takes effect upon the entry into force for the United States of the Hague Convention on Protection of Children and Co-operation in Respect of Intercountry Adoption [April 1, 2008].

CROSS REFERENCES
This section is referred to in 42 USCS § 14902.

RESEARCH GUIDE
Am Jur:
2 Am Jur 2d, Adoption § 46.

Other Treatises:
2 Adoption Law and Practice (Matthew Bender), ch 11, Intercountry Adoption: Legal Requirements and Practical Considerations § 11.07.

GENERAL PROVISIONS

§ 14951. Recognition of Convention adoptions

Subject to Article 24 of the Convention, adoptions concluded between two other Convention countries that meet the requirements of Article 23 of the Convention and that became final before the date of entry into force of the Convention for the United States shall be recognized thereafter in the United States and given full effect. Such recognition shall include the specific effects described in Article 26 of the Convention.
(Oct. 6, 2000, P. L. 106-279, Title V, § 501, 114 Stat. 843.)

HISTORY; ANCILLARY LAWS AND DIRECTIVES
Effective date of section:
Pursuant to § 505 of Act Oct. 6, 2000, P. L. 106-279, which appears as 42 USCS § 14901 note, this section takes effect upon the entry into force for the United States of the Hague Convention on Protection of Children and Co-operation in Respect of Intercountry Adoption [April 1, 2008].

CODE OF FEDERAL REGULATIONS
Department of State—Accreditation of agencies and approval of persons under the Intercountry Adoption Act of 2000 (IAA), 22 CFR 96.1 et seq.
Department of State—Issuance of adoption certificates and custody declarations in Hague Convention adoption cases, 22 CFR 97.1 et seq.
Department of State—Intercountry adoption—Convention record preservation, 22 CFR 98.1 et seq.
Department of State—Reporting on Convention and non-Convention adoptions of emigrating children, 22 CFR 99.1 et seq.

RESEARCH GUIDE
Other Treatises:
2 Adoption Law and Practice (Matthew Bender), ch 16, Liability of Adoption Agencies and Attorneys for Misconduct in the Disclosure of Health-Related Information § 16.03A.

§ 14952. Special rules for certain cases

(a) Authority to establish alternative procedures for adoption of children by relatives. To the extent consistent with the Convention, the Secretary may establish by regulation alternative procedures for the adoption of children by individuals related to them by blood, marriage, or adoption, in cases subject to the Convention.

(b) Waiver authority. (1) In general. Notwithstanding any other provision of this Act, to the extent consistent with the Convention, the Secretary may, on a case-by-case basis, waive applicable requirements of this Act or regulations issued under this Act, in the interests of justice or to prevent grave physical harm to the child.

(2) Nondelegation. The authority provided by paragraph (1) may not be delegated.

(Oct. 6, 2000, P. L. 106-279, Title V, § 502, 114 Stat. 843.)

HISTORY; ANCILLARY LAWS AND DIRECTIVES

References in text:

"This Act", referred to in this section, is Act Oct. 6, 2000, P. L. 106-279, popularly known as the Intercountry Adoption Act of 2000, which appears generally as 42 USCS §§ 14901 et seq. For full classification of such Act, consult USCS Tables volumes.

Effective date of section:

Pursuant to § 505 of Act Oct. 6, 2000, P. L. 106-279, which appears as 42 USCS § 14901 note, this section takes effect upon the entry into force for the United States of the Hague Convention on Protection of Children and Co-operation in Respect of Intercountry Adoption [April 1, 2008].

RESEARCH GUIDE

Am Jur:

2 Am Jur 2d, Adoption § 47.

Other Treatises:

2 Adoption Law and Practice (Matthew Bender), ch 11, Intercountry Adoption: Legal Requirements and Practical Considerations § 11.07.

§ 14953. Relationship to other laws

(a) Preemption of inconsistent State law. The Convention and this Act shall not be construed to preempt any provision of the law of any State or political subdivision thereof, or prevent a State or political subdivision thereof from enacting any provision of law with respect to the subject matter of the Convention or this Act, except to the extent that such provision of State law is inconsistent with the Convention or this Act, and then only to the extent of the inconsistency.

(b) Applicability of the Indian Child Welfare Act. The Convention and this Act shall not be construed to affect the application of the Indian Child Welfare Act of 1978 (25 U.S.C. 1901 et seq.).

(c) Relationship to other laws. Sections 3506(c), 3507, and 3512 of title 44,

United States Code, shall not apply to information collection for purposes of sections 104, 202(b)(4), and 303(d) of this Act [42 USCS §§ 14914, 14922(b)(4), and 14932(d)] or for use as a Convention record as defined in this Act.

(Oct. 6, 2000, P. L. 106-279, Title V, § 503, 114 Stat. 843.)

HISTORY; ANCILLARY LAWS AND DIRECTIVES

References in text:

"This Act", referred to in this section, is Act Oct. 6, 2000, P. L. 106-279, popularly known as the Intercountry Adoption Act of 2000, which appears generally as 42 USCS §§ 14901 et seq. For full classification of such Act, consult USCS Tables volumes.

Effective date of section:

This section took effect on October 6, 2000, pursuant to § 505 of Act Oct. 6, 2000, P. L. 106-279, which appears as 42 USCS § 14901 note.

RESEARCH GUIDE

Other Treatises:

2 Adoption Law and Practice (Matthew Bender), ch 11, Intercountry Adoption: Legal Requirements and Practical Considerations § 11.07.

§ 14954.   No private right of action

The Convention and this Act shall not be construed to create a private right of action to seek administrative or judicial relief, except to the extent expressly provided in this Act.

(Oct. 6, 2000, P. L. 106-279, Title V, § 504, 114 Stat. 843.)

HISTORY; ANCILLARY LAWS AND DIRECTIVES

References in text:

"This Act", referred to in this section, is Act Oct. 6, 2000, P. L. 106-279, popularly known as the Intercountry Adoption Act of 2000, which appears generally as 42 USCS §§ 14901 et seq. For full classification of such Act, consult USCS Tables volumes.

Effective date of section:

Pursuant to § 505 of Act Oct. 6, 2000, P. L. 106-279, which appears as 42 USCS § 14901 note, this section takes effect upon the entry into force for the United States of the Hague Convention on Protection of Children and Co-operation in Respect of Intercountry Adoption [April 1, 2008].

RESEARCH GUIDE

Am Jur:

2 Am Jur 2d, Adoption § 46.

CHAPTER 144. DEVELOPMENTAL DISABILITIES ASSISTANCE AND BILL OF RIGHTS

PROGRAMS FOR INDIVIDUALS WITH DEVELOPMENTAL DISABILITIES

General Provisions

CROSS REFERENCES

This Act (42 USCS §§ 15001 et seq.) is referred to in 29 USCS §§ 762, 781, 794e; 40 USCS § 14502; 42 USCS §§ 280i-1, 300a-7, 3013.

PROGRAMS FOR INDIVIDUALS WITH DEVELOPMENTAL DISABILITIES

CROSS REFERENCES

This title (42 USCS §§ 15001 et seq.) is referred to in 42 USCS § 15114.

General Provisions

§ 15001.   Findings, purposes, and policy

(a) Findings. Congress finds that—

(1) disability is a natural part of the human experience that does not diminish the right of individuals with developmental disabilities to live independently, to exert control and choice over their own lives, and to fully participate in and contribute to their communities through full integration and inclusion in the economic, political, social, cultural, and educational mainstream of United States society;

(2) in 1999, there were between 3,200,000 and 4,500,000 individuals with developmental disabilities in the United States, and recent studies indicate that individuals with developmental disabilities comprise between 1.2 and 1.65 percent of the United States population;

(3) individuals whose disabilities occur during their developmental period frequently have severe disabilities that are likely to continue indefinitely;

(4) individuals with developmental disabilities often encounter discrimina-

tion in the provision of critical services, such as services in the areas of emphasis (as defined in section 102 [42 USCS § 15002]);

(5) individuals with developmental disabilities are at greater risk than the general population of abuse, neglect, financial and sexual exploitation, and the violation of their legal and human rights;

(6) a substantial portion of individuals with developmental disabilities and their families do not have access to appropriate support and services, including access to assistive technology, from generic and specialized service systems, and remain unserved or underserved;

(7) individuals with developmental disabilities often require lifelong community services, individualized supports, and other forms of assistance, that are most effective when provided in a coordinated manner;

(8) there is a need to ensure that services, supports, and other assistance are provided in a culturally competent manner, that ensures that individuals from racial and ethnic minority backgrounds are fully included in all activities provided under this title [42 USCS §§ 15001 et seq.];

(9) family members, friends, and members of the community can play an important role in enhancing the lives of individuals with developmental disabilities, especially when the family members, friends, and community members are provided with the necessary community services, individualized supports, and other forms of assistance;

(10) current research indicates that 88 percent of individuals with developmental disabilities live with their families or in their own households;

(11) many service delivery systems and communities are not prepared to meet the impending needs of the 479,862 adults with developmental disabilities who are living at home with parents who are 60 years old or older and who serve as the primary caregivers of the adults;

(12) in almost every State, individuals with developmental disabilities are waiting for appropriate services in their communities, in the areas of emphasis;

(13) the public needs to be made more aware of the capabilities and competencies of individuals with developmental disabilities, particularly in cases in which the individuals are provided with necessary services, supports, and other assistance;

(14) as increasing numbers of individuals with developmental disabilities are living, learning, working, and participating in all aspects of community life, there is an increasing need for a well trained workforce that is able to provide the services, supports, and other forms of direct assistance required to enable the individuals to carry out those activities;

(15) there needs to be greater effort to recruit individuals from minority backgrounds into professions serving individuals with developmental disabilities and their families;

(16) the goals of the Nation properly include a goal of providing individuals with developmental disabilities with the information, skills, opportunities, and support to—

    (A) make informed choices and decisions about their lives;

(B) live in homes and communities in which such individuals can exercise their full rights and responsibilities as citizens;

(C) pursue meaningful and productive lives;

(D) contribute to their families, communities, and States, and the Nation;

(E) have interdependent friendships and relationships with other persons;

(F) live free of abuse, neglect, financial and sexual exploitation, and violations of their legal and human rights; and

(G) achieve full integration and inclusion in society, in an individualized manner, consistent with the unique strengths, resources, priorities, concerns, abilities, and capabilities of each individual; and

(17) as the Nation, States, and communities maintain and expand community living options for individuals with developmental disabilities, there is a need to evaluate the access to those options by individuals with developmental disabilities and the effects of those options on individuals with developmental disabilities.

(b) Purpose. The purpose of this title [42 USCS §§ 15001 et seq.] is to assure that individuals with developmental disabilities and their families participate in the design of and have access to needed community services, individualized supports, and other forms of assistance that promote self-determination, independence, productivity, and integration and inclusion in all facets of community life, through culturally competent programs authorized under this title [42 USCS §§ 15001 et seq.], including specifically—

(1) State Councils on Developmental Disabilities in each State to engage in advocacy, capacity building, and systemic change activities that—

(A) are consistent with the purpose described in this subsection and the policy described in subsection (c); and

(B) contribute to a coordinated, consumer- and family-centered, consumer- and family-directed, comprehensive system that includes needed community services, individualized supports, and other forms of assistance that promote self-determination for individuals with developmental disabilities and their families;

(2) protection and advocacy systems in each State to protect the legal and human rights of individuals with developmental disabilities;

(3) University Centers for Excellence in Developmental Disabilities Education, Research, and Service—

(A) to provide interdisciplinary pre-service preparation and continuing education of students and fellows, which may include the preparation and continuing education of leadership, direct service, clinical, or other personnel to strengthen and increase the capacity of States and communities to achieve the purpose of this title [42 USCS §§ 15001 et seq.];

(B) to provide community services—

(i) that provide training and technical assistance for individuals with developmental disabilities, their families, professionals, paraprofessionals, policymakers, students, and other members of the community; and

(ii) that may provide services, supports, and assistance for the persons described in clause (i) through demonstration and model activities;

(C) to conduct research, which may include basic or applied research, evaluation, and the analysis of public policy in areas that affect or could affect, either positively or negatively, individuals with developmental disabilities and their families; and

(D) to disseminate information related to activities undertaken to address the purpose of this title [42 USCS §§ 15001 et seq.], especially dissemination of information that demonstrates that the network authorized under this subtitle is a national and international resource that includes specific substantive areas of expertise that may be accessed and applied in diverse settings and circumstances; and

(4) funding for—

(A) national initiatives to collect necessary data on issues that are directly or indirectly relevant to the lives of individuals with developmental disabilities;

(B) technical assistance to entities who engage in or intend to engage in activities consistent with the purpose described in this subsection or the policy described in subsection (c); and

(C) other nationally significant activities.

(c) Policy. It is the policy of the United States that all programs, projects, and activities receiving assistance under this title [42 USCS §§ 15001 et seq.] shall be carried out in a manner consistent with the principles that—

(1) individuals with developmental disabilities, including those with the most severe developmental disabilities, are capable of self-determination, independence, productivity, and integration and inclusion in all facets of community life, but often require the provision of community services, individualized supports, and other forms of assistance;

(2) individuals with developmental disabilities and their families have competencies, capabilities, and personal goals that should be recognized, supported, and encouraged, and any assistance to such individuals should be provided in an individualized manner, consistent with the unique strengths, resources, priorities, concerns, abilities, and capabilities of such individuals;

(3) individuals with developmental disabilities and their families are the primary decisionmakers regarding the services and supports such individuals and their families receive, including regarding choosing where the individuals live from available options, and play decisionmaking roles in policies and programs that affect the lives of such individuals and their families;

(4) services, supports, and other assistance should be provided in a manner that demonstrates respect for individual dignity, personal preferences, and cultural differences;

(5) specific efforts must be made to ensure that individuals with developmental disabilities from racial and ethnic minority backgrounds and their families enjoy increased and meaningful opportunities to access and use community services, individualized supports, and other forms of assistance available to other individuals with developmental disabilities and their families;

(6) recruitment efforts in disciplines related to developmental disabilities

relating to pre-service training, community training, practice, administration, and policymaking must focus on bringing larger numbers of racial and ethnic minorities into the disciplines in order to provide appropriate skills, knowledge, role models, and sufficient personnel to address the growing needs of an increasingly diverse population;

(7) with education and support, communities can be accessible to and responsive to the needs of individuals with developmental disabilities and their families and are enriched by full and active participation in community activities, and contributions, by individuals with developmental disabilities and their families;

(8) individuals with developmental disabilities have access to opportunities and the necessary support to be included in community life, have interdependent relationships, live in homes and communities, and make contributions to their families, communities, and States, and the Nation;

(9) efforts undertaken to maintain or expand community-based living options for individuals with disabilities should be monitored in order to determine and report to appropriate individuals and entities the extent of access by individuals with developmental disabilities to those options and the extent of compliance by entities providing those options with quality assurance standards;

(10) families of children with developmental disabilities need to have access to and use of safe and appropriate child care and before-school and after-school programs, in the most integrated settings, in order to enrich the participation of the children in community life;

(11) individuals with developmental disabilities need to have access to and use of public transportation, in order to be independent and directly contribute to and participate in all facets of community life; and

(12) individuals with developmental disabilities need to have access to and use of recreational, leisure, and social opportunities in the most integrated settings, in order to enrich their participation in community life.

(Oct. 30, 2000, P. L. 106-402, Title I, Subtitle A, § 101, 114 Stat. 1678.)

HISTORY; ANCILLARY LAWS AND DIRECTIVES

Short title:
Act Oct. 30, 2000, P. L. 106-402, § 1, 114 Stat. 1677, provides: "This Act [42 USCS §§ 15001 et seq. generally; for full classification, consult USCS Tables volumes] may be cited as the 'Developmental Disabilities Assistance and Bill of Rights Act of 2000'.".

Act Oct. 30, 2000, P. L. 106-402, Title II, § 201, 114 Stat. 1728, provides: "This title [42 USCS §§ 15091 et seq.] may be cited as the 'Families of Children With Disabilities Support Act of 2000'.".

Other provisions:
Ex. Or. No. 11776 (superseded). Ex. Or. No. 11776 of March 28, 1974, 39 Fed. Reg. 11865; Ex. Or. No. 12608 of Sept. 9, 1987, § 15, 52 Fed. Reg. 34617, which provided for continuation of the President's Committee on Mental Retardation, was superseded by Ex. Or. No. 12994 of March 21, 1996, 61 Fed. Reg. 130471.

Ex. Or. No. 11973 (revoked). Ex. Or. No. 11973 of Feb. 17, 1977, 42 Fed. Reg. 10677, which related to the President's Commission on Mental Health, was revoked by Ex. Or. No. 12110 of Dec. 28, 1978, 44 Fed. Reg. 1069, effective 12/31/78.

Continuance of the President's Committee on Mental Retardation until Dec. 31, 1982. The President's Committee on Mental Retardation was continued until Dec. 31, 1982, by Ex. Or. No. 12258 of Dec. 31, 1980, § 101(e), 46 Fed Reg. 1251.

Continuance of the President's Committee on Mental Retardation until Sept. 30, 1984. The President's Committee on Mental Retardation was continued until Sept. 30, 1984, by Ex. Or. No. 12399 of Dec. 31, 1982.

Continuance of the President's Committee on Mental Retardation until Sept. 30, 1985. The President's Committee on Mental Retardation was continued until Sept. 30, 1985, by Ex. Or. No. 12489 of Sept. 28, 1984.

Continuance of the President's Committee on Mental Retardation until Sept. 30, 1987. The President's Committee on Mental Retardation was continued until Sept. 30, 1987, by Ex. Or. No. 12534 of Sept. 30, 1985.

Continuance of the President's Committee on Mental Retardation until Sept. 30, 1989. The President's Committee on Mental Retardation was continued until Sept. 30, 1989, by Ex. Or. No. 12610 of Sept. 30, 1987.

Continuance of the President's Committee on Mental Retardation until Sept. 30, 1991. The President's Committee on Mental Retardation was continued until Sept. 30, 1991, by Ex. Or. No. 12692 of Sept. 29, 1989.

Continuance of the President's Committee on Mental Retardation until Sept. 30, 1993. The President's Committee on Mental Retardation was continued until Sept. 30, 1993, by Ex. Or. No. 12774 of Sept. 27, 1991.

Continuance of the President's Committee on Mental Retardation until Sept. 30, 1995. The President's Committee on Mental Retardation was continued until Sept. 30, 1995, by Ex. Or. No. 12869 of Sept. 30, 1993.

Continuance of President's Committee on Mental Retardation and broadening of its membership and responsibilities. Ex. Or. No. 12994 of March 21, 1996, 61 Fed. Reg. 13047; Ex. Or. No. 13309 of July 25, 2003, 68 Fed. Reg. 44851; as amended by § 5 of Ex. Or. No. 13446 of Sept. 28, 2007, 72 Fed. Reg. 56175, effective 9/30/2007, provides:

"By the authority vested in me as President by the Constitution and the laws of the United States of America, and in order to promote full participation of people with intellectual disabilities in their communities, it is hereby ordered as follows:

"Section 1. Committee Continued and Responsibilities Expanded. The President's Committee on Mental Retardation, with expanded membership and expanded responsibilities, and renamed the President's Committee for People with Intellectual Disabilities (Committee), is hereby continued in operation.

"Sec. 2. Composition of Committee. (a) The Committee shall be composed of the following members:

"(1) The Attorney General;
"(2) The Secretary of the Interior;
"(3) The Secretary of Commerce;
"(4) The Secretary of Labor;
"(5) The Secretary of Health and Human Services;

"(6) The Secretary of Housing and Urban Development;

"(7) The Secretary of Transportation;

"(8) The Secretary of Education;

"(9) The Secretary of Homeland Security;

"(10) The Chief Executive Officer of the Corporation for National and Community Service;

"(11) The Commissioner of Social Security;

"(12) The Chairman of the Equal Employment Opportunity Commission;

"(13) The Chairperson of the National Council on Disability; and

"(14) No more than 21 other members who shall be appointed to the Committee by the President. These citizen members shall consist of individuals who represent a broad spectrum of perspectives, experience, and expertise on intellectual disabilities; persons with intellectual disabilities and members of families with a child or adult with intellectual disabilities; and persons employed in either the public or the private sector. Except as the President may from time to time otherwise direct, appointees under this paragraph shall serve for two-year terms, except that an appointment made to fill a vacancy occurring before the expiration of a term shall be made for the balance of the unexpired term.

"(b) The President shall designate the Chair of the Committee from the 21 citizen members. The Chair shall preside over meetings of the Committee and represent the Committee on appropriate occasions.

"Sec. 3. Functions of the Committee. (a) Consistent with subsection (c) of this section, the Committee shall:

"(1) provide such advice concerning intellectual disabilities as the President or the Secretary of Health and Human Services may request; and

"(2) provide advice to the President concerning the following for people with intellectual disabilities:

"(A) expansion of educational opportunities;

"(B) promotion of homeownership;

"(C) assurance of workplace integration;

"(D) improvement of transportation options;

"(E) expansion of full access to community living; and

"(F) increasing access to assistive and universally designed technologies.

"(b) The Committee shall provide an annual report to the President through the Secretary of Health and Human Services. Such additional reports may be made as the President may direct or as the Committee may deem appropriate.

"(c) The members shall advise the President and carry out their advisory role consistent with the requirements of the Federal Advisory Committee Act, as amended (5 U.S.C. App.).

"Sec. 4. Cooperation by Agencies. The heads of Federal departments and agencies shall:

"(a) designate, when requested by the Secretary of Health and Human Services, an officer or employee of such department or agency to serve as a liaison with the Committee; and

"(b) furnish such information and assistance to the Committee, to the extent permitted by law, as the Secretary of Health and Human Services may request to assist the Committee in performing its functions under this order.

"Sec. 5. Administration. (a) The Department of Health and Human Services shall provide the Committee with necessary staff support, administrative services and facilities, and funding, to the extent permitted by law.

"(b) Each member of the Committee, except any member who receives other compensation from the United States Government, may receive compensation for each day engaged in the work of the Committee, as authorized by law (5 U.S.C. 3109), and may also receive travel expenses, including per diem in lieu of subsistence, as authorized by law (5 U.S.C. 5701–5707), for persons employed intermittently in the Government service. Committee members with disabilities may be compensated for attendant expenses, consistent with Government procedures and practices.

"(c) The Secretary of Health and Human Services shall perform such other functions with respect to the Committee as may be required by the Federal Advisory Committee Act, as amended (5 U.S.C. App.), except that of reporting to the Congress.

"Sec. 6. General. (a) Nothing in this order shall be construed as subjecting any Federal agency, or any function vested by law in, or assigned pursuant to law to, any Federal agency, to the authority of the Committee or as abrogating or restricting any such function in any manner.

"(b) This order is not intended to, and does not, create any right or benefit, substantive or procedural, enforceable at law or in equity by any party against the United States, its departments, agencies, instrumentalities, or entities, its officers or employees, or any other person.".

Continuance of the President's Committee on Mental Retardation until Sept. 30, 1997. The President's Committee on Mental Retardation was continued until Sept. 30, 1997, by Ex. Or. No. 12974 of Sept. 29, 1995, which formerly appeared as 5 USCS Appx § 14 note.

Continuance of the President's Committee on Mental Retardation until Sept. 30, 1999. The President's Committee on Mental Retardation was continued until Sept. 30, 1999, by Ex. Or. No. 13062 of Sept. 29, 1997, which formerly appeared as 5 USCS Appx § 14 note.

Continuance of the President's Committee on Mental Retardation until Sept. 30, 2001. The President's Committee on Mental Retardation was continued until September 30, 2001, by § 1(l) of Ex. Or. No. 13138 of Sept. 30, 1999, which appears as 5 USCS Appx § 14 note.

Continuance of the President's Committee on Mental Retardation until Sept. 30, 2003. The President's Committee on Mental Retardation was continued until September 30, 2003, by Ex. Or. No. 13225 of Sept. 28, 2001, which formerly appeared as 5 USCS Appx § 14 note.

Renaming the President's Committee on Mental Retardation as the President's Committee for People with Intellectual Disabilities; continuance of Committee. Ex. Or. No. 13309 of July 25, 2003, 68 Fed. Reg. 44851, provides:

"By the authority vested in me as President by the Constitution and the laws of the United States of America, and in order to change the name of the 'President's Committee on Mental Retardation' to the 'President's Committee for People with Intellectual Disabilities' (the 'Committee') and expand the membership of the Committee, it is hereby ordered as follows:

"Section 1. The President's Committee on Mental Retardation is hereby renamed the President's Committee for People with Intellectual Disabilities.

"Secs. 2–4. [Omitted—These sections amended Ex. Or. No. 12994 (note to this section).]

"Sec. 5. The Committee is continued until September 30, 2005.".

Continuance of the President's Committee for People with Intellectual Disabilities until Sept. 30, 2007. The President's Committee for People with Intellectual Disabilities was continued until September 30, 2007, by § 1(g) of Ex. Or. No. 13385 of Sept. 29, 2005, which appears as 5 USCS Appx § 14 note.

Continuance of the President's Committee for People with Intellectual Disabilities until Sept. 30, 2009. The President's Committee for People with Intellectual Disabilities was continued until September 30, 2009, by § 1(g) of Ex. Or. No. 13446 of Sept. 28, 2007, which appears as 5 USCS Appx § 14 note.

Continuance of the President's Committee for People with Intellectual Disabilities until Sept. 30, 2011. The President's Committee for People with Intellectual Disabilities was continued until September 30, 2011, by § 1(g) of Ex. Or. No. 13511 of Sept. 29, 2009, which appears as 5 USCS Appx § 14 note.

Special Olympics Sport and Empowerment Act of 2004. Act Oct. 30, 2004, P. L. 108-406, 118 Stat. 2294, provides:

"Section 1. Short title.

"This Act may be cited as the 'Special Olympics Sport and Empowerment Act of 2004'.

"Sec. 2. Findings and purpose.

"(a) Findings. Congress finds the following:

"(1) Special Olympics celebrates the possibilities of a world where everybody matters, everybody counts, every person has value, and every person has worth.

"(2) The Government and the people of the United States recognize the dignity and value the giftedness of children and adults with an intellectual disability.

"(3) The Government and the people of the United States are determined to end the isolation and stigmatization of people with an intellectual disability.

"(4) For more than 36 years, Special Olympics has encouraged skill, sharing, courage, and joy through year-round sports training and athletic competition for children and adults with intellectual disabilities.

"(5) Special Olympics provides year-round sports training and competitive opportunities to 1,500,000 athletes with intellectual disabilities in 26 sports and plans to expand the joy of participation through sport to hundreds of thousands of people with intellectual disabilities within the United States and worldwide over the next 5 years.

"(6) Special Olympics has demonstrated its ability to provide a major positive effect on the quality of life of people with intellectual disabilities, improving their health and physical well-being, building their confidence and self-esteem, and giving them a voice to become active and productive members of their communities.

"(7) In society as a whole, Special Olympics has become a vehicle and platform for breaking down artificial barriers, improving public health, changing negative attitudes in education, and helping athletes overcome the prejudice that people with intellectual disabilities face in too many places.

"(8) The Government of the United States enthusiastically supports Special Olympics, recognizes its importance in improving the lives of people with intellectual disabilities, and recognizes Special Olympics as a valued and important component of the global community.

"(b) Purpose. The purposes of this Act are to—

"(1) provide support to Special Olympics to increase athlete participation in and public awareness about the Special Olympics movement;

"(2) dispel negative stereotypes about people with intellectual disabilities;

"(3) build athletic and family involvement through sport; and

"(4) promote the extraordinary gifts of people with intellectual disabilities.

"Sec. 3. Assistance for Special Olympics.

"(a) Education activities. The Secretary of Education may award grants to, or enter into contracts or cooperative agreements with, Special Olympics to carry out the following:

"(1) Activities to promote the expansion of Special Olympics, including activities to increase the participation of individuals with intellectual disabilities within the United States.

"(2) The design and implementation of Special Olympics education programs, including character education and volunteer programs that support the purposes of this Act, that can be integrated into classroom instruction and are consistent with academic content standards.

"(b) International activities. The Secretary of State may award grants to, or enter into contracts or cooperative agreements with, Special Olympics to carry out the following:

"(1) Activities to increase the participation of individuals with intellectual disabilities in Special Olympics outside of the United States.

"(2) Activities to improve the awareness outside of the United States of the abilities and unique contributions that individuals with intellectual disabilities can make to society.

"(c) Healthy athletes. (1) In general. The Secretary of Health and Human Services may award grants to, or enter into contracts or cooperative agreements with, Special Olympics for the implementation of on-site health assessments, screening for health problems, health education, data collection, and referrals to direct health care services.

"(2) Coordination. Activities under paragraph (1) shall be coordinated with private health providers, existing authorized programs of State and local jurisdictions, or the Department of Health and Human Services, as applicable.

"(d) Limitation. Amounts appropriated to carry out this section shall not be used for direct treatment of diseases, medical conditions, or mental health conditions. Nothing in the preceding sentence shall be construed to limit the use of non-Federal funds by Special Olympics.

"Sec. 4. Application and annual report.

"(a) Application. (1) In general. To be eligible for a grant, contract, or cooperative agreement under subsection (a), (b), or (c) of section 3, Special Olympics shall submit an application at such time, in such manner, and containing such information as the Secretary of Education, Secretary of State, or Secretary of Health and Human Services, as applicable, may require.

"(2) Content. At a minimum, an application under this subsection shall contain the following:

"(A) Activities. A description of activities to be carried out with the grant, contract, or cooperative agreement.

"(B) Measurable goals. Information on specific measurable goals and objectives to be achieved through activities carried out with the grant, contract, or cooperative agreement.

"(b) Annual Report. (1) In general. As a condition on receipt of any funds under subsection (a), (b), or (c) of section 3, Special Olympics shall agree to submit an annual report at such time, in such manner, and containing such information as the Secretary of Education, Secretary of State, or Secretary of Health and Human Services, as applicable, may require.

"(2) Content. At a minimum, each annual report under this subsection shall describe the degree to which progress has been made toward meeting the goals and objectives described in the applications submitted under subsection (a).

"Sec. 5. Authorization of appropriations.

"There are authorized to be appropriated—

"(1) for grants, contracts, or cooperative agreements under section 3(a), $5,500,000 for fiscal year 2005, and such sums as may be necessary for each of the 4 succeeding fiscal years;

"(2) for grants, contracts, or cooperative agreements under section 3(b), $3,500,000 for fiscal year 2005, and such sums as may be necessary for each of the 4 succeeding fiscal years; and

"(3) for grants, contracts, or cooperative agreements under section 3(c), $6,000,000 for each of fiscal years 2005 through 2009.".

CROSS REFERENCES

This section is referred to in 42 USCS §§ 15004, 15009, 15021, 15025, 15064, 15114.

RESEARCH GUIDE

Am Jur:

79 Am Jur 2d, Welfare § 49.

Annotations:

Validity, Construction, and Operation of Developmental Disabilities Assistance and Bill of Rights Act. 193 ALR Fed 513.

Vacating on Public Policy Grounds Arbitration Awards Reinstating Discharged Employees—State Cases. 112 ALR5th 263.

Other Treatises:

5 Rapp, Education Law (Matthew Bender), ch 13, Education Records Management and Retention § 13.04.

INTERPRETIVE NOTES AND DECISIONS

Claim under Developmentally Disabled Assistance and Bill of Rights Act (DDABRA), 42 USCS §§ 15001 et seq., by advocate for developmentally disabled adult against care provider whose employee physically abused her ward was dismissed; although DDABRA provided funding for state programs, provider was not state actor under 42 USCS § 1983. Karaahmetoglu v Res-Care, Inc. (2007, DC Dist Col) 480 F Supp 2d 183 (criticized in Harvey v Mohammed (2012, DC Dist Col) 2012 US Dist LEXIS 9574).

§ 15002. Definitions

In this title [42 USCS §§ 15001 et seq.]:

(1) American Indian consortium. The term "American Indian Consortium" means any confederation of 2 or more recognized American Indian tribes, created through the official action of each participating tribe, that has a combined total resident population of 150,000 enrolled tribal members and a contiguous territory of Indian lands in 2 or more States.

(2) Areas of emphasis. The term "areas of emphasis" means the areas related to quality assurance activities, education activities and early intervention activities, child care-related activities, health-related activities, employment-related activities, housing-related activities, transportation-related activities, recreation-related activities, and other services available or offered to individuals in a community, including formal and informal community supports, that affect their quality of life.

(3) Assistive technology device. The term "assistive technology device" means any item, piece of equipment, or product system, whether acquired commercially, modified or customized, that is used to increase, maintain, or improve functional capabilities of individuals with developmental disabilities.

(4) Assistive technology service. The term "assistive technology service" means any service that directly assists an individual with a developmental disability in the selection, acquisition, or use of an assistive technology device. Such term includes—

(A) conducting an evaluation of the needs of an individual with a developmental disability, including a functional evaluation of the individual in the individual's customary environment;

(B) purchasing, leasing, or otherwise providing for the acquisition of an assistive technology device by an individual with a developmental disability;

(C) selecting, designing, fitting, customizing, adapting, applying, maintaining, repairing or replacing an assistive technology device;

(D) coordinating and using another therapy, intervention, or service with an assistive technology device, such as a therapy, intervention, or service associated with an education or rehabilitation plan or program;

(E) providing training or technical assistance for an individual with a developmental disability, or, where appropriate, a family member, guardian, advocate, or authorized representative of an individual with a developmental disability; and

(F) providing training or technical assistance for professionals (including individuals providing education and rehabilitation services), employers, or other individuals who provide services to, employ, or are otherwise substantially involved in the major life functions of, an individual with developmental disabilities.

(5) Center. The term "Center" means a University Center for Excellence in Developmental Disabilities Education, Research, and Service established under subtitle D [42 USCS §§ 15061 et seq.].

(6) Child care-related activities. The term "child care-related activities" means advocacy, capacity building, and systemic change activities that result in families of children with developmental disabilities having access to and use of child care services, including before-school, after-school, and out-of-school services, in their communities.

(7) Culturally competent. The term "culturally competent", used with respect to services, supports, or other assistance, means services, supports, or other assistance that is conducted or provided in a manner that is responsive to the beliefs, interpersonal styles, attitudes, language, and behaviors of individuals who are receiving the services, supports, or other assistance, and in a manner that has the greatest likelihood of ensuring their maximum participation in the program involved.

(8) Developmental disability. (A) In general. The term "developmental disability" means a severe, chronic disability of an individual that—

(i) is attributable to a mental or physical impairment or combination of mental and physical impairments;

(ii) is manifested before the individual attains age 22;

(iii) is likely to continue indefinitely;

(iv) results in substantial functional limitations in 3 or more of the following areas of major life activity:

(I) Self-care.

(II) Receptive and expressive language.

(III) Learning.

(IV) Mobility.

(V) Self-direction.

(VI) Capacity for independent living.

(VII) Economic self-sufficiency; and

(v) reflects the individual's need for a combination and sequence of special, interdisciplinary, or generic services, individualized supports, or other forms of assistance that are of lifelong or extended duration and are individually planned and coordinated.

(B) Infants and young children. An individual from birth to age 9, inclusive, who has a substantial developmental delay or specific congenital or acquired condition, may be considered to have a developmental disability without meeting 3 or more of the criteria described in clauses (i) through (v) of subparagraph (A) if the individual, without services and supports, has a high probability of meeting those criteria later in life.

(9) Early intervention activities. The term "early intervention activities" means advocacy, capacity building, and systemic change activities provided to individuals described in paragraph (8)(B) and their families to enhance—

(A) the development of the individuals to maximize their potential; and

(B) the capacity of families to meet the special needs of the individuals.

(10) Education activities. The term "education activities" means advocacy, capacity building, and systemic change activities that result in individuals with developmental disabilities being able to access appropriate supports and modifications when necessary, to maximize their educational potential, to benefit from lifelong educational activities, and to be integrated and included in all facets of student life.

(11) Employment-related activities. The term "employment-related activities" means advocacy, capacity building, and systemic change activities that result in individuals with developmental disabilities acquiring, retaining, or advancing in paid employment, including supported employment or self-employment, in integrated settings in a community.

(12) Family support services. (A) In general. The term "family support services" means services, supports, and other assistance, provided to families with members who have developmental disabilities, that are designed to—

(i) strengthen the family's role as primary caregiver;

(ii) prevent inappropriate out-of-the-home placement of the members and maintain family unity; and

(iii) reunite families with members who have been placed out of the home whenever possible.

(B) Specific services. Such term includes respite care, provision of rehabilitation technology and assistive technology, personal assistance services, parent training and counseling, support for families headed by aging caregivers, vehicular and home modifications, and assistance with extraordinary expenses, associated with the needs of individuals with developmental disabilities.

(13) Health-related activities. The term "health-related activities" means advocacy, capacity building, and systemic change activities that result in individuals with developmental disabilities having access to and use of coordinated health, dental, mental health, and other human and social services, including prevention activities, in their communities.

(14) Housing-related activities. The term "housing-related activities" means advocacy, capacity building, and systemic change activities that result in individuals with developmental disabilities having access to and use of housing and housing supports and services in their communities, including assistance related to renting, owning, or modifying an apartment or home.

(15) Inclusion. The term "inclusion", used with respect to individuals with developmental disabilities, means the acceptance and encouragement of the presence and participation of individuals with developmental disabilities, by individuals without disabilities, in social, educational, work, and community activities, that enables individuals with developmental disabilities to—

(A) have friendships and relationships with individuals and families of their own choice;

(B) live in homes close to community resources, with regular contact with individuals without disabilities in their communities;

(C) enjoy full access to and active participation in the same community activities and types of employment as individuals without disabilities; and

(D) take full advantage of their integration into the same community resources as individuals without disabilities, living, learning, working, and enjoying life in regular contact with individuals without disabilities.

(16) Individualized supports. The term "individualized supports" means supports that—

(A) enable an individual with a developmental disability to exercise self-determination, be independent, be productive, and be integrated and included in all facets of community life;

(B) are designed to—

(i) enable such individual to control such individual's environment, permitting the most independent life possible;

(ii) prevent placement into a more restrictive living arrangement than is necessary; and

(iii) enable such individual to live, learn, work, and enjoy life in the community; and

(C) include—

(i) early intervention services;

(ii) respite care;

(iii) personal assistance services;

(iv) family support services;

(v) supported employment services;

(vi) support services for families headed by aging caregivers of individuals with developmental disabilities; and

(vii) provision of rehabilitation technology and assistive technology, and assistive technology services.

(17) Integration. The term "integration", used with respect to individuals with developmental disabilities, means exercising the equal right of individuals with developmental disabilities to access and use the same community resources as are used by and available to other individuals.

(18) Not-for-profit. The term "not-for-profit", used with respect to an agency, institution, or organization, means an agency, institution, or organization that is owned or operated by 1 or more corporations or associations, no part of the net earnings of which inures, or may lawfully inure, to the benefit of any private shareholder or individual.

(19) Personal assistance services. The term "personal assistance services" means a range of services, provided by 1 or more individuals, designed to assist an individual with a disability to perform daily activities, including activities on or off a job that such individual would typically perform if such individual did not have a disability. Such services shall be designed to increase such individual's control in life and ability to perform everyday activities, including activities on or off a job.

(20) Prevention activities. The term "prevention activities" means activities that address the causes of developmental disabilities and the exacerbation of functional limitation, such as activities that—

(A) eliminate or reduce the factors that cause or predispose individuals to developmental disabilities or that increase the prevalence of developmental disabilities;

(B) increase the early identification of problems to eliminate circumstances that create or increase functional limitations; and

(C) mitigate against the effects of developmental disabilities throughout the lifespan of an individual.

(21) Productivity. The term "productivity" means—

(A) engagement in income-producing work that is measured by increased income, improved employment status, or job advancement; or

(B) engagement in work that contributes to a household or community.

(22) Protection and advocacy system. The term "protection and advocacy system" means a protection and advocacy system established in accordance with section 143 [42 USCS § 15043].

(23) Quality assurance activities. The term "quality assurance activities" means advocacy, capacity building, and systemic change activities that result in improved consumer- and family-centered quality assurance and that result in systems of quality assurance and consumer protection that—

(A) include monitoring of services, supports, and assistance provided to an individual with developmental disabilities that ensures that the individual—

(i) will not experience abuse, neglect, sexual or financial exploitation, or violation of legal or human rights; and

(ii) will not be subject to the inappropriate use of restraints or seclusion;

(B) include training in leadership, self-advocacy, and self-determination for individuals with developmental disabilities, their families, and their guardians to ensure that those individuals—

(i) will not experience abuse, neglect, sexual or financial exploitation, or violation of legal or human rights; and

(ii) will not be subject to the inappropriate use of restraints or seclusion; or

(C) include activities related to interagency coordination and systems integration that result in improved and enhanced services, supports, and other assistance that contribute to and protect the self-determination, independence, productivity, and integration and inclusion in all facets of community life, of individuals with developmental disabilities.

(24) Recreation-related activities. The term "recreation-related activities" means advocacy, capacity building, and systemic change activities that result in individuals with developmental disabilities having access to and use of recreational, leisure, and social activities, in their communities.

(25) Rehabilitation technology. The term "rehabilitation technology" means the systematic application of technologies, engineering methodologies, or scientific principles to meet the needs of, and address the barriers confronted by, individuals with developmental disabilities in areas that include education, rehabilitation, employment, transportation, independent living, and

recreation. Such term includes rehabilitation engineering, and the provision of assistive technology devices and assistive technology services.

(26) Secretary. The term "Secretary" means the Secretary of Health and Human Services.

(27) Self-determination activities. The term "self-determination activities" means activities that result in individuals with developmental disabilities, with appropriate assistance, having—

(A) the ability and opportunity to communicate and make personal decisions;

(B) the ability and opportunity to communicate choices and exercise control over the type and intensity of services, supports, and other assistance the individuals receive;

(C) the authority to control resources to obtain needed services, supports, and other assistance;

(D) opportunities to participate in, and contribute to, their communities; and

(E) support, including financial support, to advocate for themselves and others, to develop leadership skills, through training in self-advocacy, to participate in coalitions, to educate policymakers, and to play a role in the development of public policies that affect individuals with developmental disabilities.

(28) State. The term "State", except as otherwise provided, includes, in addition to each of the several States of the United States, the District of Columbia, the Commonwealth of Puerto Rico, the United States Virgin Islands, Guam, American Samoa, and the Commonwealth of the Northern Mariana Islands.

(29) State Council on Developmental Disabilities. The term "State Council on Developmental Disabilities" means a Council established under section 125 [42 USCS § 15025].

(30) Supported employment services. The term "supported employment services" means services that enable individuals with developmental disabilities to perform competitive work in integrated work settings, in the case of individuals with developmental disabilities—

(A)(i) for whom competitive employment has not traditionally occurred; or

(ii) for whom competitive employment has been interrupted or intermittent as a result of significant disabilities; and

(B) who, because of the nature and severity of their disabilities, need intensive supported employment services or extended services in order to perform such work.

(31) Transportation-related activities. The term "transportation-related activities" means advocacy, capacity building, and systemic change activities that result in individuals with developmental disabilities having access to and use of transportation.

(32) Unserved and underserved. The term "unserved and underserved" includes populations such as individuals from racial and ethnic minority

backgrounds, disadvantaged individuals, individuals with limited English proficiency, individuals from underserved geographic areas (rural or urban), and specific groups of individuals within the population of individuals with developmental disabilities, including individuals who require assistive technology in order to participate in and contribute to community life.

(Oct. 30, 2000, P. L. 106-402, Title I, Subtitle A, § 102, 114 Stat. 1682.)

CROSS REFERENCES

This section is referred to in 25 USCS § 4103; 29 USCS § 3002; 42 USCS §§ 280j, 1437a, 1471, 8013, 9877, 11382, 15001, 15112, 15461.

RESEARCH GUIDE

Am Jur:

79 Am Jur 2d, Welfare § 49.

§ 15003. Records and audits

(a) Records. Each recipient of assistance under this title [42 USCS §§ 15001 et seq.] shall keep such records as the Secretary shall prescribe, including—

(1) records that fully disclose—

(A) the amount and disposition by such recipient of the assistance;

(B) the total cost of the project or undertaking in connection with which such assistance is given or used; and

(C) the amount of that portion of the cost of the project or undertaking that is supplied by other sources; and

(2) such other records as will facilitate an effective audit.

(b) Access. The Secretary and the Comptroller General of the United States, or any of their duly authorized representatives, shall have access for the purpose of audit and examination to any books, documents, papers, and records of the recipients of assistance under this title [42 USCS §§ 15001 et seq.] that are pertinent to such assistance.

(Oct. 30, 2000, P. L. 106-402, Title I, Subtitle A, § 103, 114 Stat. 1688.)

RESEARCH GUIDE

Am Jur:

79 Am Jur 2d, Welfare § 49.

§ 15004. Responsibilities of the Secretary

(a) Program accountability. (1) In general. In order to monitor entities that received funds under this Act to carry out activities under subtitles B, C, and D [42 USCS §§ 15021 et seq., 15041 et seq., 15061 et seq.] and determine the extent to which the entities have been responsive to the purpose of this title [42 USCS §§ 15001 et seq.] and have taken actions consistent with the policy described in section 101(c) [42 USCS § 15001(c)], the Secretary shall develop and implement an accountability process as described in this subsection, with respect to activities conducted after October 1, 2001.

(2) Areas of emphasis. The Secretary shall develop a process for identifying

and reporting (pursuant to section 105 [42 USCS § 15005]) on progress achieved through advocacy, capacity building, and systemic change activities, undertaken by the entities described in paragraph (1), that resulted in individuals with developmental disabilities and their families participating in the design of and having access to needed community services, individualized supports, and other forms of assistance that promote self-determination, independence, productivity, and integration and inclusion in all facets of community life. Specifically, the Secretary shall develop a process for identifying and reporting on progress achieved, through advocacy, capacity building, and systemic change activities, by the entities in the areas of emphasis.

(3) Indicators of progress. (A) In general. In identifying progress made by the entities described in paragraph (1) in the areas of emphasis, the Secretary, in consultation with the Commissioner of the Administration on Developmental Disabilities and the entities, shall develop indicators for each area of emphasis.

(B) Proposed indicators. Not later than 180 days after the date of enactment of this Act [enacted Oct. 30, 2000], the Secretary shall develop and publish in the Federal Register for public comment proposed indicators of progress for monitoring how entities described in paragraph (1) have addressed the areas of emphasis described in paragraph (2) in a manner that is responsive to the purpose of this title [42 USCS §§ 15001 et seq.] and consistent with the policy described in section 101(c) [42 USCS § 15001(c)].

(C) Final indicators. Not later than October 1, 2001, the Secretary shall revise the proposed indicators of progress, to the extent necessary based on public comment, and publish final indicators of progress in the Federal Register.

(D) Specific measures. At a minimum, the indicators of progress shall be used to describe and measure—

(i) the satisfaction of individuals with developmental disabilities with the advocacy, capacity building, and systemic change activities provided under subtitles B, C, and D [42 USCS §§ 15021 et seq., 15041 et seq., 15061 et seq.];

(ii) the extent to which the advocacy, capacity building, and systemic change activities provided through subtitles B, C, and D [42 USCS §§ 15021 et seq., 15041 et seq., 15061 et seq.] result in improvements in—

(I) the ability of individuals with developmental disabilities to make choices and exert control over the type, intensity, and timing of services, supports, and assistance that the individuals have used;

(II) the ability of individuals with developmental disabilities to participate in the full range of community life with persons of the individuals' choice; and

(III) the ability of individuals with developmental disabilities to access services, supports, and assistance in a manner that ensures that such an individual is free from abuse, neglect, sexual and financial

exploitation, violation of legal and human rights, and the inappropriate use of restraints and seclusion; and

(iii) the extent to which the entities described in paragraph (1) collaborate with each other to achieve the purpose of this title [42 USCS
§§ 15001 et seq.] and the policy described in section 101(c) [42 USCS
§ 15001(c)].

(4) Time line for compliance with indicators of progress. The Secretary shall
require entities described in paragraph (1) to meet the indicators of progress
described in paragraph (3). For fiscal year 2002 and each year thereafter, the
Secretary shall apply the indicators in monitoring entities described in
paragraph (1), with respect to activities conducted after October 1, 2001.

(b) Time line for regulations. Except as otherwise expressly provided in this
title [42 USCS §§ 15001 et seq.], the Secretary, not later than 1 year after the
date of enactment of this Act [enacted Oct. 30, 2000], shall promulgate such
regulations as may be required for the implementation of this title [42 USCS
§§ 15001 et seq.].

(c) Interagency committee. (1) In general. The Secretary shall maintain the
interagency committee authorized in (42 U.S.C. 6007) as in effect on the day
before the date of enactment of this Act [enacted Oct. 30, 2000], except as
otherwise provided in this subsection.

(2) Composition. The interagency committee shall be composed of representatives of—

(A) the Administration on Developmental Disabilities, the Administration
on Children, Youth, and Families, the Administration on Aging, and the
Health Resources and Services Administration, of the Department of
Health and Human Services; and

(B) such other Federal departments and agencies as the Secretary of
Health and Human Services considers to be appropriate.

(3) Duties. Such interagency committee shall meet regularly to coordinate
and plan activities conducted by Federal departments and agencies for
individuals with developmental disabilities.

(4) Meetings. Each meeting of the interagency committee (except for any
meetings of any subcommittees of the committee) shall be open to the public.
Notice of each meeting, and a statement of the agenda for the meeting, shall
be published in the Federal Register not later than 14 days before the date
on which the meeting is to occur.

(Oct. 30, 2000, P. L. 106-402, Title I, Subtitle A, § 104, 114 Stat. 1688.)

HISTORY; ANCILLARY LAWS AND DIRECTIVES

References in text:

"This Act", referred to in subsec. (a)(1), is Act Oct. 30, 2000, P. L. 106-
402, which appears generally as 42 USCS §§ 15001 et seq. For full classification of such Act, consult USCS Tables volumes.

"Section 108 of the Developmental Disabilities Assistance and Bill of
Rights Act", referred to in subsec. (c)(1), is § 108 of Act Oct. 31, 1963,
P. L. 88-164, which formerly appeared as 42 USCS § 6007 prior to its

repeal by Act Oct. 30, 2000, P. L. 106-402, Title IV, § 401(a), 114 Stat. 1737.

CROSS REFERENCES

This section is referred to in 42 USCS §§ 15024–15026, 15064.

RESEARCH GUIDE

Am Jur:

79 Am Jur 2d, Welfare § 49.

§ 15005. Reports of the Secretary

At least once every 2 years, the Secretary, using information submitted in the reports and information required under subtitles B, C, D, and E [42 USCS §§ 15021 et seq., 15041 et seq., 15061 et seq., 15081 et seq.], shall prepare and submit to the President, Congress, and the National Council on Disability, a report that describes the goals and outcomes of programs supported under subtitles B, C, D, and E [42 USCS §§ 15021 et seq., 15041 et seq., 15061 et seq., 15081 et seq.]. In preparing the report, the Secretary shall provide—

(1) meaningful examples of how the councils, protection and advocacy systems, centers, and entities funded under subtitles B, C, D, and E [42 USCS §§ 15021 et seq., 15041 et seq., 15061 et seq., 15081 et seq.], respectively—

(A) have undertaken coordinated activities with each other;

(B) have enhanced the ability of individuals with developmental disabilities and their families to participate in the design of and have access to needed community services, individualized supports, and other forms of assistance that promote self-determination, independence, productivity, and integration and inclusion in all facets of community life;

(C) have brought about advocacy, capacity building, and systemic change activities (including policy reform), and other actions on behalf of individuals with developmental disabilities and their families, including individuals who are traditionally unserved or underserved, particularly individuals who are members of ethnic and racial minority groups and individuals from underserved geographic areas; and

(D) have brought about advocacy, capacity building, and systemic change activities that affect individuals with disabilities other than individuals with developmental disabilities;

(2) information on the extent to which programs authorized under this title [42 USCS §§ 15001 et seq.] have addressed—

(A) protecting individuals with developmental disabilities from abuse, neglect, sexual and financial exploitation, and violations of legal and human rights, so that those individuals are at no greater risk of harm than other persons in the general population; and

(B) reports of deaths of and serious injuries to individuals with developmental disabilities; and

(3) a summary of any incidents of noncompliance of the programs authorized under this title [42 USCS §§ 15001 et seq.] with the provisions of this title

[42 USCS §§ 15001 et seq.], and corrections made or actions taken to obtain compliance.
(Oct. 30, 2000, P. L. 106-402, Title I, Subtitle A, § 105, 114 Stat. 1690.)

CROSS REFERENCES
This section is referred to in 42 USCS §§ 10824, 15004.

RESEARCH GUIDE
Am Jur:
79 Am Jur 2d, Welfare § 49.

§ 15006. State control of operations
Except as otherwise specifically provided, nothing in this title [42 USCS §§ 15001 et seq.] shall be construed as conferring on any Federal officer or employee the right to exercise any supervision or control over the administration, personnel, maintenance, or operation of any programs, services, and supports for individuals with developmental disabilities with respect to which any funds have been or may be expended under this title [42 USCS §§ 15001 et seq.].
(Oct. 30, 2000, P. L. 106-402, Title I, Subtitle A, § 106, 114 Stat. 1691.)

RESEARCH GUIDE
Am Jur:
79 Am Jur 2d, Welfare § 49.

§ 15007. Employment of individuals with disabilities
As a condition of providing assistance under this title [42 USCS §§ 15001 et seq.], the Secretary shall require that each recipient of such assistance take affirmative action to employ and advance in employment qualified individuals with disabilities on the same terms and conditions required with respect to the employment of such individuals under the provisions of title V of the Rehabilitation Act of 1973 (29 U.S.C. 791 et seq.) and the Americans with Disabilities Act of 1990 (42 U.S.C. 12101 et seq.), that govern employment.
(Oct. 30, 2000, P. L. 106-402, Title I, Subtitle A, § 107, 114 Stat. 1691.)

RESEARCH GUIDE
Am Jur:
79 Am Jur 2d, Welfare § 49.

§ 15008. Construction
Nothing in this title [42 USCS §§ 15001 et seq.] shall be construed to preclude an entity funded under this title [42 USCS §§ 15001 et seq.] from engaging in advocacy, capacity building, and systemic change activities for individuals with developmental disabilities that may also have a positive impact on individuals with other disabilities.
(Oct. 30, 2000, P. L. 106-402, Title I, Subtitle A, § 108, 114 Stat. 1692.)

RESEARCH GUIDE
Am Jur:
79 Am Jur 2d, Welfare § 49.

§ 15009.   Rights of individuals with developmental disabilities

(a) In general. Congress makes the following findings respecting the rights of individuals with developmental disabilities:

(1) Individuals with developmental disabilities have a right to appropriate treatment, services, and habilitation for such disabilities, consistent with section 101(c) [42 USCS § 15001(c)].

(2) The treatment, services, and habitation [habilitation] for an individual with developmental disabilities should be designed to maximize the potential of the individual and should be provided in the setting that is least restrictive of the individual's personal liberty.

(3) The Federal Government and the States both have an obligation to ensure that public funds are provided only to institutional programs, residential programs, and other community programs, including educational programs in which individuals with developmental disabilities participate, that—

(A) provide treatment, services, and habilitation that are appropriate to the needs of such individuals; and

(B) meet minimum standards relating to—

(i) provision of care that is free of abuse, neglect, sexual and financial exploitation, and violations of legal and human rights and that subjects individuals with developmental disabilities to no greater risk of harm than others in the general population;

(ii) provision to such individuals of appropriate and sufficient medical and dental services;

(iii) prohibition of the use of physical restraint and seclusion for such an individual unless absolutely necessary to ensure the immediate physical safety of the individual or others, and prohibition of the use of such restraint and seclusion as a punishment or as a substitute for a habilitation program;

(iv) prohibition of the excessive use of chemical restraints on such individuals and the use of such restraints as punishment or as a substitute for a habilitation program or in quantities that interfere with services, treatment, or habilitation for such individuals; and

(v) provision for close relatives or guardians of such individuals to visit the individuals without prior notice.

(4) All programs for individuals with developmental disabilities should meet standards—

(A) that are designed to assure the most favorable possible outcome for those served; and

(B)(i) in the case of residential programs serving individuals in need of comprehensive health-related, habilitative, assistive technology or rehabilitative services, that are at least equivalent to those standards applicable to intermediate care facilities for the mentally retarded, promulgated in regulations of the Secretary on June 3, 1988, as appropriate, taking into account the size of the institutions and the service delivery arrangements of the facilities of the programs;

(ii) in the case of other residential programs for individuals with developmental disabilities, that assure that—

(I) care is appropriate to the needs of the individuals being served by such programs;

(II) the individuals admitted to facilities of such programs are individuals whose needs can be met through services provided by such facilities; and

(III) the facilities of such programs provide for the humane care of the residents of the facilities, are sanitary, and protect their rights; and

(iii) in the case of nonresidential programs, that assure that the care provided by such programs is appropriate to the individuals served by the programs.

(b) Clarification. The rights of individuals with developmental disabilities described in findings made in this section shall be considered to be in addition to any constitutional or other rights otherwise afforded to all individuals.

(Oct. 30, 2000, P. L. 106-402, Title I, Subtitle A, § 109, 114 Stat. 1692.)

HISTORY; ANCILLARY LAWS AND DIRECTIVES

Explanatory notes:

The bracketed word "habilitation" has been inserted in subsec. (a)(2) to indicate the word probably intended by Congress.

CROSS REFERENCES

This section is referred to in 42 USCS §§ 15024, 15114.

RESEARCH GUIDE

Am Jur:

79 Am Jur 2d, Welfare § 49.

Federal Assistance to State Councils on Developmental Disabilities

CROSS REFERENCES

This subtitle (42 USCS §§ 15021 et seq.) is referred to in 42 USCS §§ 14403, 15004, 15005, 15043, 15081, 15083.

§ 15021. Purpose

The purpose of this subtitle [42 USCS §§ 15021 et seq.] is to provide for allotments to support State Councils on Developmental Disabilities (referred to individually in this subtitle [42 USCS §§ 15021 et seq.] as a "Council") in each State to—

(1) engage in advocacy, capacity building, and systemic change activities that are consistent with the purpose described in section 101(b) [42 USCS § 15001(b)] and the policy described in section 101(c) [42 USCS § 15001(c)]; and

(2) contribute to a coordinated, consumer- and family-centered, consumer- and family-directed, comprehensive system of community services, individualized supports, and other forms of assistance that enable individuals with developmental disabilities to exercise self-determination, be independent, be productive, and be integrated and included in all facets of community life.

(Oct. 30, 2000, P. L. 106-402, Title I, Subtitle B, § 121, 114 Stat. 1693.)

RESEARCH GUIDE

Annotations:
Validity, Construction, and Operation of Developmental Disabilities Assistance and Bill of Rights Act. 193 ALR Fed 513.

§ 15022. State allotments

(a) Allotments. (1) In general. (A) Authority. For each fiscal year, the Secretary shall, in accordance with regulations and this paragraph, allot the sums appropriated for such year under section 129 [42 USCS § 15029] among the States on the basis of—

(i) the population;

(ii) the extent of need for services for individuals with developmental disabilities; and

(iii) the financial need,

of the respective States.

(B) Use of funds. Sums allotted to the States under this section shall be used to pay for the Federal share of the cost of carrying out projects in accordance with State plans approved under section 124 [42 USCS § 15024] for the provision under such plans of services for individuals with developmental disabilities.

(2) Adjustments. The Secretary may make adjustments in the amounts of State allotments based on clauses (i), (ii), and (iii) of paragraph (1)(A) not more often than annually. The Secretary shall notify each State of any adjustment made under this paragraph and the percentage of the total sums appropriated under section 129 [42 USCS § 15029] that the adjusted allotment represents not later than 6 months before the beginning of the fiscal year in which such adjustment is to take effect.

(3) Minimum allotment for appropriations less than or equal to $70,000,000.

(A) In general. Except as provided in paragraph (4), for any fiscal year the allotment under this section—

(i) to each of American Samoa, Guam, the United States Virgin Islands, or the Commonwealth of the Northern Mariana Islands may not be less than $210,000; and

(ii) to any State not described in clause (i) may not be less than $400,000, the amount received by the State for the previous year, or the amount of Federal appropriations received in fiscal year 2000, 2001, or 2002, whichever is greater.

(B) Reduction of allotment. Notwithstanding subparagraph (A), if the aggregate of the amounts to be allotted to the States pursuant to subparagraph (A) for any fiscal year exceeds the total amount appropriated under section 129 [42 USCS § 15029] for such fiscal year, the amount to be allotted to each State for such fiscal year shall be proportionately reduced.

(4) Minimum allotment for appropriations in excess of $70,000,000. (A) In general. In any case in which the total amount appropriated under section

129 [42 USCS § 15029] for a fiscal year is more than $70,000,000, the allotment under this section for such fiscal year—

(i) to each of American Samoa, Guam, the United States Virgin Islands, or the Commonwealth of the Northern Mariana Islands may not be less than $220,000; and

(ii) to any State not described in clause (i) may not be less than $450,000, the amount received by the State for the previous year, or the amount of Federal appropriations received in fiscal year 2000, 2001, or 2002, whichever is greater.

(B) Reduction of allotment. The requirements of paragraph (3)(B) shall apply with respect to amounts to be allotted to States under subparagraph (A), in the same manner and to the same extent as such requirements apply with respect to amounts to be allotted to States under paragraph (3)(A).

(5) State supports, services, and other activities. In determining, for purposes of paragraph (1)(A)(ii), the extent of need in any State for services for individuals with developmental disabilities, the Secretary shall take into account the scope and extent of the services, supports, and assistance described, pursuant to section 124(c)(3)(A) [42 USCS § 15024(c)(3)(A)], in the State plan of the State.

(6) Increase in allotments. In any year in which the total amount appropriated under section 129 [42 USCS § 15029] for a fiscal year exceeds the total amount appropriated under such section (or a corresponding provision) for the preceding fiscal year by a percentage greater than the most recent percentage change in the Consumer Price Index published by the Secretary of Labor under section 100(c)(1) of the Rehabilitation Act of 1973 (29 U.S.C. 720(c)(1)) (if the percentage change indicates an increase), the Secretary shall increase each of the minimum allotments described in paragraphs (3) and (4). The Secretary shall increase each minimum allotment by an amount that bears the same ratio to the amount of such minimum allotment (including any increases in such minimum allotment under this paragraph (or a corresponding provision) for prior fiscal years) as the amount that is equal to the difference between—

(A) the total amount appropriated under section 129 [42 USCS § 15029] for the fiscal year for which the increase in the minimum allotment is being made; minus

(B) the total amount appropriated under section 129 [42 USCS § 15029] (or a corresponding provision) for the immediately preceding fiscal year, bears to the total amount appropriated under section 129 [42 USCS § 15029] (or a corresponding provision) for such preceding fiscal year.

(b) Unobligated funds. Any amount paid to a State for a fiscal year and remaining unobligated at the end of such year shall remain available to such State for the next fiscal year for the purposes for which such amount was paid.

(c) Obligation of funds. For the purposes of this subtitle [42 USCS §§ 15021 et seq.], State Interagency Agreements are considered valid obligations for the purpose of obligating Federal funds allotted to the State under this subtitle [42 USCS §§ 15021 et seq.].

(d) Cooperative efforts between States. If a State plan approved in accordance with section 124 [42 USCS § 15024] provides for cooperative or joint effort between or among States or agencies, public or private, in more than 1 State, portions of funds allotted to 1 or more States described in this subsection may be combined in accordance with the agreements between the States or agencies involved.

(e) Reallotments. (1) In general. If the Secretary determines that an amount of an allotment to a State for a period (of a fiscal year or longer) will not be required by the State during the period for the purpose for which the allotment was made, the Secretary may reallot the amount.

(2) Timing. The Secretary may make such a reallotment from time to time, on such date as the Secretary may fix, but not earlier than 30 days after the Secretary has published notice of the intention of the Secretary to make the reallotment in the Federal Register.

(3) Amounts. The Secretary shall reallot the amount to other States with respect to which the Secretary has not made that determination. The Secretary shall reallot the amount in proportion to the original allotments of the other States for such fiscal year, but shall reduce such proportionate amount for any of the other States to the extent the proportionate amount exceeds the sum that the Secretary estimates the State needs and will be able to use during such period.

(4) Reallotment of reductions. The Secretary shall similarly reallot the total of the reductions among the States whose proportionate amounts were not so reduced.

(5) Treatment. Any amount reallotted to a State under this subsection for a fiscal year shall be deemed to be a part of the allotment of the State under subsection (a) for such fiscal year.

(Oct. 30, 2000, P. L. 106-402, Title I, Subtitle B, § 122, 114 Stat. 1693; Dec. 3, 2003, P. L. 108-154, § 3(a), 117 Stat. 1934.)

HISTORY; ANCILLARY LAWS AND DIRECTIVES

Amendments:

2003. Act Dec. 3, 2003 (effective and applicable as provided by § 3(b) of such Act, which appears as a note to this section), in subsec. (a), in paras. (3)(A)(ii) and (4)(A)(ii), inserted ", the amount received by the State for the previous year, or the amount of Federal appropriations received in fiscal year 2000, 2001, or 2002, whichever is greater".

Other provisions:

Effective date and application of Dec. 3, 2003 amendments. Act Dec. 3, 2003, P. L. 108-154, § 3(b), 117 Stat. 1934, provides: "The amendments made by subsection (a) [amending subsec. (a)(3)(A)(ii), (4)(A)(ii) of this section] shall take effect on October 1, 2003 and apply to allotments beginning in fiscal year 2004.".

CROSS REFERENCES

This section is referred to in 42 USCS §§ 15023, 15024, 15026, 15027, 15029, 15042.

§ 15023. Payments to the States for planning, administration, and services

(a) State plan expenditures. From each State's allotments for a fiscal year under section 122 [42 USCS § 15022], the Secretary shall pay to the State the Federal share of the cost, other than the cost for construction, incurred during such year for activities carried out under the State plan approved under section 124 [42 USCS § 15024]. The Secretary shall make such payments from time to time in advance on the basis of estimates by the Secretary of the sums the State will expend for the cost under the State plan. The Secretary shall make such adjustments as may be necessary to the payments on account of previously made underpayments or overpayments under this section.

(b) Designated State agency expenditures. The Secretary may make payments to a State for the portion described in section 124(c)(5)(B)(vi) [42 USCS § 15024(c)(5)(B)(vi)] in advance or by way of reimbursement, and in such installments as the Secretary may determine.

(Oct. 30, 2000, P. L. 106-402, Title I, Subtitle B, § 123, 114 Stat. 1696.)

INTERPRETIVE NOTES AND DECISIONS

Where Virginia Office for Protection and Advocacy sued state official, alleging that refusal to produce records violated Developmental Disabilities Assistance and Bill of Rights Act of 2000 and Protection and Advocacy for Individuals with Mental Illness Act, Ex parte Young exception to sovereign immunity applied because, inter alia, suit satisfied straightforward inquiry and sought prospective relief, and state law created agency and gave it power to sue state officials. Va. Office for Prot. & Advocacy v Stewart (2011, US) 131 S Ct 1632, 179 L Ed 2d 675, 22 FLW Fed S 935.

§ 15024. State plan

(a) In general. Any State desiring to receive assistance under this subtitle [42 USCS §§ 15021 et seq.] shall submit to the Secretary, and obtain approval of, a 5-year strategic State plan under this section.

(b) Planning cycle. The plan described in subsection (a) shall be updated as appropriate during the 5-year period.

(c) State plan requirements. In order to be approved by the Secretary under this section, a State plan shall meet each of the following requirements:

(1) State Council. The plan shall provide for the establishment and maintenance of a Council in accordance with section 125 [42 USCS § 15025] and describe the membership of such Council.

(2) Designated State agency. The plan shall identify the agency or office within the State designated to support the Council in accordance with this section and section 125(d) [42 USCS § 15025(d)] (referred to in this subtitle [42 USCS §§ 15021 et seq.] as a "designated State agency").

(3) Comprehensive review and analysis. The plan shall describe the results of a comprehensive review and analysis of the extent to which services, supports, and other assistance are available to individuals with developmental disabilities and their families, and the extent of unmet needs for services, supports, and other assistance for those individuals and their families, in the State. The results of the comprehensive review and analysis shall include—

(A) a description of the services, supports, and other assistance being provided to individuals with developmental disabilities and their families under other federally assisted State programs, plans, and policies under which the State operates and in which individuals with developmental disabilities are or may be eligible to participate, including particularly programs relating to the areas of emphasis, including—

(i) medical assistance, maternal and child health care, services for children with special health care needs, children's mental health services, comprehensive health and mental health services, and institutional care options;

(ii) job training, job placement, worksite accommodation, and vocational rehabilitation, and other work assistance programs; and

(iii) social, child welfare, aging, independent living, and rehabilitation and assistive technology services, and such other services as the Secretary may specify;

(B) a description of the extent to which agencies operating such other federally assisted State programs, including activities authorized under section 4 or 5 of the Assistive Technology Act of 1998 [29 USCS § 3003 or 3004], pursue interagency initiatives to improve and enhance community services, individualized supports, and other forms of assistance for individuals with developmental disabilities;

(C) an analysis of the extent to which community services and opportunities related to the areas of emphasis directly benefit individuals with developmental disabilities, especially with regard to their ability to access and use services provided in their communities, to participate in opportunities, activities, and events offered in their communities, and to contribute to community life, identifying particularly—

(i) the degree of support for individuals with developmental disabilities that are attributable to either physical impairment, mental impairment, or a combination of physical and mental impairments;

(ii) criteria for eligibility for services, including specialized services and special adaptation of generic services provided by agencies within the State, that may exclude individuals with developmental disabilities from receiving services described in this clause;

(iii) the barriers that impede full participation of members of unserved and underserved groups of individuals with developmental disabilities and their families;

(iv) the availability of assistive technology, assistive technology services, or rehabilitation technology, or information about assistive technology, assistive technology services, or rehabilitation technology to individuals with developmental disabilities;

(v) the numbers of individuals with developmental disabilities on waiting lists for services described in this subparagraph;

(vi) a description of the adequacy of current resources and projected availability of future resources to fund services described in this subparagraph;

(vii) a description of the adequacy of health care and other services, supports, and assistance that individuals with developmental disabilities who are in facilities receive (based in part on each independent review (pursuant to section 1902(a)(30)(C) of the Social Security Act (42 U.S.C. 1396a(a)(30)(C))) of an Intermediate Care Facility (Mental Retardation) within the State, which the State shall provide to the Council not later than 30 days after the availability of the review); and

(viii) to the extent that information is available, a description of the adequacy of health care and other services, supports, and assistance that individuals with developmental disabilities who are served through home and community-based waivers (authorized under section 1915(c) of the Social Security Act (42 U.S.C. 1396n(c))) receive;

(D) a description of how entities funded under subtitles C and D [42 USCS §§ 15041 et seq., 15061 et seq.], through interagency agreements or other mechanisms, collaborated with the entity funded under this subtitle [42 USCS §§ 15021 et seq.] in the State, each other, and other entities to contribute to the achievement of the purpose of this subtitle [42 USCS §§ 15021 et seq.]; and

(E) the rationale for the goals related to advocacy, capacity building, and systemic change to be undertaken by the Council to contribute to the achievement of the purpose of this subtitle [42 USCS §§ 15021 et seq.].

(4) Plan goals. The plan shall focus on Council efforts to bring about the purpose of this subtitle [42 USCS §§ 15021 et seq.], by—

(A) specifying 5-year goals, as developed through data driven strategic planning, for advocacy, capacity building, and systemic change related to the areas of emphasis, to be undertaken by the Council, that—

(i) are derived from the unmet needs of individuals with developmental disabilities and their families identified under paragraph (3); and

(ii) include a goal, for each year of the grant, to—

(I) establish or strengthen a program for the direct funding of a State self-advocacy organization led by individuals with developmental disabilities;

(II) support opportunities for individuals with developmental disabilities who are considered leaders to provide leadership training to individuals with developmental disabilities who may become leaders; and

(III) support and expand participation of individuals with developmental disabilities in cross-disability and culturally diverse leadership coalitions; and

(B) for each year of the grant, describing—

(i) the goals to be achieved through the grant, which, beginning in fiscal year 2002, shall be consistent with applicable indicators of progress described in section 104(a)(3) [42 USCS § 15004(a)(3)];

(ii) the strategies to be used in achieving each goal; and

(iii) the method to be used to determine if each goal has been achieved.

(5) Assurances. (A) In general. The plan shall contain or be supported by assurances and information described in subparagraphs (B) through (N) that are satisfactory to the Secretary.

(B) Use of funds. With respect to the funds paid to the State under section 122 [42 USCS § 15022], the plan shall provide assurances that—

(i) not less than 70 percent of such funds will be expended for activities related to the goals described in paragraph (4);

(ii) such funds will contribute to the achievement of the purpose of this subtitle [42 USCS §§ 15021 et seq.] in various political subdivisions of the State;

(iii) such funds will be used to supplement, and not supplant, the non-Federal funds that would otherwise be made available for the purposes for which the funds paid under section 122 [42 USCS § 15022] are provided;

(iv) such funds will be used to complement and augment rather than duplicate or replace services for individuals with developmental disabilities and their families who are eligible for Federal assistance under other State programs;

(v) part of such funds will be made available by the State to public or private entities;

(vi) at the request of any State, a portion of such funds provided to such State under this subtitle [42 USCS §§ 15021 et seq.] for any fiscal year shall be available to pay up to $1/2$ (or the entire amount if the Council is the designated State agency) of the expenditures found to be necessary by the Secretary for the proper and efficient exercise of the functions of the designated State agency, except that not more than 5 percent of such funds provided to such State for any fiscal year, or $50,000, whichever is less, shall be made available for total expenditures for such purpose by the designated State agency; and

(vii) not more than 20 percent of such funds will be allocated to the designated State agency for service demonstrations by such agency that—

(I) contribute to the achievement of the purpose of this subtitle [42 USCS §§ 15021 et seq.]; and

(II) are explicitly authorized by the Council.

(C) State financial participation. The plan shall provide assurances that there will be reasonable State financial participation in the cost of carrying out the plan.

(D) Conflict of interest. The plan shall provide an assurance that no member of such Council will cast a vote on any matter that would provide direct financial benefit to the member or otherwise give the appearance of a conflict of interest.

(E) Urban and rural poverty areas. The plan shall provide assurances that special financial and technical assistance will be given to organizations that provide community services, individualized supports, and other forms of assistance to individuals with developmental disabilities who live in areas designated as urban or rural poverty areas.

(F) Program accessibility standards. The plan shall provide assurances that programs, projects, and activities funded under the plan, and the buildings in which such programs, projects, and activities are operated, will meet standards prescribed by the Secretary in regulations and all applicable Federal and State accessibility standards, including accessibility requirements of the Americans with Disabilities Act of 1990 (42 U.S.C. 12101 et seq.), section 508 of the Rehabilitation Act of 1973 (29 U.S.C. 794d), and the Fair Housing Act (42 U.S.C. 3601 et seq.).

(G) Individualized services. The plan shall provide assurances that any direct services provided to individuals with developmental disabilities and funded under the plan will be provided in an individualized manner, consistent with the unique strengths, resources, priorities, concerns, abilities, and capabilities of such individual.

(H) Human rights. The plan shall provide assurances that the human rights of the individuals with developmental disabilities (especially individuals without familial protection) who are receiving services under programs assisted under this subtitle [42 USCS §§ 15021 et seq.] will be protected consistent with section 109 [42 USCS § 15009] (relating to rights of individuals with developmental disabilities).

(I) Minority participation. The plan shall provide assurances that the State has taken affirmative steps to assure that participation in programs funded under this subtitle [42 USCS §§ 15021 et seq.] is geographically representative of the State, and reflects the diversity of the State with respect to race and ethnicity.

(J) Employee protections. The plan shall provide assurances that fair and equitable arrangements (as determined by the Secretary after consultation with the Secretary of Labor) will be provided to protect the interests of employees affected by actions taken under the plan to provide community living activities, including arrangements designed to preserve employee rights and benefits and provide training and retraining of such employees where necessary, and arrangements under which maximum efforts will be made to guarantee the employment of such employees.

(K) Staff assignments. The plan shall provide assurances that the staff and other personnel of the Council, while working for the Council, will be responsible solely for assisting the Council in carrying out the duties of the Council under this subtitle [42 USCS §§ 15021 et seq.] and will not be assigned duties by the designated State agency, or any other agency, office, or entity of the State.

(L) Noninterference. The plan shall provide assurances that the designated State agency, and any other agency, office, or entity of the State, will not interfere with the advocacy, capacity building, and systemic change activities, budget, personnel, State plan development, or plan implementation of the Council, except that the designated State agency shall have the authority necessary to carry out the responsibilities described in section 125(d)(3) [42 USCS § 15025(d)(3)].

(M) State quality assurance. The plan shall provide assurances that the Council will participate in the planning, design or redesign, and monitoring of State quality assurance systems that affect individuals with developmental disabilities.

(N) Other assurances. The plan shall contain such additional information and assurances as the Secretary may find necessary to carry out the provisions (including the purpose) of this subtitle [42 USCS §§ 15021 et seq.].

(d) Public input and review, submission, and approval. (1) Public input and review. The plan shall be based on public input. The Council shall make the plan available for public review and comment, after providing appropriate and sufficient notice in accessible formats of the opportunity for such review and comment. The Council shall revise the plan to take into account and respond to significant comments.

(2) Consultation with the designated State agency. Before the plan is submitted to the Secretary, the Council shall consult with the designated State agency to ensure that the State plan is consistent with State law and to obtain appropriate State plan assurances.

(3) Plan approval. The Secretary shall approve any State plan and, as appropriate, amendments of such plan that comply with the provisions of subsections (a), (b), and (c) and this subsection. The Secretary may take final action to disapprove a State plan after providing reasonable notice and an opportunity for a hearing to the State.

(Oct. 30, 2000, P. L. 106-402, Title I, Subtitle B, § 124, 114 Stat. 1696; Oct. 25, 2004, P. L. 108-364, § 3(a)(1), 118 Stat. 1736.)

HISTORY; ANCILLARY LAWS AND DIRECTIVES
Amendments:
2004. Act Oct. 25, 2004, in subsec. (c)(3)(B), substituted "section 4 or 5 of the Assistive Technology Act of 1998" for "section 101 or 102 of the Assistive Technology Act of 1998 (29 U.S.C. 3011, 3012)".

CROSS REFERENCES
This section is referred to in 42 USCS §§ 15022, 15023, 15025, 15026, 15027, 15028, 15044, 15064.

INTERPRETIVE NOTES AND DECISIONS

Where Virginia Office for Protection and Advocacy sued state official, alleging that refusal to produce records violated Developmental Disabilities Assistance and Bill of Rights Act of 2000 and Protection and Advocacy for Individuals with Mental Illness Act, Ex parte Young exception to sovereign immunity applied because, inter alia, suit satisfied straightforward inquiry and sought prospective relief, and state law created agency and gave it power to sue state officials. Va. Office for Prot. & Advocacy v Stewart (2011, US) 131 S Ct 1632, 179 L Ed 2d 675, 22 FLW Fed S 935.

§ 15025. State Councils on Developmental Disabilities and designated State agencies

(a) In general. Each State that receives assistance under this subtitle [42 USCS §§ 15021 et seq.] shall establish and maintain a Council to undertake advocacy, capacity building, and systemic change activities (consistent with subsections (b) and (c) of section 101 [42 USCS § 15001]) that contribute to a coordinated, consumer- and family-centered, consumer- and family-directed, comprehensive system of community services, individualized supports, and other forms of assistance that contribute to the achievement of the purpose of this subtitle [42

USCS §§ 15021 et seq.]. The Council shall have the authority to fulfill the responsibilities described in subsection (c).

(b) Council membership. (1) Council appointments. (A) In general. The members of the Council of a State shall be appointed by the Governor of the State from among the residents of that State.

(B) Recommendations. The Governor shall select members of the Council, at the discretion of the Governor, after soliciting recommendations from organizations representing a broad range of individuals with developmental disabilities and individuals interested in individuals with developmental disabilities, including the non-State agency members of the Council. The Council may, at the initiative of the Council, or on the request of the Governor, coordinate Council and public input to the Governor regarding all recommendations.

(C) Representation. The membership of the Council shall be geographically representative of the State and reflect the diversity of the State with respect to race and ethnicity.

(2) Membership rotation. The Governor shall make appropriate provisions to rotate the membership of the Council. Such provisions shall allow members to continue to serve on the Council until such members' successors are appointed. The Council shall notify the Governor regarding membership requirements of the Council, and shall notify the Governor when vacancies on the Council remain unfilled for a significant period of time.

(3) Representation of individuals with developmental disabilities. Not less than 60 percent of the membership of each Council shall consist of individuals who are—

(A)(i) individuals with developmental disabilities;

(ii) parents or guardians of children with developmental disabilities; or

(iii) immediate relatives or guardians of adults with mentally impairing developmental disabilities who cannot advocate for themselves; and

(B) not employees of a State agency that receives funds or provides services under this subtitle [42 USCS §§ 15021 et seq.], and who are not managing employees (as defined in section 1126(b) of the Social Security Act (42 U.S.C. 1320a-5(b)) of any other entity that receives funds or provides services under this subtitle [42 USCS §§ 15021 et seq.].

(4) Representation of agencies and organizations. (A) In general. Each Council shall include—

(i) representatives of relevant State entities, including—

(I) State entities that administer funds provided under Federal laws related to individuals with disabilities, including the Rehabilitation Act of 1973 (29 U.S.C. 701 et seq.), the Individuals with Disabilities Education Act (20 U.S.C. 1400 et seq.), the Older Americans Act of 1965 (42 U.S.C. 3001 et seq.), and titles V and XIX of the Social Security Act (42 U.S.C. 701 et seq. and 1396 et seq.);

(II) Centers in the State; and

(III) the State protection and advocacy system; and

(ii) representatives, at all times, of local and nongovernmental agencies, and private nonprofit groups concerned with services for individuals with developmental disabilities in the State in which such agencies and groups are located.

(B) Authority and limitations. The representatives described in subparagraph (A) shall—

(i) have sufficient authority to engage in policy planning and implementation on behalf of the department, agency, or program such representatives represent; and

(ii) recuse themselves from any discussion of grants or contracts for which such representatives' departments, agencies, or programs are grantees, contractors, or applicants and comply with the conflict of interest assurance requirement under section 124(c)(5)(D) [42 USCS § 15024(c)(5)(D)].

(5) Composition of membership with developmental disabilities. Of the members of the Council described in paragraph (3)—

(A) $1/3$ shall be individuals with developmental disabilities described in paragraph (3)(A)(i);

(B) $1/3$ shall be parents or guardians of children with developmental disabilities described in paragraph (3)(A)(ii), or immediate relatives or guardians of adults with developmental disabilities described in paragraph (3)(A)(iii); and

(C) $1/3$ shall be a combination of individuals described in paragraph (3)(A).

(6) Institutionalized individuals. (A) In general. Of the members of the Council described in paragraph (5), at least 1 shall be an immediate relative or guardian of an individual with a developmental disability who resides or previously resided in an institution or shall be an individual with a developmental disability who resides or previously resided in an institution.

(B) Limitation. Subparagraph (A) shall not apply with respect to a State if such an individual does not reside in that State.

(c) **Council responsibilities.** (1) In general. A Council, through Council members, staff, consultants, contractors, or subgrantees, shall have the responsibilities described in paragraphs (2) through (10).

(2) Advocacy, capacity building, and systemic change activities. The Council shall serve as an advocate for individuals with developmental disabilities and conduct or support programs, projects, and activities that carry out the purpose of this subtitle [42 USCS §§ 15021 et seq.].

(3) Examination of goals. At the end of each grant year, each Council shall—

(A) determine the extent to which each goal of the Council was achieved for that year;

(B) determine to the extent that each goal was not achieved, the factors that impeded the achievement;

(C) determine needs that require amendment of the 5-year strategic State plan required under section 124 [42 USCS § 15024];

(D) separately determine the information on the self-advocacy goal described in section 124(c)(4)(A)(ii) [42 USCS § 15024(c)(4)(A)(ii)]; and

(E) determine customer satisfaction with Council supported or conducted activities.

(4) State plan development. The Council shall develop the State plan and submit the State plan to the Secretary after consultation with the designated State agency under the State plan. Such consultation shall be solely for the purposes of obtaining State assurances and ensuring consistency of the plan with State law.

(5) State plan implementation. (A) In general. The Council shall implement the State plan by conducting and supporting advocacy, capacity building, and systemic change activities such as those described in subparagraphs (B) through (L).

(B) Outreach. The Council may support and conduct outreach activities to identify individuals with developmental disabilities and their families who otherwise might not come to the attention of the Council and assist and enable the individuals and families to obtain services, individualized supports, and other forms of assistance, including access to special adaptation of generic community services or specialized services.

(C) Training. The Council may support and conduct training for persons who are individuals with developmental disabilities, their families, and personnel (including professionals, paraprofessionals, students, volunteers, and other community members) to enable such persons to obtain access to, or to provide, community services, individualized supports, and other forms of assistance, including special adaptation of generic community services or specialized services for individuals with developmental disabilities and their families. To the extent that the Council supports or conducts training activities under this subparagraph, such activities shall contribute to the achievement of the purpose of this subtitle [42 USCS §§ 15021 et seq.].

(D) Technical assistance. The Council may support and conduct technical assistance activities to assist public and private entities to contribute to the achievement of the purpose of this subtitle [42 USCS §§ 15021 et seq.].

(E) Supporting and educating communities. The Council may support and conduct activities to assist neighborhoods and communities to respond positively to individuals with developmental disabilities and their families—

(i) by encouraging local networks to provide informal and formal supports;

(ii) through education; and

(iii) by enabling neighborhoods and communities to offer such individuals and their families access to and use of services, resources, and opportunities.

(F) Interagency collaboration and coordination. The Council may support and conduct activities to promote interagency collaboration and coordination to better serve, support, assist, or advocate for individuals with developmental disabilities and their families.

(G) Coordination with related councils, committees, and programs. The Council may support and conduct activities to enhance coordination of services with—

(i) other councils, entities, or committees, authorized by Federal or State law, concerning individuals with disabilities (such as the State interagency coordinating council established under part C of the Individuals with Disabilities Education Act (20 U.S.C. 1431 et seq.), the State Rehabilitation Council and the Statewide Independent Living Council established under the Rehabilitation Act of 1973 (29 U.S.C. 701 et seq.), the State mental health planning council established under subtitle B of title XIX of the Public Health Service Act (42 U.S.C. 300x-1 et seq.), and the activities authorized under section 4 or 5 of the Assistive Technology Act of 1998 [29 USCS § 3003 or 3004], and entities carrying out other similar councils, entities, or committees);

(ii) parent training and information centers under part D of the Individuals with Disabilities Education Act (20 U.S.C. 1451 et seq.) and other entities carrying out federally funded projects that assist parents of children with disabilities; and

(iii) other groups interested in advocacy, capacity building, and systemic change activities to benefit individuals with disabilities.

(H) Barrier elimination, systems design and redesign. The Council may support and conduct activities to eliminate barriers to access and use of community services by individuals with developmental disabilities, enhance systems design and redesign, and enhance citizen participation to address issues identified in the State plan.

(I) Coalition development and citizen participation. The Council may support and conduct activities to educate the public about the capabilities, preferences, and needs of individuals with developmental disabilities and their families and to develop and support coalitions that support the policy agenda of the Council, including training in self-advocacy, education of policymakers, and citizen leadership skills.

(J) Informing policymakers. The Council may support and conduct activities to provide information to policymakers by supporting and conducting studies and analyses, gathering information, and developing and disseminating model policies and procedures, information, approaches, strategies, findings, conclusions, and recommendations. The Council may provide the information directly to Federal, State, and local policymakers, including Congress, the Federal executive branch, the Governors, State legislatures, and State agencies, in order to increase the ability of such policymakers to offer opportunities and to enhance or adapt generic services to meet the needs of, or provide specialized services to, individuals with developmental disabilities and their families.

(K) Demonstration of new approaches to services and supports. (i) In general. The Council may support and conduct, on a time-limited basis, activities to demonstrate new approaches to serving individuals with developmental disabilities that are a part of an overall strategy for systemic change. The strategy may involve the education of policymakers and the public about how to deliver effectively, to individuals with developmental disabilities and their families, services, supports, and assistance that contribute to the achievement of the purpose of this subtitle [42 USCS §§ 15021 et seq.].

(ii) Sources of funding. The Council may carry out this subparagraph by supporting and conducting demonstration activities through sources of funding other than funding provided under this subtitle [42 USCS §§ 15021 et seq.], and by assisting entities conducting demonstration activities to develop strategies for securing funding from other sources.

(L) Other activities. The Council may support and conduct other advocacy, capacity building, and systemic change activities to promote the development of a coordinated, consumer- and family-centered, consumer- and family-directed, comprehensive system of community services, individualized supports, and other forms of assistance that contribute to the achievement of the purpose of this subtitle [42 USCS §§ 15021 et seq.].

(6) Review of designated State agency. The Council shall periodically review the designated State agency and activities carried out under this subtitle [42 USCS §§ 15021 et seq.] by the designated State agency and make any recommendations for change to the Governor.

(7) Reports. Beginning in fiscal year 2002, the Council shall annually prepare and transmit to the Secretary a report. Each report shall be in a form prescribed by the Secretary by regulation under section 104(b) [42 USCS § 15004(b)]. Each report shall contain information about the progress made by the Council in achieving the goals of the Council (as specified in section 124(c)(4) [42 USCS § 15024(c)(4)]), including—

(A) a description of the extent to which the goals were achieved;

(B) a description of the strategies that contributed to achieving the goals;

(C) to the extent to which the goals were not achieved, a description of factors that impeded the achievement;

(D) separate information on the self-advocacy goal described in section 124(c)(4)(A)(ii) [42 USCS § 15024(c)(4)(A)(ii)];

(E)(i) as appropriate, an update on the results of the comprehensive review and analysis described in section 124(c)(3) [42 USCS § 15024(c)(3)]; and

(ii) information on consumer satisfaction with Council supported or conducted activities;

(F)(i) a description of the adequacy of health care and other services, supports, and assistance that individuals with developmental disabilities in Intermediate Care Facilities (Mental Retardation) receive; and

(ii) a description of the adequacy of health care and other services, supports, and assistance that individuals with developmental disabilities served through home and community-based waivers (authorized under section 1915(c) of the Social Security Act (42 U.S.C. 1396n(c)) receive;

(G) an accounting of the manner in which funds paid to the State under this subtitle [42 USCS §§ 15021 et seq.] for a fiscal year were expended;

(H) a description of—

(i) resources made available to carry out activities to assist individuals with developmental disabilities that are directly attributable to Council actions; and

(ii) resources made available for such activities that are undertaken by the Council in collaboration with other entities; and

(I) a description of the method by which the Council will widely disseminate the annual report to affected constituencies and the general public and will assure that the report is available in accessible formats.

(8) Budget. Each Council shall prepare, approve, and implement a budget using amounts paid to the State under this subtitle [42 USCS §§ 15021 et seq.] to fund and implement all programs, projects, and activities carried out under this subtitle [42 USCS §§ 15021 et seq.], including—

(A)(i) conducting such hearings and forums as the Council may determine to be necessary to carry out the duties of the Council; and

(ii) as determined in Council policy—

(I) reimbursing members of the Council for reasonable and necessary expenses (including expenses for child care and personal assistance services) for attending Council meetings and performing Council duties;

(II) paying a stipend to a member of the Council, if such member is not employed or must forfeit wages from other employment, to attend Council meetings and perform other Council duties;

(III) supporting Council member and staff travel to authorized training and technical assistance activities including in-service training and leadership development activities; and

(IV) carrying out appropriate subcontracting activities;

(B) hiring and maintaining such numbers and types of staff (qualified by training and experience) and obtaining the services of such professional, consulting, technical, and clerical staff (qualified by training and experience), consistent with State law, as the Council determines to be necessary to carry out the functions of the Council under this subtitle [42 USCS §§ 15021 et seq.], except that such State shall not apply hiring freezes, reductions in force, prohibitions on travel, or other policies to the staff of the Council, to the extent that such policies would impact the staff or functions funded with Federal funds, or would prevent the Council from carrying out the functions of the Council under this subtitle [42 USCS §§ 15021 et seq.]; and

(C) directing the expenditure of funds for grants, contracts, interagency agreements that are binding contracts, and other activities authorized by the State plan approved under section 124 [42 USCS § 15024].

(9) Staff hiring and supervision. The Council shall, consistent with State law, recruit and hire a Director of the Council, should the position of Director become vacant, and supervise and annually evaluate the Director. The Director shall hire, supervise, and annually evaluate the staff of the Council. Council recruitment, hiring, and dismissal of staff shall be conducted in a manner consistent with Federal and State nondiscrimination laws. Dismissal of personnel shall be conducted in a manner consistent with State law and personnel policies.

(10) Staff assignments. The staff of the Council, while working for the Council, shall be responsible solely for assisting the Council in carrying out the duties of the Council under this subtitle [42 USCS §§ 15021 et seq.] and shall not be assigned duties by the designated State agency or any other agency or entity of the State.

(11) Construction. Nothing in this title [42 USCS §§ 15001 et seq.] shall be construed to authorize a Council to direct, control, or exercise any policy-making authority or administrative authority over any program assisted under the Rehabilitation Act of 1973 (29 U.S.C. 701 et seq.) or the Individuals with Disabilities Education Act (20 U.S.C. 1400 et seq.).

(d) Designated State agency. (1) In general. Each State that receives assistance under this subtitle [42 USCS §§ 15021 et seq.] shall designate a State agency that shall, on behalf of the State, provide support to the Council. After the date of enactment of the Developmental Disabilities Assistance and Bill of Rights Act Amendments of 1994 (Public Law 103-230) [enacted April 6, 1994], any designation of a State agency under this paragraph shall be made in accordance with the requirements of this subsection.

(2) Designation. (A) Type of agency. Except as provided in this subsection, the designated State agency shall be—

(i) the Council if such Council may be the designated State agency under the laws of the State;

(ii) a State agency that does not provide or pay for services for individuals with developmental disabilities; or

(iii) a State office, including the immediate office of the Governor of the State or a State planning office.

(B) Conditions for continuation of State service agency designation. (i) Designation before enactment. If a State agency that provides or pays for services for individuals with developmental disabilities was a designated State agency for purposes of part B of the Developmental Disabilities Assistance and Bill of Rights Act [42 USCS §§ 6021 et seq.] on the date of enactment of the Developmental Disabilities Assistance and Bill of Rights Act Amendments of 1994 [enacted April 6, 1994], and the Governor of the State (or the legislature, where appropriate and in accordance with State law) determines prior to June 30, 1994, not to change the designation of such agency, such agency may continue to be a designated State agency for purposes of this subtitle [42 USCS §§ 15021 et seq.].

(ii) Criteria for continued designation. The determination, at the discretion of the Governor (or the legislature, as the case may be), shall be made after—

(I) the Governor has considered the comments and recommendations of the general public and a majority of the non-State agency members of the Council with respect to the designation of such State agency; and

(II) the Governor (or the legislature, as the case may be) has made an independent assessment that the designation of such agency will not interfere with the budget, personnel, priorities, or other action of the Council, and the ability of the Council to serve as an independent advocate for individuals with developmental disabilities.

(C) Review of designation. The Council may request a review of and change in the designation of the designated State agency by the Governor (or the legislature, as the case may be). The Council shall provide documentation concerning the reason the Council desires a change to be made and make a recommendation to the Governor (or the legislature, as the case may be) regarding a preferred designated State agency.

(D) Appeal of designation. After the review is completed under subparagraph (C), a majority of the non-State agency members of the Council may appeal to the Secretary for a review of and change in the designation of the designated State agency if the ability of the Council to serve as an independent advocate is not assured because of the actions or inactions of the designated State agency.

(3) Responsibilities. (A) In general. The designated State agency shall, on behalf of the State, have the responsibilities described in subparagraphs (B) through (G).

(B) Support services. The designated State agency shall provide required assurances and support services as requested by and negotiated with the Council.

(C) Fiscal responsibilities. The designated State agency shall—

(i) receive, account for, and disburse funds under this subtitle [42 USCS §§ 15021 et seq.] based on the State plan required in section 124 [42 USCS § 15024]; and

(ii) provide for such fiscal control and fund accounting procedures as may be necessary to assure the proper disbursement of, and accounting for, funds paid to the State under this subtitle [42 USCS §§ 15021 et seq.].

(D) Records, access, and financial reports. The designated State agency shall keep and provide access to such records as the Secretary and the Council may determine to be necessary. The designated State agency, if other than the Council, shall provide timely financial reports at the request of the Council regarding the status of expenditures, obligations, and liquidation by the agency or the Council, and the use of the Federal and non-Federal shares described in section 126 [42 USCS § 15026], by the agency or the Council.

(E) Non-Federal share. The designated State agency, if other than the Council, shall provide the required non-Federal share described in section 126(c) [42 USCS § 15026(c)].

(F) Assurances. The designated State agency shall assist the Council in obtaining the appropriate State plan assurances and in ensuring that the plan is consistent with State law.

(G) Memorandum of understanding. On the request of the Council, the designated State agency shall enter into a memorandum of understanding with the Council delineating the roles and responsibilities of the designated State agency.

(4) Use of funds for designated State agency responsibilities. (A) Condition for Federal funding. (i) In general. The Secretary shall provide amounts to a State under section 124(c)(5)(B)(vi) [42 USCS § 15024(c)(5)(B)(vi)] for a fiscal year only if the State expends an amount from State sources for carrying out the responsibilities of the

designated State agency under paragraph (3) for the fiscal year that is not less than the total amount the State expended from such sources for carrying out similar responsibilities for the previous fiscal year.

(ii) Exception. Clause (i) shall not apply in a year in which the Council is the designated State agency.

(B) Support services provided by other agencies. With the agreement of the designated State agency, the Council may use or contract with agencies other than the designated State agency to perform the functions of the designated State agency.

(Oct. 30, 2000, P. L. 106-402, Title I, Subtitle B, § 125, 114 Stat. 1701; Oct. 25, 2004, P. L. 108-364, § 3(a)(2), 118 Stat. 1736; Dec. 3, 2004, P. L. 108-446, Title III, § 305(n)(1), 118 Stat. 2806.)

HISTORY; ANCILLARY LAWS AND DIRECTIVES

Amendments:

2004. Act Oct. 25, 2004, in subsec. (c)(5)(G)(i), substituted "section 4 or 5 of the Assistive Technology Act of 1998" for "section 101 or 102 of the Assistive Technology Act of 1998 (29 U.S.C. 3011, 3012)".

Act Dec. 3, 2004, in subsec. (c)(5)(G)(i), substituted "part C" for "subtitle C".

CROSS REFERENCES

This section is referred to in 29 USCS § 725; 42 USCS §§ 1396u, 15002, 15024, 15026, 15027.

§ 15026. Federal and non-Federal share

(a) **Aggregate cost.** (1) In general. Except as provided in paragraphs (2) and (3), the Federal share of the cost of all projects in a State supported by an allotment to the State under this subtitle [42 USCS §§ 15021 et seq.] may not be more than 75 percent of the aggregate necessary cost of such projects, as determined by the Secretary.

(2) Urban or rural poverty areas. In the case of projects whose activities or products target individuals with developmental disabilities who live in urban or rural poverty areas, as determined by the Secretary, the Federal share of the cost of all such projects may not be more than 90 percent of the aggregate necessary cost of such projects, as determined by the Secretary.

(3) State plan activities. In the case of projects undertaken by the Council or Council staff to implement State plan activities, the Federal share of the cost of all such projects may be not more than 100 percent of the aggregate necessary cost of such activities.

(b) **Nonduplication.** In determining the amount of any State's Federal share of the cost of such projects incurred by such State under a State plan approved under section 124 [42 USCS § 15024], the Secretary shall not consider—

(1) any portion of such cost that is financed by Federal funds provided under any provision of law other than section 122 [42 USCS § 15022]; and

(2) the amount of any non-Federal funds required to be expended as a condition of receipt of the Federal funds described in paragraph (1).

(c) Non-Federal share. (1) In-kind contributions. The non-Federal share of the cost of any project supported by an allotment under this subtitle [42 USCS §§ 15021 et seq.] may be provided in cash or in kind, fairly evaluated, including plant, equipment, or services.

(2) Contributions of political subdivisions and public or private entities. (A) In general. Contributions to projects by a political subdivision of a State or by a public or private entity under an agreement with the State shall, subject to such limitations and conditions as the Secretary may by regulation prescribe under section 104(b) [42 USCS § 15004(b)], be considered to be contributions by such State, in the case of a project supported under this subtitle [42 USCS §§ 15021 et seq.].

(B) State contributions. State contributions, including contributions by the designated State agency to provide support services to the Council pursuant to section 125(d)(4) [42 USCS § 15025(d)(4)], may be counted as part of such State's non-Federal share of the cost of projects supported under this subtitle [42 USCS §§ 15021 et seq.].

(3) Variations of the non-Federal share. The non-Federal share required of each recipient of a grant from a Council under this subtitle [42 USCS §§ 15021 et seq.] may vary.

(Oct. 30, 2000, P. L. 106-402, Title I, Subtitle B, § 126, 114 Stat. 1710.)

CROSS REFERENCES

This section is referred to in 42 USCS § 15025.

§ 15027. Withholding of payments for planning, administration, and services

Whenever the Secretary, after providing reasonable notice and an opportunity for a hearing to the Council and the designated State agency, finds that—

(1) the Council or agency has failed to comply substantially with any of the provisions required by section 124 [42 USCS § 15024] to be included in the State plan, particularly provisions required by paragraphs (4)(A) and (5)(B)(vii) of section 124(c) [42 USCS § 15024(c)], or with any of the provisions required by section 125(b)(3) [42 USCS § 15025(b)(3)]; or

(2) the Council or agency has failed to comply substantially with any regulations of the Secretary that are applicable to this subtitle [42 USCS §§ 15021 et seq.],

the Secretary shall notify such Council and agency that the Secretary will not make further payments to the State under section 122 [42 USCS § 15022] (or, in the discretion of the Secretary, that further payments to the State under section 122 [42 USCS § 15022] for activities for which there is such failure), until the Secretary is satisfied that there will no longer be such failure. Until the Secretary is so satisfied, the Secretary shall make no further payments to the State under section 122 [42 USCS § 15022], or shall limit further payments under section 122 [42 USCS § 15022] to such State to activities for which there is no such failure.

(Oct. 30, 2000, P. L. 106-402, Title I, Subtitle B, § 127, 114 Stat. 1711.)

CROSS REFERENCES
This section is referred to in 42 USCS § 15028.

§ 15028. Appeals by States

(a) Appeal. If any State is dissatisfied with the Secretary's action under section 124(d)(3) or 127 [42 USCS § 15024(d)(3) or 15027], such State may appeal to the United States court of appeals for the circuit in which such State is located, by filing a petition with such court not later than 60 days after such action.

(b) Filing. The clerk of the court shall transmit promptly a copy of the petition to the Secretary, or any officer designated by the Secretary for that purpose. The Secretary shall file promptly with the court the record of the proceedings on which the Secretary based the action, as provided in section 2112 of title 28, United States Code.

(c) Jurisdiction. Upon the filing of the petition, the court shall have jurisdiction to affirm the action of the Secretary or to set the action aside, in whole or in part, temporarily or permanently. Until the filing of the record, the Secretary may modify or set aside the order of the Secretary relating to the action.

(d) Findings and remand. The findings of the Secretary about the facts, if supported by substantial evidence, shall be conclusive, but the court, for good cause shown, may remand the case involved to the Secretary for further proceedings to take further evidence. On remand, the Secretary may make new or modified findings of fact and may modify the previous action of the Secretary, and shall file with the court the record of the further proceedings. Such new or modified findings of fact shall likewise be conclusive if supported by substantial evidence.

(e) Finality. The judgment of the court affirming or setting aside, in whole or in part, any action of the Secretary shall be final, subject to review by the Supreme Court of the United States upon certiorari or certification as provided in section 1254 of title 28, United States Code.

(f) Effect. The commencement of proceedings under this section shall not, unless so specifically ordered by a court, operate as a stay of the Secretary's action.

(Oct. 30, 2000, P. L. 106-402, Title I, Subtitle B, § 128, 114 Stat. 1711.)

§ 15029. Authorization of appropriations

(a) Funding for State allotments. Except as described in subsection (b), there are authorized to be appropriated for allotments under section 122 [42 USCS § 15022] $76,000,000 for fiscal year 2001 and such sums as may be necessary for each of fiscal years 2002 through 2007.

(b) Reservation for technical assistance. (1) Lower appropriation years. For any fiscal year for which the amount appropriated under subsection (a) is less than $76,000,000, the Secretary shall reserve funds in accordance with section 163(c) [42 USCS § 15083(c)] to provide technical assistance to entities funded under this subtitle [42 USCS §§ 15021 et seq.].

(2) Higher appropriation years. For any fiscal year for which the amount appropriated under subsection (a) is not less than $76,000,000, the Secretary shall reserve not less than $300,000 and not more than 1 percent of the amount appropriated under subsection (a) to provide technical assistance to entities funded under this subtitle [42 USCS §§ 15021 et seq.].
(Oct. 30, 2000, P. L. 106-402, Title I, Subtitle B, § 129, 114 Stat. 1712.)

CROSS REFERENCES
This section is referred to in 42 USCS §§ 15022, 15081, 15083, 15461, 15462.

Protection and Advocacy of Individual Rights

CROSS REFERENCES
This subtitle (42 USCS §§ 15041 et seq.) is referred to in 29 USCS §§ 794e, 3002, 3004; 42 USCS §§ 1396r, 1396u, 3058g, 10802, 14404, 15004, 15024, 15083, 15461, 15462.

§ 15041. Purpose

The purpose of this subtitle [42 USCS §§ 15041 et seq.] is to provide for allotments to support a protection and advocacy system (referred to in this subtitle [42 USCS §§ 15041 et seq.] as a "system") in each State to protect the legal and human rights of individuals with developmental disabilities in accordance with this subtitle [42 USCS §§ 15041 et seq.].
(Oct. 30, 2000, P. L. 106-402, Title I, Subtitle C, § 141, 114 Stat. 1712.)

RESEARCH GUIDE
Annotations:
Validity, Construction, and Operation of Developmental Disabilities Assistance and Bill of Rights Act. 193 ALR Fed 513.

§ 15042. Allotments and payments

(a) **Allotments.** (1) In general. To assist States in meeting the requirements of section 143(a) [42 USCS § 15043(a)], the Secretary shall allot to the States the amounts appropriated under section 145 [42 USCS § 15045] and not reserved under paragraph (6). Allotments and reallotments of such sums shall be made on the same basis as the allotments and reallotments are made under subsections (a)(1)(A) and (e) of section 122 [42 USCS § 15022], except as provided in paragraph (2).
(2) Minimum allotments. In any case in which—
   (A) the total amount appropriated under section 145 [42 USCS § 15045] for a fiscal year is not less than $20,000,000, the allotment under paragraph (1) for such fiscal year—
      (i) to each of American Samoa, Guam, the United States Virgin Islands, and the Commonwealth of the Northern Mariana Islands may not be less than $107,000; and
      (ii) to any State not described in clause (i) may not be less than $200,000; or
   (B) the total amount appropriated under section 145 [42 USCS § 15045]

for a fiscal year is less than $20,000,000, the allotment under paragraph (1) for such fiscal year—

(i) to each of American Samoa, Guam, the United States Virgin Islands, and the Commonwealth of the Northern Mariana Islands may not be less than $80,000; and

(ii) to any State not described in clause (i) may not be less than $150,000.

(3) Reduction of allotment. Notwithstanding paragraphs (1) and (2), if the aggregate of the amounts to be allotted to the States pursuant to such paragraphs for any fiscal year exceeds the total amount appropriated for such allotments under section 145 [42 USCS § 15045] for such fiscal year, the amount to be allotted to each State for such fiscal year shall be proportionately reduced.

(4) Increase in allotments. In any year in which the total amount appropriated under section 145 [42 USCS § 15045] for a fiscal year exceeds the total amount appropriated under such section (or a corresponding provision) for the preceding fiscal year by a percentage greater than the most recent percentage change in the Consumer Price Index published by the Secretary of Labor under section 100(c)(1) of the Rehabilitation Act of 1973 (29 U.S.C. 720(c)(1)) (if the percentage change indicates an increase), the Secretary shall increase each of the minimum allotments described in subparagraphs (A) and (B) of paragraph (2). The Secretary shall increase each minimum allotment by an amount that bears the same ratio to the amount of such minimum allotment (including any increases in such minimum allotment under this paragraph (or a corresponding provision) for prior fiscal years) as the amount that is equal to the difference between—

(A) the total amount appropriated under section 145 [42 USCS § 15045] for the fiscal year for which the increase in the minimum allotment is being made; minus

(B) the total amount appropriated under section 145 [42 USCS § 15045] (or a corresponding provision) for the immediately preceding fiscal year,

bears to the total amount appropriated under section 145 [42 USCS § 15045] (or a corresponding provision) for such preceding fiscal year.

(5) Monitoring the administration of the system. In a State in which the system is housed in a State agency, the State may use not more than 5 percent of any allotment under this subsection for the costs of monitoring the administration of the system required under section 143(a) [42 USCS § 15043(a)].

(6) Technical assistance and American Indian consortium. In any case in which the total amount appropriated under section 145 [42 USCS § 15045] for a fiscal year is more than $24,500,000, the Secretary shall—

(A) use not more than 2 percent of the amount appropriated to provide technical assistance to eligible systems with respect to activities carried out under this subtitle [42 USCS §§ 15041 et seq.] (consistent with requests by such systems for such assistance for the year); and

(B) provide a grant in accordance with section 143(b) [42 USCS § 15043(b)], and in an amount described in paragraph (2)(A)(i), to an American Indian consortium to provide protection and advocacy services.

(b) Payment to systems. Notwithstanding any other provision of law, the Secretary shall pay directly to any system in a State that complies with the provisions of this subtitle [42 USCS §§ 15041 et seq.] the amount of the allotment made for the State under this section, unless the system specifies otherwise.

(c) Unobligated funds. Any amount paid to a system under this subtitle [42 USCS §§ 15041 et seq.] for a fiscal year and remaining unobligated at the end of such year shall remain available to such system for the next fiscal year, for the purposes for which such amount was paid.

(Oct. 30, 2000, P. L. 106-402, Title I, Subtitle C, § 142, 114 Stat. 1712.)

CROSS REFERENCES

This section is referred to in 42 USCS §§ 15043, 15045.

INTERPRETIVE NOTES AND DECISIONS

Where Virginia Office for Protection and Advocacy sued state official, alleging that refusal to produce records violated Developmental Disabilities Assistance and Bill of Rights Act of 2000 and Protection and Advocacy for Individuals with Mental Illness Act, Ex parte Young exception to sovereign immunity applied because, inter alia, suit satisfied straightforward inquiry and sought prospective relief, and state law created agency and gave it power to sue state officials. Va. Office for Prot. & Advocacy v Stewart (2011, US) 131 S Ct 1632, 179 L Ed 2d 675, 22 FLW Fed S 935.

§ 15043. System required

(a) System required. In order for a State to receive an allotment under subtitle B or this subtitle [42 USCS §§ 15021 et seq. or 15041 et seq.]—

(1) the State shall have in effect a system to protect and advocate the rights of individuals with developmental disabilities;

(2) such system shall—

(A) have the authority to—

(i) pursue legal, administrative, and other appropriate remedies or approaches to ensure the protection of, and advocacy for, the rights of such individuals within the State who are or who may be eligible for treatment, services, or habilitation, or who are being considered for a change in living arrangements, with particular attention to members of ethnic and racial minority groups; and

(ii) provide information on and referral to programs and services addressing the needs of individuals with developmental disabilities;

(B) have the authority to investigate incidents of abuse and neglect of individuals with developmental disabilities if the incidents are reported to the system or if there is probable cause to believe that the incidents occurred;

(C) on an annual basis, develop, submit to the Secretary, and take action with regard to goals (each of which is related to 1 or more areas of emphasis) and priorities, developed through data driven strategic planning, for the system's activities;

(D) on an annual basis, provide to the public, including individuals with developmental disabilities attributable to either physical impairment, mental impairment, or a combination of physical and mental impairment, and their representatives, and as appropriate, non-State agency representatives of the State Councils on Developmental Disabilities, and Centers, in the State, an opportunity to comment on—

(i) the goals and priorities established by the system and the rationale for the establishment of such goals; and

(ii) the activities of the system, including the coordination of services with the entities carrying out advocacy programs under the Rehabilitation Act of 1973 (29 U.S.C. 701 et seq.), the Older Americans Act of 1965 (42 U.S.C. 3001 et seq.), and the Protection and Advocacy for Mentally Ill Individuals Act of 1986 (42 U.S.C. 10801 et seq.), and with entities carrying out other related programs, including the parent training and information centers funded under the Individuals with Disabilities Education Act (20 U.S.C. 1400 et seq.), and activities authorized under section 4 or 5 of the Assistive Technology Act of 1998 [29 USCS § 3003 or 3004];

(E) establish a grievance procedure for clients or prospective clients of the system to ensure that individuals with developmental disabilities have full access to services of the system;

(F) not be administered by the State Council on Developmental Disabilities;

(G) be independent of any agency that provides treatment, services, or habilitation to individuals with developmental disabilities;

(H) have access at reasonable times to any individual with a developmental disability in a location in which services, supports, and other assistance are provided to such an individual, in order to carry out the purpose of this subtitle [42 USCS §§ 15041 et seq.];

(I) have access to all records of—

(i) any individual with a developmental disability who is a client of the system if such individual, or the legal guardian, conservator, or other legal representative of such individual, has authorized the system to have such access;

(ii) any individual with a developmental disability, in a situation in which—

(I) the individual, by reason of such individual's mental or physical condition, is unable to authorize the system to have such access;

(II) the individual does not have a legal guardian, conservator, or other legal representative, or the legal guardian of the individual is the State; and

(III) a complaint has been received by the system about the individual with regard to the status or treatment of the individual or, as a result of monitoring or other activities, there is probable cause to believe that such individual has been subject to abuse or neglect; and

(iii) any individual with a developmental disability, in a situation in which—

(I) the individual has a legal guardian, conservator, or other legal representative;

(II) a complaint has been received by the system about the individual with regard to the status or treatment of the individual or, as a result of monitoring or other activities, there is probable cause to believe that such individual has been subject to abuse or neglect;

(III) such representative has been contacted by such system, upon receipt of the name and address of such representative;

(IV) such system has offered assistance to such representative to resolve the situation; and

(V) such representative has failed or refused to act on behalf of the individual;

(J)(i) have access to the records of individuals described in subparagraphs (B) and (I), and other records that are relevant to conducting an investigation, under the circumstances described in those subparagraphs, not later than 3 business days after the system makes a written request for the records involved; and

(ii) have immediate access, not later than 24 hours after the system makes such a request, to the records without consent from another party, in a situation in which services, supports, and other assistance are provided to an individual with a developmental disability—

(I) if the system determines there is probable cause to believe that the health or safety of the individual is in serious and immediate jeopardy; or

(II) in any case of death of an individual with a developmental disability;

(K) hire and maintain sufficient numbers and types of staff (qualified by training and experience) to carry out such system's functions, except that the State involved shall not apply hiring freezes, reductions in force, prohibitions on travel, or other policies to the staff of the system, to the extent that such policies would impact the staff or functions of the system funded with Federal funds or would prevent the system from carrying out the functions of the system under this subtitle [42 USCS §§ 15041 et seq.];

(L) have the authority to educate policymakers; and

(M) provide assurances to the Secretary that funds allotted to the State under section 142 [42 USCS § 15042] will be used to supplement, and not supplant, the non-Federal funds that would otherwise be made available for the purposes for which the allotted funds are provided;

(3) to the extent that information is available, the State shall provide to the system—

(A) a copy of each independent review, pursuant to section 1902(a)(30)(C) of the Social Security Act (42 U.S.C. 1396a(a)(30)(C)), of an Intermediate Care Facility (Mental Retardation) within the State, not later than 30 days after the availability of such a review; and

(B) information about the adequacy of health care and other services, supports, and assistance that individuals with developmental disabilities who are served through home and community-based waivers (authorized under section 1915(c) of the Social Security Act (42 U.S.C. 1396n(c))) receive; and

(4) the agency implementing the system shall not be redesignated unless—

(A) there is good cause for the redesignation;

(B) the State has given the agency notice of the intention to make such redesignation, including notice regarding the good cause for such redesignation, and given the agency an opportunity to respond to the assertion that good cause has been shown;

(C) the State has given timely notice and an opportunity for public comment in an accessible format to individuals with developmental disabilities or their representatives; and

(D) the system has an opportunity to appeal the redesignation to the Secretary, on the basis that the redesignation was not for good cause.

(b) American Indian consortium. Upon application to the Secretary, an American Indian consortium established to provide protection and advocacy services under this subtitle [42 USCS §§ 15041 et seq.], shall receive funding pursuant to section 142(a)(6) [42 USCS § 15042(a)(6)] to provide the services. Such consortium shall be considered to be a system for purposes of this subtitle [42 USCS §§ 15041 et seq.] and shall coordinate the services with other systems serving the same geographic area. The tribal council that designates the consortium shall carry out the responsibilities and exercise the authorities specified for a State in this subtitle [42 USCS §§ 15041 et seq.], with regard to the consortium.

(c) Record. In this section, the term "record" includes—

(1) a report prepared or received by any staff at any location at which services, supports, or other assistance is provided to individuals with developmental disabilities;

(2) a report prepared by an agency or staff person charged with investigating reports of incidents of abuse or neglect, injury, or death occurring at such location, that describes such incidents and the steps taken to investigate such incidents; and

(3) a discharge planning record.

(Oct. 30, 2000, P. L. 106-402, Title I, Subtitle C, § 143, 114 Stat. 1714; Oct. 25, 2004, P. L. 108-364, § 3(a)(3), 118 Stat. 1736.)

HISTORY; ANCILLARY LAWS AND DIRECTIVES

References in text:

The "Protection and Advocacy for Mentally Ill Individuals Act of 1986", referred to in subsec. (a)(2)(D)(ii), was Act May 23, 1986, P. L. 99-319. Such Act was renamed the Protection and Advocacy for Individuals with Mental Illness Act by Act Oct. 17, 2000, P. L. 106-310, Div B, Title XXXII, § 3206(a), 114 Stat. 1193, and appears generally as 42 USCS §§ 10801 et seq. For full classification of such Act, consult USCS Tables volumes.

Amendments:

2004. Act Oct. 25, 2004, in subsec. (a)(2)(D)(ii), substituted "section 4 or 5 of the Assistive Technology Act of 1998" for "section 101 or 102 of the Assistive Technology Act of 1998 (29 U.S.C. 3011, 3012)".

CROSS REFERENCES
This section is referred to in 42 USCS §§ 15002, 15042, 15044, 15064.

RESEARCH GUIDE
Other Treatises:
5 Rapp, Education Law (Matthew Bender), ch 13, Education Records Management and Retention § 13.04.

SHEPARD'S® Citations Service. For further research of authorities referenced here, use SHEPARD'S to be sure your case or statute is still good law and to find additional authorities that support your position. SHEPARD'S is available exclusively from LexisNexis®.

INTERPRETIVE NOTES AND DECISIONS

1. Construction
2. Relationship to other laws
3. Access to records
4. Investigations
5. Other particular cases

1. Construction

To find that protection and advocacy (P&A) systems has authority to access service location under 42 USCS § 15043(a)(2)(H) only for purpose of investigating specific incident—right conferred by § 15043(a)(2)(B)—would render § 15043(a)(2)(H) meaningless because it would authorize only those activities authorized by § 15043(a)(2)(B); Second Circuit declines to read statute in way that would create redundancy. Conn. Office of Prot. & Advocacy for Persons with Disabilities v Hartford Bd. of Educ. (2006, CA2 Conn) 464 F3d 229 (criticized in Disability Law Ctr. of Alaska, Inc. v Anchorage Sch. Dist. (2007, DC Alaska) 2007 US Dist LEXIS 72300).

Developmental Disabilities Assistance and Bill of Rights Act of 2000 (DD Act) and Protection and Advocacy for Individuals with Mental Illness Act (PAIMI), 42 USCS §§ 10801–10851, distinguish between protection and advocacy (P&A) system's authority to speak with individual and its authority to obtain individual's records; 42 USCS § 15043(a)(2)(H) provides that P&A system must have reasonable access to individuals, and 42 USCS § 10805(a)(3) provides that P&A system must have reasonable access to individuals in facilities that provide care or treatment for individuals with mental illness; nothing in statutory language of either DD Act or PAIMI conditions this access on consent of individual's parents or guardians. Conn. Office of Prot. & Advocacy for Persons with Disabilities v Hartford Bd. of Educ. (2006, CA2 Conn) 464 F3d 229 (criticized in Disability Law Ctr. of Alaska, Inc. v Anchorage Sch. Dist. (2007, DC Alaska) 2007 US Dist LEXIS 72300).

Because protection and advocacy agencies had authority to investigate past incidents, the district court erred in holding that probable cause under the Development Disabilities Act required some showing that abuse and neglect were ongoing or likely to recur; thus, the fact that the offending teacher and aide had been removed from the classroom did not defeat plaintiff law center's showing of probable cause. Disability Law Ctr. of Alaska, Inc. v Anchorage Sch. Dist. (2009, CA9 Alaska) 581 F3d 936.

Identical language in regulations promulgated pursuant to Protection and Advocacy for Mentally Ill Individuals Act (PAMII) and Developmental Disabilities Assistance and Bill of Rights Act (DD Act), specifically, 45 CFR § 1386.22 (2004) and 42 CFR § 51.43 (2003), supported interpretation of phrase "upon receipt of name and address of such representative" as authorizing request by protection and advocacy system for names and addresses of students for whom there was requisite degree of probable cause to demand records under PAMII and DD Act; upon receipt of such information, system was permitted to attempt to contact legal representatives of such individuals in order to obtain express permission to act on their behalf. Conn. Office of Prot. & Advocacy for Persons with Disabilities v Hartford Bd. of Educ. (2005, DC Conn) 355 F Supp 2d 649, affd (2006, CA2 Conn) 464 F3d 229 and (criticized in Disability Law Ctr. of Alaska, Inc. v Anchorage Sch. Dist. (2007, DC Alaska) 2007 US Dist LEXIS 72300).

2. Relationship to other laws

Development Disabilities Act expressly contemplates that a school or other facility will provide contact information to a protection and advocacy agency in order to allow the protection and advocacy agency to carry out its responsibility to investigate abuse or neglect; the Federal Educational Rights and Privacy Act does not bar a protection and advocacy agency from obtaining access to the name of and contact information for a parent, guardian, or other legal representative. Disability Law Ctr. of Alaska, Inc. v Anchorage Sch. Dist. (2009, CA9 Alaska) 581 F3d 936.

Advocacy agency's motion for contempt against psychiatric institution for its failure to provide list of residents of institution along with names and addresses of residents' respective guardians or other legal representatives was denied because agency's claim that 42 USCS §§ 10804, 10805, and 15043 required requested disclosures was misplaced where no complaint or probable cause determination had been made about residents. Iowa Prot. & Advocacy Servs. v Gerard Treatment Programs, L.L.C. (2003, ND Iowa) 274 F Supp 2d 1063.

Advocacy agency's motion for contempt against psychiatric institution for its failure to provide list of residents of institution along with names and addresses of residents' respective guardians or other legal representatives was denied because agency's claim that 42 C.F.R. § 51.42(e) required disclosure was misplaced because on its face, regulation was silent about any responsibility of institution to produce information demanded by agency. Iowa Prot. & Advocacy Servs. v Gerard Treatment Programs, L.L.C. (2003, ND Iowa) 274 F Supp 2d 1063.

Privacy rule, 45 CFR § 160.103, did not bar state hospital and training school from disclosing protected health information to designated protection and advocacy system without individual's authorization if such disclosures were required by Protection and Advocacy for Individual Rights Act, 29 USCS § 794e, Developmental Disabilities Assistance and Bill of Rights Act, 42 USCS §§ 15001 et seq., or Protection and Advocacy for Individuals with Mental Illness Act, 42 USCS §§ 10801 et seq., and designated system had complied with requirements set forth in respective Act. Prot. & Advocacy Sys. v Freudenthal (2006, DC Wyo) 412 F Supp 2d 1211.

State hospital and training school did not violate confidentiality provisions of Medicaid Act and regulations by disclosing records to designated protection and advocacy system for mentally ill so long as disclosure was required by Protection and Advocacy for Individual Rights Act, 29 USCS § 794e, Developmental Disabilities Assistance and Bill of Rights Act, 42 USCS §§ 15001 et seq., or Protection and Advocacy for Individuals with Mental Illness Act, 42 USCS §§ 10801 et seq., and disclosure requirements were met. Prot. & Advocacy Sys. v Freudenthal (2006, DC Wyo) 412 F Supp 2d 1211.

3. Access to records

Where Virginia Office for Protection and Advocacy sued state official, alleging that refusal to produce records violated Developmental Disabilities Assistance and Bill of Rights Act of 2000 and Protection and Advocacy for Individuals with Mental Illness Act, Ex parte Young exception to sovereign immunity applied because, inter alia, suit satis-

fied straightforward inquiry and sought prospective relief, and state law created agency and gave it power to sue state officials. Va. Office for Prot. & Advocacy v Stewart (2011, US) 131 S Ct 1632, 179 L Ed 2d 675, 22 FLW Fed S 935.

District court properly entered permanent injunction requiring school district to release to state-created protection and advocacy (P&A) system directory of students at learning academy for emotionally disturbed students along with contact information for their parents or guardians after parents complained about inappropriate use of physical restraints and seclusion at academy; to extent that P&A system made requisite probable cause determination, it had clear right to contact information for students' parents or guardians under record-access provisions of 42 USCS § 10805(a)(4)(C), part of Protection and Advocacy for Individuals with Mental Illness Act, 42 USCS §§ 10801–10851, and 42 USCS § 15043(a)(2)(I). Conn. Office of Prot. & Advocacy for Persons with Disabilities v Hartford Bd. of Educ. (2006, CA2 Conn) 464 F3d 229 (criticized in Disability Law Ctr. of Alaska, Inc. v Anchorage Sch. Dist. (2007, DC Alaska) 2007 US Dist LEXIS 72300).

Ex parte Young authorized suit by plaintiff designated mental health advocacy agency (AA)for prospective relief against defendants, officials of state social services agency, that alleged officials obstructed access to records under Protection and Advocacy for Individuals with Mental Illness Act of 1986, ongoing violation of federal law; Indiana's use of AA's status as independent state agency, as set forth in Ind. Code § 12-28-1-6(a)(1), to support reliance on Eleventh Amendment to block lawsuit was unfair, as Congress had taken steps in Act to ensure such designees were independent, as set forth in 42 USCS §§ 10802(2), 10805(a)(1)(B),15043(a)(2)(K). Ind. Prot. & Advocacy Servs. v Ind. Family & Soc. Servs. Admin. (2010, CA7 Ind) 603 F3d 365, cert den (2011, US) 131 S Ct 2149, 179 L Ed 2d 952.

4. Investigations

District court erred when it denied request by state agency authorized to investigate alleged incidents of abuse or neglect of people with mental or physical disabilities in state to compel state Department of Public Instruction (DPI) to disclose records uncovered in its investigation into use of "time out" or seclusion rooms for disciplining students; federal statutes, Developmental Disabilities and Bill of Rights Act, Protection and Advocacy for Mentally Ill Individuals Act of 1986, supplied state protection and advocacy agencies with broad investigatory authority, including access to certain records, and requiring protection and advocacy agency to obtain authorization before it could learn names of students with mental or physical disabilities that DPI believed were abused or neglected violated both spirit and letter of statutes. Disability Rights Wis., Inc. v State

Dep't of Pub. Instruction (2006, CA7 Wis) 463 F3d 719 (criticized in Disability Law Ctr. of Alaska, Inc. v Anchorage Sch. Dist. (2007, DC Alaska) 2007 US Dist LEXIS 72300).

Advocacy center for individuals with disabilities was not entitled to temporary restraining order that would have prohibited guardian from interfering with center's investigation of alleged abuse and neglect of ward under 42 USCS § 15043(a)(2)(B) where center, at best, alleged mere prospect that guardian might interfere at some time in unknown manner with wholly prospective investigation; further, complaint failed to establish any basis to pre-liminarily conclude that steps authorized by Florida were abusive or neglectful and failed to demonstrate both substantial likelihood of success on merits and substantial threat that center would suffer irreparable harm or that any harm to center outweighed harm to others, including guardian, ward, and public as re-quired by U.S. Dist. Ct., M.D. Fla., R. 4.05(b)(4). Advocacy Ctr. for Persons with Disabilities, Inc. v Schiavo (2003, MD Fla) 17 FLW Fed D 291.

5. Other particular cases

District court properly entered permanent injunc-tion requiring school district to allow state-created protection and advocacy system access to learning academy for emotionally disturbed students during school hours to observe and interview students after parents complained about inappropriate use of physi-cal restraints and seclusion at academy; 42 USCS § 10805(a)(3), 42 USCS § 15043(a)(2)(H), and 29 USCS § 794e(f) authorized such access for investi-gatory and monitoring purposes. Conn. Office of Prot. & Advocacy for Persons with Disabilities v Hartford Bd. of Educ. (2006, CA2 Conn) 464 F3d 229 (criticized in Disability Law Ctr. of Alaska, Inc. v Anchorage Sch. Dist. (2007, DC Alaska) 2007 US Dist LEXIS 72300).

Advocacy system, which was established under 42 USCS § 15043 of Developmental Disabilities Assis-tance and Bill of Rights Act, could not bring federal court suit against state hospital, state agency, and state officials to obtain patient records under 42 USCS §§ 10805(a)(4) and 10806, Protection and Advocacy for Individuals with Mental Illness Act, 42 USCS §§ 10801–10851; §§ 10805 and 10806 lacked right of action, system could not sue under 42 USCS § 1983 because it was public agency, and Eleventh Amendment barred action. Ind. Prot. & Advocacy Servs. v Ind. Family & Soc. Servs. Ad-min. (2009, CA7 Ind) 573 F3d 548.

Organization that had duty under 42 USCS § 15043(a)(2)(A)(i) to advocate for persons who were in need of services did not entitle organization to intervene as of right under Fed. R. Civ. P. 24(a)(2) in suit concerning closure of intermediate care facil-ity for mentally retarded persons and transfer of facility's former residents; court's orders in case did not impair organization's legal interests in protecting and advocating for former residents and in advocat-ing for continued integration of all institutionalized persons. Alexander v Rendell (2007, WD Pa) 246 FRD 220, summary judgment gr, motion den, judg-ment entered (2009, WD Pa) 2009 US Dist LEXIS 1540.

Motion to dismiss action brought under Develop-mental Disabilities Assistance and Bill of Rights Act, 42 USCS §§ 15001 et seq., was denied because state agency was charged with responsibility to comply with federal law, including responsibility to carry out conditions of compliance, such as pursuing legal remedies, 42 USCS § 15043(a)(2)(A)(I), and "bringing lawsuits in its own right" when neces-sary. Haw. Disability Rights Ctr. v Cheung (2007, DC Hawaii) 513 F Supp 2d 1185.

§ 15044. Administration

(a) Governing board. In a State in which the system described in section 143 [42 USCS § 15043] is organized as a private nonprofit entity with a multimem-ber governing board, or a public system with a multimember governing board, such governing board shall be selected according to the policies and procedures of the system, except that—

    (1)(A) the governing board shall be composed of members who broadly represent or are knowledgeable about the needs of the individuals served by the system;

    (B) a majority of the members of the board shall be—

        (i) individuals with disabilities, including individuals with developmen-tal disabilities, who are eligible for services, or have received or are receiving services through the system; or

        (ii) parents, family members, guardians, advocates, or authorized representatives of individuals referred to in clause (i); and

    (C) the board may include a representative of the State Council on

Developmental Disabilities, the Centers in the State, and the self-advocacy organization described in section 124(c)(4)(A)(ii)(I) [42 USCS § 15024(c)(4)(A)(ii)(I)];

(2) not more than 1/3 of the members of the governing board may be appointed by the chief executive officer of the State involved, in the case of any State in which such officer has the authority to appoint members of the board;

(3) the membership of the governing board shall be subject to term limits set by the system to ensure rotating membership;

(4) any vacancy in the board shall be filled not later than 60 days after the date on which the vacancy occurs; and

(5) in a State in which the system is organized as a public system without a multimember governing or advisory board, the system shall establish an advisory council—

   (A) that shall advise the system on policies and priorities to be carried out in protecting and advocating the rights of individuals with developmental disabilities; and

   (B) on which a majority of the members shall be—

      (i) individuals with developmental disabilities who are eligible for services, or have received or are receiving services, through the system; or

      (ii) parents, family members, guardians, advocates, or authorized representatives of individuals referred to in clause (i).

(b) Legal action. (1) In general. Nothing in this title [42 USCS §§ 15001 et seq.] shall preclude a system from bringing a suit on behalf of individuals with developmental disabilities against a State, or an agency or instrumentality of a State.

(2) Use of amounts from judgment. An amount received pursuant to a suit described in paragraph (1) through a court judgment may only be used by the system to further the purpose of this subtitle [42 USCS §§ 15041 et seq.] and shall not be used to augment payments to legal contractors or to award personal bonuses.

(3) Limitation. The system shall use assistance provided under this subtitle [42 USCS §§ 15041 et seq.] in a manner consistent with section 5 of the Assisted Suicide Funding Restriction Act of 1997 (42 U.S.C. 14404).

(c) Disclosure of information. For purposes of any periodic audit, report, or evaluation required under this subtitle [42 USCS §§ 15041 et seq.], the Secretary shall not require an entity carrying out a program to disclose the identity of, or any other personally identifiable information related to, any individual requesting assistance under such program.

(d) Public notice of Federal onsite review. The Secretary shall provide advance public notice of any Federal programmatic or administrative onsite review of a system conducted under this subtitle [42 USCS §§ 15041 et seq.] and solicit public comment on the system through such notice. The Secretary shall prepare an onsite visit report containing the results of such review, which shall be distributed to the Governor of the State and to other interested public and private parties. The comments received in response to the public comment solicitation notice shall be included in the onsite visit report.

(e) Reports. Beginning in fiscal year 2002, each system established in a State pursuant to this subtitle [42 USCS §§ 15041 et seq.] shall annually prepare and transmit to the Secretary a report that describes the activities, accomplishments, and expenditures of the system during the preceding fiscal year, including a description of the system's goals, the extent to which the goals were achieved, barriers to their achievement, the process used to obtain public input, the nature of such input, and how such input was used.

(Oct. 30, 2000, P. L. 106-402, Title I, Subtitle C, § 144, 114 Stat. 1717.)

INTERPRETIVE NOTES AND DECISIONS

Where Virginia Office for Protection and Advocacy sued state official, alleging that refusal to produce records violated Developmental Disabilities Assistance and Bill of Rights Act of 2000 and Protection and Advocacy for Individuals with Mental Illness Act, Ex parte Young exception to sovereign immunity applied because, inter alia, suit satisfied straightforward inquiry and sought prospective relief, and state law created agency and gave it power to sue state officials. Va. Office for Prot. & Advocacy v Stewart (2011, US) 131 S Ct 1632, 179 L Ed 2d 675, 22 FLW Fed S 935.

Ex parte Young authorized suit by plaintiff designated mental health advocacy agency (AA) for prospective relief against defendants, officials of state social services agency, that alleged officials obstructed access to records under Protection and Advocacy for Individuals with Mental Illness Act of 1986, ongoing violation of federal law; Indiana had chosen under 42 USCS § 15044(a) for AA to be independent agency, and to use that status, as set forth in Ind. Code § 12-28-1-6(a)(1), to support reliance on Eleventh Amendment to block lawsuit was unfair, as Congress had taken steps in Act to ensure such designees were independent, as set forth in 42 USCS §§ 10802(2), 10805(a)(1)(B),15043(a)(2)(K). Ind. Prot. & Advocacy Servs. v Ind. Family & Soc. Servs. Admin. (2010, CA7 Ind) 603 F3d 365, cert den (2011, US) 131 S Ct 2149, 179 L Ed 2d 952.

§ 15045. Authorization of appropriations

For allotments under section 142 [42 USCS § 15042], there are authorized to be appropriated $32,000,000 for fiscal year 2001 and such sums as may be necessary for each of fiscal years 2002 through 2007.

(Oct. 30, 2000, P. L. 106-402, Title I, Subtitle C, § 145, 114 Stat. 1718.)

CROSS REFERENCES

This section is referred to in 42 USCS § 15042.

National Network of University Centers for Excellence in Developmental Disabilities Education, Research, and Service

CROSS REFERENCES

This subtitle (42 USCS §§ 15061 et seq.) is referred to in 29 USCS § 3005; 42 USCS §§ 14403, 15002, 15004, 15005, 15024, 15081, 15083.

§ 15061. Grant authority

(a) National network. From appropriations authorized under section 156(a)(1) [42 USCS § 15066(a)(1)], the Secretary shall make 5-year grants to entities in each State designated as University Centers for Excellence in Developmental Disabilities Education, Research, and Service to carry out activities described in section 153(a) [42 USCS § 15063(a)].

(b) National training initiatives. From appropriations authorized under section 156(a)(1) [42 USCS § 15066(a)(1)] and reserved under section 156(a)(2) [42 USCS § 15066(a)(2)], the Secretary shall make grants to Centers to carry out activities described in section 153(b) [42 USCS § 15063(b)].

(c) Technical assistance. From appropriations authorized under section 156(a)(1) [42 USCS § 15066(a)(1)] and reserved under section 156(a)(3) [42 USCS § 15066(a)(3)] (or from funds reserved under section 163 [42 USCS § 15083], as appropriate), the Secretary shall enter into 1 or more cooperative agreements or contracts for the purpose of providing technical assistance described in section 153(c) [42 USCS § 15063(c)].

(Oct. 30, 2000, P. L. 106-402, Title I, Subtitle D, § 151, 114 Stat. 1719.)

CROSS REFERENCES
This section is referred to in 42 USCS §§ 15062, 15063, 15064.

RESEARCH GUIDE
Annotations:
Validity, Construction, and Operation of Developmental Disabilities Assistance and Bill of Rights Act. 193 ALR Fed 513.

§ 15062. Grant awards

(a) Existing Centers. (1) In general. In awarding and distributing grant funds under section 151(a) [42 USCS § 15061(a)] for a fiscal year, the Secretary, subject to the availability of appropriations and the condition specified in subsection (d), shall award and distribute grant funds in equal amounts of $500,000 (adjusted in accordance with subsection (b)), to each Center that existed during the preceding fiscal year and that meets the requirements of this subtitle [42 USCS §§ 15061 et seq.], prior to making grants under subsection (c) or (d).

(2) Reduction of award. Notwithstanding paragraph (1), if the aggregate of the funds to be awarded to the Centers pursuant to paragraph (1) for any fiscal year exceeds the total amount appropriated under section 156 [42 USCS § 15066] for such fiscal year, the amount to be awarded to each Center for such fiscal year shall be proportionately reduced.

(b) Adjustments. Subject to the availability of appropriations, for any fiscal year following a year in which each Center described in subsection (a) received a grant award of not less than $500,000 under subsection (a) (adjusted in accordance with this subsection), the Secretary shall adjust the awards to take into account the most recent percentage change in the Consumer Price Index published by the Secretary of Labor under section 100(c)(1) of the Rehabilitation Act of 1973 (29 U.S.C. 720(c)(1)) (if the percentage change indicates an increase), prior to making grants under subsection (c) or (d).

(c) National training initiatives on critical and emerging needs. Subject to the availability of appropriations, for any fiscal year in which each Center described in subsection (a) receives a grant award of not less than $500,000, under subsection (a) (adjusted in accordance with subsection (b)), after making the grant awards, the Secretary shall make grants under section 151(b) [42 USCS § 15061(b)] to Centers to pay for the Federal share of the cost of training initiatives related to the unmet needs of individuals with developmental disabilities and their families, as described in section 153(b) [42 USCS § 15063(b)].

(d) Additional grants. For any fiscal year in which each Center described in subsection (a) receives a grant award of not less than $500,000 under subsection (a) (adjusted in accordance with subsection (b)), after making the grant awards, the Secretary may make grants under section 151(a) [42 USCS § 15061(a)] for activities described in section 153(a) [42 USCS § 15063(a)] to additional Centers, or additional grants to Centers, for States or populations that are unserved or underserved by Centers due to such factors as—

(1) population;

(2) a high concentration of rural or urban areas; or

(3) a high concentration of unserved or underserved populations.

(Oct. 30, 2000, P. L. 106-402, Title I, Subtitle D, § 152, 114 Stat. 1719.)

CROSS REFERENCES
This section is referred to in 42 USCS § 15066.

§ 15063. Purpose and scope of activities

(a) National network of University Centers for Excellence in Developmental Disabilities Education, Research, and Service. (1) In general. In order to provide leadership in, advise Federal, State, and community policymakers about, and promote opportunities for individuals with developmental disabilities to exercise self-determination, be independent, be productive, and be integrated and included in all facets of community life, the Secretary shall award grants to eligible entities designated as Centers in each State to pay for the Federal share of the cost of the administration and operation of the Centers. The Centers shall be interdisciplinary education, research, and public service units of universities (as defined by the Secretary) or public or not-for-profit entities associated with universities that engage in core functions, described in paragraph (2), addressing, directly or indirectly, 1 or more of the areas of emphasis.

(2) Core functions. The core functions referred to in paragraph (1) shall include the following:

(A) Provision of interdisciplinary pre-service preparation and continuing education of students and fellows, which may include the preparation and continuing education of leadership, direct service, clinical, or other personnel to strengthen and increase the capacity of States and communities to achieve the purpose of this title [42 USCS §§ 15001 et seq.].

(B) Provision of community services—

(i) that provide training or technical assistance for individuals with developmental disabilities, their families, professionals, paraprofessionals, policymakers, students, and other members of the community; and

(ii) that may provide services, supports, and assistance for the persons described in clause (i) through demonstration and model activities.

(C) Conduct of research, which may include basic or applied research, evaluation, and the analysis of public policy in areas that affect or could affect, either positively or negatively, individuals with developmental disabilities and their families.

(D) Dissemination of information related to activities undertaken to address the purpose of this title [42 USCS §§ 15001 et seq.], especially dissemination of information that demonstrates that the network authorized under this subtitle [42 USCS §§ 15061 et seq.] is a national and international resource that includes specific substantive areas of expertise that may be accessed and applied in diverse settings and circumstances.

(b) National training initiatives on critical and emerging needs. (1) Supplemental grants. After consultation with relevant, informed sources, including individuals with developmental disabilities and their families, the Secretary shall award, under section 151(b) [42 USCS § 15061(b)], supplemental grants to Centers to pay for the Federal share of the cost of training initiatives related to the unmet needs of individuals with developmental disabilities and their families. The Secretary shall make the grants on a competitive basis, and for periods of not more than 5 years.

(2) Establishment of consultation process by the secretary. Not later than 1 year after the date of enactment of this Act [enacted Oct. 30, 2000], the Secretary shall establish a consultation process that, on an ongoing basis, allows the Secretary to identify and address, through supplemental grants authorized under paragraph (1), training initiatives related to the unmet needs of individuals with developmental disabilities and their families.

(c) Technical assistance. In order to strengthen and support the national network of Centers, the Secretary may enter into 1 or more cooperative agreements or contracts to—

(1) assist in national and international dissemination of specific information from multiple Centers and, in appropriate cases, other entities whose work affects the lives of individuals with developmental disabilities;

(2) compile, analyze, and disseminate state-of-the-art training, research, and demonstration results policies, and practices from multiple Centers and, in appropriate cases, other entities whose work affects the lives of persons with developmental disabilities;

(3) convene experts from multiple Centers to discuss and make recommendations with regard to national emerging needs of individuals with developmental disabilities;

(4)(A) develop portals that link users with every Center's website; and

(B) facilitate electronic information sharing using state-of-the-art Internet technologies such as real-time online discussions, multipoint video conferencing, and web-based audio/video broadcasts, on emerging topics that impact individuals with disabilities and their families;

(5) serve as a research-based resource for Federal and State policymakers on information concerning and issues impacting individuals with developmental disabilities and entities that assist or serve those individuals; or

(6) undertake any other functions that the Secretary determines to be appropriate;

to promote the viability and use of the resources and expertise of the Centers nationally and internationally.

(Oct. 30, 2000, P. L. 106-402, Title I, Subtitle D, § 153, 114 Stat. 1720.)

CROSS REFERENCES
This section is referred to in 42 USCS §§ 15061, 15062, 15064, 15066, 15083.

§ 15064. Applications

(a) Applications for core Center grants. (1) In general. To be eligible to receive a grant under section 151(a) [42 USCS § 15061(a)] for a Center, an entity shall submit to the Secretary, and obtain approval of, an application at such time, in such manner, and containing such information, as the Secretary may require.

(2) Application contents. Each application described in paragraph (1) shall describe a 5-year plan, including a projected goal related to 1 or more areas of emphasis for each of the core functions described in section 153(a) [42 USCS § 15063(a)].

(3) Assurances. The application shall be approved by the Secretary only if the application contains or is supported by reasonable assurances that the entity designated as the Center will—

(A) meet regulatory standards as established by the Secretary for Centers;

(B) address the projected goals, and carry out goal-related activities, based on data driven strategic planning and in a manner consistent with the objectives of this subtitle [42 USCS §§ 15061 et seq.], that—

(i) are developed in collaboration with the consumer advisory committee established pursuant to subparagraph (E);

(ii) are consistent with, and to the extent feasible complement and further, the Council goals contained in the State plan submitted under section 124 [42 USCS § 15024] and the system goals established under section 143 [42 USCS § 15043]; and

(iii) will be reviewed and revised annually as necessary to address emerging trends and needs;

(C) use the funds made available through the grant to supplement, and not supplant, the funds that would otherwise be made available for activities described in section 153(a) [42 USCS § 15063(a)];

(D) protect, consistent with the policy specified in section 101(c) [42 USCS § 15001(c)] (relating to rights of individuals with developmental disabilities), the legal and human rights of all individuals with developmental disabilities (especially those individuals under State guardianship) who are involved in activities carried out under programs assisted under this subtitle [42 USCS §§ 15061 et seq.];

(E) establish a consumer advisory committee—

(i) of which a majority of the members shall be individuals with developmental disabilities and family members of such individuals;

(ii) that is comprised of—

(I) individuals with developmental disabilities and related disabilities;

(II) family members of individuals with developmental disabilities;
(III) a representative of the State protection and advocacy system;
(IV) a representative of the State Council on Developmental Disabilities;
(V) a representative of a self-advocacy organization described in section 124(c)(4)(A)(ii)(I) [42 USCS § 15024(c)(4)(A)(ii)(I)]; and
(VI) representatives of organizations that may include parent training and information centers assisted under section 671 or 672 of the Individuals with Disabilities Education Act [20 USCS § 1471 or 1472], entities carrying out activities authorized under section 4 or 5 of the Assistive Technology Act of 1998 [29 USCS § 3003 or 3004], relevant State agencies, and other community groups concerned with the welfare of individuals with developmental disabilities and their families;
(iii) that reflects the racial and ethnic diversity of the State; and
(iv) that shall—
(I) consult with the Director of the Center regarding the development of the 5-year plan, and shall participate in an annual review of, and comment on, the progress of the Center in meeting the projected goals contained in the plan, and shall make recommendations to the Director of the Center regarding any proposed revisions of the plan that might be necessary; and
(II) meet as often as necessary to carry out the role of the committee, but at a minimum twice during each grant year;
(F) to the extent possible, utilize the infrastructure and resources obtained through funds made available under the grant to leverage additional public and private funds to successfully achieve the projected goals developed in the 5-year plan;
(G)(i) have a director with appropriate academic credentials, demonstrated leadership, expertise regarding developmental disabilities, significant experience in managing grants and contracts, and the ability to leverage public and private funds; and
(ii) allocate adequate staff time to carry out activities related to each of the core functions described in section 153(a) [42 USCS § 15063(a)]; and
(H) educate, and disseminate information related to the purpose of this title [42 USCS §§ 15001 et seq.] to, the legislature of the State in which the Center is located, and to Members of Congress from such State.

(b) Supplemental grant applications pertaining to national training initiatives in critical and emerging needs. To be eligible to receive a supplemental grant under section 151(b) [42 USCS § 15061(b)], a Center may submit a supplemental application to the Secretary at such time, in such manner, and containing such information as the Secretary may require, pursuant to the terms and conditions set by the Secretary consistent with section 153(b) [42 USCS § 15063(b)].

(c) Peer review. (1) In general. The Secretary shall require that all applications submitted under this subtitle [42 USCS §§ 15061 et seq.] be subject to technical and qualitative review by peer review groups established under paragraph (2). The Secretary may approve an application under this subtitle [42 USCS §§ 15061 et seq.] only if such application has been recommended by a peer review group that has conducted the peer review required under this paragraph. In conducting the review, the group may conduct onsite visits or inspections of related activities as necessary.

(2) Establishment of peer review groups. (A) In general. The Secretary, acting through the Commissioner of the Administration on Developmental Disabilities, may, notwithstanding—

(i) the provisions of title 5, United States Code, concerning appointments to the competitive service; and

(ii) the provisions of chapter 51, and subchapter III of chapter 53 of title 5, United States Code [5 USCS §§ 5101 et seq., 5331 et seq.], concerning classification and General Schedule pay rates;

establish such peer review groups and appoint and set the rates of pay of members of such groups.

(B) Composition. Each peer review group shall include such individuals with disabilities and parents, guardians, or advocates of or for individuals with developmental disabilities, as are necessary to carry out this subsection.

(3) Waivers of approval. The Secretary may waive the provisions of paragraph (1) with respect to review and approval of an application if the Secretary determines that exceptional circumstances warrant such a waiver.

(d) **Federal share.** (1) In general. The Federal share of the cost of administration or operation of a Center, or the cost of carrying out a training initiative, supported by a grant made under this subtitle [42 USCS §§ 15061 et seq.] may not be more than 75 percent of the necessary cost of such project, as determined by the Secretary.

(2) Urban or rural poverty areas. In the case of a project whose activities or products target individuals with developmental disabilities who live in an urban or rural poverty area, as determined by the Secretary, the Federal share of the cost of the project may not be more than 90 percent of the necessary costs of the project, as determined by the Secretary.

(3) Grant expenditures. For the purpose of determining the Federal share with respect to the project, expenditures on that project by a political subdivision of a State or by a public or private entity shall, subject to such limitations and conditions as the Secretary may by regulation prescribe under section 104(b) [42 USCS § 15004(b)], be considered to be expenditures made by a Center under this subtitle [42 USCS §§ 15061 et seq.].

(e) **Annual report.** Each Center shall annually prepare and transmit to the Secretary a report containing—

(1) information on progress made in achieving the projected goals of the Center for the previous year, including—

(A) the extent to which the goals were achieved;

(B) a description of the strategies that contributed to achieving the goals;

(C) to the extent to which the goals were not achieved, a description of factors that impeded the achievement; and

(D) an accounting of the manner in which funds paid to the Center under this subtitle [42 USCS §§ 15061 et seq.] for a fiscal year were expended;

(2) information on proposed revisions to the goals; and

(3) a description of successful efforts to leverage funds, other than funds made available under this subtitle [42 USCS §§ 15061 et seq.], to pursue goals consistent with this subtitle [42 USCS §§ 15061 et seq.].

(Oct. 30, 2000, P. L. 106-402, Title I, Subtitle D, § 154, 114 Stat. 1722; Oct. 25, 2004, P. L. 108-364, § 3(a)(4), 118 Stat. 1737; Dec. 3, 2004, P. L. 108-446, Title III, § 305(n)(2), 118 Stat. 2806.)

HISTORY; ANCILLARY LAWS AND DIRECTIVES

References in text:

"Provisions of title 5, United States Code, concerning appointments to the competitive service", referred to in this section, are classified to 5 USCS §§ 3301 et seq.

Amendments:

2004. Act Oct. 25, 2004, in subsec. (a)(3)(E)(ii)(VI), substituted "section 4 or 5 of the Assistive Technology Act of 1998" for "section 101 or 102 of the Assistive Technology Act of 1998 (29 U.S.C. 3011, 3012)".

Act Dec. 3, 2004, in subsec. (a)(3)(E)(ii)(VI), substituted "671 or 672" for "682 or 683", and deleted "(20 U.S.C. 1482, 1483)" following "Education Act".

§ 15065.　Definition

In this subtitle [42 USCS §§ 15061 et seq.], the term "State" means each of the several States of the United States, the District of Columbia, the Commonwealth of Puerto Rico, the United States Virgin Islands, and Guam.

(Oct. 30, 2000, P. L. 106-402, Title I, Subtitle D, § 155, 114 Stat. 1725.)

§ 15066.　Authorization of appropriations

(a) **Authorization and reservations.** (1) Authorization. There are authorized to be appropriated to carry out this subtitle [42 USCS §§ 15061 et seq.] (other than section 153(c)(4) [42 USCS § 15063(c)(4)]) $30,000,000 for fiscal year 2001 and such sums as may be necessary for each of fiscal years 2002 through 2007.

(2) Reservation for training initiatives. From any amount appropriated for a fiscal year under paragraph (1) and remaining after each Center described in section 152(a) [42 USCS § 15062(a)] has received a grant award of not less than $500,000, as described in section 152 [42 USCS § 15062], the Secretary shall reserve funds for the training initiatives authorized under section 153(b) [42 USCS § 15063(b)].

(3) Reservation for technical assistance. (A) Years before appropriation trigger. For any covered year, the Secretary shall reserve funds in accordance with section 163(c) [42 USCS § 15083(c)] to fund technical assistance

activities under section 153(c) [42 USCS § 15063(c)] (other than section 153(c)(4) [42 USCS § 15063(c)(4)]).

(B) Years after appropriation trigger. For any fiscal year that is not a covered year, the Secretary shall reserve not less than $300,000 and not more than 2 percent of the amount appropriated under paragraph (1) to fund technical assistance activities under section 153(c) [42 USCS § 15063(c)] (other than section 153(c)(4) [42 USCS § 15063(c)(4)]).

(C) Covered year. In this paragraph, the term "covered year" means a fiscal year prior to the first fiscal year for which the amount appropriated under paragraph (1) is not less than $20,000,000.

(b) Limitation. The Secretary may not use, for peer review or other activities directly related to peer review conducted under this subtitle [42 USCS §§ 15061 et seq.]—

(1) for fiscal year 2001, more than $300,000 of the funds made available under subsection (a); and

(2) for any succeeding fiscal year, more than the amount of funds used for the peer review and related activities in fiscal year 2001, adjusted to take into account the most recent percentage change in the Consumer Price Index published by the Secretary of Labor under section 100(c)(1) of the Rehabilitation Act of 1973 (29 U.S.C. 720(c)(1)) (if the percentage change indicates an increase).

(Oct. 30, 2000, P. L. 106-402, Title I, Subtitle D, § 156, 114 Stat. 1725.)

CROSS REFERENCES

This section is referred to in 42 USCS §§ 15061, 15062, 15081, 15083.

Projects of National Significance

CROSS REFERENCES

This subtitle (42 USCS §§ 15081 et seq.) is referred to in 42 USCS §§ 14403, 15005.

§ 15081. Purpose

The purpose of this subtitle [42 USCS §§ 15081 et seq.] is to provide grants, contracts, or cooperative agreements for projects of national significance that—

(1) create opportunities for individuals with developmental disabilities to directly and fully contribute to, and participate in, all facets of community life; and

(2) support the development of national and State policies that reinforce and promote, with the support of families, guardians, advocates, and communities, of individuals with developmental disabilities, the self-determination, independence, productivity, and integration and inclusion in all facets of community life of such individuals through—

(A) family support activities;

(B) data collection and analysis;

(C) technical assistance to entities funded under subtitles B and D [42 USCS §§ 15021 et seq., 15061 et seq.], subject to the limitations described in sections 129(b), 156(a)(3), and 163(c) [42 USCS §§ 15029(b), 15066(a)(3), 15083(c)]; and

(D) other projects of sufficient size and scope that hold promise to expand or improve opportunities for such individuals, including—

(i) projects that provide technical assistance for the development of information and referral systems;

(ii) projects that provide technical assistance to self-advocacy organizations of individuals with developmental disabilities;

(iii) projects that provide education for policymakers;

(iv) Federal interagency initiatives;

(v) projects that enhance the participation of racial and ethnic minorities in public and private sector initiatives in developmental disabilities;

(vi) projects that provide aid to transition youth with developmental disabilities from school to adult life, especially in finding employment and postsecondary education opportunities and in upgrading and changing any assistive technology devices that may be needed as a youth matures;

(vii) initiatives that address the development of community quality assurance systems and the training related to the development, implementation, and evaluation of such systems, including training of individuals with developmental disabilities and their families;

(viii) initiatives that address the needs of aging individuals with developmental disabilities and aging caregivers of adults with developmental disabilities in the community;

(ix) initiatives that create greater access to and use of generic services systems, community organizations, and associations, and initiatives that assist in community economic development;

(x) initiatives that create access to increased living options;

(xi) initiatives that address the challenging behaviors of individuals with developmental disabilities, including initiatives that promote positive alternatives to the use of restraints and seclusion; and

(xii) initiatives that address other areas of emerging need.

(Oct. 30, 2000, P. L. 106-402, Title I, Subtitle E, § 161, 114 Stat. 1725.)

CROSS REFERENCES

This section is referred to in 42 USCS §§ 15082, 15083.

RESEARCH GUIDE

Annotations:

Validity, Construction, and Operation of Developmental Disabilities Assistance and Bill of Rights Act. 193 ALR Fed 513.

§ 15082. Grant authority

(a) **In general.** The Secretary shall award grants, contracts, or cooperative agreements to public or private nonprofit entities for projects of national significance relating to individuals with developmental disabilities to carry out activities described in section 161(2) [42 USCS § 15081(2)].

(b) Federal interagency initiatives. (1) In general. (A) Authority. The Secretary may—

(i) enter into agreements with Federal agencies to jointly carry out activities described in section 161(2) [42 USCS § 15081(2)] or to jointly carry out activities of common interest related to the objectives of such section; and

(ii) transfer to such agencies for such purposes funds appropriated under this subtitle [42 USCS §§ 15081 et seq.], and receive and use funds from such agencies for such purposes.

(B) Relation to program purposes. Funds transferred or received pursuant to this paragraph shall be used only in accordance with statutes authorizing the appropriation of such funds. Such funds shall be made available through grants, contracts, or cooperative agreements only to recipients eligible to receive such funds under such statutes.

(C) Procedures and criteria. If the Secretary enters into an agreement under this subsection for the administration of a jointly funded project—

(i) the agreement shall specify which agency's procedures shall be used to award grants, contracts, or cooperative agreements and to administer such awards;

(ii) the participating agencies may develop a single set of criteria for the jointly funded project, and may require applicants to submit a single application for joint review by such agencies; and

(iii) unless the heads of the participating agencies develop joint eligibility requirements, an applicant for an award for the project shall meet the eligibility requirements of each program involved.

(2) Limitation. The Secretary may not construe the provisions of this subsection to take precedence over a limitation on joint funding contained in an applicable statute.

(Oct. 30, 2000, P. L. 106-402, Title I, Subtitle E, § 162, 114 Stat. 1727.)

CROSS REFERENCES
This section is referred to in 42 USCS § 15083.

§ 15083. Authorization of appropriations

(a) In general. There are authorized to be appropriated to carry out the projects specified in this section $16,000,000 for fiscal year 2001, and such sums as may be necessary for each of fiscal years 2002 through 2007.

(b) Use of funds. (1) Grants, contracts, and agreements. Except as provided in paragraph (2), the amount appropriated under subsection (a) for each fiscal year shall be used to award grants, or enter into contracts, cooperative agreements, or other agreements, under section 162 [42 USCS § 15082].

(2) Administrative costs. Not more than 1 percent of the amount appropriated under subsection (a) for each fiscal year may be used to provide for the administrative costs (other than compensation of Federal employees) of the Administration on Developmental Disabilities for administering this subtitle [42 USCS §§ 15081 et seq.] and subtitles B, C, and D [42 USCS §§ 15021

et seq., 15041 et seq., 15061 et seq.], including monitoring the performance of and providing technical assistance to, entities that receive funds under this title [42 USCS §§ 15001 et seq.].

(c) Technical assistance for Councils and Centers. (1) In general. For each covered year, the Secretary shall expend, to provide technical assistance for entities funded under subtitle B or D [42 USCS §§ 15021 et seq. or 15061 et seq.], an amount from funds appropriated under subsection (a) that is not less than the amount the Secretary expended on technical assistance for entities funded under that subtitle (or a corresponding provision) in the previous fiscal year.

(2) Covered year. In this subsection, the term "covered year" means—

(A) in the case of an expenditure for entities funded under subtitle B [42 USCS §§ 15021 et seq.], a fiscal year for which the amount appropriated under section 129(a) [42 USCS § 15029(a)] is less than $76,000,000; and

(B) in the case of an expenditure for entities funded under subtitle D [42 USCS §§ 15061 et seq.], a fiscal year prior to the first fiscal year for which the amount appropriated under section 156(a)(1) [42 USCS § 15066(a)(1)] is not less than $20,000,000.

(3) References. References in this subsection to subtitle D [42 USCS §§ 15061 et seq.] shall not be considered to include section 153(c)(4) [42 USCS § 15063(c)(4)].

(d) Technical assistance on electronic information sharing. In addition to any funds reserved under subsection (c), the Secretary shall reserve $100,000 from the amount appropriated under subsection (a) for each fiscal year to carry out section 153(c)(4) [42 USCS § 15063(c)(4)].

(e) Limitation. For any fiscal year for which the amount appropriated under subsection (a) is not less than $10,000,000, not more than 50 percent of such amount shall be used for activities carried out under section 161(2)(A) [42 USCS § 15081(2)(A)].

(Oct. 30, 2000, P. L. 106-402, Title I, Subtitle E, § 163, 114 Stat. 1727.)

CROSS REFERENCES

This section is referred to in 42 USCS §§ 15029, 15061, 15066, 15081.

FAMILY SUPPORT

§ 15091. Findings, purposes, and policy

(a) Findings. Congress makes the following findings:

(1) It is in the best interest of our Nation to preserve, strengthen, and maintain the family.

(2) Families of children with disabilities provide support, care, and training to their children that can save States millions of dollars. Without the efforts of family caregivers, many persons with disabilities would receive care through State-supported out-of-home placements.

(3) Most families of children with disabilities, especially families in unserved

and underserved populations, do not have access to family-centered and family-directed services to support such families in their efforts to care for such children at home.

(4) Medical advances and improved health care have increased the life span of many people with disabilities, and the combination of the longer life spans and the aging of family caregivers places a continually increasing demand on the finite service delivery systems of the States.

(5) In 1996, 49 States provided family support initiatives in response to the needs of families of children with disabilities. Such initiatives included the provision of cash subsidies, respite care, and other forms of support. There is a need in each State, however, to strengthen, expand, and coordinate the activities of a system of family support services for families of children with disabilities that is easily accessible, avoids duplication, uses resources efficiently, and prevents gaps in services to families in all areas of the State.

(6) The goals of the Nation properly include the goal of providing to families of children with disabilities the family support services necessary—

(A) to support the family;

(B) to enable families of children with disabilities to nurture and enjoy their children at home;

(C) to enable families of children with disabilities to make informed choices and decisions regarding the nature of supports, resources, services, and other assistance made available to such families; and

(D) to support family caregivers of adults with disabilities.

(b) Purposes. The purposes of this title [42 USCS §§ 15091 et seq.] are—

(1) to promote and strengthen the implementation of comprehensive State systems of family support services, for families with children with disabilities, that are family-centered and family-directed, and that provide families with the greatest possible decisionmaking authority and control regarding the nature and use of services and support;

(2) to promote leadership by families in planning, policy development, implementation, and evaluation of family support services for families of children with disabilities;

(3) to promote and develop interagency coordination and collaboration between agencies responsible for providing the services; and

(4) to increase the availability of, funding for, access to, and provision of family support services for families of children with disabilities.

(c) Policy. It is the policy of the United States that all programs, projects, and activities funded under this title [42 USCS §§ 15091 et seq.] shall be family-centered and family-directed, and shall be provided in a manner consistent with the goal of providing families of children with disabilities with the support the families need to raise their children at home.

(Oct. 30, 2000, P. L. 106-402, Title II, § 202, 114 Stat. 1728.)

CROSS REFERENCES

This section is referred to in 42 USCS §§ 15098, 15100.

§ 15092. Definitions and special rule

(a) Definitions. In this title [42 USCS §§ 15091 et seq.]:

(1) Child with a disability. The term "child with a disability" means an individual who—

(A) has a significant physical or mental impairment, as defined pursuant to State policy to the extent that such policy is established without regard to type of disability; or

(B) is an infant or a young child from birth through age 8 and has a substantial developmental delay or specific congenital or acquired condition that presents a high probability of resulting in a disability if services are not provided to the infant or child.

(2) Family. (A) In general. Subject to subparagraph (B), for purposes of the application of this title [42 USCS §§ 15091 et seq.] in a State, the term "family" has the meaning given the term by the State.

(B) Exclusion of employees. The term does not include an employee who, acting in a paid employment capacity, provides services to a child with a disability in an out-of-home setting such as a hospital, nursing home, personal care home, board and care home, group home, or other facility.

(3) Family support for families of children with disabilities. The term "family support for families of children with disabilities" means supports, resources, services, and other assistance provided to families of children with disabilities pursuant to State policy that are designed to—

(A) support families in the efforts of such families to raise their children with disabilities in the home;

(B) strengthen the role of the family as primary caregiver for such children;

(C) prevent involuntary out-of-the-home placement of such children and maintain family unity; and

(D) reunite families with children with disabilities who have been placed out of the home, whenever possible.

(4) Secretary. The term "Secretary" means the Secretary of Health and Human Services.

(5) State. The term "State" means each of the 50 States of the United States, the District of Columbia, the Commonwealth of Puerto Rico, the United States Virgin Islands, Guam, American Samoa, and the Commonwealth of the Northern Mariana Islands.

(6) Systems change activities. The term "systems change activities" means efforts that result in laws, regulations, policies, practices, or organizational structures—

(A) that are family-centered and family-directed;

(B) that facilitate and increase access to, provision of, and funding for, family support services for families of children with disabilities; and

(C) that otherwise accomplish the purposes of this title [42 USCS §§ 15091 et seq.].

(b) Special rule. References in this title [42 USCS §§ 15091 et seq.] to a child with a disability shall be considered to include references to an individual who is not younger than age 18 who—

(1) has a significant impairment described in subsection (a)(1)(A); and

(2) is residing with and receiving assistance from a family member.

(Oct. 30, 2000, P. L. 106-402, Title II, § 203, 114 Stat. 1729.)

§ 15093. Grants to States

(a) In general. The Secretary shall make grants to States on a competitive basis, in accordance with the provisions of this title [42 USCS §§ 15091 et seq.], to support systems change activities designed to assist States to develop and implement, or expand and enhance, a statewide system of family support services for families of children with disabilities that accomplishes the purposes of this title [42 USCS §§ 15091 et seq.].

(b) Award period and grant limitation. No grant shall be awarded under this section for a period of more than 3 years. No State shall be eligible for more than 1 grant under this section.

(c) Amount of grants. (1) Grants to States. (A) Federal matching share. From amounts appropriated under section 212(a) [42 USCS § 15101(a)], the Secretary shall pay to each State that has an application approved under section 205 [42 USCS § 15094], for each year of the grant period, an amount that is—

(i) equal to not more than 75 percent of the cost of the systems change activities to be carried out by the State; and

(ii) not less than $100,000 and not more than $500,000.

(B) Non-Federal share. The non-Federal share of the cost of the systems change activities may be in cash or in kind, fairly evaluated, including plant, equipment, or services.

(2) Calculation of amounts. The Secretary shall calculate a grant amount described in paragraph (1) on the basis of—

(A) the amounts available for making grants under this section; and

(B) the child population of the State concerned.

(d) Priority for previously participating States. For the second and third fiscal years for which amounts are appropriated to carry out this section, the Secretary, in providing payments under this section, shall give priority to States that received payments under this section during the preceding fiscal year.

(e) Priorities for distribution. To the extent practicable, the Secretary shall award grants to States under this section in a manner that—

(1) is geographically equitable;

(2) distributes the grants among States that have differing levels of development of statewide systems of family support services for families of children with disabilities; and

(3) distributes the grants among States that attempt to meet the needs of unserved and underserved populations, such as individuals from racial and ethnic minority backgrounds, disadvantaged individuals, individuals with limited English proficiency, and individuals from underserved geographic areas (rural or urban).

(Oct. 30, 2000, P. L. 106-402, Title II, § 204, 114 Stat. 1730.)

CROSS REFERENCES
This section is referred to in 42 USCS §§ 15095, 15096.

RESEARCH GUIDE
Am Jur:
79 Am Jur 2d, Welfare § 49.

§ 15094. Application

To be eligible to receive a grant under this title [42 USCS §§ 15091 et seq.], a State shall submit an application to the Secretary at such time, in such manner, and containing such information and assurances as the Secretary may require, including information about the designation of a lead entity, a description of available State resources, and assurances that systems change activities will be family-centered and family-directed.

(Oct. 30, 2000, P. L. 106-402, Title II, § 205, 114 Stat. 1731.)

CROSS REFERENCES
This section is referred to in 42 USCS §§ 15093, 15095.

RESEARCH GUIDE
Am Jur:
79 Am Jur 2d, Welfare § 49.

§ 15095. Designation of the lead entity

(a) Designation. The Chief Executive Officer of a State that desires to receive a grant under section 204 [42 USCS § 15093], shall designate the office or entity (referred to in this title [42 USCS §§ 15091 et seq.] as the "lead entity") responsible for—

(1) submitting the application described in section 205 [42 USCS § 15094] on behalf of the State;

(2) administering and supervising the use of the amounts made available under the grant;

(3) coordinating efforts related to and supervising the preparation of the application;

(4) coordinating the planning, development, implementation (or expansion and enhancement), and evaluation of a statewide system of family support services for families of children with disabilities among public agencies and between public agencies and private agencies, including coordinating efforts related to entering into interagency agreements;

(5) coordinating efforts related to the participation by families of children with disabilities in activities carried out under a grant made under this title [42 USCS §§ 15091 et seq.]; and

(6) submitting the report described in section 208 [42 USCS § 15097] on behalf of the State.

(b) Qualifications. In designating the lead entity, the Chief Executive Officer may designate—

(1) an office of the Chief Executive Officer;

(2) a commission appointed by the Chief Executive Officer;

(3) a public agency;

(4) a council established under Federal or State law; or

(5) another appropriate office, agency, or entity.

(Oct. 30, 2000, P. L. 106-402, Title II, § 206, 114 Stat. 1731.)

§ 15096. Authorized activities

(a) **In general.** A State that receives a grant under section 204 [42 USCS § 15093] shall use the funds made available through the grant to carry out systems change activities that accomplish the purposes of this title [42 USCS §§ 15091 et seq.].

(b) **Special rule.** In carrying out activities authorized under this title [42 USCS §§ 15091 et seq.], a State shall ensure that such activities address the needs of families of children with disabilities from unserved or underserved populations.

(Oct. 30, 2000, P. L. 106-402, Title II, § 207, 114 Stat. 1732.)

RESEARCH GUIDE

Am Jur:

79 Am Jur 2d, Welfare § 49.

§ 15097. Reporting

A State that receives a grant under this title [42 USCS §§ 15091 et seq.] shall prepare and submit to the Secretary, at the end of the grant period, a report containing the results of State efforts to develop and implement, or expand and enhance, a statewide system of family support services for families of children with disabilities.

(Oct. 30, 2000, P. L. 106-402, Title II, § 208, 114 Stat. 1732.)

CROSS REFERENCES

This section is referred to in 42 USCS § 15095.

§ 15098. Technical assistance

(a) **In general.** The Secretary shall enter into contracts or cooperative agreements with appropriate public or private agencies and organizations, including institutions of higher education, with documented experience, expertise, and capacity, for the purpose of providing technical assistance and information with respect to the development and implementation, or expansion and enhancement, of a statewide system of family support services for families of children with disabilities.

(b) **Purpose.** An agency or organization that provides technical assistance and information under this section in a State that receives a grant under this title [42 USCS §§ 15091 et seq.] shall provide the technical assistance and information to the lead entity of the State, family members of children with disabilities, organizations, service providers, and policymakers involved with children with disabilities and their families. Such an agency or organization may also provide technical assistance and information to a State that does not receive a grant under this title [42 USCS §§ 15091 et seq.].

(c) **Reports to the Secretary.** An entity providing technical assistance and information under this section shall prepare and submit to the Secretary periodic reports regarding Federal policies and procedures identified within the States that facilitate or impede the delivery of family support services to families of children with disabilities. The report shall include recommendations to the Secretary regarding the delivery of services, coordination with other programs, and integration of the policies described in section 202 [42 USCS § 15091] in Federal law, other than this title [42 USCS §§ 15091 et seq.].

(Oct. 30, 2000, P. L. 106-402, Title II, § 209, 114 Stat. 1732.)

CROSS REFERENCES

This section is referred to in 42 USCS § 15101.

§ 15099. Evaluation

(a) **In general.** The Secretary shall conduct a national evaluation of the program of grants to States authorized by this title [42 USCS §§ 15091 et seq.].

(b) **Purpose.** (1) In general. The Secretary shall conduct the evaluation under subsection (a) to assess the status and effects of State efforts to develop and implement, or expand and enhance, statewide systems of family support services for families of children with disabilities in a manner consistent with the provisions of this title [42 USCS §§ 15091 et seq.]. In particular, the Secretary shall assess the impact of such efforts on families of children with disabilities, and recommend amendments to this title [42 USCS §§ 15091 et seq.] that are necessary to assist States to accomplish fully the purposes of this title [42 USCS §§ 15091 et seq.].

(2) Information systems. The Secretary shall work with the States to develop an information system designed to compile and report, from information provided by the States, qualitative and quantitative descriptions of the impact of the program of grants to States authorized by this title [42 USCS §§ 15091 et seq.] on—

   (A) families of children with disabilities, including families from unserved and underserved populations;

   (B) access to and funding for family support services for families of children with disabilities;

   (C) interagency coordination and collaboration between agencies responsible for providing the services; and

   (D) the involvement of families of children with disabilities at all levels of the statewide systems.

(c) **Report to Congress.** Not later than 2¹/₂ years after the date of enactment of this Act [enacted Oct. 30, 2000], the Secretary shall prepare and submit to the appropriate committees of Congress a report concerning the results of the evaluation conducted under this section.

(Oct. 30, 2000, P. L. 106-402, Title II, § 210, 114 Stat. 1733.)

CROSS REFERENCES
This section is referred to in 42 USCS § 15101.

§ 15100. Projects of national significance

(a) Study by the Secretary. The Secretary shall review Federal programs to determine the extent to which such programs facilitate or impede access to, provision of, and funding for family support services for families of children with disabilities, consistent with the policies described in section 202 [42 USCS § 15091].

(b) Projects of national significance. The Secretary shall make grants or enter into contracts for projects of national significance to support the development of national and State policies and practices related to the development and implementation, or expansion and enhancement, of family-centered and family-directed systems of family support services for families of children with disabilities.

(Oct. 30, 2000, P. L. 106-402, Title II, § 211, 114 Stat. 1733.)

CROSS REFERENCES
This section is referred to in 42 USCS § 15101.

§ 15101. Authorization of appropriations

(a) In general. There are authorized to be appropriated to carry out this title [42 USCS §§ 15091 et seq.] such sums as may be necessary for each of fiscal years 2001 through 2007.

(b) Reservation. (1) In general. The Secretary shall reserve for each fiscal year 10 percent, or $400,000 (whichever is greater), of the amount appropriated pursuant to subsection (a) to carry out—

(A) section 209 [42 USCS § 15098] (relating to the provision of technical assistance and information to States); and

(B) section 210 [42 USCS § 15099] (relating to the conduct of evaluations).

(2) Special rule. For each year that the amount appropriated pursuant to subsection (a) is $10,000,000 or greater, the Secretary may reserve 5 percent of such amount to carry out section 211 [42 USCS § 15100].

(Oct. 30, 2000, P. L. 106-402, Title II, § 212, 114 Stat. 1734.)

CROSS REFERENCES
This section is referred to in 42 USCS § 15093.

PROGRAM FOR DIRECT SUPPORT WORKERS WHO ASSIST INDIVIDUALS WITH DEVELOPMENTAL DISABILITIES

§ 15111. Findings

Congress finds that—

(1) direct support workers, especially young adults, have played essential

roles in providing the support needed by individuals with developmental disabilities and expanding community options for those individuals;

(2) 4 factors have contributed to a decrease in the available pool of direct support workers, specifically—

(A) the small population of individuals who are age 18 through 25, an age group that has been attracted to direct support work in the past;

(B) the rapid expansion of the service sector, which attracts individuals who previously would have elected to pursue employment as direct support workers;

(C) the failure of wages in the human services sector to keep pace with wages in other service sectors; and

(D) the lack of quality training and career advancement opportunities available to direct support workers; and

(3) individuals with developmental disabilities benefit from assistance from direct support workers who are well trained, and benefit from receiving services from professionals who have spent time as direct support workers.

(Oct. 30, 2000, P. L. 106-402, Title III, § 301, 114 Stat. 1734.)

§ 15112. Definitions

In this title [42 USCS §§ 15111 et seq.]:

(1) Developmental disability. The term "developmental disability" has the meaning given the term in section 102 [42 USCS § 15002].

(2) Institution of higher education. The term "institution of higher education" has the meaning given the term in section 1201 of the Higher Education Act of 1965 (20 U.S.C. 1141).

(3) Secretary. The term "Secretary" means the Secretary of Health and Human Services.

(Oct. 30, 2000, P. L. 106-402, Title III, § 302, 114 Stat. 1734.)

HISTORY; ANCILLARY LAWS AND DIRECTIVES

References in text:

"Section 1201 of the Higher Education Act of 1965 (20 U.S.C. 1141)", referred to in para. (2), was repealed by Act Oct. 7, 1998, P. L. 105-244, Title I, § 101(b), Title VII, § 702, 112 Stat. 1616, 1803. However, the term "institution of higher education" is defined in 20 USCS § 1001.

§ 15113. Reaching up scholarship program

(a) Program authorization. The Secretary may award grants to eligible entities, on a competitive basis, to enable the entities to carry out scholarship programs by providing vouchers for postsecondary education to direct support workers who assist individuals with developmental disabilities residing in diverse settings. The Secretary shall award the grants to pay for the Federal share of the cost of providing the vouchers.

(b) Eligible entity. To be eligible to receive a grant under this section, an entity shall be—

(1) an institution of higher education;

(2) a State agency; or

(3) a consortium of such institutions or agencies.

(c) Application requirements. To be eligible to receive a grant under this section, an eligible entity shall submit to the Secretary an application at such time, in such manner, and containing such information as the Secretary may require, including a description of—

(1) the basis for awarding the vouchers;

(2) the number of individuals to receive the vouchers; and

(3) the amount of funds that will be made available by the eligible entity to pay for the non-Federal share of the cost of providing the vouchers.

(d) Selection criteria. In awarding a grant under this section for a scholarship program, the Secretary shall give priority to an entity submitting an application that—

(1) specifies that individuals who receive vouchers through the program will be individuals—

(A) who are direct support workers who assist individuals with developmental disabilities residing in diverse settings, while pursuing postsecondary education; and

(B) each of whom verifies, prior to receiving the voucher, that the worker has completed 250 hours as a direct support worker in the past 90 days;

(2) states that the vouchers that will be provided through the program will be in amounts of not more than $2,000 per year;

(3) provides an assurance that the eligible entity (or another specified entity that is not a voucher recipient) will contribute the non-Federal share of the cost of providing the vouchers; and

(4) meets such other conditions as the Secretary may specify.

(e) Federal share. The Federal share of the cost of providing the vouchers shall be not more than 80 percent.

(Oct. 30, 2000, P. L. 106-402, Title III, § 303, 114 Stat. 1735.)

CROSS REFERENCES

This section is referred to in 42 USCS § 15115.

§ 15114.   Staff development curriculum authorization

(a) Funding. (1) In general. The Secretary shall award funding, on a competitive basis, through a grant, cooperative agreement, or contract, to a public or private entity or a combination of such entities, for the development, evaluation, and dissemination of a staff development curriculum, and related guidelines, for computer-assisted, competency-based, multimedia, interactive instruction, relating to service as a direct support worker.

(2) Participants. The curriculum shall be developed for individuals who—

(A) seek to become direct support workers who assist individuals with developmental disabilities or are such direct support workers; and

(B) seek to upgrade their skills and competencies related to being a direct support worker.

(b) Application requirements. To be eligible to receive an award under this section, an entity shall submit to the Secretary an application at such time, in such manner, and containing such information as the Secretary may require, including—

(1) a comprehensive analysis of the content of direct support roles;

(2) information identifying an advisory group that—

(A) is comprised of individuals with experience and expertise with regard to the support provided by direct support workers, and effective ways to provide the support, for individuals with developmental disabilities in diverse settings; and

(B) will advise the entity throughout the development, evaluation, and dissemination of the staff development curriculum and guidelines;

(3) information describing how the entity will—

(A) develop, field test, and validate a staff development curriculum that—

(i) relates to the appropriate reading level for direct service workers who assist individuals with disabilities;

(ii) allows for multiple levels of instruction;

(iii) provides instruction appropriate for direct support workers who work in diverse settings; and

(iv) is consistent with subsections (b) and (c) of section 101 [42 USCS § 15001] and section 109 [42 USCS § 15009];

(B) develop, field test, and validate guidelines for the organizations that use the curriculum that provide for—

(i) providing necessary technical and instructional support to trainers and mentors for the participants;

(ii) ensuring easy access to and use of such curriculum by workers that choose to participate in using, and agencies that choose to use, the curriculum;

(iii) evaluating the proficiency of the participants with respect to the content of the curriculum;

(iv) providing necessary support to the participants to assure that the participants have access to, and proficiency in using, a computer in order to participate in the development, testing, and validation process;

(v) providing necessary technical and instructional support to trainers and mentors for the participants in conjunction with the development, testing, and validation process;

(vi) addressing the satisfaction of participants, individuals with developmental disabilities and their families, providers of services for such individuals and families, and other relevant entities with the curriculum; and

(vii) developing methods to maintain a record of the instruction completed, and the content mastered, by each participant under the curriculum; and

(C) nationally disseminate the curriculum and guidelines, including dissemination through—

(i) parent training and information centers funded under part D of the Individuals with Disabilities Education Act (20 U.S.C. 1451 et seq.);

(ii) community-based organizations of and for individuals with developmental disabilities and their families;

(iii) entities funded under title I [42 USCS §§ 15001 et seq.];

(iv) centers for independent living;

(v) State educational agencies and local educational agencies;

(vi) entities operating appropriate medical facilities;

(vii) postsecondary education entities; and

(viii) other appropriate entities; and

(4) such other information as the Secretary may require.

(Oct. 30, 2000, P. L. 106-402, Title III, § 304, 114 Stat. 1735.)

CROSS REFERENCES

This section is referred to in 42 USCS § 15115.

§ 15115. Authorization of appropriations

(a) Scholarships. There are authorized to be appropriated to carry out section 303 [42 USCS § 15113] $800,000 for fiscal year 2001 and such sums as may be necessary for each of fiscal years 2002 through 2007.

(b) Staff development curriculum. There are authorized to be appropriated to carry out section 304 [42 USCS § 15114] $800,000 for fiscal year 2001 and such sums as may be necessary for each of fiscal years 2002 and 2003.

(Oct. 30, 2000, P. L. 106-402, Title III, § 305, 114 Stat. 1737.)

CHAPTER 145. PUBLIC SAFETY OFFICER MEDAL OF VALOR AND TRIBUTES

§ 15201. Authorization of Medal

After September 1, 2001, the President may award, and present in the name of Congress, a Medal of Valor of appropriate design, with ribbons and appurtenances, to a public safety officer who is cited by the Attorney General, upon the recommendation of the Medal of Valor Review Board, for extraordinary valor above and beyond the call of duty. The Public Safety Medal of Valor shall be the highest national award for valor by a public safety officer.
(May 30, 2001, P. L. 107-12, § 2, 115 Stat. 20.)

HISTORY; ANCILLARY LAWS AND DIRECTIVES
Short title:
Act May 30, 2001, P. L. 107-12, § 1, 115 Stat. 20, provides: "This Act [classified to 15 USCS § 2214 and 42 USCS §§ 15201 et seq.] may be cited as the 'Public Safety Officer Medal of Valor Act of 2001'.".

§ 15202. Medal of Valor Board

(a) Establishment of Board. There is established a Medal of Valor Review

Board (hereinafter in this Act referred to as the "Board"), which shall be composed of 11 members appointed in accordance with subsection (b) and shall conduct its business in accordance with this Act.

(b) Membership. (1) Members. The members of the Board shall be individuals with knowledge or expertise, whether by experience or training, in the field of public safety, of which—

    (A) two shall be appointed by the majority leader of the Senate;

    (B) two shall be appointed by the minority leader of the Senate;

    (C) two shall be appointed by the Speaker of the House of Representatives;

    (D) two shall be appointed by the minority leader of the House of Representatives; and

    (E) three shall be appointed by the President, including one with experience in firefighting, one with experience in law enforcement, and one with experience in emergency services.

(2) Term. The term of a Board member shall be 4 years.

(3) Vacancies. Any vacancy in the membership of the Board shall not affect the powers of the Board and shall be filled in the same manner as the original appointment.

(4) Operation of the Board. (A) Chairman. The Chairman of the Board shall be elected by the members of the Board from among the members of the Board.

    (B) Meetings. The Board shall conduct its first meeting not later than 90 days after the appointment of the last member appointed of the initial group of members appointed to the Board. Thereafter, the Board shall meet at the call of the Chairman of the Board. The Board shall meet not less often than twice each year.

    (C) Voting and rules. A majority of the members shall constitute a quorum to conduct business, but the Board may establish a lesser quorum for conducting hearings scheduled by the Board. The Board may establish by majority vote any other rules for the conduct of the Board's business, if such rules are not inconsistent with this Act or other applicable law.

(c) Duties. The Board shall select candidates as recipients of the Medal of Valor from among those applications received by the National Medal of Valor Office. Not more often than once each year, the Board shall present to the Attorney General the name or names of those it recommends as Medal of Valor recipients. In a given year, the Board shall not be required to select any recipients but may not select more than 5 individuals, or groups of individuals, as recipients. The Attorney General may in extraordinary cases increase the number of recipients in a given year. The Board shall set an annual timetable for fulfilling its duties under this Act.

(d) Hearings. (1) In general. The Board may hold such hearings, sit and act at such times and places, administer such oaths, take such testimony, and receive such evidence as the Board considers advisable to carry out its duties.

(2) Witness expenses. Witnesses requested to appear before the Board may

be paid the same fees as are paid to witnesses under section 1821 of title 28, United States Code. The per diem and mileage allowances for witnesses shall be paid from funds appropriated to the Board.

(e) Information from Federal agencies. The Board may secure directly from any Federal department or agency such information as the Board considers necessary to carry out its duties. Upon the request of the Board, the head of such department or agency may furnish such information to the Board.

(f) Information to be kept confidential. The Board shall not disclose any information which may compromise an ongoing law enforcement investigation or is otherwise required by law to be kept confidential.

(May 30, 2001, P. L. 107-12, § 3, 115 Stat. 20; Jan. 5, 2006, P. L. 109-162, Title XI, Subtitle B, Ch. 1, § 1112, 119 Stat. 3103.)

HISTORY; ANCILLARY LAWS AND DIRECTIVES

References in text:
"This Act", referred to in this section, is Act May 30, 2001, P. L. 107-12, popularly known as the Public Safety Officer Medal of Valor Act of 2001, which appears generally as 42 USCS §§ 15201 et seq. For full classification of such Act, consult USCS Tables volumes.

Amendments:
2006. Act Jan. 5, 2006, in subsec. (c), substituted "more than 5 individuals, or groups of individuals, as recipients" for "more than 5 recipients".

§ 15203. Board personnel matters

(a) Compensation of members. (1) Except as provided in paragraph (2), each member of the Board shall be compensated at a rate equal to the daily equivalent of the annual rate of basic pay prescribed for level IV of the Executive Schedule under section 5315 of title 5, United States Code, for each day (including travel time) during which such member is engaged in the performance of the duties of the Board.

(2) All members of the Board who serve as officers or employees of the United States, a State, or a local government, shall serve without compensation in addition to that received for those services.

(b) Travel expenses. The members of the Board shall be allowed travel expenses, including per diem in lieu of subsistence, at rates authorized for employees of agencies under subchapter I of chapter 57 of title 5 [5 USCS §§ 5701 et seq.], United States Code, while away from their homes or regular places of business in the performance of service for the Board.

(May 30, 2001, P. L. 107-12, § 4, 115 Stat. 21.)

§ 15204. Definitions

In this Act:

(1) Public safety officer. The term "public safety officer" means a person serving a public agency, with or without compensation, as a firefighter, law enforcement officer, or emergency services officer, as determined by the At-

torney General. For the purposes of this paragraph, the term "law enforcement officer" includes a person who is a corrections or court officer or a civil defense officer.

(2) State. The term "State" means each of the several States of the United States, the District of Columbia, the Commonwealth of Puerto Rico, the Virgin Islands, Guam, American Samoa, and the Commonwealth of the Northern Mariana Islands.

(May 30, 2001, P. L. 107-12, § 5, 115 Stat. 22.)

HISTORY; ANCILLARY LAWS AND DIRECTIVES

References in text:
"This Act", referred to in this section, is Act May 30, 2001, P. L. 107-12, popularly known as the Public Safety Officer Medal of Valor Act of 2001, which appears generally as 42 USCS §§ 15201 et seq. For full classification of such Act, consult USCS Tables volumes.

§ 15205. Authorization of appropriations

There are authorized to be appropriated to the Attorney General such sums as may be necessary to carry out this Act.

(May 30, 2001, P. L. 107-12, § 6, 115 Stat. 22.)

HISTORY; ANCILLARY LAWS AND DIRECTIVES

References in text:
"This Act", referred to in this section, is Act May 30, 2001, P. L. 107-12, popularly known as the Public Safety Officer Medal of Valor Act of 2001, which appears generally as 42 USCS §§ 15201 et seq. For full classification of such Act, consult USCS Tables volumes.

§ 15206. National Medal of Valor Office

There is established within the Department of Justice a National Medal of Valor Office. The Office shall provide staff support to the Board to establish criteria and procedures for the submission of recommendations of nominees for the Medal of Valor and for the final design of the Medal of Valor.

(May 30, 2001, P. L. 107-12, § 7, 115 Stat. 22.)

§ 15207. Consultation requirement

The Board shall consult with the Institute of Heraldry within the Department of Defense regarding the design and artistry of the Medal of Valor. The Board may also consider suggestions received by the Department of Justice regarding the design of the medal, including those made by persons not employed by the Department.

(May 30, 2001, P. L. 107-12, § 9, 115 Stat. 22.)

§ 15208. Law enforcement tribute acts

(a) Short title. This section may be cited as the "Law Enforcement Tribute Act".

(b) Findings. Congress finds the following:

(1) The well-being of all citizens of the United States is preserved and enhanced as a direct result of the vigilance and dedication of law enforcement and public safety personnel.

(2) More than 700,000 law enforcement officers, both men and women, at great risk to their personal safety, serve their fellow citizens as guardians of peace.

(3) Nationwide, 51 law enforcement officers were killed in the line of duty in 2000, according to statistics released by the Federal Bureau of Investigation. This number is an increase of 9 from the 1999 total of 42.

(4) In 1999, 112 firefighters died while on duty, an increase of 21 deaths from the previous year.

(5) Every year, 1 in 9 peace officers is assaulted, 1 in 25 is injured, and 1 in 4,400 is killed in the line of duty.

(6) In addition, recent statistics indicate that 83 officers were accidentally killed in the performance of their duties in 2000, an increase of 18 from the 65 accidental deaths in 1999.

(7) A permanent tribute is a powerful means of honoring the men and women who have served our Nation with distinction. However, many law enforcement and public safety agencies lack the resources to honor their fallen colleagues.

(c) Program authorized. From amounts made available to carry out this section, the Attorney General may make grants to States, units of local government, and Indian tribes to carry out programs to honor, through permanent tributes, men and women of the United States who were killed or disabled while serving as law enforcement or public safety officers.

(d) Uses of funds. Grants awarded under this section shall be distributed directly to the State, unit of local government, or Indian tribe, and shall be used for the purposes specified in subsection (c).

(e) $150,000 limitation. A grant under this section may not exceed $150,000 to any single recipient.

(f) Matching funds. (1) The Federal portion of the costs of a program provided by a grant under this section may not exceed 50 percent.

(2) Any funds appropriated by Congress for the activities of any agency of an Indian tribal government or the Bureau of Indian Affairs performing law enforcement or public safety functions on any Indian lands may be used to provide the non-Federal share of a matching requirement funded under this subsection.

(g) Applications. To request a grant under this section, the chief executive of a State, unit of local government, or Indian tribe shall submit an application to the Attorney General at such time, in such manner, and accompanied by such information as the Attorney General may require.

(h) Annual report to Congress. Not later than November 30 of each year, the Attorney General shall submit a report to the Congress regarding the activities carried out under this section. Each such report shall include, for the preceding fiscal year, the number of grants funded under this section, the amount of funds provided under those grants, and the activities for which those funds were used.

(i) Authorization of appropriations. There are authorized to be appropriated to carry out this section $3,000,000 for each of fiscal years 2002 through 2009. (Nov. 2, 2002, P. L. 107-273, Div C, Title I, Subtitle A, § 11001, 116 Stat. 1815; Jan. 5, 2006, P. L. 109-162, Title XI, Subtitle C, § 1185, 119 Stat. 3127.)

HISTORY; ANCILLARY LAWS AND DIRECTIVES

Explanatory notes:
This section was enacted as part of Act Nov. 2, 2002, P. L. 107-273, and not as part of Act May 30, 2001, P. L. 107-12, which generally comprises this chapter.

Amendments:
2006. Act Jan. 5, 2006, in subsec. (i), substituted "2009" for "2006".

CHAPTER 145A.   LAW ENFORCEMENT CONGRESSIONAL BADGE OF BRAVERY

§ 15231.   Definitions

In this Act [42 USCS §§ 15231 et seq.]:

(1) Federal agency head. The term "Federal agency head" means the head of any executive, legislative, or judicial branch Government entity that employs Federal law enforcement officers.

(2) Federal Board. The term "Federal Board" means the Federal Law Enforcement Congressional Badge of Bravery Board established under section 103(a) [42 USCS § 15243(a)].

(3) Federal Board members. The term "Federal Board members" means the members of the Federal Board appointed under section 103(c) [42 USCS § 15243(c)].

(4) Federal Law Enforcement Badge. The term "Federal Law Enforcement Badge" means the Federal Law Enforcement Congressional Badge of Bravery described in section 101 [42 USCS § 15241].

(5) Federal law enforcement officer. The term "Federal law enforcement officer"—

    (A) means a Federal employee—

        (i) who has statutory authority to make arrests or apprehensions;

        (ii) who is authorized by the agency of the employee to carry firearms; and

        (iii) whose duties are primarily—

            (I) engagement in or supervision of the prevention, detection, investigation, or prosecution of, or the incarceration of any person for, any violation of law; or

            (II) the protection of Federal, State, local, or foreign government officials against threats to personal safety; and

    (B) includes a law enforcement officer employed by the Amtrak Police Department or Federal Reserve.

(6) Office. The term "Office" means the Congressional Badge of Bravery Office established under section 301(a) [42 USCS § 15261(a)].

(7) State and Local Board. The term "State and Local Board" means the State and Local Law Enforcement Congressional Badge of Bravery Board established under section 203(a) [42 USCS § 15253(a)].

(8) State and Local Board members. The term "State and Local Board members" means the members of the State and Local Board appointed under section 203(c) [42 USCS § 15253(c)].

(9) State and Local Law Enforcement Badge. The term "State and Local Law Enforcement Badge" means the State and Local Law Enforcement Congressional Badge of Bravery described in section 201 [42 USCS § 15251].

(10) State or local agency head. The term "State or local agency head" means the head of any executive, legislative, or judicial branch entity of a State or local government that employs State or local law enforcement officers.

(11) State or local law enforcement officer. The term "State or local law enforcement officer" means an employee of a State or local government—

    (A) who has statutory authority to make arrests or apprehensions;

    (B) who is authorized by the agency of the employee to carry firearms; and

(C) whose duties are primarily—

(i) engagement in or supervision of the prevention, detection, investigation, or prosecution of, or the incarceration of any person for, any violation of law; or

(ii) the protection of Federal, State, local, or foreign government officials against threats to personal safety.

(July 31, 2008, P. L. 110-298, § 2, 122 Stat. 2985.)

HISTORY; ANCILLARY LAWS AND DIRECTIVES

Short title:

Act July 31, 2008, P. L. 110-298, § 1, 122 Stat. 2985, provides: "This Act [42 USCS §§ 15231 et seq.] may be cited as the 'Law Enforcement Congressional Badge of Bravery Act of 2008'.".

FEDERAL LAW ENFORCEMENT CONGRESSIONAL BADGE OF BRAVERY

§ 15241. Authorization of a badge

The Attorney General may award, and a Member of Congress or the Attorney General may present, in the name of Congress a Federal Law Enforcement Congressional Badge of Bravery to a Federal law enforcement officer who is cited by the Attorney General, upon the recommendation of the Federal Board, for performing an act of bravery while in the line of duty.

(July 31, 2008, P. L. 110-298, Title I, § 101, 122 Stat. 2986.)

§ 15242. Nominations

(a) In general. A Federal agency head may nominate for a Federal Law Enforcement Badge an individual—

(1) who is a Federal law enforcement officer working within the agency of the Federal agency head making the nomination; and

(2) who—

(A)(i) sustained a physical injury while—

(I) engaged in the lawful duties of the individual; and

(II) performing an act characterized as bravery by the Federal agency head making the nomination; and

(ii) put the individual at personal risk when the injury described in clause (i) occurred; or

(B) while not injured, performed an act characterized as bravery by the Federal agency head making the nomination that placed the individual at risk of serious physical injury or death.

(b) Contents. A nomination under subsection (a) shall include—

(1) a written narrative, of not more than 2 pages, describing the circumstances under which the nominee performed the act of bravery described in subsection (a) and how the circumstances meet the criteria described in such subsection;

(2) the full name of the nominee;

(3) the home mailing address of the nominee;

(4) the agency in which the nominee served on the date when such nominee performed the act of bravery described in subsection (a);

(5) the occupational title and grade or rank of the nominee;

(6) the field office address of the nominee on the date when such nominee performed the act of bravery described in subsection (a); and

(7) the number of years of Government service by the nominee as of the date when such nominee performed the act of bravery described in subsection (a).

(c) **Submission deadline.** A Federal agency head shall submit each nomination under subsection (a) to the Office not later than February 15 of the year following the date on which the nominee performed the act of bravery described in subsection (a).

(July 31, 2008, P. L. 110-298, Title I, § 102, 122 Stat. 2986.)

§ 15243. Federal Law Enforcement Congressional Badge of Bravery Board

(a) **Establishment.** There is established within the Department of Justice a Federal Law Enforcement Congressional Badge of Bravery Board.

(b) **Duties.** The Federal Board shall do the following:

(1) Design the Federal Law Enforcement Badge with appropriate ribbons and appurtenances.

(2) Select an engraver to produce each Federal Law Enforcement Badge.

(3) Recommend recipients of the Federal Law Enforcement Badge from among those nominations timely submitted to the Office.

(4) Annually present to the Attorney General the names of Federal law enforcement officers who the Federal Board recommends as Federal Law Enforcement Badge recipients in accordance with the criteria described in section 102(a) [42 USCS § 15242(a)].

(5) After approval by the Attorney General—

(A) procure the Federal Law Enforcement Badges from the engraver selected under paragraph (2);

(B) send a letter announcing the award of each Federal Law Enforcement Badge to the Federal agency head who nominated the recipient of such Federal Law Enforcement Badge;

(C) send a letter to each Member of Congress representing the congressional district where the recipient of each Federal Law Enforcement Badge resides to offer such Member an opportunity to present such Federal Law Enforcement Badge; and

(D) make or facilitate arrangements for presenting each Federal Law Enforcement Badge in accordance with section 104 [42 USCS § 15244].

(6) Set an annual timetable for fulfilling the duties described in this subsection.

(c) **Membership.** (1) Number and appointment. The Federal Board shall be composed of 7 members appointed as follows:

(A) One member jointly appointed by the majority leader and minority leader of the Senate.

(B) One member jointly appointed by the Speaker and minority leader of the House of Representatives.

(C) One member from the Department of Justice appointed by the Attorney General.

(D) Two members of the Federal Law Enforcement Officers Association appointed by the Executive Board of the Federal Law Enforcement Officers Association.

(E) Two members of the Fraternal Order of Police appointed by the Executive Board of the Fraternal Order of Police.

(2) Limitation. Not more than—

(A) 2 Federal Board members may be members of the Federal Law Enforcement Officers Association; and

(B) 2 Federal Board members may be members of the Fraternal Order of Police.

(3) Qualifications. Federal Board members shall be individuals with knowledge or expertise, whether by experience or training, in the field of Federal law enforcement.

(4) Terms and vacancies. Each Federal Board member shall be appointed for 2 years and may be reappointed. A vacancy in the Federal Board shall not affect the powers of the Federal Board and shall be filled in the same manner as the original appointment.

(d) Operations. (1) Chairperson. The Chairperson of the Federal Board shall be a Federal Board member elected by a majority of the Federal Board.

(2) Meetings. The Federal Board shall conduct its first meeting not later than 90 days after the appointment of a majority of Federal Board members. Thereafter, the Federal Board shall meet at the call of the Chairperson, or in the case of a vacancy of the position of Chairperson, at the call of the Attorney General.

(3) Voting and rules. A majority of Federal Board members shall constitute a quorum to conduct business, but the Federal Board may establish a lesser quorum for conducting hearings scheduled by the Federal Board. The Federal Board may establish by majority vote any other rules for the conduct of the business of the Federal Board, if such rules are not inconsistent with this title [42 USCS §§ 15241 et seq.] or other applicable law.

(e) Powers. (1) Hearings. (A) In general. The Federal Board may hold hearings, sit and act at times and places, take testimony, and receive evidence as the Federal Board considers appropriate to carry out the duties of the Federal Board under this title [42 USCS §§ 15241 et seq.]. The Federal Board may administer oaths or affirmations to witnesses appearing before it.

(B) Witness expenses. Witnesses requested to appear before the Federal Board may be paid the same fees as are paid to witnesses under section 1821 of title 28, United States Code. The per diem and mileage allowances for witnesses shall be paid from funds appropriated to the Federal Board.

(2) Information from Federal agencies. Subject to sections 552, 552a, and 552b of title 5, United States Code [5 USCS §§ 552, 552a, and 552b]—

(A) the Federal Board may secure directly from any Federal department or agency information necessary to enable it to carry out this title [42 USCS §§ 15241 et seq.]; and

(B) upon request of the Federal Board, the head of that department or agency shall furnish the information to the Federal Board.

(3) Information to be kept confidential. The Federal Board shall not disclose any information which may compromise an ongoing law enforcement investigation or is otherwise required by law to be kept confidential.

(f) **Compensation.** (1) In general. Except as provided in paragraph (2), each Federal Board member shall be compensated at a rate equal to the daily equivalent of the annual rate of basic pay prescribed for level IV of the Executive Schedule under section 5315 of title 5, United States Code, for each day (including travel time) during which such Federal Board member is engaged in the performance of the duties of the Federal Board.

(2) Prohibition of compensation for government employees. Federal Board members who serve as officers or employees of the Federal Government or a State or a local government may not receive additional pay, allowances, or benefits by reason of their service on the Federal Board.

(3) Travel expenses. Each Federal Board member shall receive travel expenses, including per diem in lieu of subsistence, in accordance with applicable provisions under subchapter I of chapter 57 of title 5, United States Code [5 USCS §§ 5701 et seq.].

(July 31, 2008, P. L. 110-298, Title I, § 103, 122 Stat. 2987.)

§ 15244. Presentation of Federal Law Enforcement Badges

(a) **Presentation by Member of Congress.** A Member of Congress may present a Federal Law Enforcement Badge to any Federal Law Enforcement Badge recipient who resides in such Member's congressional district. If both a Senator and Representative choose to present a Federal Law Enforcement Badge, such Senator and Representative shall make a joint presentation.

(b) **Presentation by Attorney General.** If no Member of Congress chooses to present the Federal Law Enforcement Badge as described in subsection (a), the Attorney General, or a designee of the Attorney General, shall present such Federal Law Enforcement Badge.

(c) **Presentation arrangements.** The office of the Member of Congress presenting each Federal Law Enforcement Badge may make arrangements for the presentation of such Federal Law Enforcement Badge, and if a Senator and Representative choose to participate jointly as described in subsection (a), the Members shall make joint arrangements. The Federal Board shall facilitate any such presentation arrangements as requested by the congressional office presenting the Federal Law Enforcement Badge and shall make arrangements in cases not undertaken by Members of Congress.

(July 31, 2008, P. L. 110-298, Title I, § 104, 122 Stat. 2989.)

STATE AND LOCAL LAW ENFORCEMENT CONGRESSIONAL BADGE
OF BRAVERY

§ 15251. Authorization of a Badge

The Attorney General may award, and a Member of Congress or the Attorney
General may present, in the name of Congress a State and Local Law Enforcement Congressional Badge of Bravery to a State or local law enforcement officer who is cited by the Attorney General, upon the recommendation of the
State and Local Board, for performing an act of bravery while in the line of
duty.

(July 31, 2008, P. L. 110-298, Title II, § 201, 122 Stat. 2990.)

§ 15252. Nominations

(a) In general. A State or local agency head may nominate for a State and Local Law Enforcement Badge an individual—

(1) who is a State or local law enforcement officer working within the agency
of the State or local agency head making the nomination; and

(2) who—

(A)(i) sustained a physical injury while—

(I) engaged in the lawful duties of the individual; and

(II) performing an act characterized as bravery by the State or local
agency head making the nomination; and

(ii) put the individual at personal risk when the injury described in
clause (i) occurred; or

(B) while not injured, performed an act characterized as bravery by the
State or local agency head making the nomination that placed the
individual at risk of serious physical injury or death.

(b) Contents. A nomination under subsection (a) shall include—

(1) a written narrative, of not more than 2 pages, describing the circumstances under which the nominee performed the act of bravery described in
subsection (a) and how the circumstances meet the criteria described in such
subsection;

(2) the full name of the nominee;

(3) the home mailing address of the nominee;

(4) the agency in which the nominee served on the date when such nominee
performed the act of bravery described in subsection (a);

(5) the occupational title and grade or rank of the nominee;

(6) the field office address of the nominee on the date when such nominee
performed the act of bravery described in subsection (a); and

(7) the number of years of government service by the nominee as of the date
when such nominee performed the act of bravery described in subsection (a).

(c) Submission deadline. A State or local agency head shall submit each
nomination under subsection (a) to the Office not later than February 15 of the
year following the date on which the nominee performed the act of bravery
described in subsection (a).

(July 31, 2008, P. L. 110-298, Title II, § 202, 122 Stat. 2990.)

§ 15253. State and Local Law Enforcement Congressional Badge of Bravery Board

(a) **Establishment.** There is established within the Department of Justice a State and Local Law Enforcement Congressional Badge of Bravery Board.

(b) **Duties.** The State and Local Board shall do the following:

(1) Design the State and Local Law Enforcement Badge with appropriate ribbons and appurtenances.

(2) Select an engraver to produce each State and Local Law Enforcement Badge.

(3) Recommend recipients of the State and Local Law Enforcement Badge from among those nominations timely submitted to the Office.

(4) Annually present to the Attorney General the names of State or local law enforcement officers who the State and Local Board recommends as State and Local Law Enforcement Badge recipients in accordance with the criteria described in section 202(a) [42 USCS § 15252(a)].

(5) After approval by the Attorney General—

(A) procure the State and Local Law Enforcement Badges from the engraver selected under paragraph (2);

(B) send a letter announcing the award of each State and Local Law Enforcement Badge to the State or local agency head who nominated the recipient of such State and Local Law Enforcement Badge;

(C) send a letter to each Member of Congress representing the congressional district where the recipient of each State and Local Law Enforcement Badge resides to offer such Member an opportunity to present such State and Local Law Enforcement Badge; and

(D) make or facilitate arrangements for presenting each State and Local Law Enforcement Badge in accordance with section 204 [42 USCS § 15254].

(6) Set an annual timetable for fulfilling the duties described in this subsection.

(c) **Membership.** (1) Number and appointment. The State and Local Board shall be composed of 9 members appointed as follows:

(A) One member jointly appointed by the majority leader and minority leader of the Senate.

(B) One member jointly appointed by the Speaker and minority leader of the House of Representatives.

(C) One member from the Department of Justice appointed by the Attorney General.

(D) Two members of the Fraternal Order of Police appointed by the Executive Board of the Fraternal Order of Police.

(E) One member of the National Association of Police Organizations appointed by the Executive Board of the National Association of Police Organizations.

(F) One member of the National Organization of Black Law Enforcement Executives appointed by the Executive Board of the National Organization of Black Law Enforcement Executives.

(G) One member of the International Association of Chiefs of Police appointed by the Board of Officers of the International Association of Chiefs of Police.

(H) One member of the National Sheriffs' Association appointed by the Executive Committee of the National Sheriffs' Association.

(2) Limitation. Not more than 5 State and Local Board members may be members of the Fraternal Order of Police.

(3) Qualifications. State and Local Board members shall be individuals with knowledge or expertise, whether by experience or training, in the field of State and local law enforcement.

(4) Terms and vacancies. Each State and Local Board member shall be appointed for 2 years and may be reappointed. A vacancy in the State and Local Board shall not affect the powers of the State and Local Board and shall be filled in the same manner as the original appointment.

(d) **Operations.** (1) Chairperson. The Chairperson of the State and Local Board shall be a State and Local Board member elected by a majority of the State and Local Board.

(2) Meetings. The State and Local Board shall conduct its first meeting not later than 90 days after the appointment of a majority of State and Local Board members. Thereafter, the State and Local Board shall meet at the call of the Chairperson, or in the case of a vacancy of the position of Chairperson, at the call of the Attorney General.

(3) Voting and rules. A majority of State and Local Board members shall constitute a quorum to conduct business, but the State and Local Board may establish a lesser quorum for conducting hearings scheduled by the State and Local Board. The State and Local Board may establish by majority vote any other rules for the conduct of the business of the State and Local Board, if such rules are not inconsistent with this title [42 USCS §§ 15251 et seq.] or other applicable law.

(e) **Powers.** (1) Hearings. (A) In general. The State and Local Board may hold hearings, sit and act at times and places, take testimony, and receive evidence as the State and Local Board considers appropriate to carry out the duties of the State and Local Board under this title [42 USCS §§ 15251 et seq.]. The State and Local Board may administer oaths or affirmations to witnesses appearing before it.

(B) Witness expenses. Witnesses requested to appear before the State and Local Board may be paid the same fees as are paid to witnesses under section 1821 of title 28, United States Code. The per diem and mileage allowances for witnesses shall be paid from funds appropriated to the State and Local Board.

(2) Information from Federal agencies. Subject to sections 552, 552a, and 552b of title 5, United States Code [5 USCS §§ 552, 552a, and 552b]—

(A) the State and Local Board may secure directly from any Federal department or agency information necessary to enable it to carry out this title [42 USCS §§ 15251 et seq.]; and

(B) upon request of the State and Local Board, the head of that department or agency shall furnish the information to the State and Local Board.

(3) Information to be kept confidential. The State and Local Board shall not disclose any information which may compromise an ongoing law enforcement investigation or is otherwise required by law to be kept confidential.

(f) Compensation. (1) In general. Except as provided in paragraph (2), each State and Local Board member shall be compensated at a rate equal to the daily equivalent of the annual rate of basic pay prescribed for level IV of the Executive Schedule under section 5315 of title 5, United States Code, for each day (including travel time) during which such State and Local Board member is engaged in the performance of the duties of the State and Local Board.

(2) Prohibition of compensation for government employees. State and Local Board members who serve as officers or employees of the Federal Government or a State or a local government may not receive additional pay, allowances, or benefits by reason of their service on the State and Local Board.

(3) Travel expenses. Each State and Local Board member shall receive travel expenses, including per diem in lieu of subsistence, in accordance with applicable provisions under subchapter I of chapter 57 of title 5, United States Code [5 USCS §§ 5701 et seq.].

(July 31, 2008, P. L. 110-298, Title II, § 203, 122 Stat. 2991.)

§ 15254. Presentation of State and Local Law Enforcement Badges

(a) Presentation by Member of Congress. A Member of Congress may present a State and Local Law Enforcement Badge to any State and Local Law Enforcement Badge recipient who resides in such Member's congressional district. If both a Senator and Representative choose to present a State and Local Law Enforcement Badge, such Senator and Representative shall make a joint presentation.

(b) Presentation by Attorney General. If no Member of Congress chooses to present the State and Local Law Enforcement Badge as described in subsection (a), the Attorney General, or a designee of the Attorney General, shall present such State and Local Law Enforcement Badge.

(c) Presentation arrangements. The office of the Member of Congress presenting each State and Local Law Enforcement Badge may make arrangements for the presentation of such State and Local Law Enforcement Badge, and if a Senator and Representative choose to participate jointly as described in subsection (a), the Members shall make joint arrangements. The State and Local Board shall facilitate any such presentation arrangements as requested by the congressional office presenting the State and Local Law Enforcement Badge and shall make arrangements in cases not undertaken by Members of Congress.

(July 31, 2008, P. L. 110-298, Title II, § 204, 122 Stat. 2993.)

CONGRESSIONAL BADGE OF BRAVERY OFFICE

§ 15261. Congressional Badge of Bravery Office

(a) Establishment. There is established within the Department of Justice a Congressional Badge of Bravery Office.

(b) Duties. The Office shall—

(1) receive nominations from Federal agency heads on behalf of the Federal Board and deliver such nominations to the Federal Board at Federal Board meetings described in section 103(d)(2) [42 USCS § 15243(d)(2)];

(2) receive nominations from State or local agency heads on behalf of the State and Local Board and deliver such nominations to the State and Local Board at State and Local Board meetings described in section 203(d)(2) [42 USCS § 15253(d)(2)]; and

(3) provide staff support to the Federal Board and the State and Local Board to carry out the duties described in section 103(b) [42 USCS § 15243(b)] and section 203(b) [42 USCS § 15253(b)], respectively.

(July 31, 2008, P. L. 110-298, Title III, § 301, 122 Stat. 2994.)

CHAPTER 146.   ELECTION ADMINISTRATION IMPROVEMENT

PAYMENTS TO STATES FOR ELECTION ADMINISTRATION IMPROVEMENTS AND REPLACEMENT OF PUNCH CARD AND LEVER VOTING MACHINES

COMMISSION

ESTABLISHMENT AND GENERAL ORGANIZATION

Election Assistance Commission

CROSS REFERENCES

This Act (42 USCS §§ 15301 et seq.) is referred to in 2 USCS § 8; 29 USCS § 3001; 42 USCS §§ 405, 1973ff-1.

PAYMENTS TO STATES FOR ELECTION ADMINISTRATION IMPROVEMENTS AND REPLACEMENT OF PUNCH CARD AND LEVER VOTING MACHINES

CROSS REFERENCES
This title (42 USCS §§ 15301 et seq.) is referred to in 42 USCS §§ 15404, 15545.

§ 15301. Payments to States for activities to improve administration of elections

(a) **In general.** Not later than 45 days after the date of the enactment of this Act [enacted Oct. 29, 2002], the Administrator of General Services (in this title [42 USCS §§ 15301 et seq.] referred to as the "Administrator") shall establish a program under which the Administrator shall make a payment to each State in which the chief executive officer of the State, or designee, in consultation and coordination with the chief State election official, notifies the Administrator not later than 6 months after the date of the enactment of this Act [enacted Oct. 29, 2002] that the State intends to use the payment in accordance with this section.

(b) **Use of payment.** (1) In general. A State shall use the funds provided under a payment made under this section to carry out one or more of the following activities:

(A) Complying with the requirements under title III [42 USCS §§ 15481 et seq.].

(B) Improving the administration of elections for Federal office.

(C) Educating voters concerning voting procedures, voting rights, and voting technology.

(D) Training election officials, poll workers, and election volunteers.

(E) Developing the State plan for requirements payments to be submitted under part 1 of subtitle D of title II [42 USCS §§ 15401 et seq.].

(F) Improving, acquiring, leasing, modifying, or replacing voting systems and technology and methods for casting and counting votes.

(G) Improving the accessibility and quantity of polling places, including providing physical access for individuals with disabilities, providing nonvisual access for individuals with visual impairments, and providing assistance to Native Americans, Alaska Native citizens, and to individuals with limited proficiency in the English language.

(H) Establishing toll-free telephone hotlines that voters may use to report possible voting fraud and voting rights violations, to obtain general election information, and to access detailed automated information on their own voter registration status, specific polling place locations, and other relevant information.

(2) Limitation. A State may not use the funds provided under a payment made under this section—

(A) to pay costs associated with any litigation, except to the extent that such costs otherwise constitute permitted uses of a payment under this section; or

(B) for the payment of any judgment.

(c) Use of funds to be consistent with other laws and requirements. In order to receive a payment under the program under this section, the State shall provide the Administrator with certifications that—

(1) the State will use the funds provided under the payment in a manner that is consistent with each of the laws described in section 906 [42 USCS § 15545], as such laws relate to the provisions of this Act; and

(2) the proposed uses of the funds are not inconsistent with the requirements of title III [42 USCS §§ 15481 et seq.].

(d) Amount of payment. (1) In general. Subject to section 103(b) [42 USCS § 15303(b)], the amount of payment made to a State under this section shall be the minimum payment amount described in paragraph (2) plus the voting age population proportion amount described in paragraph (3).

(2) Minimum payment amount. The minimum payment amount described in this paragraph is—

(A) in the case of any of the several States or the District of Columbia, one-half of 1 percent of the aggregate amount made available for payments under this section; and

(B) in the case of the Commonwealth of Puerto Rico, Guam, American Samoa, or the United States Virgin Islands, one-tenth of 1 percent of such aggregate amount.

(3) Voting age population proportion amount. The voting age population proportion amount described in this paragraph is the product of—

(A) the aggregate amount made available for payments under this section minus the total of all of the minimum payment amounts determined under paragraph (2); and

(B) the voting age population proportion for the State (as defined in paragraph (4)).

(4) Voting age population proportion defined. The term "voting age population proportion" means, with respect to a State, the amount equal to the quotient of—

(A) the voting age population of the State (as reported in the most recent decennial census); and

(B) the total voting age population of all States (as reported in the most recent decennial census).

(Oct. 29, 2002, P. L. 107-252, Title I, § 101, 116 Stat. 1668.)

HISTORY; ANCILLARY LAWS AND DIRECTIVES

References in text:

"This Act", referred to in this section, is Act Oct. 29, 2002, P. L. 107-252, popularly known as the Help America Vote Act of 2002, which appears generally as 42 USCS §§ 15301 et seq. For full classification of such Act, consult USCS Tables volumes.

Short title:

Act Oct. 29, 2002, P. L. 107-252, § 1(a), 116 Stat. 1666, provides: "This Act [42 USCS §§ 15301 et seq. generally; for full classification, consult

USCS Tables volumes] may be cited as the 'Help America Vote Act of 2002'.''.

CROSS REFERENCES

This section is referred to in 42 USCS §§ 15303, 15304.

RESEARCH GUIDE

Am Jur:

25 Am Jur 2d, Elections § 5.

26 Am Jur 2d, Elections § 303.

Annotations:

Construction and Application of Provisional Balloting Provisions of the Help America Vote Act, Pub. L. 107-252, Title III, § 302, 116 Stat. 1706 (codified at 42 U.S.C.A. §§ 15301 et seq. [42 USCS §§ 15301 et seq.]). 10 ALR Fed 2d 643.

Preemption of State Election Laws By Help America Vote Act. 47 ALR Fed 2d 81.

Law Review Articles:

Tokaji. The Paperless Chase: Electronic Voting and Democratic Values. 73 Fordham L Rev 1711, March 2005.

Tokaji. Early Returns on Election Reform: Discretion, Disenfranchisement, and the Help America Vote Act. 73 Geo Wash L Rev 1206, August 2005.

Waterstone. Civil Rights and the Administration of Elections—Toward Secret Ballots and Polling Place Access. 8 J Gender Race & Just 101, Spring 2004.

Tokaji; Colker. Facilitating Voting As People Age: Implications of Cognitive Impairment: Article: Absentee Voting By People with Disabilities: Promoting Access and Integrity. 38 McGeorge L Rev 1015, 2007.

Overton. Voter Identification. 105 Mich L Rev 631, February 2007.

Ramirez; Organick. Taking Voting Rights Seriously: Race and the Integrity of Democracy in America. 27 N Ill U L Rev 427, Summer 2007.

Anderson; Berger; Robson. Presidential Elections — The Right to Vote and Access to the Ballot. 29 Nova L Rev 571, Spring, 2005.

Shambon; Abouchar. Trapped by Precincts? The Help America Vote Act's Provisional Ballots and the Problem of Precincts. 10 NYU J Legis & Pub Pol'y 133, 2006/2007.

Elmendorf. Representation Reinforcement Through Advisory Commissions: The Case of Election Law. 80 NYU L Rev 1366, November 2005.

Wang. Competing Values or False Choices: Coming to Consensus on the Election Reform Debate in Washington State and the Country. 29 Seattle Univ L R 353, Winter 2005.

Waterstone. Constitutional and Statutory Voting Rights for People with Disabilities. 14 Stan L & Pol'y Rev 353, 2003.

Wassom. The Help America Vote Act of 2002 and Selected Issues in Election Law Reform. 29 T Marshall L Rev 357, Spring 2004.

Daniels. A Vote Delayed Is a Vote Denied: A Preemptive Approach to Eliminating Election Administration Legislation that Disenfranchises Unwanted Voters. 47 U Louisville L Rev 57, Fall, 2008.

Magpantay. Two Steps Forward, One Step Back, and a Side Step: Asian Americans and the Federal Help America Vote Act. 10 UCLA Asian Pac Am LJ 31, 2005.

Saphire; Moke. Litigating Bush v. Gore in the States: Dual Voting Systems and the Fourteenth Amendment. 51 Vill L Rev 229, 2006.

Siegel. Congressional Power Over Presidential Elections: The Constitutionality of the Help America Vote Act under Article II, Section 1. 28 Vt L Rev 373, Winter 2004.

SHEPARD'S® Citations Service. For further research of authorities referenced here, use SHEPARD'S to be sure your case or statute is still good law and to find additional authorities that support your position. SHEPARD'S is available exclusively from LexisNexis®.

INTERPRETIVE NOTES AND DECISIONS

1. Generally
2. Constitutionality
3. Private right of action
4. Fees and costs

1. Generally

Help America Vote Act of 2002, 42 USCS §§ 15301 et seq., guarantees that voters casting provisional ballots will have their votes counted if election officials can verify their eligibility in accordance with state law. Bay County Democratic Party v Land (2004, ED Mich) 340 F Supp 2d 802, motion den, injunction gr, in part, injunction den, in part (2004, ED Mich) 347 F Supp 2d 404 (criticized in Fla. Democratic Party v Hood (2004, ND Fla) 342 F Supp 2d 1073, 17 FLW Fed D 1196).

2. Constitutionality

Texas Election Code's system of providing defendant Secretary of State discretion to choose from three signature validation methods, as to petitions submitted by all potential independent gubernatorial candidates, was not unreasonable burden on plaintiff voters' First and Fourteenth Amendment rights; it satisfied legitimate interest in determining how best to assure plaintiff potential candidate was truly independent serious contender with satisfactory level of community support; 2006 general election was to be first statewide election in Texas pursuant to Help America Vote Act of 2002, 42 USCS §§ 15301–15545, and for first time, official list of registered voters against which petition signatures would be checked would be maintained by Secretary of State's office, and Secretary had submitted testimony that advances in law and technology had made checking every signature most accurate, efficient and practicable option, particularly in light of fact that in 2006 election there was possibility that several independents would file petitions, likelihood of duplicate signatures, and other circumstances surrounding 2006 general election, and thus, based on totality of circumstances related to 2006 general election, statutory system, which provided Secretary discretion to

choose from three methods to validate petition signatures, one of which was statistical sampling, did not place unreasonable burden on voters' First and Fourteenth Amendment rights. Strayhorn v Williams (2006, WD Tex) 430 F Supp 2d 661.

3. Private right of action

Because of "close" answer to question of whether Congress intended to create federal right under Help America Vote Act (HAVA), 42 USCS § 15301 et seq., together with reality that all of other risks of error supported Republican Party weighed in favor of denying Secretary of State's motion to stay temporary restraining order which directed Secretary to ensure compliance with matching requirements of HAVA. Ohio Republican Party v Brunner (2008, CA6) 544 F3d 711, 2008 FED App 374P.

Ohio's Secretary of State failed to meet high standard under Fed. R. Civ. P. 62(a) for granting stay of preliminary injunction requiring Secretary to prepare directive that complied with Help America Vote Act's (HAVA), 42 USCS §§ 15301 et seq., provisional voting rights where (1) Secretary did not have substantial likelihood of prevailing on merits with respect to issue of whether plaintiffs had private right of action to enforce HAVA's provisional voting rights and, although issue of whether provisional voting could occur in precinct in which voter was registered was somewhat closer question, mere possibility of different result did not amount to substantial likelihood of success; (2) Ohio's election process would not be irreparably harmed because drafting of HAVA-sufficient directive would not be difficult; (3) no one would suffer irreparable injury because task would not be difficult; and (4) public interest favored denial of stay because there was risk that mere passage of time would impede, if not defeat, HAVA's effective implementation unless HAVA-sufficient directive was ready and set to be distributed at earliest possible and appropriate time. Sandusky County Democratic Party v Blackwell (2004, ND Ohio) 340 F Supp 2d 810.

Section 301 of Help America Vote Act, 42 USCS

§ 15301, imposes obligation on states and local jurisdictions to put in place voting system that meets certain criteria; voters as whole may benefit from mandates of § 301; that is insufficient, however, to create Federal right of action under § 301, and voters were therefore not entitled to preliminary injunction to enjoin use of touch screen voting machines. Taylor v Onorato (2006, WD Pa) 428 F Supp 2d 384.

Congress does not intend to provide for private right of action to enforce § 301 of Help America Vote Act, 42 USCS § 15301; rather, Congress has empowered Attorney General of United States to enforce it. Taylor v Onorato (2006, WD Pa) 428 F Supp 2d 384.

4. Fees and costs

Where plaintiffs succeeded on all but one issue on their claim that state Secretary of State violated Help America Vote Act, 42 USCS §§ 15301 et seq., plaintiffs were entitled to full award of attorneys' fees and costs under 42 USCS § 1988 because such issue was not predominant focus of either parties' or court's attention; fact that such issue gained significant amount of notoriety with media did not make it focus of what case was all about. Sandusky County Democratic Party v Blackwell (2005, ND Ohio) 361 F Supp 2d 688, affd (2006, CA6 Ohio) 191 Fed Appx 397, 2006 FED App 538N.

§ 15302. Replacement of punch card or lever voting machines

(a) **Establishment of program.** (1) In general. Not later than 45 days after the date of the enactment of this Act [enacted Oct. 29, 2002], the Administrator shall establish a program under which the Administrator shall make a payment to each State eligible under subsection (b) in which a precinct within that State used a punch card voting system or a lever voting system to administer the regularly scheduled general election for Federal office held in November 2000 (in this section referred to as a "qualifying precinct").

(2) Use of funds. A State shall use the funds provided under a payment under this section (either directly or as reimbursement, including as reimbursement for costs incurred on or after January 1, 2001, under multiyear contracts) to replace punch card voting systems or lever voting systems (as the case may be) in qualifying precincts within that State with a voting system (by purchase, lease, or such other arrangement as may be appropriate) that—

(A) does not use punch cards or levers;

(B) is not inconsistent with the requirements of the laws described in section 906 [42 USCS § 15545]; and

(C) meets the requirements of section 301 [42 USCS § 15481].

(3) Deadline. (A) In general. Except as provided in subparagraph (B), a State receiving a payment under the program under this section shall ensure that all of the punch card voting systems or lever voting systems in the qualifying precincts within that State have been replaced in time for the regularly scheduled general election for Federal office to be held in November 2004.

(B) Waiver. If a State certifies to the Administrator not later than January 1, 2004, that the State will not meet the deadline described in subparagraph (A) for good cause and includes in the certification the reasons for the failure to meet such deadline, the State shall ensure that all of the punch card voting systems or lever voting systems in the qualifying precincts within that State will be replaced in time for the first election for Federal office held after November 1, 2010.

(b) **Eligibility.** (1) In general. A State is eligible to receive a payment under the program under this section if it submits to the Administrator a notice not later than the date that is 6 months after the date of the enactment of this Act [enacted Oct. 29, 2002] (in such form as the Administrator may require) that contains—

(A) certifications that the State will use the payment (either directly or as reimbursement, including as reimbursement for costs incurred on or after January 1, 2001, under multiyear contracts) to replace punch card voting systems or lever voting systems (as the case may be) in the qualifying precincts within the State by the deadline described in subsection (a)(3);

(B) certifications that the State will continue to comply with the laws described in section 906 [42 USCS § 15545];

(C) certifications that the replacement voting systems will meet the requirements of section 301 [42 USCS § 15481]; and

(D) such other information and certifications as the Administrator may require which are necessary for the administration of the program.

(2) Compliance of States that require changes to State law. In the case of a State that requires State legislation to carry out an activity covered by any certification submitted under this subsection, the State shall be permitted to make the certification notwithstanding that the legislation has not been enacted at the time the certification is submitted and such State shall submit an additional certification once such legislation is enacted.

(c) **Amount of payment.** (1) In general. Subject to paragraph (2) and section 103(b) [42 USCS § 15303(b)], the amount of payment made to a State under the program under this section shall be equal to the product of—

(A) the number of the qualifying precincts within the State; and

(B) $4,000.

(2) Reduction. If the amount of funds appropriated pursuant to the authority of section 104(a)(2) [42 USCS § 15304(a)(2)] is insufficient to ensure that each State receives the amount of payment calculated under paragraph (1), the Administrator shall reduce the amount specified in paragraph (1)(B) to ensure that the entire amount appropriated under such section is distributed to the States.

(d) **Repayment of funds for failure to meet deadlines.** (1) In general. If a State receiving funds under the program under this section fails to meet the deadline applicable to the State under subsection (a)(3), the State shall pay to the Administrator an amount equal to the noncompliant precinct percentage of the amount of the funds provided to the State under the program.

(2) Noncompliant precinct percentage defined. In this subsection, the term "noncompliant precinct percentage" means, with respect to a State, the amount (expressed as a percentage) equal to the quotient of—

(A) the number of qualifying precincts within the State for which the State failed to meet the applicable deadline; and

(B) the total number of qualifying precincts in the State.

(e) **Punch card voting system defined.** For purposes of this section, a "punch card voting system" includes any of the following voting systems:

(1) C.E.S.

(2) Datavote.

(3) PBC Counter.

(4) Pollstar.

(5) Punch Card.

(6) Vote Recorder.

(7) Votomatic.

(Oct. 29, 2002, P. L. 107-252, Title I, § 102, 116 Stat. 1670; May 25, 2007, P. L. 110-28, Title VI, Ch. 3, § 6301(a), 121 Stat. 171; March 11, 2009, P. L. 111-8, Div D, Title VI, § 625(a), 123 Stat. 678.)

HISTORY; ANCILLARY LAWS AND DIRECTIVES

Amendments:

2007. Act May 25, 2007 (effective as if included in the enactment of Act Oct. 29, 2002, as provided by § 6301(b) of the 2007 Act, which appears as a note to this section), in subsec. (a)(3)(B, substituted "March 1, 2008" for "January 1, 2006".

2009. Act March 11, 2009 (effective as if included in the enactment of Act Oct. 29, 2002, as provided by § 625(b) of the 2009 Act, which appears as a note to this section), in subsec. (a)(3)(B), substituted "November 1, 2010" for "March 1, 2008".

Other provisions:

Effective date of May 25, 2007 amendment. Act May 25, 2007, P. L. 110-28, Title VI, Ch. 3, § 6301(b), 121 Stat. 171, provides: "The amendment made by subsection (a) [amending subsec. (a)(3)(B) of this section] shall take effect as if included in the enactment of the Help America Vote Act of 2002 [Act Oct. 29, 2002, P. L. 107-252].".

Effective date of March 11, 2009 amendment. Act March 11, 2009, P. L. 111-8, Div D, Title VI, § 625(b), 123 Stat. 678, provides: "The amendment made by subsection (a) [amending subsec. (a)(3)(B) of this section] shall take effect as if included in the enactment of the Help America Vote Act of 2002 [Act Oct. 29, 2002, P. L. 107-252].".

CROSS REFERENCES

This section is referred to in 42 USCS §§ 15303, 15304.

RESEARCH GUIDE

Am Jur:

26 Am Jur 2d, Elections § 281.

Law Review Articles:

Tokaji. The Paperless Chase: Electronic Voting and Democratic Values. 73 Fordham L Rev 1711, March 2005.

Tokaji. Early Returns on Election Reform: Discretion, Disenfranchisement, and the Help America Vote Act. 73 Geo Wash L Rev 1206, August 2005.

Wang. Competing Values or False Choices: Coming to Consensus on the Election Reform Debate in Washington State and the Country. 29 Seattle Univ L R 353, Winter 2005.

Waterstone. Constitutional and Statutory Voting Rights for People with Disabilities. 14 Stan L & Pol'y Rev 353, 2003.

Wassom. The Help America Vote Act of 2002 and Selected Issues in Election Law Reform. 29 T Marshall L Rev 357, Spring 2004.

Magpantay. Two Steps Forward, One Step Back, and a Side Step: Asian
Americans and the Federal Help America Vote Act. 10 UCLA Asian Pac
Am LJ 31, 2005.
Saphire; Moke. Litigating Bush v. Gore in the States: Dual Voting Systems
and the Fourteenth Amendment. 51 Vill L Rev 229, 2006.

§ 15303. Guaranteed minimum payment amount

(a) In general. In addition to any other payments made under this title [42
USCS §§ 15301 et seq.], the Administrator shall make a payment to each State
to which a payment is made under either section 101 or 102 [42 USCS § 15301
or 15302] and with respect to which the aggregate amount paid under such
sections is less than $5,000,000 in an amount equal to the difference between
the aggregate amount paid to the State under sections 101 and 102 [42 USCS
§§ 15301, 15302] and $5,000,000. In the case of the Commonwealth of Puerto
Rico, Guam, American Samoa, and the United States Virgin Islands, the previous sentence shall be applied as if each reference to "$5,000,000" were a
reference to "$1,000,000".

(b) Pro rata reductions. The Administrator shall make such pro rata reductions to the amounts described in sections 101(d) and 102(c) [42 USCS
§§ 15301(d), 15302(c)] as are necessary to comply with the requirements of
subsection (a).
(Oct. 29, 2002, P. L. 107-252, Title I, § 103, 116 Stat. 1672.)

CROSS REFERENCES
This section is referred to in 42 USCS §§ 15301, 15302.

RESEARCH GUIDE
Law Review Articles:
Wassom. The Help America Vote Act of 2002 and Selected Issues in Elec-
tion Law Reform. 29 T Marshall L Rev 357, Spring 2004.

§ 15304. Authorization of appropriations

(a) In general. There are authorized to be appropriated for payments under this
title [42 USCS §§ 15301 et seq.] $650,000,000, of which—
   (1) 50 percent shall be for payments under section 101 [42 USCS § 15301];
   and
   (2) 50 percent shall be for payments under section 102 [42 USCS § 15302].

(b) Continuing availability of funds after appropriation. Any payment made
to a State under this title [42 USCS §§ 15301 et seq.] shall be available to the
State without fiscal year limitation (subject to subsection (c)(2)(B)).

**(c) Use of returned funds and funds remaining unexpended for require-
ments payments.** (1) In general. The amounts described in paragraph (2)
shall be transferred to the Election Assistance Commission (established
under title II [42 USCS §§ 15321 et seq.]) and used by the Commission to
make requirements payments under part 1 of subtitle D of title II [42 USCS
§§ 15401 et seq.].

(2) Amounts described. The amounts referred to in this paragraph are as follows:

(A) Any amounts paid to the Administrator by a State under section 102(d)(1) [42 USCS § 15302(d)(1)].

(B) Any amounts appropriated for payments under this title [42 USCS §§ 15301 et seq.] which remain unobligated as of September 1, 2003.

(d) Deposit of amounts in State election fund. When a State has established an election fund described in section 254(b) [42 USCS § 15404(b)], the State shall ensure that any funds provided to the State under this title [42 USCS §§ 15301 et seq.] are deposited and maintained in such fund.

(e) Authorization of appropriations for Administrator. In addition to the amounts authorized under subsection (a), there are authorized to be appropriated to the Administrator such sums as may be necessary to administer the programs under this title [42 USCS §§ 15301 et seq.].

(Oct. 29, 2002, P. L. 107-252, Title I, § 104, 116 Stat. 1672.)

CROSS REFERENCES

This section is referred to in 42 USCS §§ 15302, 15407.

RESEARCH GUIDE

Law Review Articles:

Tokaji. The Paperless Chase: Electronic Voting and Democratic Values. 73 Fordham L Rev 1711, March 2005.

Waterstone. Constitutional and Statutory Voting Rights for People with Disabilities. 14 Stan L & Pol'y Rev 353, 2003.

Wassom. The Help America Vote Act of 2002 and Selected Issues in Election Law Reform. 29 T Marshall L Rev 357, Spring 2004.

Saphire; Moke. Litigating Bush v. Gore in the States: Dual Voting Systems and the Fourteenth Amendment. 51 Vill L Rev 229, 2006.

§ 15305. Administration of programs

In administering the programs under this title [42 USCS §§ 15301 et seq.], the Administrator shall take such actions as the Administrator considers appropriate to expedite the payment of funds to States.

(Oct. 29, 2002, P. L. 107-252, Title I, § 105, 116 Stat. 1673.)

RESEARCH GUIDE

Law Review Articles:

Wassom. The Help America Vote Act of 2002 and Selected Issues in Election Law Reform. 29 T Marshall L Rev 357, Spring 2004.

§ 15306. Effective date

The Administrator shall implement the programs established under this title [42 USCS §§ 15301 et seq.] in a manner that ensures that the Administrator is able to make payments under the program not later than the expiration of the 45-day period which begins on the date of the enactment of this Act [enacted Oct. 29, 2002].

(Oct. 29, 2002, P. L. 107-252, Title I, § 106, 116 Stat. 1673.)

RESEARCH GUIDE
Law Review Articles:
Wassom. The Help America Vote Act of 2002 and Selected Issues in Election Law Reform. 29 T Marshall L Rev 357, Spring 2004.

COMMISSION

CROSS REFERENCES
This subchapter is referred to in 42 USCS §§ 15304, 15481, 15545.

ESTABLISHMENT AND GENERAL ORGANIZATION

Election Assistance Commission

§ 15321.   Establishment

There is hereby established as an independent entity the Election Assistance Commission (hereafter in this title [42 USCS §§ 15321 et seq.] referred to as the "Commission"), consisting of the members appointed under this part. Additionally, there is established the Election Assistance Commission Standards Board (including the Executive Board of such Board) and the Election Assistance Commission Board of Advisors under part 2 [42 USCS §§ 15341 et seq.] (hereafter in this part [42 USCS §§ 15321 et seq.] referred to as the "Standards Board" and the "Board of Advisors", respectively) and the Technical Guidelines Development Committee under part 3 [42 USCS §§ 15361 et seq.].

(Oct. 29, 2002, P. L. 107-252, Title II, Subtitle A, Part 1, § 201, 116 Stat. 1673.)

CROSS REFERENCES
This section is referred to in 42 USCS §§ 15531, 15532.

RESEARCH GUIDE
Am Jur:
25 Am Jur 2d, Elections § 5.

Law Review Articles:
Tokaji. The Paperless Chase: Electronic Voting and Democratic Values. 73 Fordham L Rev 1711, March 2005.

Ramirez; Organick. Taking Voting Rights Seriously: Race and the Integrity of Democracy in America. 27 N Ill U L Rev 427, Summer 2007.

Elmendorf. Representation Reinforcement Through Advisory Commissions: The Case of Election Law. 80 NYU L Rev 1366, November 2005.

Wang. Competing Values or False Choices: Coming to Consensus on the Election Reform Debate in Washington State and the Country. 29 Seattle Univ L R 353, Winter 2005.

Wassom. The Help America Vote Act of 2002 and Selected Issues in Election Law Reform. 29 T Marshall L Rev 357, Spring 2004.

Magpantay. Two Steps Forward, One Step Back, and a Side Step: Asian Americans and the Federal Help America Vote Act. 10 UCLA Asian Pac Am LJ 31, 2005.

Saphire; Moke. Litigating Bush v. Gore in the States: Dual Voting Systems and the Fourteenth Amendment. 51 Vill L Rev 229, 2006.

§ 15322. Duties

The Commission shall serve as a national clearinghouse and resource for the compilation of information and review of procedures with respect to the administration of Federal elections by—

(1) carrying out the duties described in part 3 [42 USCS §§ 15361 et seq.] (relating to the adoption of voluntary voting system guidelines), including the maintenance of a clearinghouse of information on the experiences of State and local governments in implementing the guidelines and in operating voting systems in general;

(2) carrying out the duties described in subtitle B [42 USCS §§ 15371 et seq.] (relating to the testing, certification, decertification, and recertification of voting system hardware and software);

(3) carrying out the duties described in subtitle C [42 USCS §§ 15381 et seq.] (relating to conducting studies and carrying out other activities to promote the effective administration of Federal elections);

(4) carrying out the duties described in subtitle D [42 USCS §§ 15401 et seq.] (relating to election assistance), and providing information and training on the management of the payments and grants provided under such subtitle;

(5) carrying out the duties described in subtitle B of title III [42 USCS §§ 15501 et seq.] (relating to the adoption of voluntary guidance); and

(6) developing and carrying out the Help America Vote College Program under title V [42 USCS §§ 15521 et seq.].

(Oct. 29, 2002, P. L. 107-252, Title II, Subtitle A, Part 1, § 202, 116 Stat. 1673.)

RESEARCH GUIDE

Law Review Articles:

Tokaji. The Paperless Chase: Electronic Voting and Democratic Values. 73 Fordham L Rev 1711, March 2005.

Tokaji. Early Returns on Election Reform: Discretion, Disenfranchisement, and the Help America Vote Act. 73 Geo Wash L Rev 1206, August 2005.

Ramirez; Organick. Taking Voting Rights Seriously: Race and the Integrity of Democracy in America. 27 N Ill U L Rev 427, Summer 2007.

Wang. Competing Values or False Choices: Coming to Consensus on the Election Reform Debate in Washington State and the Country. 29 Seattle Univ L R 353, Winter 2005.

Waterstone. Constitutional and Statutory Voting Rights for People with Disabilities. 14 Stan L & Pol'y Rev 353, 2003.

Wassom. The Help America Vote Act of 2002 and Selected Issues in Election Law Reform. 29 T Marshall L Rev 357, Spring 2004.

Saphire; Moke. Litigating Bush v. Gore in the States: Dual Voting Systems and the Fourteenth Amendment. 51 Vill L Rev 229, 2006.

§ 15323. Membership and appointment

(a) **Membership.** (1) In general. The Commission shall have four members appointed by the President, by and with the advice and consent of the Senate.

(2) Recommendations. Before the initial appointment of the members of the Commission and before the appointment of any individual to fill a vacancy on the Commission, the Majority Leader of the Senate, the Speaker of the House of Representatives, the Minority Leader of the Senate, and the Minority Leader of the House of Representatives shall each submit to the President a candidate recommendation with respect to each vacancy on the Commission affiliated with the political party of the Member of Congress involved.

(3) Qualifications. Each member of the Commission shall have experience with or expertise in election administration or the study of elections.

(4) Date of appointment. The appointments of the members of the Commission shall be made not later than 120 days after the date of the enactment of this Act [enacted Oct. 29, 2002].

(b) Term of service. (1) In general. Except as provided in paragraphs (2) and (3), members shall serve for a term of 4 years and may be reappointed for not more than one additional term.

(2) Terms of initial appointees. As designated by the President at the time of nomination, of the members first appointed—

    (A) two of the members (not more than one of whom may be affiliated with the same political party) shall be appointed for a term of 2 years; and

    (B) two of the members (not more than one of whom may be affiliated with the same political party) shall be appointed for a term of 4 years.

(3) Vacancies. (A) In general. A vacancy on the Commission shall be filled in the manner in which the original appointment was made and shall be subject to any conditions which applied with respect to the original appointment.

    (B) Expired terms. A member of the Commission shall serve on the Commission after the expiration of the member's term until the successor of such member has taken office as a member of the Commission.

    (C) Unexpired terms. An individual appointed to fill a vacancy shall be appointed for the unexpired term of the member replaced.

(c) Chair and vice chair. (1) In general. The Commission shall select a chair and vice chair from among its members for a term of 1 year, except that the chair and vice chair may not be affiliated with the same political party.

(2) Number of terms. A member of the Commission may serve as the chairperson and vice chairperson for only 1 term each during the term of office to which such member is appointed.

(d) Compensation. (1) In general. Each member of the Commission shall be compensated at the annual rate of basic pay prescribed for level IV of the Executive Schedule under section 5315 of title 5, United States Code.

(2) Other activities. No member appointed to the Commission under subsection (a) may engage in any other business, vocation, or employment while serving as a member of the Commission and shall terminate or liquidate such business, vocation, or employment before sitting as a member of the Commission.

(Oct. 29, 2002, P. L. 107-252, Title II, Subtitle A, Part 1, § 203, 116 Stat. 1674.)

CROSS REFERENCES
This section is referred to in 42 USCS § 15534.

RESEARCH GUIDE
Law Review Articles:
Tokaji. Early Returns on Election Reform: Discretion, Disenfranchisement, and the Help America Vote Act. 73 Geo Wash L Rev 1206, August 2005.
Ramirez; Organick. Taking Voting Rights Seriously: Race and the Integrity of Democracy in America. 27 N Ill U L Rev 427, Summer 2007.
Elmendorf. Representation Reinforcement Through Advisory Commissions: The Case of Election Law. 80 NYU L Rev 1366, 2005.
Wang. Competing Values or False Choices: Coming to Consensus on the Election Reform Debate in Washington State and the Country. 29 Seattle Univ L R 353, Winter 2005.
Wassom. The Help America Vote Act of 2002 and Selected Issues in Election Law Reform. 29 T Marshall L Rev 357, Spring 2004.

§ 15324. Staff

(a) Executive Director, General Counsel, and other staff. (1) Executive Director. The Commission shall have an Executive Director, who shall be paid at a rate not to exceed the rate of basic pay for level V of the Executive Schedule under section 5316 of title 5, United States Code.

(2) Term of service for Executive Director. The Executive Director shall serve for a term of 4 years. An Executive Director may serve for a longer period only if reappointed for an additional term or terms by a vote of the Commission.

(3) Procedure for appointment. (A) In general. When a vacancy exists in the position of the Executive Director, the Standards Board and the Board of Advisors shall each appoint a search committee to recommend at least three nominees for the position.

(B) Requiring consideration of nominees. Except as provided in subparagraph (C), the Commission shall consider the nominees recommended by the Standards Board and the Board of Advisors in appointing the Executive Director.

(C) Interim service of General Counsel. If a vacancy exists in the position of the Executive Director, the General Counsel of the Commission shall serve as the acting Executive Director until the Commission appoints a new Executive Director in accordance with this paragraph.

(D) Special rules for interim Executive Director. (i) Convening of search committees. The Standards Board and the Board of Advisors shall each appoint a search committee and recommend nominees for the position of Executive Director in accordance with subparagraph (A) as soon as practicable after the appointment of their members.

(ii) Interim initial appointment. Notwithstanding subparagraph (B), the Commission may appoint an individual to serve as an interim Executive Director prior to the recommendation of nominees for the position by the Standards Board or the Board of Advisors, except that such individual's term of service may not exceed 6 months. Nothing in the previous sentence may be construed to prohibit the individual serving as the interim Executive Director from serving any additional term.

(4) General Counsel. The Commission shall have a General Counsel, who shall be appointed by the Commission and who shall serve under the Executive Director. The General Counsel shall serve for a term of 4 years, and may serve for a longer period only if reappointed for an additional term or terms by a vote of the Commission.

(5) Other staff. Subject to rules prescribed by the Commission, the Executive Director may appoint and fix the pay of such additional personnel as the Executive Director considers appropriate.

(6) Applicability of certain civil service laws. The Executive Director, General Counsel, and staff of the Commission may be appointed without regard to the provisions of title 5, United States Code, governing appointments in the competitive service, and may be paid without regard to the provisions of chapter 51 and subchapter III of chapter 53 of that title [5 USCS §§ 5101 et seq., 5331 et seq.] relating to classification and General Schedule pay rates, except that an individual so appointed may not receive pay in excess of the annual rate of basic pay for level V of the Executive Schedule under section 5316 of that title.

(b) Experts and consultants. Subject to rules prescribed by the Commission, the Executive Director may procure temporary and intermittent services under section 3109(b) of title 5, United States Code, by a vote of the Commission.

(c) Staff of Federal agencies. Upon request of the Commission, the head of any Federal department or agency may detail, on a reimbursable basis, any of the personnel of that department or agency to the Commission to assist it in carrying out its duties under this Act.

(d) Arranging for assistance for Board of Advisors and Standards Board. At the request of the Board of Advisors or the Standards Board, the Commission may enter into such arrangements as the Commission considers appropriate to make personnel available to assist the Boards with carrying out their duties under this title [42 USCS §§ 15321 et seq.] (including contracts with private individuals for providing temporary personnel services or the temporary detailing of personnel of the Commission).

(e) Consultation with Board of Advisors and Standards Board on certain matters. In preparing the program goals, long-term plans, mission statements, and related matters for the Commission, the Executive Director and staff of the Commission shall consult with the Board of Advisors and the Standards Board. (Oct. 29, 2002, P. L. 107-252, Title II, Subtitle A, Part 1, § 204, 116 Stat. 1675.)

HISTORY; ANCILLARY LAWS AND DIRECTIVES

References in text:
"This Act", referred to in this section, is Act Oct. 29, 2002, P. L. 107-252, popularly known as the Help America Vote Act of 2002, which appears generally as 42 USCS §§ 15301 et seq. For full classification of such Act, consult USCS Tables volumes.

The "provisions of title 5, United States Code, governing appointments in the competitive service", referred to in this section, appear generally as 5 USCS §§ 3301 et seq.

RESEARCH GUIDE

Law Review Articles:
Wassom. The Help America Vote Act of 2002 and Selected Issues in Election Law Reform. 29 T Marshall L Rev 357, Spring 2004.

§ 15325. Powers

(a) Hearings and sessions. The Commission may hold such hearings for the purpose of carrying out this Act, sit and act at such times and places, take such testimony, and receive such evidence as the Commission considers advisable to carry out this Act. The Commission may administer oaths and affirmations to witnesses appearing before the Commission.

(b) Information from Federal agencies. The Commission may secure directly from any Federal department or agency such information as the Commission considers necessary to carry out this Act. Upon request of the Commission, the head of such department or agency shall furnish such information to the Commission.

(c) Postal services. The Commission may use the United States mails in the same manner and under the same conditions as other departments and agencies of the Federal Government.

(d) Administrative support services. Upon the request of the Commission, the Administrator of General Services shall provide to the Commission, on a reimbursable basis, the administrative support services that are necessary to enable the Commission to carry out its duties under this Act.

(e) Contracts. The Commission may contract with and compensate persons and Federal agencies for supplies and services without regard to section 3709 of the Revised Statutes of the United States (41 U.S.C. 5) [41 USCS § 6101].
(Oct. 29, 2002, P. L. 107-252, Title II, Subtitle A, Part 1, § 205, 116 Stat. 1677.)

HISTORY; ANCILLARY LAWS AND DIRECTIVES

References in text:
"This Act", referred to in this section, is Act Oct. 29, 2002, P. L. 107-252, popularly known as the Help America Vote Act of 2002, which appears generally as 42 USCS §§ 15301 et seq. For full classification of such Act, consult USCS Tables volumes.

Explanatory notes:
In subsec. (e), "41 USCS § 6101" has been inserted in brackets pursuant to § 6(c) of Act Jan. 4, 2011, P. L. 111-350, which appears as a note preceding 41 USCS § 101. Section 3 of such Act enacted Title 41 as positive law, and and § 6(c) of such Act provided that a reference to a law replaced by such Act is deemed to refer to the corresponding provision enacted by such Act.

RESEARCH GUIDE

Law Review Articles:
Wassom. The Help America Vote Act of 2002 and Selected Issues in Election Law Reform. 29 T Marshall L Rev 357, Spring 2004.

§ 15326. Dissemination of information

In carrying out its duties, the Commission shall, on an ongoing basis, disseminate to the public (through the Internet, published reports, and such other methods as the Commission considers appropriate) in a manner that is consistent with the requirements of chapter 19 of title 44, United States Code [44 USCS §§ 1901 et seq.], information on the activities carried out under this Act.

(Oct. 29, 2002, P. L. 107-252, Title II, Subtitle A, Part 1, § 206, 116 Stat. 1677.)

HISTORY; ANCILLARY LAWS AND DIRECTIVES

References in text:
"This Act", referred to in this section, is Act Oct. 29, 2002, P. L. 107-252, popularly known as the Help America Vote Act of 2002, which appears generally as 42 USCS §§ 15301 et seq. For full classification of such Act, consult USCS Tables volumes.

RESEARCH GUIDE

Law Review Articles:
Wassom. The Help America Vote Act of 2002 and Selected Issues in Election Law Reform. 29 T Marshall L Rev 357, Spring 2004.
Saphire; Moke. Litigating Bush v. Gore in the States: Dual Voting Systems and the Fourteenth Amendment. 51 Vill L Rev 229, 2006.

§ 15327. Annual report

Not later than January 31 of each year (beginning with 2004), the Commission shall submit a report to the Committee on House Administration of the House of Representatives and the Committee on Rules and Administration of the Senate detailing its activities during the fiscal year which ended on September 30 of the previous calendar year, and shall include in the report the following information:

(1) A detailed description of activities conducted with respect to each program carried out by the Commission under this Act, including information on each grant or other payment made under such programs.

(2) A copy of each report submitted to the Commission by a recipient of such grants or payments which is required under such a program, including reports submitted by States receiving requirements payments under part 1 of subtitle D [42 USCS §§ 15401 et seq.], and each other report submitted to the Commission under this Act.

(3) Information on the voluntary voting system guidelines adopted or modified by the Commission under part 3 [42 USCS §§ 15361 et seq.] and information on the voluntary guidance adopted under subtitle B of title III [42 USCS §§ 15501 et seq.].

(4) All votes taken by the Commission.

(5) Such other information and recommendations as the Commission considers appropriate.

(Oct. 29, 2002, P. L. 107-252, Title II, Subtitle A, Part 1, § 207, 116 Stat. 1677.)

HISTORY; ANCILLARY LAWS AND DIRECTIVES

References in text:

"This Act", referred to in this section, is Act Oct. 29, 2002, P. L. 107-252, popularly known as the Help America Vote Act of 2002, which appears generally as 42 USCS §§ 15301 et seq. For full classification of such Act, consult USCS Tables volumes.

CROSS REFERENCES

This section is referred to in 42 USCS §§ 15441, 15451.

RESEARCH GUIDE

Law Review Articles:

Wassom. The Help America Vote Act of 2002 and Selected Issues in Election Law Reform. 29 T Marshall L Rev 357, Spring 2004.

§ 15328. Requiring majority approval for actions

Any action which the Commission is authorized to carry out under this Act may be carried out only with the approval of at least three of its members.

(Oct. 29, 2002, P. L. 107-252, Title II, Subtitle A, Part 1, § 208, 116 Stat. 1678.)

HISTORY; ANCILLARY LAWS AND DIRECTIVES

References in text:

"This Act", referred to in this section, is Act Oct. 29, 2002, P. L. 107-252, popularly known as the Help America Vote Act of 2002, which appears generally as 42 USCS §§ 15301 et seq. For full classification of such Act, consult USCS Tables volumes.

RESEARCH GUIDE

Law Review Articles:

Tokaji. Early Returns on Election Reform: Discretion, Disenfranchisement, and the Help America Vote Act. 73 Geo Wash L Rev 1206, August 2005.

Ramirez; Organick. Taking Voting Rights Seriously: Race and the Integrity of Democracy in America. 27 N Ill U L Rev 427, Summer 2007.

Elmendorf. Representation Reinforcement Through Advisory Commissions: The Case of Election Law. 80 NYU L Rev 1366, November 2005.

Wassom. The Help America Vote Act of 2002 and Selected Issues in Election Law Reform. 29 T Marshall L Rev 357, Spring 2004.

§ 15329. Limitation on rulemaking authority

The Commission shall not have any authority to issue any rule, promulgate any regulation, or take any other action which imposes any requirement on any State or unit of local government, except to the extent permitted under section 9(a) of the National Voter Registration Act of 1993 (42 U.S.C. 1973gg-7(a)).

(Oct. 29, 2002, P. L. 107-252, Title II, Subtitle A, Part 1, § 209, 116 Stat. 1678.)

§ 15330. Authorization of appropriations

In addition to the amounts authorized for payments and grants under this title [42 USCS §§ 15321 et seq.] and the amounts authorized to be appropriated for the program under section 503 [42 USCS § 15523], there are authorized to be appropriated for each of the fiscal years 2003 through 2005 such sums as may be necessary (but not to exceed $10,000,000 for each such year) for the Commission to carry out this title [42 USCS §§ 15321 et seq.].

(Oct. 29, 2002, P. L. 107-252, Title II, Subtitle A, Part 1, § 210, 116 Stat. 1678.)

Election Assistance Commission Standards Board and Board of Advisors

§ 15341. Establishment

There are hereby established the Election Assistance Commission Standards Board (hereafter in this title [42 USCS §§ 15321 et seq.] referred to as the "Standards Board") and the Election Assistance Commission Board of Advisors (hereafter in this title [42 USCS §§ 15321 et seq.] referred to as the "Board of Advisors").

(Oct. 29, 2002, P. L. 107-252, Title II, Subtitle A, Part 2, § 211, 116 Stat. 1678.)

§ 15342. Duties

The Standards Board and the Board of Advisors shall each, in accordance with the procedures described in part 3 [42 USCS §§ 15361 et seq.], review the voluntary voting system guidelines under such part, the voluntary guidance

under title III [42 USCS §§ 15481 et seq.], and the best practices recommendations contained in the report submitted under section 242(b) [42 USCS
§ 15382(b)].
(Oct. 29, 2002, P. L. 107-252, Title II, Subtitle A, Part 2, § 212, 116 Stat. 1678.)

RESEARCH GUIDE

Law Review Articles:
Waterstone. Constitutional and Statutory Voting Rights for People with
Disabilities. 14 Stan L & Pol'y Rev 353, 2003.
Wassom. The Help America Vote Act of 2002 and Selected Issues in Elec-
tion Law Reform. 29 T Marshall L Rev 357, Spring 2004.

§ 15343. Membership of Standards Board

(a) **Composition.** (1) In general. Subject to certification by the chair of the
Federal Election Commission under subsection (b), the Standards Board shall
be composed of 110 members as follows:

(A) Fifty-five shall be State election officials selected by the chief State
election official of each State.

(B) Fifty-five shall be local election officials selected in accordance with
paragraph (2).

(2) List of local election officials. Each State's local election officials,
including the local election officials of Puerto Rico and the United States
Virgin Islands, shall select (under a process supervised by the chief election
official of the State) a representative local election official from the State for
purposes of paragraph (1)(B). In the case of the District of Columbia, Guam,
and American Samoa, the chief election official shall establish a procedure
for selecting an individual to serve as a local election official for purposes
of such paragraph, except that under such a procedure the individual selected
may not be a member of the same political party as the chief election official.

(3) Requiring mix of political parties represented. The two members of the
Standards Board who represent the same State may not be members of the
same political party.

(b) **Procedures for notice and certification of appointment.** (1) Notice to
chair of Federal Election Commission. Not later than 90 days after the date
of the enactment of this Act [enacted Oct. 29, 2002], the chief State election
official of the State shall transmit a notice to the chair of the Federal Election Commission containing—

(A) the name of the State election official who agrees to serve on the
Standards Board under this title [42 USCS §§ 15321 et seq.]; and

(B) the name of the representative local election official from the State
selected under subsection (a)(2) who agrees to serve on the Standards
Board under this title [42 USCS §§ 15321 et seq.].

(2) Certification. Upon receiving a notice from a State under paragraph (1),
the chair of the Federal Election Commission shall publish a certification
that the selected State election official and the representative local election

official are appointed as members of the Standards Board under this title [42 USCS §§ 15321 et seq.].

(3) Effect of failure to provide notice. If a State does not transmit a notice to the chair of the Federal Election Commission under paragraph (1) within the deadline described in such paragraph, no representative from the State may participate in the selection of the initial Executive Board under subsection (c).

(4) Role of Commission. Upon the appointment of the members of the Election Assistance Commission, the Election Assistance Commission shall carry out the duties of the Federal Election Commission under this subsection.

(c) **Executive Board.** (1) In general. Not later than 60 days after the last day on which the appointment of any of its members may be certified under subsection (b), the Standards Board shall select nine of its members to serve as the Executive Board of the Standards Board, of whom—

(A) not more than five may be State election officials;

(B) not more than five may be local election officials; and

(C) not more than five may be members of the same political party.

(2) Terms. Except as provided in paragraph (3), members of the Executive Board of the Standards Board shall serve for a term of 2 years and may not serve for more than 3 consecutive terms.

(3) Staggering of initial terms. Of the members first selected to serve on the Executive Board of the Standards Board—

(A) three shall serve for 1 term;

(B) three shall serve for 2 consecutive terms; and

(C) three shall serve for 3 consecutive terms,

as determined by lot at the time the members are first appointed.

(4) Duties. In addition to any other duties assigned under this title [42 USCS §§ 15321 et seq.], the Executive Board of the Standards Board may carry out such duties of the Standards Board as the Standards Board may delegate.

(Oct. 29, 2002, P. L. 107-252, Title II, Subtitle A, Part 2, § 213, 116 Stat. 1678.)

RESEARCH GUIDE

Law Review Articles:

Tokaji. The Paperless Chase: Electronic Voting and Democratic Values. 73 Fordham L Rev 1711, March 2005.

Wassom. The Help America Vote Act of 2002 and Selected Issues in Election Law Reform. 29 T Marshall L Rev 357, Spring 2004.

§ 15344. Membership of Board of Advisors

(a) **In general.** The Board of Advisors shall be composed of 37 members appointed as follows:

(1) Two members appointed by the National Governors Association.

(2) Two members appointed by the National Conference of State Legislatures.

(3) Two members appointed by the National Association of Secretaries of State.

(4) Two members appointed by the National Association of State Election Directors.

(5) Two members appointed by the National Association of Counties.

(6) Two members appointed by the National Association of County Recorders, Election Administrators, and Clerks [National Association of County Recorders, Election Officials and Clerks].

(7) Two members appointed by the United States Conference of Mayors.

(8) Two members appointed by the Election Center.

(9) Two members appointed by the International Association of County Recorders, Election Officials, and Treasurers [International Association of Clerks, Recorders, Election Officials and Treasurers].

(10) Two members appointed by the United States Commission on Civil Rights.

(11) Two members appointed by the Architectural and Transportation Barrier [Barriers] Compliance Board under section 502 of the Rehabilitation Act of 1973 (29 U.S.C. 792).

(12) The chief of the Office of Public Integrity of the Department of Justice, or the chief's designee.

(13) The chief of the Voting Section of the Civil Rights Division of the Department of Justice or the chief's designee.

(14) The director of the Federal Voting Assistance Program of the Department of Defense.

(15) Four members representing professionals in the field of science and technology, of whom—

(A) one each shall be appointed by the Speaker and the Minority Leader of the House of Representatives; and

(B) one each shall be appointed by the Majority Leader and the Minority Leader of the Senate.

(16) Eight members representing voter interests, of whom—

(A) four members shall be appointed by the Committee on House Administration of the House of Representatives, of whom two shall be appointed by the chair and two shall be appointed by the ranking minority member; and

(B) four members shall be appointed by the Committee on Rules and Administration of the Senate, of whom two shall be appointed by the chair and two shall be appointed by the ranking minority member.

(b) Manner of appointments. Appointments shall be made to the Board of Advisors under subsection (a) in a manner which ensures that the Board of Advisors will be bipartisan in nature and will reflect the various geographic regions of the United States.

(c) Term of service; vacancy. Members of the Board of Advisors shall serve for a term of 2 years, and may be reappointed. Any vacancy in the Board of Advisors shall be filled in the manner in which the original appointment was made.

(d) Chair. The Board of Advisors shall elect a Chair from among its members.

(Oct. 29, 2002, P. L. 107-252, Title II, Subtitle A, Part 2, § 214, 116 Stat. 1680.)

HISTORY; ANCILLARY LAWS AND DIRECTIVES

References in text:

In subsec. (a)(12), "Office of Public Integrity of the Department of Justice" is probably a reference to the Public Integrity Section of the Criminal Division of the Department of Justice.

Explanatory notes:

In subsec. (a)(6), "National Association of County Recorders, Election Officials and Clerks" has been inserted in brackets to indicate the name probably intended by Congress.

In subsec. (a)(9), "International Association of Clerks, Recorders, Election Officials and Treasurers" has been inserted in brackets to indicatethe name probably intended by Congress.

The bracketed word "Barriers" has been inserted in subsec. (a)(11) to indicate the word probably intended by Congress.

RESEARCH GUIDE

Law Review Articles:

Tokaji. The Paperless Chase: Electronic Voting and Democratic Values. 73 Fordham L Rev 1711, March 2005.

Wassom. The Help America Vote Act of 2002 and Selected Issues in Election Law Reform. 29 T Marshall L Rev 357, Spring 2004.

§ 15345. Powers of Boards; no compensation for service

(a) Hearings and sessions. (1) In general. To the extent that funds are made available by the Commission, the Standards Board (acting through the Executive Board) and the Board of Advisors may each hold such hearings for the purpose of carrying out this Act, sit and act at such times and places, take such testimony, and receive such evidence as each such Board considers advisable to carry out this title [42 USCS §§ 15321 et seq.], except that the Boards may not issue subpoenas requiring the attendance and testimony of witnesses or the production of any evidence.

(2) Meetings. The Standards Board and the Board of Advisors shall each hold a meeting of its members—

(A) not less frequently than once every year for purposes of voting on the voluntary voting system guidelines referred to it under section 222 [42 USCS § 15362];

(B) in the case of the Standards Board, not less frequently than once every 2 years for purposes of selecting the Executive Board; and

(C) at such other times as it considers appropriate for purposes of conducting such other business as it considers appropriate consistent with this title [42 USCS §§ 15321 et seq.].

(b) Information from Federal agencies. The Standards Board and the Board of Advisors may each secure directly from any Federal department or agency such information as the Board considers necessary to carry out this Act. Upon request of the Executive Board (in the case of the Standards Board) or the

Chair (in the case of the Board of Advisors), the head of such department or agency shall furnish such information to the Board.

(c) **Postal services.** The Standards Board and the Board of Advisors may use the United States mails in the same manner and under the same conditions as a department or agency of the Federal Government.

(d) **Administrative support services.** Upon the request of the Executive Board (in the case of the Standards Board) or the Chair (in the case of the Board of Advisors), the Administrator of the General Services Administration shall provide to the Board, on a reimbursable basis, the administrative support services that are necessary to enable the Board to carry out its duties under this title [42 USCS §§ 15321 et seq.].

(e) **No compensation for service.** Members of the Standards Board and members of the Board of Advisors shall not receive any compensation for their service, but shall be paid travel expenses, including per diem in lieu of subsistence, at rates authorized for employees of agencies under subchapter I of chapter 57 of title 5, United States Code [5 USCS §§ 5701 et seq.], while away from their homes or regular places of business in the performance of services for the Board.

(Oct. 29, 2002, P. L. 107-252, Title II, Subtitle A, Part 2, § 215, 116 Stat. 1681.)

HISTORY; ANCILLARY LAWS AND DIRECTIVES

References in text:
"This Act", referred to in this section, is Act Oct. 29, 2002, P. L. 107-252, popularly known as the Help America Vote Act of 2002, which appears generally as 42 USCS §§ 15301 et seq. For full classification of such Act, consult USCS Tables volumes.

RESEARCH GUIDE

Law Review Articles:
Wassom. The Help America Vote Act of 2002 and Selected Issues in Election Law Reform. 29 T Marshall L Rev 357, Spring 2004.

§ 15346. Status of Boards and members for purposes of claims against Board.

(a) **In general.** The provisions of chapters 161 and 171 of title 28, United States Code [28 USCS §§ 2401 et seq., 2671 et seq.], shall apply with respect to the liability of the Standards Board, the Board of Advisors, and their members for acts or omissions performed pursuant to and in the course of the duties and responsibilities of the Board.

(b) **Exception for criminal acts and other willful conduct.** Subsection (a) may not be construed to limit personal liability for criminal acts or omissions, willful or malicious misconduct, acts or omissions for private gain, or any other act or omission outside the scope of the service of a member of the Standards Board or the Board of Advisors.

(Oct. 29, 2002, P. L. 107-252, Title II, Subtitle A, Part 2, § 216, 116 Stat. 1681.)

RESEARCH GUIDE

Law Review Articles:

Wassom. The Help America Vote Act of 2002 and Selected Issues in Election Law Reform. 29 T Marshall L Rev 357, Spring 2004.

Technical Guidelines Development Committee

CROSS REFERENCES

This part (42 USCS §§ 15361 et seq.) is referred to in 42 USCS §§ 15321, 15322, 15327, 15342, 15371, 15441, 15451.

§ 15361. Technical Guidelines Development Committee

(a) Establishment. There is hereby established the Technical Guidelines Development Committee (hereafter in this part [42 USCS §§ 15361 et seq.] referred to as the "Development Committee").

(b) Duties. (1) In general. The Development Committee shall assist the Executive Director of the Commission in the development of the voluntary voting system guidelines.

(2) Deadline for initial set of recommendations. The Development Committee shall provide its first set of recommendations under this section to the Executive Director of the Commission not later than 9 months after all of its members have been appointed.

(c) Membership. (1) In general. The Development Committee shall be composed of the Director of the National Institute of Standards and Technology (who shall serve as its chair), together with a group of 14 other individuals appointed jointly by the Commission and the Director of the National Institute of Standards and Technology, consisting of the following:

(A) An equal number of each of the following:

(i) Members of the Standards Board.

(ii) Members of the Board of Advisors.

(iii) Members of the Architectural and Transportation Barrier Compliance Board under section 502 of the Rehabilitation Act of 1973 (29 U.S.C. 792).

(B) A representative of the American National Standards Institute.

(C) A representative of the Institute of Electrical and Electronics Engineers.

(D) Two representatives of the National Association of State Election Directors selected by such Association who are not members of the Standards Board or Board of Advisors, and who are not of the same political party.

(E) Other individuals with technical and scientific expertise relating to voting systems and voting equipment.

(2) Quorum. A majority of the members of the Development Committee shall constitute a quorum, except that the Development Committee may not conduct any business prior to the appointment of all of its members.

(d) No compensation for service. Members of the Development Committee shall not receive any compensation for their service, but shall be paid travel expenses, including per diem in lieu of subsistence, at rates authorized for employees of agencies under subchapter I of chapter 57 of title 5, United States Code [5 USCS §§ 5701 et seq.], while away from their homes or regular places of business in the performance of services for the Development Committee.

(e) Technical support from National Institute of Standards and Technology. (1) In general. At the request of the Development Committee, the Director of the National Institute of Standards and Technology shall provide the Development Committee with technical support necessary for the Development Committee to carry out its duties under this subtitle [42 USCS §§ 15321 et seq.].

(2) Technical support. The technical support provided under paragraph (1) shall include intramural research and development in areas to support the development of the voluntary voting system guidelines under this part [42 USCS §§ 15361 et seq.], including—

(A) the security of computers, computer networks, and computer data storage used in voting systems, including the computerized list required under section 303(a) [42 USCS § 15483(a)];

(B) methods to detect and prevent fraud;

(C) the protection of voter privacy;

(D) the role of human factors in the design and application of voting systems, including assistive technologies for individuals with disabilities (including blindness) and varying levels of literacy; and

(E) remote access voting, including voting through the Internet.

(3) No private sector intellectual property rights in guidelines. No private sector individual or entity shall obtain any intellectual property rights to any guideline or the contents of any guideline (or any modification to any guideline) adopted by the Commission under this Act.

(f) Publication of recommendations in Federal Register. At the time the Commission adopts any voluntary voting system guideline pursuant to section 222 [42 USCS § 15362], the Development Committee shall cause to have published in the Federal Register the recommendations it provided under this section to the Executive Director of the Commission concerning the guideline adopted.

(Oct. 29, 2002, P. L. 107-252, Title II, Subtitle A, Part 3, § 221, 116 Stat. 1682.)

HISTORY; ANCILLARY LAWS AND DIRECTIVES

References in text:
"This Act", referred to in this section, is Act Oct. 29, 2002, P. L. 107-252, popularly known as the Help America Vote Act of 2002, which appears generally as 42 USCS §§ 15301 et seq. For full classification of such Act, consult USCS Tables volumes.

CROSS REFERENCES
This section is referred to in 42 USCS § 15362.

RESEARCH GUIDE
Law Review Articles:
Tokaji. The Paperless Chase: Electronic Voting and Democratic Values. 73 Fordham L Rev 1711, March 2005.

Waterstone. Constitutional and Statutory Voting Rights for People with Disabilities. 14 Stan L & Pol'y Rev 353, 2003.
Wassom. The Help America Vote Act of 2002 and Selected Issues in Election Law Reform. 29 T Marshall L Rev 357, Spring 2004.
Saphire; Moke. Litigating Bush v. Gore in the States: Dual Voting Systems and the Fourteenth Amendment. 51 Vill L Rev 229, 2006.

§ 15362. Process for adoption

(a) General requirement for notice and comment. Consistent with the requirements of this section, the final adoption of the voluntary voting system guidelines (or modification of such a guideline) shall be carried out by the Commission in a manner that provides for each of the following:

(1) Publication of notice of the proposed guidelines in the Federal Register.

(2) An opportunity for public comment on the proposed guidelines.

(3) An opportunity for a public hearing on the record.

(4) Publication of the final guidelines in the Federal Register.

(b) Consideration of recommendations of Development Committee; submission of proposed guidelines to Board of Advisors and Standards Board. (1) Consideration of recommendations of Development Committee. In developing the voluntary voting system guidelines and modifications of such guidelines under this section, the Executive Director of the Commission shall take into consideration the recommendations provided by the Technical Guidelines Development Committee under section 221 [42 USCS § 15361].

(2) Board of Advisors. The Executive Director of the Commission shall submit the guidelines proposed to be adopted under this part [42 USCS §§ 15361 et seq.] (or any modifications to such guidelines) to the Board of Advisors.

(3) Standards Board. The Executive Director of the Commission shall submit the guidelines proposed to be adopted under this part [42 USCS §§ 15361 et seq.] (or any modifications to such guidelines) to the Executive Board of the Standards Board, which shall review the guidelines (or modifications) and forward its recommendations to the Standards Board.

(c) Review. Upon receipt of voluntary voting system guidelines described in subsection (b) (or a modification of such guidelines) from the Executive Director of the Commission, the Board of Advisors and the Standards Board shall each review and submit comments and recommendations regarding the guideline (or modification) to the Commission.

(d) Final adoption. (1) In general. A voluntary voting system guideline described in subsection (b) (or modification of such a guideline) shall not be considered to be finally adopted by the Commission unless the Commission votes to approve the final adoption of the guideline (or modification), taking into consideration the comments and recommendations submitted by the Board of Advisors and the Standards Board under subsection (c).

(2) Minimum period for consideration of comments and recommendations. The Commission may not vote on the final adoption of a guideline described

in subsection (b) (or modification of such a guideline) until the expiration of the 90-day period which begins on the date the Executive Director of the Commission submits the proposed guideline (or modification) to the Board of Advisors and the Standards Board under subsection (b).

(e) Special rule for initial set of guidelines. Notwithstanding any other provision of this part [42 USCS §§ 15361 et seq.], the most recent set of voting system standards adopted by the Federal Election Commission prior to the date of the enactment of this Act [enacted Oct. 29, 2002] shall be deemed to have been adopted by the Commission as of the date of the enactment of this Act [enacted Oct. 29, 2002] as the first set of voluntary voting system guidelines adopted under this part [42 USCS §§ 15361 et seq.].

(Oct. 29, 2002, P. L. 107-252, Title II, Subtitle A, Part 3, § 222, 116 Stat. 1683.)

CROSS REFERENCES
This section is referred to in 42 USCS §§ 15345, 15361.

RESEARCH GUIDE
Law Review Articles:
Wassom. The Help America Vote Act of 2002 and Selected Issues in Election Law Reform. 29 T Marshall L Rev 357, Spring 2004.
Saphire; Moke. Litigating Bush v. Gore in the States: Dual Voting Systems and the Fourteenth Amendment. 51 Vill L Rev 229, 2006.

TESTING, CERTIFICATION, DECERTIFICATION, AND RECERTIFICATION OF VOTING SYSTEM HARDWARE AND SOFTWARE

CROSS REFERENCES
This subtitle (42 USCS §§ 15371 et seq.) is referred to in 42 USCS § 15322.

§ 15371. Certification and testing of voting systems

(a) Certification and testing. (1) In general. The Commission shall provide for the testing, certification, decertification, and recertification of voting system hardware and software by accredited laboratories.

(2) Optional use by States. At the option of a State, the State may provide for the testing, certification, decertification, or recertification of its voting system hardware and software by the laboratories accredited by the Commission under this section.

(b) Laboratory accreditation. (1) Recommendations by National Institute of Standards and Technology. Not later than 6 months after the Commission first adopts voluntary voting system guidelines under part 3 of subtitle A [42 USCS §§ 15361 et seq.], the Director of the National Institute of Standards and Technology shall conduct an evaluation of independent, non-Federal laboratories and shall submit to the Commission a list of those laboratories the Director proposes to be accredited to carry out the testing, certification, decertification, and recertification provided for under this section.

(2) Approval by Commission. (A) In general. The Commission shall vote on the accreditation of any laboratory under this section, taking into consideration the list submitted under paragraph (1), and no laboratory may be

accredited for purposes of this section unless its accreditation is approved
by a vote of the Commission.

(B) Accreditation of laboratories not on Director list. The Commission
shall publish an explanation for the accreditation of any laboratory not
included on the list submitted by the Director of the National Institute of
Standards and Technology under paragraph (1).

(c) Continuing review by National Institute of Standards and Technology.
(1) In general. In cooperation with the Commission and in consultation with
the Standards Board and the Board of Advisors, the Director of the National
Institute of Standards and Technology shall monitor and review, on an ongoing basis, the performance of the laboratories accredited by the Commission
under this section, and shall make such recommendations to the Commission
as it considers appropriate with respect to the continuing accreditation of
such laboratories, including recommendations to revoke the accreditation of
any such laboratory.

(2) Approval by Commission required for revocation. The accreditation of a
laboratory for purposes of this section may not be revoked unless the revocation is approved by a vote of the Commission.

(d) Transition. Until such time as the Commission provides for the testing,
certification, decertification, and recertification of voting system hardware and
software by accredited laboratories under this section, the accreditation of
laboratories and the procedure for the testing, certification, decertification, and
recertification of voting system hardware and software used as of the date of
the enactment of this Act [enacted Oct. 29, 2002] shall remain in effect.
(Oct. 29, 2002, P. L. 107-252, Title II, Subtitle B, § 231, 116 Stat. 1684.)

RESEARCH GUIDE
Law Review Articles:
Tokaji. The Paperless Chase: Electronic Voting and Democratic Values. 73
Fordham L Rev 1711, March 2005.

STUDIES AND OTHER ACTIVITIES TO PROMOTE EFFECTIVE
ADMINISTRATION OF FEDERAL ELECTIONS

CROSS REFERENCES
This subtitle (42 USCS §§ 15381 et seq.) is referred to in 42 USCS § 15322.

§ 15381. Periodic studies of election administration issues

(a) In general. On such periodic basis as the Commission may determine, the
Commission shall conduct and make available to the public studies regarding
the election administration issues described in subsection (b), with the goal of
promoting methods of voting and administering elections which—

(1) will be the most convenient, accessible, and easy to use for voters,
including members of the uniformed services and overseas voters, individuals with disabilities, including the blind and visually impaired, and voters
with limited proficiency in the English language;

(2) will yield the most accurate, secure, and expeditious system for voting
and tabulating election results;

(3) will be nondiscriminatory and afford each registered and eligible voter an equal opportunity to vote and to have that vote counted; and

(4) will be efficient and cost-effective for use.

(b) Election administration issues described. For purposes of subsection (a), the election administration issues described in this subsection are as follows:

(1) Methods and mechanisms of election technology and voting systems used in voting and counting votes in elections for Federal office, including the over-vote and under-vote notification capabilities of such technology and systems.

(2) Ballot designs for elections for Federal office.

(3) Methods of voter registration, maintaining secure and accurate lists of registered voters (including the establishment of a centralized, interactive, statewide voter registration list linked to relevant agencies and all polling sites), and ensuring that registered voters appear on the voter registration list at the appropriate polling site.

(4) Methods of conducting provisional voting.

(5) Methods of ensuring the accessibility of voting, registration, polling places, and voting equipment to all voters, including individuals with disabilities (including the blind and visually impaired), Native American or Alaska Native citizens, and voters with limited proficiency in the English language.

(6) Nationwide statistics and methods of identifying, deterring, and investigating voting fraud in elections for Federal office.

(7) Identifying, deterring, and investigating methods of voter intimidation.

(8) Methods of recruiting, training, and improving the performance of poll workers.

(9) Methods of educating voters about the process of registering to vote and voting, the operation of voting mechanisms, the location of polling places, and all other aspects of participating in elections.

(10) The feasibility and advisability of conducting elections for Federal office on different days, at different places, and during different hours, including the advisability of establishing a uniform poll closing time and establishing—

(A) a legal public holiday under section 6103 of title 5, United States Code, as the date on which general elections for Federal office are held;

(B) the Tuesday next after the 1st Monday in November, in every even numbered year, as a legal public holiday under such section;

(C) a date other than the Tuesday next after the 1st Monday in November, in every even numbered year as the date on which general elections for Federal office are held; and

(D) any date described in subparagraph (C) as a legal public holiday under such section.

(11) Federal and State laws governing the eligibility of persons to vote.

(12) Ways that the Federal Government can best assist State and local authorities to improve the administration of elections for Federal office and what levels of funding would be necessary to provide such assistance.

(13)(A) The laws and procedures used by each State that govern—
(i) recounts of ballots cast in elections for Federal office;
(ii) contests of determinations regarding whether votes are counted in such elections; and
(iii) standards that define what will constitute a vote on each type of voting equipment used in the State to conduct elections for Federal office.

(B) The best practices (as identified by the Commission) that are used by States with respect to the recounts and contests described in clause (i).

(C) Whether or not there is a need for more consistency among State recount and contest procedures used with respect to elections for Federal office.

(14) The technical feasibility of providing voting materials in eight or more languages for voters who speak those languages and who have limited English proficiency.

(15) Matters particularly relevant to voting and administering elections in rural and urban areas.

(16) Methods of voter registration for members of the uniformed services and overseas voters, and methods of ensuring that such voters receive timely ballots that will be properly and expeditiously handled and counted.

(17) The best methods for establishing voting system performance benchmarks, expressed as a percentage of residual vote in the Federal contest at the top of the ballot.

(18) Broadcasting practices that may result in the broadcast of false information concerning the location or time of operation of a polling place.

(19) Such other matters as the Commission determines are appropriate.

(c) **Reports.** The Commission shall submit to the President and to the Committee on House Administration of the House of Representatives and the Committee on Rules and Administration of the Senate a report on each study conducted under subsection (a) together with such recommendations for administrative and legislative action as the Commission determines is appropriate.

(Oct. 29, 2002, P. L. 107-252, Title II, Subtitle C, § 241, 116 Stat. 1686.)

HISTORY; ANCILLARY LAWS AND DIRECTIVES

Other provisions:
Election Assistance Commission; administrative provisions. Act Dec. 26, 2007, P. L. 110-161, Div D, Title V, § 501, 121 Stat. 1997, provides:
"(a) Election data collection grants. Not later than March 30, 2008, the Election Assistance Commission (in this section referred to as the 'Commission') shall establish an election data collection grant program (in this section referred to as the 'program') to provide a grant of $2,000,000 to 5 eligible States to improve the collection of data relating to the regularly scheduled general election for Federal office held in November 2008. For purposes of this section, the term 'State' has the meaning given such term in section 901 of the Help America Vote Act of 2002 (42 U.S.C. 15541).

"(b) Eligibility. A State is eligible to receive a grant under the program if it submits to the Commission, at such time and in such form as the Commission may require, an application containing the following information and assurances:

"(1) A plan for the use of the funds provided by the grant which will expand and improve the collection of the election data described in subsection (a) at the precinct level and will provide for the collection of such data in a common electronic format (as determined by the Commission).

"(2) An assurance that the State will comply with all requests made by the Commission for the compilation and submission of the data.

"(3) An assurance that the State will provide the Commission with such information as the Commission may require to prepare and submit the report described in subsection (d).

"(4) Such other information and assurances as the Commission may require.

"(c) Timing of grants; availability. (1) Timing. The Commission shall award grants under the program to eligible States not later than 60 days after the date on which the Commission establishes the program.

"(2) Availability of funds. Amounts provided by a grant under the program shall remain available without fiscal year limitation until expended.

"(d) Report to Congress. (1) Report. Not later than June 30, 2009, the Commission, in consultation with the States receiving grants under the program and the Election Assistance Commission Board of Advisors, shall submit a report to Congress on the impact of the program on the collection of the election data described in subsection (a).

"(2) Recommendations. The Commission shall include in the report submitted under paragraph (1) such recommendations as the Commission considers appropriate to improve the collection of data relating to regularly scheduled general elections for Federal office in all States, including recommendations for changes in Federal law or regulations and the Commission's estimate of the amount of funding necessary to carry out such changes.".

RESEARCH GUIDE

Law Review Articles:

Tokaji. The Paperless Chase: Electronic Voting and Democratic Values. 73 Fordham L Rev 1711, March 2005.

Shambon; Abouchar. Trapped by Precincts? The Help America Vote Act's Provisional Ballots and the Problem of Precincts. 10 NYU J Legis & Pub Pol'y 133, 2006/2007.

Elmendorf. Representation Reinforcement Through Advisory Commissions: The Case of Election Law. 80 NYU L Rev 1366, November 2005.

Wassom. The Help America Vote Act of 2002 and Selected Issues in Election Law Reform. 29 T Marshall L Rev 357, Spring 2004.

§ 15382. Study, report, and recommendations on best practices for facilitating military and overseas voting

(a) Study. (1) In general. The Commission, in consultation with the Secretary of Defense, shall conduct a study on the best practices for facilitating voting by absent uniformed services voters (as defined in section 107(1) of the Uniformed and Overseas Citizens Absentee Voting Act [unclassified]) and overseas voters (as defined in section 107(5) of such Act [unclassified]).

(2) Issues considered. In conducting the study under paragraph (1) the Commission shall consider the following issues:

(A) The rights of residence of uniformed services voters absent due to military orders.

(B) The rights of absent uniformed services voters and overseas voters to register to vote and cast absentee ballots, including the right of such voters to cast a secret ballot.

(C) The rights of absent uniformed services voters and overseas voters to submit absentee ballot applications early during an election year.

(D) The appropriate preelection deadline for mailing absentee ballots to absent uniformed services voters and overseas voters.

(E) The appropriate minimum period between the mailing of absentee ballots to absent uniformed services voters and overseas voters and the deadline for receipt of such ballots.

(F) The timely transmission of balloting materials to absent uniformed services voters and overseas voters.

(G) Security and privacy concerns in the transmission, receipt, and processing of ballots from absent uniformed services voters and overseas voters, including the need to protect against fraud.

(H) The use of a single application by absent uniformed services voters and overseas voters for absentee ballots for all Federal elections occurring during a year.

(I) The use of a single application for voter registration and absentee ballots by absent uniformed services voters and overseas voters.

(J) The use of facsimile machines and electronic means of transmission of absentee ballot applications and absentee ballots to absent uniformed services voters and overseas voters.

(K) Other issues related to the rights of absent uniformed services voters and overseas voters to participate in elections.

(b) Report and recommendations. Not later than the date that is 18 months after the date of the enactment of this Act [enacted Oct. 29, 2002], the Commission shall submit to the President and Congress a report on the study conducted under subsection (a)(1) together with recommendations identifying the best practices used with respect to the issues considered under subsection (a)(2).

(Oct. 29, 2002, P. L. 107-252, Title II, Subtitle C, § 242, 116 Stat. 1688.)

CROSS REFERENCES
This section is referred to in 42 USCS § 15342.

RESEARCH GUIDE
Law Review Articles:
Wassom. The Help America Vote Act of 2002 and Selected Issues in Election Law Reform. 29 T Marshall L Rev 357, Spring 2004.

§ 15383. Report on human factor research

Not later than 1 year after the date of the enactment of this Act [enacted Oct. 29, 2002], the Commission, in consultation with the Director of the National Institute of Standards and Technology, shall submit a report to Congress which assesses the areas of human factor research, including usability engineering and human-computer and human-machine interaction, which feasibly could be applied to voting products and systems design to ensure the usability and accuracy of voting products and systems, including methods to improve access for individuals with disabilities (including blindness) and individuals with limited proficiency in the English language and to reduce voter error and the number of spoiled ballots in elections.
(Oct. 29, 2002, P. L. 107-252, Title II, Subtitle C, § 243, 116 Stat. 1688.)

RESEARCH GUIDE

Law Review Articles:
Tokaji. The Paperless Chase: Electronic Voting and Democratic Values. 73 Fordham L Rev 1711, March 2005.
Wassom. The Help America Vote Act of 2002 and Selected Issues in Election Law Reform. 29 T Marshall L Rev 357, Spring 2004.

§ 15384. Study and report on voters who register by mail and use of Social Security information

(a) **Registration by mail.** (1) Study. (A) In general. The Commission shall conduct a study of the impact of section 303(b) [42 USCS § 15483(b)] on voters who register by mail.

(B) Specific issues studied. The study conducted under subparagraph (A) shall include—

(i) an examination of the impact of section 303(b) [42 USCS § 15483(b)] on first time mail registrant voters who vote in person, including the impact of such section on voter registration;

(ii) an examination of the impact of such section on the accuracy of voter rolls, including preventing ineligible names from being placed on voter rolls and ensuring that all eligible names are placed on voter rolls; and

(iii) an analysis of the impact of such section on existing State practices, such as the use of signature verification or attestation procedures to verify the identity of voters in elections for Federal office, and an analysis of other changes that may be made to improve the voter registration process, such as verification or additional information on the registration card.

(2) Report. Not later than 18 months after the date on which section 303(b)(2) [42 USCS § 15483(b)(2)] takes effect, the Commission shall submit a report to the President and Congress on the study conducted under paragraph (1)(A) together with such recommendations for administrative and legislative action as the Commission determines is appropriate.

(b) **Use of Social Security information.** Not later than 18 months after the date on which section 303(a)(5) [42 USCS § 15483(a)(5)] takes effect, the Commission, in consultation with the Commissioner of Social Security, shall study and report to Congress on the feasibility and advisability of using Social Security identification numbers or other information compiled by the Social Security Administration to establish voter registration or other election law eligibility or identification requirements, including the matching of relevant information specific to an individual voter, the impact of such use on national security issues, and whether adequate safeguards or waiver procedures exist to protect the privacy of an individual voter.

(Oct. 29, 2002, P. L. 107-252, Title II, Subtitle C, § 244, 116 Stat. 1689.)

HISTORY; ANCILLARY LAWS AND DIRECTIVES

References in text:

With respect to the "date on which section 303(b)(2) takes effect", referred to in this section, see 42 USCS § 15483(d)(2).

RESEARCH GUIDE

Law Review Articles:

Wassom. The Help America Vote Act of 2002 and Selected Issues in Election Law Reform. 29 T Marshall L Rev 357, Spring 2004.

§ 15385. Study and report on electronic voting and the electoral process

(a) Study. (1) In general. The Commission shall conduct a thorough study of issues and challenges, specifically to include the potential for election fraud, presented by incorporating communications and Internet technologies in the Federal, State, and local electoral process.

(2) Issues to be studied. The Commission may include in the study conducted under paragraph (1) an examination of—

(A) the appropriate security measures required and minimum standards for certification of systems or technologies in order to minimize the potential for fraud in voting or in the registration of qualified citizens to register and vote;

(B) the possible methods, such as Internet or other communications technologies, that may be utilized in the electoral process, including the use of those technologies to register voters and enable citizens to vote online, and recommendations concerning statutes and rules to be adopted in order to implement an online or Internet system in the electoral process;

(C) the impact that new communications or Internet technology systems for use in the electoral process could have on voter participation rates, voter education, public accessibility, potential external influences during the elections process, voter privacy and anonymity, and other issues related to the conduct and administration of elections;

(D) whether other aspects of the electoral process, such as public availability of candidate information and citizen communication with candidates, could benefit from the increased use of online or Internet technologies;

(E) the requirements for authorization of collection, storage, and processing of electronically generated and transmitted digital messages to permit any eligible person to register to vote or vote in an election, including applying for and casting an absentee ballot;

(F) the implementation cost of an online or Internet voting or voter registration system and the costs of elections after implementation (including a comparison of total cost savings for the administration of the electoral process by using Internet technologies or systems);

(G) identification of current and foreseeable online and Internet technologies for use in the registration of voters, for voting, or for the purpose of reducing election fraud, currently available or in use by election authorities;

(H) the means by which to ensure and achieve equity of access to online or Internet voting or voter registration systems and address the fairness of such systems to all citizens; and

(I) the impact of technology on the speed, timeliness, and accuracy of vote counts in Federal, State, and local elections.

(b) Report. (1) Submission. Not later than 20 months after the date of the enactment of this Act [enacted Oct. 29, 2002], the Commission shall transmit to the Committee on House Administration of the House of Representatives and the Committee on Rules and Administration of the Senate a report on the results of the study conducted under subsection (a), including such legislative recommendations or model State laws as are required to address the findings of the Commission.

(2) Internet posting. In addition to the dissemination requirements under chapter 19 of title 44, United States Code [44 USCS §§ 1901 et seq.], the Election Administration Commission shall post the report transmitted under paragraph (1) on an Internet website.

(Oct. 29, 2002, P. L. 107-252, Title II, Subtitle C, § 245, 116 Stat. 1690.)

RESEARCH GUIDE

Law Review Articles:

Tokaji. The Paperless Chase: Electronic Voting and Democratic Values. 73 Fordham L Rev 1711, March 2005.

Wassom. The Help America Vote Act of 2002 and Selected Issues in Election Law Reform. 29 T Marshall L Rev 357, Spring 2004.

§ 15386. Study and report on free absentee ballot postage

(a) Study on the establishment of a free absentee ballot postage program.
(1) In general. The Commission, in consultation with the Postal Service, shall conduct a study on the feasibility and advisability of the establishment of a program under which the Postal Service shall waive or otherwise reduce the amount of postage applicable with respect to absentee ballots submitted by voters in general elections for Federal office (other than balloting materials mailed under section 3406 of title 39, United States Code) that does not apply with respect to the postage required to send the absentee ballots to voters.

(2) Public survey. As part of the study conducted under paragraph (1), the Commission shall conduct a survey of potential beneficiaries under the program described in such paragraph, including the elderly and disabled, and shall take into account the results of such survey in determining the feasibility and advisability of establishing such a program.

(b) Report. (1) Submission. Not later than the date that is 1 year after the date of the enactment of this Act [enacted Oct. 29, 2002], the Commission shall submit to Congress a report on the study conducted under subsection (a)(1) together with recommendations for such legislative and administrative action as the Commission determines appropriate.

(2) Costs. The report submitted under paragraph (1) shall contain an estimate of the costs of establishing the program described in subsection (a)(1).

(3) Implementation. The report submitted under paragraph (1) shall contain an analysis of the feasibility of implementing the program described in subsection (a)(1) with respect to the absentee ballots to be submitted in the general election for Federal office held in 2004.

(4) Recommendations regarding the elderly and disabled. The report submitted under paragraph (1) shall—

(A) include recommendations on ways that program described in subsection (a)(1) would target elderly individuals and individuals with disabilities; and

(B) identify methods to increase the number of such individuals who vote in elections for Federal office.

(c) Postal Service defined. The term "Postal Service" means the United States Postal Service established under section 201 of title 39, United States Code.
(Oct. 29, 2002, P. L. 107-252, Title II, Subtitle C, § 246, 116 Stat. 1691.)

RESEARCH GUIDE
Law Review Articles:
Wassom. The Help America Vote Act of 2002 and Selected Issues in Election Law Reform. 29 T Marshall L Rev 357, Spring 2004.

§ 15387. Consultation with Standards Board and Board of Advisors

The Commission shall carry out its duties under this subtitle [42 USCS §§ 15381 et seq.] in consultation with the Standards Board and the Board of Advisors.
(Oct. 29, 2002, P. L. 107-252, Title II, Subtitle C, § 247, 116 Stat. 1692.)

RESEARCH GUIDE
Law Review Articles:
Wassom. The Help America Vote Act of 2002 and Selected Issues in Election Law Reform. 29 T Marshall L Rev 357, Spring 2004.

ELECTION ASSISTANCE

CROSS REFERENCES
This subtitle (42 USCS §§ 15401 et seq.) is referred to in 42 USCS §§ 15322, 15461.

CROSS REFERENCES

This part (42 USCS §§ 15401 et seq.) is referred to in 42 USCS §§ 15301, 15304, 15327.

§ 15401. Requirements payments

(a) In general. The Commission shall make a requirements payment each year in an amount determined under section 252 [42 USCS § 15402] to each State which meets the conditions described in section 253 [42 USCS § 15403] for the year.

(b) Use of funds. (1) In general. Except as provided in paragraphs (2) and (3), a State receiving a requirements payment shall use the payment only to meet the requirements of title III [42 USCS §§ 15481 et seq.].

(2) Other activities. A State may use a requirements payment to carry out other activities to improve the administration of elections for Federal office if the State certifies to the Commission that—

    (A) the State has implemented the requirements of title III [42 USCS §§ 15481 et seq.]; or

    (B) the amount expended with respect to such other activities does not exceed an amount equal to the minimum payment amount applicable to the State under section 252(c) [42 USCS § 15402(c)].

(3) Activities under Uniformed and Overseas Citizens Absentee Voting Act. A State shall use a requirements payment made using funds appropriated pursuant to the authorization under section 257(a)(4) [42 USCS § 15407(a)(4)] only to meet the requirements under the Uniformed and Overseas Citizens Absentee Voting Act imposed as a result of the provisions of and amendments made by the Military and Overseas Voter Empowerment Act.

(c) Retroactive payments. (1) In general. Notwithstanding any other provision of this subtitle [42 USCS §§ 15401 et seq.], including the maintenance of effort requirements of section 254(a)(7) [42 USCS § 15404(a)(7)], a State may use a requirements payment as a reimbursement for costs incurred in obtaining voting equipment which meets the requirements of section 301 [42 USCS § 15481] if the State obtains the equipment after the regularly scheduled general election for Federal office held in November 2000.

(2) Special rule regarding multiyear contracts. A State may use a requirements payment for any costs for voting equipment which meets the requirements of section 301 [42 USCS § 15481] that, pursuant to a multiyear contract, were incurred on or after January 1, 2001, except that the amount that the State is otherwise required to contribute under the maintenance of effort requirements of section 254(a)(7) [42 USCS § 15404(a)(7)] shall be increased by the amount of the payment made with respect to such multiyear contract.

(d) Adoption of Commission guidelines and guidance not required to receive payment. Nothing in this part [42 USCS §§ 15401 et seq.] may be construed to require a State to implement any of the voluntary voting system guidelines or any of the voluntary guidance adopted by the Commission with respect to any matter as a condition for receiving a requirements payment.

(e) Schedule of payments. As soon as practicable after the initial appointment of all members of the Commission (but in no event later than 6 months thereafter), and not less frequently than once each calendar year thereafter, the Commission shall make requirements payments to States under this part [42 USCS §§ 15401 et seq.].

(f) Limitation. A State may not use any portion of a requirements payment—
　(1) to pay costs associated with any litigation, except to the extent that such costs otherwise constitute permitted uses of a requirements payment under this part [42 USCS §§ 15401 et seq.]; or
　(2) for the payment of any judgment.

(Oct. 29, 2002, P. L. 107-252, Title II, Subtitle D, Part 1, § 251, 116 Stat. 1692; Oct. 28, 2009, P. L. 111-84, Div A, Title V, Subtitle H, § 588(a), 123 Stat. 2333.)

HISTORY; ANCILLARY LAWS AND DIRECTIVES

References in text:

The "Uniformed and Overseas Citizens Absentee Voting Act", referred to in subsec. (b)(3), is Act Aug. 28, 1986, P. L. 99-410, which appears generally as 42 USCS §§ 1973ff et seq. For full classification of such Act, consult USCS Tables volumes.

The "Military and Overseas Voter Empowerment Act", referred to in subsec. (b)(3), is Subtitle H of Title V of Div A of Act Oct. 28, 2009, P. L. 111-84. For full classification of such Act, consult USCS Tables volumes.

Amendments:

2009. Act Oct. 28, 2009, in subsec. (b), in para. (1), substituted "paragraphs (2) and (3)" for "paragraph (2)", and added para. (3).

CROSS REFERENCES

This section is referred to in 42 USCS §§ 15403, 15404, 15406, 15542.

RESEARCH GUIDE

Law Review Articles:

Waterstone. Constitutional and Statutory Voting Rights for People with Disabilities. 14 Stan L & Pol'y Rev 353, 2003.

Wassom. The Help America Vote Act of 2002 and Selected Issues in Election Law Reform. 29 T Marshall L Rev 357, Spring 2004.

Magpantay. Two Steps Forward, One Step Back, and a Side Step: Asian Americans and the Federal Help America Vote Act. 10 UCLA Asian Pac Am LJ 31, 2005.

Saphire; Moke. Litigating Bush v. Gore in the States: Dual Voting Systems and the Fourteenth Amendment. 51 Vill L Rev 229, 2006.

INTERPRETIVE NOTES AND DECISIONS

It is within Election Assistance Commission's legitimate range of discretion to determine that payments made to states under Help America Vote Act of 2002 (HAVA), 42 USCS § 15401, are available to fund replacement of HAVA-compliant voting systems, originally purchased with HAVA funds, with different kind of HAVA-compliant voting system. Matter of: Election Assistance Comm'n—Availability of Funds for Purchase of Replacement Voting Equip. (2008, Comp Gen) 2008 US Comp Gen LEXIS 52.

§ 15402. Allocation of funds

(a) In general. Subject to subsection (c), the amount of a requirements payment made to a State for a year shall be equal to the product of—

(1) the total amount appropriated for requirements payments for the year pursuant to the authorization under section 257 [42 USCS § 15407]; and

(2) the State allocation percentage for the State (as determined under subsection (b)).

(b) State allocation percentage defined. The "State allocation percentage" for a State is the amount (expressed as a percentage) equal to the quotient of—

(1) the voting age population of the State (as reported in the most recent decennial census); and

(2) the total voting age population of all States (as reported in the most recent decennial census).

(c) Minimum amount of payment. The amount of a requirements payment made to a State for a year may not be less than—

(1) in the case of any of the several States or the District of Columbia, one-half of 1 percent of the total amount appropriated for requirements payments for the year under section 257 [42 USCS § 15407]; or

(2) in the case of the Commonwealth of Puerto Rico, Guam, American Samoa, or the United States Virgin Islands, one-tenth of 1 percent of such total amount.

(d) Pro rata reductions. The Administrator [Commission] shall make such pro rata reductions to the allocations determined under subsection (a) as are necessary to comply with the requirements of subsection (c).

(e) Continuing availability of funds after appropriation. A requirements payment made to a State under this part [42 USCS §§ 15401 et seq.] shall be available to the State without fiscal year limitation.

(Oct. 29, 2002, P. L. 107-252, Title II, Subtitle D, Part 1, § 252, 116 Stat. 1693.)

HISTORY; ANCILLARY LAWS AND DIRECTIVES

Explanatory notes:
The bracketed word "Commission" has been inserted in subsec. (d) to indicate the word probably intended by Congress.

CROSS REFERENCES
This section is referred to in 42 USCS § 15401.

Law Review Articles:
Tokaji. The Paperless Chase: Electronic Voting and Democratic Values. 73
Fordham L Rev 1711, March 2005.
Wassom. The Help America Vote Act of 2002 and Selected Issues in Election Law Reform. 29 T Marshall L Rev 357, Spring 2004.

§ 15403. Condition for receipt of funds

(a) In general. A State is eligible to receive a requirements payment for a fiscal year if the chief executive officer of the State, or designee, in consultation and coordination with the chief State election official, has filed with the Commission a statement certifying that the State is in compliance with the requirements referred to in subsection (b). A State may meet the requirement of the previous sentence by filing with the Commission a statement which reads as follows: "_____ hereby certifies that it is in compliance with the requirements referred to in section 253(b) of the Help America Vote Act of 2002." (with the blank to be filled in with the name of the State involved).

(b) State plan requirement; certification of compliance with applicable laws and requirements. The requirements referred to in this subsection are as follows:

(1) The State has filed with the Commission a State plan covering the fiscal year which the State certifies—

(A) contains each of the elements described in section 254(a) [42 USCS § 15404(a)] (or, for purposes of determining the eligibility of a State to receive a requirements payment appropriated pursuant to the authorization provided under section 257(a)(4) [42 USCS § 15407(a)(4)], contains the element described in paragraph (14) of such section) with respect to the fiscal year;

(B) is developed in accordance with section 255 [42 USCS § 15405]; and

(C) meets the public notice and comment requirements of section 256 [42 USCS § 15406].

(2)(A) Subject to subparagraph (B), the State has filed with the Commission a plan for the implementation of the uniform, nondiscriminatory administrative complaint procedures required under section 402 [42 USCS § 15512] (or has included such a plan in the State plan filed under paragraph (1)), and has such procedures in place for purposes of meeting the requirements of such section. If the State does not include such an implementation plan in the State plan filed under paragraph (1), the requirements of sections 255(b) and 256 [42 USCS §§ 15405(b), 15406] shall apply to the implementation plan in the same manner as such requirements apply to the State plan.

(B) Subparagraph (A) shall not apply for purposes of determining the eligibility of a State to receive a requirements payment appropriated pursuant to the authorization provided under section 257(a)(4) [42 USCS § 15407(a)(4)].

(3) The State is in compliance with each of the laws described in section 906 [42 USCS § 15545], as such laws apply with respect to this Act.

(4) To the extent that any portion of the requirements payment is used for

activities other than meeting the requirements of title III [42 USCS §§ 15481 et seq.]—

    (A) the State's proposed uses of the requirements payment are not inconsistent with the requirements of title III [42 USCS §§ 15481 et seq.]; and

    (B) the use of the funds under this paragraph is consistent with the requirements of section 251(b) [42 USCS § 15401(b)].

  (5)(A) Subject to subparagraph (B), the State has appropriated funds for carrying out the activities for which the requirements payment is made in an amount equal to 5 percent of the total amount to be spent for such activities (taking into account the requirements payment and the amount spent by the State) and, in the case of a State that uses a requirements payment as a reimbursement under section 251(c)(2) [42 USCS § 15401(c)(2)], an additional amount equal to the amount of such reimbursement.

  (B) Subparagraph (A) shall not apply for purposes of determining the eligibility of a State to receive a requirements payment appropriated pursuant to the authorization provided under section 257(a)(4) [42 USCS § 15407(a)(4)] for fiscal year 2010, except that if the State does not appropriate funds in accordance with subparagraph (A) prior to the last day of fiscal year 2011, the State shall repay to the Commission the requirements payment which is appropriated pursuant to such authorization.

(c) Methods of compliance left to discretion of State. The specific choices on the methods of complying with the elements of a State plan shall be left to the discretion of the State.

(d) Timing for filing of certification. A State may not file a statement of certification under subsection (a) until the expiration of the 45-day period (or, in the case of a fiscal year other than the first fiscal year for which a requirements payment is made to the State under this subtitle [42 USCS §§ 15401 et seq.], the 30-day period) which begins on the date notice of the State plan under this subtitle [42 USCS §§ 15401 et seq.] is published in the Federal Register pursuant to section 255(b) [42 USCS § 15405(b)].

(e) Chief State election official defined. In this subtitle [42 USCS §§ 15401 et seq.], the "chief State election official" of a State is the individual designated by the State under section 10 of the National Voter Registration Act of 1993 (42 U.S.C. 1973gg-8) to be responsible for coordination of the State's responsibilities under such Act.

(Oct. 29, 2002, P. L. 107-252, Title II, Subtitle D, Part 1, § 253, 116 Stat. 1693; Oct. 28, 2009, P. L. 111-84, Div A, Title V, Subtitle H, § 588(b)(1)(B)–(3), 123 Stat. 2333; Dec. 23, 2011, P. L. 112-74, Div C, Title VI, § 622(2), 125 Stat. 927.)

HISTORY; ANCILLARY LAWS AND DIRECTIVES

References in text:

"This Act", referred to in this section, is Act Oct. 29, 2002, P. L. 107-252, popularly known as the Help America Vote Act of 2002, which appears generally as 42 USCS §§ 15301 et seq. For full classification of such Act, consult USCS Tables volumes.

Amendments:
2009. Act Oct. 28, 2009, in subsec. (b), in para. (1)(A), substituted "section 254(a) (or, for purposes of determining the eligibility of a State to receive a requirements payment appropriated pursuant to the authorization provided under section 257(a)(4), contains the element described in paragraph (14) of such section)" for "section 254", and in paras. (2) and (5), designated the existing provisions as subpara. (A), substituted "Subject to subparagraph (B), the State" for "The State", and added subpara. (B).
2011. Act Dec. 23, 2011, in subsec. (d), inserted "notice of".

CROSS REFERENCES
This section is referred to in 42 USCS § 15401.

RESEARCH GUIDE
Law Review Articles:
Tokaji. Early Returns on Election Reform: Discretion, Disenfranchisement, and the Help America Vote Act. 73 Geo Wash L Rev 1206, August 2005.
Wassom. The Help America Vote Act of 2002 and Selected Issues in Election Law Reform. 29 T Marshall L Rev 357, Spring 2004.
Saphire; Moke. Litigating Bush v. Gore in the States: Dual Voting Systems and the Fourteenth Amendment. 51 Vill L Rev 229, 2006.

§ 15404. State plan

(a) In general. The State plan shall contain a description of each of the following:
(1) How the State will use the requirements payment to meet the requirements of title III [42 USCS §§ 15481 et seq.], and, if applicable under section 251(a)(2) [42 USCS § 15401(a)(2)], to carry out other activities to improve the administration of elections.
(2) How the State will distribute and monitor the distribution of the requirements payment to units of local government or other entities in the State for carrying out the activities described in paragraph (1), including a description of—
  (A) the criteria to be used to determine the eligibility of such units or entities for receiving the payment; and
  (B) the methods to be used by the State to monitor the performance of the units or entities to whom the payment is distributed, consistent with the performance goals and measures adopted under paragraph (8).
(3) How the State will provide for programs for voter education, election official education and training, and poll worker training which will assist the State in meeting the requirements of title III [42 USCS §§ 15481 et seq.].
(4) How the State will adopt voting system guidelines and processes which are consistent with the requirements of section 301 [42 USCS § 15481].
(5) How the State will establish a fund described in subsection (b) for purposes of administering the State's activities under this part [42 USCS §§ 15401 et seq.], including information on fund management.
(6) The State's proposed budget for activities under this part [42 USCS §§ 15401 et seq.], based on the State's best estimates of the costs of such

activities and the amount of funds to be made available, including specific information on—

(A) the costs of the activities required to be carried out to meet the requirements of title III [42 USCS §§ 15481 et seq.];

(B) the portion of the requirements payment which will be used to carry out activities to meet such requirements; and

(C) the portion of the requirements payment which will be used to carry out other activities.

(7) How the State, in using the requirements payment, will maintain the expenditures of the State for activities funded by the payment at a level that is not less than the level of such expenditures maintained by the State for the fiscal year ending prior to November 2000.

(8) How the State will adopt performance goals and measures that will be used by the State to determine its success and the success of units of local government in the State in carrying out the plan, including timetables for meeting each of the elements of the plan, descriptions of the criteria the State will use to measure performance and the process used to develop such criteria, and a description of which official is to be held responsible for ensuring that each performance goal is met.

(9) A description of the uniform, nondiscriminatory State-based administrative complaint procedures in effect under section 402 [42 USCS § 15512].

(10) If the State received any payment under title I [42 USCS §§ 15301 et seq.], a description of how such payment will affect the activities proposed to be carried out under the plan, including the amount of funds available for such activities.

(11) How the State will conduct ongoing management of the plan, except that the State may not make any material change in the administration of the plan unless notice of the change—

(A) is developed and published in the Federal Register in accordance with section 255 [42 USCS § 15405] in the same manner as the State plan;

(B) is subject to public notice and comment in accordance with section 256 [42 USCS § 15406] in the same manner as the State plan; and

(C) takes effect only after the expiration of the 30-day period which begins on the date notice of the change is published in the Federal Register in accordance with subparagraph (A).

(12) In the case of a State with a State plan in effect under this subtitle [42 USCS §§ 15401 et seq.] during the previous fiscal year, a description of how the plan reflects changes from the State plan for the previous fiscal year and of how the State succeeded in carrying out the State plan for such previous fiscal year.

(13) A description of the committee which participated in the development of the State plan in accordance with section 255 [42 USCS § 15405] and the procedures followed by the committee under such section and section 256 [42 USCS § 15406].

(14) How the State will comply with the provisions and requirements of and amendments made by the Military and Overseas Voter Empowerment Act.

(b) Requirements for election fund. (1) Election fund described. For purposes of subsection (a)(5), a fund described in this subsection with respect to a State is a fund which is established in the treasury of the State government, which is used in accordance with paragraph (2), and which consists of the following amounts:

(A) Amounts appropriated or otherwise made available by the State for carrying out the activities for which the requirements payment is made to the State under this part [42 USCS §§ 15401 et seq.].

(B) The requirements payment made to the State under this part [42 USCS §§ 15401 et seq.].

(C) Such other amounts as may be appropriated under law.

(D) Interest earned on deposits of the fund.

(2) Use of fund. Amounts in the fund shall be used by the State exclusively to carry out the activities for which the requirements payment is made to the State under this part [42 USCS §§ 15401 et seq.].

(3) Treatment of States that require changes to State law. In the case of a State that requires State legislation to establish the fund described in this subsection, the Commission shall defer disbursement of the requirements payment to such State until such time as legislation establishing the fund is enacted.

(c) Protection against actions based on information in plan. (1) In general. No action may be brought under this Act against a State or other jurisdiction on the basis of any information contained in the State plan filed under this part [42 USCS §§ 15401 et seq.].

(2) Exception for criminal acts. Paragraph (1) may not be construed to limit the liability of a State or other jurisdiction for criminal acts or omissions.

(Oct. 29, 2002, P. L. 107-252, Title II, Subtitle D, Part 1, § 254, 116 Stat. 1694; Oct. 28, 2009, P. L. 111-84, Div A, Title V, Subtitle H, § 588(b)(1)(A), 123 Stat. 2333; Dec. 23, 2011, P. L. 112-74, Div C, Title VI, § 622(3), (4), 125 Stat. 927.)

HISTORY; ANCILLARY LAWS AND DIRECTIVES

References in text:

"This Act", referred to in this section, is Act Oct. 29, 2002, P. L. 107-252, popularly known as the Help America Vote Act of 2002, which appears generally as 42 USCS §§ 15301 et seq. For full classification of such Act, consult USCS Tables volumes.

The "Military and Overseas Voter Empowerment Act", referred to in subsec. (a)(14), is Subtitle H of Title V of Div A of Act Oct. 28, 2009, P. L. 111-84. For full classification of such Act, consult USCS Tables volumes.

Amendments:

2009. Act Oct. 28, 2009, added subsec. (a)(14).

2011. Act Dec. 23, 2011, in subsec. (a)(11), in the introductory matter and in subpara. (C), inserted "notice of".

CROSS REFERENCES

This section is referred to in 42 USCS §§ 15304, 15401, 15403, 15408.

RESEARCH GUIDE
Law Review Articles:
Wassom. The Help America Vote Act of 2002 and Selected Issues in Election Law Reform. 29 T Marshall L Rev 357, Spring 2004.
Magpantay. Two Steps Forward, One Step Back, and a Side Step: Asian Americans and the Federal Help America Vote Act. 10 UCLA Asian Pac Am LJ 31, 2005.

§ 15405. Process for development and filing of plan; publication by Commission

(a) In general. The chief State election official shall develop the State plan under this subtitle [42 USCS §§ 15401 et seq.] through a committee of appropriate individuals, including the chief election officials of the two most populous jurisdictions within the States, other local election officials, stake holders (including representatives of groups of individuals with disabilities), and other citizens, appointed for such purpose by the chief State election official.

(b) Publication of plan by Commission. After receiving the State plan of a State under this subtitle [42 USCS §§ 15401 et seq.], the Commission shall cause to have the plan posted on the Commission's website with a notice published in the Federal Register.
(Oct. 29, 2002, P. L. 107-252, Title II, Subtitle D, Part 1, § 255, 116 Stat. 1697; Dec. 23, 2011, P. L. 112-74, Div C, Title VI, § 622(1), 125 Stat. 926.)

HISTORY; ANCILLARY LAWS AND DIRECTIVES
Amendments:
2011. Act Dec. 23, 2011, in subsec. (b), inserted "posted on the Commission's website with a notice".

CROSS REFERENCES
This section is referred to in 42 USCS §§ 15403, 15404.

RESEARCH GUIDE
Law Review Articles:
Wassom. The Help America Vote Act of 2002 and Selected Issues in Election Law Reform. 29 T Marshall L Rev 357, Spring 2004.

§ 15406. Requirement for public notice and comment

For purposes of section 251(a)(1)(C) [253(b)(1)(C)] [42 USCS § 15403(b)(1)(C)], a State plan meets the public notice and comment requirements of this section if—

(1) not later than 30 days prior to the submission of the plan, the State made a preliminary version of the plan available for public inspection and comment;

(2) the State publishes notice that the preliminary version of the plan is so available; and

(3) the State took the public comments made regarding the preliminary ver-

sion of the plan into account in preparing the plan which was filed with the Commission.

(Oct. 29, 2002, P. L. 107-252, Title II, Subtitle D, Part 1, § 256, 116 Stat. 1697.)

HISTORY; ANCILLARY LAWS AND DIRECTIVES
Explanatory notes:
The bracketed section designator "253(b)(1)(C)" has been inserted in this section to indicate the reference probably intended by Congress.

CROSS REFERENCES
This section is referred to in 42 USCS §§ 15403, 15404.

RESEARCH GUIDE
Law Review Articles:
Wassom. The Help America Vote Act of 2002 and Selected Issues in Election Law Reform. 29 T Marshall L Rev 357, Spring 2004.

§ 15407. Authorization of appropriations

(a) In general. In addition to amounts transferred under section 104(c) [42 USCS § 15304(c)], there are authorized to be appropriated for requirements payments under this part [42 USCS §§ 15401 et seq.] the following amounts:

(1) For fiscal year 2003, $1,400,000,000.

(2) For fiscal year 2004, $1,000,000,000.

(3) For fiscal year 2005, $600,000,000.

(4) For fiscal year 2010 and subsequent fiscal years, such sums as are necessary for purposes of making requirements payments to States to carry out the activities described in section 251(b)(3) [42 USCS § 15401(b)(3)].

(b) Availability. Any amounts appropriated pursuant to the authority of subsection (a) shall remain available without fiscal year limitation until expended.

(Oct. 29, 2002, P. L. 107-252, Title II, Subtitle D, Part 1, § 257, 116 Stat. 1697; Oct. 28, 2009, P. L. 111-84, Div A, Title V, Subtitle H, § 588(c), 123 Stat. 2334.)

HISTORY; ANCILLARY LAWS AND DIRECTIVES
Amendments:
2009. Act Oct. 28, 2009, added subsec. (a)(4).

CROSS REFERENCES
This section is referred to in 42 USCS § 15402.

RESEARCH GUIDE
Law Review Articles:
Tokaji. The Paperless Chase: Electronic Voting and Democratic Values. 73 Fordham L Rev 1711, March 2005.

Waterstone. Constitutional and Statutory Voting Rights for People with Disabilities. 14 Stan L & Pol'y Rev 353, 2003.

Wassom. The Help America Vote Act of 2002 and Selected Issues in Election Law Reform. 29 T Marshall L Rev 357, Spring 2004.

§ 15408. Reports

Not later than 6 months after the end of each fiscal year for which a State received a requirements payment under this part [42 USCS §§ 15401 et seq.], the State shall submit a report to the Commission on the activities conducted with the funds provided during the year, and shall include in the report—

(1) a list of expenditures made with respect to each category of activities described in section 251(b) [42 USCS § 15401(b)];

(2) the number and type of articles of voting equipment obtained with the funds; and

(3) an analysis and description of the activities funded under this part [42 USCS §§ 15401 et seq.] to meet the requirements of this Act and an analysis and description of how such activities conform to the State plan under section 254 [42 USCS § 15404].

(Oct. 29, 2002, P. L. 107-252, Title II, Subtitle D, Part 1, § 258, 116 Stat. 1697.)

HISTORY; ANCILLARY LAWS AND DIRECTIVES

References in text:

"This Act", referred to in this section, is Act Oct. 29, 2002, P. L. 107-252, popularly known as the Help America Vote Act of 2002, which appears generally as 42 USCS §§ 15301 et seq. For full classification of such Act, consult USCS Tables volumes.

RESEARCH GUIDE

Law Review Articles:

Wassom. The Help America Vote Act of 2002 and Selected Issues in Election Law Reform. 29 T Marshall L Rev 357, Spring 2004.

Payments to States and Units of Local Government To Assure Access for Individuals With Disabilities

§ 15421. Payments to States and units of local government to assure access for individuals with disabilities.

(a) **In general.** The Secretary of Health and Human Services shall make a payment to each eligible State and each eligible unit of local government (as described in section 263 [42 USCS § 15423]).

(b) **Use of funds.** An eligible State and eligible unit of local government shall use the payment received under this part [42 USCS §§ 15421 et seq.] for—

(1) making polling places, including the path of travel, entrances, exits, and voting areas of each polling facility, accessible to individuals with disabilities, including the blind and visually impaired, in a manner that provides the same opportunity for access and participation (including privacy and independence) as for other voters; and

(2) providing individuals with disabilities and the other individuals described in paragraph (1) with information about the accessibility of polling places, including outreach programs to inform the individuals about the availability of accessible polling places and training election officials, poll workers, and election volunteers on how best to promote the access and participation of individuals with disabilities in elections for Federal office.

(c) Schedule of payments. As soon as practicable after the date of the enactment of this Act [enacted Oct. 29, 2002] (but in no event later than 6 months thereafter), and not less frequently than once each calendar year thereafter, the Secretary shall make payments under this part [42 USCS §§ 15421 et seq.].
(Oct. 29, 2002, P. L. 107-252, Title II, Subtitle D, Part 2, § 261, 116 Stat. 1698.)

CROSS REFERENCES
This section is referred to in 42 USCS § 15425.

RESEARCH GUIDE
Law Review Articles:
Waterstone. Civil Rights and the Administration of Elections—Toward Secret Ballots and Polling Place Access. 8 J Gender Race & Just 101, Spring 2004.
Waterstone. Constitutional and Statutory Voting Rights for People with Disabilities. 14 Stan L & Pol'y Rev 353, 2003.
Wassom. The Help America Vote Act of 2002 and Selected Issues in Election Law Reform. 29 T Marshall L Rev 357, Spring 2004.
Magpantay. Two Steps Forward, One Step Back, and a Side Step: Asian Americans and the Federal Help America Vote Act. 10 UCLA Asian Pac Am LJ 31, 2005.

§ 15422. Amount of payment

(a) In general. The amount of a payment made to an eligible State or an eligible unit of local government for a year under this part [42 USCS §§ 15421 et seq.] shall be determined by the Secretary.

(b) Continuing availability of funds after appropriation. A payment made to an eligible State or eligible unit of local government under this part [42 USCS §§ 15421 et seq.] shall be available without fiscal year limitation.
(Oct. 29, 2002, P. L. 107-252, Title II, Subtitle D, Part 2, § 262, 116 Stat. 1698.)

RESEARCH GUIDE
Law Review Articles:
Wassom. The Help America Vote Act of 2002 and Selected Issues in Election Law Reform. 29 T Marshall L Rev 357, Spring 2004.

§ 15423. Requirements for eligibility

(a) Application. Each State or unit of local government that desires to receive a payment under this part [42 USCS §§ 15421 et seq.] for a fiscal year shall submit an application for the payment to the Secretary at such time and in such manner and containing such information as the Secretary shall require.

(b) Contents of application. Each application submitted under subsection (a) shall—

(1) describe the activities for which assistance under this section is sought; and

(2) provide such additional information and certifications as the Secretary determines to be essential to ensure compliance with the requirements of this part [42 USCS §§ 15421 et seq.].

(c) Protection against actions based on information in application. (1) In general. No action may be brought under this Act against a State or unit of local government on the basis of any information contained in the application submitted under subsection (a).

(2) Exception for criminal acts. Paragraph (1) may not be construed to limit the liability of a State or unit of local government for criminal acts or omissions.

(Oct. 29, 2002, P. L. 107-252, Title II, Subtitle D, Part 2, § 263, 116 Stat. 1698.)

HISTORY; ANCILLARY LAWS AND DIRECTIVES

References in text:
"This Act", referred to in this section, is Act Oct. 29, 2002, P. L. 107-252, popularly known as the Help America Vote Act of 2002, which appears generally as 42 USCS §§ 15301 et seq. For full classification of such Act, consult USCS Tables volumes.

CROSS REFERENCES
This section is referred to in 42 USCS § 15421.

RESEARCH GUIDE

Law Review Articles:
Waterstone. Constitutional and Statutory Voting Rights for People with Disabilities. 14 Stan L & Pol'y Rev 353, 2003.
Wassom. The Help America Vote Act of 2002 and Selected Issues in Election Law Reform. 29 T Marshall L Rev 357, Spring 2004.

§ 15424. Authorization of appropriations

(a) In general. There are authorized to be appropriated to carry out the provisions of this part [42 USCS §§ 15421 et seq.] the following amounts:

(1) For fiscal year 2003, $50,000,000.

(2) For fiscal year 2004, $25,000,000.

(3) For fiscal year 2005, $25,000,000.

(b) Availability. Any amounts appropriated pursuant to the authority of subsection (a) shall remain available without fiscal year limitation until expended.

(Oct. 29, 2002, P. L. 107-252, Title II, Subtitle D, Part 2, § 264, 116 Stat. 1699.)

RESEARCH GUIDE
Law Review Articles:
Waterstone. Constitutional and Statutory Voting Rights for People with Disabilities. 14 Stan L & Pol'y Rev 353, 2003.
Wassom. The Help America Vote Act of 2002 and Selected Issues in Election Law Reform. 29 T Marshall L Rev 357, Spring 2004.

§ 15425. Reports

(a) Reports by recipients. Not later than [the] 6 months after the end of each fiscal year for which an eligible State or eligible unit of local government received a payment under this part [42 USCS §§ 15421 et seq.], the State or unit shall submit a report to the Secretary on the activities conducted with the funds provided during the year, and shall include in the report a list of expenditures made with respect to each category of activities described in section 261(b) [42 USCS § 15421(b)].

(b) Report by Secretary to Committees. With respect to each fiscal year for which the Secretary makes payments under this part [42 USCS §§ 15421 et seq.], the Secretary shall submit a report on the activities carried out under this part to the Committee on House Administration of the House of Representatives and the Committee on Rules and Administration of the Senate.

(Oct. 29, 2002, P. L. 107-252, Title II, Subtitle D, Part 2, § 265, 116 Stat. 1699.)

HISTORY; ANCILLARY LAWS AND DIRECTIVES

Explanatory notes:

The word "the" has been enclosed in brackets in subsec. (a) to indicate the probable intent of Congress to delete it.

RESEARCH GUIDE

Law Review Articles:

Wassom. The Help America Vote Act of 2002 and Selected Issues in Election Law Reform. 29 T Marshall L Rev 357, Spring 2004.

Grants for Research on Voting Technology Improvements

§ 15441.   Grants for research on voting technology improvements

(a) In general. The Commission shall make grants to assist entities in carrying out research and development to improve the quality, reliability, accuracy, accessibility, affordability, and security of voting equipment, election systems, and voting technology.

(b) Eligibility. An entity is eligible to receive a grant under this part [42 USCS §§ 15441 et seq.] if it submits to the Commission (at such time and in such form as the Commission may require) an application containing—

(1) certifications that the research and development funded with the grant will take into account the need to make voting equipment fully accessible for individuals with disabilities, including the blind and visually impaired, the need to ensure that such individuals can vote independently and with privacy, and the need to provide alternative language accessibility for individuals with limited proficiency in the English language (consistent with the requirements of the Voting Rights Act of 1965 [42 USCS §§ 1973 et seq.]); and

(2) such other information and certifications as the Commission may require.

(c) Applicability of regulations governing patent rights in inventions made with Federal assistance. Any invention made by the recipient of a grant under this part [42 USCS §§ 15441 et seq.] using funds provided under this part [42 USCS §§ 15441 et seq.] shall be subject to chapter 18 of title 35, United States Code [35 USCS §§ 200 et seq.] (relating to patent rights in inventions made with Federal assistance).

(d) Recommendation of topics for research. (1) In general. The Director of the National Institute of Standards and Technology (hereafter in this section referred to as the "Director") shall submit to the Commission an annual list of the Director's suggestions for issues which may be the subject of research funded with grants awarded under this part [42 USCS §§ 15441 et seq.] during the year.

(2) Review of grant applications received by Commission. The Commission shall submit each application it receives for a grant under this part [42 USCS §§ 15441 et seq.] to the Director, who shall review the application and provide the Commission with such comments as the Director considers appropriate.

(3) Monitoring and adjustment of grant activities at request of Commission. After the Commission has awarded a grant under this part [42 USCS §§ 15441 et seq.], the Commission may request that the Director monitor the grant, and (to the extent permitted under the terms of the grant as awarded) the Director may recommend to the Commission that the recipient of the grant modify and adjust the activities carried out under the grant.

(4) Evaluation of grants at request of Commission. (A) In general. In the case of a grant for which the Commission submits the application to the Director under paragraph (2) or requests that the Director monitor the grant under paragraph (3), the Director shall prepare and submit to the Commission an evaluation of the grant and the activities carried out under the grant.

(B) Inclusion in reports. The Commission shall include the evaluations submitted under subparagraph (A) for a year in the report submitted for the year under section 207 [42 USCS § 15327].

(e) **Provision of information on projects.** The Commission may provide to the Technical Guidelines Development Committee under part 3 of subtitle A [42 USCS §§ 15361 et seq.] such information regarding the activities funded under this part [42 USCS §§ 15441 et seq.] as the Commission deems necessary to assist the Committee in carrying out its duties.

(Oct. 29, 2002, P. L. 107-252, Title II, Subtitle D, Part 3, § 271, 116 Stat. 1699.)

RESEARCH GUIDE

Law Review Articles:

Tokaji. Early Returns on Election Reform: Discretion, Disenfranchisement, and the Help America Vote Act. 73 Geo Wash L Rev 1206, August 2005.

Wassom. The Help America Vote Act of 2002 and Selected Issues in Election Law Reform. 29 T Marshall L Rev 357, Spring 2004.

§ 15442. Report

(a) **In general.** Each entity which receives a grant under this part [42 USCS §§ 15441 et seq.] shall submit to the Commission a report describing the activities carried out with the funds provided under the grant.

(b) **Deadline.** An entity shall submit a report required under subsection (a) not later than 60 days after the end of the fiscal year for which the entity received the grant which is the subject of the report.

(Oct. 29, 2002, P. L. 107-252, Title II, Subtitle D, Part 3, § 272, 116 Stat. 1700.)

RESEARCH GUIDE

Law Review Articles:

Wassom. The Help America Vote Act of 2002 and Selected Issues in Election Law Reform. 29 T Marshall L Rev 357, Spring 2004.

§ 15443. Authorization of appropriations

(a) In general. There are authorized to be appropriated for grants under this part [42 USCS §§ 15441 et seq.] $20,000,000 for fiscal year 2003.

(b) Availability of funds. Amounts appropriated pursuant to the authorization under this section shall remain available, without fiscal year limitation, until expended.

(Oct. 29, 2002, P. L. 107-252, Title II, Subtitle D, Part 3, § 273, 116 Stat. 1700.)

RESEARCH GUIDE

Law Review Articles:

Wassom. The Help America Vote Act of 2002 and Selected Issues in Election Law Reform. 29 T Marshall L Rev 357, Spring 2004.

Pilot Program for Testing of Equipment and Technology

§ 15451. Pilot program

(a) In general. The Commission shall make grants to carry out pilot programs under which new technologies in voting systems and equipment are tested and implemented on a trial basis so that the results of such tests and trials are reported to Congress.

(b) Eligibility. An entity is eligible to receive a grant under this part [42 USCS §§ 15451 et seq.] if it submits to the Commission (at such time and in such form as the Commission may require) an application containing—

(1) certifications that the pilot programs funded with the grant will take into account the need to make voting equipment fully accessible for individuals with disabilities, including the blind and visually impaired, the need to ensure that such individuals can vote independently and with privacy, and the need to provide alternative language accessibility for individuals with limited proficiency in the English language (consistent with the requirements of the Voting Rights Act of 1965 [42 USCS §§ 1973 et seq.] and the requirements of this Act); and

(2) such other information and certifications as the Commission may require.

(c) Recommendation of topics for pilot programs. (1) In general. The Director of the National Institute of Standards and Technology (hereafter in this section referred to as the "Director") shall submit to the Commission an annual list of the Director's suggestions for issues which may be the subject of pilot programs funded with grants awarded under this part [42 USCS §§ 15451 et seq.] during the year.

(2) Review of grant applications received by Commission. The Commission

shall submit each application it receives for a grant under this part [42 USCS §§ 15451 et seq.] to the Director, who shall review the application and provide the Commission with such comments as the Director considers appropriate.

(3) Monitoring and adjustment of grant activities at request of Commission. After the Commission has awarded a grant under this part [42 USCS §§ 15451 et seq.], the Commission may request that the Director monitor the grant, and (to the extent permitted under the terms of the grant as awarded) the Director may recommend to the Commission that the recipient of the grant modify and adjust the activities carried out under the grant.

(4) Evaluation of grants at request of Commission. (A) In general. In the case of a grant for which the Commission submits the application to the Director under paragraph (2) or requests that the Director monitor the grant under paragraph (3), the Director shall prepare and submit to the Commission an evaluation of the grant and the activities carried out under the grant.

(B) Inclusion in reports. The Commission shall include the evaluations submitted under subparagraph (A) for a year in the report submitted for the year under section 207 [42 USCS § 15327].

(d) **Provision of information on projects.** The Commission may provide to the Technical Guidelines Development Committee under part 3 of subtitle A [42 USCS §§ 15361 et seq.] such information regarding the activities funded under this part [42 USCS §§ 15451 et seq.] as the Commission deems necessary to assist the Committee in carrying out its duties.

(Oct. 29, 2002, P. L. 107-252, Title II, Subtitle D, Part 4, § 281, 116 Stat. 1701.)

HISTORY; ANCILLARY LAWS AND DIRECTIVES

References in text:
"This Act", referred to in this section, is Act Oct. 29, 2002, P. L. 107-252, popularly known as the Help America Vote Act of 2002, which appears generally as 42 USCS §§ 15301 et seq. For full classification of such Act, consult USCS Tables volumes.

RESEARCH GUIDE

Law Review Articles:
Wassom. The Help America Vote Act of 2002 and Selected Issues in Election Law Reform. 29 T Marshall L Rev 357, Spring 2004.

§ 15452. Report

(a) **In general.** Each entity which receives a grant under this part [42 USCS §§ 15451 et seq.] shall submit to the Commission a report describing the activities carried out with the funds provided under the grant.

(b) **Deadline.** An entity shall submit a report required under subsection (a) not later than 60 days after the end of the fiscal year for which the entity received the grant which is the subject of the report.

(Oct. 29, 2002, P. L. 107-252, Title II, Subtitle D, Part 4, § 282, 116 Stat. 1702.)

RESEARCH GUIDE
Law Review Articles:
Wassom. The Help America Vote Act of 2002 and Selected Issues in Election Law Reform. 29 T Marshall L Rev 357, Spring 2004.

§ 15453. Authorization of appropriations

(a) In general. There are authorized to be appropriated for grants under this part [42 USCS §§ 15451 et seq.] $10,000,000 for fiscal year 2003.

(b) Availability of funds. Amounts appropriated pursuant to the authorization under this section shall remain available, without fiscal year limitation, until expended.

(Oct. 29, 2002, P. L. 107-252, Title II, Subtitle D, Part 4, § 283, 116 Stat. 1703.)

RESEARCH GUIDE
Law Review Articles:
Wassom. The Help America Vote Act of 2002 and Selected Issues in Election Law Reform. 29 T Marshall L Rev 357, Spring 2004.

Protection and Advocacy Systems

§ 15461. Payments for protection and advocacy systems

(a) In general. In addition to any other payments made under this subtitle [42 USCS §§ 15401 et seq.], the Secretary of Health and Human Services shall pay the protection and advocacy system (as defined in section 102 of the Developmental Disabilities Assistance and Bill of Rights Act of 2000 (42 U.S.C. 15002)) of each State to ensure full participation in the electoral process for individuals with disabilities, including registering to vote, casting a vote and accessing polling places. In providing such services, protection and advocacy systems shall have the same general authorities as they are afforded under subtitle C of title I of the Developmental Disabilities Assistance and Bill of Rights Act of 2000 (42 U.S.C. 15041 et seq.).

(b) Minimum grant amount. The minimum amount of each grant to a protection and advocacy system shall be determined and allocated as set forth in subsections (c)(3), (c)(4), (c)(5), (e), and (g) of section 509 of the Rehabilitation Act of 1973 (29 U.S.C. 794e), except that the amount of the grants to systems referred to in subsections (c)(3)(B) and (c)(4)(B) of that section shall be not less than $70,000 and $35,000, respectively.

(c) Training and technical assistance program. (1) In general. Not later than 90 days after the date on which the initial appropriation of funds for a fiscal year is made pursuant to the authorization under section 292 [42 USCS § 15462], the Secretary shall set aside 7 percent of the amount appropriated under such section and use such portion to make payments to eligible entities to provide training and technical assistance with respect to the activities carried out under this section.

(2) Use of funds. A recipient of a payment under this subsection may use the payment to support training in the use of voting systems and technologies, and to demonstrate and evaluate the use of such systems and technolo-

gies, by individuals with disabilities (including blindness) in order to assess the availability and use of such systems and technologies for such individuals. At least one of the recipients under this subsection shall use the payment to provide training and technical assistance for nonvisual access.

(3) Eligibility. An entity is eligible to receive a payment under this subsection if the entity—

   (A) is a public or private nonprofit entity with demonstrated experience in voting issues for individuals with disabilities;

   (B) is governed by a board with respect to which the majority of its members are individuals with disabilities or family members of such individuals or individuals who are blind; and

   (C) submits to the Secretary an application at such time, in such manner, and containing such information as the Secretary may require.

(Oct. 29, 2002, P. L. 107-252, Title II, Subtitle D, Part 5, § 291, 116 Stat. 1702.)

CROSS REFERENCES

This section is referred to in 42 USCS § 15462.

RESEARCH GUIDE

Law Review Articles:
Waterstone. Constitutional and Statutory Voting Rights for People with Disabilities. 14 Stan L & Pol'y Rev 353, 2003.
Wassom. The Help America Vote Act of 2002 and Selected Issues in Election Law Reform. 29 T Marshall L Rev 357, Spring 2004.

§ 15462. Authorization of appropriations

(a) In general. In addition to any other amounts authorized to be appropriated under this subtitle [42 USCS §§ 15401 et seq.], there are authorized to be appropriated $10,000,000 for each of the fiscal years 2003, 2004, 2005, and 2006, and for each subsequent fiscal year such sums as may be necessary, for the purpose of making payments under section 291(a) [42 USCS § 15461(a)]; except that none of the funds provided by this subsection shall be used to initiate or otherwise participate in any litigation related to election-related disability access, notwithstanding the general authorities that the protection and advocacy systems are otherwise afforded under subtitle C of title I of the Developmental Disabilities Assistance and Bill of Rights Act of 2000 (42 U.S.C. 15041 et seq.).

(b) Availability. Any amounts appropriated pursuant to the authority of this section shall remain available until expended.

(Oct. 29, 2002, P. L. 107-252, Title II, Subtitle D, Part 5, § 292, 116 Stat. 1703.)

CROSS REFERENCES

This section is referred to in 42 USCS § 15461.

RESEARCH GUIDE

Law Review Articles:
Waterstone. Constitutional and Statutory Voting Rights for People with Disabilities. 14 Stan L & Pol'y Rev 353, 2003.

Wassom. The Help America Vote Act of 2002 and Selected Issues in Election Law Reform. 29 T Marshall L Rev 357, Spring 2004.

National Student and Parent Mock Election

§ 15471. National Student and Parent Mock Election

(a) In general. The Election Assistance Commission is authorized to award grants to the National Student and Parent Mock Election, a national nonprofit, nonpartisan organization that works to promote voter participation in American elections to enable it to carry out voter education activities for students and their parents. Such activities may—

(1) include simulated national elections at least 5 days before the actual election that permit participation by students and parents from each of the 50 States in the United States, its territories, the District of Columbia, and United States schools overseas; and

(2) consist of—

(A) school forums and local cable call-in shows on the national issues to be voted upon in an "issues forum";

(B) speeches and debates before students and parents by local candidates or stand-ins for such candidates;

(C) quiz team competitions, mock press conferences, and speech writing competitions;

(D) weekly meetings to follow the course of the campaign; or

(E) school and neighborhood campaigns to increase voter turnout, including newsletters, posters, telephone chains, and transportation.

(b) Requirement. The National Student and Parent Mock Election shall present awards to outstanding student and parent mock election projects.
(Oct. 29, 2002, P. L. 107-252, Title II, Subtitle D, Part 6, § 295, 116 Stat. 1703.)

§ 15472. Authorization of appropriations

There are authorized to be appropriated to carry out the provisions of this subtitle $200,000 for fiscal year 2003 and such sums as may be necessary for each of the 6 succeeding fiscal years.
(Oct. 29, 2002, P. L. 107-252, Title II, Subtitle D, Part 6, § 296, 116 Stat. 1704.)

HISTORY; ANCILLARY LAWS AND DIRECTIVES

References in text:
The reference in this section to "this subtitle" should probably read "this part", i.e., Part 6 of Subtitle D of Title II of Act Oct. 29, 2002, P. L. 107-252 (42 USCS §§ 15471 et seq.).

UNIFORM AND NONDISCRIMINATORY ELECTION TECHNOLOGY AND ADMINISTRATION REQUIREMENTS

CROSS REFERENCES

This title (42 USCS §§ 15481 et seq.) is referred to in 42 USCS §§ 15301, 15342, 15401, 15403, 15404, 15512.

§ 15481. Voting systems standards

(a) Requirements. Each voting system used in an election for Federal office shall meet the following requirements:

    (1) In general. (A) Except as provided in subparagraph (B), the voting system (including any lever voting system, optical scanning voting system, or direct recording electronic system) shall—

        (i) permit the voter to verify (in a private and independent manner) the votes selected by the voter on the ballot before the ballot is cast and counted;

        (ii) provide the voter with the opportunity (in a private and independent manner) to change the ballot or correct any error before the ballot is cast and counted (including the opportunity to correct the error through the issuance of a replacement ballot if the voter was otherwise unable to change the ballot or correct any error); and

        (iii) if the voter selects votes for more than one candidate for a single office—

            (I) notify the voter that the voter has selected more than one candidate for a single office on the ballot;

            (II) notify the voter before the ballot is cast and counted of the effect of casting multiple votes for the office; and

            (III) provide the voter with the opportunity to correct the ballot before the ballot is cast and counted.

    (B) A State or jurisdiction that uses a paper ballot voting system, a punch card voting system, or a central count voting system (including mail-in absentee ballots and mail-in ballots), may meet the requirements of subparagraph (A)(iii) by—

        (i) establishing a voter education program specific to that voting system that notifies each voter of the effect of casting multiple votes for an office; and

        (ii) providing the voter with instructions on how to correct the ballot before it is cast and counted (including instructions on how to correct the error through the issuance of a replacement ballot if the voter was otherwise unable to change the ballot or correct any error).

    (C) The voting system shall ensure that any notification required under this paragraph preserves the privacy of the voter and the confidentiality of the ballot.

    (2) Audit capacity. (A) In general. The voting system shall produce a record with an audit capacity for such system.

    (B) Manual audit capacity. (i) The voting system shall produce a permanent paper record with a manual audit capacity for such system.

        (ii) The voting system shall provide the voter with an opportunity to change the ballot or correct any error before the permanent paper record is produced.

(iii) The paper record produced under subparagraph (A) shall be available as an official record for any recount conducted with respect to any election in which the system is used.

(3) Accessibility for individuals with disabilities. The voting system shall—

(A) be accessible for individuals with disabilities, including nonvisual accessibility for the blind and visually impaired, in a manner that provides the same opportunity for access and participation (including privacy and independence) as for other voters;

(B) satisfy the requirement of subparagraph (A) through the use of at least one direct recording electronic voting system or other voting system equipped for individuals with disabilities at each polling place; and

(C) if purchased with funds made available under title II [42 USCS §§ 15321 et seq.] on or after January 1, 2007, meet the voting system standards for disability access (as outlined in this paragraph).

(4) Alternative language accessibility. The voting system shall provide alternative language accessibility pursuant to the requirements of section 203 of the Voting Rights Act of 1965 (42 U.S.C. 1973aa-1a).

(5) Error rates. The error rate of the voting system in counting ballots (determined by taking into account only those errors which are attributable to the voting system and not attributable to an act of the voter) shall comply with the error rate standards established under section 3.2.1 of the voting systems standards issued by the Federal Election Commission which are in effect on the date of the enactment of this Act [enacted Oct. 29, 2002].

(6) Uniform definition of what constitutes a vote. Each State shall adopt uniform and nondiscriminatory standards that define what constitutes a vote and what will be counted as a vote for each category of voting system used in the State.

(b) Voting system defined. In this section, the term "voting system" means—

(1) the total combination of mechanical, electromechanical, or electronic equipment (including the software, firmware, and documentation required to program, control, and support the equipment) that is used—

(A) to define ballots;

(B) to cast and count votes;

(C) to report or display election results; and

(D) to maintain and produce any audit trail information; and

(2) the practices and associated documentation used—

(A) to identify system components and versions of such components;

(B) to test the system during its development and maintenance;

(C) to maintain records of system errors and defects;

(D) to determine specific system changes to be made to a system after the initial qualification of the system; and

(E) to make available any materials to the voter (such as notices, instructions, forms, or paper ballots).

(c) Construction. (1) In general. Nothing in this section shall be construed to prohibit a State or jurisdiction which used a particular type of voting system in the elections for Federal office held in November 2000 from using the same type of system after the effective date of this section, so long as the system meets or is modified to meet the requirements of this section.

(2) Protection of paper ballot voting systems. For purposes of subsection (a)(1)(A)(i), the term "verify" may not be defined in a manner that makes it impossible for a paper ballot voting system to meet the requirements of such subsection or to be modified to meet such requirements.

(d) Effective date. Each State and jurisdiction shall be required to comply with the requirements of this section on and after January 1, 2006.

(Oct. 29, 2002, P. L. 107-252, Title III, Subtitle A, § 301, 116 Stat. 1704.)

CROSS REFERENCES

This section is referred to in 42 USCS §§ 15302, 15401, 15404, 15501, 15511.

RESEARCH GUIDE

Am Jur:

25 Am Jur 2d, Elections § 5.

Annotations:

Electronic Voting Systems. 12 ALR6th 523.

Law Review Articles:

Tanner. Effective Monitoring of Polling Places. 61 Baylor L Rev 50, Winter, 2009.

Tokaji. The Paperless Chase: Electronic Voting and Democratic Values. 73 Fordham L Rev 1711, March 2005.

Tokaji. Early Returns on Election Reform: Discretion, Disenfranchisement, and the Help America Vote Act. 73 Geo Wash L Rev 1206, August 2005.

Waterstone. Civil Rights and the Administration of Elections—Toward Secret Ballots and Polling Place Access. 8 J Gender Race & Just 101, Spring 2004.

Ramirez; Organick. Taking Voting Rights Seriously: Race and the Integrity of Democracy in America. 27 N Ill U L Rev 427, Summer 2007.

Shambon; Abouchar. Trapped by Precincts? The Help America Vote Act's Provisional Ballots and the Problem of Precincts. 10 NYU J Legis & Pub Pol'y 133, 2006/2007.

Wang. Competing Values or False Choices: Coming to Consensus on the Election Reform Debate in Washington State and the Country. 29 Seattle Univ L R 353, Winter 2005.

Waterstone. Constitutional and Statutory Voting Rights for People with Disabilities. 14 Stan L & Pol'y Rev 353, 2003.

Wassom. The Help America Vote Act of 2002 and Selected Issues in Election Law Reform. 29 T Marshall L Rev 357, Spring 2004.

Magpantay. Two Steps Forward, One Step Back, and a Side Step: Asian Americans and the Federal Help America Vote Act. 10 UCLA Asian Pac Am LJ 31, 2005.

Saphire; Moke. Litigating Bush v. Gore in the States: Dual Voting Systems and the Fourteenth Amendment. 51 Vill L Rev 229, 2006.

Siegel. Congressional Power Over Presidential Elections: The Constitutionality of the Help America Vote Act under Article II, Section 1. 28 Vt L Rev 373, Winter 2004.

INTERPRETIVE NOTES AND DECISIONS

1. Generally
2. Individuals with disabilities

1. Generally

National Voting Rights Act, in 42 USCS §§ 1973gg-2, 1973gg-9(b), applied only to federal elections, as did Help America Vote Act, under 42 USCS §§ 15481, 15482(a); thus, plaintiff property owners' challenge against defendants, State of Texas, incorporating committee, and its chairman, to municipal incorporation election failed. Broyles v Texas (2009, SD Tex) 618 F Supp 2d 661, judgment entered, claim dismissed (2009, SD Tex) 2009 US Dist LEXIS 56942, costs/fees proceeding, request den (2009, SD Tex) 2009 US Dist LEXIS 64080, affd (2010, CA5 Tex) 381 Fed Appx 370.

2. Individuals with disabilities

Where disabled voters asserted claims under 42 USCS § 12133 and 29 USCS § 794, based on inac-

cessible voting machines, court of appeals found that 42 USCS § 15481(a)(3) and 28 CFR § 35.151(b) did not provide for private cause of action against state election officials, and their injunction was dissolved. Am. Ass'n of People with Disabilities v Harris (2010, CA11 Fla) 605 F3d 1124, 22 FLW Fed C 795, substituted op, adhered to, on reh (2011, CA11 Fla) 647 F3d 1093, 25 AD Cas 467, 23 FLW Fed C 159.

Disabled voters' claims that California Secretary of State would not be able to offer voters with disabilities accessible voting equipment under Help America Vote Act's (HAVA), 42 USCS § 15481, requirement were not ripe because no evidence was presented to establish that it was impossible, or even difficult, for manufacturers of direct recording electronic voting systems to comply with HAVA's effective date. Am. Ass'n of People with Disabilities v Shelley (2004, CD Cal) 324 F Supp 2d 1120, 12 ALR6th 885.

§ 15482. Provisional voting and voting information requirements

(a) Provisional voting requirements. If an individual declares that such individual is a registered voter in the jurisdiction in which the individual desires to vote and that the individual is eligible to vote in an election for Federal office, but the name of the individual does not appear on the official list of eligible voters for the polling place or an election official asserts that the individual is not eligible to vote, such individual shall be permitted to cast a provisional ballot as follows:

(1) An election official at the polling place shall notify the individual that the individual may cast a provisional ballot in that election.

(2) The individual shall be permitted to cast a provisional ballot at that polling place upon the execution of a written affirmation by the individual before an election official at the polling place stating that the individual is—

(A) a registered voter in the jurisdiction in which the individual desires to vote; and

(B) eligible to vote in that election.

(3) An election official at the polling place shall transmit the ballot cast by the individual or the voter information contained in the written affirmation executed by the individual under paragraph (2) to an appropriate State or local election official for prompt verification under paragraph (4).

(4) If the appropriate State or local election official to whom the ballot or voter information is transmitted under paragraph (3) determines that the individual is eligible under State law to vote, the individual's provisional ballot shall be counted as a vote in that election in accordance with State law.

(5)(A) At the time that an individual casts a provisional ballot, the appropriate State or local election official shall give the individual written information that states that any individual who casts a provisional ballot will be able to ascertain under the system established under subparagraph (B) whether the vote was counted, and, if the vote was not counted, the reason that the vote was not counted.

(B) The appropriate State or local election official shall establish a free access system (such as a toll-free telephone number or an Internet website) that any individual who casts a provisional ballot may access to discover whether the vote of that individual was counted, and, if the vote was not counted, the reason that the vote was not counted.

States described in section 4(b) of the National Voter Registration Act of 1993 (42 U.S.C. 1973gg-2(b)) may meet the requirements of this subsection using voter registration procedures established under applicable State law. The appropriate State or local official shall establish and maintain reasonable procedures necessary to protect the security, confidentiality, and integrity of personal information collected, stored, or otherwise used by the free access system established under paragraph (5)(B). Access to information about an individual provisional ballot shall be restricted to the individual who cast the ballot.

(b) **Voting information requirements.** (1) Public posting on Election Day. The appropriate State or local election official shall cause voting information to be publicly posted at each polling place on the day of each election for Federal office.

(2) Voting information defined. In this section, the term "voting information" means—

(A) a sample version of the ballot that will be used for that election;

(B) information regarding the date of the election and the hours during which polling places will be open;

(C) instructions on how to vote, including how to cast a vote and how to cast a provisional ballot;

(D) instructions for mail-in registrants and first-time voters under section 303(b) [42 USCS § 15483(b)];

(E) general information on voting rights under applicable Federal and State laws, including information on the right of an individual to cast a provisional ballot and instructions on how to contact the appropriate officials if these rights are alleged to have been violated; and

(F) general information on Federal and State laws regarding prohibitions on acts of fraud and misrepresentation.

(c) **Voters who vote after the polls close.** Any individual who votes in an election for Federal office as a result of a Federal or State court order or any other order extending the time established for closing the polls by a State law in effect 10 days before the date of that election may only vote in that election by casting a provisional ballot under subsection (a). Any such ballot cast under the preceding sentence shall be separated and held apart from other provisional ballots cast by those not affected by the order.

(d) **Effective date for provisional voting and voting information.** Each State

and jurisdiction shall be required to comply with the requirements of this section on and after January 1, 2004.
(Oct. 29, 2002, P. L. 107-252, Title III, Subtitle A, § 302, 116 Stat. 1706.)

CROSS REFERENCES

This section is referred to in 42 USCS §§ 15483, 15501, 15511.

RESEARCH GUIDE

Annotations:

Construction and Application of Provisional Balloting Provisions of the
Help America Vote Act, Pub. L. 107-252, Title III, § 302, 116 Stat. 1706
(codified at 42 U.S.C.A. §§ 15301 et seq. [42 USCS §§ 15301 et seq.]). 10
ALR Fed 2d 643.

Preemption of State Election Laws By Help America Vote Act. 47 ALR
Fed 2d 81.

Law Review Articles:

Tokaji. The Paperless Chase: Electronic Voting and Democratic Values. 73
Fordham L Rev 1711, March 2005.

Tokaji. Early Returns on Election Reform: Discretion, Disenfranchisement,
and the Help America Vote Act. 73 Geo Wash L Rev 1206, August 2005.

Overton. Voter Identification. 105 Mich L Rev 631, February 2007.

Ramirez; Organick. Taking Voting Rights Seriously: Race and the Integrity
of Democracy in America. 27 N Ill U L Rev 427, Summer 2007.

Shambon; Abouchar. Trapped by Precincts? The Help America Vote Act's
Provisional Ballots and the Problem of Precincts. 10 NYU J Legis & Pub
Pol'y 133, 2006/2007.

Wang. Competing Values or False Choices: Coming to Consensus on the
Election Reform Debate in Washington State and the Country. 29 Seattle
Univ L R 353, Winter 2005.

Wassom. The Help America Vote Act of 2002 and Selected Issues in Election Law Reform. 29 T Marshall L Rev 357, Spring 2004.

Magpantay. Two Steps Forward, One Step Back, and a Side Step: Asian
Americans and the Federal Help America Vote Act. 10 UCLA Asian Pac
Am LJ 31, 2005.

Siegel. Congressional Power Over Presidential Elections: The Constitutionality of the Help America Vote Act under Article II, Section 1. 28 Vt L Rev
373, Winter 2004.

SHEPARD'S® Citations Service. For further research of authorities
referenced here, use SHEPARD'S to be sure your case or statute is still
good law and to find additional authorities that support your position.
SHEPARD'S is available exclusively from LexisNexis®.

INTERPRETIVE NOTES AND DECISIONS

1. Generally
2. Construction
3. Relationship to state laws

4. Private right of action
5. Fees and costs
6. Miscellaneous

1. Generally

Right created by 42 USCS § 15482(a), part of federal Help America Vote Act, Pub. L. 107-252, Title III, § 302, 116 Stat. 1706 (codified at 42 USCS §§ 15301 et seq.), to cast provisional ballot in federal elections is enforceable under 42 USCS § 1983. Sandusky County Democratic Party v Blackwell (2004, CA6) 386 F3d 815, reported in full (2004, CA6 Ohio) 387 F3d 565, 10 ALR Fed 2d 869.

2. Construction

Federal Help America Vote Act, Pub. L. 107-252, Title III, § 302, 116 Stat. 1706 (codified at 42 USCS §§ 15301 et seq.), does not require that voter's provisional ballot be counted as valid ballot if it is cast anywhere in county in which voter resides, even if it is cast outside precinct in which voter resides. Sandusky County Democratic Party v Blackwell (2004, CA6) 386 F3d 815, reported in full (2004, CA6 Ohio) 387 F3d 565, 10 ALR Fed 2d 869.

3. Relationship to state laws

Ohio Secretary of State Directive 2004-33 violates federal Help America Vote Act, Pub. L. 107-252, Title III, § 302, 116 Stat. 1706 (codified at 42 USCS §§ 15301 et seq.), to extent that it fails to ensure that any individual affirming that he or she is registered voter in jurisdiction in which he or she desires to vote and eligible to vote in federal election is permitted to cast provisional ballot as required by 42 USCS § 15482(a). Sandusky County Democratic Party v Blackwell (2004, CA6) 386 F3d 815, reported in full (2004, CA6 Ohio) 387 F3d 565, 10 ALR Fed 2d 869.

Upon review, "provisional" ballots cast in precinct where voter does not reside and which would be invalid under Ohio Rev. Code Ann. § 3503.01, were not required by Help America Vote Act to be considered legal votes. Sandusky County Democratic Party v Blackwell (2004, CA6 Ohio) 387 F3d 565, 10 ALR Fed 2d 869.

Help American Vote Act of 2002 allowed states to choose if they would effectively waive voter registration requirement for provisional ballots, and Florida's decision in Fla. Stat. §§ 97.053(6), 97.041(1)(a)(5), (b)(3), to not do so did not conflict with 42 USCS §§ 15482(a), 15483(b)(2)(B); contrary to plaintiff minority voter organizations' arguments, Fla. Stat. § 97.053(6) was not preempted and preliminary injunction against defendant Florida Secretary of State was reversed. Fla. State Conf. of the NAACP v Browning (2008, CA11 Fla) 522 F3d 1153, 21 FLW Fed C 523, 47 ALR Fed 2d 591, injunction den (2008, ND Fla) 569 F Supp 2d 1237, 48 ALR6th 613.

4. Private right of action

Individual enforcement, under 42 USCS § 1983, of Help America Vote Act's (HAVA) provisional ballot right, 42 USCS § 15482(a), is not precluded by either explicit language of HAVA or by comprehensive enforcement scheme incompatible with individual enforcement. Sandusky County Democratic Party v Blackwell (2004, CA6 Ohio) 387 F3d 565, 10 ALR Fed 2d 869.

Language of 42 USCS § 15482, which was intended to benefit voters who were turned away from polls, is type of unmistakable rights-focused language that Supreme Court has found to establish private right of action in other contexts; in addition, statutory language clearly created obligation on local election officials to allow provisional voting and right could easily be enforced; moreover, there was no indication that enforcement mechanisms that were included in Help America Vote Act's, 42 USCS §§ 15301 et seq., were meant to be exclusive. Bay County Democratic Party v Land (2004, ED Mich) 347 F Supp 2d 404 (criticized in Fla. Democratic Party v Hood (2004, ND Fla) 342 F Supp 2d 1073, 17 FLW Fed D 1196).

5. Fees and costs

Enactment of Ohio Rev. Code Ann. § 3509.09 mooted case, but voters were still prevailing parties who were entitled to attorney fees because when court granted motion for permanent injunction this materially altered legal relationship among parties and case still presented live controversy regarding whether state violated 42 USCS § 15482(a), which guaranteed right of registered voters to cast provisional ballots in "federal" elections when they had previously requested absentee ballot. White v Blackwell (2006, ND Ohio) 418 F Supp 2d 988.

6. Miscellaneous

Preliminary injunction was granted in part, so voters who affirmed that they were registered to vote had right to cast provisional ballot at wrong polling location; however, vote would be counted only if it had been cast in accord with State law. Fla. Democratic Party v Hood (2004, ND Fla) 342 F Supp 2d 1073, 17 FLW Fed D 1196.

Although state election officials may enforce precinct-based voting system, pursuant to 42 USCS § 15482, they may not do so in manner that abridges right of voter to have counted votes for federal offices on provisional ballot that was cast in voter's proper jurisdiction once voter eligibility was verified; directives from state director of elections prohibiting tabulation of all out-of-precinct provisional ballots, if enforced, would have abridged that right, which was enforceable under 42 USCS § 1983, and, therefore, plaintiffs established likelihood of success on merits of their claim. Bay County Democratic Party v Land (2004, ED Mich) 347 F Supp 2d 404 (criticized in Fla. Democratic Party v Hood (2004, ND Fla) 342 F Supp 2d 1073, 17 FLW Fed D 1196).

National Voting Rights Act, in 42 USCS §§ 1973gg-2, 1973gg-9(b), applied only to federal elections, as did Help America Vote Act, under 42

USCS §§ 15481, 15482(a); thus, plaintiff property owners' challenge against defendants, State of Texas, incorporating committee, and its chairman, to municipal incorporation election failed. Broyles v Texas (2009, SD Tex) 618 F Supp 2d 661, judgment entered, claim dismissed (2009, SD Tex) 2009 US Dist LEXIS 56942, costs/fees proceeding, request den (2009, SD Tex) 2009 US Dist LEXIS 64080, affd (2010, CA5 Tex) 381 Fed Appx 370.

Help America Vote Act of 2002 (HAVA), 42 USCS §§ 15301 et seq., did not warrant vacating consent decree that prohibited Republican National Committee from engaging in pre-election ballot security initiatives that targeted minority voters because 42 USCS § 15483(a) imposed several measures that decreased danger of voter fraud and provisional ballot mechanism required by 42 USCS § 15482(a) was not reliable means of assuring that ballots cast by voters whose eligibility was wrongly challenged were counted. Democratic Nat'l Comm. v Republican Nat'l Comm. (2009, DC NJ) 671 F Supp 2d 575, affd (2012, CA3 NJ) 2012 US App LEXIS 4859.

§ 15483. Computerized statewide voter registration list requirements and requirements for voters who register by mail

(a) **Computerized statewide voter registration list requirements.** (1) Implementation. (A) In general. Except as provided in subparagraph (B), each State, acting through the chief State election official, shall implement, in a uniform and nondiscriminatory manner, a single, uniform, official, centralized, interactive computerized statewide voter registration list defined, maintained, and administered at the State level that contains the name and registration information of every legally registered voter in the State and assigns a unique identifier to each legally registered voter in the State (in this subsection referred to as the "computerized list"), and includes the following:

(i) The computerized list shall serve as the single system for storing and managing the official list of registered voters throughout the State.

(ii) The computerized list contains the name and registration information of every legally registered voter in the State.

(iii) Under the computerized list, a unique identifier is assigned to each legally registered voter in the State.

(iv) The computerized list shall be coordinated with other agency databases within the State.

(v) Any election official in the State, including any local election official, may obtain immediate electronic access to the information contained in the computerized list.

(vi) All voter registration information obtained by any local election official in the State shall be electronically entered into the computerized list on an expedited basis at the time the information is provided to the local official.

(vii) The chief State election official shall provide such support as may be required so that local election officials are able to enter information as described in clause (vi).

(viii) The computerized list shall serve as the official voter registration list for the conduct of all elections for Federal office in the State.

(B) Exception. The requirement under subparagraph (A) shall not apply to a State in which, under a State law in effect continuously on and after the date of the enactment of this Act [enacted Oct. 29, 2002], there is no voter registration requirement for individuals in the State with respect to elections for Federal office.

(2) Computerized list maintenance. (A) In general. The appropriate State or local election official shall perform list maintenance with respect to the computerized list on a regular basis as follows:

(i) If an individual is to be removed from the computerized list, such individual shall be removed in accordance with the provisions of the National Voter Registration Act of 1993 (42 U.S.C. 1973gg et seq.), including subsections (a)(4), (c)(2), (d), and (e) of section 8 of such Act (42 U.S.C. 1973gg-6).

(ii) For purposes of removing names of ineligible voters from the official list of eligible voters—

(I) under section 8(a)(3)(B) of such Act (42 U.S.C. 1973gg-6(a)(3)(B)), the State shall coordinate the computerized list with State agency records on felony status; and

(II) by reason of the death of the registrant under section 8(a)(4)(A) of such Act (42 U.S.C. 1973gg-6(a)(4)(A)), the State shall coordinate the computerized list with State agency records on death.

(iii) Notwithstanding the preceding provisions of this subparagraph, if a State is described in section 4(b) of the National Voter Registration Act of 1993 (42 U.S.C. 1973gg-2(b)), that State shall remove the names of ineligible voters from the computerized list in accordance with State law.

(B) Conduct. The list maintenance performed under subparagraph (A) shall be conducted in a manner that ensures that—

(i) the name of each registered voter appears in the computerized list;

(ii) only voters who are not registered or who are not eligible to vote are removed from the computerized list; and

(iii) duplicate names are eliminated from the computerized list.

(3) Technological security of computerized list. The appropriate State or local official shall provide adequate technological security measures to prevent the unauthorized access to the computerized list established under this section.

(4) Minimum standard for accuracy of State voter registration records. The State election system shall include provisions to ensure that voter registration records in the State are accurate and are updated regularly, including the following:

(A) A system of file maintenance that makes a reasonable effort to remove registrants who are ineligible to vote from the official list of eligible voters. Under such system, consistent with the National Voter Registration Act of 1993 (42 U.S.C. 1973gg et seq.), registrants who have not responded to a notice and who have not voted in 2 consecutive general elections for Federal office shall be removed from the official list of eligible voters, except that no registrant may be removed solely by reason of a failure to vote.

(B) Safeguards to ensure that eligible voters are not removed in error from the official list of eligible voters.

(5) Verification of voter registration information. (A) Requiring provision of

certain information by applicants. (i) In general. Except as provided in clause (ii), notwithstanding any other provision of law, an application for voter registration for an election for Federal office may not be accepted or processed by a State unless the application includes—

(I) in the case of an applicant who has been issued a current and valid driver's license, the applicant's driver's license number; or

(II) in the case of any other applicant (other than an applicant to whom clause (ii) applies), the last 4 digits of the applicant's social security number.

(ii) Special rule for applicants without driver's license or social security number. If an applicant for voter registration for an election for Federal office has not been issued a current and valid driver's license or a social security number, the State shall assign the applicant a number which will serve to identify the applicant for voter registration purposes. To the extent that the State has a computerized list in effect under this subsection and the list assigns unique identifying numbers to registrants, the number assigned under this clause shall be the unique identifying number assigned under the list.

(iii) Determination of validity of numbers provided. The State shall determine whether the information provided by an individual is sufficient to meet the requirements of this subparagraph, in accordance with State law.

(B) Requirements for State officials. (i) Sharing information in databases. The chief State election official and the official responsible for the State motor vehicle authority of a State shall enter into an agreement to match information in the database of the statewide voter registration system with information in the database of the motor vehicle authority to the extent required to enable each such official to verify the accuracy of the information provided on applications for voter registration.

(ii) Agreements with Commissioner of Social Security. The official responsible for the State motor vehicle authority shall enter into an agreement with the Commissioner of Social Security under section 205(r)(8) of the Social Security Act [42 USCS § 405(r)(8)] (as added by subparagraph (C)).

(C) [Omitted]

(D) Special rule for certain States. In the case of a State which is permitted to use social security numbers, and provides for the use of social security numbers, on applications for voter registration, in accordance with section 7 of the Privacy Act of 1974 (5 U.S.C. 552a note), the provisions of this paragraph shall be optional.

(b) Requirements for voters who register by mail. (1) In general. Notwithstanding section 6(c) of the National Voter Registration Act of 1993 (42 U.S.C. 1973gg-4(c)) and subject to paragraph (3), a State shall, in a uniform and nondiscriminatory manner, require an individual to meet the requirements of paragraph (2) if—

(A) the individual registered to vote in a jurisdiction by mail; and

(B)(i) the individual has not previously voted in an election for Federal office in the State; or

(ii) the individual has not previously voted in such an election in the jurisdiction and the jurisdiction is located in a State that does not have a computerized list that complies with the requirements of subsection (a).

(2) Requirements. (A) In general. An individual meets the requirements of this paragraph if the individual—

(i) in the case of an individual who votes in person—

(I) presents to the appropriate State or local election official a current and valid photo identification; or

(II) presents to the appropriate State or local election official a copy of a current utility bill, bank statement, government check, paycheck, or other government document that shows the name and address of the voter; or

(ii) in the case of an individual who votes by mail, submits with the ballot—

(I) a copy of a current and valid photo identification; or

(II) a copy of a current utility bill, bank statement, government check, paycheck, or other government document that shows the name and address of the voter.

(B) Fail-safe voting. (i) In person. An individual who desires to vote in person, but who does not meet the requirements of subparagraph (A)(i), may cast a provisional ballot under section 302(a) [42 USCS § 15482(a)].

(ii) By mail. An individual who desires to vote by mail but who does not meet the requirements of subparagraph (A)(ii) may cast such a ballot by mail and the ballot shall be counted as a provisional ballot in accordance with section 302(a) [42 USCS § 15482(a)].

(3) Inapplicability. Paragraph (1) shall not apply in the case of a person—

(A) who registers to vote by mail under section 6 of the National Voter Registration Act of 1993 (42 U.S.C. 1973gg-4) and submits as part of such registration either—

(i) a copy of a current and valid photo identification; or

(ii) a copy of a current utility bill, bank statement, government check, paycheck, or government document that shows the name and address of the voter;

(B)(i) who registers to vote by mail under section 6 of the National Voter Registration Act of 1993 (42 U.S.C. 1973gg-4) and submits with such registration either—

(I) a driver's license number; or

(II) at least the last 4 digits of the individual's social security number; and

(ii) with respect to whom a State or local election official matches the information submitted under clause (i) with an existing State identification record bearing the same number, name and date of birth as provided in such registration; or

(C) who is—

(i) entitled to vote by absentee ballot under the Uniformed and Overseas Citizens Absentee Voting Act (42 U.S.C. 1973ff-1 et seq.);

(ii) provided the right to vote otherwise than in person under section 3(b)(2)(B)(ii) of the Voting Accessibility for the Elderly and Handicapped Act (42 U.S.C. 1973ee-1(b)(2)(B)(ii)); or

(iii) entitled to vote otherwise than in person under any other Federal law.

(4) Contents of mail-in registration form. (A) In general. The mail voter registration form developed under section 6 of the National Voter Registration Act of 1993 (42 U.S.C. 1973gg-4) shall include the following:

(i) The question "Are you a citizen of the United States of America?" and boxes for the applicant to check to indicate whether the applicant is or is not a citizen of the United States.

(ii) The question "Will you be 18 years of age on or before election day?" and boxes for the applicant to check to indicate whether or not the applicant will be 18 years of age or older on election day.

(iii) The statement "If you checked 'no' in response to either of these questions, do not complete this form.".

(iv) A statement informing the individual that if the form is submitted by mail and the individual is registering for the first time, the appropriate information required under this section must be submitted with the mail-in registration form in order to avoid the additional identification requirements upon voting for the first time.

(B) Incomplete forms. If an applicant for voter registration fails to answer the question included on the mail voter registration form pursuant to subparagraph (A)(i), the registrar shall notify the applicant of the failure and provide the applicant with an opportunity to complete the form in a timely manner to allow for the completion of the registration form prior to the next election for Federal office (subject to State law).

(5) Construction. Nothing in this subsection shall be construed to require a State that was not required to comply with a provision of the National Voter Registration Act of 1993 (42 U.S.C. 1973gg et seq.) before the date of the enactment of this Act [enacted Oct. 29, 2002] to comply with such a provision after such date.

(c) **Permitted use of last 4 digits of social security numbers.** The last 4 digits of a social security number described in subsections (a)(5)(A)(i)(II) and (b)(3)(B)(i)(II) shall not be considered to be a social security number for purposes of section 7 of the Privacy Act of 1974 (5 U.S.C. 552a note).

(d) **Effective date.** (1) Computerized statewide voter registration list requirements. (A) In general. Except as provided in subparagraph (B), each State and jurisdiction shall be required to comply with the requirements of subsection (a) on and after January 1, 2004.

(B) Waiver. If a State or jurisdiction certifies to the Commission not later than January 1, 2004, that the State or jurisdiction will not meet the deadline described in subparagraph (A) for good cause and includes in the certification the reasons for the failure to meet such deadline, subparagraph (A) shall apply to the State or jurisdiction as if the reference in such subparagraph to "January 1, 2004" were a reference to "January 1, 2006".

(2) Requirement for voters who register by mail. (A) In general. Each State and jurisdiction shall be required to comply with the requirements of subsection (b) on and after January 1, 2004, and shall be prepared to receive registration materials submitted by individuals described in subparagraph (B) on and after the date described in such subparagraph.

(B) Applicability with respect to individuals. The provisions of subsection (b) shall apply to any individual who registers to vote on or after January 1, 2003.

(Oct. 29, 2002, P. L. 107-252, Title III, Subtitle A, § 303, 116 Stat. 1708.)

HISTORY; ANCILLARY LAWS AND DIRECTIVES

Explanatory notes:
Subsec. (a)(5)(C), which has been omitted, added 42 USCS § 405(r)(8).

CROSS REFERENCES

This section is referred to in 42 USCS §§ 15361, 15384, 15482, 15501, 15511, 15545.

RESEARCH GUIDE

Annotations:
Construction and Application of Provisional Balloting Provisions of the Help America Vote Act, Pub. L. 107-252, Title III, § 302, 116 Stat. 1706 (codified at 42 U.S.C.A. §§ 15301 et seq. [42 USCS §§ 15301 et seq.]). 10 ALR Fed 2d 643.
Preemption of State Election Laws By Help America Vote Act. 47 ALR Fed 2d 81.

Law Review Articles:
Tokaji. The Paperless Chase: Electronic Voting and Democratic Values. 73 Fordham L Rev 1711, March 2005.
Tokaji. Early Returns on Election Reform: Discretion, Disenfranchisement, and the Help America Vote Act. 73 Geo Wash L Rev 1206, August 2005.
Benson. Voter Fraud Or Voter Defrauded? Highlighting An Inconsistent Consideration of Election Fraud. 44 Harv CR-CL L Rev 1, Winter, 2009.
Overton. Voter Identification. 105 Mich L Rev 631, February 2007.
Ramirez; Organick. Taking Voting Rights Seriously: Race and the Integrity of Democracy in America. 27 N Ill U L Rev 427, Summer 2007.
Shambon; Abouchar. Trapped by Precincts? The Help America Vote Act's Provisional Ballots and the Problem of Precincts. 10 NYU J Legis & Pub Pol'y 133, 2006/2007.
Wang. Competing Values or False Choices: Coming to Consensus on the Election Reform Debate in Washington State and the Country. 29 Seattle Univ L R 353, Winter 2005.
Wassom. The Help America Vote Act of 2002 and Selected Issues in Election Law Reform. 29 T Marshall L Rev 357, Spring 2004.
Magpantay. Two Steps Forward, One Step Back, and a Side Step: Asian

Americans and the Federal Help America Vote Act. 10 UCLA Asian Pac Am LJ 31, 2005.

Saphire; Moke. Litigating Bush v. Gore in the States: Dual Voting Systems and the Fourteenth Amendment. 51 Vill L Rev 229, 2006.

Siegel. Congressional Power Over Presidential Elections: The Constitutionality of the Help America Vote Act under Article II, Section 1. 28 Vt L Rev 373, Winter 2004.

INTERPRETIVE NOTES AND DECISIONS

1. Removal of ineligible registrants
2. Verification
3. Registration by mail
4. Miscellaneous

1. Removal of ineligible registrants

Help America Vote Act of 2002 (HAVA), 42 USCS §§ 15301 et seq., did not warrant vacating consent decree that prohibited Republican National Committee from engaging in pre-election ballot security initiatives that targeted minority voters because 42 USCS § 15483(a) imposed several measures that decreased danger of voter fraud and provisional ballot mechanism required by 42 USCS § 15482(a) was not reliable means of assuring that ballots cast by voters whose eligibility was wrongly challenged were counted. Democratic Nat'l Comm. v Republican Nat'l Comm. (2009, DC NJ) 671 F Supp 2d 575, affd (2012, CA3 NJ) 2012 US App LEXIS 4859.

Colorado's 20-day Rule, codified in Colo. Rev. Stat. § 1-2-509(3), conformed with Congress's mandates under Help America Vote Act of 2002, 42 USCS §§ 15301–15545, to facilitate and ensure that all eligible registration applicants were added to Colorado's statewide voter registration database on expedited basis and that database be monitored and maintained so that ineligible or "not registered" voters were removed from it. Common Cause of Colo. v Buescher (2010, DC Colo) 750 F Supp 2d 1259.

2. Verification

Contrary to plaintiff minority voter organizations' arguments, Fla. Stat. § 97.053(6) did not conflict with 42 USCS § 15483(a) because even if they were right that § 15483(a)(5) did not impose matching as requirement of voter registration, it also did not seem to prohibit states from implementing it, as § 15483(a)(5)(A)(iii) provided that state was to determine whether information provided by individual was sufficient to meet requirements of § 15483(a) in accordance with state law and injunction against defendant Florida Secretary of State was reversed. Fla. State Conf. of the NAACP v Browning (2008, CA11 Fla) 522 F3d 1153, 21 FLW Fed C 523, 47 ALR Fed 2d 591, injunction den (2008, ND Fla) 569 F Supp 2d 1237, 48 ALR6th 613.

On reconsideration, based on consideration of

state constitution, National Voter Registration Act of 1993, 42 USCS § 1973gg et seq., and Help America Vote Act of 2002, 42 USCS §§ 15301 et seq., court found that procedure authorized by Md. Code Ann., Elec. Law § 3-504(f), which allowed purging of voters from active roll if they failed to confirm that they had not moved, violated Md. Const. art. I, § 2. Md. Green Party v Md. Bd. of Elections (2003) 377 Md 127, 832 A2d 214.

In action under 42 USCS § 1983, political party was entitled to temporary restraining order under Fed. R. Civ. P. 65(b) mandating that Ohio Secretary of State (SOS) comply with matching and verification requirements under Help America Vote Act (HAVA), 42 USCS § 15483(a)(5)(B)(i), because it demonstrated likelihood of success on its claim that SOS was not in compliance with HAVA's requirement to match and verify voter registration information prior to counting absentee ballots of new registrants; although SOS entered into agreement to match information with Ohio Bureau of Motor Vehicles, she did not establish feasible method for county boards of elections to access and resolve any mismatches. Ohio Republican Party v Brunner (2008, SD Ohio) 582 F Supp 2d 957, motion gr, in part, injunction gr (2008, SD Ohio) 71 FR Serv 3d 1115 and vacated, stay gr (2008) 555 US 5, 129 S Ct 5, 172 L Ed 2d 4, 21 FLW Fed S 545.

Help America Vote Act, 42 USCS § 15483(a)(5)(B)(i), requires matching for purpose of verifying identity and eligibility of voter before counting that person's vote. Ohio Republican Party v Brunner (2008, SD Ohio) 582 F Supp 2d 957, motion gr, in part, injunction gr (2008, SD Ohio) 71 FR Serv 3d 1115 and vacated, stay gr (2008) 555 US 5, 129 S Ct 5, 172 L Ed 2d 4, 21 FLW Fed S 545.

3. Registration by mail

Help American Vote Act of 2002 allowed states to choose if they would effectively waive voter registration requirement for provisional ballots, and Florida's decision in Fla. Stat. §§ 97.053(6), 97.041(1)(a)(5), (b)(3), to not do so did not conflict with 42 USCS §§ 15482(a), 15483(b)(2)(B); contrary to plaintiff minority voter organizations' arguments, Fla. Stat. § 97.053(6) was not preempted and preliminary injunction against defendant Florida Secretary of State was reversed. Fla. State Conf. of the NAACP v Browning (2008, CA11 Fla) 522 F3d

1153, 21 FLW Fed C 523, 47 ALR Fed 2d 591, injunction den (2008, ND Fla) 569 F Supp 2d 1237, 48 ALR6th 613.

If first-time voter who registered by mail cannot comply with requirement of § 303(b)(2)(A)(i) (42 USCS § 15483(b)(2)(A)(i)) of Help America Vote Act, 42 USCS § 15301 et seq., at polls on election day, that person may cast provisional ballot, which will be tabulated if person can furnish requisite identification within six days thereafter. Bay County Democratic Party v Land (2004, ED Mich) 347 F Supp 2d 404 (criticized in Fla. Democratic Party v Hood (2004, ND Fla) 342 F Supp 2d 1073, 17 FLW Fed D 1196).

Materiality provision of Voting Rights Act, 42 USCS § 1971(a)(2)(B), was not violated because checking check-box was not duplicative of signing oath on voter application because check boxes contained specific affirmations of specific qualifications and oath contained general affirmation of eligibility;

further, check-boxes were not immaterial, as supported by 42 USCS § 15483(b)(4)(A), part of Help America Vote Act. Diaz v Cobb (2006, SD Fla) 435 F Supp 2d 1206, 19 FLW Fed D 734.

4. Miscellaneous

Political party had standing to challenge Ohio Secretary of State's compliance with matching and verification process under Help America Vote Act (HAVA), 42 USCS § 15483(a)(5)(B)(i); HAVA created federal right enforceable against state officials under 42 USCS § 1983, and 42 USCS §§ 15511, 15512 did not indicate congressional intention to shut door to federal judicial review of state actions. Ohio Republican Party v Brunner (2008, SD Ohio) 582 F Supp 2d 957, motion gr, in part, injunction gr (2008, SD Ohio) 71 FR Serv 3d 1115 and vacated, stay gr (2008) 555 US 5, 129 S Ct 5, 172 L Ed 2d 4, 21 FLW Fed S 545.

§ 15484. Minimum requirements

The requirements established by this title [42 USCS §§ 15481 et seq.] are minimum requirements and nothing in this title [42 USCS §§ 15481 et seq.] shall be construed to prevent a State from establishing election technology and administration requirements that are more strict than the requirements established under this title [42 USCS §§ 15481 et seq.] so long as such State requirements are not inconsistent with the Federal requirements under this title [42 USCS §§ 15481 et seq.] or any law described in section 906 [42 USCS § 15545].

(Oct. 29, 2002, P. L. 107-252, Title III, Subtitle A, § 304, 116 Stat. 1714.)

RESEARCH GUIDE

Law Review Articles:

Magpantay. Two Steps Forward, One Step Back, and a Side Step: Asian Americans and the Federal Help America Vote Act. 10 UCLA Asian Pac Am LJ 31, 2005.

INTERPRETIVE NOTES AND DECISIONS

By adding entirely new voter-intent language to N.M. Stat. Ann. § 1-9-4.2(B)(4), Legislature intended to delegate discretion to Secretary of State to implement regulations for determining what constituted "voter intent," and to diminish chances for voter disenfranchisement by broadening universe of valid ballot markings; this was consistent with U.S. Supreme Court's equal protection analysis in Bush

v. Gore, as well as 42 USCS §§ 15484 and 15485 of Help America Vote Act of 2005, 42 USCS §§ 15301–15545, and as such, voter organization's emergency petition for writ of mandamus was granted. State ex rel. League of Women Voters v Herrera (2009) 2009 NMSC 3, 145 NM 563, 203 P3d 94.

§ 15485. Methods of implementation left to discretion of State

The specific choices on the methods of complying with the requirements of this title [42 USCS §§ 15481 et seq.] shall be left to the discretion of the State.

(Oct. 29, 2002, P. L. 107-252, Title III, Subtitle A, § 305, 116 Stat. 1714.)

RESEARCH GUIDE

Law Review Articles:

Wang. Competing Values or False Choices: Coming to Consensus on the Election Reform Debate in Washington State and the Country. 29 Seattle Univ L R 353, Winter 2005.

INTERPRETIVE NOTES AND DECISIONS

By adding entirely new voter-intent language to N.M. Stat. Ann. § 1-9-4.2(B)(4), Legislature intended to delegate discretion to Secretary of State to implement regulations for determining what constituted "voter intent," and to diminish chances for voter disenfranchisement by broadening universe of valid ballot markings; this was consistent with U.S. Supreme Court's equal protection analysis in Bush v. Gore, as well as 42 USCS §§ 15484 and 15485 of Help America Vote Act of 2005, 42 USCS §§ 15301–15545, and as such, voter organization's emergency petition for writ of mandamus was granted. State ex rel. League of Women Voters v Herrera (2009) 2009 NMSC 3, 145 NM 563, 203 P3d 94.

VOLUNTARY GUIDANCE

CROSS REFERENCES

This subtitle (42 USCS §§ 15501 et seq.) is referred to in 42 USCS §§ 15322, 15327.

§ 15501.   Adoption of voluntary guidance by Commission

(a) In general. To assist States in meeting the requirements of subtitle A [42 USCS §§ 15481 et seq.], the Commission shall adopt voluntary guidance consistent with such requirements in accordance with the procedures described in section 312 [42 USCS § 15502].

(b) Deadlines. The Commission shall adopt the recommendations under this section not later than—

(1) in the case of the recommendations with respect to section 301 [42 USCS § 15481], January 1, 2004;

(2) in the case of the recommendations with respect to section 302 [42 USCS § 15482], October 1, 2003; and

(3) in the case of the recommendations with respect to section 303 [42 USCS § 15483], October 1, 2003.

(c) Quadrennial update. The Commission shall review and update recommendations adopted with respect to section 301 [42 USCS § 15481] no less frequently than once every 4 years.

(Oct. 29, 2002, P. L. 107-252, Title III, Subtitle B, § 311, 116 Stat. 1715.)

RESEARCH GUIDE

Law Review Articles:

Tokaji. Early Returns on Election Reform: Discretion, Disenfranchisement, and the Help America Vote Act. 73 Geo Wash L Rev 1206, August 2005.

§ 15502.   Process for adoption

The adoption of the voluntary guidance under this subtitle [42 USCS §§ 15501 et seq.] shall be carried out by the Commission in a manner that provides for each of the following:

(1) Publication of notice of the proposed recommendations in the Federal Register.

(2) An opportunity for public comment on the proposed recommendations.

(3) An opportunity for a public hearing on the record.

(4) Publication of the final recommendations in the Federal Register.

(Oct. 29, 2002, P. L. 107-252, Title III, Subtitle B, § 312, 116 Stat. 1715.)

CROSS REFERENCES

This section is referred to in 42 USCS § 15501.

ENFORCEMENT

§ 15511. Actions by the Attorney General for declaratory and injunctive relief

The Attorney General may bring a civil action against any State or jurisdiction in an appropriate United States District Court for such declaratory and injunctive relief (including a temporary restraining order, a permanent or temporary injunction, or other order) as may be necessary to carry out the uniform and nondiscriminatory election technology and administration requirements under sections 301, 302, and 303 [42 USCS §§ 15481, 15482, 15483].

(Oct. 29, 2002, Title IV, § 401, 116 Stat. 1715.)

RESEARCH GUIDE

Am Jur:

25 Am Jur 2d, Elections § 5.

26 Am Jur 2d, Elections § 449.

Law Review Articles:

Waterstone. Civil Rights and the Administration of Elections—Toward Secret Ballots and Polling Place Access. 8 J Gender Race & Just 101, Spring 2004.

Ramirez; Organick. Taking Voting Rights Seriously: Race and the Integrity of Democracy in America. 27 N Ill U L Rev 427, Summer 2007.

Waterstone. Constitutional and Statutory Voting Rights for People with Disabilities. 14 Stan L & Pol'y Rev 353, 2003.

Magpantay. Two Steps Forward, One Step Back, and a Side Step: Asian Americans and the Federal Help America Vote Act. 10 UCLA Asian Pac Am LJ 31, 2005.

Saphire; Moke. Litigating Bush v. Gore in the States: Dual Voting Systems and the Fourteenth Amendment. 51 Vill L Rev 229, 2006.

Siegel. Congressional Power Over Presidential Elections: The Constitutionality of the Help America Vote Act under Article II, Section 1. 28 Vt L Rev 373, Winter 2004.

INTERPRETIVE NOTES AND DECISIONS

Political party had standing to challenge Ohio Secretary of State's compliance with matching and verification process under Help America Vote Act (HAVA), 42 USCS § 15483(a)(5)(B)(i); HAVA created federal right enforceable against state officials under 42 USCS § 1983, and 42 USCS §§ 15511,

15512 did not indicate congressional intention to shut door to federal judicial review of state actions. Ohio Republican Party v Brunner (2008, SD Ohio) 582 F Supp 2d 957, motion gr, in part, injunction gr

(2008, SD Ohio) 71 FR Serv 3d 1115 and vacated, stay gr (2008) 555 US 5, 129 S Ct 5, 172 L Ed 2d 4, 21 FLW Fed S 545.

§ 15512. Establishment of State-based administrative complaint procedures to remedy grievances

(a) **Establishment of State-based administrative complaint procedures to remedy grievances.** (1) Establishment of procedures as condition of receiving funds. If a State receives any payment under a program under this Act, the State shall be required to establish and maintain State-based administrative complaint procedures which meet the requirements of paragraph (2).

(2) Requirements for procedures. The requirements of this paragraph are as follows:

(A) The procedures shall be uniform and nondiscriminatory.

(B) Under the procedures, any person who believes that there is a violation of any provision of title III [42 USCS §§ 15481 et seq.] (including a violation which has occurred, is occurring, or is about to occur) may file a complaint.

(C) Any complaint filed under the procedures shall be in writing and notarized, and signed and sworn by the person filing the complaint.

(D) The State may consolidate complaints filed under subparagraph (B).

(E) At the request of the complainant, there shall be a hearing on the record.

(F) If, under the procedures, the State determines that there is a violation of any provision of title III [42 USCS §§ 15481 et seq.], the State shall provide the appropriate remedy.

(G) If, under the procedures, the State determines that there is no violation, the State shall dismiss the complaint and publish the results of the procedures.

(H) The State shall make a final determination with respect to a complaint prior to the expiration of the 90-day period which begins on the date the complaint is filed, unless the complainant consents to a longer period for making such a determination.

(I) If the State fails to meet the deadline applicable under subparagraph (H), the complaint shall be resolved within 60 days under alternative dispute resolution procedures established for purposes of this section. The record and other materials from any proceedings conducted under the complaint procedures established under this section shall be made available for use under the alternative dispute resolution procedures.

(b) **Requiring Attorney General approval of compliance plan for States not receiving funds.** (1) In general. Not later than January 1, 2004, each nonparticipating State shall elect—

(A) to certify to the Commission that the State meets the requirements of subsection (a) in the same manner as a State receiving a payment under this Act; or

(B) to submit a compliance plan to the Attorney General which provides detailed information on the steps the State will take to ensure that it meets the requirements of title III [42 USCS §§ 15481 et seq.].

(2) States without approved plan deemed out of compliance. A nonparticipating State (other than a State which makes the election described in paragraph (1)(A)) shall be deemed to not meet the requirements of title III [42 USCS §§ 15481 et seq.] if the Attorney General has not approved a compliance plan submitted by the State under this subsection.

(3) Nonparticipating State defined. In this section, a "nonparticipating State" is a State which, during 2003, does not notify any office which is responsible for making payments to States under any program under this Act of its intent to participate in, and receive funds under, the program.

(Oct. 29, 2002, Title IV, § 402, 116 Stat. 1715.)

HISTORY; ANCILLARY LAWS AND DIRECTIVES

References in text:
"This Act", referred to in this section, is Act Oct. 29, 2002, P. L. 107-252, popularly known as the Help America Vote Act of 2002, which appears generally as 42 USCS §§ 15301 et seq. For full classification of such Act, consult USCS Tables volumes.

CROSS REFERENCES

This section is referred to in 42 USCS §§ 15403, 15404.

RESEARCH GUIDE

Law Review Articles:
Waterstone. Civil Rights and the Administration of Elections—Toward Secret Ballots and Polling Place Access. 8 J Gender Race & Just 101, Spring 2004.

Ramirez; Organick. Taking Voting Rights Seriously: Race and the Integrity of Democracy in America. 27 N Ill U L Rev 427, Summer 2007.

Waterstone. Constitutional and Statutory Voting Rights for People with Disabilities. 14 Stan L & Pol'y Rev 353, 2003.

Magpantay. Two Steps Forward, One Step Back, and a Side Step: Asian Americans and the Federal Help America Vote Act. 10 UCLA Asian Pac Am LJ 31, 2005.

Saphire; Moke. Litigating Bush v. Gore in the States: Dual Voting Systems and the Fourteenth Amendment. 51 Vill L Rev 229, 2006.

INTERPRETIVE NOTES AND DECISIONS

Political party had standing to challenge Ohio Secretary of State's compliance with matching and verification process under Help America Vote Act (HAVA), 42 USCS § 15483(a)(5)(B)(i); HAVA created federal right enforceable against state officials under 42 USCS § 1983, and 42 USCS §§ 15511, 15512 did not indicate congressional intention to shut door to federal judicial review of state actions. Ohio Republican Party v Brunner (2008, SD Ohio) 582 F Supp 2d 957, motion gr, in part, injunction gr (2008, SD Ohio) 71 FR Serv 3d 1115 and vacated, stay gr (2008) 555 US 5, 129 S Ct 5, 172 L Ed 2d 4, 21 FLW Fed S 545.

HELP AMERICA VOTE COLLEGE PROGRAM

CROSS REFERENCES

This title (42 USCS §§ 15521 et seq.) is referred to in 42 USCS § 15322.

§ 15521. Establishment of Program

(a) In general. Not later than 1 year after the appointment of its members, the Election Assistance Commission shall develop a program to be known as the "Help America Vote College Program" (hereafter in this title [42 USCS §§ 15521 et seq.] referred to as the "Program").

(b) Purposes of Program. The purpose of the Program shall be—

(1) to encourage students enrolled at institutions of higher education (including community colleges) to assist State and local governments in the administration of elections by serving as nonpartisan poll workers or assistants; and

(2) to encourage State and local governments to use the services of the students participating in the Program.

(Oct. 29, 2002, P. L. 107-252, Title V, § 501, 116 Stat. 1717.)

CROSS REFERENCES

This section is referred to in 42 USCS § 15522.

RESEARCH GUIDE

Am Jur:

25 Am Jur 2d, Elections § 5.

Law Review Articles:

Magpantay. Two Steps Forward, One Step Back, and a Side Step: Asian Americans and the Federal Help America Vote Act. 10 UCLA Asian Pac Am LJ 31, 2005.

Saphire; Moke. Litigating Bush v. Gore in the States: Dual Voting Systems and the Fourteenth Amendment. 51 Vill L Rev 229, 2006.

§ 15522. Activities under Program

(a) In general. In carrying out the Program, the Commission (in consultation with the chief election official of each State) shall develop materials, sponsor seminars and workshops, engage in advertising targeted at students, make grants, and take such other actions as it considers appropriate to meet the purposes described in section 501(b) [42 USCS § 15521(b)].

(b) Requirements for grant recipients. In making grants under the Program, the Commission shall ensure that the funds provided are spent for projects and activities which are carried out without partisan bias or without promoting any particular point of view regarding any issue, and that each recipient is governed in a balanced manner which does not reflect any partisan bias.

(c) Coordination with institutions of higher education. The Commission shall encourage institutions of higher education (including community colleges) to participate in the Program, and shall make all necessary materials and other

assistance (including materials and assistance to enable the institution to hold workshops and poll worker training sessions) available without charge to any institution which desires to participate in the Program.
(Oct. 29, 2002, P. L. 107-252, TItle V, § 502, 116 Stat. 1717.)

RESEARCH GUIDE

Law Review Articles:
Saphire; Moke. Litigating Bush v. Gore in the States: Dual Voting Systems and the Fourteenth Amendment. 51 Vill L Rev 229, 2006.

§ 15523. Authorization of appropriations

In addition to any funds authorized to be appropriated to the Commission under section 210 [42 USCS § 15330], there are authorized to be appropriated to carry out this title [42 USCS §§ 15521 et seq.]—
   (1) $5,000,000 for fiscal year 2003; and
   (2) such sums as may be necessary for each succeeding fiscal year.
(Oct. 29, 2002, P. L. 107-252, TItle V, § 503, 116 Stat. 1717.)

CROSS REFERENCES
This section is referred to in 42 USCS § 15330.

TRANSFER TO COMMISSION OF FUNCTIONS UNDER CERTAIN LAWS

§ 15531. Transfer of functions of Office of Election Administration of Federal Election Commission

There are transferred to the Election Assistance Commission established under section 201 [42 USCS § 15321] all functions which the Office of Election Administration, established within the Federal Election Commission, exercised before the date of the enactment of this Act [enacted Oct. 29, 2002].
(Oct. 29, 2002, P. L. 107-252, Title VIII, Subtitle A, § 801(a), 116 Stat. 1725.)

§ 15532. Transfer of functions

There are transferred to the Election Assistance Commission established under section 201 [42 USCS § 15321] all functions which the Federal Election Commission exercised under section 9(a) of the National Voter Registration Act of 1993 (42 U.S.C. 1973gg-7(a)) before the date of the enactment of this Act [enacted Oct. 29, 2002].
(Oct. 29, 2002, P. L. 107-252, Title VIII, Subtitle A, § 802(a), 116 Stat. 1726.)

CODE OF FEDERAL REGULATIONS
Election Assistance Commission—National Voter Registration Act (42 U.S.C. 1973gg-1 et seq.), 11 CFR 9428.1 et seq.

§ 15533. Transfer of property, records, and personnel

(a) Property and records. The contracts, liabilities, records, property, and other assets and interests of, or made available in connection with, the offices and functions of the Federal Election Commission which are transferred by this subtitle are transferred to the Election Assistance Commission for appropriate allocation.

(b) Personnel. (1) In general. The personnel employed in connection with the offices and functions of the Federal Election Commission which are transferred by this subtitle are transferred to the Election Assistance Commission. (2) Effect. Any full-time or part-time personnel employed in permanent positions shall not be separated or reduced in grade or compensation because of the transfer under this subsection during the 1-year period beginning on the date of the enactment of this Act [enacted Oct. 29, 2002].

(Oct. 29, 2002, P. L. 107-252, Title VIII, Subtitle A, § 803, 116 Stat. 1726.)

HISTORY; ANCILLARY LAWS AND DIRECTIVES

References in text:

"This subtitle", referred to in this section is Subtitle A of Title VIII of Act Oct. 29, 2002, P. L. 107-252, which appears generally as 42 USCS §§ 15531 et seq. For full classification of such Subtitle, consult USCS Tables volumes.

§ 15534. Effective date; transition

(a) Effective date. This title and the amendments made by this title shall take effect upon the appointment of all members of the Election Assistance Commission under section 203 [42 USCS § 15323].

(b) Transition. With the consent of the entity involved, the Election Assistance Commission is authorized to utilize the services of such officers, employees, and other personnel of the entities from which functions have been transferred to the Election Assistance Commission under this title or the amendments made by this title for such period of time as may reasonably be needed to facilitate the orderly transfer of such functions.

(c) No effect on authorities of Office of Election Administration prior to appointment of members of Commission. During the period which begins on the date of the enactment of this Act [enacted Oct. 29, 2002] and ends on the effective date described in subsection (a), the Office of Election Administration of the Federal Election Commission shall continue to have the authority to carry out any of the functions (including the development of voluntary standards for voting systems and procedures for the certification of voting systems) which it has the authority to carry out as of the date of the enactment of this Act [enacted Oct. 29, 2002].

(Oct. 29, 2002, P. L. 107-252, Title VIII, Subtitle A, § 804, 116 Stat. 1726.)

HISTORY; ANCILLARY LAWS AND DIRECTIVES

References in text:

"This title", referred to in this section, is Title VIII of Act Oct. 29, 2002, which appears generally as 42 USCS §§ 15531 et seq. For full classification of such Title, consult USCS Tables volumes.

MISCELLANEOUS PROVISIONS

§ 15541.   State defined

In this Act, the term "State" includes the District of Columbia, the Commonwealth of Puerto Rico, Guam, American Samoa, and the United States Virgin Islands.
(Oct. 29, 2002, P. L. 107-252, Title IX, § 901, 116 Stat. 1727.)

HISTORY; ANCILLARY LAWS AND DIRECTIVES

References in text:
"This Act", referred to in this section, is Act Oct. 29, 2002, P. L. 107-252, popularly known as the Help America Vote Act of 2002, which appears generally as 42 USCS §§ 15301 et seq. For full classification of such Act, consult USCS Tables volumes.

§ 15542.   Audits and repayment of funds

(a) Recordkeeping requirement. Each recipient of a grant or other payment made under this Act shall keep such records with respect to the payment as are consistent with sound accounting principles, including records which fully disclose the amount and disposition by such recipient of funds, the total cost of the project or undertaking for which such funds are used, and the amount of that portion of the cost of the project or undertaking supplied by other sources, and such other records as will facilitate an effective audit.

(b) Audits and examinations. (1) Audits and examinations. Except as provided in paragraph (5), each office making a grant or other payment under this Act, or any duly authorized representative of such office, may audit or examine any recipient of the grant or payment and shall have access for the purpose of audit and examination to any books, documents, papers, and records of the recipient which in the opinion of the entity may be related or pertinent to the grant or payment.

(2) Recipients of assistance subject to provisions of section. The provisions of this section shall apply to all recipients of grants or other payments under this Act, whether by direct grant, cooperative agreement, or contract under this Act or by subgrant or subcontract from primary grantees or contractors under this Act.

(3) Mandatory audit. In addition to audits conducted pursuant to paragraph (1), all funds provided under this Act shall be subject to mandatory audit by the Comptroller General at least once during the lifetime of the program involved. For purposes of an audit under this paragraph, the Comptroller General shall have access to books, documents, papers, and records of recipients of funds in the same manner as the office making the grant or payment involved has access to such books, documents, papers, and records under paragraph (1).

(4) Special rule for payments by general services administration. With respect to any grant or payment made under this Act by the Administrator of General Services, the Election Assistance Commission shall be deemed to be the office making the grant or payment for purposes of this section.

(5) Special rule. In the case of grants or payments made under section 251 [42 USCS § 15401], audits and examinations conducted under paragraph (1) shall be performed on a regular basis (as determined by the Commission).

(6) Special rules for audits by the commission. In addition to the audits described in paragraph (1), the Election Assistance Commission may conduct a special audit or special examination of a recipient described in paragraph (1) upon a vote of the Commission.

(c) Recoupment of funds. If the Comptroller General determines as a result of an audit conducted under subsection (b) that—

(1) a recipient of funds under this Act is not in compliance with each of the requirements of the program under which the funds are provided; or

(2) an excess payment has been made to the recipient under the program,

the recipient shall pay to the office which made the grant or payment involved a portion of the funds provided which reflects the proportion of the requirements with which the recipient is not in compliance, or the extent to which the payment is in excess, under the program involved.

(Oct. 29, 2002, P. L. 107-252, Title IX, § 902, 116 Stat. 1727.)

HISTORY; ANCILLARY LAWS AND DIRECTIVES

References in text:

"This Act", referred to in this section, is Act Oct. 29, 2002, P. L. 107-252, popularly known as the Help America Vote Act of 2002, which appears generally as 42 USCS §§ 15301 et seq. For full classification of such Act, consult USCS Tables volumes.

INTERPRETIVE NOTES AND DECISIONS

Comptroller General need not make determination under 42 USCS § 15542(c) before agency making payments may take corrective action on questioned costs. Matter of: Help Am. Vote Act of 2002: Audits & Recovery of Funds (2006, Comp Gen) 2006 US Comp Gen LEXIS 40.

42 USCS § 15542(c) applies only to Comptroller General audits conducted under § 15542(b), not to other audits conducted under § 15542(b) or other authorities. Matter of: Help Am. Vote Act of 2002: Audits & Recovery of Funds (2006, Comp Gen) 2006 US Comp Gen LEXIS 40.

Recovery provision of 42 USCS § 15542(c) does not supersede various preexisting authorities of agencies awarding federal funds to take corrective action, as § 15542 can be construed consistently with such preexisting authorities and there is no evidence that in statute or legislative history that Congress intended for statute to supersede such authorities. Matter of: Help Am. Vote Act of 2002: Audits & Recovery of Funds (2006, Comp Gen) 2006 US Comp Gen LEXIS 40.

§ 15543. Review and report on adequacy of existing electoral fraud statutes and penalties

(a) Review. The Attorney General shall conduct a review of existing criminal statutes concerning election offenses to determine—

(1) whether additional statutory offenses are needed to secure the use of the Internet for election purposes; and

(2) whether existing penalties provide adequate punishment and deterrence with respect to such offenses.

(b) Report. The Attorney General shall submit a report to the Committees on the Judiciary of the Senate and House of Representatives, the Committee on Rules and Administration of the Senate, and the Committee on House Administration of the House of Representatives on the review conducted under subsection (a) together with such recommendations for legislative and administrative action as the Attorney General determines appropriate.

(Oct. 29, 2002, P. L. 107-252, Title IX, § 904, 116 Stat. 1729.)

§ 15544. Other criminal penalties

(a) Conspiracy to deprive voters of a fair election. Any individual who knowingly and willfully gives false information in registering or voting in violation of section 11(c) of the National Voting Rights Act of 1965 (42 U.S.C. 1973i(c)), or conspires with another to violate such section, shall be fined or imprisoned, or both, in accordance with such section.

(b) False information in registering and voting. Any individual who knowingly commits fraud or knowingly makes a false statement with respect to the naturalization, citizenry, or alien registry of such individual in violation of section 1015 of title 18, United States Code, shall be fined or imprisoned, or both, in accordance with such section.

(Oct. 29, 2002, P. L. 107-252, Title IX, § 905, 116 Stat. 1729.)

§ 15545. No effect on other laws

(a) In general. Except as specifically provided in section 303(b) of this Act [42 USCS § 15483(b)] with regard to the National Voter Registration Act of 1993 (42 U.S.C. 1973gg et seq.), nothing in this Act may be construed to authorize or require conduct prohibited under any of the following laws, or to supersede, restrict, or limit the application of such laws:

    (1) The Voting Rights Act of 1965 (42 U.S.C. 1973 et seq.).

    (2) The Voting Accessibility for the Elderly and Handicapped Act (42 U.S.C. 1973ee et seq.).

    (3) The Uniformed and Overseas Citizens Absentee Voting Act (42 U.S.C. 1973ff et seq.).

    (4) The National Voter Registration Act of 1993 (42 U.S.C. 1973gg et seq.).

    (5) The Americans with Disabilities Act of 1990 (42 U.S.C. 12101 et seq.).

    (6) The Rehabilitation Act of 1973 (29 U.S.C. 701 et seq.).

(b) No effect on preclearance or other requirements under Voting Rights Act. The approval by the Administrator or the Commission of a payment or grant application under title I or title II [42 USCS §§ 15301 et seq. or 15321 et seq.], or any other action taken by the Commission or a State under such title, shall not be considered to have any effect on requirements for preclearance under section 5 of the Voting Rights Act of 1965 (42 U.S.C. 1973c) or any other requirements of such Act.

(Oct. 29, 2002, P. L. 107-252, Title IX, § 906, 116 Stat. 1729.)

HISTORY; ANCILLARY LAWS AND DIRECTIVES

References in text:

"This Act", referred to in this section, is Act Oct. 29, 2002, P. L. 107-252, popularly known as the Help America Vote Act of 2002, which appears generally as 42 USCS §§ 15301 et seq. For full classification of such Act, consult USCS Tables volumes.

CROSS REFERENCES

This section is referred to in 42 USCS §§ 15301, 15302, 15403, 15484.

CHAPTER 147. PRISON RAPE ELIMINATION

§ 15601. Findings

Congress makes the following findings:

(1) 2,100,146 persons were incarcerated in the United States at the end of 2001: 1,324,465 in Federal and State prisons and 631,240 in county and local jails. In 1999, there were more than 10,000,000 separate admissions to and discharges from prisons and jails.

(2) Insufficient research has been conducted and insufficient data reported on the extent of prison rape. However, experts have conservatively estimated that at least 13 percent of the inmates in the United States have been sexually assaulted in prison. Many inmates have suffered repeated assaults. Under this estimate, nearly 200,000 inmates now incarcerated have been or will be the victims of prison rape. The total number of inmates who have been sexually assaulted in the past 20 years likely exceeds 1,000,000.

(3) Inmates with mental illness are at increased risk of sexual victimization. America's jails and prisons house more mentally ill individuals than all of the Nation's psychiatric hospitals combined. As many as 16 percent of inmates in State prisons and jails, and 7 percent of Federal inmates, suffer from mental illness.

(4) Young first-time offenders are at increased risk of sexual victimization. Juveniles are 5 times more likely to be sexually assaulted in adult rather than juvenile facilities—often within the first 48 hours of incarceration.

(5) Most prison staff are not adequately trained or prepared to prevent, report, or treat inmate sexual assaults.

(6) Prison rape often goes unreported, and inmate victims often receive inadequate treatment for the severe physical and psychological effects of sexual assault—if they receive treatment at all.

(7) HIV and AIDS are major public health problems within America's correctional facilities. In 2000, 25,088 inmates in Federal and State prisons were known to be infected with HIV/AIDS. In 2000, HIV/AIDS accounted for more than 6 percent of all deaths in Federal and State prisons. Infection rates for other sexually transmitted diseases, tuberculosis, and hepatitis B and C are also far greater for prisoners than for the American population as a whole. Prison rape undermines the public health by contributing to the spread of these diseases, and often giving a potential death sentence to its victims.

(8) Prison rape endangers the public safety by making brutalized inmates more likely to commit crimes when they are released—as 600,000 inmates are each year.

(9) The frequently interracial character of prison sexual assaults significantly exacerbates interracial tensions, both within prison and, upon release of perpetrators and victims from prison, in the community at large.

(10) Prison rape increases the level of homicides and other violence against inmates and staff, and the risk of insurrections and riots.

(11) Victims of prison rape suffer severe physical and psychological effects that hinder their ability to integrate into the community and maintain stable employment upon their release from prison. They are thus more likely to become homeless and/or require government assistance.

(12) Members of the public and government officials are largely unaware of the epidemic character of prison rape and the day-to-day horror experienced by victimized inmates.

(13) The high incidence of sexual assault within prisons involves actual and potential violations of the United States Constitution. In Farmer v. Brennan, 511 U.S. 825 [128 L. Ed. 2d 811] (1994), the Supreme Court ruled that deliberate indifference to the substantial risk of sexual assault violates prisoners' rights under the Cruel and Unusual Punishments Clause of the Eighth Amendment. The Eighth Amendment rights of State and local prisoners are protected through the Due Process Clause of the Fourteenth Amendment. Pursuant to the power of Congress under Section Five of the Fourteenth Amendment, Congress may take action to enforce those rights in States where officials have demonstrated such indifference. States that do not take basic steps to abate prison rape by adopting standards that do not generate significant additional expenditures demonstrate such indifference. Therefore, such States are not entitled to the same level of Federal benefits as other States.

(14) The high incidence of prison rape undermines the effectiveness and efficiency of United States Government expenditures through grant programs such as those dealing with health care; mental health care; disease prevention; crime prevention, investigation, and prosecution; prison construction, maintenance, and operation; race relations; poverty; unemployment and homelessness. The effectiveness and efficiency of these federally funded grant programs are compromised by the failure of State officials to adopt policies and procedures that reduce the incidence of prison rape in that the high incidence of prison rape—

(A) increases the costs incurred by Federal, State, and local jurisdictions to administer their prison systems;

(B) increases the levels of violence, directed at inmates and at staff, within prisons;

(C) increases health care expenditures, both inside and outside of prison systems, and reduces the effectiveness of disease prevention programs by substantially increasing the incidence and spread of HIV, AIDS, tuberculosis, hepatitis B and C, and other diseases;

(D) increases mental health care expenditures, both inside and outside of prison systems, by substantially increasing the rate of post-traumatic stress disorder, depression, suicide, and the exacerbation of existing mental illnesses among current and former inmates;

(E) increases the risks of recidivism, civil strife, and violent crime by individuals who have been brutalized by prison rape; and

(F) increases the level of interracial tensions and strife within prisons and, upon release of perpetrators and victims, in the community at large.

(15) The high incidence of prison rape has a significant effect on interstate commerce because it increases substantially—

(A) the costs incurred by Federal, State, and local jurisdictions to administer their prison systems;

(B) the incidence and spread of HIV, AIDS, tuberculosis, hepatitis B and C, and other diseases, contributing to increased health and medical expenditures throughout the Nation;

(C) the rate of post-traumatic stress disorder, depression, suicide, and the exacerbation of existing mental illnesses among current and former inmates, contributing to increased health and medical expenditures throughout the Nation; and

(D) the risk of recidivism, civil strife, and violent crime by individuals who have been brutalized by prison rape.

(Sept. 4, 2003, P. L. 108-79, § 2, 117 Stat. 972.)

HISTORY; ANCILLARY LAWS AND DIRECTIVES

Short title:

Act Sept. 4, 2003, P. L. 108-79, § 1(a), 117 Stat. 972, provides: "This Act [42 USCS §§ 15601 et seq.] may be cited as the 'Prison Rape Elimination Act of 2003'.".

RESEARCH GUIDE

Law Review Articles:

Corlew. Congress Attempts to Shine a Light on a Dark Problem: An In-Depth Look at the Prison Rape Elimination Act of 2003. 33 Am J Crim L 157, Spring 2006.

White. The Concept of "Less Eligibility" and the Social Function of Prison Violence in Class Society. 56 Buffalo L Rev 737, 2008.

Ristroph. Prison and Punishment: Sexual Punishments. 15 Colum J Gender & L 139, 2006.

Smith. Prison and Punishment: Rethinking Prison Sex: Self-Expression and Safety. 15 Colum J Gender & L 185, 2006.

DeBraux. Prison Rape: Have We Done Enough? A Deep Look Into the Adequacy of the Prison Rape Elimination Act. 50 How LJ 203, Fall 2006.

Sigler. By the Light of Virtue: Prison Rape and the Corruption of Character. 91 Iowa L Rev 561, January 2006.

Dumond. The Impact of Prisoner Sexual Violence: Challenges of Implementing Public Law 108-79 The Prison Rape Elimination Act of 2003. 32 J Legis 142, 2006.

Mair; Frattaroli; Teret. Part III: National Challenges in Population Health: New Hope for Victims of Prison Sexual Assault. 31 JL Med & Ethics 602, Winter 2003.

Robertson. Compassionate Conservatism and Prison Rape: the Prison Rape Elimination Act of 2003. 30 NE J on Crim & Civ Con 1, Winter 2004.

Robertson. A Punk's Song About Prison Reform. 24 Pace L Rev 527, Spring 2004.

Jenness; Smyth. Prison Policy: the Passage and Implementation of the Prison Rape Elimination Act: Legal Endogeneity and the Uncertain Road From Symbolic Law to Instrumental Effects. 22 Stan L & Pol'y Rev 489, 2011.

§ 15602. Purposes

The purposes of this Act [42 USCS §§ 15601 et seq.] are to—

(1) establish a zero-tolerance standard for the incidence of prison rape in prisons in the United States;

(2) make the prevention of prison rape a top priority in each prison system;

(3) develop and implement national standards for the detection, prevention, reduction, and punishment of prison rape;

(4) increase the available data and information on the incidence of prison rape, consequently improving the management and administration of correctional facilities;

(5) standardize the definitions used for collecting data on the incidence of prison rape;

(6) increase the accountability of prison officials who fail to detect, prevent, reduce, and punish prison rape;

(7) protect the Eighth Amendment rights of Federal, State, and local prisoners;

(8) increase the efficiency and effectiveness of Federal expenditures through grant programs such as those dealing with health care; mental health care; disease prevention; crime prevention, investigation, and prosecution; prison construction, maintenance, and operation; race relations; poverty; unemployment; and homelessness; and

(9) reduce the costs that prison rape imposes on interstate commerce.

(Sept. 4, 2003, P. L. 108-79, § 3, 117 Stat. 974.)

RESEARCH GUIDE

Law Review Articles:

Corlew. Congress Attempts to Shine a Light on a Dark Problem: An In-Depth Look at the Prison Rape Elimination Act of 2003. 33 Am J Crim L 157, Spring 2006.

Ristroph. Prison and Punishment: Sexual Punishments. 15 Colum J Gender & L 139, 2006.

Smith. Prison and Punishment: Rethinking Prison Sex: Self-Expression and Safety. 15 Colum J Gender & L 185, 2006.

DeBraux. Prison Rape: Have We Done Enough? A Deep Look Into the Adequacy of the Prison Rape Elimination Act. 50 How LJ 203, Fall 2006.

Sigler. By the Light of Virtue: Prison Rape and the Corruption of Character. 91 Iowa L Rev 561, January 2006.

Dumond. The Impact of Prisoner Sexual Violence: Challenges of Implementing Public Law 108-79 The Prison Rape Elimination Act of 2003. 32 J Legis 142, 2006.

Mair; Frattaroli; Teret. Part III: National Challenges in Population Health: New Hope for Victims of Prison Sexual Assault. 31 JL Med & Ethics 602, Winter 2003.

Robertson. Compassionate Conservatism and Prison Rape: the Prison Rape Elimination Act of 2003. 30 NE J on Crim & Civ Con 1, Winter 2004.

Robertson. A Punk's Song About Prison Reform. 24 Pace L Rev 527, Spring 2004.

§ 15603. National prison rape statistics, data, and research

(a) **Annual comprehensive statistical review.** (1) In general. The Bureau of Justice Statistics of the Department of Justice (in this section referred to as the "Bureau") shall carry out, for each calendar year, a comprehensive statistical review and analysis of the incidence and effects of prison rape.

The statistical review and analysis shall include, but not be limited to the identification of the common characteristics of—

(A) both victims and perpetrators of prison rape; and

(B) prisons and prison systems with a high incidence of prison rape.

(2) Considerations. In carrying out paragraph (1), the Bureau shall consider—

(A) how rape should be defined for the purposes of the statistical review and analysis;

(B) how the Bureau should collect information about staff-on-inmate sexual assault;

(C) how the Bureau should collect information beyond inmate self-reports of prison rape;

(D) how the Bureau should adjust the data in order to account for differences among prisons as required by subsection (c)(3);

(E) the categorization of prisons as required by subsection (c)(4); and

(F) whether a preliminary study of prison rape should be conducted to inform the methodology of the comprehensive statistical review.

(3) Solicitation of views. The Bureau of Justice Statistics shall solicit views from representatives of the following: State departments of correction; county and municipal jails; juvenile correctional facilities; former inmates; victim advocates; researchers; and other experts in the area of sexual assault.

(4) Sampling techniques. The review and analysis under paragraph (1) shall be based on a random sample, or other scientifically appropriate sample, of not less than 10 percent of all Federal, State, and county prisons, and a representative sample of municipal prisons. The selection shall include at least one prison from each State. The selection of facilities for sampling shall be made at the latest practicable date prior to conducting the surveys and shall not be disclosed to any facility or prison system official prior to the time period studied in the survey. Selection of a facility for sampling during any year shall not preclude its selection for sampling in any subsequent year.

(5) Surveys. In carrying out the review and analysis under paragraph (1), the Bureau shall, in addition to such other methods as the Bureau considers appropriate, use surveys and other statistical studies of current and former inmates from a sample of Federal, State, county, and municipal prisons. The Bureau shall ensure the confidentiality of each survey participant, except as authorized in paragraph (7).

(6) Participation in survey. Federal, State, or local officials or facility administrators that receive a request from the Bureau under subsection (a)(4) or (5) will be required to participate in the national survey and provide access to any inmates under their legal custody.

(7) Reporting on child abuse and neglect. Nothing in section 304 or 812 of title I of the Omnibus Crime Control and Safe Streets Act of 1968 (42 U.S.C. 3735, 3789g) or any other provision of law, including paragraph (5), shall prevent the Bureau (including its agents), in carrying out the review and analysis under paragraph (1), from reporting to the designated public of-

ficials such information (and only such information) regarding child abuse or child neglect with respect to which the statutes or regulations of a State (or a political subdivision thereof) require prompt reporting.

(b) Review Panel on Prison Rape. (1) Establishment. To assist the Bureau in carrying out the review and analysis under subsection (a), there is established, within the Department of Justice, the Review Panel on Prison Rape (in this section referred to as the "Panel").

(2) Membership. (A) Composition. The Panel shall be composed of 3 members, each of whom shall be appointed by the Attorney General, in consultation with the Secretary of Health and Human Services.

(B) Qualifications. Members of the Panel shall be selected from among individuals with knowledge or expertise in matters to be studied by the Panel.

(3) Public hearings. (A) In general. The duty of the Panel shall be to carry out, for each calendar year, public hearings concerning the operation of the three prisons with the highest incidence of prison rape and the two prisons with the lowest incidence of prison rape in each category of facilities identified under subsection (c)(4). The Panel shall hold a separate hearing regarding the three Federal or State prisons with the highest incidence of prison rape. The purpose of these hearings shall be to collect evidence to aid in the identification of common characteristics of both victims and perpetrators of prison rape, and the identification of common characteristics of prisons and prison systems with a high incidence of prison rape, and the identification of common characteristics of prisons and prison systems that appear to have been successful in deterring prison rape.

(B) Testimony at hearings. (i) Public officials. In carrying out the hearings required under subparagraph (A), the Panel shall request the public testimony of Federal, State, and local officials (and organizations that represent such officials), including the warden or director of each prison, who bears responsibility for the prevention, detection, and punishment of prison rape at each entity, and the head of the prison system encompassing such prison.

(ii) Victims. The Panel may request the testimony of prison rape victims, organizations representing such victims, and other appropriate individuals and organizations.

(C) Subpoenas. (i) Issuance. The Panel may issue subpoenas for the attendance of witnesses and the production of written or other matter.

(ii) Enforcement. In the case of contumacy or refusal to obey a subpoena, the Attorney General may in a Federal court of appropriate jurisdiction obtain an appropriate order to enforce the subpoena.

(c) Reports. (1) In general. Not later than June 30 of each year, the Attorney General shall submit a report on the activities of the Bureau and the Review Panel, with respect to prison rape, for the preceding calendar year to—

(A) Congress; and

(B) the Secretary of Health and Human Services.

(2) Contents. The report required under paragraph (1) shall include—

(A) with respect to the effects of prison rape, statistical, sociological, and psychological data;

(B) with respect to the incidence of prison rape—

(i) statistical data aggregated at the Federal, State, prison system, and prison levels;

(ii) a listing of those institutions in the representative sample, separated into each category identified under subsection (c)(4) and ranked according to the incidence of prison rape in each institution; and

(iii) an identification of those institutions in the representative sample that appear to have been successful in deterring prison rape; and

(C) a listing of any prisons in the representative sample that did not cooperate with the survey conducted pursuant to section 4.

(3) Data adjustments. In preparing the information specified in paragraph (2), the Attorney General shall use established statistical methods to adjust the data as necessary to account for differences among institutions in the representative sample, which are not related to the detection, prevention, reduction and punishment of prison rape, or which are outside the control of the State, prison, or prison system, in order to provide an accurate comparison among prisons. Such differences may include the mission, security level, size, and jurisdiction under which the prison operates. For each such adjustment made, the Attorney General shall identify and explain such adjustment in the report.

(4) Categorization of prisons. The report shall divide the prisons surveyed into three categories. One category shall be composed of all Federal and State prisons. The other two categories shall be defined by the Attorney General in order to compare similar institutions.

(d) Contracts and grants. In carrying out its duties under this section, the Attorney General may—

(1) provide grants for research through the National Institute of Justice; and

(2) contract with or provide grants to any other entity the Attorney General deems appropriate.

(e) Authorization of appropriations. There are authorized to be appropriated $15,000,000 for each of fiscal years 2004 through 2010 to carry out this section.

(Sept. 4, 2003, P. L. 108-79, § 4, 117 Stat. 975; Nov. 22, 2005, P. L. 109-108, Title I, § 113(a), 119 Stat. 2305.)

HISTORY; ANCILLARY LAWS AND DIRECTIVES

Amendments:

2005. Act Nov. 22, 2005, in subsec. (a), in para. (5), inserted ", except as authorized in paragraph (7)", and added para. (7).

CROSS REFERENCES

This section is referred to in 42 USCS § 15607.

RESEARCH GUIDE
Law Review Articles:

Corlew. Congress Attempts to Shine a Light on a Dark Problem: An In-Depth Look at the Prison Rape Elimination Act of 2003. 33 Am J Crim L 157, Spring 2006.

Ristroph. Prison and Punishment: Sexual Punishments. 15 Colum J Gender & L 139, 2006.

Smith. Prison and Punishment: Rethinking Prison Sex: Self-Expression and Safety. 15 Colum J Gender & L 185, 2006.

DeBraux. Prison Rape: Have We Done Enough? A Deep Look Into the Adequacy of the Prison Rape Elimination Act. 50 How LJ 203, Fall 2006.

Sigler. By the Light of Virtue: Prison Rape and the Corruption of Character. 91 Iowa L Rev 561, January 2006.

Dumond. The Impact of Prisoner Sexual Violence: Challenges of Implementing Public Law 108-79 The Prison Rape Elimination Act of 2003. 32 J Legis 142, 2006.

Mair; Frattaroli; Teret. Part III: National Challenges in Population Health: New Hope for Victims of Prison Sexual Assault. 31 JL Med & Ethics 602, Winter 2003.

Robertson. Compassionate Conservatism and Prison Rape: the Prison Rape Elimination Act of 2003. 30 NE J on Crim & Civ Con 1, Winter 2004.

Robertson. A Punk's Song About Prison Reform. 24 Pace L Rev 527, Spring 2004.

§ 15604. Prison rape prevention and prosecution

(a) **Information and assistance.** (1) National clearinghouse. There is established within the National Institute of Corrections a national clearinghouse for the provision of information and assistance to Federal, State, and local authorities responsible for the prevention, investigation, and punishment of instances of prison rape.

(2) Training and education. The National Institute of Corrections shall conduct periodic training and education programs for Federal, State, and local authorities responsible for the prevention, investigation, and punishment of instances of prison rape.

(b) **Reports.** (1) In general. Not later than September 30 of each year, the National Institute of Corrections shall submit a report to Congress and the Secretary of Health and Human Services. This report shall be available to the Director of the Bureau of Justice Statistics.

(2) Contents. The report required under paragraph (1) shall summarize the activities of the Department of Justice regarding prison rape abatement for the preceding calendar year.

(c) **Authorization of appropriations.** There are authorized to be appropriated $5,000,000 for each of fiscal years 2004 through 2010 to carry out this section.
(Sept. 4, 2003, P. L. 108-79, § 5, 117 Stat. 978.)

CROSS REFERENCES
This section is referred to in 42 USCS § 15605.

RESEARCH GUIDE

Law Review Articles:

Corlew. Congress Attempts to Shine a Light on a Dark Problem: An In-Depth Look at the Prison Rape Elimination Act of 2003. 33 Am J Crim L 157, Spring 2006.

Ristroph. Prison and Punishment: Sexual Punishments. 15 Colum J Gender & L 139, 2006.

Smith. Prison and Punishment: Rethinking Prison Sex: Self-Expression and Safety. 15 Colum J Gender & L 185, 2006.

DeBraux. Prison Rape: Have We Done Enough? A Deep Look Into the Adequacy of the Prison Rape Elimination Act. 50 How LJ 203, Fall 2006.

Sigler. By the Light of Virtue: Prison Rape and the Corruption of Character. 91 Iowa L Rev 561, January 2006.

Dumond. The Impact of Prisoner Sexual Violence: Challenges of Implementing Public Law 108-79 The Prison Rape Elimination Act of 2003. 32 J Legis 142, 2006.

Mair; Frattaroli; Teret. Part III: National Challenges in Population Health: New Hope for Victims of Prison Sexual Assault. 31 JL Med & Ethics 602, Winter 2003.

Robertson. Compassionate Conservatism and Prison Rape: the Prison Rape Elimination Act of 2003. 30 NE J on Crim & Civ Con 1, Winter 2004.

Robertson. A Punk's Song About Prison Reform. 24 Pace L Rev 527, Spring 2004.

§ 15605. Grants to protect inmates and safeguard communities

(a) Grants authorized. From amounts made available for grants under this section, the Attorney General shall make grants to States to assist those States in ensuring that budgetary circumstances (such as reduced State and local spending on prisons) do not compromise efforts to protect inmates (particularly from prison rape) and to safeguard the communities to which inmates return. The purpose of grants under this section shall be to provide funds for personnel, training, technical assistance, data collection, and equipment to prevent and prosecute prisoner rape.

(b) Use of grant amounts. Amounts received by a grantee under this section may be used by the grantee, directly or through subgrants, only for one or more of the following activities:

    (1) Protecting inmates. Protecting inmates by—
        (A) undertaking efforts to more effectively prevent prison rape;
        (B) investigating incidents of prison rape; or
        (C) prosecuting incidents of prison rape.
    (2) Safeguarding communities. Safeguarding communities by—
        (A) making available, to officials of State and local governments who are considering reductions to prison budgets, training and technical assistance in successful methods for moderating the growth of prison populations without compromising public safety, including successful methods used by other jurisdictions;
        (B) developing and utilizing analyses of prison populations and risk assessment instruments that will improve State and local governments' understanding of risks to the community regarding release of inmates in the prison population;

(C) preparing maps demonstrating the concentration, on a community-by-community basis, of inmates who have been released, to facilitate the efficient and effective—

(i) deployment of law enforcement resources (including probation and parole resources); and

(ii) delivery of services (such as job training and substance abuse treatment) to those released inmates;

(D) promoting collaborative efforts, among officials of State and local governments and leaders of appropriate communities, to understand and address the effects on a community of the presence of a disproportionate number of released inmates in that community; or

(E) developing policies and programs that reduce spending on prisons by effectively reducing rates of parole and probation revocation without compromising public safety.

(c) **Grant requirements.** (1) Period. A grant under this section shall be made for a period of not more than 2 years.

(2) Maximum. The amount of a grant under this section may not exceed $1,000,000.

(3) Matching. The Federal share of a grant under this section may not exceed 50 percent of the total costs of the project described in the application submitted under subsection (d) for the fiscal year for which the grant was made under this section.

(d) **Applications.** (1) In general. To request a grant under this section, the chief executive of a State shall submit an application to the Attorney General at such time, in such manner, and accompanied by such information as the Attorney General may require.

(2) Contents. Each application required by paragraph (1) shall—

(A) include the certification of the chief executive that the State receiving such grant—

(i) has adopted all national prison rape standards that, as of the date on which the application was submitted, have been promulgated under this Act [42 USCS §§ 15601 et seq.]; and

(ii) will consider adopting all national prison rape standards that are promulgated under this Act [42 USCS §§ 15601 et seq.] after such date;

(B) specify with particularity the preventative, prosecutorial, or administrative activities to be undertaken by the State with the amounts received under the grant; and

(C) in the case of an application for a grant for one or more activities specified in paragraph (2) of subsection (b)—

(i) review the extent of the budgetary circumstances affecting the State generally and describe how those circumstances relate to the State's prisons;

(ii) describe the rate of growth of the State's prison population over the preceding 10 years and explain why the State may have difficulty sustaining that rate of growth; and

(iii) explain the extent to which officials (including law enforcement officials) of State and local governments and victims of crime will be consulted regarding decisions whether, or how, to moderate the growth of the State's prison population.

(e) Reports by grantee. (1) In general. The Attorney General shall require each grantee to submit, not later than 90 days after the end of the period for which the grant was made under this section, a report on the activities carried out under the grant. The report shall identify and describe those activities and shall contain an evaluation of the effect of those activities on—

(A) the number of incidents of prison rape, and the grantee's response to such incidents; and

(B) the safety of the prisons, and the safety of the communities in which released inmates are present.

(2) Dissemination. The Attorney General shall ensure that each report submitted under paragraph (1) is made available under the national clearinghouse established under section 5 [42 USCS § 15604].

(f) State defined. In this section, the term "State" includes the District of Columbia, the Commonwealth of Puerto Rico, and any other territory or possession of the United States.

(g) Authorization of appropriations. (1) In general. There are authorized to be appropriated for grants under this section $40,000,000 for each of fiscal years 2004 through 2010.

(2) Limitation. Of amounts made available for grants under this section, not less than 50 percent shall be available only for activities specified in paragraph (1) of subsection (b).

(Sept. 4, 2003, P. L. 108-79, § 6, 117 Stat. 978.)

RESEARCH GUIDE

Law Review Articles:

Corlew. Congress Attempts to Shine a Light on a Dark Problem: An In-Depth Look at the Prison Rape Elimination Act of 2003. 33 Am J Crim L 157, Spring 2006.

Ristroph. Prison and Punishment: Sexual Punishments. 15 Colum J Gender & L 139, 2006.

Smith. Prison and Punishment: Rethinking Prison Sex: Self-Expression and Safety. 15 Colum J Gender & L 185, 2006.

DeBraux. Prison Rape: Have We Done Enough? A Deep Look Into the Adequacy of the Prison Rape Elimination Act. 50 How LJ 203, Fall 2006.

Sigler. By the Light of Virtue: Prison Rape and the Corruption of Character. 91 Iowa L Rev 561, January 2006.

Dumond. The Impact of Prisoner Sexual Violence: Challenges of Implementing Public Law 108-79 The Prison Rape Elimination Act of 2003. 32 J Legis 142, 2006.

Mair; Frattaroli; Teret. Part III: National Challenges in Population Health: New Hope for Victims of Prison Sexual Assault. 31 JL Med & Ethics 602, Winter 2003.

Robertson. Compassionate Conservatism and Prison Rape: the Prison Rape Elimination Act of 2003. 30 NE J on Crim & Civ Con 1, Winter 2004.

Robertson. A Punk's Song About Prison Reform. 24 Pace L Rev 527, Spring 2004.

§ 15606.   National Prison Rape Elimination Commission

(a) **Establishment.** There is established a commission to be known as the National Prison Rape Elimination Commission (in this section referred to as the "Commission").

(b) **Members.** (1) In general. The Commission shall be composed of 9 members, of whom—

(A) 3 shall be appointed by the President;

(B) 2 shall be appointed by the Speaker of the House of Representatives, unless the Speaker is of the same party as the President, in which case 1 shall be appointed by the Speaker of the House of Representatives and 1 shall be appointed by the minority leader of the House of Representatives;

(C) 1 shall be appointed by the minority leader of the House of Representatives (in addition to any appointment made under subparagraph (B));

(D) 2 shall be appointed by the majority leader of the Senate, unless the majority leader is of the same party as the President, in which case 1 shall be appointed by the majority leader of the Senate and 1 shall be appointed by the minority leader of the Senate; and

(E) 1 member appointed by the minority leader of the Senate (in addition to any appointment made under subparagraph (D)).

(2) Persons eligible. Each member of the Commission shall be an individual who has knowledge or expertise in matters to be studied by the Commission.

(3) Consultation required. The President, the Speaker and minority leader of the House of Representatives, and the majority leader and minority leader of the Senate shall consult with one another prior to the appointment of the members of the Commission to achieve, to the maximum extent possible, fair and equitable representation of various points of view with respect to the matters to be studied by the Commission.

(4) Term. Each member shall be appointed for the life of the Commission.

(5) Time for initial appointments. The appointment of the members shall be made not later than 60 days after the date of enactment of this Act [enacted Sept. 4, 2003].

(6) Vacancies. A vacancy in the Commission shall be filled in the manner in which the original appointment was made, and shall be made not later than 60 days after the date on which the vacancy occurred.

(c) **Operation.** (1) Chairperson. Not later than 15 days after appointments of all the members are made, the President shall appoint a chairperson for the Commission from among its members.

(2) Meetings. The Commission shall meet at the call of the chairperson. The initial meeting of the Commission shall take place not later than 30 days after the initial appointment of the members is completed.

(3) Quorum. A majority of the members of the Commission shall constitute

a quorum to conduct business, but the Commission may establish a lesser quorum for conducting hearings scheduled by the Commission.

(4) Rules. The Commission may establish by majority vote any other rules for the conduct of Commission business, if such rules are not inconsistent with this Act [42 USCS §§ 15601 et seq.] or other applicable law.

(d) **Comprehensive study of the impacts of prison rape.** (1) In general. The Commission shall carry out a comprehensive legal and factual study of the penalogical, physical, mental, medical, social, and economic impacts of prison rape in the United States on—

(A) Federal, State, and local governments; and

(B) communities and social institutions generally, including individuals, families, and businesses within such communities and social institutions.

(2) Matters included. The study under paragraph (1) shall include—

(A) a review of existing Federal, State, and local government policies and practices with respect to the prevention, detection, and punishment of prison rape;

(B) an assessment of the relationship between prison rape and prison conditions, and of existing monitoring, regulatory, and enforcement practices that are intended to address any such relationship;

(C) an assessment of pathological or social causes of prison rape;

(D) an assessment of the extent to which the incidence of prison rape contributes to the spread of sexually transmitted diseases and to the transmission of HIV;

(E) an assessment of the characteristics of inmates most likely to commit prison rape and the effectiveness of various types of treatment or programs to reduce such likelihood;

(F) an assessment of the characteristics of inmates most likely to be victims of prison rape and the effectiveness of various types of treatment or programs to reduce such likelihood;

(G) an assessment of the impacts of prison rape on individuals, families, social institutions and the economy generally, including an assessment of the extent to which the incidence of prison rape contributes to recidivism and to increased incidence of sexual assault;

(H) an examination of the feasibility and cost of conducting surveillance, undercover activities, or both, to reduce the incidence of prison rape;

(I) an assessment of the safety and security of prison facilities and the relationship of prison facility construction and design to the incidence of prison rape;

(J) an assessment of the feasibility and cost of any particular proposals for prison reform;

(K) an identification of the need for additional scientific and social science research on the prevalence of prison rape in Federal, State, and local prisons;

(L) an assessment of the general relationship between prison rape and prison violence;

(M) an assessment of the relationship between prison rape and levels of training, supervision, and discipline of prison staff; and

(N) an assessment of existing Federal and State systems for reporting incidents of prison rape, including an assessment of whether existing systems provide an adequate assurance of confidentiality, impartiality and the absence of reprisal.

(3) Report. (A) Distribution. Not later than 5 years after the date of the initial meeting of the Commission, the Commission shall submit a report on the study carried out under this subsection to—

(i) the President;

(ii) the Congress;

(iii) the Attorney General;

(iv) the Secretary of Health and Human Services;

(v) the Director of the Federal Bureau of Prisons;

(vi) the chief executive of each State; and

(vii) the head of the department of corrections of each State.

(B) Contents. The report under subparagraph (A) shall include—

(i) the findings and conclusions of the Commission;

(ii) recommended national standards for reducing prison rape;

(iii) recommended protocols for preserving evidence and treating victims of prison rape; and

(iv) a summary of the materials relied on by the Commission in the preparation of the report.

(e) **Recommendations.** (1) In general. In conjunction with the report submitted under subsection (d)(3), the Commission shall provide the Attorney General and the Secretary of Health and Human Services with recommended national standards for enhancing the detection, prevention, reduction, and punishment of prison rape.

(2) Matters included. The information provided under paragraph (1) shall include recommended national standards relating to—

(A) the classification and assignment of prisoners, using proven standardized instruments and protocols, in a manner that limits the occurrence of prison rape;

(B) the investigation and resolution of rape complaints by responsible prison authorities, local and State police, and Federal and State prosecution authorities;

(C) the preservation of physical and testimonial evidence for use in an investigation of the circumstances relating to the rape;

(D) acute-term trauma care for rape victims, including standards relating to—

(i) the manner and extent of physical examination and treatment to be provided to any rape victim; and

(ii) the manner and extent of any psychological examination, psychiatric care, medication, and mental health counseling to be provided to any rape victim;

(E) referrals for long-term continuity of care for rape victims;

(F) educational and medical testing measures for reducing the incidence of HIV transmission due to prison rape;

(G) post-rape prophylactic medical measures for reducing the incidence of transmission of sexual diseases;

(H) the training of correctional staff sufficient to ensure that they understand and appreciate the significance of prison rape and the necessity of its eradication;

(I) the timely and comprehensive investigation of staff sexual misconduct involving rape or other sexual assault on inmates;

(J) ensuring the confidentiality of prison rape complaints and protecting inmates who make complaints of prison rape;

(K) creating a system for reporting incidents of prison rape that will ensure the confidentiality of prison rape complaints, protect inmates who make prison rape complaints from retaliation, and assure the impartial resolution of prison rape complaints;

(L) data collection and reporting of—

(i) prison rape;

(ii) prison staff sexual misconduct; and

(iii) the resolution of prison rape complaints by prison officials and Federal, State, and local investigation and prosecution authorities; and

(M) such other matters as may reasonably be related to the detection, prevention, reduction, and punishment of prison rape.

(3) Limitation. The Commission shall not propose a recommended standard that would impose substantial additional costs compared to the costs presently expended by Federal, State, and local prison authorities.

(f) Consultation with accreditation organizations. In developing recommended national standards for enhancing the detection, prevention, reduction, and punishment of prison rape, the Commission shall consider any standards that have already been developed, or are being developed simultaneously to the deliberations of the Commission. The Commission shall consult with accreditation organizations responsible for the accreditation of Federal, State, local or private prisons, that have developed or are currently developing standards related to prison rape. The Commission will also consult with national associations representing the corrections profession that have developed or are currently developing standards related to prison rape.

(g) Hearings. (1) In general. The Commission shall hold public hearings. The Commission may hold such hearings, sit and act at such times and places, take such testimony, and receive such evidence as the Commission considers advisable to carry out its duties under this section.

(2) Witness expenses. Witnesses requested to appear before the Commission shall be paid the same fees as are paid to witnesses under section 1821 of title 28, United States Code. The per diem and mileage allowances for witnesses shall be paid from funds appropriated to the Commission.

(h) Information from Federal or State agencies. The Commission may secure directly from any Federal department or agency such information as the Commission considers necessary to carry out its duties under this section. The Commission may request the head of any State or local department or agency to furnish such information to the Commission.

(i) Personnel matters. (1) Travel expenses. The members of the Commission shall be allowed travel expenses, including per diem in lieu of subsistence, at rates authorized for employees of agencies under subchapter I of chapter 57 of title 5, United States Code [5 USCS §§ 5701 et seq.], while away from their homes or regular places of business in the performance of service for the Commission.

(2) Detail of Federal employees. With the affirmative vote of 2/3 of the Commission, any Federal Government employee, with the approval of the head of the appropriate Federal agency, may be detailed to the Commission without reimbursement, and such detail shall be without interruption or loss of civil service status, benefits, or privileges.

(3) Procurement of temporary and intermittent services. Upon the request of the Commission, the Attorney General shall provide reasonable and appropriate office space, supplies, and administrative assistance.

(j) Contracts for research. (1) National Institute of Justice. With a 2/3 affirmative vote, the Commission may select nongovernmental researchers and experts to assist the Commission in carrying out its duties under this Act [42 USCS §§ 15601 et seq.]. The National Institute of Justice shall contract with the researchers and experts selected by the Commission to provide funding in exchange for their services.

(2) Other organizations. Nothing in this subsection shall be construed to limit the ability of the Commission to enter into contracts with other entities or organizations for research necessary to carry out the duties of the Commission under this section.

(k) Subpoenas. (1) Issuance. The Commission may issue subpoenas for the attendance of witnesses and the production of written or other matter.

(2) Enforcement. In the case of contumacy or refusal to obey a subpoena, the Attorney General may in a Federal court of appropriate jurisdiction obtain an appropriate order to enforce the subpoena.

(3) Confidentiality of documentary evidence. Documents provided to the Commission pursuant to a subpoena issued under this subsection shall not be released publicly without the affirmative vote of 2/3 of the Commission.

(l) Authorization of appropriations. There are authorized to be appropriated such sums as may be necessary to carry out this section.

(m) Termination. The Commission shall terminate on the date that is 60 days after the date on which the Commission submits the reports required by this section.

(n) Exemption. The Commission shall be exempt from the Federal Advisory Committee Act [5 USCS Appx].

(Sept. 4, 2003, P. L. 108-79, § 7, 117 Stat. 980; Dec. 8, 2004, P. L. 108-447, Div B, Title I, § 123(1), 118 Stat. 2871; Nov. 22, 2005, P. L. 109-108, Title I, § 113(b), 119 Stat. 2305; Jan. 5, 2006, P. L. 109-162, Title XI, Subtitle C, § 1181, 119 Stat. 3126; April 9, 2008, P. L. 110-199, Title II, Subtitle C, Ch. 4, § 261, 122 Stat. 694.)

HISTORY; ANCILLARY LAWS AND DIRECTIVES

Amendments:

2004. Act Dec. 8, 2004, in the section heading and in subsec. (a), substituted "Elimination" for "Reduction".

2005. Act Nov. 22, 2005, in subsec. (d)(3)(A), in the introductory matter, substituted "3 years" for "2 years".

2006. Act Jan. 5, 2006 purported to amend subsec. (d)(3)(A) by striking "2 years" and inserting "3 years"; however, because of a prior amendment, this amendment could not be executed.

2008. Act April 9, 2008, in subsec. (d)(3)(A), in the introductory matter, substituted "5 years" for "3 years".

Other provisions:

Construction of April 9, 2008 amendments. For construction of amendments by Act April 9, 2008, P. L. 110-199 and requirements for grants made under such amendments, see 42 USCS § 17504.

CROSS REFERENCES

This section is referred to in 42 USCS § 15607.

RESEARCH GUIDE

Law Review Articles:

Dolovich. Strategic Segregation in the Modern Prison. 48 Am Crim L Rev 1, Winter, 2011.

Corlew. Congress Attempts to Shine a Light on a Dark Problem: An In-Depth Look at the Prison Rape Elimination Act of 2003. 33 Am J Crim L 157, Spring 2006.

Ristroph. Prison and Punishment: Sexual Punishments. 15 Colum J Gender & L 139, 2006.

Smith. Prison and Punishment: Rethinking Prison Sex: Self-Expression and Safety. 15 Colum J Gender & L 185, 2006.

DeBraux. Prison Rape: Have We Done Enough? A Deep Look Into the Adequacy of the Prison Rape Elimination Act. 50 How LJ 203, Fall 2006.

Sigler. By the Light of Virtue: Prison Rape and the Corruption of Character. 91 Iowa L Rev 561, January 2006.

Dumond. The Impact of Prisoner Sexual Violence: Challenges of Implementing Public Law 108-79 The Prison Rape Elimination Act of 2003. 32 J Legis 142, 2006.

Mair; Frattaroli; Teret. Part III: National Challenges in Population Health: New Hope for Victims of Prison Sexual Assault. 31 JL Med & Ethics 602, Winter 2003.

Robertson. Compassionate Conservatism and Prison Rape: the Prison Rape Elimination Act of 2003. 30 NE J on Crim & Civ Con 1, Winter 2004.

Robertson. A Punk's Song About Prison Reform. 24 Pace L Rev 527, Spring 2004.

§ 15607. Adoption and effect of national standards

(a) Publication of proposed standards. (1) Final rule. Not later than 1 year after receiving the report specified in section 7(d)(3) [42 USCS § 15606(d)(3)], the Attorney General shall publish a final rule adopting national standards for the detection, prevention, reduction, and punishment of prison rape.

(2) Independent judgment. The standards referred to in paragraph (1) shall be based upon the independent judgment of the Attorney General, after giving due consideration to the recommended national standards provided by the Commission under section 7(e) [42 USCS § 15606(e)], and being informed by such data, opinions, and proposals that the Attorney General determines to be appropriate to consider.

(3) Limitation. The Attorney General shall not establish a national standard under this section that would impose substantial additional costs compared to the costs presently expended by Federal, State, and local prison authorities. The Attorney General may, however, provide a list of improvements for consideration by correctional facilities.

(4) Transmission to States. Within 90 days of publishing the final rule under paragraph (1), the Attorney General shall transmit the national standards adopted under such paragraph to the chief executive of each State, the head of the department of corrections of each State, and to the appropriate authorities in those units of local government who oversee operations in one or more prisons.

(b) **Applicability to Federal Bureau of Prisons.** The national standards referred to in subsection (a) shall apply to the Federal Bureau of Prisons immediately upon adoption of the final rule under subsection (a)(4).

(c) **Eligibility for Federal funds.** (1) Covered programs. (A) In general. For purposes of this subsection, a grant program is covered by this subsection if, and only if—

(i) the program is carried out by or under the authority of the Attorney General; and

(ii) the program may provide amounts to States for prison purposes.

(B) List. For each fiscal year, the Attorney General shall prepare a list identifying each program that meets the criteria of subparagraph (A) and provide that list to each State.

(2) Adoption of national standards. For each fiscal year, any amount that a State would otherwise receive for prison purposes for that fiscal year under a grant program covered by this subsection shall be reduced by 5 percent, unless the chief executive of the State submits to the Attorney General—

(A) a certification that the State has adopted, and is in full compliance with, the national standards described in section 8(a) [subsec. (a) of this section]; or

(B) an assurance that not less than 5 percent of such amount shall be used only for the purpose of enabling the State to adopt, and achieve full compliance with, those national standards, so as to ensure that a certification under subparagraph (A) may be submitted in future years.

(3) Report on noncompliance. Not later than September 30 of each year, the Attorney General shall publish a report listing each grantee that is not in compliance with the national standards adopted pursuant to section 8(a) [subsec. (a) of this section].

(4) Cooperation with survey. For each fiscal year, any amount that a State receives for that fiscal year under a grant program covered by this subsection shall not be used for prison purposes (and shall be returned to the grant program if no other authorized use is available), unless the chief executive of the State submits to the Attorney General a certification that neither the State, nor any political subdivision or unit of local government within the State, is listed in a report issued by the Attorney General pursuant to section 4(c)(2)(C) [42 USCS § 15603(c)(2)(C)].

(5) Redistribution of amounts. Amounts under a grant program not granted by reason of a reduction under paragraph (2), or returned by reason of the prohibition in paragraph (4), shall be granted to one or more entities not subject to such reduction or such prohibition, subject to the other laws governing that program.

(6) Implementation. The Attorney General shall establish procedures to implement this subsection, including procedures for effectively applying this subsection to discretionary grant programs.

(7) Effective date. (A) Requirement of adoption of standards. The first grants to which paragraph (2) applies are grants for the second fiscal year beginning after the date on which the national standards under section 8(a) [subsec. (a) of this section] are finalized.

(B) Requirement for cooperation. The first grants to which paragraph (4) applies are grants for the fiscal year beginning after the date of the enactment of this Act [enacted Sept. 4, 2003].

(Sept. 4, 2003, P. L. 108-79, § 8, 117 Stat. 985.)

CROSS REFERENCES

This section is referred to in 42 USCS § 15608.

RESEARCH GUIDE

Law Review Articles:

Corlew. Congress Attempts to Shine a Light on a Dark Problem: An In-Depth Look at the Prison Rape Elimination Act of 2003. 33 Am J Crim L 157, Spring 2006.

Ristroph. Prison and Punishment: Sexual Punishments. 15 Colum J Gender & L 139, 2006.

Smith. Prison and Punishment: Rethinking Prison Sex: Self-Expression and Safety. 15 Colum J Gender & L 185, 2006.

DeBraux. Prison Rape: Have We Done Enough? A Deep Look Into the Adequacy of the Prison Rape Elimination Act. 50 How LJ 203, Fall 2006.

Sigler. By the Light of Virtue: Prison Rape and the Corruption of Character. 91 Iowa L Rev 561, January 2006.

Dumond. The Impact of Prisoner Sexual Violence: Challenges of Implementing Public Law 108-79 The Prison Rape Elimination Act of 2003. 32 J Legis 142, 2006.

Mair; Frattaroli; Teret. Part III: National Challenges in Population Health: New Hope for Victims of Prison Sexual Assault. 31 JL Med & Ethics 602, Winter 2003.

Robertson. Compassionate Conservatism and Prison Rape: the Prison Rape Elimination Act of 2003. 30 NE J on Crim & Civ Con 1, Winter 2004.

Robertson. A Punk's Song About Prison Reform. 24 Pace L Rev 527, Spring 2004.

§ 15608. Requirement that accreditation organizations adopt accreditation standards.

(a) Eligibility for Federal grants. Notwithstanding any other provision of law, an organization responsible for the accreditation of Federal, State, local, or private prisons, jails, or other penal facilities may not receive any new Federal grants during any period in which such organization fails to meet any of the requirements of subsection (b).

(b) Requirements. To be eligible to receive Federal grants, an accreditation organization referred to in subsection (a) must meet the following requirements:

(1) At all times after 90 days after the date of enactment of this Act [enacted Sept. 4, 2003], the organization shall have in effect, for each facility that it is responsible for accrediting, accreditation standards for the detection, prevention, reduction, and punishment of prison rape.

(2) At all times after 1 year after the date of the adoption of the final rule under section 8(a)(4) [42 USCS § 15607(a)(4)], the organization shall, in addition to any other such standards that it may promulgate relevant to the detection, prevention, reduction, and punishment of prison rape, adopt accreditation standards consistent with the national standards adopted pursuant to such final rule.

(Sept. 4, 2003, P. L. 108-79, § 9, 117 Stat. 987.)

RESEARCH GUIDE

Law Review Articles:

Corlew. Congress Attempts to Shine a Light on a Dark Problem: An In-Depth Look at the Prison Rape Elimination Act of 2003. 33 Am J Crim L 157, Spring 2006.

Ristroph. Prison and Punishment: Sexual Punishments. 15 Colum J Gender & L 139, 2006.

Smith. Prison and Punishment: Rethinking Prison Sex: Self-Expression and Safety. 15 Colum J Gender & L 185, 2006.

DeBraux. Prison Rape: Have We Done Enough? A Deep Look Into the Adequacy of the Prison Rape Elimination Act. 50 How LJ 203, Fall 2006.

Sigler. By the Light of Virtue: Prison Rape and the Corruption of Character. 91 Iowa L Rev 561, January 2006.

Dumond. The Impact of Prisoner Sexual Violence: Challenges of Implementing Public Law 108-79 The Prison Rape Elimination Act of 2003. 32 J Legis 142, 2006.

Mair; Frattaroli; Teret. Part III: National Challenges in Population Health: New Hope for Victims of Prison Sexual Assault. 31 JL Med & Ethics 602, Winter 2003.

Robertson. Compassionate Conservatism and Prison Rape: the Prison Rape Elimination Act of 2003. 30 NE J on Crim & Civ Con 1, Winter 2004.

Robertson. A Punk's Song About Prison Reform. 24 Pace L Rev 527, Spring 2004.

§ 15609. Definitions

In this Act [42 USCS §§ 15601 et seq.], the following definitions shall apply:

(1) Carnal knowledge. The term "carnal knowledge" means contact between the penis and the vulva or the penis and the anus, including penetration of any sort, however slight.

(2) Inmate. The term "inmate" means any person incarcerated or detained in any facility who is accused of, convicted of, sentenced for, or adjudicated delinquent for, violations of criminal law or the terms and conditions of parole, probation, pretrial release, or diversionary program.

(3) Jail. The term "jail" means a confinement facility of a Federal, State, or local law enforcement agency to hold—

    (A) persons pending adjudication of criminal charges; or

    (B) persons committed to confinement after adjudication of criminal charges for sentences of 1 year or less.

(4) HIV. The term "HIV" means the human immunodeficiency virus.

(5) Oral sodomy. The term "oral sodomy" means contact between the mouth and the penis, the mouth and the vulva, or the mouth and the anus.

(6) Police lockup. The term "police lockup" means a temporary holding facility of a Federal, State, or local law enforcement agency to hold—

    (A) inmates pending bail or transport to jail;

    (B) inebriates until ready for release; or

    (C) juveniles pending parental custody or shelter placement.

(7) Prison. The term "prison" means any confinement facility of a Federal, State, or local government, whether administered by such government or by a private organization on behalf of such government, and includes—

    (A) any local jail or police lockup; and

    (B) any juvenile facility used for the custody or care of juvenile inmates.

(8) Prison rape. The term "prison rape" includes the rape of an inmate in the actual or constructive control of prison officials.

(9) Rape. The term "rape" means—

    (A) the carnal knowledge, oral sodomy, sexual assault with an object, or sexual fondling of a person, forcibly or against that person's will;

    (B) the carnal knowledge, oral sodomy, sexual assault with an object, or sexual fondling of a person not forcibly or against the person's will, where the victim is incapable of giving consent because of his or her youth or his or her temporary or permanent mental or physical incapacity; or

    (C) the carnal knowledge, oral sodomy, sexual assault with an object, or sexual fondling of a person achieved through the exploitation of the fear or threat of physical violence or bodily injury.

(10) Sexual assault with an object. The term "sexual assault with an object" means the use of any hand, finger, object, or other instrument to penetrate, however slightly, the genital or anal opening of the body of another person.

(11) Sexual fondling. The term "sexual fondling" means the touching of the private body parts of another person (including the genitalia, anus, groin, breast, inner thigh, or buttocks) for the purpose of sexual gratification.

(12) Exclusions. The terms and conditions described in paragraphs (9) and (10) shall not apply to—

(A) custodial or medical personnel gathering physical evidence, or engaged in other legitimate medical treatment, in the course of investigating prison rape;

(B) the use of a health care provider's hands or fingers or the use of medical devices in the course of appropriate medical treatment unrelated to prison rape; or

(C) the use of a health care provider's hands or fingers and the use of instruments to perform body cavity searches in order to maintain security and safety within the prison or detention facility, provided that the search is conducted in a manner consistent with constitutional requirements.

(Sept. 4, 2003, P. L. 108-79, § 10, 117 Stat. 987.)

RESEARCH GUIDE

Law Review Articles:

Corlew. Congress Attempts to Shine a Light on a Dark Problem: An In-Depth Look at the Prison Rape Elimination Act of 2003. 33 Am J Crim L 157, Spring 2006.

Ristroph. Prison and Punishment: Sexual Punishments. 15 Colum J Gender & L 139, 2006.

Smith. Prison and Punishment: Rethinking Prison Sex: Self-Expression and Safety. 15 Colum J Gender & L 185, 2006.

DeBraux. Prison Rape: Have We Done Enough? A Deep Look Into the Adequacy of the Prison Rape Elimination Act. 50 How LJ 203, Fall 2006.

Sigler. By the Light of Virtue: Prison Rape and the Corruption of Character. 91 Iowa L Rev 561, January 2006.

Dumond. The Impact of Prisoner Sexual Violence: Challenges of Implementing Public Law 108-79 The Prison Rape Elimination Act of 2003. 32 J Legis 142, 2006.

Mair; Frattaroli; Teret. Part III: National Challenges in Population Health: New Hope for Victims of Prison Sexual Assault. 31 JL Med & Ethics 602, Winter 2003.

Robertson. Compassionate Conservatism and Prison Rape: the Prison Rape Elimination Act of 2003. 30 NE J on Crim & Civ Con 1, Winter 2004.

Robertson. A Punk's Song About Prison Reform. 24 Pace L Rev 527, Spring 2004.

CHAPTER 148. WINDSTORM IMPACT REDUCTION

§ 15701. Findings

The Congress finds the following:

(1) Hurricanes, tropical storms, tornadoes, and thunderstorms can cause significant loss of life, injury, destruction of property, and economic and social disruption. All States and regions are vulnerable to these hazards.

(2) The United States currently sustains several billion dollars in economic damages each year due to these windstorms. In recent decades, rapid development and population growth in high-risk areas has greatly increased overall vulnerability to windstorms.

(3) Improved windstorm impact reduction measures have the potential to reduce these losses through—

(A) cost-effective and affordable design and construction methods and practices;

(B) effective mitigation programs at the local, State, and national level;

(C) improved data collection and analysis and impact prediction methodologies;

(D) engineering research on improving new structures and retrofitting existing ones to better withstand windstorms, atmospheric-related research to better understand the behavior and impact of windstorms on the built environment, and subsequent application of those research results; and

(E) public education and outreach.

(4) There is an appropriate role for the Federal Government in supporting

windstorm impact reduction. An effective Federal program in windstorm impact reduction will require interagency coordination, and input from individuals, academia, the private sector, and other interested non-Federal entities.

(Oct. 25, 2004, P. L. 108-360, Title II, § 202, 118 Stat. 1675.)

HISTORY; ANCILLARY LAWS AND DIRECTIVES

Short title:
Act Oct. 25, 2004, P. L. 108-360, Title II, § 201, 118 Stat. 1675, provides: "This Act [title] [classified to 42 USCS §§ 1885d(a) and 15701 et seq.] may be cited as the 'National Windstorm Impact Reduction Act of 2004'.".

§ 15702. Definitions

In this title:

(1) Director. The term "Director" means the Director of the Office of Science and Technology Policy.

(2) Program. The term "Program" means the National Windstorm Impact Reduction Program established by section 204(a) [42 USCS § 15703(a)].

(3) State. The term "State" means each of the States of the United States, the District of Columbia, the Commonwealth of Puerto Rico, the United States Virgin Islands, Guam, American Samoa, the Commonwealth of the Northern Mariana Islands, and any other territory or possession of the United States.

(4) Windstorm. The term "windstorm" means any storm with a damaging or destructive wind component, such as a hurricane, tropical storm, tornado, or thunderstorm.

(Oct. 25, 2004, P. L. 108-360, Title II, § 203, 118 Stat. 1676.)

HISTORY; ANCILLARY LAWS AND DIRECTIVES

References in text:
"This title", referred to in this section, is Title II of Act Oct. 25, 2004, P. L. 108-360, which appears generally as 42 USCS §§ 15701 et seq. For full classification of such Title, consult USCS Tables volumes.

§ 15703. National Windstorm Impact Reduction Program

(a) Establishment. There is established the National Windstorm Impact Reduction Program.

(b) Objective. The objective of the Program is the achievement of major measurable reductions in losses of life and property from windstorms. The objective is to be achieved through a coordinated Federal effort, in cooperation with other levels of government, academia, and the private sector, aimed at improving the understanding of windstorms and their impacts and developing and encouraging implementation of cost-effective mitigation measures to reduce those impacts.

(c) Interagency Working Group. Not later than 90 days after the date of enactment of this Act [enacted Oct. 25, 2004], the Director shall establish an Interagency Working Group consisting of representatives of the National Science Foundation, the National Oceanic and Atmospheric Administration, the National Institute of Standards and Technology, the Federal Emergency Management Agency, and other Federal agencies as appropriate. The Director shall designate an agency to serve as Chair of the Working Group and be responsible for the planning, management, and coordination of the Program, including budget coordination. Specific agency roles and responsibilities under the Program shall be defined in the implementation plan required under subsection (e). General agency responsibilities shall include the following:

(1) The National Institute of Standards and Technology shall support research and development to improve building codes and standards and practices for design and construction of buildings, structures, and lifelines.

(2) The National Science Foundation shall support research in engineering and the atmospheric sciences to improve the understanding of the behavior of windstorms and their impact on buildings, structures, and lifelines.

(3) The National Oceanic and Atmospheric Administration shall support atmospheric sciences research to improve the understanding of the behavior of windstorms and their impact on buildings, structures, and lifelines.

(4) The Federal Emergency Management Agency shall support the development of risk assessment tools and effective mitigation techniques, windstorm-related data collection and analysis, public outreach, information dissemination, and implementation of mitigation measures consistent with the Agency's all-hazards approach.

(d) **Program components.** (1) In general. The Program shall consist of three primary mitigation components: improved understanding of windstorms, windstorm impact assessment, and windstorm impact reduction. The components shall be implemented through activities such as data collection and analysis, risk assessment, outreach, technology transfer, and research and development. To the extent practicable, research activities authorized under this title shall be peer-reviewed, and the components shall be designed to be complementary to, and avoid duplication of, other public and private hazard reduction efforts.

(2) Understanding of windstorms. Activities to enhance the understanding of windstorms shall include research to improve knowledge of and data collection on the impact of severe wind on buildings, structures, and infrastructure.

(3) Windstorm impact assessment. Activities to improve windstorm impact assessment shall include—

(A) development of mechanisms for collecting and inventorying information on the performance of buildings, structures, and infrastructure in windstorms and improved collection of pertinent information from sources, including the design and construction industry, insurance companies, and building officials;

(B) research, development, and technology transfer to improve loss estimation and risk assessment systems; and

(C) research, development, and technology transfer to improve simulation and computational modeling of windstorm impacts.

(4) Windstorm impact reduction. Activities to reduce windstorm impacts shall include—

(A) development of improved outreach and implementation mechanisms to translate existing information and research findings into cost-effective and affordable practices for design and construction professionals, and State and local officials;

(B) development of cost-effective and affordable windstorm-resistant systems, structures, and materials for use in new construction and retrofit of existing construction; and

(C) outreach and information dissemination related to cost-effective and affordable construction techniques, loss estimation and risk assessment methodologies, and other pertinent information regarding windstorm phenomena to Federal, State, and local officials, the construction industry, and the general public.

(e) Implementation plan. Not later than 1 year after date of enactment of this title [enacted Oct. 25, 2004], the Interagency Working Group shall develop and transmit to the Congress an implementation plan for achieving the objectives of the Program. The plan shall include—

(1) an assessment of past and current public and private efforts to reduce windstorm impacts, including a comprehensive review and analysis of windstorm mitigation activities supported by the Federal Government;

(2) a description of plans for technology transfer and coordination with natural hazard mitigation activities supported by the Federal Government;

(3) a statement of strategic goals and priorities for each Program component area;

(4) a description of how the Program will achieve such goals, including detailed responsibilities for each agency; and

(5) a description of plans for cooperation and coordination with interested public and private sector entities in each program component area.

(f) Biennial report. The Interagency Working Group shall, on a biennial basis, and not later than 180 days after the end of the preceding 2 fiscal years, transmit a report to the Congress describing the status of the windstorm impact reduction program, including progress achieved during the preceding two fiscal years. Each such report shall include any recommendations for legislative and other action the Interagency Working Group considers necessary and appropriate. In developing the biennial report, the Interagency Working Group shall consider the recommendations of the Advisory Committee established under section 205 [42 USCS § 15704].

(Oct. 25, 2004, P. L. 108-360, Title II, § 204, 118 Stat. 1676.)

HISTORY; ANCILLARY LAWS AND DIRECTIVES

References in text:

"This title", referred to in this section, is Title II of Act Oct. 25, 2004, P. L. 108-360, which appears generally as 42 USCS §§ 15701 et seq. For full classification of such Title, consult USCS Tables volumes.

Transfer of functions:
For transfer of all functions, personnel, assets, components, authorities, grant programs, and liabilities of the Federal Emergency Management Agency, including the functions of the Under Secretary for Federal Emergency Management relating thereto, to the Federal Emergency Management Agency, see 6 USCS § 315(a)(1).

CROSS REFERENCES
This section is referred to in 42 USCS §§ 15702, 15704.

§ 15704. National Advisory Committee on Windstorm Impact Reduction

(a) Establishment. The Director shall establish a National Advisory Committee on Windstorm Impact Reduction, consisting of not less than 11 and not more than 15 non-Federal members representing a broad cross section of interests such as the research, technology transfer, design and construction, and financial communities; materials and systems suppliers; State, county, and local governments; the insurance industry; and other representatives as designated by the Director.

(b) Assessment. The Advisory Committee shall assess—
(1) trends and developments in the science and engineering of windstorm impact reduction;
(2) the effectiveness of the Program in carrying out the activities under section 204(d) [42 USCS § 15703(d)];
(3) the need to revise the Program; and
(4) the management, coordination, implementation, and activities of the Program.

(c) Biennial report. At least once every two years, the Advisory Committee shall report to Congress and the Interagency Working Group on the assessment carried out under subsection (b).

(d) Sunset exemption. Section 14 of the Federal Advisory Committee Act [5 USCS Appx] shall not apply to the Advisory Committee established under this section.

(Oct. 25, 2004, P. L. 108-360, Title II, § 205, 118 Stat. 1678.)

CROSS REFERENCES
This section is referred to in 42 USCS § 15703.

§ 15705. Savings clause

Nothing in this title supersedes any provision of the National Manufactured Housing Construction and Safety Standards Act of 1974 [42 USCS §§ 5401 et seq.]. No design, construction method, practice, technology, material, mitigation methodology, or hazard reduction measure of any kind developed under this title shall be required for a home certified under section 616 of the National Manufactured Housing Construction and Safety Standards Act of 1974 (42 U.S.C. 5415), pursuant to standards issued under such Act, without being subject to the consensus development process and rulemaking procedures of that Act.

(Oct. 25, 2004, P. L. 108-360, Title II, § 206, 118 Stat. 1679.)

HISTORY; ANCILLARY LAWS AND DIRECTIVES

References in text:
"This title", referred to in this section, is Title II of Act Oct. 25, 2004, P. L. 108-360, which appears generally as 42 USCS §§ 15701 et seq. For full classification of such Title, consult USCS Tables volumes.

§ 15706. Authorization of appropriations

(a) Federal Emergency Management Agency. There are authorized to be appropriated to the Federal Emergency Management Agency for carrying out this title—

(1) $8,700,000 for fiscal year 2006;

(2) $9,400,000 for fiscal year 2007; and

(3) $9,400,000 for fiscal year 2008.

(b) National Science Foundation. There are authorized to be appropriated to the National Science Foundation for carrying out this title—

(1) $8,700,000 for fiscal year 2006;

(2) $9,400,000 for fiscal year 2007; and

(3) $9,400,000 for fiscal year 2008.

(c) National Institute of Standards and Technology. There are authorized to be appropriated to the National Institute of Standards and Technology for carrying out this title—

(1) $3,000,000 for fiscal year 2006;

(2) $4,000,000 for fiscal year 2007; and

(3) $4,000,000 for fiscal year 2008.

(d) National Oceanic and Atmospheric Administration. There are authorized to be appropriated to the National Oceanic and Atmospheric Administration for carrying out this title—

(1) $2,100,000 for fiscal year 2006;

(2) $2,200,000 for fiscal year 2007; and

(3) $2,200,000 for fiscal year 2008.

(Oct. 25, 2004, P. L. 108-360, Title II, § 207, 118 Stat. 1679.)

HISTORY; ANCILLARY LAWS AND DIRECTIVES

References in text:
"This title", referred to in this section, is Title II of Act Oct. 25, 2004, P. L. 108-360, which appears generally as 42 USCS §§ 15701 et seq. For full classification of such Title, consult USCS Tables volumes.

Transfer of functions:
For transfer of all functions, personnel, assets, components, authorities, grant programs, and liabilities of the Federal Emergency Management Agency, including the functions of the Under Secretary for Federal Emergency Management relating thereto, to the Federal Emergency Management Agency, see 6 USCS § 315(a)(1).

§ 15707. Coordination

The Secretary of Commerce, the Director of the National Institute of Standards and Technology, the Director of the Office of Science and Technology Policy and the heads of other Federal departments and agencies carrying out activities under this title and the statutes amended by this title shall work together to ensure that research, technologies, and response techniques are shared among the programs authorized in this title in order to coordinate the Nation's efforts to reduce vulnerability to the hazards described in this title.
(Oct. 25, 2004, P. L. 108-360, Title II, § 209, 118 Stat. 1680.)

HISTORY; ANCILLARY LAWS AND DIRECTIVES

References in text:
"This title", referred to in this section, is Title II of Act Oct. 25, 2004, P. L. 108-360, which appears generally as 42 USCS §§ 15701 et seq. For full classification of such Title, consult USCS Tables volumes.